Labor Law

LABOR LAW

Nicholas S. Falcone, M.A., L.L.M.

MEMBER OF THE NEW YORK BAR

ASSOCIATE PROFESSOR OF LABOR ECONOMICS

AND INDUSTRIAL RELATIONS

FORDHAM UNIVERSITY

John Wiley and Sons, Inc., New York and London

Library of Congress Catalog Card Number: 62-18352
Printed in the United States of America

TO MY WIFE AND DAUGHTER

Elizabeth and Patricia

Preface

This book attempts to present a historical development of labor law in its strictest sense. Although minimum wage laws, workmen's compensation laws, factory laws, and the social security act are all part of the vast subject of labor law, I have deliberately chosen to concentrate on that body of common, statutory, and administrative law which governs the collective-bargaining process, a device evolving in those democratic societies where employers and labor unions are allowed maximum freedom of economic action.

This is not, however, a history book. It is my belief that contemporary labor law can be best understood only after the student has assimilated a knowledgeable background. Every important labor law, as well as leading court decisions on them all, is covered in this book, and the lawyer along with the student should find the treatment of modern labor legislation and related decisions of practical value. A word of caution is necessary. Government labor policy is ever changing. Conflicting decisions in the lower courts are not uncommon. Decisions of the National Labor Relations Board sometimes conflict with federal court decisions, and the United States Supreme Court has not passed on every labor law issue. Therefore, the reader ought not to rest his case on any single textbook. A careful study of federal and state court decisions and administrative rulings must never cease.

Since learning is a slow process, it is essential that the student "travel to the river by way of the streams." It is therefore wise to start at the beginning and digest small morsels at a time.

This book is divided into two parts. The first deals with the evolution of labor law in England; the second part covers the complete development of labor law in the United States. Because the doctrines of criminal conspiracy, civil conspiracy, and contract interference are important creations of English common law that were later adopted by American courts, a study of English labor law should prove to be useful.

Cases covering every period in the development of American labor law, and legislation, including the 1959 Landrum-Griffin Act, are presented in this book because cases bring clarity and give life to the law.

The rules under which industrial strife is waged regulate strikes, picketing, and boycotts. Several chapters deal with these weapons, and all key issues have been selected and are studied. Emphasis has been laid on current problems of interest. In the last chapter I have discussed arbitration, a device proven effective in resolving labor disputes and minimizing conflict within the employer-employee relationship.

The complexity of labor law increases with each passing year as new laws and new decisions are made. Although this book includes every important facet of the subject, the more significant matters have been treated, I hope, in a comprehensive fashion. A broad knowledge of labor law is useful, yet other disciplines such as economics and government will allow the student to appraise objectively labor laws and the interpretations placed on them by courts and administrative agencies.

NICHOLAS S. FALCONE

July, 1962
New York, N.Y.

Contents

Introduction

LAW, in its most general and comprehensive sense, signifies a rule of action prescribed by some superior which the inferior is bound to obey. We may define the law also as a rule of civil conduct prescribed by the supreme power in a state, decreeing which conduct is right and prohibiting the wrong. Labor law is part of a great body of substantive law. Since law seeks to regulate human activities, we shall learn that labor law is enmeshed in, and has become an inseparable part of, common law, constitutional law, the law of associations, criminal law, equity law, and the law of torts.

The first English labor law was enacted by Parliament in the fourteenth century, and in the following centuries Parliament continued to legislate in this area. The English courts independently established common law doctrines which became universal rules of conduct regulating the employer-employee relationship. Since our legal system clearly manifests our heritage of English common and statute law, we must realize that one of our most important sources of labor law is England.

The law of the United States may with propriety be divided into two kinds; common law, and statute law.

COMMON LAW. Common law rests primarily on custom, because in deciding cases the judges seek to give effect to the prevailing customs of people in their relations and dealings with each other. But when a point of law has once been decided, judges in the same jurisdiction follow it as a precedent, and the point is said to be decisively settled. This is known as the doctrine of stare decisis, the doctrine that courts must stand by decided cases, uphold precedents, and maintain former adjudications. With the lapse of time, the greater number of ordinary questions that may arise have been settled and the common law has been established. Occasionally courts do overrule precedent. Appeals based on social or psychological changes have sometimes influenced our courts to reform long-standing principles of the common law. We seek the law in the printed reports of court decisions.

STATUTE LAW. Statute law consists of the enactments of legislatures. These enactments may have the purpose of changing some rule established by the courts, when, for example, the society's development makes the old rule inexpedient, or of codifying into a brief statute rules scattered through hundreds or even thousands of volumes of reported cases. The whole law of negotiable instruments has been codified in most of our American states. An outstanding example of statute law is the famous Statute of Frauds, enacted in England in 1676, which provides in part that all contracts covering the sale of real property must be in writing and signed by the party to be charged. Most of our states have adopted this statute, which was designed to prevent frauds and perjuries. The Wagner Act of 1935, another example of statute law, guarantees workers the right to join a labor union, previously nonexistent as a legal right.

Another important source of labor law is the United States Constitution. Most federal labor laws are based on the language found in Article I, Section 8 of the Constitution, which authorizes Congress to regulate commerce between this nation and foreign nations as well as commerce flowing among the several American states. The guarantee of free speech is part of the First Amendment, and a great deal of decision law concerning picketing has this source. In a leading labor case involving picketing, a jurist commented that picketing is the "workingman's means of communication." The Fifth and Fourteenth Amendments are invoked frequently on the legality of specific picketing activities, on strikes, and on labor contracts.

Each of the fifty states has a constitution which is consistent with the federal constitution and provides the states with authority to promote the general welfare and to maintain peace and tranquility within their boundaries. Should pickets become disorderly and damage private property during a strike, the state may, through the exercise of this police power, seek to restore order and, through its courts, punish the wrongdoers. About eighteen states have enacted state labor relations laws which are concerned with labor relations in noninterstate commerce. The avowed purpose of these state acts has been to diminish the causes of labor disputes and to guarantee the right of collective bargaining. When labor activities penetrate into the much broader field of interstate commerce and foreign commerce, they usually come under exclusive federal regulation. The federal labor board may, however, decline to assert jurisdiction over labor disputes that do not affect interstate commerce substantially. In those cases the states may assume jurisdiction.

In addition to this narrow type of labor law, states may enact such laws in the broad area of social legislation as antidiscrimination laws, child labor laws, minimum wage laws, and other laws affecting the general welfare. This legislative power comes from the broad principle that the state is the supreme guardian over the general health and welfare of its citizens. The courts, both federal and state, administer and enforce the laws, whether they are enacted by legislatures or result from rulings which through custom and practice have become binding on society.

STATE COURTS. The courts of each state consist of law courts and equity courts. Law courts are organized tribunals for the trial of cases and the hearing of appeals. Each state has trial courts and at least one court to which appeals may be taken. Trial courts usually consist of a judge and a jury. Under certain conditions a jury trial may be waived, and the case is heard by a judge alone. Appellate courts consist of a bench of judges without a jury.

The trial courts are generally classified as follows:

(1) A court of general jurisdiction, before which most cases may be brought.

(2) Courts of limited or local jurisdiction for the trial of small cases, such as those held in county courts, city courts, municipal courts, and courts held by justices of the peace.

(3) Courts for the administration of estates of the deceased called surrogate courts, probate courts, orphan courts, etc.

The appellate courts are those to which appeals are taken from the trial courts and it is called, in most states, the supreme court. In New York, however, the highest appellate court is called the court of appeals, and the trial court of general jurisdiction is called the supreme court. Owing to the large number of appeals in New York, there is an intermediate court called the appellate division of the supreme court.

FEDERAL COURTS. In the federal jurisdiction, the trial court is the district court, found in each federal judicial district of the United States. The intermediate appellate court is the circuit court of appeals, and the highest appellate court is the Supreme Court of the United States.

Side by side with common law courts there grew up in England a separate court known as the equity court or the chancery court. This court, which consisted of a judge without a jury, was intended to give relief in hard cases, where, by some rigid rules of the common law courts, none could be had. In a few of our states such separate equity courts still exist, but generally the powers of the common law court and the equity court have been combined in one that administers both law and equity. Where the courts operate separately, the law court is the proper tribunal for seeking pecuniary damages. When the relief sought is the legal construction of a will or the desire to reform a deed upon the ground that a mistake had been made in its drafting, the proper tribunal is the equity court. In those states where the courts have been combined, it is possible to recover money damages and obtain equitable relief in the same action. Under the federal court system, the district court has concurrent common law and equity jurisdiction.

Under ordinary circumstances, cases which originate in a state court may be appealed only to the state appellate courts. However, when a question involving the federal constitution arises in a proceeding initiated in a state court, appeals are permitted from the highest appellate state court directly to the United States Supreme Court, but only on its consent to review.

The issue of states' rights has arisen from time to time in matters concerning labor law. States have sought zealously to retain jurisdiction over cases involving intrastate commerce or concerned with the exercise of state police power. It is not always easy to decide whether commerce is interstate or intrastate. Yet in labor law this problem of federal-state jurisdiction is far less serious than, for example, the issue of state and federal jurisdiction over civil rights.

Major court decisions in recent years have done much to settle the question of jurisdiction in specific labor cases. When pure labor law questions affecting commerce are concerned, the general rule allows the federal courts and federal administrative agencies to preempt the field. The national government, given power to regulate interstate commerce by the Constitution, has by express statute assumed jurisdiction over such commerce when it is substantially affected by labor activities. Despite the preemption doctrine, under which the federal power may assert superior jurisdictional rights, state courts and state administrative agencies have been permitted in certain cases to take jurisdiction if the federal government fails to act, and in other cases if by statute, or by consent of federal authorities, the state is permitted to take control of a labor case. A more detailed analysis of this federal-state jurisdictional question is made in Chapter 10.

ADMINISTRATIVE AGENCIES. Under modern legislation labor cases are processed by administrative agencies such as the National Labor Relations Board and the state labor relations boards. The National Labor Relations Board, created under the original National Labor Relations Act of 1935, is empowered to prevent any person from engaging in any unfair labor practice affecting commerce. The public right and duty of the board is not only the prevention of unfair labor practices by the employer and by unions in the future but also the prevention of their enjoying any advantage which they have gained by violation of the act. The jurisdiction of the board is limited to that conferred on it by the statute, and it enjoys a wide discretion in determining the procedure necessary to insure the fair and free choice of bargaining representatives by employees. In short, the board is a quasi-judicial body given power to issue subpoenas requiring the attendance of witnesses at hearings. Its proceedings must be conducted, so far as practicable, in accordance with the rules of civil procedure for the federal district courts. The National Labor Relations Board appraises conflicting and circumstantial evidence and the credibility of testimony, and its orders must be based on the preponderance of the testimony taken. At the conclusion of a board hearing, it is authorized to issue appropriate orders, yet it is given no power to enforce these orders. The federal statute authorizes the board to petition the United States circuit court of appeals for enforcement of its orders. The board alone is permitted to initiate court proceedings to enforce its orders. We can say that the National Labor Relations Board is a fact-finding tribunal with inquisitorial powers in labor controversies similar to those of a grand jury in criminal cases. The authority and procedure before state labor relations boards are substantially those of the federal labor relations board.

A great source of substantive labor law is the rulings handed down by the National Labor Relations Boards. On a state level the appropriate boards, wherever they exist, provide substantive rulings which govern only in the state where the ruling has been made. Administrative rulings of the federal and state boards are subject to challenge by court petition. Whenever the courts review the rulings of a board, the court decision becomes the rule of law; and where the board rulings remain unchallenged, they become valuable precedents and guideposts, until a court reverses or modifies the board decision.

During the last twenty years another source of labor law has been developing. It has come through arbitration. Although not of major importance at this time, the arbitration of labor controversies has contributed to the development of what might be called industrial jurisprudence. Arbitration of labor dispute cases is resorted to only when collective-bargaining contracts provide for it. The awards of arbitrators do not come within the doctrine of stare decisis and therefore do not have the binding effect given to court decisions. Perhaps after the passage of time arbitration awards may come to enjoy some degree of precedent status. If this were to occur, the awards could well become another major source of labor law. To avoid any misapprehension, we should note here that decisions rendered through the arbitration process are enforcible on the parties through legal action instituted in federal and state courts.

Before we consider the common law and statutory rulings that govern labor activities and labor controversies, let us devote some attention to two questions.

How do controversies between employers and employees or labor unions come before courts and administrative agencies?

Let us assume that a wage dispute develops between Employer A and Union B. Most of these controversies are resolved by private negotiation between the parties, i.e., through the medium of collective bargaining.

But at times a deadlock occurs, and a meeting of minds cannot be achieved. When such an impasse has been reached there are various possible techniques for the settlement of the controversy; for example, mediation or arbitration. However, we shall assume that before a settlement has occurred, the deadlocked parties resort to their respective self-help devices, used singly or in combination.

What self-help devices are available to the disputants? First, we shall consider labor-serving techniques. Labor's traditional self-help devices are the

> strike,
> picket-line, and
> boycott.

Union B is hopeful that the use of any, or all, of these means will cut off Employer A from the

> labor market,
> raw material market,
> service market (transportation), and
> consumer market.

The withholding of labor services by members of Union B, and their influencing prospective strike-replacements to withhold their labor, may result in an effective blockade that could cause enough economic damage to Employer A to compel him to make concessions to Union B. Of course, if the concessions would render the business unprofitable, Employer A would choose either to hold out with the hope that Union B would take less or to go out of business entirely.

Under certain conditions Union B, in addition to the use of self-help devices, seeks relief from an administrative agency. Perhaps Union B predicated its wage demand on a belief that Employer A's business was very profitable. If Employer A denied its ability to meet the wage demand, it is certain Union B would request the employer to produce business records to support its position. Assuming Employer A refused to produce his records, Union B could file a complaint with the National Labor Relations Board, or with a state labor relations board, charging the employer with failing to bargain in good faith. If the labor board upheld the charge, it would issue a cease and desist order to compel Employer A to produce its records and bargain in good faith.

We may now examine the self-help devices available to Employer A, and let us assume that he has decided to seek such remedies as may be given to him from courts, or from administrative agencies. What are the possibilities open to him? This is our second question. At common law Employer A would have been permitted to use

strikebreakers,
the lock-out, and the
blacklist.

Present statutory enactments proscribe the use of professional strike-breakers and the blacklist. Under certain conditions, Employer A could use the lock-out which is a refusal to furnish work to his employees in an effort to obtain more desirable terms for himself. Of course, Employer A would have the right to replace the strikers with new workers. We could say that these devices have been made available to Employer A to balance the economic power resulting from the techniques made available to Union B. In reality, the only objectives gained by Employer A have been a shutdown of his plant or a replacement of his labor force. He is still faced with possible economic damage resulting from the Union's picket line and boycott.

What legal remedies does Employer A have? They are contingent on the conduct of the picket line and the boycott. If the pickets engage in violence which damages or threatens to damage the employer's plant, or if the union exerts secondary-boycott pressure, or if the union enters into agreements with secondary employers to inflict economic damage on Employer A, the following remedies are available:

(1) A damage suit against Union B to recover losses suffered as a result of the union's violent action.

(2) A damage suit based on the use of the secondary boycott.

(3) To request law enforcement agents to prosecute at criminal law those responsible for the property damage.

(4) A treble damage suit under the Sherman Act against the union and the secondary employers for the illegal restraint of trade.

(5) Request the National Labor Relations Board under the Taft-Hartley Law to seek injunctive relief against the use of the secondary boycott.

(6) Request the Department of Justice under the antitrust laws to enjoin the illegal restraint of trade activities carried on by Union B and the secondary employer conspiracy.

(7) Request the Department of Justice under the antitrust laws to institute criminal proceedings against those charged with an illegal restraint of trade.

(8) File with the National Labor Relations Board unfair labor practice charges against the union for the use of the secondary boycott.

Actions for damages against labor unions are time-consuming and cumbersome, and the collection of a judgment may be uncertain. At common law a labor union had no legal status, and was not a legal entity, apart from its members. Property owned by the union was in fact the property of the members, and it could sue and be sued only in the names of its members. By statute in most states, unions may now sue and be sued in the association name.

Whenever possible, Employer A would seek to invoke equity power to prevent damage to his business. He would apply for an injunction. An injunctive order is usually prohibitory and compels a defendant to refrain from specific conduct. At times, it is mandatory and requires the defendant to perform an affirmative act. Disobedience of this restraining order can lead to fine or imprisonment. Since 1932 statutory restrictions have been placed on the federal and state courts that limit the issuance of injunctions in cases involving labor disputes.

The choice of self-help devices presents little difficulty for Employer A and Union B. Serious problems frequently develop when the parties must decide which legal remedy should be used so that a peaceful solution will result.

We may now begin our formal study of labor law.

PART ONE

CHAPTER ONE

Development of the Law of Labor in England

THE English medieval period may well be characterized as one of total restriction for the workingman struggling to improve his economic and social position. In the fourteenth century, even when acting alone, he faced harsh punitive laws. A breakdown in the feudal system and the devastating bubonic plague stimulated the natural drive for better working conditions. The plague, having depopulated about two-thirds of Europe, encouraged surviving serfs and freemen to leave estates and manors to which they had been attached for centuries and to seek work in the growing commerce of the towns. The bargaining position of the worker in towns hard hit by the labor shortage allowed him to demand higher wages and improved working conditions. The worker understood the operation of the natural law of supply and demand, especially when he witnessed employers bidding against each other for his services. The dreams of workers for fair wages and decent job conditions were short-lived. Employers immediately petitioned Parliament for relief. It came with the passage of the first English labor law, the Ordinance of Laborers,[1] in 1349, enacted quickly to meet what employers considered an urgent situation. In 1351 a more studied law called the Statute of Laborers [2] was passed.

In essence these laws required every able-bodied man and woman under 60 years of age without independent means of support to work on the demand of an employer at wages fixed by law. Refusal to work on terms unilaterally established by the employer resulted in fine or imprisonment. The law also imposed penalties on any employer who voluntarily improved wages or working conditions, which penalties discouraged employer competition for workers. The importance of these

1. 23 Edw. 3, c. 1.
2. 25 Edw. 3, c. 1.

first laws is in their shattering the workers' hope for improved living conditions. Since unions were nonexistent during the period, the laws condemned only the individual worker who attempted to exploit his bargaining power.

The effectiveness of these early statutes is evident; two hundred years passed before a more general labor law was enacted in 1548.[3] This was the first law pushed through Parliament directed against developing unions, then called workingmen's associations; it condemned attempts by workers to bargain collectively. It provided serious criminal penalties upon

. . . "any artificers, workmen or laborers who conspire, covenant or promise together, or make any oaths that they shall not make or do their work but at a certain price, or shall not enterprise or take upon them to finish that another hath begun, or shall do but a certain work in a day, or shall not work but at certain hours and times."

A union was a criminal conspiracy, and members were liable to serious punishment. In 1562 all prior statutes were consolidated into a longer act called "An Act Containing Divers Orders for Artificers, Laborers, Servants of Husbandry, and Apprentices,"[4] more often referred to as the Statute of Elizabeth. It reiterated the main provisions of the 1351 Statute of Laborers requiring workers to labor on the request of another. The hours of work were fixed, and judges were given power to establish wages to be paid laborers. Elaborate rules were made regulating apprenticeship, with a minimum period of 7 years for journeyman status. The most significant feature of this law, which was not formally repealed until 1875, was the continued condemnation of workers' attempts to bargain collectively. The 1562 act labeled a combination of workers a criminal conspiracy, each member of the combine liable to a severe jail sentence. If the act of a single person is against the law of 1349, went the rationale behind the statute of 1562, the crime is grossly aggravated when he joins with others to perform the same act. Despite the severity of the criminal conspiracy laws, workers did combine secretly. Frequently the combinations were exposed and their members punished, sometimes harshly. This doctrine of criminal conspiracy harassed labor unions until 1824.

Although the seventeenth century ushered in a greater wave of industrial activity than had been witnessed in any previous period, no statute innovations were created during this century, nor was there any relaxing of the fixed attitudes of the ruling economic class toward releasing the worker from his historic duty to perform obligatory labor. The obligation to work for legally fixed wages continued, and the la-

3. 2 & 3 Edw. 6, c. 15.
4. 5 Eliz. 1, c. 4.

borer remained frustrated in his human desire to improve his economic position.

The eighteenth century is of considerable historical significance to students of labor law; during this period many important statutes harassing labor activity were enacted. England had now developed into a highly industrial state. Her mercantilist economy was showing great profits, her colonial expansion program had been very successful, her merchant fleet was increasing rapidly, and she had access to great stores of raw materials awaiting transportation from her colonies. The invention of the steam engine was the great stimulant in developing rich colonies. The Industrial Revolution was in full swing.

The more formal relationship between the employer and the employee which had existed for centuries in preindustrial England was swept away with the introduction of the factory system. The powerful guild system, with its master, journeyman, and apprentice relationship, was losing its strong economic position. Under the guild economy the journeyman and the apprentice were members of the master's household. The shop and home comprised one distinguishable economic unit in which production was started and completed.

The factory system was a radical innovation that separated the shop from the home. Now each worker completed only a small operation in producing a commodity, and his skill was necessarily limited. With division of labor a new relationship developed. The worker no longer dealt directly with the owner of the business. When the factory system introduced the foreman the laborer lost his owner contact and was required to deal with the supervisor exclusively.

The French Revolution had dealt a death blow to the remnants of feudalism and had acclaimed equality for all. Freedom of movement and freedom of contract were great social gains that resulted. Workers could bargain individually with employers, and occasionally a valid and enforcible contract was entered into between the parties. In the eighteenth century freedom of contract was largely theoretical, since employers unilaterally established wage rates and other terms of employment. Although labor was no longer obligatory, the worker had no choice other than to accept employment on the employers' terms.

Protective labor legislation, including collective-bargaining rights, was not to come until the nineteenth century. The laissez-faire economic philosophy of the English government during the eighteenth century brought few, if any, tangible comforts to the great mass of industrial workers. Realizing that his individual freedom provided him with little or no bargaining power to deal on any equitable basis with the resourceful employer, the worker joined his fellow workers to bring concerted pressure against the employer. Their objective was bilateral bargaining. These worker combinations were regarded as criminal conspiracies under existing law. A criminal conspiracy was a combination of two or more persons seeking by concerted action to accomplish an unlawful purpose or seeking a lawful purpose by criminal means. To the workers collective bargaining rights were a paramount good, and they were willing to risk indictments and convictions under the criminal conspiracy doctrine to obtain them, for they knew that economic justice could become a reality only through the collective process.

One outstanding eighteenth-century case illustrating the application of the doctrine of criminal conspiracy is that of Rex v. Journeymen Taylors of Cambridge,[5] in which several tailors were indicted for conspiracy among themselves to raise their wages. In finding the defendants guilty the court held that their combining constituted conspiracy, a common law offense. More than sixty years later there occurred another leading case on this point. This was Rex v. Eccles,[6] again involving several journeymen tailors, who combined and sought wage increases from their employers. Once more the tailors were found guilty. A famous jurist of the period, Lord Mansfield, participating in the decision, said:

. . . The illegal combination is the gist of the offense; persons in possession of any articles of trade may sell them at such prices as they may individually please, but if they confederate and agree not to sell them under certain prices, it is conspiracy; so, every man may work at what price he pleases, but a combination not to work under certain prices, is an indictable offense.

It is interesting to note from the cited portion of Mansfield's opinion that the individual worker had by this time gained the freedom to refuse work when he was dissatisfied with the wages offered or other working conditions. This became possible in 1783, even though the 1351 Statute of Laborers was still law and was not repealed until 1875. Yet the worker was not free to join his fellow workers for the purpose of bargaining collectively.

Traditionally under English law combinations of individuals were frowned on, even when employers made up the alliances. In 1779 an act directed against combines of both employers and workers was passed. Although there appears to be no record of prosecutions against combinations of employers, the antistrike, antipicketing and anticombination features of previous laws and decisions were restated. There were also frequent court proceedings initiated against workers, and criminal conspiracy was the basis of the charges.

The harshness and discriminatory features of the 1799 act resulted in the passage of a slightly milder anticombination law in 1800, but several

5. 8 Mod. 10 (1721).
6. Leach C. C. 274 (1783).

worker combinations were prosecuted after 1800. Despite the severe punishment given to workmen who were proven to have violated either the 1800 statute or the common law doctrine of conspiracy, workmen pressed for recognition, realizing that their economic survival and betterment could come only through collective action. When the law of supply and demand favored the worker and brought higher wages, food prices increased immediately and wiped out the wage gains. In addition, employers sought out and hired women and children; the adult male could not compete with their cheap labor and faced long periods of unemployment with unbearable social conditions. The workers' main objective was to obtain statutory recognition of their right to combine as trade unionists and to carry on collective bargaining without fear of molestation. Lacking this recognition, the worker could expect nothing but deterioration in living standards, and with it slums, disease, and human degradation.

Delegations of workers supported by a few aristocratic friends carried pleas to Parliament seeking legislative relief, some of which came with the passage of the act of 1824.[7] Although the workers' Magna Charta was not to come until the twentieth century, this new law was a great triumph for all workers; it recognized their right to organize unions and to strike.

History is replete with examples of the excessive and sometimes violent enthusiasm of people who gain freedom for the first time. In 1825 workers called strikes with questionable provocation, and the strikes were followed by much disorder and destruction of property. The few unions that existed at the time were led by inexperienced leaders with few or none of the funds needed to carry on industrial disputes. Since the necessary discipline and loyalty of membership were missing, disorganized workers engaged in destructive strikes and vandalism, which brought swift action by Parliament to restore domestic tranquility and maintain British leadership in the markets of the world. Parliament passed the act of 1825,[8] which almost nullified the concessions given workers under the law of 1824. Although the new law restored some of the old oppressions, it did recognize the right of the workers to join unions and to consummate legally binding collective-bargaining contracts. Once the door to freedom has been opened people inevitably fight hard to keep it open, and they slowly demand greater freedom of action, even when the lawmakers seek to maintain a rigid status quo. Recognition of the trade union movement once given, some progress developed, in spite of the legal harassments that developed later under common law. For example, recognition of labor union activity was conditioned on the legality of the means used by such organizations in at-

7. 5 Geo. 4, c. 95.
8. 6 Geo. 4, c. 129.

taining objectives. The lawfulness of the objectives themselves was carefully scrutinized. What constitutes a lawful means? What constitutes a legal end? These are not easy questions to answer, as we shall see.

At this period of English history, members of courts were drawn from aristocracy exclusively, and upon them alone rested the judicial responsibility of deciding cases involving property rights. It is sometimes said that the environment in which a person is born, his education, his associates, and the amount of wealth he controls influences his philosophical development. In determining the legality of worker activity, the nineteenth-century judge was certainly very exacting in the interpretation and application of existing law. Throughout the remainder of the nineteenth century, all gains made by the workers resulted from statutory enactment. The common law was against the worker from its beginning, and it constantly harassed him until Parliament modified or abrogated the common law restrictions.

The nineteenth and early twentieth centuries prove quite conclusively that any economic and social progress made by laborers came only when Parliament acted favorably. Cognizant of this fact, workers in most countries of the world—the United States may be a qualified exception—have concentrated on control of the legislature with which to obtain favorable labor laws. The student of labor organization is likely to go even further and declare that legislative control is still the chief vehicle for seeking improved labor conditions, particularly in Europe.

A mild form of picketing was sanctioned by another law of Parliament called the Molestation of Workmen Act of 1859.[9] If the picketing influenced other workers to breach employment contracts, the picketing was illegal and might be enjoined. Inducing a breach of an employment contract became the basis for use of the "yellow-dog" contract, which scholars report was not widely used in England to harass workers but did become one favorite method of American employers in curbing union organizational campaigns. We shall hear more about the "yellow-dog" contract when the American development of labor law is discussed.

The next legislative improvement came in 1869 with the passage of the Trades Union Funds Protection Act,[10] which removed the protection formerly given to a larcenous union treasurer. The common law had provided that a union member who stole union funds could not be prosecuted, on the theory that union funds belonged to all union members. Therefore a member who stole union money was really taking his own funds and could not be legally charged with larceny. Along with the act of 1824, the act of 1875 [11] highlights the greatest legislative gain

9. 22 Vict., c. 34.
10. 31 & 32 Vict., c. 116.
11. 38 & 39 Vict., c. 86.

made by labor during the century. The 1875 act repealed the Statute of Laborers of 1351. It redefined picketing and placed a broader interpretation on its use by workers. Labor unions were free to engage in all those activities which if engaged in by a single person did not constitute a crime. The legal status of labor unions was no longer in doubt.

Even with all these legislative improvements, final victory did not come during the nineteenth century. Certain aspects of common law still plagued the trade union movement. In the latter part of the century the doctrine of civil conspiracy hindered trade union progress.

Justice Oliver Wendell Holmes defined civil conspiracy as the intentional infliction of damage by concerted action upon another without just cause or excuse. Although this doctrine was applicable to all combinations which "wronged" another, there has been considerable doubt that the law was impartially applied when labor unions engaged in industrial warfare with business firms.

In 1794 [12] one of the earliest civil conspiracy cases was tried in England, the case of Tarleton v. McGauley.

For a long period the defendant in this case, McGauley, had sailed the ship *Othello* from England laden with English goods for trading with African natives of Cameroon. The trader enjoyed a monopolistic position and presumably earned handsome profits in his dealings with these unsophisticated natives. The plaintiff, Tarleton, learning of McGauley's good fortune and hoping to share in this profitable trade, sailed his ship to Africa and anchored a short distance from the *Othello*. While it was lying at anchor, canoes with natives aboard visited Tarleton's ship for the purpose of trading. McGauley, seeking to discourage the natives from trading with Tarleton and hoping to reestablish his monopoly, fired a cannon from the *Othello*. The natives having heard nothing as loud before, and believing the rumble to be ominous, scurried back to shore for protection. In the melee a few natives were drowned. The defendant's act deterred and discouraged the natives

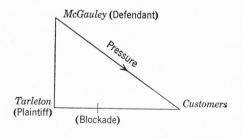

Figure 1

12. Tarleton v. McGauley (1794) Nisi Prius, Peake, N.F. Cas. 270.

from continuing to trade with Tarleton, and thus promoted a secondary boycott.

Tarleton sued McGauley seeking damages for loss of profits and used the doctrine of civil conspiracy as the basis for his suit. McGauley contended that the damage suffered by Tarleton, although intentional, could be justified on the ground that the defendant had a right to protect his monopolistic trade position, a lawful end. The court rendered judgment to Tarleton and ruled that the end sought by McGauley was lawful but that the means used (violence) was unlawful. English policy as expressed in this case encouraged monopolies and cartels to restrain trade, but the courts frowned on the use of any violent means to effectuate their monopolistic practices.

With this introduction to the doctrine of civil conspiracy, we are ready to consider three famous cases called the Trilogy, each passed on by the House of Lords, England's highest court. In 1889 [13] the first case arose. The twenty-four defendants made up one of the most powerful British cartels, or aggregates of monopolies.

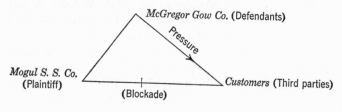

Figure 2

McGregor Gow Company and the other defendants used the secondary boycott as a means of denying to the Mogul Company a share of the customers' business. Each cartel member enjoyed a monopoly on at least one trade route running between England and the Far East. They had faced no serious competition until the Mogul Company, a newly organized firm with modern facilities, announced that it was prepared to carry passengers and freight between English ports and the Far East. The defendants desired no competition and laid plans to destroy the Mogul Company by economic warfare. No direct pressure was used against Mogul, but only because asking Mogul to abandon commercial activities on routes the defendants felt were exclusively theirs would have brought from Mogul a retort that the seas and the available trade were big enough for all, including Mogul. The defendants notified their customers that they were not to deal with Mogul, and that Mogul would in a short time be bankrupt. The customers were warned that any who chose to deal with Mogul would be forever

13. Mogul S. S. Co. v. McGregor Gow and Co., L.R. 23 Q.B.D. 598 (1899).

blacklisted after the destruction of Mogul. All shippers were offered rebates in consideration of remaining loyal customers of the defendants. We might assume that this new company, hoping to compete with the giant cartel, had something to offer which the monopolistic firms lacked. Perhaps its ships were more modern and faster, making quicker deliveries, a feature that shippers of perishables particularly would find invaluable. There must have been other advantages offered by this new company since it knew that the powerful combine made up of the defendants would not accept this new challenge passively.

The threat of boycotting and blacklisting discouraged customers from dealing with Mogul, and resulted in a successful blockade between the customers and Mogul. The ultimate objective of the secondary boycott in this case was to starve Mogul and put the firm out of business. The Mogul Company had a fleet of good ships, well manned and prepared to serve shippers, but it had no customers. The customers were not averse to dealing with Mogul, but they were fearful of the economic power held over them by the giant combine.

Mogul sued the combination, seeking damages for loss of profits and an injunction to restrain the defendants from using the boycott. What Mogul needed more than money damages was a lifting of the blockade brought about by the use of secondary pressure. Civil conspiracy was the theory on which Mogul initiated court action, pleading that the great damage inflicted on its company was compensable because the defendants had had no excuse or justification for dealing out that kind of economic punishment.

The defendants admitted that they were responsible for the damage done to Mogul, but they contended that their conduct was proper since it was motivated by self-interest. They sought only to discourage competition and thereby protect their monopolistic position in the shipping business. At this point, we should note that in this and the two other cases making up the Trilogy, violence, an important factor in the Tarleton decision, was completely absent.

The House of Lords, holding for the defendants, said that the damage which the combine inflicted on Mogul through the exertion of economic pressure (secondary boycott and blacklisting) was permissible so long as it was done for self-advancement and in pursuit of pecuniary profit and so long as violence, or threat of violence, was absent. The Court said in part:

The acts of the defendants which are complained of here were intentional and were also calculated, no doubt, to do the plaintiffs damage in their trade. But in order to see whether they were wrongful we have to discuss the question whether they were done without any just cause or excuse. Such just cause or excuse the defendants on their side assert to be found in their own positive right to carry on their own trade freely in the mode and manner that best suits them, and which they think best calculated to secure their own advantage.

The court then asked the following question, What, then are the limitations which the law imposes on a trader in the conduct of his business as between himself and other traders? It answers its question in the following words, His right to trade freely is a right which the law recognizes and encourages, but it is one which places him at no special disadvantage as compared with others. No man, whether trader or not, can, however, justify damaging another in his commercial business by fraud or misrepresentation. Intimidation, obstruction, and molestation are forbidden; so is the intentional procurement of a violation of individual rights, contractural or other, assuming always that there is no just cause for it. The intentional driving away of customers by show of violence; the obstruction of actors on the stage by preconcerted hissing; the disturbance of wild fowl in decoys by the firing of guns; the impeding or threatening servants or workmen; the inducing of persons under personal contracts to break their contracts; all are instances of such forbidden acts. But the defendants have been guilty of none of these acts. They have done nothing more against the plaintiffs than pursue to the bitter end a war of competition waged in the interest of their own trade. Competition, however, severe and egotistical, if unattended by circumstances of dishonesty, intimidation, molestation, or such other illegalities, gives rise to no cause of action at common law.

What is the direct purpose of the combination? The answer determines the legality or illegality of the act. Not all the injuries that may be inflicted on third parties render an act unlawful. When a combination acts in a nonviolent manner causing damage to another person, that damage is not actionable if the direct purpose of the combination is self-interest. Therefore the Mogul case teaches that when the principal object of a combine is to injure or damage third parties, it is a conspiracy, but when the damage is merely incidental to the protection of self-interest, the combination does not constitute a conspiracy.

The secondary boycott used here had devastating effect, giving business cartels a weapon against which no competitor had any defense at the time. Most would agree that this case illustrates business activity at its worst. The advantages of competition to business firms and to customers are completely subordinated to the pursuit of profit by the combination of monopolies. Some legal scholars have attributed the decline of the British Empire to the prominent position held by monopolies in England. Without risk of competition, private monopolies seem to have a tendency toward complacency, leading eventually after a period of vulnerability to deterioration when strongly challenged. This challenge came in the twentieth century not from domestic companies but from modern merchant fleets and industrial plants developed in rival European countries.

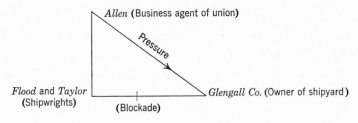

Figure 3

The second and third cases of the Trilogy concerned themselves with civil conspiracy and trade union activity.

The second case [14] concerned members of the boilermaker's union at the Glengall shipyard, who objected to the employment of shipwrights on ironwork. The union requested the employer to discharge two shipwrights, Flood and Taylor, who were known to have worked as ironworkers on a previous job and threatened to call a strike of forty boilermakers unless they were fired. The ironworkers were trying to end the practice of shipwrights performing the work of boilermakers. The employer complied with the request of the union and discharged the two shipwrights.

Flood and Taylor sued Allen, a union delegate, for maliciously and wrongfully intending to injure them and for inducing the employer to break its contract with the plaintiffs. The contract with Flood and Taylor was one at will and one which either the employer or the workers might terminate at any time. The jury returned a verdict in favor of Flood and Taylor and a judgment of £20 was entered for them. Allen appealed the verdict, and ultimately the appeal reached the House of Lords. The highest appellate court in the kingdom reversed the judgment, and Lord Herschell said:

> The company in declining to employ the plaintiffs was violating no contract—they were doing nothing wrongful in the eyes of the law. The course which they took was dictated by self-interest . . . . the object which the ironworkers had in view was that they should be freed from the presence of men with whom they disliked working, or to prevent what they deemed an unfair interference with their rights by men who did not belong to their craft doing the work in which they had been trained . . . . it was entirely within the right of the ironworkers to take any steps, not unlawful, to prevent any of the work which they regarded as legitimately theirs being intrusted to other hands. . . .

Lord Shand, citing the Mogul case and supporting the verdict for the defendants, said:

14. Allen v. Flood, [1898] A.C. 1.

I can find no reason for saying that a workman is not within his legal rights in resolving that he will decline to work in the same employment with certain other persons, and in intimating that resolution to his employers.

Lord Watson dissented from the majority opinion and pointed out:

In my opinion there was evidence that the defendant acted without legal excuse or justification in invading the right of the plaintiffs to exercise their calling without hindrance; and there was evidence to go to the jury that the defendant intimidated and coerced or maliciously induced the Glengall Co. not to enter into new contracts with the plaintiffs.

The victory labor secured in the Allen case was celebrated widely and it was the accepted view that labor organizations were on a par with commercial firms when it came to the use of economic power and pressures. Was the decision consistent with that rendered in the Mogul case? The answer rests upon the union's motivation. Were the ironworkers trying to bring about a destruction of Flood and Taylor's rights to work in this specific shipyard, or was the union ultimately and solely striving to control all the jobs in the shipyard by demanding that card holders only be hired? There is no question that the closed shop gives a union maximum security for job protection and that the closed shop may discriminate against and exclude the nonunion person from working. This case clearly displays the potent exclusiveness of the closed shop. In upholding the closed shop, the court justified it by the obvious strength it gives to the union. The damage suffered by the shipwrights, according to the court, was merely incidental and therefore not actionable.

The joy of labor, however, was short-lived when the decision in the last case of the Trilogy came down. This was Quinn v. Leathem.[15]

Quinn, a business agent, was treasurer of a butchers' union, one of the rules of which was that all members had the duty of assisting their fel-

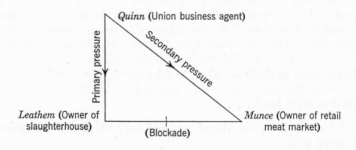

Figure 4

15. [1901] A.C. 495, 23.

low unionists to obtain employment in preference to nonunion men. Leathem was a slaughterer who employed nonunion workers. The union brought primary pressure against Leathem to employ only union workers. Leathem attended a union meeting at the invitation of one of the union officers, offered to pay all fines, debts, and demands against his men, and asked to have them admitted to the union. This offer was refused; the union insisted that Leathem fire his nonunion workers and promised that union replacements would be furnished him. When Leathem refused to comply with this request, the union brought secondary pressure against him upon one Munce, a retailer who employed union men exclusively; it got Munce to agree reluctantly to accept no more meat from Leathem. Munce had purchased meat from Leathem's slaughterhouse for more than 20 years; at the trial he testified that Leathem's product was of high quality and his prices were reasonable.

Leathem, basing his action on the doctrine of civil conspiracy, sued the union for damages resulting from the secondary boycott. He contended that Allen's actions were motivated by malice and sought to injure Leathem's business. The union, relying on the two earlier decisions, claimed that organizing the Leathem firm would substantially strengthen it and that any losses sustained by Leathem were merely incidental to the over-all objective. One of the questions submitted to the jury was, "Did the defendants wrongfully and maliciously induce the customers of the plaintiff named in the evidence to refuse to deal with the plaintiff?" Another question submitted was, "Did the defendants publish a blacklist with intent to injure the plaintiff in his business, and if so, did the publication so injure him?" The jury answered both questions in the affirmative and returned a verdict of £250, of which £50 was for damages on the cause of action relating to the blacklist and £200 was for damages on the other causes of action. The judge had told the jury

that it had to consider whether the intent and actions of the defendants went beyond the limits which would not be actionable, namely, securing or advancing their own interests or those of their trade by reasonable means, including lawful combinations, or whether their acts were intended and calculated to injure the plaintiff in his trade through a combination and with a common purpose to prevent the free action of his customers in dealing with him, and with the effect of actually injuring him, as distinguished from acts legitimately done to secure or advance their own interests.

The House of Lords, in affirming the decision of the lower courts, said:

Here we have no such defense as legitimate trade competition. The acts of the defendants were wrongful and malicious in the sense found by the jury—that is to say, they acted by conspiracy, not for any purpose of advancing their own interests as workmen, but for the sole purpose of injuring the plaintiff in his trade. The law prohibits such acts as unjustifiable and illegal; that by so acting the defendants were guilty of a clear violation of the rights of the plaintiff, with the result of causing serious injury to him, and that the case of Allen v. Flood, as a case of legitimate competition in the labor market is essentially different, and gives no ground for the defendant's argument.

. . . It is at all times a painful thing for any individual to be the object of the hatred, spite, and ill-will of any one who seeks to do him harm. But that is nothing compared to the danger and alarm created by a conspiracy formed by a number of unscrupulous enemies acting under an illegal compact, together and separately, as often as opportunity occurs regardless of law, and actuated by malevolence, to injure him and all who stand by him. Such a conspiracy is a powerful and dangerous engine, which in this case has, I think been employed by the defendants for the perpetration of organized and ruinous oppression.

The decision in the Quinn case seems to have been based on the finding that the acts of the butchers' union were inspired not by strengthening the union but rather by injuring Leathem's business. Did the union try to destroy the Leathem firm? What real gain could be made by the union through Leathem's destruction? In the Allen case just discussed, Flood and Taylor lost their jobs only because they lacked membership in the ironworkers union. The union members found their presence distasteful and made this known to the employer, who discharged the men at the request of the union.

The Quinn case would never have arisen had the union accepted the nonunion members. However, a question arises. Were Leathem's workers eligible for membership in the butchers' union? The case does not reveal this. However, it is traditional that membership in skilled trade unions is reserved for those who have undergone apprenticeship training under union supervision. Leathem's workers lacked this training and were therefore ineligible for membership. Had the union prevailed in this case it would have gained closed-shop conditions in the Leathem establishment,[16] and the economic strength of the union would have been measurably increased.

When the Quinn decision came down in 1901 the composition of the House of Lords had changed, and a more firm policy prevailed. Some might say that in both the Quinn and the Allen cases the conduct of the trade unionists was vindictive, but others might feel that the 1901

16. In 1924 an English court supported the validity of the closed-shop agreement when it held that such an agreement is not actionable conspiracy and that a worker who loses his job and cannot find another as a result of not being a union member cannot claim redress by way of injunction or damages against those operating the closed-shop agreement. This ruling was made in Reynolds v. Shipping Federation, 1 Ch. 28 (1924).

decision rested on the fact that there were several defendants, and not only one as in the Allen case. It was held in some later cases that industrial conduct which did not give rise to a cause of action against an individual might nevertheless be actionable conspiracy if originating in an agreement or combination between two or more persons.

The tort of conspiracy developed in the eighteenth century largely in connection with trade disputes; it was to some extent based on a common law belief that two are stronger and therefore more powerful than one.

It should be observed that as a result of the Leathem decision the courts applied principles to industrial relations which they had since the Mogul case disclaimed in matters of business competition and monopoly. This court attitude is well documented in a speech made in 1911 in the House of Commons by Sir Winston Churchill, when he said:

> The courts hold justly a high, and I think, unequalled prominence in the respect of the world in criminal cases, and in civil cases between man and man no doubt they deserve and command the respect and admiration of all classes of the community, but where class issues are involved, it is impossible to pretend that the courts command the same degree of general confidence.

In 1941 [17] the House of Lords in a fundamental decision extended the principles of the Mogul decision of 1892 to labor disputes. Thus the double standard of conduct came to an end. In the Crofter case it was made clear that courts would not intervene as long as the parties were engaged in a conflict of interest, and therefore the settlement of the conflict could be pursued through persuasion or economic pressure. The hairline distinction which the House of Lords made in the Trilogy and the confusion which followed it became academic after the 1941 ruling.

In 1901 [18] labor unions suffered a surprise defeat when, during a railway strike, pickets seriously damaged railroad property. An injunction was issued against the strikers, and an action for damages was instituted against the union rather than against the union members responsible for the damage suffered. The House of Lords ruled that union funds were liable for the wrongs committed by union members. Labor unions realized that this ruling could result in more than harassment. Union treasuries were now vulnerable whenever a strike was called and one or more pickets became disorderly and damaged an employer's property. The unions, seeking the relief of having their funds immunized from employer suits, intensified their political activity. During the election of 1906, labor was successful in electing twenty-nine candidates to Parlia-

17. Crofter Hand Woven Harris Tweed Co. v. Veitch, [1941] A.C. 425.
18. Taff Vale Ry. Co. v. Amalgamated Soc. of Ry. Servants, [1901] A.C. 426.

ment. They joined with a powerful group of liberals and were able to get the Trades Disputes Act of 1906 [19] enacted. This law truly represented a Bill of Rights for all English workers. The legality of labor unions was reiterated. The act provided for peaceful picketing and barred civil actions against unions for damages alleged to have resulted from acts committed by or on behalf of a trade union; the Taff Vale decision was nullified. One provision of the 1906 statute read that an

Act done by a person in contemplation or furtherance of a trade dispute shall not be actionable on the ground only that it induces some other person to break a contract of employment or that it is an interference with the trade, business or employment of some other person, or with the right of some other person to dispose of his capital or his labor as he wills.

This section barred suits against unions based on the common law principle that created liability on a person who, or a combination which, induces another person to break a valid contract. The "yellow-dog" contract, under which a worker agrees he will not join a union, was a natural outgrowth of this legal principle. Another important provision of this act legalized the use of the secondary boycott by labor unions.

The Trades Disputes Act of 1913 [20] permitted the use of union funds for the furtherance of political objectives, and affected chiefly the political rather than the industrial activities of unions.

In 1915 Parliament enacted the Munitions of War Act,[21] which required compulsory arbitration of labor disputes, and although it persisted during World War II, the law was revoked by the Industrial Dispute Order of 1958.[22]

After a 1926 general strike in England, the act of 1927 [23] outlawing this type of strike was passed. The 1927 act also barred the closed shop; this provision was repealed in 1946.[24]

This survey of labor law development in England began with complete governmental intolerance against the attempt of the single worker to improve his working conditions, and traced how this suppression later prevented the development of labor unions. Nineteenth-century statutes provided some relief and gave encouragement for the expression of the natural desire of men to improve themselves. The small improvement resulting from this favorable legislation was impeded somewhat by the rigid application of the common law principle of civil conspiracy. It was not until 1906 that labor attained its most complete legislative vic-

19. 6 Edw. 7, c. 47.
20. 2 & 3 Geo. 5, c. 30.
21. 5 & 6 Geo. 5, c. 54.
22. Stat. Inst. No. 1796.
23. 17 & 18 Geo. 5, c. 22.
24. 9 & 10 Geo. 6, c. 52.

tory, which gave unions a preferred status and legalized picketing and boycotts. Protection of union funds from certain types of civil suits was also afforded.

Although labor suffered some setbacks in 1915 and again in 1927, subsequent court decisions and legislative enactments restored unions to their position of freedom of action as long as the public interest was not imperiled by the exercise of this freedom.[25] In contrast with the United States, where statutory enactments have imposed strict limitations on unions and their activities, the English labor union today has been generously supplied with a freedom unparalleled in any other country. The rights and obligations of unions as well as those of employers have been legislatively defined, and conflict has been reduced to a minimum.

25. For an excellent summary of English labor laws, see Ginsburg, *Law and Opinion in England in the 20th Century*, (1956) Stevens Publication, British Information Service (304 G37).

PART TWO

PART TWO

CHAPTER TWO

Development of the Law of Labor in the United States

L ABOR law in the United States differs somewhat from that of England. The economic and social climate at the time of the Revolution was quite at variance with that existing in England. The mercantilist expansion policy and its consequent laissez-faire philosophy near the close of the seventeenth century in England had little if any effect on the position of labor in early eighteenth-century America. The colonies, struggling for survival and hoping for independence, could afford no luxuries such as international trade, world markets, and expensive navies. English industrialism before 1776 constituted a delicate mechanism, dependent on a meticulous coordination of all the factors of production. Her raw materials were borne over hostile seas from far-away lands, deposited in England, converted into finished goods, and in turn exported to the far corners of the world. In return, gold flowed into England. Labor played a highly important role in this well-integrated commercialism, but it was weighted down with historical impediments, some going back to the feudal period. Aristocratic industrialism dominated the English scene. The worker had been long the subject of unscrupulous exploitation, and it should surprise no one that the English harassed and degraded workers through the application of harsh common law decisions and statutory enactments.

In early American commercial history, labor never reached the abyss reached by the laboring classes of England, and this was despite our inheritance of English common law. The early Americans were not in the race for world commercial supremacy that was being carried on in England and on the continent.

American industrialism developed more slowly than the English. The competitive industrial wars raging throughout Europe during the seventeenth and eighteenth centuries necessitated a highly geared machine powered by a submissive working force; any attempt by labor to disturb this essential equilibrium was met with smashing instruments of the law.

Period of Antagonism

On gaining independence, the United States started on a road of great industrial development. It was only natural and expedient that we adopted the common law of England. During the latter part of the eighteenth century, and throughout most of the nineteenth century, the English doctrines of conspiracy and illegal restraint of trade were used quite effectively in retarding the development of American labor unions. The laissez-faire philosophy of economics harmonized well with the American industrial system, and this doctrine merged completely with our legal system. As in England, our early judges came principally from the propertied class, and their decisions generally favored members of their own group.

The first American experience with a labor problem originated in the Mayor's Court of Philadelphia in 1806. In this case a group of shoemakers was indicted; they were charged with criminal conspiracy. These workers had been charged with the following activities:

(1) Agreeing among themselves that they would work only in those shops where the employees were all members of the group or combine.

(2) Agreeing among themselves that they would not work for any wage below the wage scale established by the group.

Commonwealth v. Pullis [1]

RECORDER LEVY. This prosecution has been commenced, not from any private pique, or personal resentment, but solely with a view to promote the common good of the community; and to prevent in future the pernicious combinations of misguided men to effect purposes not only injurious to themselves, but mischievous to society. Yet infinite pains have been taken to represent this prosecution as founded in very improper motives. Not only in private conversation, and in public taverns, but even the press has been employed in the work of misrepresentations. . . .

Let it be well understood that the present action is not intended to introduce the doctrine that a man is not at liberty to fix any price whatso-

1. This case, known as the Case of the Philadelphia Cordwainers, is most easily accessible in Commons and Gilmore's *Documentary History of American Industiral Society*, Vol. 3 (1910), pp. 59–236.

ever upon his own labour; we disclaim the idea in the most unqualified terms; we declare that every man has a right to fix any price upon his commodities or his labour which he deems proper. We have no design to prevent him. We disclaim any such design. If any one of the defendants had thought proper to charge $100.00 for making a pair of boots, nobody would interfere if he could get his employer to give it, or could compel the payment. He would have a legal right to do so and our complaint is not of that kind.

Our position is that no man is at liberty to combine, conspire, confederate and unlawfully agree to regulate the whole body of workmen in the city. The defendants are not indicted for regulating their own individual wages, but for undertaking by a combination, to regulate the price of the labour of others as well as their own. . . .

When the testimony and arguments were completed, the Recorder, in charging the jury, made the following observations:

An attempt has been made to show that the spirit of the revolution and the principle of the common law, are opposite in this case. That the common law, if applied in this case, would operate an attack upon the rights of men. The inquiry on that point, was unnecessary and improper. Nothing more was required than to ascertain what the law is. The law is the permanent rule, it is the will of the whole community. After that is discovered, whatever may be its spirit or tendency, it must be executed, and the most imperious duty demands our submission to it. . . .

It is proper to consider, is such a combination consistent with the principles of our law, and injurious to the public welfare? The usual means by which the prices of work are regulated, are the demand for the article and the excellence of its fabric. Where the work is well done, and the demand is considerable, the prices will necessarily be high. Where the work is ill done, and the demand is inconsiderable, they will unquestionably be low. If there are many to consume, and few to work, the price of the article will be high; but if there are few to consume, and many to work, the article must be low. Much will depend too, upon these circumstances, whether the materials are plenty or scarce; the price of the commodity, will in consequence be higher or lower. These are the means by which prices are regulated in the natural course of things. To make an artificial regulation, is not to regard the excellence of the work or quality of the material, but to fix a positive and arbitrary price, governed by no standard, controlled by no impartial person, but dependent on the will of the few who are interested; this is the unnatural way of raising the price of goods or work. This is independent of the number of customers, or of the quality of the material, or of the number who are to do the work. It is an unnatural, artificial means of raising the price of work beyond its standard, and taking an undue advantage of the public. Is the rule of law bottomed upon such principles, as to permit or protect such conduct? Consider it on the footing of the general commerce of the city. Is there any man who can calculate (if this is tolerated) at what price he may safely contract to deliver articles, for which he may receive orders, if he is to be regulated by the journeymen in an arbitrary jump from one price to another? It renders it impossible for a man, making a contract for a large quantity of such goods, to know whether he shall lose or gain by it. If he makes a large contract for goods today, for delivery at three, six, or nine months, hence, can he calculate what the prices will be then, if the journeymen in the intermediate time, are permitted to meet and raise their prices, according to their caprice or pleasure? Can he fix the price of his commondity for a future day? It is impossible that any man can carry on commerce in this way. There cannot be a large contract entered into, but what the contractor will make at his peril. He may be ruined by the difference of prices made by the journeymen in the intermediate time. What then is the operation of this kind of conduct upon the commerce of the city? It exposes it to inconveniences, if not to ruin; therefore, it is against the public welfare. . . .

Consider these circumstances as they affect trade generally. Does this measure tend to make good workmen? No: it puts the botch incapable of doing justice to his work, on the level with the best tradesman. The master must give the same wages to each. Such a practice would take away all the excitement to excel in workmanship or industry. Consider the effect it would have upon the whole community. If the masters say they will not sell under certain prices, as the journeymen declare they will not work at certain wages, they, if persisted in, would put the whole body of the people into their power. Shoes and boots are articles of the first necessity. If they could stand out three or four weeks in winter, they might raise the price of boots to thirty, forty, or fifty dollars a pair, at least for some time, and until a competent supply could be got from other places. In every point of view, this measure is pregnant with public mischief and private injury, tends to demoralize the workmen, destroy the trade of the city, and leaves the pockets of the whole community to the discretion of the concerned. If these evils were unprovided for by the law now existing, it would be necessary that laws should be made to restrain them.

What has been the conduct of the defendants in this instance? They belong to an association, the object of which is that every person who follows the trade of a journeyman shoemaker must be a member of their body. The apprentice immediately upon becoming free, and the journeyman who comes here from distant places, are all considered members of this institution. If they do not join the body, a term of reproach is fixed upon them. The members of the body will not work with them, and they refuse to board or lodge with them. The consequence is, that every one is compelled to join the society. It is in evidence, that the defendants in this action all took a part in the last attempt to raise their wages; . . . Keimer was their secretary, and the others were employed in giving notice, and were of the tramping committee. If the purpose of the association is well understood, it will be found they leave no individual at liberty to join the society or reject it. They compel him to become a member. Is there any reason to suppose that the laws are not competent to redress an evil of this magnitude? The laws of this society are grievous to those not inclined to become members . . . They are injurious to the community, but they are not the laws of Pennsylvania. We live in a community where the people in their collective capacity give the first momentum, and their representatives pass laws on circumstances, and occasions, which require their interference, as they arise. . . .

It is in the volumes of the common law we are to seek for information in the far greater number, as well as the most important causes that come before our tribunals . . . Those who know it, know that it regulates with a sound discretion most of our concerns in civil and social life. Its rules are the result of the wisdom of ages. It says there may be cases in which what one man may do with(out) offence, many combined may not do with impunity. It distinguishes between the object so aimed at in different transactions. If the purpose to be obtained, be an object of individual interest, it may be fairly attempted by an individual. . . . Many are prohibited from combining for the attainment of it.

What is the case now before us? . . . A combination of workmen to raise their wages may be considered in a two-fold point of view; One is to benefit themselves . . . the other is to injure those who do not join their society. The rule of law condemns both. If the rule be clear, we are bound to conform to it even though we do not comprehend the principle upon which it is founded. We are not to reject it because we do not see the reason of it. It is enough, that it is the will of the majority. It is law because it is their will—if it is law, there may be good reasons for it though we cannot find them out. But the rule in this case is repugnant with sound sense and all the authorities are clear upon the subject. Hawkins, the greatest authority on the criminal law, has laid it down, that a combination to maintain one another, carrying a particular object, whether true or false, is criminal . . . the authority cited does not rest merely upon the reputation of that book. He gives you other authorities to which he refers. It is adopted by Blackstone, and laid down as the law by Lord Mansfield in 1793, that an act innocent in an individual, is rendered criminal by a confederacy to effect it. . . .

It is of no consequence whether the prosecutors are two or three, or whether the defendants are ten thousand; their numbers are not to prevent the execution of our laws . . . though we acknowledge it is the hard hand of labour that promises the wealth of a nation; though we acknowledge the usefulness of such a large body of tradesmen and agree they should have everything to which they are legally entitled; yet, we conceive they ought to ask nothing more. They should neither be the slaves nor the governors of the community. . . .

The sentiments of the court, not an individual of which is connected either with the masters or the journeymen, all stand independent of both parties, are unanimous. They have given you the rule as they have found it in the book and it is now for you to say whether the defendants are guilty or not. The rule they consider as fixed, they cannot change. It is now, therefore, left to you upon the law, and the evidence to find the verdict. If you can reconcile it to your consciences to find the defendants not guilty, you will do so; if not, the alternative that remains is a verdict of guilty.

VERDICT. We find the defendants guilty of a combination to raise their wages. . . . And the Court fined the defendants eight dollars each, with costs of the suit, and to stand committed till paid.

This decision is replete with references to English common law. One of the authorities relied upon by Judge Levy was Rex v. Eccles,[2] a decision rendered by Lord Mansfield in which he declared that a worker acting alone might charge whatever price he pleased for his services, but that when he combined with other workers seeking to establish a wage scale, i.e., a minimum wage, the combination constituted a conspiracy.

The conspiracy doctrine was based on a general acceptance that a combination of persons possesses a power to commit serious wrongs which individuals as such do not have. In the Pullis case the intrinsic evil was the combination, frowned on by the common law. The courts of that period assumed that all combinations sought ends which, left undisturbed, would unlawfully destroy the rights of others. Many years were to pass before courts would rule that there was nothing evil per se in labor combinations, and realizing that their objectives could be lawful as well as unlawful. Judge Levy was probably aware of the advantages which workers might gain through combination, yet he asserted clearly that the welfare of society was a paramount right. What Judge Levy really said in this case was this: A worker has a right to get a good price for his labor but he must get it solely on his own individual bargaining strength; at the moment he joins other workers who seek good prices for their labor, he and the other members of the combine become criminals. The fallaciousness of his reasoning ought to be obvious. If any act when done by a single individual is intrinsically good, its virtuous character ought to be unassailable when done together by two or five thousand persons. In our complex modern society it is well recognized that under special conditions the mass exercise of an act intrinsically good might have to be suspended when it could result in irreparable damage to a large part of a society. For example, a strike which would result in a complete shutdown of electric power in the city of New York could not be tolerated even where the workers individually have legitimate grievances and might properly quit their jobs. However, there is no evidence that these special conditions existed in 1806 when the Pullis case was decided.

As late as 1886, a New York court found a combination of workers objectionable. In this case,[3] the court said:

A combination of men is a very serious matter. No man can stand up against a combination; he may successfully defend himself against a single adversary, but when his foes are combined and numerous he must fall.

2. Leach C. C. 274 (1783).
3. 4 N.Y. Crim. 403 (1886).

There is no doubt that the courts regarded trade unions as a menace not only to nonunion workers but also to society generally. It was the accepted opinion that if men were permitted to agree among themselves not to work with persons who lacked membership, the impoverishment of the nonunion workers would result. When a labor combination forced up wages, the early courts felt that prices would naturally rise and the general public would suffer.

The English judicial attitude is again manifested in the Melvin case [4] decided in the state of New York. The decision is in line with that in the Pullis case. The court points out the dangers inherent in combinations and the damage which they might do to individuals and to the community. The indictment follows.

The first count states that the defendants, being workmen and journeymen in the art, mystery and manual occupation of cordwainers, on October 18, 1809, unlawfully, pernicously and deceitfully designing and intending to form and unite themselves into an unlawful club and combination, and to make and ordain unlawful by-laws, rules and orders among themselves, and thereby to govern themselves and other workmen in the said art, and unlawfully and unjustly to extort great sums of money by means thereof, on the day and year aforesaid, with force and arms, together with divers other workmen and journeymen in the same art, did unlawfully assemble and meet together, being so, did then and there, unjustly and corruptly conspire, combine, confederate and agree together, that none of them, after the said October 18th, would work for any master or person whatsoever, in the said art etc., who should employ any workman or journeyman, not being a member of said club or combination, after notice given to discharge such workman. . . .

THE CHARGE OF THE COURT. We observed there were two points of view in which the offense of conspiracy might be considered; the one where there existed a combination to do an act unlawful in itself, to the prejudice of other persons; the other where the act done or the object of it was not unlawful, but unlawful means were used to accomplish it. As to the first, there could be no doubt that a combination to do an unlawful act was a conspiracy. The second depended on the common principle that the goodness of the end would not justify improper means to obtain it. If, therefore, in the present case the defendants had confederated either to do an unlawful act to the injury of others, or to make use of unlawful means to obtain their ends, they would be liable to the charge of conspiracy. The Court did not mean to say, nor did the facts in the case require them to decide, whether an agreement not to work, except for certain wages, would amount to this offense without any unlawful means taken to enforce it. . . .

The injury produced by unlawful combinations might affect any person or number of persons, as in the present case the master workmen or the fellow journeymen of the defendants, or any other individuals. It appeared in evidence that the society of journeymen, of which the defendants were

4. People v. Melvin, 7 N.Y. Common Law Reports 153 (1809).

members, had established a constitution, or certain rules for its government, to which the defendants had assented, and which they had endeavored to enforce. These rules were made to operate on all the members of the Society, on others of their trade who were not members, and through them on the master workmen, and all were coerced to submit, or else the members of the Society which comprehended the best workmen in the City, were to stop the work of their employers. One of the regulations even required that every person of their trade whom they thought worthy of notice, should become a member of the Society, and of course become subject to its rules, and in case of neglect or refusal, it imposed fines on the person guilty of disobedience. When the Society determined on any measure, it found no difficulty in carrying it into execution. If its ordinary functions failed, it enforced obedience by decreeing what was called a strike against a particular shop that had transgressed, or a general turnout against all the shops in the City; terms which had been explained by the witnesses, and were sufficiently understood. These steps were generally decisive, and compelled submission to all concerned.

Whatever might be the motives of the defendants, or their object, the means thus employed were arbitrary and unlawful, and their having been directed against several individuals in the present case, it was brought in the opinion of the court, within one of the descriptions of the offense which has been given.

The jury retired and shortly after returned a verdict against the defendants.

The sentence was then passed by His Honor the Mayor, who observed to the defendants that the novelty of the case, and the general conduct of their body, composed of members useful in the community, inclined the court to believe that they had erred from a mistake of the law and from supposing that they had rights upon which to found their proceedings. . . .

The defendants were fined each $1, with costs of the suit.[5]

In this case the court was quite sympathetic with the desire of the workers to improve their wages and felt that they might properly have sought this end individually, but when they combined for the purpose of attaining this lawful end the means were disapproved. Another point of interest in this case is the attempt on the part of the workers to organize closed shops so as to establish a uniform wage scale. The court held that the closed shop was an unlawful means. Under the closed shop only union members may be hired by an employer. In other words, union membership is a prerequisite of employment. Even today the validity of the closed shop has not been firmly settled. Although present federal law proscribes the closed shop, many states, like New York, permit it.

5. See Nelles, 32 *Colum. L. Rev.* 1128, 1166 (1932) for a series of criminal conspiracy cases decided between 1806 and 1845.

Period of Benign Toleration

Commonwealth v. Hunt

The archaic doctrine of criminal conspiracy demonstrated in the cases discussed up to this point was overthrown in the case of Commonwealth v. Hunt.[6] A new era in the development of labor law commences with this decision. The facts in this case are no different from those in the previous cases. Seven journeymen members of the Boston Bootmakers' Society were indicted, tried, and found guilty of criminal conspiracy. The defendants appealed and Chief Justice Shaw of the Massachusetts Supreme Court delivered his historic decision. Before considering Shaw's opinion, let us become acquainted with the salient facts. Jeremiah Horne was fined by the society for accepting wages below the scale it had established. When Horne refused to pay the fine, the society demanded that his employer, one Isaac Wait, discharge Horne. After Horne was fired, he complained to the district attorney, who was successful in getting a five-count indictment voted by the grand jury against the society. One of the counts set forth

. . . that the defendants and other formed themselves into a society, and agreed not to work for any person who should employ any journeyman or other person, not a member of such society, after notice given him to discharge such workman.

In setting aside the convictions and dismissing the indictment, Justice Shaw said:

. . . the manifest intent of the association is to induce all those engaged in the same occupation to become members of it. Such a purpose is not unlawful. It would give them a power which might be exerted for useful and honorable purposes, or for dangerous and pernicious ones. If the latter were the real and actual object, and susceptible of proof, it should have been specially charged. Such an association might be used to afford each other assistance in times of poverty, sickness and distress; or to raise their intellectual, moral and social condition; or to make improvement in their art; or for other proper purposes. Or the association might be designed for purposes of oppression and injustice. But in order to charge all those who become members of an association with the guilt of a criminal conspiracy, it must be averred and proved that the actual if not the avowed object of the association was criminal. . . . Nor can we perceive that the objects of this association, whatever they may have been, were to be attained by criminal means. The means which they proposed to employ, as averred in

6. 45 Mass. 111 (1842).

this count, and which, as we are now to presume, were established by the proof, were that they would not work for a person, who, after due notice, should employ a journeyman not a member of their society. Supposing the object of the association to be laudable and lawful, or at least not unlawful, are these means criminal? The case supposes that these persons are not bound by contract, but are free to work for whom they please, or not to work, if they so prefer. In this state of things we cannot perceive that it is criminal for men to agree together to exercise their own acknowledged rights, in such manner as best to subserve their own interests. One way to test this is to consider the effect of such an agreement, where the object of the association is acknowledged on all hands to be a laudable one. Suppose a class of workmen, impressed with the manifold evils of intemperance, should agree with each other not to work in a shop in which ardent spirit was furnished, or not to work in a shop with any one who used it, or not to work for an employer, who should, after notice, employ a journeyman who habitually used it. The consequences might be the same. A workman, who should still persist in the use of ardent spirit, would find it more difficult to get employment; a master employing such a one, might, at times, experience inconvenience in his work, in losing the services of a skillful but intemperate workman. Still it seems to us, that as the object would be lawful, and the means not unlawful, such agreement could not be pronounced a criminal conspiracy.

Shaw suggested that if the defendants had been under contract with their employer to work for a stated period, the breach of which would have been actionable, then a collective walkout during such contract period would have represented the use of unlawful means. On this point, he said:

If a large number of men, engaged for a certain time, should combine together to violate their contract, and quit their employment together, it would present a very different question. Suppose a farmer, employing a large number of men, engaged for the year, at fair monthly wages, and suppose that just at the moment that his crops were ready to harvest, they should all combine to quit his service, unless he would advance their wages, at a time when other laborers could not be obtained. It would surely be a conspiracy to do an unlawful act though of such a character, that if done by an individual, it would lay the foundation of a civil action only, and not of a criminal prosecution. It would be a case very different from that stated in this court.

The substance of the second count charged that the defendants had conspired not to work for any master who employed a nonmember of the society, or anyone who broke society rules, unless such worker paid the society a stipulated fine: "and that by means of said conspiracy they did compel one Isaac B. Wait, a master cordwainer, to turn out of his employ one Jeremiah Horne, a journeyman bootmaker."

Shaw could see nothing serious in this charge, declaring,

It sets forth no illegal or criminal purpose . . . nor any illegal or criminal means. . . . It was an agreement, as to the manner in which they would exercise an acknowledged right to contract with others for their labor. It does not aver a conspiracy or even an intention to raise their wages. . . .

Then he continued his remarks:

But further; if this is to be considered as a substantive charge, it would depend altogether upon the force of the word "compel," which may be used in a sense of coercion, or duress, by force or fraud. It would, therefore, depend upon the context and the connexion with other words, to determine the sense in which it was used in the indictment. If, for instance, the indictment had averred a conspiracy, by the defendants, to compel Wait to turn Horne out of his employment, and to accomplish that object by the use of force or fraud, it would have been a very different case; especially if it might be fairly construed, as perhaps, in that case it might have been, that Wait was under obligation, by contract, for an unexpired term of time, to employ and pay Horne. . . . But whatever might be the force of the word "compel," unexplained by its connexion, it is disarmed and rendered harmless by the precise statement of the means, by which such compulsion was to be effected. It was the agreement not to work for him, by which they compelled Wait to decline employing Horne longer. On both of these grounds, we are of opinion that the statement made in this second count, that the unlawful agreement was carried into execution makes no essential difference between this and the first count.

The third count, according to Shaw, alleged "A wicked and unlawful intent to impoverish one Jeremiah Horne, and hinder him from following his trade as a bootmaker." But Shaw thought this count was deficient in not having stated or averred either illegal means or objective. He pointed out:

. . . that associations may be entered into, the object of which is to adopt measures that may have a tendency to impoverish another, that is, to diminish his gains and profits, and yet so far from being criminal or unlawful, the object may be highly meritorious and public spirited. The legality of such an association will therefore depend upon the means to be used for its accomplishment. If it is to be carried into effect by fair or honorable and lawful means, it is, to say the least, innocent; if by falsehood or force, it may be stamped with the character of conspiracy.

Shaw considered the following two counts of the indictment repetitious, and adequately covered by his preceding remarks. He then noted that the defendants requested instructions to the jury concerning the inadequacy of the indictment and the trial court's refusal to give it. He then summarized the trial court statement to the jury and concluded as follows:

In this opinion of the learned judge, this court, for the reasons stated, cannot concur. Whatever illegal purpose can be found in the constitution of the Bootmakers' Society, it not being clearly set forth in the indictment, cannot be relied upon to support this conviction. So if any facts were disclosed at the trial, which, if properly averred, would have given a different character to the indictment, they do not appear in the bill of exceptions, nor could they, after verdict, aid the indictment. But looking solely at the material allegations, and confining ourselves to facts so averred as to be capable of being traversed and put in issue, we cannot perceive that it charges a criminal conspiracy punishable by law. The exceptions must, therefore, be sustained, and the judgment arrested.

The Hunt case became the first authority to support the right of workers to combine into associations, now called trade unions; to engage in peaceful strikes, and to press for the closed shop. At this period, the Massachusetts Supreme Court was regarded by legal scholars and judges in all the existing states as a leader in formulating American common law. Excepting New Jersey, all states followed the ruling in the Hunt case.

No one can be certain of the reasons that influenced Judge Shaw in refusing to apply the doctrine of criminal conspiracy in this case. We might, however, speculate on them by examining the language appearing in his opinion and reasonably arrive at certain conclusions. Shaw said that the society could be used to help the poor and sick members and to help raise their moral and social conditions. These early worker associations were weak, unaggressive, and financially poor. Employer hostility and the doctrine of criminal conspiracy forced most unions to conduct their affairs in secret. Most unions operated along the lines of fraternal organizations, and it was therefore quite common for them to help rescue a brother member from the vices of alcoholism or gambling. At other times they financed funerals of deceased members and contributed financial aid to the widows and children of the deceased. Many similar social services were provided. Justice Shaw was probably aware of these socially desirable services initiated by the early unions. Organized charities and government subsidies to the poor and unemployed were nonexistent. There appear good grounds for attributing a social awareness to this courageous judge who agreed that workers might combine for the purpose of combating oppression and injustice. Shaw had seen for himself the pitiful economic and social conditions prevailing in workers' quarters. It therefore appears reasonable to conclude that Shaw not only was cognizant of the distressing worker problems but was also realistic enough to concede workers the right to economic justice. Understanding the problem was not enough; means had to be devised to resolve it. Shaw noted clearly that the trade union institution was the only means through which this justice could be obtained. We can only say that Shaw was the first to legitimatize this institution.

No serious legal obstacles developed from 1842, when the Hunt decision came down, until the 1860's, when some of the states, notably Connecticut, Illinois, and Minnesota, passed legislation outlawing the closed shop.

The Injunction

The Railway Strike of 1877[7] involved for the first time the use of the injunction as a legal weapon to curb labor activity. The injunction, another English device appropriated by American courts, broke the back of this strike when the workers were enjoined from striking against a court-appointed receiver instructed to operate a railroad. The defiant workers were punished by the federal court for their contempt. In the Pullman strike of 1894, Eugene Debs, leader of the American Railway Union, and his followers were restrained from continuing the strike. When he refused to obey the mandate of the court Debs was sentenced to jail for contempt; the decision was sustained by the U.S. Supreme Court.[8]

An injunction[9] is a decree issued by an equity court commanding one or more persons to refrain from committing an act or, in the affirmative, requiring them to perform a specific act. Originally, the injunction was designed purposely for the English king who alone had the right to forbid the commission of an act rather than wait for damage to be done and later sue at law for money damages. Injunctive relief is preventive and may be sought only when no adequate law remedy is available.

The Just Cause Doctrine

Until American employers learned in the 1880's the potency and speed with which the injunction could be used to curb labor union activity, the doctrine of civil conspiracy, later modified by judicial dicta to become the doctrine of just cause, became the basis for some interesting decisions. There is a vast difference between criminal and civil conspiracy. At common law, the existence of criminal conspiracy would be established without proof of any act to further its object. In civil conspiracy on the other hand, damage is the gist of the offense; the damage must be intentional and without justification. In modern labor law, if a strike seeks a lawful objective and the means used are legal, no civil liability is incurred by the workers or their union, even if total eco-

7. King v. Ohio and Miss. R.R., 14 Fed. Cas. 539 (1877).
8. *In re* Debs, 158 U.S. 564 (1895).
9. For a comprehensive discussion of the labor injunction, see F. Frankfurter and N. Greene, *The Labor Injunction,* (1930) The Macmillan Co., New York.

nomic destruction of the owner's business results. Ruin in such case is damnum abseque injuria [10] (the damage is present but the unlawful object is absent).

No labor cases dealing with the doctrine of just cause have gone to the U.S. Supreme Court. However, state decisions do exist. State courts applied specific tests to determine the legality or illegality of labor activities. Courts also took cognizance of the motive, intent, and objectives of labor unions in passing on the legality of their actions. Sometimes the courts spoke about malice, even though admitting that its presence or absence was difficult to determine. It should not surprise us that judges interpreted the doctrine of just cause in the light of their environment, their attitudes on labor unions, and their conception of justice. One writer [11] concludes that courts adopted a double standard of conduct; one for unions and one for business. For example, the boycott is not and never has been a tool exclusive to labor unions. Business firms have used the boycott effectively, and courts have frequently justified its use, as in the Mogul case.[12] At other times, the boycott has been considered an illegal means when used by labor unions.[13]

The doctrine of just cause was first developed in Vegelahn v. Guntner,[14] and is simply stated in Justice Oliver Wendell Holmes' dissent:

> Whatever may be the law in the case of a single defendant, Rice v. Albee, 164 Mass. 88, that when a plaintiff proves that several persons have combined and conspired to injure his business, and have done acts producing that effect, he shows temporal damage and a cause of action, unless the facts disclose, or the defendants prove some ground of excuse or justification. . . . in numberless instances the law warrants the intentional infliction of temporal damage because it regards it as justified.

In his opinion, Holmes clearly observed that labor unions were not treated equally and fairly with business combinations before the law, when he said:

> One of the eternal conflicts out of which life is made up is that between the effort of every man to get the most he can for his services and that of society, disguised under the name of capital, to get his services for the least possible return. Combination on the one side is patent and powerful. Combination on the other is the necessary and desirable counterpart, if the battle is to be carried on in a fair and equal way.

10. See Schuster v. I.A.M., 293 Ill. App. 177 (1937).
11. C. O. Gregory, *Labor and the Law*, (1946) W. W. Norton and Co., New York.
12. See *supra*. For a discussion of business boycotts not involving labor unions, see Master Builders' Ass'n v. Domascio, 16 Colo. App. 25 (1901); Jackson v. Standfield, 137 Ind. 592 (1894); Schulter v. Bavarian Brew. Co., 96 Ky. 224 (1894); Bowen v. Matheson, 96 Mass. 499 (14 Allen 499) (1867).
13. Leathem v. Quinn, *supra*; Loewe v. Lawler, 208 U.S. 274 (1908); Buck's Stove and Range Co., 221 U.S. 418 (1911).
14. 167 Mass. 92 (1896).

In the just cause theory, there are involved a primary and a secondary motive. Let us assume a legal end, i.e., to increase wages to better themselves. With this end a group of workers peacefully strikes. To attain such an end, the workers engage in picketing. The picketing is intended to injure the employer; but is the injury to the employer the primary motive or reason for it? The answer would appear to be no, for the workers picket primarily to attain their end and secondarily to injure the employer economically and thereby force him to terms. On this basis the workers are seemingly justified in picketing. Yet in a series of cases [15] state courts condemned labor activity on the ground that the primary motivation for labor pressure of a nonviolent type was not to seek a lawful end, but rather to inflict damage on the employer or a third person. The courts again turned to the question of malice, a subjective thing, which in most cases is not determinable. Today it is generally accepted that the judges whose opinions then prevailed were out of sympathy with unions and their objectives and devised vague tests to narrow labor activities until impotency might result. This judgment seems to be confirmed by Justice Holmes when he wrote:

> The ground for decision really comes down to the proposition of policy of rather a delicate nature concerning the merit of the particular benefit to themselves intended by the defendants and suggest doubt whether judges with different economic sympathies might not decide a case differently when brought face to face with the same issue.[16]

A natural outgrowth of the civil conspiracy doctrine and the modified just cause theory was the doctrine of conspiracy in restraint of trade. The early conception of monopoly was a grant of an exclusive right from the crown. In the modern sense, monopoly denotes a combination whose tendency is to suppress competition with resulting harm to the general public. At common law the individual, and the public collectively, had a right to require that business be kept free from unreasonable restraints. In other words, free access to the market was theoretically assured at all times for all persons; merchant, worker, and consumer alike. Contracts which restrained trade were held to be unenforcible at common law. Later a statutory enactment [17] prescribed both criminal and civil penalties against those who restrained trade.

After examining the common law cases, we can say that American courts when dealing with the economic pressures used by labor organizations, applied the following principles of law:

(1) The intentional infliction of damage on another is not actionable, unless inflicted maliciously or without justification.

15. Carew v. Rutherford, 106 Mass. 1 (1870); Curran v. Galen, 152 N.Y. 33 (1897); Plant v. Woods, 176 Mass. 492 (1900).
16. 8 *Harv. L. Rev.* 114 (1894).
17. Act of July 2, 1890 (Sherman Act).

(2) An act which is permissible when done by an individual may be actionable when done in concert with other individuals.

(3) When a third party induces the one party to breach an existing valid contract, such interference is actionable.[18]

(4) If the object sought, or the means used, is improper, any concerted action that results in damage is actionable.

(5) Concerted action resulting in an unreasonable restrain of trade is illegal.

In order to adhere to a chronological order in the presentation of labor law development, we shall next consider the Sherman Act of 1890 and its application to various types of labor union pressures. Because of this act many celebrated labor law cases developed, which require our attention.

18. The contract interference doctrine is discussed in Chapter 4.

CHAPTER THREE

Antitrust Laws and Labor from 1890 to 1932

DURING the latter part of the nineteenth century the rapid growth of industrialism and particularly the great popularity of the corporate form of business venture resulted in small groups of men possessing enormous economic power. Monopolistic interference and its conflict with the developing philosophy of reasonable opportunity for business competition caused considerable agitation for installing curbs on unscrupulous economic warfare. Big business was concerned largely with collective elimination of uncooperative competitors and wherever possible purchased competing firms outright. The ultimate objective was to obtain strict control over the production of commodities and control over the prices charged the public for them.

Public opinion mandated Congress to stop these flagrant corporate abuses, which, if allowed to continue unchecked, might have destroyed all competitive initiative and brought into being a state controlled by a small, select group of monopolistic firms.

The Sherman Act of 1890

It was in this atmosphere that the Sherman Act [1] was introduced in the Senate in 1890. Much of the debate concerning the proposed law centered on one issue: whether or not labor organizations came within the clause, "combinations in restraint of trade." One authority [2] seems to be of the opinion that the intent of the Senate was to exclude labor from the proscriptions of the act. Historical accounts of the Senate de-

1. Act of July 2, 1890.
2. E. Berman, *Labor and the Sherman Act*, (1930) Harper and Brothers, New York.

bate indicated that attempts were made to exclude labor unions from the act and that amendments to carry out this intent were offered. An examination of what transpired during these Senate discussions appears to support the theory that the legislators intended to exempt labor unions from the restrictions placed upon "combinations." However, when finally approved by Congress, the proposed amendments to the statute were omitted. The act provides:

SECTION 1. Every contract, combination in the form of trust or otherwise, or conspiracy, in restraint of trade or commerce among the several states, or with foreign nations, is hereby declared to be illegal. Every person who shall make any such contract or engage in any such combination or conspiracy, shall be deemed guilty of a misdemeanor, and, on conviction thereof, shall be punished by fine not exceeding five thousand dollars, or by imprisonment not exceeding one year, or by both said punishments, in the discretion of the court.

SECTION 2. Every person who shall monopolize, or attempt to monopolize, or combine or conspire with any other person or persons, to monopolize any part of the trade or commerce among the several states, or with foreign nations, shall be deemed guilty of a misdemeanor, and, on conviction thereof, shall be punished by fine not exceeding five thousand dollars, or by imprisonment not exceeding one year, or by both said punishments, in the discretion of the court.

SECTION 4. The several circuit courts of the U.S. are hearby invested with jurisdiction to prevent and restrain violations of this Act; and it shall be the duty of the several district attorneys of the U.S., in their respective districts, under the direction of the Attorney General, to institute proceedings in equity to prevent and restrain such violations. Such proceedings may be by way of petition setting forth the case and praying that such violation shall be enjoined or otherwise prohibited. When the parties complained of shall have been duly notified of such petition the court shall proceed, as soon as may be, to the hearing and determination of the case; and pending such petition and before final decree, the court may at any time make such temporary restraining order or prohibition as shall be deemed just in the premises.

SECTION 7. Any person who shall be injured in his business or property by any other person or corporation by reason of anything forbidden or declared to be unlawful by this Act, may sue therefore in any circuit court of the U.S. in the district in which the defendant resides or is found, without respect to the amount in controversy, and shall recover three fold the damages by him sustained, and the costs of the suit, including a reasonable attorney's fee.

Whether labor union activity came within the purview of the Sherman Act was squarely raised for the first time in the case of United States v. Workingmen's Amalgamated Council.[3] In this case a combination of labor unions called a large-scale strike in New Orleans. In

3. 57 Fed. 85 (1893).

order to exert the greatest amount of economic pressure against the employer involved the unions organized boycotts throughout Louisiana to discourage entrance into the state of nonunion materials. The United States government filed a bill under Section 4 of the Sherman Act averring the existence of a "gigantic and widespread combination of members of a multitude of separate organizations for the purpose of restraining the commerce among the several States and with foreign countries." The labor unions set up the defense that the Sherman Act was not applicable to combinations of laborers. The district court rejected the defense, and in granting the injunction, said:

Congressional debates show that the statute had its origin in the evils of massed capital; but, when Congress came to formulating the prohibition, which is the yardstick for measuring the complainant's right to the injunction, it expressed it in these words: every contract or combination in the form of trust, or otherwise in restraint of trade or commerce among the several States or with foreign nations, is hereby declared to be illegal. The subject had so broadened in the minds of the legislators that the course of the evil was not regarded as material and the evil in its entirety is dealt with. They made the interdiction include combinations of labor, as well as of capital; in fact, all combinations in restraint of commerce, without reference to the character of the persons who entered into them. . . . It is the successful effort of the combination of the defendant to intimidate and overawe others who were at work in conducting or carrying on the commerce of the country, in which the court finds their error and their violation of the statute. One of the intended results of their combined action was the forced stagnation of all commerce which flowed through New Orleans. This intent and combined action are none the less unlawful because they included in their scope the paralysis of all other business within the City as well.

Other lower federal courts followed this decision, yet it was not until 1908 that the U.S. Supreme Court entertained for the first time a case in which this issue was presented. This was the celebrated case of Loewe v. Lawlor,[4] better known as the Danbury Hatters' case.

The Danbury Hatters' Case

The Loewe Company was nonunionized and paid wages far below the union shops, which gave the company a decided advantage in the hat market. The union attempted to organize the company, and when

4. 235 U.S. 522 (1915). In 1908 the Supreme Court heard the first case of Loewe v. Lawler, 208 U.S. 274, after the district court had ruled that unions did not come under the Sherman Act. Upon appeal, the U.S. Court of Appeals certified the following question to the Supreme Court: "Upon this state of facts can plaintiff maintain an action against defendants under Section 7 of the Anti-Trust Act of July 2, 1890?" The U.S. Supreme Court answered the question affirmatively and remanded the case for trial.

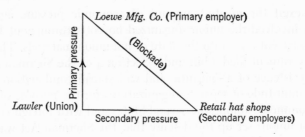

Figure 5

the conference method did not succeed, it used the strike for this purpose. This primary strike was ineffective. The union then adopted secondary pressure against retail customers of Loewe, threatening these customers with strike action if they continued to buy for retail distribution the hats manufactured by Loewe. The union also placed the name of the company on a blacklist requesting friends of the union and the general public to refrain from purchasing Loewe hats. The use of the secondary boycott and the blacklist resulted in the loss of $80,000 to the Loewe Company.

Loewe sued the union and its local membership, which numbered more than two hundred, charging them with a violation of Section 1 of the Sherman Act. Under Section 7 of the act, the company sought treble damages by reason of the illegal restraint of commerce charged against the union.

The company was successful in getting a substantial money judgment against the union. On appeal, the case reached the U.S. Supreme Court, which, speaking through Mr. Justice Holmes, said:

This is an action under the act of July 2, 1890, c. 647, sec. 7, 26 Stat. 209,210, 15 U.S.C.A. sec. 15, note, for a combination and conspiracy in restraint of commerce among the States, specifically directed against the plaintiffs (defendants in error), among others, and effectively carried out with the infliction of great damage. The declaration was held good on demurrer in Loewe v. Lawlor, 208 U.S. 274, 28 S. Ct. 301, 52 L. Ed. 488, 13 Ann. Cas. 815, where it will be found set forth at length. The substance of the charge is that the plaintiffs were hat manufacturers who employed non-union labor; that the defendants were members of the United Hatters of North America and also of the American Federation of Labor; that in furtherance of a general scheme to unionize the labor employed by manufacturers of fur hats (a purpose previously made effective against all but a few manufacturers), the defendants and other members of the United Hatters caused the American Federation of Labor to declare a boycott against the plaintiffs and against all hats sold by the plaintiffs to dealers in other States and against dealers who should deal in them; and that they carried out their plan with such success that they have restrained or destroyed the plaintiff's commerce with other States. The case now has been tried, the plaintiffs have got a verdict and the judgment of the District Court has been affirmed by the Circuit Court of Appeals, 209 F. 721, 126 CCA 445.

The grounds for discussion under the statute that were not cut away by the decision upon the demurrer have been narrowed still further since the trial by the case of Eastern States Retail Lumber Dealers' Ass'n. v. U.S., 234 U.S. 600, 34 S. Ct. 951, 58 L. Ed. 1490, L.R.A. 1915A, 788. Whatever may be the law otherwise, that case establishes that, irrespective of compulsion or even agreement to observe its intimation, the circulation of a list of "unfair dealers," manifestly intended to put the ban upon those whose names appear therein among an important body of possible customers combined with a view to joint action and in anticipation of such reports, is within the prohibitions of the Sherman Act if it is intended to restrain and restrains commerce among the States.

It requires more than the blindness of justice not to see that many branches of the United Hatters and the Federation of Labor, to both of which the defendants belonged, in pursuance of a plan emanating from headquarters made use of such lists, and of the primary and secondary boycott in their effort to subdue the plaintiffs to their demands. The union label was used and a strike of the plaintiffs' employees was ordered and carried out to the same end, and the purpose to break up the plaintiffs' commerce affected the quality of the acts. Loewe v. Lawlor, 208 U.S. 274, 299, 28 S. Ct. 301, 52 L. Ed. 488, 13 Ann. Cas. 815. We agree with the Circuit Court of Appeals that a combination and conspiracy forbidden by the statute were proved, and that the question is narrowed to the responsibility of the defendant for what was done by the sanction and procurement of the societies above named.

The court in substance instructed the jury that if these members paid their dues and continued to delegate authority to their officers unlawfully to interfere with the plaintiffs' interstate commerce in such circumstances that they knew or ought to have known, and such officers were warranted in the belief that they were acting in the matter within their delegated authority, then such members were jointly liable, and no others. It seems to us that this instruction sufficiently guarded the defendants' rights, and that the defendants got all that they were entitled to ask in not being held chargeable with knowledge as matter of law. It is a tax on credulity to ask anyone to believe that members of labor unions at that time did not know that the primary and secondary boycott and the use of the "We don't patronize" or "Unfair" list were means expected to be employed in the effort to unionize shops. Very possibly they were thought to be lawful. See Gompers v. United States, 233 U.S. 604, 34 S. Ct. 693, 58 L. Ed. 1115. By the Constitution of the United Hatters the directors are to use "all the means in their power" to bring shops "not under our jurisdiction" "into the trade." The by-laws provide a separate fund to be kept for strikes, lockouts, and agitation for the union label. Members are forbidden to sell non-union hats. The Federation of Labor with which the Hatters were affiliated had organization of labor for one of its objects, helped affiliated unions in trade disputes, and to that end, before the present trouble, had provided in its constitution for prosecuting and had prosecuted many what it called legal boycotts. Their conduct in this and former cases was made public especially among the members in every possible way. If the words of the documents on their face and without explanation did not authorize what was done, the evidence of what was done publicly and habitually showed their meaning, and how they were interpreted. The jury could not but find that by the usage of the unions the acts complained of were authorized, and authorized without regard to their interference with commerce among the States. We think it unnecessary to repeat the evidence of the publicity of this particular struggle in the common newspapers, and union prints, evidence that made it almost inconceivable that the defendants, all living in the neighborhood of the plaintiffs did not know what was done in the specific case. If they did not know that, they were bound to know the constitution of their societies, and at least well might be found to have known how the words of those constitutions had been construed in the act.

It is suggested that injustice was done by the judge speaking of "proof" that in carrying out the object of the associations unlawful means had been used with their approval. The judge cautioned the jury with special care not to take their view of what had been proved from him, going even farther than he need have gone. Graham v. United States, 231 U.S. 474, 480, 34 S. Ct. 148, 58 L. Ed. 319. But the context showed plainly that proof was used here in a popular way for evidence and must have been understood in that sense.

Damages accruing since the action began were allowed, but only such as were the consequence of acts done before and constituting part of the cause of action declared on. This was correct. New York, Lake Erie & Western R.R. v. Estill, 147 U.S. 591, 615, 616, 13 S. Ct. 444, 37 L. Ed. 292. We shall not discuss the objections to evidence separately and in detail as we find no error requiring it. The introduction of newspapers, etc., was proper in large part to show publicity in places and directions where the facts were likely to be brought home to the defendants, and also to prove an intended and detrimental consequence of the principal acts, not to speak of other grounds. The reason given by customers for ceasing to deal with sellers of the Loewe hats, including letters from dealers to Loewe & Co., were admissible. 3 Wigmore, Evidence, sec. 1729 (2). We need not repeat or add to what was said by the Circuit Court of Appeals with regard to evidence of the payment of dues after this suit was begun. And in short neither the argument nor the perusal of the voluminous brief for the plaintiffs in error shows that they suffered any injustice, or that there was any error requiring the judgment to be reversed.

The decision left no doubt that labor activities were subject to the Sherman Act, and the Supreme Court held further that the secondary boycott and the blacklisting constituted unlawful means which were used in this case to restrain commerce.[5]

5. "This was the final litigation, but it was not until two years later that a settlement was made with the Loewe Co. In the meantime, the hatters' union and the

The Loewe case struck a serious blow at labor union activity. It resulted in complete abandonment of the "unfair" list [6] of employers by the AFL. The decision deprived unions of their most potent weapon, the secondary boycott. Union treasuries were now subject to damage suits and union members were proper game under law suits. Every threat of civil action against a labor union had to result in a cautious appraisal of strike action and it was inevitable that union timidity would result. The Sherman Act, which was designed primarily to prevent the concentration of economic power with its tendency to stifle competition in the market place, became now the greatest threat to organized labor's goal of bringing economic justice to all laboring men.

The Clayton Act of 1914

Organized labor marshalled all its energy to remove itself from the restraints of the Sherman Act. Samuel Gompers, President of the AFL, after years of intensive lobbying, succeeded in 1914 in getting Congress to pass the Clayton Act,[7] described by him as labor's Magna Charta. Labor leaders were assured that the language of the act was such as to prevent another Danbury Hatters' case from developing. Complete dis-

American Federation of Labor sought by voluntary contributions to raise the funds to pay the judgment. A 'hatters' day' was staged throughout the country, all union members being asked to contribute their wages for the day to the hatters. Through these appeals the major portion of the amount was collected, and in the summer of 1917 the case was settled for a total of something over $234,000, of which amount the American Federation of Labor furnished $216,000." E. E. Witte, *The Government and Labor Disputes*, (1932) McGraw-Hill Book Co., New York, p. 135.

"The case might well be called a cause célèbre. It was fourteen years in the courts. It was twice tried by a jury, four times was it before the United States Circuit Court of Appeals on appeal, and went three times to the United States Supreme Court. . . . It resulted in the complete abandonment of the unfair list by the American Federation of Labor. It demonstrated the fact that the protest of the American people against combination of this character, which had first been stimulated in 1902, was not 'idle, impudent and impotent.' Its result found its way into the platforms of at least one of the great political parties, and a great statesman who had formerly sat on the Supreme Court was publicly heckled concerning it when stumping as a candidate for President. Probably no case, except the Dred Scott decision, ever caused greater agitation in legal and political circles, and few, if any, have exercised greater influence on our industrial institutions." W. G. Merritt, *Labor Unions and the Law*, (1926) League for Industrial Rights, New York, pp. 32–35.

6. In Buck's Stove and Range Co. v. Gompers, 221 U.S. 418 (1911), the President of the AFL was sentenced to jail for contempt of court in refusing to take the firm's name off the union's unfair list. The sentence was not served when the action was settled.

7. 38 U.S. Stat. c. 323, 15 U.S.C.A. Sec. 17, 29 U.S.C.A. Sec. 52.

appointment came when in a series of cases the U.S. Supreme Court set forth its interpretation of this new law. The relevant provisions of the act provide:

SECTION 6. That the labor of a human being is not a commodity or article of commerce. Nothing contained in the antitrust laws shall be construed to forbid the existence and operation of labor, agriculture, or horticultural organizations, instituted for the purpose of mutual help, and not having capital stock or conducted for profit, or to forbid or restrain individual members of such organizations from lawfully carrying out the legitimate objects thereof; nor shall such organizations, or the members thereof, be held or construed to be illegal combinations or conspiracies in restrain of trade, under the antitrust laws.

SECTION 20. That no restraining order or injunction shall be granted by any court of the United States, or a judge or the judges thereof, in any case between an employer and employees, or between employers and employees, or between employees, or between persons employed and persons seeking employment, involving, or growing out of a dispute concerning terms or conditions of employment, unless necessary to prevent irreparable injury to property, or to a property right, of the party making the application, for which injury there is no adequate remedy at law, and such property or prosperity right must be described with particularity in the application, which must be in writing and sworn to by the applicant or by his agent or attorney.

And no such restraining order or injunction shall prohibit any person or persons whether singly or in concert, from terminating any relation of employment, or from ceasing to perform any work or labor, or from recommending, advising, or persuading others by peaceful means so to do; or from attending at any place where such person or persons may lawfully be, for the purpose of peacefully obtaining or communicating information, or from peacefully persuading any person to work or to abstain from working; or from ceasing to patronize or to employ any party to such dispute, or from recommending, advising, or persuading others by peaceful and lawful means so to do; or from paying or giving to, or withholding from, any person engaged in such dispute, any strike benefits or other moneys or things of value; or from peaceably assembling in a lawful manner and for lawful purposes; or from doing any act or thing which might lawfully be done in the absence of such dispute by any party thereto; nor shall any of the acts specified in this paragraph be considered or held to be violations of any law of the United States.

Section 6 appeared to remove labor from the restrictions in the Sherman Act and Section 20 seemed to provide strict limitations on the use of the injunction in labor dispute cases. However, the words "lawful" and "peaceful," which appear in both sections of the act, are not defined in the statute. Therefore it is necessary to go to the common law decisions to determine whether or not a specific type of labor activity is lawful or peaceful. Since the common law condemns the secondary boycott as an unlawful means, unions did come under the antitrust laws when such means were adopted to interfere with the normal flow of interstate commerce. The act has special importance in that it permits private parties to seek injunctions against those charged with violating the antitrust laws. Under Section 4 of the Sherman Act, injunction proceedings may be initiated only by the U.S. Attorney in the name of the government.

Before discussing leading cases interpreting the Clayton Act, it is wise to discuss the far-reaching effects of the injunction. Most law suits seek to recover money by reason of the wrongful act of the defendant. An injunction, however, is sought to prevent a specific type of activity which, if committed or continued, will result in irreparable damage. A money judgment is only good if the defendant has funds or property to cover the judgment. The ordinary law suit for money damages requires months, and at times years, between the filing of a suit and the rendering of a judgment. Perhaps the greatest advantage in using the injunctive procedure is the elimination of delay and the effectiveness of the decree when issued. A restraining order issued by an equity court in an injunction proceeding must be obeyed. A flagrant violation of the decree results in a contempt proceeding in which the defendant may be punished by fine and in some cases by a jail sentence. The availability of immediate relief was the dominating factor in using the injunction process whenever possible to fight off strikes, picket lines and boycotts. In some states, as in New York, courts have concurrent equity and law jurisdiction, and petitioners frequently seek injunctions and money damages in the same action.

The Duplex, Truax, Bedford Stone, Brims, and Coronado Cases

THE DUPLEX CASE. In the first test before the U.S. Supreme Court, Duplex Printing Co. v. Deering,[8] the Clayton Act not only failed labor unions but gave to employers a new weapon, the injunction, which had formerly been reserved only for the U.S. government under the Sherman Act.

The facts and opinion were delivered by Mr. Justice Pitney.

This was a suit in equity brought by appellant in the District Court for the Southern District of New York for an injunction to restrain a course of conduct carried on by defendants in the District and vicinity in maintaining a boycott against the products of the complainant's factory, in furtherance of a conspiracy to injure and destroy its goodwill, trade and business,— especially to obstruct and destroy its interstate trade. There was also a prayer

8. 245 U.S. 445 (1921).

for damages, but this has not been pressed, and calls for no further mention. Complainant is a Michigan corporation, and manufactures printing presses at a factory in Battle Creek, in that state, employing about 200 machinists in the factory in addition to 50 office employees, traveling salesmen, and expert machinists or road men who supervise the erection of the presses for complainant's customers at their various places of business. The defendants, who were brought into court and answered the bill, are Emil J. Deering and William Bramley, sued individually and as business agents and representatives of District No. 15 of the International Association of Machinists, and Michael T. Neyland, sued individually and as business agent and representative of Local Lodge No. 328, of the same association. The District Council and the Lodge are unincorporated associations having headquarters in New York City, with numerous members resident in that city and vicinity. There were averments and proof to show that it was impracticable to bring all the members before the court, and that named defendants properly represented them; and those named were called up to defend for all, pursuant to Equity Rule 38. . . .

The jurisdiction of the Federal court was invoked both by reason of diverse citizenship and on the ground that defendants were engaged in a conspiracy to restrain complainant's interstate trade and commerce in printing presses, contrary to the Sherman Anti-Trust Act of July 2, 1890. . . . The suit was begun before, but brought to hearing after the passage of the Clayton Act of October 15, 1914. . . . Both parties invoked the provisions of the latter act, and both courts treated them as applicable. Complainant relied also upon the common law; but we shall deal first with the effect of the acts of Congress.

The facts of the case and the nature of the relief prayed are sufficiently set forth in the report of the decision of the circuit court of appeals. . . . These may be summarized as follows: Complainant conducts its business on the "open-shop" policy, without discrimination against either union or non-union men. The individual defendants and the local organizations of which they are the representatives are affiliated with the International Association of Machinists, an unincorporated association having a membership of more than 60,000 and are united in a combination, to which the International Association also is a party, having the object of compelling complainant to unionize its factory, and enforce the "closed shop," the eight-hour day, and the union scale of wages, by means of interfering with and restraining its interstate trade in the products of the factory. Complainant's principal manufacture is newspaper presses of large size and complicated mechanism, varying in weight from 10,000 to 100,000 pounds, and requiring a considerable force of labor and a considerable expenditure of time—a week or more—to handle, haul, and erect them at the point of delivery. These presses are sold throughout the United States and in foreign countries; and, as they are especially designed for the production of daily papers, there is a large market for them in and about the city of New York. They are delivered there in the ordinary course of interstate commerce, the handling, hauling, and installation work at destination being done by employees of the purchaser, under the supervision of a specially skilled machinist supplied by complainant. The acts complained of and sought to be restrained having nothing to do with the conduct or management of the factory in Michigan, but solely with the installation and operation of the presses by complainant's customers. None of the defendants is or ever was an employee of complainant, and complainant at no time has had relations with either of the organizations that they represent. In August, 1913 (eight months before the filing of the bill), the International Association called a strike at complainant's factory in Battle Creek, as a result of which union machinists to the number of about eleven in the factory, and three who supervised the erection of presses in the field, left complainant's employ. But the defection of so small a number did not materially interfere with the operation of the factory, and sales and shipments in interstate commerce continued. The acts complained of made up the details of an elaborate program adopted and carried out by defendants and their organizations in and about the city of New York as part of a country-wide program adopted by the International Association, for the purpose of enforcing a boycott of complainant's product. The acts embraced the following, with others: Warning customers that it would be better for them not to purchase, or, having purchased, not to install, presses made by complainant, and threatening them with loss should they do so; threatening customers with sympathetic strikes in other trades; notifying a trucking company usually employed by customers to haul the presses not to do so, and threatening it with trouble if it should; inciting employees of the trucking company, and other men employed by customers of complainant, to strike against their respective employers, in order to interfere with the hauling and installation of presses, and thus bring pressure to bear upon the customers; notifying repair shops not to do repair work on Duplex presses; coercing union men by threatening them with loss of union cards and with being blacklisted as "scabs" if they assisted in installing the presses; threatening an exposition company with a strike if it permitted complainant's presses to be exhibited; and resorting to a variety of other modes of preventing the sale of presses of complainant's manufacture in or about New York City, and delivery of them in interstate commerce, such as injuring and threatening to injure complainant's customers and prospective customers, and persons concerned in hauling, handling, or installing the presses. In some cases the threats were undisguised; in other cases polite in form, but none the less sinister in purpose and effect. All the judges of the circuit court of appeals concurred in the view that defendants' conduct consisted essentially of efforts to render it impossible for complainant to carry on any commerce in printing presses between Michigan and New York; and that defendants had agreed to do and were endeavoring to accomplish the very thing pronounced unlawful by this court in Loewe v. Lawlor. . . . The judges also agreed that the interference with interstate commerce was such as ought to be enjoined, unless the Clayton Act of October 15, 1914, forbade such injunction.

That act was passed after the beginning of the suit, but more than two years before it was brought to hearing. We are clear that the courts below were right in giving effect to it; the real question being, whether they gave it the proper effect. In so far as the act (a) provided for relief by injunction to private suitors, (2) imposed conditions upon granting such relief under particular circumstances, and (c) otherwise modified the Sherman Act, it was effective from the time of its passage, and applicable to pending suits for injunction. . . .

The Clayton Act, in Sec. 1, includes the Sherman Act in a definition of "anti-trust laws," and, in Sec. 16, . . . gives to private parties a right to relief by injunction in any court of the United States against threatened loss or damage by a violation of the Anti-trust Laws, under the conditions and principles regulating the granting of such relief by courts of equity. Evidently this provision was intended to supplement the Sherman Act, under which some of the Federal courts had held, as this court afterwards held, . . . that a private party could not maintain a suit for injunction.

That complainant's business of manufacturing printing presses and disposing of them in commerce is a property right, entitled to protection against unlawful injury or interference; that unrestrained access to the channels of interstate commerce is necessary for the successful conduct of the business; that a widespread combination exists, to which defendants and the associations represented by them are parties, to hinder and obstruct complainant's interstate trade and commerce by the means that have been indicated; and that, as a result of it, complainant has sustained substantial damage to its interstate trade, and is threatened with further and irreparable loss and damage in the future,—is proved by clear and undisputed evidence. Hence, the right to an injunction is clear if the threatened loss is due to a violation of the Sherman Act, as amended by the Clayton Act.

The substance of the matters here complained of is an interference with complainant's interstate trade, intended to have coercive effect upon complainant, and produced by what is commonly known as a "secondary boycott"; that is, a combination not merely to refrain from dealing with complainant, or to advise or by peaceful means persuade complainant's customers to refrain ("primary boycott"), but to exercise coercive pressure upon such customers, actual or prospective, in order to cause them to withhold or withdraw patronage from complainant through fear of loss or damage to themselves should they deal with it.

As we shall see, the recognized distinction between a primary and a secondary boycott is material to be considered upon the question of the proper construction of the Clayton Act. But, in determining the right to an injunction under that and the Sherman Act, it is of minor consequence whether either kind of boycott is lawful or unlawful at common law or under the statutes of particular states. Those acts, passed in the exercise of the power of Congress to regulate commerce among the states, are of paramount authority, and their prohibitions must be given full effect irrespective of whether the things prohibited are lawful or unlawful at common law or under local statutes.

The court discussed the significance of Loewe v. Lawlor and Eastern States Retail Lumber Dealers' Association v. United States, and then continued:

It is settled by these decisions that such a restraint produced by peaceable persuasion is as much within the prohibition as one accomplished by force or threats of force; and it is not to be justified by the fact that the participants in the combination or conspiracy may have some object beneficial to themselves or their associates which possibly they might have been at liberty to pursue in the absence of the statute.

Upon the question whether the provisions of the Clayton Act forbade the grant of an injunction under the circumstances of the present case, the circuit court of appeals was divided; the majority holding that under Sec. 20, "perhaps in conjunction with Sec. 6," there could be no injunction. . . . Defendants seek to derive from them some authority for their conduct. As to Sec. 6, it seems to us its principal importance in this discussion is for what it does not authorize, and for the limit it sets to the immunity conferred. The section assumes the normal objects of a labor organization to be legitimate, and declares that nothing in the Anti-trust Laws shall be construed to forbid the existence and operation of such organizations, or to forbid their members from lawfully carrying out their legitimate objects; and that such an organization shall not be held in itself—merely because of its existence and operation—to be an illegal combination or conspiracy in restraint of trade. But there is nothing in the section to exempt such an organization or its members from accountability where it or they depart from its normal and legitimate objects, and engage in an actual combination or conspiracy in restraint of trade. And by no fair or permissible construction can it be taken as authorizing any activity otherwise unlawful, or enabling a normally lawful organization to become a cloak for an illegal combination or conspiracy in restraint of trade, as defined by the Anti-trust Laws.

The principal reliance is upon Sec. 20. This regulates the granting of restraining orders and injunctions by the courts of the United States in a designated class of cases, with respect to (a) the terms and conditions of the relief and the practice to be pursued, and (b) the character of acts that are to be exempted from the restraint; and in the concluding words it declares (c) that none of the acts specified shall be held to be violations of any law of the United States. All its provisions are subject to a general qualification respecting the nature of the controversy and the parties affected. It is to be a "case between an employer and employees, or between employers and employees, or between employes, or between persons employed and persons seeking employment, involving or growing out of, a dispute concerning terms or conditions of employment.

The first paragraph merely puts into statutory form familiar restrictions upon the granting of injunctions already established and of general application in the equity practice of the courts of the United States. It is but declaratory of the law as it stood before. The second paragraph declares that "no such restraining order or injunction" shall prohibit certain conduct specified, —manifestly still referring to a "case between an employer and employees, . . . involving, or growing out of, a dispute concerning terms or conditions of employment," as designated in the first paragraph. It is very clear that the restriction upon the use of the injunction is in favor only of those concerned as parties to such a dispute as is described. The words defining the permitted conduct include particular qualifications consistent with the general one respecting the nature of the case and dispute intended; and the concluding words; "nor shall any of the acts specified in this paragraph be considered or held to be violations of any law of the United States," are to be read in the light of the context, and mean only that those acts are not to be so held, when committed by parties concerned in "a dispute concerning terms or conditions of employment." If the qualifying words are to have any effect, they must operate to confine the restriction upon the granting of injunctions, and also the relaxation of the provisions of the anti-trust and other laws of the United States, to parties standing in proximate relation to a controversy such as is particularly described.

The majority of the circuit court of appeals appear to have entertained the view that the words "employers and employees," as used in Sec. 20, should be treated as referring to "the business class or clan to which the parties litigant respectively belong," and that, as there had been a dispute at complainant's factory in Michigan concerning the conditions of employment there,—a dispute created, it is said, if it did not exist before, by the act of the Machinists' Union in calling a strike at the factory—Sec. 20 operated to permit members of the Machinists' Union elsewhere,—some 60,000 in number,—although standing in no relation to employment under complainant, past, present, or prospective, to make that dispute their own, and proceed to instigate sympathetic strikes, picketing, and boycotting against employers wholly unconnected with complainant's factory, and having relations with complainant only in the way of purchasing its product in the ordinary course of interstate commerce,—and this where there was no dispute between such employers and their employees respecting terms or conditions of employment.

We deem this construction altogether inadmissible. Section 20 must be given full effect according to its terms as an expression of the purpose of Congress; but it must be borne in mind that the section imposes an exceptional and extraordinary restriction upon the equity powers of the courts of the United States, and upon the general operation of the Anti-trust Laws, —a restriction in the nature of a special privilege or immunity to a particular class, with corresponding deteriment to the general public; . . . Congress had in mind particular industrial controversies, not a general class war. "Terms or conditions of employment" are the only grounds of dispute recognized as adequate to bring into play the exemptions; and it would do violence to the guarded language employed were the exemption extended beyond the parties affected in a proximate and substantial, not merely a sentimental or sympathetic, sense by the cause of dispute. Nor can Sec. 20 be regarded as bringing in all members of a labor organization as parties to a "dispute concerning terms and conditions of employment" which proximately affects only a few of them, with the result of conferring upon any and all members,—no matter how many thousands there may be, nor how remote from the actual conflict—those exemptions which Congress in terms conferred only upon parties to the dispute. That would enlarge by construction the provisions of Sec. 20, which contain no mention of labor organization, so as to produce an inconsistency with Sec. 6, which deals specifically with the subject and must be deemed to express the measure and limit of the immunity intended by Congress to be incident to mere membership in such an organization. At the same time it would virtually repeal by implication the prohibition of the Sherman Act, so far as labor organizations are concerned, notwithstanding repeals by implication are not favored . . . . the emphasis placed on the words "lawful" and "lawfully," "peaceful" and "peacefully," and the references to the dispute and the parties to it, strongly rebut a legislative intent to confer a general immunity for conduct violative of the Anti-trust Laws, or otherwise unlawful. The subject of the boycott is dealt with specifically in the "ceasing to patronize" provision, and by the clear force of the language employed the exemption is limited to pressure exerted upon a "party to such dispute" by means of "peaceful and lawful" influence upon neutrals. There is nothing here to justify defendants or the organizations they represent in using either threats or persuasion to bring about strikes or a cessation of work on the part of employees of complainant's customers or prospective customers, or of the trucking company employed by the customers, with the object of compelling such customers to withdraw or refrain from commercial relations with complainant, and of thereby constraining complainant to yield the matter in dispute. To instigate a sympathetic strike in aid of a secondary boycott cannot be deemed "peaceful and lawful" persuasion. In essence it is a threat to inflict damage upon the immediate employer, between whom and his employees no dispute exists, in order to bring him against his will into a concerted plan to inflict damage upon another employer who is in dispute with his employees. The majority of the circuit court of appeals, very properly treating the case as involving a secondary boycott, based the decision upon a view that it was the purpose of Sec. 20 to legalize the secondary boycott, "at least in so far as it rests on or consists of refusing to work for anyone who deals with the principal offender." In the case of the Clayton Act, the printed committee reports are not explicit with respect to the meaning of the "ceasing to patronize" clause . . . the report was supplemented in this regard by a spokesman of the House committee (Mr. Webb), who had the bill in charge when it was under consideration by the House. The question whether the bill legalized the secondary boycott having been raised, it was emphatically and unequivocally answered by him in the negative.

"Reaching the conclusion, as we do, that complainant has a clear right to an injunction under the Sherman Act, as amended by the Clayton Act, it becomes unnecessary to consider whether a like result would follow under the common law. . . . Decree reversed, and the cause remanded to the District Court for further proceedings in conformity with this opinion."

Justice Brandeis, who dissented, wrote a separate opinion as follows:

. . . As to the rights at common law, defendants' justification is that of self-interest. They have supported a strike at the employer's factory by a strike elsewhere against its product. They have contended that the Duplex Company has been injured not maliciously, but in self-defense. They contend that the Duplex Company's refusal to deal with the machinists' union and to observe its standards threatened the interest not only of such union members as were its factory employees, but even more of all members of the several affiliated unions employed by plaintiff's competitors, and by others whose more advanced standards the plaintiff was, in reality attacking; and that none of the defendants and no person whom they are endeavoring to induce to refrain from working in connection with the setting up of presses made by plaintiff is an outsider,—an interloper. In other words, that the contest between the company and the machinists' union involves vitally the interest of every person whose cooperation is sought. May not all with a common interest join in refusing to expend their labor upon articles whose very production constitutes an attack upon their standard of living and the institution which they are convinced supports it? Applying common-law principles the answer should, in my opinion, be: Yes, if as matter of fact those who so cooperate have a common interest. The change in the law by which strikes once illegal and even criminal are now recognized as lawful was effected in America largely without the intervention of legislation. This reversal of a common-law rule was not due to the rejection by the courts of one principle and the adoption in its stead of another, but to a better realization of the facts of industrial life. It is conceded that, although the strike of the workmen in plaintiff's factory injured its business, the strike was not an actionable wrong, because the obvious self-interest of the strike constituted a justification. . . . Formerly courts held that self-interest could not be so served. . . . But even after strikes to raise wages or reduce hours were held to be legal, because of the self-interest, some courts held that there was not sufficient causal relationship between a strike to unionize a shop and the self-interest of the strikes to justify injuries inflicted. . . . But other courts, repeating the same legal formula, found that there was justification, because they viewed the facts differently. . . . With centralization in the organization of workingmen, new facts had to be appraised. A single employer might, as in this case, threaten the standing of the whole organization and the standards of all its members; and when he did so the union, in order to protect itself, would naturally refuse to work on his materials wherever found. When such a situation was first presented to the courts, judges concluded that the intervention of the purchaser of the materials established an insulation through which the direct relationship of the employer and the workingmen did not penetrate; and the strike against the materials was considered a strike against the purchaser by unaffected third parties. . . . But other courts, with better appreciation of the facts of industry, recognized the unity of interest throughout the union, and that, in refusing to work on materials which threatened it, the union was only refusing to aid in destroying itself. . . .

This statute was the fruit of unceasing agitation, which extended over more than twenty years, and was designed to equalize before the law the position of workingmen and employer as industrial combatants. Aside from the use of the injunction, the chief source of dissatisfaction with the existing law lay in the doctrine of malicious combination, and, in many parts of the country, in the judicial declaration of the illegality at common law of picketing and persuading others to leave work. The grounds for objection to the latter are obvious. The objection to the doctrine of malicious combinations requires some explanation. By virtue of that doctrine, damage resulting from conduct such as striking or withholding patronage or persuading others to do either, which, without more, might be damnum abseque injuria because the result of trade competition, became actionable when done for a purpose which a judge considered socially or economically harmful, and therefore branded as malicious and unlawful. It was objected that, due largely to environment, the social and economic ideas of judges, which thus became translated into law, were prejudicial to a position of equality between work-ingmen and employer; that, due to this dependence upon the individual opinion of judges, great confusion existed as to what purposes were lawful and what unlawful; and that, in any event, Congress, not the judges, was the body which should declare what public policy in regard to the industrial struggle demands . . . . the Clayton Act substituted the opinion of Con-gress as to the propriety of the purpose for that of differing judges; and thereby it declared that the relations between employers of labor and workingmen were competitive relations, that organized competition was not harmful, and that it justified injuries necessarily inflicted in its course. Both the majority and the minority report of the House Committee indicate that such was the purpose. If, therefore, the act applies to the case at bar, the acts here complained of cannot "be considered or held to be violations of any law of the U.S.," and, hence, do not violate the Sherman Act. . . . Be-cause I have come to the conclusion that both the common law of the state and a statute of the U.S. declare the right of industrial combatants to push their struggle to the limits of the justification of self-interest, I do not wish to be understood as attaching any constitutional or moral sanction to that right. All rights are derived from the purposes of the society in which they exist; above all rights rises duty to the community. The conditions developed in industry may be such that those engaged in it cannot continue their struggle without danger to the community. But it is not for judges to deter-mine whether such conditions exist, nor is it their function to set the limits of permissible contest, and to declare the duties which the new situation demands. This is the function of the legislature, which, while, limiting indi-vidual and group rights of aggression and defense, may substitute processes of justice for the more primitive method of trial by combat.

The Supreme Court adhered to a strict common-law rule when it held that Section 20 of the Clayton Act limited concerted action to employees of the Duplex Company in Michigan, and that New York members of the machinists' union were too remote from the sites of the controversy to have any substantial interest. This narrow interpreta-tion of the act overlooked the self-interest motivation which the New York union had in seeking to protect union conditions which prevailed in three other press manufacturers where the 8-hour work day prevailed. At Duplex, the work day consisted of 10 hours; along with a low wage scale, it had a major competitive advantage over the unionized printing press manufacturers. In fact, the three unionized companies had informed the union of the Duplex advantage and had issued a statement to the effect that they would go nonunion unless Duplex was brought up to union standards.

In his vigorous dissent Justice Brandeis stated that Congress had, by its passage of the Clayton Act, given recognition to the "facts of industrial life." He disagreed with the majority of the court when it rejected the argument that Congress had intended to grant new rights to labor. The majority held that Congress had intended only to embody in the Clayton Act previous judicial interpretations of the Sherman Act.

Justice Brandeis indicated an excellent knowledge of basic labor economics when he noted the enormous market advantage Duplex, a nonunion firm, held over the rest of this industry comprising three union-operated shops. He felt that this margin would act not only to the disadvantage of the few union employees working for Duplex, but also as a threat to the good working standards enjoyed by all the machinists employed by the unionized press manufacturers. He was convinced also that the Duplex advantage would adversely effect the workers employed by the unionized firms that installed and serviced the printing presses. With great conviction, Justice Brandeis held that there existed a proximate economic relationship between all these workers which allowed them to adopt, under the permissive language of Section 20, the concerted action against Duplex. The motivation for this economic pressure was the advancement of their self-interest, which would have been ultimately promoted if Duplex became a union shop. Justice Brandeis maintained that none of the workers engaged in this dispute were "interlopers," but that all, without exception, had a legitimate stake which they should have been permitted to protect by participating as industrial combatants. Furthermore, he did not agree with the majority opinion that Section 20 was applicable only in those labor disputes in which there existed an employer-employee relationship. Justice Learned Hand, a member of the U.S. Circuit Court of Appeals for the Second Circuit, agreed with Justice Brandeis on this point. Sitting as a member of the Appellate Circuit Court during the Duplex appeal in 1918, Justice Hand, in a concurring opinion which denied injunctive relief to the Duplex Company, said, ". . . I do not think that the section applies only when the employer is plaintiff and his present or former employees are the defendants. Further, I think that the dispute here under any definition included the conditions of employment."

Although the labor supporters had thought in 1914 that the Clayton Act would prove to be a true Magna Carta, this decision brought them complete disillusionment.

By this decision employers were stimulated to greater opposition to unions, and encouraged to apply for injunctions. Professor Gregory explains the confusion concerning the Clayton Act as follows: [9]

> Ever since this first interpretation of Section 20 of the Clayton Act, almost all educated opinion in this country has been that the Supreme Court sold organized labor down the river when it construed this section. . . . Several astute lawyers thought that Congress was the body which had betrayed the labor unions when it enacted Section 20. They believed that Congress deliberately made this section ambiguous, with the surface appearance of going very far indeed, but nevertheless using restrictive words like "employee" in close juxtaposition with the word "employer" and craftily inserting words like "lawful" and "peaceful," so that labor people would think, after a hasty reading that they had achieved something substantial. . . . Evidence tending to support this belief was found in some of the Congressional committee reports on this section, indicating that Congress had no intention of going so far as to allow the secondary boycott. It is only fair to Congress, however, to remember that an understanding of concepts like the secondary boycott was even less clear in 1914 than it is today. Quite possibly none of the members of the committee knew what was being talked about when the group disclaimed all intention to legalize such a technique.

Labor's great disappointment with the setback suffered at the hands of the Supreme Court convinced it of the need for more definite legislation defining its rights in clear terms, so that unions might proceed to carry out what they believed to be their legitimate objectives. The new law did not come for more than ten years, during which time labor became enmeshed in two additional cases which further restricted the permissible area of lawful labor activity. In 1921 the Supreme Court was asked to construe a state statute paralleling the federal Clayton Act. The case was Truax v. Corrigan.[10]

THE TRUAX CASE. William Truax and William A. Truax were the owners of a restaurant called The English Kitchen. It was a fair-sized restaurant located on the main street of Bisbee, Ariz., employing about ten cooks and waiters. In April 1916, William Truax informed his employees that their wages would be cut and their daily hours would be increased. The change was supposed to take place on April 9. The workers belonged to the Cooks' and Waiters' Union of Bisbee. The un-

9. C. O. Gregory, *Labor and the Law*, (1946 ed.) W. W. Norton and Co., New York, p. 170. For a revealing article on the events leading to the drafting of the act, see D. L. Jones, The Enigma of the Clayton Act, *Ind. and Lab. Rel. Rev.*, Jan. 1957.
10. 257 U.S. 312 (1921). In another Supreme Court decision, Am. Steel Foundries v. Tri-City Central Trades Council, 257 U.S. 184 (1921) the application of the Clayton Act was further narrowed by limiting the number of pickets as well as restricting the right to picket to employees exclusively. Strangers who felt a unity of interest with the workers directly engaged in the dispute were barred from picketing.

ion communicated with Truax and urged him not to change the working conditions, but he refused. On April 10, the day following the change, the cooks and waiters of The English Kitchen went out on strike. They were supported in their strike by the Warren District Trade Assembly.

The union waged a hot campaign against Truax. Donkeys draped with banners publicizing the strike were driven about the town for several days. Various handbills and circulars attacking Truax's methods of treating the workers were distributed. One circular charged Truax with chasing the employees down the street with a butcher knife. Another circular referred to him as "12-hours Bill Truax." Some circulars stated that Truax's prices were higher and his food worse than in the other Bisbee restaurants. Other circulars imaginatively speculated about Truax's ambitions and stated that he wanted to hasten the day when he would have made his pile and could return to that "dear Los Angeles, perhaps with a Japanese valet, a Chinese cook and an imported Jamaica chauffeur." During business hours pickets paraded up and down in front of the restaurant with large banners publicizing their strike against Truax. Often sympathizers gathered near The English Kitchen and discussed the strike situation in loud voices. There was no violence and the picketing was peaceful.

The plaintiff claimed that the action of the strikers caused irreparable injury to his business. The defendants relied for immunity on Paragraph 1464 of the Revised Statutes of Arizona, enacted in 1913 and almost identical in language with the federal Clayton Act of 1914. The statute provided that no injunction should be granted in any case between employer and employees, involving or growing out of conditions of employment, unless irreparable injury to a property right was threatened. The plaintiff urged that this statute was unconstitutional and asked for an injunction. A lower state court declined to issue it, and this decision was sustained by the Supreme Court of Arizona. The case was appealed to the Supreme Court of the United States.

Mr. Chief Justice Taft delivered the opinion of the U.S. Supreme Court.

The complaint and its exhibits make this case:
The defendants conspire to injure and destroy plaintiffs' business by inducing their heretofore willing patrons and would-be patrons not to patronize them and they influenced these to withdraw or withhold their patronage:
(1) By having the agents of the union walk forward and back constantly during all business hours in front of plantiffs' restaurant and within five feet thereof, displaying a banner announcing in large letters that the restaurant was unfair to cooks and waiters and their union.
(2) By having agents attend at or near the entrance of the restaurant during all business hours and continuously announcing in a loud voice,

audible for a great distance, that the restaurant was unfair to the labor union.

(3) By characterizing the employees of the plaintiffs as scab Mexican labor, and using opprobrious epithets concerning them in handbills continously distributed in front of the restaurant to would-be customers.

(4) By applying in such handbills abusive epithets to Truax, the senior member of plaintiffs' firm, and making libelous charges against him, to the effect that he was tyrannical with his help, and chased them down the street with a butcher knife, that he broke his contract and repudiated his pledged words; that he had made attempts to force cooks and waiters to return to work by attacks on men and women; that a friend of Truax assaulted a woman and pleaded guilty; that plaintiff was known by his friends, and that Truax's treatment of his employees was explained by his friend's assault; that he was a "bad actor."

(5) By seeking to disparage plaintiff's restaurant, charging that the prices were higher and the food worse than in any other restaurant, and that assaults and slugging were a regular part of the bill of fare, with police indifferent.

(6) By attacking the character of those who did patronize, saying that their mental calibre and moral fibre fell far below the American average, and inquiring of the would-be patrons— Can you patronize such a place and look the world in the face?

(7) By threats of similar injury to the would-be patrons by such expressions as "all ye who enter here leave all hope behind." "Don't be a traitor to humanity"; by offering a reward for any of the ex-members of the union caught eating in the restaurant; by saying in the handbills: "We are also aware that handbills and banners in front of a business house on the main street give the town a bad name, but they are permanent institutions until William Truax agrees to the eight-hour day."

(8) By warning any person wishing to purchase the business from the Truax firm that a donation would be necessary, amount to be fixed by the District Trades Assembly, before the picketing and boycotting would be given up.

The result of this campaign was to reduce the business of the plaintiffs from more than $55,000 a year to $12,000.

Plaintiffs' business is a property right. . . . and free access for employees, owner, and customers to his place of business is incident to such right. Intentional injury caused to either right or both by a conspiracy is a tort (a wrong punishable by damages). Concert of action is a conspiracy if its object is unlawful or if the means used are unlawful. *. . .* Intention to inflict the loss and the actual loss caused are clear. The real question here is, were the means used illegal? The above recital of what the defendants did can leave no doubt of that. The libelous attacks upon the plaintiffs, their business, their employees, and their customers, and the abusive epithets applied to them were palpable wrongs. They were uttered in aid of the plan to induce plaintiffs' customers and would-be customers to refrain from patronizing the plaintiffs. The patrolling of defendants immediately in front of the restaurant on the main street and within five feet of the plaintiffs' premises continuously during business hours, with the banners announcing plaintiffs' unfairness; the attendance by the picketers at the entrance to the restaurant and their insistent and loud appeals all day long, the constant circulation by them of the libels and epithets applied to employees, plaintiffs and customers, and the threats of injurious consequences to future customers, all linked together in a campaign, were an unlawful annoyance and a hurtful nuisance in respect of the free access to the plaintiffs' place of business. It was not lawful persuasion or inducing. It was not a mere appeal to the sympathetic aid of would-be customers by a simple statement of the fact of the strike and a request to withhold patronage. It was compelling every customer or would-be customer to run the gauntlet of most uncomfortable publicity, aggressive and annoying importunity, libelous attacks and fear of injurious consequences, illegally inflicted, to his reputation and standing in the community. No wonder that a business of $50,000 was reduced to only one-fourth of its former extent. Violence could not have been more effective. It was moral coercion by illegal annoyance and obstruction and it thus was plainly a conspiracy.

A law which operates to make lawful such a wrong as is described in plaintiffs' complaint deprives the owner of the business and the premises of his property without due process, and cannot be held valid under the Fourteenth Amendment.

. . . It is true that no one has a vested right in any particular rule of the common law, but it is also true that the legislative power of a State can only be exerted in subordination to the fundamental principles of right and justice which the guaranty of due process in the Fourteenth Amendment is intended to preserve, and that a purely arbitrary or capricious exercise of that power whereby a wrongful and highly injurious invasion of property rights, as here, is practically sanctioned and the owner stripped of all real remedy, is wholly at variance with those principles.

It is to be observed that this is not the mere case of a peaceful secondary boycott as to the illegality of which courts have differed and States have adopted different statutory provisions. A secondary boycott of this kind is where many combine to injure one in his business by coercing third persons against their will to cease patronizing him by threats of similar injury. In such a case the many have a legal right to withdraw their trade from the one, they have the legal right to withdraw their trade from third persons, and they have the right to advise third persons of their intention to do so when each act is considered singly. The question in such cases is whether the moral coercion exercised over a stranger to the original controversy by steps in themselves legal becomes a legal wrong. But here the illegality of the means used is without doubt and fundamental. The means used are the libelous and the abusive attacks on the plaintiffs' reputation, like attacks on the employees and customers, threats of such attacks on would-be customers, picketing and patrolling of the entrance to their place of business, and the consequent obstruction of free access thereto—all with the purpose of depriving the plaintiffs of their business. To give operation to a statute whereby serious losses inflicted by such unlawful means are in effect made remediless, is, we think, to disregard fundamental rights of liberty and property and to deprive the person suffering the loss of due process of law. . . .

This brings us to consider the effect in this case of that provision of the Fourteenth Amendment which forbids any State to deny to any person the equal protection of the laws. The clause is associated in the Amendment with the due process clause and it is customary to consider them together. It may be that they overlap, that a violation of one may involve at times the violation of the other, but the spheres of the protection they offer are not coterminous. The due process clause, brought down from Magna Charta, was found in the early state constitutions, and later in the Fifth Amendment to the Federal Constitution as a limitation upon the executive, legislative, and judicial powers of the Federal Government, while the equality clause does not appear in the Fifth Amendment and so does not apply to congressional legislation. The due process clause requires that every man shall have the protection of his day in court, and the benefit of the general law, a law which hears before it condemns, which proceeds not arbitrarily or capriciously but upon inquiry, and renders judgment only after trial, so that every citizen shall hold his life, liberty, property and immunities under the protection of the general rules which govern society. It, of course, tends to secure equality of law in the sense that it makes a required minimum of protection for every one's right of life, liberty and property, which the Congress or the legislature may not withhold. Our whole system of law is predicated on the general, fundamental principle of equality of application of the law. . . .

The judgment of the Supreme Court of Arizona is reversed.

Mr. Justice Holmes, in his dissenting opinion, stated:

. . . By calling business "property" you make it seem like land and lead up to the conclusion that a statute cannot substantially cut down the advantages of ownership existing before the statute was passed. An established business no doubt may have pecuniary value and commonly is protected by law against various unjustified injuries. But you cannot give it definiteness of contour by calling it a thing. It is a course of conduct and like other conduct is subject to substantial modification according to time and circumstance both in itself and in regard to what shall justify doing it a harm. I cannot understand the notion that it would be unconstitutional to authorize boycotts and the like in aid of the employees' or the employers' interest by statute when the same result has been reached consitutionally without statute by Courts with whom I agree. . . . Legislation may begin where an evil begins. If, as many intelligent people believe, there is more danger that the injunction will be abused in labor cases than elsewhere, I can feel no doubt of the power of the legislature to deny it in such cases. . . . I must add one general consideration. There is nothing that I more deprecate than the use of the Fourteenth Amendment beyond the absolute compulsion of its words to prevent the making of social experiments that an important part of the community desires, in the insulated chambers afforded by the several States, even though the experiments may seem futile or even noxious to me and those whose judgment I most respect . . .

Justice Holmes stated succinctly that the federal Constitution ought not to be used as a bar when states sought to restrict the use of injunctions in labor dispute cases. He questioned the right of the Supreme

Court to interfere with a state's attempt to regulate industrial relations, and he believed that a state was within its rights to permit social changes. When the Supreme Court adhered to the traditional doctrine of inviolability of property rights, unions became convinced that it could not look to this court for any help in advancing worker objectives. More and more, unions were certain that federal judicial power would override any gains labor might seek through the machinery of state legislatures. Although labor's case seemed hopeless with the decision in Truax v. Corrigan, and perhaps it was at this time, unions were certain that any relief had to come from the federal legislature. Before real relief came, labor was due to suffer many more defeats.

Justice Brandeis, in his dissent, presented a valuable sociological survey of the long struggle of the worker seeking to improve his conditions. His principal argument affirmed the right of Arizona to abridge by statute the issuance of injunctions in cases involving labor disputes. He believed states had inherent power to limit the equity authority of their courts provided the abridgement [sic] was not done unreasonably or arbitrarily.

His dissenting opinion follows:

The first legislature of the State of Arizona adopted in 1913 a Civil Code. By Title 6, c. III, it sets forth conditions and circumstances under which the courts of the State may or may not grant injunctions. Paragraph 1464 contains, among other things, a prohibition against interfering by injunction between employers and employees, in any case growing out of a dispute concerning terms or conditions of employment, unless interposition by injunction is necessary to protect property from injury through violence. Its main purpose was doubtless to prohibit the courts from enjoining peaceful picketing and the boycott. With the wisdom of the statute we have no concern. Whether Arizona in enacting this statute transgressed limitations imposed upon the power of the States by the Fourteenth Amendment is the question presented for decision.

The employer has, of course, a legal right to carry on his business for profit; and incidentally the subsidiary rights to secure and retain customers, to fix such prices for his product as he deems proper, and to buy merchandise and labor at such prices as he chooses to pay. This right to carry on business—be it called liberty or property—has value; and, he who interferes with the right without cause renders himself liable. But for cause the right may be interfered with and even be destroyed. Such cause exists when, in the pursuit of an equal right to further their several interests, his competitors make inroads upon his trade, or when suppliers of merchandise or of labor make inroads upon his profits. What methods and means are permissible in this struggle of contending forces is determined in part by decisions of the courts, in part by acts of the legislatures. The rules governing the contest necessarily change from time to time. For conditions change; and, furthermore, the rules evolved, being merely experiments in government, must be discarded when they prove to be failures.

to the means by which, and also as to the persons through whom, and upon whom pressure might permissibly be exerted in order to induce the employer to yield to the demands of the workingmen. Courts were required, in the absence of legislation, to determine what the public welfare demanded;—whether it would not be best subserved by leaving the contestants free to resort to any means not involving a breach of the peace or injury to tangible property; whether it was consistent with the public interest that the contestants should be permitted to invoke the aid of others not directly interested in the matter in controversy; and to what extent incidental injury to persons not parties to the controversy should be held justifiable.

The earliest reported American decision on peaceful picketing appears to have been rendered in 1888, the earliest on boycotting in 1886. By no great majority the prevailing judicial opinion in America declares the boycott as commonly practiced an illegal means (see Duplex Printing Press Co. v. Deering, 254 U.S. 443, 41 S. Ct. 172, 65 L. Ed. 349, 16 A.L.R. 196), while it inclines towards the legality of peaceful picketing. See American Steel Foundaries v. Tri-City Central Trades Council, ante (257 U.S. 184, 42 S. Ct. 72, 66 L. Ed. 189, 27 A.L.R. 360). But in some of the States, notably New York, both peaceful picketing and the boycott are declared permissible. Judges, being thus called upon to exercise a quasi-legislative function and weigh relative social values, naturally differed in their conclusions on such questions.

In England, observance of the rules of the contest has been enforced by the courts almost wholly through the criminal law or through actions at law for compensation. An injunction was granted in a labor dispute as early as 1868. But in England resort to the injunction has not been frequent and it has played no appreciable part there in the conflict between capital and labor. In America the injunction did not secure recognition as a possible remedy until 1888. When a few years later its use became extensive and conspicuous, the controversy over the remedy overshadowed in bitterness the question of the relative substantive rights of the parties. In the storms of protest against this use many thoughtful lawyers joined. The equitable remedy, although applied in accordance with established practice, involved incidents which, it was asserted, endangered the personal liberty of wage-earners. The acts enjoined were frequently, perhaps usually, acts which were already crimes at common law or had been made so by statutes. The issues in litigation arising out of trade disputes related largely to questions of fact. But in equity issues of fact as of law were tried by a single judge, sitting without a jury. Charges of violating an injunction were often heard on affidavits merely, without the opportunity of confronting or cross-examining witnesses. Men found guilty of contempt were committed in the judge's discretion, without either a statutory limit upon the length of the imprisonment, or the opportunity of effective review on appeal, or the right to release on bail pending possible revisory proceedings. The effect of the proceeding upon the individual was substantially the same as if he had been successfully prosecuted for a crime; but he was denied, in the course of the equity proceedings, those rights which by the Constitution are commonly secured to persons charged with a crime.

It was asserted that in these proceedings an alleged danger to property, always incidental and at times insignificant, was often laid hold of to enable the penalties of the criminal law to be enforced expeditiously without that protection to the liberty of the individual which the Bill of Rights was designed to afford; that through such proceedings a single judge often usurped the functions not only of the jury but of the police department; that, in prescribing the conditions under which strikes were permissible and how they might be carried out, he usurped also the powers of the legis-lature; and that incidentally he abridged the constitutional rights of indi-viduals to free speech, to a free press and to peaceful assembly.

It was urged that the real motive in seeking the injunction was not ordi-narily to prevent property from being injured nor to protect the owner in its use, but to endow property with active, militant power which would make it dominant over men. In other words, that, under the guise of pro-tecting property rights, the employer was seeking sovereign power. And many disinterested men, solicitous only for the public welfare, believed that the law of property was not appropriate for dealing with the forces beneath social unrest; that in this vast struggle it was unwise to throw the power of the State on one side or the other according to principles deducted from that law; that the problem of the control and conduct of industry demanded a solution of its own; and that, pending the ascertainment of new principles to govern industry, it was wiser for the State not to interfere in industrial struggles by the issuance of an injunction.

After the constitutionality and the propriety of the use of the injunction in labor disputes was established judicially, those who opposed the practice sought the aid of Congress and of state legislatures. The bills introduced varied in character and in scope. Many dealt merely with rights; and, of these, some declared, in effect, that no act done in furtherance of a labor dispute by a combination of workingmen should be held illegal, unless it would have been so if done by a single individual; while others purported to legalize specific practices, like boycotting or picketing. Other bills dealt merely with the remedy; and of these some undertook practically to abolish the use of the injunction in labor disputes, while some merely limited its use either by prohibiting its issue under certain conditions or by denying power to restrain certain acts. Some bills undertook to modify both rights and remedies. These legislative proposals occupied the attention of Congress during every session but one in the twenty years between 1894 and 1914. Reports recommending such legislation were repeatedly made by the Judi-ciary Committee of the House or that of the Senate; and at some sessions by both. Prior to 1914, legislation of this character had at several sessions passed the House; and in that year Congress passed and the President ap-proved the Clayton Act, Sec. 20 of which is substantially the same as Para-graph 1464 of the Arizona Civil Code. Act of October 15, 1914, c. 323, 38 Stat. 730, 738, 29 U.S.C.A. sec. 52.

Such was the diversity of view concerning peaceful picketing and the boycott expressed in judicial decisions and legislation in English-speaking countries when in 1913 the new State of Arizona, in establishing its judi-cial system, limited the use of the injunction and when in 1918 its Supreme Court was called upon to declare for the first time the law of Arizona on these subjects. The case of Truax v. Bisbee Local No. 380, Cooks' & Waiters' Union, 19 Ariz. 379, 171 P. 121, presented facts identical with those of the case at bar. In that case the Supreme Court made its decision on four controverted points of law. In the first place, it held that the officials of the union were not outsiders with no justification for their acts (19 Ariz. 379, 390). In the second place, rejecting the view held by the federal courts and the majority of the state courts on the illegality of the boycott, it specifically accepted the law of New York, Montana and California, citing the decisions of those States (19 Ariz. 379, 388, 390). In the third place, it rejected the law of New Jersey, Minnesota and Pennsylvania that it is illegal to circularize an employer's customers, and again adopted the rule declared in the decisions of the courts of New York, Montana, California and Connecticut (19 Ariz. 379, 389). In deciding these three points the Supreme Court of Arizona made a choice between well-established precedents laid down on either side by some of the strongest courts in the country. Can this court say that thereby it deprived the plaintiff of his property without due process of law?

The fourth question requiring decision was whether peaceful picketing should be deemed legal. Here, too, each of the opposing views had the support of decisions of strong courts. If the Arizona court had decided that by the common law of the State the defendants might peacefully picket the plaintiffs, its decision, like those of the courts of Ohio, Minnesota, Montana, New York, Oklahoma and New Hampshire, would surely not have been open to objection under the Federal Constitution; for this court has recently held that peaceful picketing is not unlawful. American Steel Foundries v. Tri-City Central Trades Council, *supra*. The Supreme Court of Arizona found it unnecessary to determine what was the common law of the State on that subject, because it construed Paragraph 1464 of the Civil Code as declaring peaceful picketing to be legal. In the case at bar, commenting on the earlier case, the court said "The statute adopts the view of a number of courts which have held 'picketing,' if peaceably carried on for a lawful purpose, to be no violation of any legal right of the party whose place of business is 'picketed,' and whether as a fact the picketing is carried on by peaceful means, as against the other view, taken by the federal courts and many of the state courts, that picketing is per se unlawful." Shortly before that decision the Criminal Court of Appeals of Oklahoma had placed a similar construction upon a statute of that State, declaring that "the doctrine (that picketing is not per se unlawful) represents the trend of legal thought of modern times, and is specifically reflected in the statute above construed." Ex parte Sweitzer, 13 Okl. Cr. 154, 160, 162 P. 1134. See City of St. Louis v. Gloner, 210 Mo. 502, 109 S.W. 30, 15 L.R.A., N.S., 973, 124 Am. St. Rep. 750. A State which despite the Fourteenth Amendment possesses the power to impose on employers without fault unlimited liability for injuries suffered by employees, and to limit the freedom of contract of some employers and not of others, surely does not lack the power to select for its citizens that one of conflicting views on boycott by peaceful picketing which its legislature and highest court consider will best meet its conditions and secure the public welfare.

The Supreme Court of Arizona, having held as a rule of substantive law that the boycott as here practiced was legal at common law; and that the picketing was peaceful and, hence, legal under the statute (whether or not it was legal at common law), necessarily denied the injunction, since, in its opinion, the defendants had committed no legal wrong and were threatening none. But even if this court should hold that an employer has a constitutional right to be free from interference by such a boycott or that the picketing practiced was not in fact peaceful, it does not follow that Arizona would lack the power to refuse to protect that right by injunction. For it is clear that the refusal of an equitable remedy for a tort is not necessarily a denial of due process of law. And it seems to be equally clear that such refusal is not necessarily arbitrary and unreasonable when applied to incidents of the relation of employer and employee. The considerations which show that the refusal is not arbitrary or unreasonable show likewise that such refusal does not necessarily constitute a denial of equal protection of the laws merely because some, or even the same, property rights which are excluded by this statute from protection by injunction, receive such protection under other circumstances or between persons standing in different relations. The acknowledged legislative discretion exerted in classification, so frequently applied in defining rights, extends equally to the grant of remedies. It is for the legislature to say—within the broad limits of the discretion which it possesses—whether or not the remedy for a wrong shall be both criminal and civil and whether or not it shall be both at law and in equity.

A State is free since the adoption of the Fourteenth Amendment, as it was before, not only to determine what system of law shall prevail in it, but, also, by what processes legal rights may be asserted, and in what courts they may be enforced. Missouri v. Lewis, 101 U.S. 22, 31, 25 L. Ed. 989; Iowa Central Ry. Co. v. Iowa, 160 U.S. 389, 16 S. Ct. 344, 40 L. Ed. 467. As a State may adopt or reject trial by jury, Walker v. Sauvinet, 92 U.S. 90, 23 L. Ed. 678; or adopting it may retain or discard its customary incidents, Hayes v. Missouri, 120 U.S. 68, 7 S. Ct. 350, 30 L. Ed. 578; Brown v. New Jersey, 175 U.S. 172, 20 S. Ct. 77, 44 L. Ed. 119; Maxwell v. Dow, 176 U.S. 581, 20 S. Ct. 448, 494, 44 L. Ed. 597; as a State may grant or withhold review of a decision by appeal, Reetz v. Michigan, 188 U.S. 505, 23 S. Ct. 390, 47 L. Ed. 563; so it may determine for itself, from time to time, whether the protection which it affords to property rights through its courts shall be given by means of the preventive remedy or exclusively by an action at law for compensation.

Nor is a State obliged to protect all property rights by injunction merely because it protects some, even if the attending circumstances are in some respects similar. The restraining power of equity might conceivably be applied to every intended violation of a legal right. On grounds of expediency its application is commonly denied in cases where there is a remedy at law which is deemed legally adequate. But an injunction has been denied on grounds of expediency in many cases where the remedy at law is confessedly not adequate. This occurs whenever a dominant public interest is deemed to require that the preventive remedy, otherwise available for the protection of private rights, be refused and the injured party left to such remedy as courts of law may afford. Thus, courts ordinarily refuse, perhaps in the interest of free speech, to restrain actionable libels. Boston Diatite Co. v. Florence Mfg. Co., 114 Mass. 69, 19 Am. Rep. 310; Prudential Insurance Co. v. Knott, L.R. 10 Ch. App. 142. In the interest of personal liberty they ordinarily refuse to enforce specifically, by mandatory injunction or otherwise, obligations involving personal service. Arthur v. Oakes, 63 F. 310, 318, 11 C.C.A. 209, 25 L.R.A. 414; Davis v. Foreman (1894) 3 Ch. 654, 657; Gossard v. Crosby, 132 Iowa 155, 163, 164, 109 N.W. 483, 6 L.R.A., N.S., 1115. In the desire to preserve the separation of governmental powers they have declined to protect by injunction mere political rights, Giles v. Harris, 189 U.S. 475, 23 S. Ct. 639, 47 L. Ed. 909; and have refused to interfere with the operations of the police department. Davis v. American Society for the Prevention of Cruelty to Animals, 75 N.Y. 362; Delaney v. Flood, 183 N.Y. 323, 76 N.E. 209, 2 L.R.A., N.S., 678, 111 Am. St. Rev. 759, 5 Ann. Cas. 480; compare Bisbee v. Arizona Insurance Agency, 14 Ariz. 313, 127 P. 722. Instances are numerous where protection to property by way of injunction has been refused solely on the ground that serious public inconvenience would result from restraining the act complained of. Such, for example, was the case where a neighboring land owner sought to restrain a smelter from polluting the air, but that relief, if granted would have necessitated shutting down the plant and this would have destroyed the business and impaired the means of livelihood of a large community. There are also numerous instances where the circumstances would, according to general equity practice, have justified the issue of an injunction, but it was refused solely because the right sought to be enforced was created by statute, and the courts, applying a familiar rule, held that the remedy provided by the statute was exclusive.

Such limitations upon the use of the injunction for the protection of private rights have ordinarily been imposed in the interest of the public by the court acting in the exercise of its broad discretion. But, in some instances, the denial of the preventive remedy because of a public interest deemed paramount, has been expressly commanded by statute. Thus, the courts of the United States have been prohibited from staying proceedings in any court of a State, Judicial Code, sec. 265, 28 U.S.C.A. sec. 371; and also from enjoining the illegal assessment and collection of taxes. Revised Statutes, sec. 3224; Snyder v. Marks, 109 U.S. 189, 3 S. Ct. 157, 27 L. Ed. 901; Dodge v. Osborn, 240 U.S. 118, 36 S. Ct. 275, 60 L. Ed. 557. What Congress can do in curtailing the equity power of the federal courts, state legislatures may do in curtailing equity powers of the state court; unless prevented by the constitution of the State. In other words States are free since the adoption of the Fourteenth Amendment as they were before, either to expand or to contract their equity jurisdiction. The denial of the more adequate equitable remedy for private wrongs is in essence an exercise of the police power, by which, in the interest of the public and in order to preserve the liberty and the property of the great majority of the citizens of a State, rights of property and the liberty of the individual must be remoulded, from time to time, to meet the changing needs of society.

For these reasons, as well as for others stated by Mr. Justice Holmes and Mr. Justice Pitney, in which I concur, the judgment of the Supreme Court of Arizona should, in my opinion, be affirmed:—first, because in permitting damage to be inflicted by means of boycott and peaceful picketing Arizona did not deprive the plaintiffs of property without due process of law or deny them equal protection of the laws; and secondly, because, if Arizona was constitutionally prohibited from adopting this rule of substantive law, it was still free to restrict the extraordinary remedies of equity where it considered their exercise to be detrimental to the public welfare, since such restriction was not a denial to the employer either of due process of law or of equal protection of the laws.

THE BEDFORD STONE CASE. A more restrictive application of the Sherman and Clayton antitrust laws came in 1927 with the decision in Bedford Cut Stone Co. v. Journeymen Stone Cutters' Ass'n.[11] For some years the union and the producers of Indiana limestone maintained cordial relations. In 1921 twenty-four of these employers combined and refused to deal with the union. They locked out all the union workers, hired nonunion workers, and required them to join a company union. The union, believing that the lockout sought to bring about its destruction, advised its 5000 members not to work on any stone originating from the Associated Indiana Quarries. Under the union constitution all members were bound not to handle any stone which had been cut by men working in opposition to the union. The employers, aware that the union stonecutters working on buildings throughout the country were refusing to work on stone quarried by nonunion men, proceeded under Section 20 of the Clayton Act and applied for an injunction restraining the union members from carrying out their announced boycott. The action was brought in the name of the Bedford Cut Stone Company a member of the Indiana combine.

The U.S. Supreme Court, sustaining a verdict for the employers, said:

. . . Respondents' chief contention is that "their sole and only purpose . . . was to unionize the cutters and carvers of stone at the quarries." . . . A restraint of interstate commerce cannot be justified by the fact that the ultimate object of the participants was to secure an ulterior benefit which they might have been at liberty to pursue by means not involving such restraint. . . .
With a few changes in respect of the product involved, dates, names and incidents, which would have no effect upon the principles established, the opinion in Duplex Co. v. Deering (254 U.S. 443) . . . , might serve as an opinion in this case. The object of the boycott there was precisely the same as it is here, and the interferences with interstate commerce, while they were more numerous and more drastic, did not differ in essential character from the interferences here.
Whatever may be said as to the motives of the respondents or their gen-

11. 274 U.S. 37 (1927).

eral right to combine for the purpose of redressing alleged grievances of their fellow craftsmen or of protecting themselves or their organizations, the present combination deliberately adopted a course of conduct which directly and substantially curtailed, or threatened thus to curtail, the natural flow in interstate commerce of a very large proportion of the building limestone production of the entire country, to the gravely probable disadvantage of producers, purchasers and the public; and it must be held to be a combination in undue and unreasonable restraint of such commerce within the meaning of the Anti-Trust Act as interpreted by this court. An act which lawfully might be done by one, may when done by many acting in concert take on the form of a conspiracy and become a public wrong, and may be prohibited if the result be hurtful to the public or to individuals against whom such concerted action is directed. . . .

. . . That the organizations, in general purpose and in and of themselves, were lawful and that the ultimate result aimed at may not have been illegal in itself, are beside the point. Where the means adopted are unlawful, the innocent general character of the organizations adopting them or the lawfulness of the ultimate end sought to be attained, cannot serve as a justification.

Mr. Justice Brandeis, dissenting, said:

"The plaintiffs are not weak employers opposed by a mighty union. They have large financial resources. Together, they ship 70 per cent of all the cut stone in the country. They are not isolated concerns. They had combined in a local employers' organization. And their organization is affiliated with the national employers' organization, called "International Cut Stone & Quarrymen's Association." Standing alone, each of the 150 Journeymen's locals is weak. The average number of members in a local union is only 33. The locals are widely scattered throughout the country. Strong employers could destroy a local "by importing scabs" from other cities. And many of the builders by whom the stonecutters were employed in different cities, are strong. It is only through combining the 5000 organized stonecutters in a national union, and developing loyalty to it, that the individual stonecutter anywhere can protect his own job. . . .

The manner in which the Journeymen's unions acted was also clearly legal. The combination complained of is the cooperation of persons wholly of the same craft, united in a national union, solely for self-protection. No outsider—be he quarrier, dealer, builder or laborer—was a party to the combination. No purpose was to be subserved except to promote the trade interests of members of the Journeymen's Association. There was no attempt by the unions to boycott the plaintiffs. There was no attempt to seek the aid of members of any other craft, by a sympathetic strike or otherwise. The contest was not a class struggle. It was a struggle between particular employers and their employees. . . .

Members of the Journeymen Stone Cutters' Association could not work any where on stone which has been cut at the quarries by "men working in opposition" to it, without aiding and abetting the enemy. Observance by each member of the provision of their constitution which forbids such action was essential to his own self-protection. It was demanded of each by loyalty to the organization and to his fellows. If, on the undisputed facts of this case, refusal to work can be enjoined, Congress created by the Sherman Law and the Clayton Act an instrument for imposing restraints upon labor which reminds of involuntary servitude. The Sherman Law was held in United States v. United States Steel Corporation (251 U.S. 417), to permit capitalists to combine in a single corporation 50 per cent of the steel industry of the United States dominating the trade through its vast resources. The Sherman Law was held in United States v. United Shoe Machinery Co. (247 U.S. 32), to permit capitalists to combine in another corporation practically the whole shoe machinery industry of the country, necessarily giving it a position of dominance over shoe-manufacturing in America. It would, indeed, be strange if Congress had by the same Act willed to deny to members of a small craft of workingmen the right to cooperate in simply refraining from work, when that course was the only means of self-protection against a combination of militant and powerful employers. I cannot believe that Congress did so.

Mr. Justice Holmes concurs in this opinion.

The protection which labor expected from the Clayton Act was completely lacking in the majority decision in the Bedford case. After the Duplex decision, where economic pressure exerted by nonemployees of the company was condemned, labor felt confident that strikes involving employees in direct relationship with the struck employer would receive legal sanction. The Supreme Court's test of reasonable restraint of trade which established a guide for business when confronted with antitrust charges did not apparently apply to labor activities. The Bedford decision prohibited members of the same union from cooperating with their international in refusing to handle or work on a product which had originated from a struck employer.

Unions accepted this decision as bringing them to a new low in their attempts to organize nonunion plants. Frustrated also was their intense desire to protect union-negotiated wages and working conditions. To deny workers the right to boycott nonunion products in effect compels union workers to strengthen the antilabor position of the nonunion employer whom the union feels will eventually seek to destroy, or at least weaken, union organization.

THE BRIMS CASE. An important antitrust case [12] with a new flavor was decided in 1926 by the U.S. Supreme Court. The issue involved a contract between building contractors, manufacturers of millwork, and the Carpenters' Union. The agreement provided that the contractors and the manufacturers would employ union carpenters only, and in turn that the carpenters would not install millwork produced under nonunion conditions. The carpenters' agreement is sometimes referred to

12. U.S. v. Brims, 272 U.S. 549 (1926).

as a lateral boycott, a variation of the secondary boycott. It is quite evident from the agreement that all the parties had everything to gain. By excluding nonunion products from the rich Chicago market the carpenters would force unionization of the nonunion mills, and the manufacturers no longer would have to meet competition from low-wage-paying firms. The contractors were to enjoy liberal discounts on their purchases from union millwork houses.

In 1921 a federal grand jury indicted all the parties, charging them with conspiracy to violate Section 1 of the Sherman Act. All were found guilty. The U.S. Supreme Court, upholding the convictions by a unanimous decision, declared that,

. . . as intended by all the parties, the so-called outside competition was cut-down and thereby interstate commerce directly and materially impeded. The local manufacturers, relieved from the competition that came through interstate commerce, increased their output and profits; they gave special discounts to local contractors; more union carpenters secured employment in Chicago and their wages were increased. These were the incentives which brought about the combination. The non-union mills outside of the city found their Chicago market greatly circumscribed or destroyed; the price of buildings was increased; and, as usual under such circumstances, the public paid excessive prices. . . . It is a matter of no consequence that the purpose was to shut out non-union millwork made within Illinois as well as that made without. The crime of restraining interstate commerce through combination is not condoned by the inclusion of intrastate commerce as well. . . .

The essence of the crime in this case was a restraint of commerce by the joint venture entered into by business firms and the labor union. In a later chapter we shall take up some antitrust cases holding that a union may lawfully engage in activities similar to those of the Carpenters' Union in the Brims case, so long as the union does not join hands with business groups in bringing about the restraining effect upon commerce.

THE CORONADO CASES. Labor, though considerably weakened by the series of decisions under the antitrust acts, realized more than ever that its survival and progress depended on its ability to encourage Congress to enact a new statute which would render it invulnerable to successful employer attacks in the courts. The legislation did come in 1932, but not before labor suffered further setbacks under the antitrust laws and under the common law. The last serious defeat under the antitrust laws came with the Supreme Court's decision in the Coronado case.[13]

This was a suit for damages charging a conspiracy of the defendants unlawfully to restrain and prevent plaintiff's interstate trade in coal in

13. Coronado Coal Co. v. U.M.W., 268 U.S. 295 (1925). In the first Coronado case, 259 U.S. 344, the Supreme Court reversed a verdict in favor of the mine workers and ordered a new trial.

violation of the Sherman Act. The charge was that the defendants in 1914 destroyed valuable mining properties of the plaintiffs. Treble damages and an attorney's fee were asked under Section 7 of the act.

There were two legal questions involved. The first legal issue was: May the unions be sued in their own name?

On this issue the Supreme Court said:

Undoubtedly at common law, an unincorporated association of persons was not recognized as having any other character than a partnership in whatever was done, and it could only sue or be sued in the names of its members, and their liability had to be enforced against each member. . . . Trade unions have been recognized as lawful by the Clayton Act; they have been tendered formal incorporation as National Unions by the Act of Congress approved June 29, 1886.

. . . In this state of federal jurisdiction, we think that such organizations are suable in the federal courts for their acts, and that funds accumulated to be expended in conducting strikes are subject to execution in suits committed by such unions in strikes.

The second legal issue was:

Does the complaint state a cause of action under the Sherman Act?

In the first Coronado case the Supreme Court held that the reduction in shipment of coal by reason of the strike was small and there appeared no evidence to show that the union had in mind interference with interstate commerce or competition when it interfered with plaintiffs' attempt to operate their mines with nonunion workers.

In the second Coronado case the Supreme Court reversed its position and although dismissing the complaint against the international union, held the local unions liable for damages under Section 7 of the Sherman Act. The court justified this reversal in the following words:

New and more elaborate evidence was also introduced in the second trial as to the capacity of the Bache-Denman mines under the open shop. In our previous opinion we declined to hold that the mere elimination from interstate trade of 5000 tons a week, which we took to be the practical limit of capacity of the plaintiffs, was significant in the total tonnage of the country or state or that its stoppage furnished a basis of itself for inferring a palpable and intentional restraint of interstate trade with which the defendants could be charged even though coal could be produced at a reduced cost under non-union conditions. . . . In a petition for a rehearing, plaintiffs urged upon us that this was an error and that the Denman Company in that region, nine in number, was 5000 tons a day rather than 5000 tons a week. In the view we took of the evidence then before us, we had only the isolated circumstances of the reduction in shipment of the normal product of the four mines destroyed, without the other evidence to show an actual intent and plan on the part of the defendants thereby to restrain interstate commerce. . . .

The mere reduction in the supply of an article to be shipped in interstate commerce by the illegal or tortious prevention of its manufacture or production is ordinarily an indirect and remote obstruction to that commerce. But when the intent of those unlawfully preventing the manufacture or production is shown to be to restrain or control the supply entering and moving in interstate commerce, or the price of it in interstate markets, their action is a direct violation of the Anti-Trust Act. . . . We think there was substantial evidence at the second trial in this case tending to show that the purpose of the destruction of the mines was to stop production of non-union coal and prevent its shipment to markets of other States than Arkansas, where it would by competition tend to reduce the price of the commodity and affect injuriously the maintenance of wages for union labor in competing mines and that the direction of the District Judge to return a verdict for the defendants other than the International Union was erroneous. We affirm the judgment of the District Court and the Circuit Court of Appeals in favor of the International Union, and reverse that in favor of District No. 21 and the other local unions and the individual defendant and remand the cause as to them for a new trial.

The third trial ended in a jury disagreement. During the fourth Coronado case and while the action was being tried, District 21 settled and paid $27,000 to the mine owners.

This decision presented a perplexing problem for unions generally. Almost every strike affects shipments of goods in interstate commerce. If the major union weapon, the strike, could be broken by the use of processes under the antitrust laws, the labor movement would necessarily become little more than a social experiment. It is true that the strike itself was not condemned. The violation occurred when the strike unreasonably restrained commerce, said the court. What is an unreasonable restraint of commerce is a matter exclusively for the courts. This far-reaching and disturbing ruling became academic after 1940 when the celebrated Apex case [14] and others were decided by the Supreme Court. We shall study these decisions in Chapter 7 after the Norris-LaGuardia Act resulted in different interpretations of the antitrust laws.

14. Apex Hosiery Co. v. Leader, 310 U.S. 469 (1940).

CHAPTER FOUR

The Contract
Interference Doctrine

W E must return to a consideration of common law development. In the middle of the nineteenth century, English courts created a new common law doctrine which American employers adopted and used effectively to hinder the growth of labor union organizations. The doctrine recognized a new tort or civil wrong which the courts permitted to be used as the basis for equitable relief in the form of an injunction. This common law principle is applicable where one party induces another party to breach a contract which it has with a third party, and the principle is often called the "contract interference" doctrine.

Three English Cases Involving Contract Interference

The new legal theory of contract interference first developed in the English case of Lumley v. Gye.[1] Although a labor union was not involved in this case, the common law doctrine which came out of it had great effects on the organizational campaigns of American labor unions at the turn of the twentieth century and plagued unions until 1932. More particularly, the doctrine laid the basis for the enforcement of "yellow-dog" contracts, by which an employee agreed, as a condition of employment, that he would not join or support a union during his tenure of employment. A more detailed discussion of this type of contract will take place when we study the Hitchman case, which appears later in this chapter.

Mr. Lumley, a theatre manager, and Miss Wagner, a singer, entered into a personal service contract. Mr. Gye, the defendant, persuaded Miss

1. Q.B. (1853) 2 EL and BL 216.

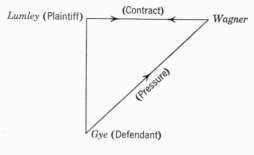

Figure 6

Wagner to breach her contract with Lumley and enter into a new contract with Gye.

The court's presentation of the facts and its decision follow:

Lumley alleges a contract made between himself and Johanna Wagner for her to perform in his theatre in operas for a specified time on certain terms, and among these, are that she was not during the time to sing or use her talents elsewhere than in his theatre without his written authority. He then complains that the defendant Gye, knowing the promises and maliciously intending to injure him and to prevent Wagner from performing according to her contract enticed and procured her to default in her performance and to abandon her contract. Lumley sued for special damages.

. . . It must now be considered clear law that a person who wrongfully and maliciously interrupts the relations subsisting between master and servant by procuring the servant to depart from the master's service, whereby the master is injured, commits a wrongful act for which he is responsible in law: The rule applies wherever the wrongful interruption operates to prevent service during the time for which the parties have contracted that the service shall continue; the relation of master and servant subsists during the time for which there is a binding contract of hiring and service between the parties.

Lumley deviated from the legal procedure formerly used in cases of this type. There are at least two other legal theories upon which Lumley might have proceeded. First, proceeding in equity for injunctive relief, he might have sought to enjoin Miss Wagner from performing under Gye's auspices. This procedure might have restored the contractual relations between Lumley and Wagner, and encouraged her to live up to her contract. Secondly, Lumley might have sued Miss Wagner for damages resulting from her breach of contract. Had Lumley adopted either of these two procedures, the case would have been buried in the law books as just another routine law suit. When Lumley proceeded against Gye seeking damages for his wrongful interference in bringing about a breach of the agreement, the case created new law. The contract interference doctrine became the backdrop for the use of the "yellow-dog" agreement in the United States.

There are two other English cases dealing with this new tort, or contract interference. One deals with a moral issue which resulted in the court's approval of an inducement to breach a contract. This was the case of Brimelow v. Casson.[2] In this case the actor's union was sued for inducing chorus girls to breach their contracts with a theatrical promoter. The union, for its defense, sought to condone the breach upon the ground that the promoter was paying the girls a substandard wage which they were forced to supplement by immoral activities. Justice Russell, giving the verdict to the actors' union, said:

. . . My task here is to decide whether, in the circumstances of this case, justification existed for the acts done. The plaintiff is carrying on a business which involves the employment for wage of persons engaged in the theatrical calling, a calling in which numberless persons of both sexes are engaged in different classes of work throughout the country. The unions, or associations, formed for the purpose of representing and advancing the interests of those persons in connection with their different classes of work, and the interests of the calling as a whole, have ascertained by experience, and no one could doubt the fact, that it is essential for the safeguarding of those interests that there should be no sweating by employers. They have found by experience that the payment of less than a living wage to chorus girls frequently drives them to supplement their insufficient earnings by indulging in misconduct for gain, thus ruining themselves in morals and bringing discredit to the theatrical calling. . . . They find that the plaintiff is paying to his chorus girls wages on which no girl could with decency, feed, clothe, and lodge herself, wages far below the minimum fixed by the Actors' Association. They have had previous experience of the plaintiff, and they caused fresh inquiries to be made, with the result that they are satisfied that many, if not all, the results anticipated by them to flow from such underpayment are present in the plaintiff's company. They desire in the interest of the theatrical calling and the members thereof to stop such underpayment with its evil consequences. The only way they can do so is by inducing the proprietors of theaters not to allow persons like the plaintiff the use of their theaters, either by breaking contracts already made or by refusing to enter into contracts. . . . But have they in law justification for those acts? As has been pointed out, no general rule can be laid down as a general guide in such cases, but I confess that if justification does not exist here I can hardly conceive of the case in which it would be present. . . . The result is that the action is dismissed with costs.

In this case the sanctity of the employment contract is justifiably withheld upon moral grounds. To enforce the contracts in this case would in effect encourage immoral conduct necessitated by the sweat shop conditions imposed upon the chorus girls.

2. 33 Ch. 302 (1924).

The last English case[3] concerned with this doctrine of contract interference was extended from third-party interference in a commercial matter to a situation where a union called out its own members in order to maintain decent conditions of employment. The employers were successful in obtaining damages from the union. The House of Lords entertained a case in which the Glamorgan Coal Company and seventy-three other plaintiffs, owners of collieries in South Wales, brought an action against the South Wales Miners' Federation, its trustees and officers, and several members of its executive council, claiming damages for wrongfully and maliciously procuring and inducing workmen in the collieries to break their contracts of service with the plaintiffs, and alternatively for wrongfully and maliciously conspiring to do so.

Briefly, the facts were as follows: The federation, which was a registered trade union, was formed (*inter alia*) to consider trade and wages, to protect the workmen and regulate the relation between them and employers, and to call conferences. The wages were paid on a sliding scale, rising and falling with the price of coal. In November 1900 the council of the federation, fearing that the action of the merchants and middlemen would reduce the price of coal and consequently the rate of wages, resolved to order a "stop day" on November 9 and informed the workmen. This order was obeyed by over 100,000 men, who took a holiday and thereby broke their contracts of service. Four other like holidays were later taken.

In support of the judgment for the mine owners, Lord MacNaughten, speaking for the House of Lords, said:

My Lords, I agree in the motion which my noble and learned friend the Lord Chancellor proposes, and I also agree with him in thinking that the question before your Lordships lies in a very narrow compass.

It is not disputed now—it never was disputed seriously—that the union known as the South Wales Miners' Federation, acting by its executive, induced and procured a vast body of workmen, members of the union, who were at the time in the employment of the plaintiffs, to break their contracts of service, and thus the federation acting by its executive knowingly and intentionally inflicted pecuniary loss on the plaintiffs. It is not disputed that the federation committed an actionable wrong. It is no defence to say that there was no malice or ill-will against the masters on the part of the federation or on the part of the workmen at any of the collieries thrown out of work by the action of the federation. It is settled now that malice is not the gist of such an action as that which the plaintiffs have instituted. Still less is it a defence to say that if the masters had only known their own interest they would have welcomed the interference of the federation.

It was argued—and that was the only argument—that although the thing

3. South Wales Miners' Fed'n v. Glamorgan Coal Co., [1905] A.C. 239.

done was prima facie an actionable wrong, it was justifiable under the circumstances. That there may be justification for that which in itself is an actionable wrong I do not for a moment doubt. And I do not think it would be difficult to give instances putting aside altogether cases complicated by the introduction of moral considerations. But what is the alleged justification in the present case? It was said that the council—the executive of the federation—had a duty cast upon them to protect the interest of the members of the union, and that they could not be made legally responsible for the consequences of their action if they acted honestly in good faith and without any sinister or indirect motive. The case was argued with equal candor and ability. But it seems to me that the argument may be disposed of by two simple questions. How was the duty created? What in fact was the alleged duty? The alleged duty was created by the members of the union themselves, who elected or appointed the officials of the union to guide and direct their action; and then it was contended that the body to whom the members of the union have thus committed their individual freedom of action are not responsible for what they do if they act according to their honest judgment in furtherance of what they consider to be the interest of their constituents. It seems to me that if that plea were admitted there would be an end to all responsibility. It would be idle to sue the workmen, the individual wrong-doers, even if it were practicable to do so. Their counsellors and protectors, the real authors of the mischief, would be safe from legal proceedings. The only other question is, What is the alleged duty set up by the federation? I do not think it can be better described than it was by Mr. Lush. It comes to this—it is the duty on all proper occasions, of which the federation or their officials are to be the sole judges, to counsel and procure a breach of duty."

Presumably it might have been argued that the union was justified in pursuing a course of action which led to the breach of contracts between the workmen and the mine owners, on the ground that the wages received by the workers were substandard and that to continue to work for indecent wages might have tempted the men to engage in stealing or other types of immoral activities so as to increase their income. As in the Brimelow case, it would not have been too far fetched to have pleaded that coal miners, like chorus girls, are subject to the temptations of immoral conduct when their wages are insufficient to provide the necessaries. There is some fragmentary evidence that this argument was pursued by counsel for the miners. One important fact must be noted; the Brimelow case was decided in 1924, twenty-four years after the miners' case had been adjudicated. Even had the Brimelow case come prior to 1900, there is no certainty that the House of Lords would have accepted this lower-court ruling as a binding precedent. We might note also that in most societies, courts have generally been considerably more solicitous to protect the virtue of womanhood than to preserve that of man, presumably on some notion that the worst penalty that can befall a poorly paid male worker is starvation, an honorable although unpleasant end.

The "Yellow-Dog" Contract

The English decisions laid the necessary foundation for effective use of the "yellow-dog" contract by American employers to frustrate union organizational campaigns.[4]

The right to join a union did not become legally enforcible until 1935, when the Wagner Act was enacted. At common law, employers were allowed to lay down arbitrary conditions of employment on the premise that ownership of property carried with it an exclusive right to determine working conditions. The Fourteenth Amendment implemented these arbitrary employer rights when a state attempted to make unenforcible the "yellow-dog" contract. In Coppage v. Kansas [5] the Supreme Court declared unconstitutional a Kansas statute of 1903 which made illegal the exaction by an employer from a worker of a pledge not to join a union. The court declared that an employer had a constitutional right to require his workers to sign antiunion contracts and depriving the employer of that right interfered with his freedom of contract and violated the Fourteenth Amendment.[6]

The Hitchman Case, 1917

Before the Hitchman decision [7] "yellow-dog" contracts were not enforcible in courts of equity. The legal action adopted in this case was based upon the old common law doctrine which provided that an actionable civil wrong resulted when a third party induced or sought to induce another to breach a valid contract.

In the Hitchman case the employer (represented in our figure by E), who had exacted "yellow-dog" contracts from its employees (W), sought an injunction to restrain the UMW (U) from inducing the workers to breach their contracts.

Mr. Justice Pitney delivered the opinion of the court.

4. *See* E. E. Witte, Yellow-dog Contracts, 6 *Wis. L. Rev.* 26 (1930).
5. 236 U.S. 1 (1915).
6. *See* Adair v. U.S., 208 U.S. 161 (1908), where the Supreme Court declared unconstitutional Sec. 10 of the Erdman Act of 1898, which made it unlawful for an interstate carrier to discharge a worker because of his union membership.
7. Hitchman Coal Co. v. Mitchell, 245 U.S. 229 (1917).

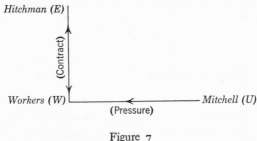

Figure 7

This was a suit in equity, commenced October 24, 1907, in the United States Circuit (afterwards District) Court for the Northern District of West Virginia, by the Hitchman Coal & Coke Company, a corporation organized under the laws of the state of West Virginia, against certain citizens of the state of Ohio, sued individually and also as officers of the United Mine Workers of America . . .

Plaintiff owns about 5000 acres of coal lands situate at or near Benwood, in Marshall county, West Virginia, and within what is known as the "Pan Handle District" of that state, and operates a coal mine thereon, employing between 200 and 300 men, and having an annual output, in and before 1907, of about 300,000 tons. At the time of the filing of the bill, and for a considerable time before and ever since, it operated its mine "non-union," under an agreement with its men to the effect that the mine should be run on a non-union basis, that the employees should not become connected with the union while employed by plaintiff, and that if they joined it their employment with plaintiff should cease. The bill set forth these facts, *inter alia,* alleged that they were known to defendants and each of them, and "that the said defendants have unlawfully and maliciously agreed together, confederated, combined and formed themselves into a conspiracy, the purpose of which they are proceeding to carry out and are now about to finally accomplish, namely: To cause your orator's mine to be shut down, its plant to remain idle, its contracts to be broken and unfulfilled, until such time as your orator shall submit to the demand of the union that it shall unionize its plant, and having submitted to such demand unionize its plant by employing only union men who shall become subject to the orders of the union," etc. The general object of the bill was to obtain an injunction to restrain defendants from interfering with the relations existing between plaintiff and its employees in order to compel plaintiff to "unionize" the mine. . . .

That the plaintiff was acting within its lawful rights in employing its men only upon terms of continuing non-membership in the United Mine Workers of America is not open to question. Plaintiff's repeated costly experiences of strikes and other interferences while attempting to "run union" were a sufficient explanation of its resolve to run "non-union," if any were needed. But neither explanation nor justification is needed. Whatever may be the advantages of "collective bargaining," it is not bargaining at all, in any just sense, unless it is voluntary on both sides. The same liberty which enables men to form unions, and through the union to enter into agreements with employers willing to agree, entitles other men to remain independent of the union and other employers to agree with them to employ no man who owes any allegiance or obligation to the union. In the latter case, as in the former, the parties are entitled to be protected by the law in the enjoyment of the benefits of any lawful agreement they make. This court repeatedly has held that the employer is as free to make nonmembership in a union a condition of employment, as the working man is free to join the union, and that this is a part of the constitutional rights of personal liberty and private property not to be taken away even by legislation, unless through some proper exercise of the paramount police power. . . .[8]

Plaintiff, having in the exercise of its undoubted rights established a working agreement between it and its employees, with the free assent of the latter, is entitled to be protected in the enjoyment of the resulting status, as in any other legal right. That the employment was "at will," and terminable by either party at any time, is of no consequence. . . .

In short, plaintiff was and is entitled to the good will of its employees, precisely as a merchant is entitled to the good will of his customers although they are under no obligation to continue to deal with him. The value of the relation lies in the reasonable probability that, by properly treating its employees, and paying them fair wages, and avoiding reasonable grounds of complaints, it will be able to retain them in its employ, and to fill vacancies occurring from time to time by the employment of other men on the same terms. The pecuniary value of such reasonable probabilities is incalculably great, and is recognized by the law in a variety of relations. . . .

We turn to the matters set up by way of justification or excuse for defendants' interference with the situation existing at plaintiff's mine.

The case involves no question of the rights of employees. Defendants have no agency for plaintiff's employees, nor do they assert any disagreement or grievance in their behalf. In fact, there is none; but, if there were, defendants could not, without agency, set up any rights that employees might have. The right of the latter to strike would not give to defendants the right to instigate a strike. The difference is fundamental.

It is suggested as a ground of criticism that plaintiff endeavored to secure a closed non-union mine through individual agreements with its employees, as if this furnished some sort of excuse for the employment of coercive measures to secure a closed union shop through a collective agreement with the union. It is a sufficient answer, in law, to repeat that plaintiff had a legal and constitutional right to exclude union men from its employ. But it may be worth while to say, in addition: First, that there was no middle ground open to plaintiffs; no option to have an "open shop" employing union men and non-union men indifferently; it was the union that insisted upon closed-shop agreements, requiring even carpenters employed about a mine to be members of the union, and making the employment of any non-

8. The court cites as its authority Coppage v. Kansas, 236 U.S. 1, 35 Sup. Ct. 240 (1915). This case is similar to Adair v. U.S., reported in this chapter.

union man a ground for a strike; and secondly, plaintiff was in the reasonable exercise of its rights in excluding all union men from its employ, having learned, from a previous experience, that unless this were done union organizers might gain access to its mine in the guise of laborers.

Defendants set up, by way of justification or excuse, the right of workingmen to form unions, and to enlarge their membership by inviting other workingmen to join. The right is freely conceded, provided the objects of the union be proper and legitimate, which we assume to be true, in a general sense, with respect to the union here in question . . . The cardinal error of defendants' position lies in the assumption that the right is so absolute that it may be exercised under any circumstances and without any qualification; whereas in truth, like other rights that exist in civilized society, it must always be exercised with reasonable regard for the conflicting rights of others. . . .

Now, assuming defendants were exercising, through Hughes, the right to invite men to join their union, still they had plain notice that plaintiff's mine was run "non-union," that none of the men had a right to remain at work there after joining the union, and that the observance of this agreement was of great importance and value both to plaintiff and to its men, who had voluntarily made the agreement and desired to continue working under it. Yet defendants, far from exercising any care to refrain from unnecessarily injuring plaintiff, deliberately and advisedly selected that method of enlarging their membership which would inflict the greatest injury upon plaintiff and its loyal employees. Every Hitchman miner who joined Hughes' "secret order" and permitted his name to be entered upon Hughes' list was guilty of a breach of his contract of employment and acted a lie whenever thereafter he entered plaintiff's mine to work. Hughes not only connived at this, but must be deemed to have caused and procured it, for it was the main feature of defendants' plan, the sine qua non of their programme. Evidently it was deemed to be necessary, in order to "organize the Panhandle by a strike movement," that at the Hitchman, for example, man after man should be persuaded to join the union, and having done so to remain at work, keeping the employer in ignorance of their number and identity, until so many had joined that by stopping work in a body they could coerce the employer and the remaining miners to "organize the mine," that is, to make an agreement that none but members of the union should be employed, that terms of employment should be determined by negotiation not with the employees but with union officers—perhaps residents of other states and employees of competing mines—and that all questions in controversy between the mine operator and the miners should likewise be settled with outsiders.

True, it is suggested that under the existing contract an employee was not called upon to leave plaintiff's employ until he actually joined the union and that the evidence shows only an attempt by Hughes to induce the men to agree to join, but no attempt to induce them to violate their contract by failing to withdraw from plaintiff's employment after actually joining. But in a court of equity, which looks to the substance and essence of things and disregards matters of form and technical nicety, it is sufficient to say that to induce men to agree to join is but a mode of inducing them to join, and that when defendants "had sixty men who had signed up or agreed to join the organization at Hitchman," and were "going to shut the mine down as soon as they got a few more men," the sixty were for practical purposes, and therefore in the sight of equity, already members of the union, and it needed no formal ritual or taking of an oath to constitute them such; their uniting with the union in the plan to subvert the system of employment at the Hitchman mine, to which they had voluntarily agreed and upon which their employer and their fellow employees were relying, was sufficient.

But the facts render it plain that what the defendants were endeavoring to do at the Hitchman mine and neighboring mines cannot be treated as a bona fide effort to enlarge the membership of the union. There is no evidence to show, nor can it be inferred, that defendants intended or desired to have the men at these mines join the union, unless they could organize the mines. Without this, the new members would be added to the number of men competing for jobs in the organized districts, while non-union men would take their places in the Panhandle mines. Except as a means to the end of compelling the owners of these mines to change their method of operation, the defendants were not seeking to enlarge the union membership.

In any aspect of the matter, it cannot be said that defendants, were pursuing their object by lawful means. The question of their intentions—of their bona fides—cannot be ignored. . . . Of course, in a court of equity, when passing upon the right of injunction, damage threatened, irremediable by action at law, is equivalent to damage done. And we cannot deem the proffered excuse to be a "just cause or excuse," where it is based, as in this case, upon an assertion of conflicting rights that are sought to be attained by unfair methods, and for the very purpose of interfering with plaintiff's rights, of which defendants have full notice.

Another fundamental error in defendants' position consists in the assumption that all measures that may be resorted to are lawful if they are "peaceable"—that is, if they stop short of physical violence, or coercion through fear of it. In our opinion, any violation of plaintiff's legal rights contrived by defendants for the purpose of inflicting damage, or having that as its necessary effect, is as plainly inhibited by the law as if it involved a breach of the peace. A combination to procure concerted breaches of contract by plaintiff's employees constitutes such a violation. . . .

The present is not a case of merely withholding from an employer an economic need—as a supply of labor—until he assents to be governed by union regulations. Defendants have no supply of labor of which plaintiff stands in need. By the statement of defendant (J.L.) Lewis himself, made in his formal report to the Indianapolis convention of 1907, out of more than 370,000 coal miners in the states of Pennsylvania, Maryland, Virginia, and West Virginia, less than 80,000 (about 22%) were members of union. Considering the Panhandle separately, doubtless the proportion was even smaller, and the supply of non-union labor ample. There is no reason to doubt that if defendants had been actuated by a genuine desire to increase the membership of the union without unnecessary injury to the known rights of plaintiff, they would have permitted their proselytes to withdraw from plaintiff's employ when and as they became affiliated with the union—as their contract of employment required them to do—and that in this event plaintiff would have been able to secure an adequate supply of non-union men to take their places. It was with knowledge of this, and because of it, that defendants, through Hughes as their agent, caused the new members to remain at work in plaintiff's mine until a sufficient number of men should be persuaded to join so as to bring about a strike and render it difficult if not practically impossible for plaintiff to continue to exercise its undoubted legal and constitutional right to run its mine "non-union."

It was one thing for plaintiff to find, from time to time comparatively small numbers of men to take vacant places in a going mine, another and a much more difficult thing to find a complete gang of new men to start up a mine shut down by a strike, when there might be a reasonable apprehension of violence at the hands of the strikers and their sympathizers. The disordered condition of a mining town in time of strike is matter of common knowledge. It was this kind of intimidation as well as that resulting from the large organized membership of the union, that defendants sought to exert upon plaintiff.

Defendants' acts cannot be justified by any analogy to competition in trade. They are not competitors of plaintiff; and if they were, their conduct exceeds the bounds of fair trade. Certainly, if a competing trader should endeavor to draw a custom from his rival, not by offering better or cheaper goods, employing more competent salesmen, or displaying more attractive advertisements, but by persuading the rival's clerks to desert him under circumstances rendering it difficult or embarrassing for him to fill their places, any court of equity would grant an injunction to restrain this as unfair competition.

Upon all the facts, we are constrained to hold that the purpose entertained by defendants to bring about a strike at plaintiff's mine in order to compel plaintiff, through fear of financial loss, to consent to the unionization of the mine as the lesser evil, was an unlawful purpose, and that the methods resorted to by Hughes—the inducing of employees to unite with the union in an effort to subvert the system of employment at the mine by concerted breaches of the contracts of employment known to be in force there, not to mention misrepresentation, deceptive statements, and threats of pecuniary loss communicated by Hughes to the men—were unlawful and malicious methods, and not to be justified as a fair exercise of the right to increase the membership of the union.

There can be no question that plaintiff was threatened with danger of an immediate strike as a result of the activities of Hughes. The effect of his arguments and representations is not to be judged from the testimony of those witnesses who rejected his overtures. Naturally, it was not easy for plaintiff to find men who could testify that they had agreed with Hughes to break their contract with plaintiff. One such did testify. But the true measure of the extent of his operations and the probability of his carrying them to success are indicated by his declaration to Myers that he had about enough names at the Hitchman to "crack off," by the statement to McKinley that 24 men at the Glendale mine had joined the organization, and 60 at the Hitchman, and by the fact that they actually succeeded in shutting down the Richland about the middle of October. The declaration made concerning the Glendale is corroborated by the evidence of what happened at that time.

That the damage resulting from a strike would be irremediable at law is too plain for discussion.

Therefore, upon the undisputed facts of the case, and the indubitable inferences from them, plaintiff is entitled to relief by injunction. Having become convinced by 3 costly strikes, occurring within a period of as many years, of the futility of attempting to operate under a closed-shop agreement with the union, it established the mine on a non-union basis, with the unanimous approval of its employees—in fact, upon their suggestions—and under a mutual agreement, assented to by every employee, that plaintiff would continue to run its mine non-union and would not recognize the United Mine Workers of America; that if any man wanted to become a member of that union he was at liberty to do so, but he could not be a member and remain in the plaintiff's employ. Under that agreement plaintiff ran its mine for a year and more, and, so far as appears, without the slightest disagreement between it and its men, and without any grievance on their part. Thereupon defendants, having full notice of the working agreement between plaintiff and its men, and acting without any agency for those men, but as representatives of an organization of mine workers in other states, and in order to subject plaintiff to such participation by the Union in the management of the mine as necessarily results from the making of a closed-shop agreement, sent their agent to the mine, who, with full notice of, and for the very purpose of subverting, the status arising from plaintiff's working agreement and subjecting the mine to the union control, proceeded, without physical violence, indeed, but by persuasion accompanied by threats of a reduction of wages and deceptive statements as to the attitude of the mine management, to induce plaintiff's employees to join the union and at the same time to break their agreement with plaintiff by remaining in its employ after joining; and this for the purpose not of enlarging the membership of the union, but of coercing plaintiff, through a strike or the threat of one, into recognition of the union.

As against the answering defendants, plaintiff's right [is clear].

Mr. Justice Brandeis, dissenting, said

The Circuit Court of Appeals, reversing the decree of the District Court, held that the United Mine Workers of America was not an unlawful organization under the laws of West Virginia, that its validity under the Federal Anti-trust Act could not be considered in this proceeding; that so long as defendants "refrained from resorting to unlawful measures to effectuate" their purpose "they could not be said to be engaged in a conspiracy to unionize plaintiff's mine"; That "the evidence failed to show that any unlawful methods were resorted to by these defendants in this instance"; and specifically, that there was nothing in the individual contracts which barred defendants from inducing the employees to join the union. With these conclusions I agree substantially.

FIRST: THE ALLEGED ILLEGALITY OF THE UNITED MINE WORK-
ERS OF AMERICA UNDER THE LAW OF WEST VIRGINIA. The United
Mine Workers of America does not appear to differ essentially in character
and purpose from other international unions which, like it, are affiliated
with the American Federation of Labor. Its membership is said to be larger
than that of any other, and it may be more powerful. But the common law
does not limit the size of unions or the degree to which individual workmen may by union increase their bargaining power. . . .

SECOND: THE ALLEGED ILLEGALITY OF THE UNITED MINE WORK-
ERS OF AMERICA UNDER THE FEDERAL ANTI-TRUST ACT. . . . the
question was not in issue in the case. It had not been raised in the bill or
by answer. Evidence bearing upon the issue . . . should have been excluded.

THIRD: THE ALLEGED CONSPIRACY AGAINST THE WEST VIRGINIA
MINES. It was doubtless the desire of the United Mine Workers to unionize every mine on the American continent and especially those in West
Virginia. . . . That desire and the purpose to effect it were not unlawful.
They were part of a reasonable effort to improve the condition of workingmen engaged in the industry by strengthening their bargaining power
through unions, and extending the field of union power. No conspiracy to
shut down or otherwise injure West Virginia was proved. . . .

FOURTH: UNIONIZING PLAINTIFF'S MINE WITHOUT PLAINTIFF'S
CONSENT. The fundamental prohibition of the injunction is against acts
done "for the purpose of unionizing plaintiff's mine without plaintiff's
consent." Unionizing a shop does not mean inducing the employees to
become members of the union. It means inducing the employer to enter into
a collective agreement with the union governing the relations of the employer
to the employees. Unionizing implies, therefore, at least formal consent of
the employer. Both plaintiff and defendants insisted upon exercising the
right to secure contracts for a closed shop. The plaintiff sought to secure
the closed non-union shop through individual agreements with employees.
The defendants sought to secure the closed union shop through a collective
agreement with the union. Since collective bargaining is legal, the fact that
the workingmen's agreement is made not by individuals directly with the
employer, but by the employees with the union and by it, on their behalf,
with the employer, is of no significance in this connection. The end being
lawful, defendants' efforts to unionize the mine can be illegal only if the
methods or means pursued were unlawful; unless indeed there is some
special significance in the expression "unionizing without plaintiff's consent."

It is urged that a union agreement curtails the liberty of the operator.
Every agreement curtails the liberty of those who enter into it. The test of
legality is not whether an agreement curtails liberty, but whether the parties
have agreed upon something which the law prohibits or declares otherwise
to be inconsistent with the public welfare. The operator by the union agreement binds himself: (1) To employ only members of the union; (2) to
negotiate with union officers instead of with employees individually the scale
of wages and the hours of work; (3) to treat with the duly constituted representatives of the union to settle disputes concerning the discharge of men

and other controversies arising out of the employment. These are the chief features of a "unionizing" by which the employer's liberty is curtailed. Each of them is legal. To obtain each of the things for which the agreement provides, why may it not strike or use equivalent economic pressure to secure an agreement to provide them?

It is also urged that defendants are seeking to "coerce" plaintiff to "unionize" its mine. But coercion, in a legal sense, is not exerted when a union merely endeavors to induce employees to join a union with the intention thereafter to order a strike unless the employer consents to unionize his shop. Such pressure is not coercion in a legal sense. The employer is free either to accept the agreement or the disadvantage. Indeed, the plaintiff's whole case is rested upon agreements secured under similar pressure of economic necessity or disadvantage. If it is coercion to threaten to strike unless plaintiff consents to a closed shop union, it is coercion also to threaten not to give one employment unless the applicant will consent to a closed non-union agreement for fear that labor may not be otherwise obtainable; the workman may sign the individual agreement, for fear that employment may not be otherwise obtainable. But such fear does not imply coercion in a legal sense.

In other words, an employer, in order to effectuate the closing of his shop to union labor, may exact an agreement to that effect from his employees. The agreement itself being a lawful one, the employer may withhold from the men an economic need—employment—until they assent to make it. Likewise an agreement closing a shop to non-union labor being lawful, the union may withhold from an employer an economic need—labor—until he assents to make it. In a legal sense an agreement entered into, under such circumstances, is voluntarily entered into; and as the agreement is in itself legal, no reason appears why the general rule that a legal end may be pursued by legal means should not be applied. Or, putting it in other words, there is nothing in the character of the agreement which should make unlawful means used to attain it which in other connections are recognized as lawful.

FIFTH: THERE WAS NO ATTEMPT TO INDUCE EMPLOYEES TO VIOLATE THEIR CONTRACTS. The contract created an employment at will; and the employee was free to leave at any time. The contract did not bind the employee not to join the union; and he was free to join it at any time. The contract merely bound him to withdraw from plaintiff's employ if he joined the union. There is evidence of an attempt to induce plaintiff's employees to agree to join the union; but none whatever of any attempt to induce them to violate their contract. Until an employee actually joined the union he was not, under the contract, called upon to leave plaintiff's employ. There consequently would be no breach of contract until the employee both joined the union and failed to withdraw from plaintiff's employ. There was no evidence that any employee was persuaded to do that, or that such a course was contemplated. What perhaps was intended was to secure agreements or assurances from individual employees that they would join the union when a large number of them should have consented to do so: with the purpose, when such time arrived, to have them join the union together and strike—unless plaintiff consented to unionize the mine. Such a course would have been clearly permissible under the contract.

SIXTH: MERELY PERSUADING EMPLOYEES TO LEAVE PLAIN-TIFF'S EMPLOY, OR OTHERS NOT TO ENTER IT, WAS NOT UNLAW-FUL. To induce third persons to leave an employment is actionable if done maliciously and without justifiable cause, although such persons are free to leave at their own will. . . . It is equally actionable so to induce others not to enter the service. The individual contracts of plaintiff with its employees added nothing to its right in this connection, since the employment was terminable at will.

As persuasion, considered merely as a means, is clearly legal, defendants were within their rights if, and only if, their interference with the relation of plaintiff to its employees was for justifiable cause. The purpose of inter-fering was confessedly in order to strengthen the union, in the belief that thereby the condition of workmen engaged in mining would be improved; the bargaining power of the individual workingman was to be strengthened by collective bargaining; and collective bargaining was to be insured by obtaining the union agreement. It should not, at this day, be doubted that to induce workingmen to leave or not to enter an employment in order to advance such a purpose is justifiable when the workmen are not bound by contract to remain in such employment.

SEVENTH: THERE WAS NO "THREAT, VIOLENCE, OR INTIMIDA-TION." The decree enjoined "threats, violence, or intimidation." Such action would, of course, be unlawful though employed in a justifiable cause. But there is no evidence that any of the defendants have resorted to such means. The propaganda among plaintiff's employees was conducted almost entirely by one man, the defendant Hughes, a district No. 6 organizer. His actions were orderly and peaceable, consisting of informal talks with the men, and a few quietly conducted public meetings in which he argued the benefits of organization and pointed out to the men that, although the com-pany was then paying them according to the union scale, there would be nothing to prevent a later reduction of wages unless the men united. He also urged upon the men that if they lost their present jobs, membership in the union was requisite to obtaining employment in the union mines of the neighboring states. But there is no suggestion that he exceeded the moderate bounds of peaceful persuasion, and indeed, if plaintiff's witnesses are to be believed, men with whom Hughes had talked, his argument made no impression on them, and they expressed to him their satisfaction with existing conditions at the mines.

When this suit was filed no right of the plaintiff had been infringed and there was no reasonable ground to believe that any of its rights would be interfered with; and, in my opinion, the Circuit Court of Appeals properly reversed the decree of the District Court, and directed that the bill be dismissed.

Under its majority decision, the Supreme Court lent legal sanctity to the "yellow-dog" contract. To call it a contract was misnomer. It could be terminated at will by either party; the employer could fire the worker at any time and for any reason and the worker was free to quit his job at his pleasure. Each man must work to live, and to force him to sign a contract under which he surrenders what many consider to be a natural right leading to justice is tantamount to telling him he may not survive unless he keeps out of a union. A fundamental requirement of every valid agreement is that each party enters into it freely and without any form of coercion. A job is one of man's most precious possessions, which, at times, he finds difficult to obtain. The "yellow-dog" agreement, however odious it might appear to a worker, was entered into by him because it was the only means offered him to avoid impoverishment. Had the court not been inspired by prejudice, it might have recognized the existence of economic coercion inherent in the "agreement" and vitiating it, just as a "shotgun" wedding would vitiate a marriage contract.

When the court declared that it would protect the personal liberty of a worker to contract away his right to join a union, it made a mockery out of liberty. All enlightened persons today concede that a coal miner has no bargaining strength in dealing with the owner of a coal mine, and that without a union a worker subjects himself to wages and working conditions unilaterally established by the employer. Real personal liberty allows a man freedom to choose between two or more equitable courses of action. If the miner exercised his freedom not to sign the "yellow-dog" contract, he remained unemployed, a completely inequitable choice.

When the court defended the property right which it said was inherent in the "yellow-dog" contract, it had to determine first that a valid agreement existed. Although this conclusion found ready support by the court's majority, few persons today would undertake to label the "yellow-dog" contract worthy of the constitutional protection afforded contracts.

The Hitchman decision was more than another major defeat for labor unions. Any widespread adoption of the "yellow-dog" contract device by employers would have threatened the very foundation of the then small organized labor movement. Legislative relief was therefore imperative and fortunately came, in 1932, with the passage of the Norris-LaGuardia Act.

THE NEW YORK COURTS. In concluding our discussion of the Hitchman case, it should be noted that in most states the courts adhered to this decision. The state of New York was an exception. In the Exchange Bakery case [9] the New York Court of Appeals refused to allow the enforcement of a "yellow-dog" contract. In Interborough Rapid Transit Company v. Green,[10] another leading New York case, an injunction

9. 245 N.Y. 260 (1927).
10. 227 N.Y. Supp. 258 (1928).

application seeking to restrain the defendant union from inducing a breach of a "yellow-dog" contract was denied on the ground that such agreements were inequitable and therefore unenforcible in the courts.

Justice Andrew's eloquent opinion on the rights of workers is set forth in the Exchange Bakery case, and it became the backdrop of the court's repudiation of the "yellow-dog" contract. He observed:

"A workman may leave his work for any cause whatever. He need make no defense, give no explanations. Whether in good or bad faith, whether with malice or without, no one can question his action. What one man may do, two may do or a dozen, so long as they act independently. If, however, any action taken is concerted; if it is planned to produce some result, it is subject to control. As always, what is done, if legal, must be to effect some lawful results by lawful means, but both a result and a means lawful in the case of an individual may be unlawful if the joint action of a number.

A combination to strike or to picket an employer's factory to the end of coercing him to commit a crime, or to pay a stale or disputed claim would be unlawful in itself although for an individual, his intent in leaving work does not make wrongful the act otherwise lawful. His wrong, if wrong there be, would consist of some threat, of something beyond the mere termination of his contract with his employer. Likewise a combination to effect many other results would be wrongful. Among them would be one to strike or picket a factory where the intent to injure rests solely on malice or ill will. Another's business may not be so injured or ruined. It may be attacked only to attain some purpose in the eye of the law thought sufficient to justify the harm that may be done to others.

The purpose of a labor union to improve the conditions under which its members do their work; to increase their wages; to assist them in other ways may justify what would otherwise be a wrong. So would an effort to increase its numbers and to unionize an entire trade or business. It may be as interested in the wages of those not members, or in the conditions under which they work as in its own members because of the influence of one upon the other. All engaged in a trade are affected by the prevailing rate of wages. All, by the principle of collective bargaining. Economic organization today is not based on the single shop. Unions believe that wages may be increased, collective bargaining maintained only if union conditions prevail, not in some single factory but generally. That they may prevail it may call a strike and picket the premises of an employer with the intent of inducing him to employ only union labor. And it may adopt either method separately. Picketing without a strike is no more unlawful than a strike without picketing. Both are based upon a lawful purpose. Resulting injury is incidental and must be endured.

Even if the end sought is lawful, the means used must be also. "Picketing" connotes no evil. It may not be accompanied, however, by violence, trespass, threats or intimidation express or implied. No crowds may be collected on or near the employer's property. The free entrance of strangers, customers or employees may not be impeded. There may be no threats—

no statements oral or written, false in fact, yet tending to injure the employer's business. We here make no attempt to enumerate all the acts that might make picketing illegal. Doubtless there are others. When the situation in a particular case comes to be reviewed by the courts there will be no difficulty in drawing the line between acts permissible and acts forbidden.

We have been speaking in terms of the workman. We might equally have spoken in terms of the employer. The rule that applies to the one also applies to the other. The latter may hire and discharge men when and where he chooses and for any reason. But again any combination must be for lawful ends secured by lawful means. If believed to be for their interests employers may agree to employ non-union men only. By proper persuasion they may induce union men to resign from their unions. They may not, however, because of mere malice or ill will, combine to limit the opportunities of any one to obtain employment. The means adopted must be lawful. No violence or intimidation, no threats, no trespass, no harmful false statements, no means that would be improper were the workman the actor.

In writing as we have done, we have in mind cases where the strike, the picketing or the lockout is made use of by associates in the same trade or business; where the end sought, therefore, directly affects those, masters or men, engaged therein. We do not consider so-called sympathetic strikes, boycotts or lockouts where interest is more remote. Questions that may arise under such circumstances are not before us. Neither do we consider strikes or lockouts not connected with labor disputes, but designed to enforce political action.

Where the end or the means are unlawful and the damage has already been done the remedy is given by a criminal prosecution or by a recovery of damages at law. Equity is to be invoked only to give protection for the future. To prevent repeated violations, threatened or probable, of the complainant's property rights, an injunction may be granted. This is no novel assumption of jurisdiction. For many years, while leaving to the law redress for single or isolated wrongs to property rights, where there is danger of their repetition, the chancellor has used this weapon to protect the innocent. The theoretical basis of this power has been said to be the avoidance of a multiplicity of actions. Whatever the basis, however, the power is undoubted. It has been exercised in many ways. Repeated trespasses have been prevented; the continued pollution of streams; the maintenance of nuisances; the misuse of a trade name. Other instances might be cited. The rule is not different where behind the facts presented to the court lies a labor dispute. Freedom to conduct a business, freedom to engage in labor, each is like a property right. Threatened and unjustified interference with either will be prevented. But the basis of permissible action by the court is the probability of such interference in the future, a conclusion only to be reached through proof contained in the record. Unless the need for protection appears, equity should decline jurisdiction.

In the case before us findings of fact were made by the Special Term resulting in a judgment for the defendants. Most of such findings were reversed by the Appellate Division. As a substitute new findings were made by that court and a sweeping injunction was granted to the plaintiff. It, therefore, becomes our duty to review these findings and to determine for ourselves whether they are sustained by the weight of the evidence.

In 1918 the plaintiff corporation was formed. From the first its intention was to employ only non-union waitresses in its restaurant. Always, with one exception, an applicant for employment was questioned as to her membership in any union and only those who denied such a connection were engaged. No contract as to this matter was then made but the applicant was hired at the rate of $8 per week for full time or $5 for half time. This hiring was at will and might be ended at any time by either party. (Cuppy v. Stollwerck Brothers, 216 N.Y. 591). Thereafter the waitresses were asked repeatedly if they had joined a union. They always denied it. If it had been discovered that their denials were untrue they would have been at once discharged. Also after beginning work each waitress signed a paper stating that it was the understanding that she was not a member of any union, pledging herself not to join one or if she did to withdraw from her employment. She further promised to make no efforts to unionize the restaurant, and says that she will attempt to adjust by individual bargaining any dispute that may arise. This paper was not a contract. It was merely a promise based upon no consideration on the part of the plaintiff. From fourteen to sixteen waitresses were employed and so far as appears the conditions of their work was [were?] satisfactory to them.

The three defendants are members of a waiters' union. Its schedule of wages is $15 a week for full time and $10 for half time. Apparently at their instigation four waitresses joined the union after employment was obtained. They had not been members on the date when they were originally engaged. The fact that they had done so was not known to the plaintiff. Efforts were also made to induce other employees to take the same course. At the same time the plaintiff was asked to unionize its restaurant, but it refused.

The Appellate Division has based its decision in part upon the theory that the defendants wrongfully attempted to persuade the plaintiff's employees to break this alleged contract. Even had it been a valid subsisting contract, however, it should be noticed that whatever rule we may finally adopt, there is as yet no precedent in this court for the conclusion that a union may not persuade its members or others to end contracts of employment where the final intent lying behind the attempt is to extend its influence. In Lamb v. Cheney & Son (227 N.Y. 418) we said that where a specific contract of employment for a definite time exists another may not intentionally, without just cause or excuse, interfere therewith.

On April 22, 1925, some of the defendants representing the union entered the plaintiff's restaurant as ordinary customers. They did this, however, with the preconceived design of causing a strike by blowing a whistle at a time inconvenient to the plaintiff when many patrons were present. In so acting they were clearly trespassers and if such trespasses were to be continued in the future they might be enjoined. It was an isolated wrong, however, and adequate compensation might be recovered in an action at law. When the strike was declared the four waitresses who had joined the union at once stopped work and left the premises. In so doing one of them threatened an officer of the plaintiff and she interfered with the access of a patron of the restaurant. A crowd collected but was soon dispersed. Again we have an isolated instance of intimidation occurring at the outset of the strike. Thereafter there was picketing which consisted of two women walking in the street close to the curb but near the premises, having placards ten by sixteen inches in size pinned to their dresses and bearing the legend: "Waitresses Strike Picket. Waiters Union Local No. 1. Affiliated with the American Federation of Labor and the United Hebrew Trades." There was no violence; no intimidation; no obstruction of entrances to the premises; no collection of crowds. This course of conduct continued for four days until it was ended by a temporary injunction.

Under such a state of facts the defendants have been enjoined from "patrolling the sidewalk and street in front of and near the plaintiff's premises, from approaching, accosting, threatening, assaulting or intimidating any person desiring to enter the premises, from blockading the entrance thereto, from collecting crowds, from exhibiting any signs or notices in the vicinity, from suggesting a boycott, and from coercing or intimidating any person seeking to enter the employment of the plaintiff." In this we think the Appellate Division has erred.

As we have indicated, the action of those defendants who entered the restaurant when the strike was called was a trespass. There is, however, no indication that such acts will be repeated. There was no contract between the plaintiff and its waitresses in regard to the union with which the defendants can be said to have interfered. There is nothing untruthful in the placards carried by the pickets, even assuming that the word "strike" is to be confined to cases where some of those who have become employees of the plaintiff have left its employment to obtain relief in a labor dispute. Such was the case here. Three of these four waitresses were employed by the plaintiff long before they became members of the union. Their reply to inquiries then made was entirely truthful. To the fourth, no questions were put. If they subsequently joined the union they might have been discharged; but until they were discharged they remained in the plaintiff's employment. Except on the one occasion the picketing was entirely lawful and for a lawful object, although the plaintiff's business might be injured thereby. It is said that the strike was not properly called because of the neglect of some preliminaries which the union rules required in such a case, and that the four waitresses referred to were not properly members of the union because their dues had not been paid. This is a question as to which the plaintiff is not interested.

It is quite true that where unlawful picketing has been continued; where violence and intimidation have been used and where misstatements as to the employers' business have been distributed, a broad injunction prohibiting all picketing may be granted. The course of conduct of the strikers has been such as to indicate the danger of injury to property if any picketing whatever is allowed. Such is not this case. Nor should a court of equity intervene where there is no evidence that wrongs have been committed or threatened on the theory that the defendant is not harmed by the prohibition of such unlawful acts.

The judgment of the Appellate Division should be reversed and that of the Special Term affirmed, with costs in this court and in the Appellate Division.

Boycotts at Common Law

The word "boycott" is not easily defined. It is frequently spoken of as merely passive, a let-alone policy, or a withdrawal of all business relations.

It has been defined more formally as "an organized effort to exclude a person from business relations with others by persuasion, intimidation and other acts which tend to violence, and thereby to coerce him, through fear or resulting injury, to submit to dictation in the management of his affairs." [11]

A primary boycott occurs when an organized union of employees by concerted action ceases dealing in a business way with the employer.

A secondary boycott occurs when such employees induce others to withhold their business relations from a former employer by threatening a like boycott against such others if they refuse to comply with their demand. It seeks to influence A by exerting economic pressure against persons who deal with A.

A backward boycott is a refusal by men in the higher processes of manufacture to work on or with material which in the next lower process of manufacture is made by nonunion workers.

The forward boycott is a refusal by union workers in the lower processes of manufacture to make material that will probably be used in the next higher process by nonunionists.

A lateral boycott is a boycott on materials, not for the purpose of organizing workers in the lower or higher processes of manufacture, but to force the employment of members of the same union on the same level of manufacture.

Boycotts first made their appearance in this country in the early 1880's. They were regarded by the courts as agreements by a combination of persons to do some unlawful act or to effect a lawful object by unlawful means. They were treated as conspiracies, and actions for damages were allowed and injunctions were granted, because they employed force and threats or intimidations.[12]

11. Bouvier's *Law Dictionary*, Third Revision (Eighth ed.), (1914) West Pub. Co., St. Paul, Minn., Vol. I, p. 385.

12. For the status of boycotts at common law, see J. H. Wigmore, The Boycott and Kindred Practices as Ground for Damages, 21 *Am. L. Rev.* 509 (1887); L. Wolman, *The Boycott in American Trade Unions*, (1916) Johns Hopkins Univ. Press, Baltimore; Strikes and Boycotts, 34 *Harv. L. Rev.* 880 (1921).

In 1922 an Iowa court [13] held that the law very generally condemned those combinations usually termed "boycotts" which were formed for the purpose of interfering, other than by lawful competition, with the affairs of others, and depriving them, by means of threats and intimidation, of the right to conduct the business in which they happened to be engaged according to the dictates of their own judgment.

A California court in 1938 [14] granted an injunction restraining secondary boycott pressure. It held unlawful an attempt to compel A to yield a legitimate benefit to B, when B demanded that C withdraw his patronage from A under the penalty of losing B's services or patronage to which he had no contract right.

Whether or not the boycott used was lawful became a difficult question at common law. Naturally the answer hinged largely on the facts in each controversy. Very frequently the issue was decided according to the philosophy of the judge who heard the matter. It was therefore not uncommon for federal judges to disagree with each other, and sometimes sharp conflicts existed between federal and state court judges. The result of this judicial difference of opinion on what constituted a legal or illegal boycott was that the combatants who participated in industrial controversies had few binding precedents available. The Iron Molders' case,[15] which follows, was an example of the conflict of opinion existing between a federal court and a state court.

The trial court had issued an injunction which forbade the union

. . . from enforcing, maintaining or aiding any legal boycott against the said company, its agents or employees; from endeavoring to illegally induce people not to deal with said company; and, from preventing or attempting to prevent by threats, intimidation, persuasion or in any other manner any person or corporation from performing work for said complainant and from doing business with it.

Chief Justice Baker refused to find the boycott illegal. He said:

. . . Appellants were aiming to prevent, and appellee to secure, the doing of certain work in which the skill of appellants' trade was necessary. Here was the ground of controversy, and here the test of endurance. If appellee had the right (and we think the right was perfect) to seek the aid of fellow foundrymen to the end that the necessary element of labor should enter into appellee's product, appellant had a reciprocal right of seeking the aid of fellow molders to prevent that end. To whatever extent employers may lawfully combine and cooperate to control the supply and the conditions of work to be done, to the same extent should be recognized the right of workmen to combine and cooperate to control the supply and the conditions

13. Ellis v. Journeyman Barbers' Int'l Union, 194 Iowa 1179 (1922).
14. Parkinson Co. v. Bldg. Trades Council, 154 Cal. 581 (1938).
15. Iron Molders' Union v. Allis-Chalmers Co., U.S. Cir. C. App., 7th Circuit, 166 F. 45 (1908). *Contra*, York Mfg. Co. v. Oberdick, 10 Pa. Dist. 463 (1901).

of the labor that is necessary to the doing of the work. In the fullest recognition of the equality and mutuality of their rights and their restrictions lies the peace of capital and labor, for so they, like nations with equally well drilled and equipped armies and navies, will make and keep treaties of peace, in the fear of the cost and consequences of war. . . .

An Illinois appellate court [16] affirmed a lower court's decision refusing to grant an injunction in a boycott case. During an attempt to organize workers employed by the complainant, a union broadcasted several statements over station WCFL. One of the statements was this:

Dental Laboratories Workers' Union No. 19,358 wishes to inform the public that Boston Dental Parlors are non-union so far as organized labor is concerned, as they will not permit collective bargaining. We would suggest that you patronize other dental parlors for your necessary dental work if you are interested in fair, impartial treatment for the working man.

The complainant sought to enjoin the radio station from continuing to broadcast this and similar statements on the ground that the broadcasts constituted a "boycott" intended to intimidate it into recognizing the defendant union. The court said:

. . . We are impelled to hold that it is not unlawful for a labor organization in a radio broadcast to express freely its honest opinion as to the fairness or unfairness of the attitude of an employer toward organized labor, and that it is not unlawful that such broadcast contain advice to the public and friends of union labor not to patronize such employer. . . .

In a Pennsylvania case [17] a labor union used the primary and the secondary boycott during a labor controversy after the employer had refused to unionize his mill. Circulars were distributed to builders and contractors declaring that the union would not handle mill work coming from nonunion mills and that plaintiff's mill was nonunion. Disciplinary action was taken against all members of the defendant union who violated the boycott. Union label stamps were provided for union mills to distinguish their products from those of nonunion mills. The trial court enjoined all these acts. On appeal, the decision was affirmed. Quoting from the opinion of the trial court, Justice Brown declared:

. . . On part of plaintiffs, it is alleged that the means used are a boycott of their business. The defendants contend that their methods were persuasive and were not accompanied with violence, threats or intimidation. No violence was used nor does any seem to have been contemplated or threatened. But acts may be coercive in character without threats or commission of violence or personal injury. When the district council with its 7000 members in the Pittsburgh district gave notice to practically all the building con-

16. Dr. Lietzman, Dentist Inc. v. Radio Broadcasting Station WCFL, 282 Ill. App. 203 (1935).
17. Purvis v. Local 500, Bhd. of Carpenters, 214 Pa. 348 (1906).

tractors of that district that the plaintiffs refused to run their mill in accordance with union rules, and calling attention to the working rule which forbids union workmen to work material from any nonunion mill, the contractors understood what the request not to patronize plaintiffs' mill meant. When the members of Local No. 500, who were willingly working material from plaintiffs' mill were visited by the business agent of the union, who called them off, they doubtless knew that it meant trial, fine or expulsion and ostracism if they continued to work. . . . In all these things the attitude of the defendants was threatening and coercive rather than persuasive.

In Pickett v. Walsh,[18] the Massachusetts Supreme Court refused to vacate an injunction when members of a labor union employed by a contractor to do work on a building, and who had no dispute with the contractor as to the work which they were performing, struck the contractor when he was doing work and employing other members of the same union to work on another building on which nonunion men were employed, not by the contractor, but by the owner of that building.

In a 1938 New York case [19] a union was enjoined from picketing restaurants selling union-made beer which had been delivered to the restaurants in a truck driven by a chauffeur who was not a member of the Teamsters' Union. The court held this to be a secondary boycott not within the protection of the laws of New York.

Labor unions have always considered the boycott one of their most effective self-help devices. At common law the courts have upheld labor's use of the primary boycott. The secondary boycott, however, has been declared unlawful on the ground that labor unions have used this means to damage parties having no relation or interest with the dispute at issue. Courts have considered the secondary boycott unlawful because it tends to restrain commerce, and because they believed it constituted an unjustifiable interference with the business of one not himself a party to a labor controversy.

The leading New York case on the legality of the secondary boycott is Goldfinger v. Feintuch,[20] in which the court denied the injunction and permitted the boycott. Although this case was decided after the enactment of Section 876(a), Civil Practice Act, frequently called the "anti-injunction" statute, there is some authority holding that this new law did not effect the substantive law relating to the status of secondary boycotts at common law.[21]

18. 192 Mass. 572 (1906).
19. Sweeney v. Doe, 255 App. Div. 893 (1938).
20. 276 N.Y. 281 (1937).
21. *See* Busch Jewelry Co. v. United Retail Union Local 830, 281 N.Y. 151 (1930), in which the Court of Appeals held that Section 876(a) was never intended to deprive the Supreme Court of New York of jurisdiction to enjoin dangerous illegal acts which constitute disorderly conduct and breach of the peace. The majority stated that, when unions deliberately and willfully, with full knowledge that their

The court justified its action in Goldfinger when it developed a "unity of interest" doctrine. Simply stated, the court allowed picketing here because it stated that a "unity of interest" existed between the struck manufacturer and the retailer who was picketed. The court insisted that the placards used by the pickets indicate clearly that it was the product and not the retailer who was being picketed. The case has considerable importance in setting forth the New York law on secondary boycotts.

Justice Finch delivered the opinion of the Court of Appeals which follows.

W. and I. Blumenthal manufacture kosher meat products which are sold under the name of "Ukor." The "Ukor" products are the only non-union made kosher products sold in the city of New York, and the salaries paid by this company range from 50 to 75 cents an hour as compared with the union scale of 95 cents to $1.25 an hour. The defendant Butchers' Union Local No. 174 endeavored to obtain a union agreement from the manufacturer of "Ukor" products. When these efforts were unsuccessful, the defendant decided to picket the non-union made products at the retail stores. Among the stores picketed was that of the plaintiff, a dealer in kosher meat products. The defendant placed pickets, sometimes one, sometimes two, in front of the plaintiff's store, carrying signs which bore the inscriptions in English and Yiddish, "This store sells delicatessen that is made in a non-union factory," and "Ukor Provision Company is unfair to Union labor. Please buy union-made delicatessen only."

The important question in this case is whether, assuming that there has been no violence, force, intimidation, breach of the peace, coercion, fraud, or unlawful threat, the act of the defendant in thus picketing the delicatessen store of the plaintiff is legal. . . .

As between an employer and an employee, the right of a union to picket peacefully is generally conceded. Its purpose must be to persuade, not to intimidate. So long as the pleas of both employer and employee are lawful, the courts have not been constituted arbiters of the fairness, justice, or wisdom of the terms demanded by either the employer or employees. J.H. & S. Theatres, Inc. v. Fay, 260 N.Y. 315, 183 N.E. 509. It is only where unlawful acts have been committed that the courts interevene to redress or prevent manifest abuse of the right to picket peacefully with a limited number of pickets. . . .

Within the limits of peaceful picketing, however, picketing may be carried on not only against the manufacturer but against a non-union product sold by one in unity of interest with the manufacturer who is in the same business for profit. Where a manufacturer pays less than union wages, both it and the retailers who sell its products are in a position to undersell competitors who pay the higher scale, and this may result in unfair reduction of the wages of union members. Concededly the defendant union would be

---

acts are illegal, advise and encourage the commission of acts that violate the law, they are not entitled to the benefits of statutes enacted to protect them in the enjoyment of their right of peaceful picketing.

entitled to picket peacefully the plant of the manufacturer. Where the manufacturer disposes of the product through retailers in unity of interest with it, unless the union may follow the product to the place where it is sold and peacefully ask the public to refrain from purchasing it, the union would be deprived of a fair and proper means of bringing its plea to the attention of the public.

An analogous principle has been applied by this court in Bossert v. Dhuy, 221 N.Y. 342, 117 N.E. 582, Ann. Cas. 1918 D, Willson & Adams Co. v. Pearce, 264 N.Y. 521, affirming 240 App. Div. 718, 265 N.Y.S. 624, and in New York Lumber Trade Ass'n v. Lacey, 269 N.Y. 595, 199 N.E. 688. The cases of Auburn Draying Co. v. Wardell, 227 N.Y. 1, 124 N.E. 97, 6 A.L.R. 901, and George F. Stuhmer & Co. v. Korman, 241 App. Div. 702, 269 N.Y.S. 788, affirmed, 265 N.Y. 481, 193 N.E. 281, are not in point. In the Wardell case all union members in the city of Auburn, regardless of industry, threatened to withdraw their patronage from any one who dealt with the plaintiff because it refused to require its employees to join a union. In the Stuhmer case the pickets made false statements, obstructed the sidewalks, created disturbances, and were guilty of other unlawful conduct which so permeated all the picketing that an injunction would have been warranted whether the picketing was at the store of a retailer or that of the nonunion manufacturer.

We do not hold more than that, where a retailer is in unity of interest with the manufacturer, the union may follow the nonunion goods and seek by peaceful picketing to persuade the consuming public to refrain from purchasing the nonunion product, whether that is at the plant of the manufacturer or at the store of the retailer in the same line of business and in unity of interest with the manufacturer. Such storekeeper may be, as in the case at bar, the sole person required to man his business. If Goldfinger, the delicatessen dealer, had employed any help, legally they could strike or refuse to work for him so long as he sold Ukor products. We have so held in Bossert v. Dhuy, *supra*. Such employees, having the right to refuse to work for the plaintiff, would likewise have the right to inform the public why they refused to work for the plaintiff. In this respect at least it has been settled that labor may aid its cause. If a union may request its members not to work upon or with materials brought from a nonunion shop or call a strike for such reasons, it is difficult to see why, under the law of this state, it may not peacefully state the grievance by placards similar to those used here. In other words, it may, in a proper manner and in a peaceful way, ask the public to refrain from purchasing products made by nonunion labor and state where the same are sold. The holding by this court that where a shopkeeper is the sole person required to run his business he is, therefore, not subject to picketing by a union which seeks to compel him to employ union labor (Luft v. Flove, 270 N.Y. 640, 1 N.E. 2d 369; Thompson v. Boekhout, 273 N.Y. 390, 7 N.E. 2d 674) is not authority to prevent peaceful picketing for the purposes in the case at bar. Here the purpose is legal. There it was unlawful.

We are thus brought to a consideration of the recently enacted statute applicable to the issuance of injunctions in labor disputes. Civil Practice

Act, Sec. 876(a) (Laws of 1935, C. 477). This provides in brief that no injunction shall issue in a labor dispute in the absence of certain enumerated findings which have been found on disputed evidence in the case at bar. . . .

It is urged, however, that Section 876(a) was never intended to apply to the conduct involved herein; that this case does not involve a "labor dispute" within the meaning of the term as used in the statute. Paragraph 10 of that section defines labor dispute. Pertinent portions thereof provide: "A case shall be held to involve or to grow out of a labor dispute when the case involves persons who are engaged in the same industry, trade, craft or occupation . . . when the case involves any conflicting or competing interests in a 'labor dispute' (as hereinafter defined) of 'persons participating or interested' therein (as hereinafter defined)." . . . The term "labor dispute" is then defined as "any controversy concerning terms or conditions of employment, or concerning the association or representation of persons in negotiating, fixing, maintaining, changing or seeking to arrange terms of conditions of employment, or concerning employment relations, or any other controversy arising out of the respective interests of employer and employee, regardless of whether or not the disputants stand in the relation of employer and employee." . . . In view of this definition it cannot be contended that the case at bar does not involve a labor dispute under Section 876(a). . . . The judgment should be modified in accordance with this opinion, and as so modified affirmed, without costs.[22]

Justice Finch contributed the following dictum in the Goldfinger case:

. . . Likewise it is illegal to picket the place of business of one who is not himself a party to an industrial dispute to persuade the public to withdraw its patronage generally from the business for the purpose of coercing the owner to take sides in a controversy in which he has no interest.[23]

There is no question that the picketing of the retail store in the Goldfinger case sought to put pressure on the manufacturer with whom the union was engaged in a controversy. If the picketing proved effective; it would be the result of customer sympathy with the objectives of the union. The customer would be expected to withhold his patronage only with respect to the commodity in dispute. Once this happened, the retailer could be expected to stop selling the disputed commodity and stock his shelves with a substitute. The continuing economic loss to the manufacturer would be expected to force him to settle its controversy on terms acceptable by the union.

22. New York courts have enjoined the picketing of third parties where no "unity of interest" existed on the ground that such picketing constituted a secondary boycott. See Weill Company v. John Doe, 5 N.Y.S. (2d) 559 (1938); City Specialty Stores v. Livingston, 23 LC 67, 664 (1953).

23. See Fortenbury v. Superior Court, 16 Cal. (2d) 405 (1940), in which the Supreme Court of California held lawful exactly what the New York court condemned in this statement.

A great deal of criticism has been directed against the Goldfinger decision. Some believe that the retailer was an innocent third party, or at least a neutral to the controversy between the manufacturer and the union, and that the picketing of the retail store influenced customers to withhold all patronage because the average customer is not sufficiently discerning when it comes to reading and interpreting the message carried on a picket's placard. The irreparable damage which could visit the retailer unless he became an ally of the union, however unwilling, was a prime factor in getting the retailer's cooperation.

It would appear therefore that the "unity of interest" doctrine is based on a court-endorsed public policy openly sympathetic to the legitimate goals of labor unions.

In this chapter we have seen how public policy, expressed through the Congress, removed the "yellow-dog" contract as an impediment to the growth of the labor movement. We might say that this public policy recognized great merit in encouraging the development of a strong labor movement which could require even the largest industries to engage in collective bargaining, the product of which could lead to economic justice for the workers and to less conflict in the field of labor relations.

The public policy manifested in the Goldfinger decision appears to be another encouragement to labor unions' attainment of what the court believed to be a desirable objective.

From 1914 to 1932 the labor injunction was for employers the most effective weapon to protect property and property rights against interference by picketing, strikes, and boycotts. During this period workers had no legal right to join unions or to engage in concerted activities. Most of the conflict developed during union organizing campaigns, and most of these drives were stopped by court injunctions.

Public policy is ever changing, and in 1932 Congress, through the Norris-LaGuardia Act, endorsed and legitimatized the self-help methods available to labor unions. This act allowed labor unions to seek legitimate objectives without court interference. Several of our states reflected the change in public policy by enacting legislation which paralleled the federal law. Between 1932 and 1947 the labor injunction constituted no threat to the legitimate and peaceful activities of labor unions.

CHAPTER FIVE

The Norris-LaGuardia Act of 1932

THE era of labor union promotion began in 1932 with the passage of the Norris-LaGuardia Act,[1] frequently called the anti-injunction law. The act was based on the power granted Congress by Article III of the United States Constitution to regulate the jurisdiction of federal courts. The relevant language of the article is:

The judicial power of the United States shall be vested in one supreme court, and in such inferior courts as the congress may, from time to time, ordain and establish. . . . The judicial power shall extend to all cases in law and equity arising under this constitution, the laws of the United States, and treaties made, or which shall be made, under their authority. . . .

The legislative history of the act indicates that it was the purpose of Congress to deprive the federal courts of jurisdiction to issue injunctions "in any case involving or growing out of any labor dispute" and to restrict the power of these courts to enjoin "other labor dispute" activities except after findings of certain facts by the court.

Since the act's restriction of the injunction powers of federal courts hinges on the existence or nonexistence of a "labor dispute," this determination is crucial. If there is no "labor dispute," none of the provisions of the Norris-LaGuardia Act apply.

In conventional usage the term "labor dispute" is applied indiscriminately to virtually any controversy between an employer and employees, or unions. But for the purposes of the act the term has a specific meaning, which is set forth in Section 13. The term "labor dispute" is quite broad and includes any dispute concerning "terms or conditions of employment." The employer-employee relationship is not required for a "labor dispute" to exist. For example, jurisdictional disputes between

1. Act of March 23, 1932, 47 Stat. 70, 29 U.S.C. 102.

two or more unions over control of jobs and union drives to organize workers have been declared to be "labor disputes."

If there is a "labor dispute," there is a complete withdrawal of the jurisdiction of federal courts with regard to enjoining nine types of activities listed in Section 4 when carried on by persons interested in the "dispute." These activities will be listed later; they include most of the usual self-help devices of employees or unions.

Even when a "labor dispute" exists as defined in Section 13, certain activities may be enjoined provided the petitioner has satisfied certain statutory requirements found in Sections 7 and 8.

In "labor disputes" undertaken in combination with nonlabor groups, and where the activity violates the antitrust laws, the Norris-LaGuardia Act protection is withdrawn.

With this background, we may consider the important statutory provisions of the act and leading cases from which have come precedent-setting decisions. The heart of the act is found in Sections 3, 4, 7, and 13.

Section 3 declares that "yellow-dog" contracts are contrary to public policy and shall not be enforcible in federal courts. The statute does not mention the term "yellow-dog," but the language used in the act clearly describes this type of agreement. Those who drafted the law were careful not to declare such contracts void or illegal. They knew the act would have to undergo the customary constitutional test, and to have declared explicitly that "yellow-dog" agreements were unlawful, might, they believed, have imperiled major provisions in the statute, or even the entire act. Such contracts have been denied legal enforcement on the legal principle that individual rights may become subject to governmental regulation when the exercise of such rights has been declared to be detrimental to the health, safety, or general welfare of society. Section 3 has been sustained by the courts on this sound principle. In abridging freedom to enter into this type of contract, the general welfare of workers and the public good are protected.

Section 4 allows workers to strike, to picket, to engage in primary and secondary boycotting, and to engage in related activities. It protects nine specific activities from the injunctive process.

(1) Concerted stoppage or refusal to work.

(2) Joining or remaining a union member.

(3) Providing financial help to persons taking part in or interested in a "labor dispute."

(4) Giving assistance to a person participating or interested in a "labor dispute" who may be involved in litigation.

(5) Publicizing the existence of a "dispute" by any method not involving violence or fraud.

(6) Assemblying peaceably to promote the interests of participants in a "labor dispute."

(7) Notifying any person of an intent to engage in those activities listed in 1 to 6 inclusive.

(8) Agreeing with others to do or not to engage in those activities listed in 1 to 6 inclusive.

(9) Inducing or advising without violence or fraud any of the above activities.

Section 7 provides that federal courts may not issue injunctions in "labor dispute" cases except after the court has made findings of all of the following:

(1) Unlawful acts have been committed or are threatened.

(2) Irreparable injury to property has been committed or is imminent.

(3) The petitioner has more to lose if the injunction is denied than will be suffered by the employees or union if the injunction is granted.

(4) The petitioner has no adequate remedy at law.

(5) The police are either unable or unwilling to protect the petitioner's property.

In addition, Section 8 requires, as another condition precedent for injunctive relief, that the petitioner must have made efforts to settle the "labor dispute."

Section 13 defines a "labor dispute" as any controversy dealing with wages, conditions of employment, or representation for bargaining purposes, and there need not be an employer-employee relationship.

Section 9 is worth mentioning. Before the Norris-LaGuardia Act was passed the omnibus or blanket injunction was often issued as a matter of course. This so-called "blanket" form of restraining order prevented specified persons and "all others" from engaging in specified activities.[2] At times the "other persons" were union lawyers, shopkeepers who refused to serve strike-breakers, and members of the community who sympathized with the cause of the strikers. Under Section 9 this broad type of order may no longer be granted by the court. The court is permitted to enjoin only specific acts expressly complained of, and which are expressly included in the court's findings.

The act's principal accomplishment was to control federal courts in issuing injunctions in "labor dispute" matters. Another important point is not what this law does for labor, but what it allows labor to do for itself. We can say this is a good example of self-help legislation.

2. This aspect of the injunction is discussed in more detail in F. Frankfurter and N. Greene, *The Labor Injunction*, (1930) The Macmillan Co., New York. See also D. Bonnett, The Origin of the Labor Injunction, 5 *So. Cal. L. Rev.* 105 (1931); J. Kerian, Injunctions in Labor Disputes, The History of the Norris-LaGuardia Act, 37 *N.D. L. Rev.*, Jan. 1960.

The Constitutionality of the Act

The Norris-LaGuardia bill was introduced in Congress in 1931, and the state of Wisconsin, interested in the subject matter, had access to the bill. It was interesting in tightening up the issuance of injunctions in labor cases by its state courts; in 1931 the legislature had passed a "baby" Norris-LaGuardia Act, making it Section 103.53 of the Wisconsin Labor Code. The constitutionality of the Wisconsin statute was upheld by the U.S. Supreme Court in 1937 when it ruled in the case of Senn v. Tile Layers Protective Union.[3] Although the federal Norris-LaGuardia Act was not directly involved, the decision in the Senn case gave constitutional approval to the federal statute which resembled Section 103.53 of the Wisconsin Labor Code.

The Senn case is one of the most provocative in labor law and it has resulted in considerable discussion on the question of constitutional freedoms.[4]

Senn, a nonunion contractor, was advised by the tilelayers' union to operate a union shop and give up his practice of working with the tools of his trade, a practice disallowed by all the union shops in Milwaukee. When Senn agreed to operate under union shop conditions, but refused to give up his right to work, his place of business was picketed. Senn petitioned a state court for an injunction, charging that the picketing was coercive and unlawful, since it was directed against his constitutional right to work. The Wisconsin courts denied him any relief. He then petitioned the U.S. Supreme Court for a review of the state court decisions. The Supreme Court upheld the constitutionality of the "baby" Norris-LaGuardia Act and thereby approved the Wisconsin Labor Code, which immunized the tilelayers' union's picketing activities.

Mr. Justice Brandeis delivered the opinion of the court.

"This case presents the question whether the provisions of the Wisconsin Labor Code which authorize giving publicity to labor disputes, declare peaceful picketing and patrolling lawful and prohibit granting of an injunction against such conduct, violate, as here construed and applied, the due process clause or equal protection clause of the Fourteenth Amendment.

. . . The following provisions of section 103.53 are directly involved on this appeal:

(1) The following acts, whether performed singly or in concert, shall be legal. . . .

3. 301 U.S. 468 (1937).
4. For interesting comment on this case, see Constitutionality of Anti-Injunction Statute, 6 *Fordham L. Rev.* 474 (1937).

(e) Giving publicity to and obtaining or communicating information regarding the existence of, or the facts involved in, any dispute, whether by advertising, speaking, patrolling any public street or any place where any person or persons may lawfully be, without intimidation or coercion, or by any other method not involving fraud, violence, breach of the peace, or threat thereof. . . .

(1) Peaceful picketing or patrolling, whether engaged in singly or in numbers, shall be legal.

(2) No court, nor any judge or judges thereof, shall have jurisdiction to issue any restraining order, or temporary or permanent injunction which, in specific or general terms, prohibits any person or persons from doing, whether singly or in concert, any of the foregoing acts.

On December 28, 1935, Senn brought this suit in the Circuit Court of Milwaukee County, against Tile Layers Protective Union, Local No. 5, Tile Layers Helpers Union, Local No. 47, and their business agents, seeking an injunction to restrain picketing, and particularly "publishing, stating or proclaiming that the plaintiff is unfair to organized labor or to the defendant unions"; and also to restrain some other acts which have since been discontinued, and are not now material. The defendants answered; and the case was heard upon extensive evidence. The trial court found the following facts.

The journeymen tile layers at Milwaukee were, to a large extent, members of Tile Layers Protective Union, Local No. 5, and the helpers, members of Tile Layers Helpers Union, Local No. 47. Senn was engaged at Milwaukee in the tile contracting business under the name of "Paul Senn & Co. Tile Contracting." His business was a small one, conducted, in the main, from his residence, with a showroom elsewhere. He employed one or two journeymen tile layers and one or two helpers, depending upon the amount of work he had contracted to do at the time. But, working with his own hands with tools of the trade, he performed personally on the jobs much work of a character commonly done by a tile layer or a helper. Neither Senn, nor any of his employees, was at the time this suit was begun a member of either union, and neither had any contractual relations with them. Indeed, Senn could not become a member of the tile layers union, since its constitution and rules require, among other things, that a journeyman tile setter shall have acquired his practical experience through an apprenticeship of not less than three years, and Senn had not served such an apprenticeship. . . .

The unions endeavored to induce Senn to become a union contractor; and requested him to execute an agreement in form substantially identical with that entered into by the Milwaukee contractors who employ union men. Senn expressed a willingness to execute the agreement provided Article III [5] was eliminated. The union declared that this was impossible, that the inclusion of the provision was essential to the unions' interest in maintaining

5. "Article III. It is definitely understood that no individual, member of a partnership or corporation engaged in the Tile Contracting Business shall work with the tools or act as Helper but that the installation of all materials claimed by the party of the second part as listed under the caption 'Classification of Work' in this agreement, shall be done by journeymen members of Tile Layers Protective Union Local 5."

wage standards and spreading work among their members; and, moreover, that to eliminate Article III from the contract with Senn would discriminate against existing union contractors, all of whom had signed agreements containing the article. As the unions declared its elimination impossible, Senn refused to sign the agreement and unionize his shop. Because of his refusal, the unions picketed his place of business. The picketing was peaceful, without violence, and without any unlawful act. The evidence was that the pickets carried one banner with the inscription "P. Senn Tile Company is unfair to the Tile Layers Protective Union," another with the inscription "Let the Union tile layer install your tile work."

The trial court denied the injunction and dismissed the bill. On the findings made, it ruled that the controversy was "a labor dispute" within the meaning of section 103.62; that the picketing, done solely in furtherance of the dispute, was "lawful" under section 193:53. . . .

The judgment of the highest court of the state establishes that both the means employed and the end sought by the unions are legal under its law. The question for our determination is whether either the means or the end sought is forbidden by the Federal Constitution.

. . . Clearly the means which the statute authorizes—picketing and publicity—are not prohibited by the Fourteenth Amendment. Members of a union might, without special statutory authorization by a state, make known the facts of a labor dispute, for freedom of speech is guaranteed by the Federal Constitution. The state may, in the exercise of its police power, regulate the methods and means of publicity as well as the use of public streets. If the end sought by the unions is not forbidden by the Federal Constitution the state may authorize working men to seek to attain it by combining as pickets, just as it permits capitalists and employers to combine in other ways to attain their desired economic ends. The Legislature of Wisconsin has declared that "peaceful picketing and patrolling" on the public streets and places shall be permissible "whether engaged in singly or in numbers" provided this is done "without intimidation or coercion" and free from "fraud, violence breach of the peace or threat thereof." The statute provides that the picketing must be peaceful; and that term as used implies not only absence of violence, but absence of any unlawful act. It precludes the intimidation of customers. It precludes any form of physical obstruction or interference with the plaintiff's business. It authorizes giving publicity to the existence of the dispute "whether by advertising, speaking, patrolling any public street or any place where any person or persons may lawfully be"; but precludes misrepresentations of the facts of the controversy. And it declares that "nothing herein shall be construed to legalize a secondary boycott."

. . . Inherently, the means authorized are clearly unobjectionable. In declaring such picketing permissible Wisconsin has put this means of publicity on a par with advertisements in the press.

The state courts found that the unions observed the limitations prescribed by the statute.

. . . The end sought by the unions is not unconstitutional. Article III, which the unions seek to have Senn accept, was found by the state courts to be not arbitrary or capricious, but a reasonable rule "adopted by the defendants out of the necessities of employment within the industry and for the protection of themselves as workers and craftsmen in the industry." That finding is amply supported by the evidence. There is no basis for a suggestion that the unions' request that Senn refrain from working with his own hands, or their employment of picketing and publicity, was malicious; or that there was a desire to injure Senn. The sole purpose of the picketing was to acquaint the public with the facts and by gaining its support to induce Senn to unionize his shop. There was no effort to induce Senn to do an unlawful thing. There was no violence, no force was applied, no molestation or interference, no coercion. There was only the persuasion incident to publicity. . . .

The unions acted, and had the right to act as they did, to protect the interests of their members against the harmful effect upon them of Senn's action. . . .

The laws of Wisconsin, as declared by its highest court, permit unions to endeavor to induce an employer, when unionizing his shop, to agree to refrain from working in his business with his own hands—so to endeavor although none of his employees is a member of a union. Whether it was wise for the state to permit the unions to do so is a question of its public policy —not our concern. The Fourteenth Amendment does not prohibit it.

. . . There is nothing in the Federal Constitution which forbids unions from competing with nonunion concerns for customers by means of picketing as freely as one merchant competes with another by means of advertisements in the press, by circulars, or by his window display. Each member of the unions, as well as Senn, has the right to strive to earn his living. Senn seeks to do so through exercise of his individual skill and planning. The union members seek to do so through combination. Earning a living is dependent upon securing work; and securing work is dependent upon public favor. To win the patronage of the public each may strive by legal means. Exercising its police power, Wisconsin has declared that in a labor dispute peaceful picketing and truthful publicity are means legal for unions. It is true that disclosure of the facts of the labor dispute may be annoying to Senn even if the method and means employed in giving the publicity are inherently unobjectionable. But such annoyance, like that often suffered from publicity in other connections, is not an invasion of the liberty guaranteed by the Constitution. . . . Affirmed.

Prior to this decision the U.S. Supreme Court considered most picketing a coercive force used unlawfully to damage property and, therefore, whenever the states attempted to protect picketing, as in the Truax case,[6] the court struck down the legislation on the ground that it was in violation of property rights protected under the Fourteenth Amendment of the Constitution. In 1937 the court appeared to deviate somewhat from this earlier attitude. The Supreme Court for the first time in the

6. *Supra.*

Senn case gave peaceful picketing the same status given to free speech under the First Amendment, leaving the states free, under their inherent police power, to regulate picketing.

Much criticism followed this five-to-four decision. Many were of the opinion that Mr. Senn should have been applauded for his willingness to work side by side with his employees. After all, did not all business start small and grow through the hard work of its principals? Most of the outcry was directed against the right of a union to use a picket line for the purpose of inducing a businessman to stop working with his own hands. The Senn decision, despite what appeared to be valid criticism at the time, might be justified on the basis of social responsibility. Certainly workers were entitled to good wages; if this objective has been reached through a union, it must necessarily follow that the union has a right to protect that which is intrinsically good. What means are available to the union for this purpose? There appears no choice other than a picket with authority to advise the general public of its objectives and appeal to it for support against one who, by his independent action, will if left free destroy that which is socially good. Left unhindered, it was inevitable that Senn's cutthroat type of competition would have reduced the number of union men he employed. If this analysis is acceptable, it should be clear that the union was compelled to act against Senn as it did. By its action, the union protected the unionized employers and at the same time protected the good wage scale and the other desirable working conditions it had gained through collective bargaining. Unquestionably there is great value in the statement that competition is good. Yet it ought to follow that all sides must have the opportunity to compete for business, or, as in the case of unions, for jobs. The Supreme Court accepted this position, stating that Senn and the tilelayers' union both had a right to compete for available work and the method of competition open to the union was public appeal; i.e., asking the public to support the union in preference to the nonunion worker. In spite of the union's appeal, the public makes the final choice, which might well have favored Senn, whose contract price was lower than that of the union shops. In a later chapter we shall have more to say on the subject of picketing as a form of free speech.

The Concept of a Labor Dispute

In the late 1930's the U.S. Supreme Court passed on two important cases in which the complainants sought injunctions to restrain picketing. The decrees were sought on the ground that no labor dispute existed within the meaning of Section 13 of the Norris-LaGuardia Act, and that therefore the picketing constituted an unlawful interference with the property rights protected under the Federal Constitution.

The first case was Lauf v. E. G. Shinner and Co.,[7] in which a union sought recognition as the bargaining representative for butchers employed in several retail markets operated by the Shinner Co. The union approached the employer asking for recognition. The employer consulted with its employees, and when it learned that none of its thirty-five workers desired to join the union, the employer refused to deal with it. The union picketed the five shops advising the public that they were nonunion shops. The picketing was orderly and completely peaceful. The company moved in the Federal District Court for an injunction charging that no labor dispute existed between it and the union, and that the picketing was an unlawful interference with the company's right to engage in business free of molestation. Both the district court and the circuit court of appeals agreed with the position of the company. The union appealed to the U.S. Supreme Court and was successful in having the judgment reversed. The case was remanded to the district court for further proceedings on questions concerning charges of unlawful picketing.

Mr. Justice Roberts delivered the opinion for the Supreme Court and said:

The respondent is a Delaware corporation maintaining five meat markets in Milwaukee, Wisconsin. The petitioners are, respectively, an unincorporated labor union and its business manager, citizens and residents of Wisconsin. The respondent's employees number about thirty-five; none of them are members of the petitioning union. The petitioners demand the respondent to require its employees, as a condition of their continued employment, to become members of the union. The respondent notified the employees that they were free to do this and that it was willing to permit them to join, but they declined and refused to join. The union had not been chosen by the employees to represent them in any matter connected with the respondent. For the purpose of coercing the respondent to require its employees to join the union and to accept it as their bargaining agent and representative, as a condition of continued employment, and for the purpose of injuring and destroying the business if the respondent refused to yield to such coercion, the petitioners conspired to do the following things, and did them: They caused false and misleading signs to be placed before the respondent's markets; caused persons who were not respondent's employees to parade and picket before the markets; falsely accused respondent of being unfair to organized labor in its dealings with employees, and, by molestation, annoyance, threats and intimidation, prevented patrons and prospective patrons of respondent from patronizing its markets; respondent suffered and will suffer irreparable injury from the continuance of the practice and customers

7. 303 U.S. 323 (1938).

will be intimidated and restrained from patronizing the stores as a consequence of petitioners' acts. . . .

The District Court held that no labor dispute, as defined by federal or state law exists between the respondent and the petitioners. . . . It entered a final decree enjoining the petitioners from seeking to coerce the respondent to discharge any of its employees for refusal to join the union or to coerce the respondent to compel employees to become members of the organization, from advertising that the respondent is unfair to organized labor, and from annoying or molesting patrons . . . not to patronize respondent's markets.

The Circuit Court of Appeals affirmed the decree . . .

. . . The District Court erred in holding that no labor dispute, as defined by the law of Wisconsin, existed between the parties . . . The District Court erred in granting an injunction in the absence of findings which the Norris-LaGuardia Act makes prerequisites to the exercise of jurisdiction . . . Section 13(c) of the act is: "The term 'labor dispute' includes any controversy concerning terms or conditions of employment, or concerning the association or representation of the persons in negotiating, fixing, maintaining, changing, or seeking to arrange terms or conditions of employment, regardless of whether or not the disputants stand in the proximate relation of employer and employee". . . .

This definition does not differ materially from that of the Wisconsin Labor Code, and the facts of the instant case bring it within both. . . .

Mr. Justice Butler dissented, holding that no labor dispute existed in this case, and therefore that the petitioning employer was not required under the mandatory provisions of the act to meet the prerequisites for issuance of an injunction.

The important point in the Shinner case was the finding by the Supreme Court that a labor dispute did exist. Even though the union represented none of the Shinner workers, the dispute arose when the union sought to represent these workers for the purpose of collective bargaining. In brief, a representation demand is sufficient to create a labor dispute under the act. It should be remembered that after the court determines a labor dispute exists, it is mandatory upon the petitioner to meet all the conditions found in Sections 7 and 8 of the Norris-LaGuardia Act before the court may issue the injunction.

The second case dealing with the concept of a labor dispute is New Negro Alliance v. Sanitary Grocery Co.[8] The New Negro Alliance was not a union. It sought social and economic improvement for the Negro. When the grocery chain opened a new store in the heart of a Negro residential area, the alliance requested the company to give job opportunities to members of this race. The company refused to employ Negroes. The alliance established a single picket advising the general public that Negroes were not allowed to work for the company, and suggested that

8. 303 U.S. 552 (1938).

patronage be withheld. The company proceeded to secure injunctive relief on the constitutional ground that the picket was violating property rights protected under the Federal Constitution. The alliance asserted that a labor dispute existed, and that the court was required to dismiss the petition. The district court granted the injunction, deciding that no labor dispute existed. The alliance appealed to the U.S. Supreme Court where the decision was reversed and the injunction vacated.

Mr. Justice Roberts, speaking for the Supreme Court, said:

The matter in controversy is whether the case made by the pleadings involves or grows out of a labor dispute within the meaning of Section 13 of the Norris-LaGuardia Act.

The following facts alleged in the bill are admitted by the answer. Respondent, a Delaware corporation, operates 255 retail grocery, meat and vegetable stores, a warehouse and a bakery in the District of Columbia and employs both white and colored persons. April 3, 1936, it opened a new store at 1936 Eleventh Street, N.W., installing personnel having acquaintance with the trade in the vicinity. Petitioner, The New Negro Alliance, is a corporation composed of colored persons, organized for the mutual improvement of its members and the promotion of civic, educational, benevolent, and charitable enterprises. . . .

. . . The bill asserts: the petitioners have made arbitrary and summary demands upon the respondent that it engage and employ colored persons in managerial and sales positions in the new store and in various other stores; it is essential to the conduct of the business that respondent employ experienced persons in its stores and compliance with the arbitrary demands of defendants would involve the discharge of white employees and their replacement with colored; it is imperative that respondent be free in the selection and control of persons employed by it without interference by the petitioners or others. . . . The case, then, as it stood for judgment, was this:

The petitioners requested the respondent to adopt a policy of employing Negro clerks in certain of its stores in the course of personnel changes; the respondent ignored the request and the petitioners caused one person to patrol in front of one of respondent's stores on one day carrying a placard which said: 'Do your part! Buy where you can Work! No Negroes Employed Here!' and caused or threatened a similar patrol of two other stores of respondent. The information borne by the placard was true. The patrolling did not coerce or intimidate respondent's customers; did not physically obstruct, interfere with, or harass persons desiring to enter the store; the picket acted in an orderly manner and his conduct did not cause crowds to gather in front of the store.

. . . The trial judge was of the view that the laws relating to labor disputes had no application to the case. . . . The Circuit Court of Appeals thought that the dispute was not a labor dispute within the Norris-LaGuardia Act. . . .

. . . We think that the conclusion that the dispute was not a labor dispute within the meaning of the act, because it did not involve terms and conditions of employment in the sense of wages, hours, unionization or betterment of working conditions is erroneous. . . . The desire for fair and equitable conditions of employment on the part of persons of any race, color, or persuasion, and the removal of discrimination against them by reason of their race or religious beliefs is quite as important to those concerned as fairness and equity in terms and conditions of employment can be to trade or craft unions or any form of labor organization or association. Race discrimination by an employer may be deemed more unfair and less excusable than discrimination against workers on the ground of union affiliation. There is no justification in the apparent purposes or the express terms of the act for limiting its definition of labor disputes and cases arising therefrom by excluding those which arise with respect to discrimination in terms and conditions of employment based upon differences of race or color. . . .

The District Court erred in not complying with the provisions of the act. . . . The decree must be reversed. . . .[9]

Does the Norris-LaGuardia Act immunize labor unions from actions under the antitrust laws? The general rule is that labor activities are not violations of these laws if they arise from a labor dispute as defined by Section 13 of the act, and if the labor group is not acting in combination with employers. This question is discussed in Chapter 7.

The New York Courts and the Concept of a Labor Dispute

There are times when issues involving picketing deal with the existence or nonexistence of a labor dispute. What constitutes a labor dispute has been a matter of judicial interpretation. Therefore a reading of the New York statute will provide little help in determining whether or not a labor dispute exists. The answer is available only from reading the decisions. Because the law in New York is quite rigid, few injunctions have been granted when a labor dispute exists. Since most of the injunctions have been granted when the court has made a determination that no labor dispute existed, we shall examine some of these cases.

When an employer and a union have entered into a valid labor con-

9. In Hughes v. Superior Court, 339 U.S. 460 (1950), a Negro association picketed a chain of stores in California demanding that it hire Negroes in proportion to the white and Negro customers who patronized the stores. The State Court granted an injunction barring the picketing. The U.S. Supreme Court affirmed, on the ground that the Fourteenth Amendment in the Constitution *does not* bar a state from using the injunctive process to prohibit picketing of a place of business solely in order to secure compliance with a demand that its employees be hired in proportion to the racial origin of its then customers.

tract, picketing by a rival union for recognition as the bargaining representative may be enjoined on the ground that no labor dispute exists.[10] But a rival union may picket to publicize the substandard wages and working conditions existing in the employer's establishment.[11]

In a leading case [12] dealing with the subject of a labor dispute, the New York Court of Appeals held that a labor dispute exists when a union undertakes to organize the employees of a particular employer, does not demand a labor contract from the employer, does not engage in violence or mass picketing, and carries truthful placards. Under such circumstances, and irrespective of the length of time it continues, the picketing is for a lawful purpose and unenjoinable.

Where an employer's premises were picketed before any employees were hired, the court granted injunctive relief on the ground that no labor dispute existed.[13]

In the following cases, injunctive relief was granted where the court found that a labor dispute did not exist or where the objectives sought by the labor union were construed as unlawful.

(1) Picketing an employer to compel him to hire negroes where an employer operated his business without outside help.[14]

(2) Picketing to force a contract on an individual proprietor of a business having no employees.[15]

(3) Picketing for organizational purposes after the employees had unanimously voted against the union in a representative election.[16]

(4) A sit-down strike or a sit-in strike is illegal and may be enjoined.[17]

(5) A strike in violation of a no-strike clause in a valid labor contract may be enjoined.[18]

(6) In another case the picketing was found to violate a no-strike, no-picketing clause and the court enjoined the picketing even though it sought to organize clerical employees not covered by the existing agreement.[19]

(7) When it was clear that picketing was conducted for an unlawful objective, the proscription of Section 876(a) did not apply.[20]

10. Fay Loevin Shops v. Harlem Labor Union, 17 LC 65,372 (1949).
11. Stern-Fair Corp. v. Moving Picture Operators' Union, 27 LC 68,927 (1955).
12. Wood v. O'Grady, 307 N.Y. 532 (1954); see Golden Horn Restaurant v. Rubin, 32 LC 70,650 (1957).
13. Amco Plastic Materials v. Sanchez, 28 LC 69,508 (1955).
14. Pappas v. Straughn, 3 LC 60,104 (1940).
15. Sanfilippo v. Barbers and Beauty Culturists of America, 26 LC 68,714 (1954).
16. Sheehy's West Side Restaurant v. Townsend, 21 LC 66,830 (1952).
17. American Safety Razor Corporation v. Local 475, U.E., 26 LC 68,806 (1954).
18. Stewart Stamping Co. v. Uprichard, 26 LC 68,731 (1954).
19. McLean Trucking Co. v. Doyle, 36 LC 65,192 (1959).
20. For cases, see Opera on Tour v. Weber, 285 N.Y. 348 (1939); Goodwins, Inc. v. Hagedorn, 303 N.Y. 300 (1952).

(8) Peaceful picketing for organizational purposes did not constitute a labor dispute under Section 876(a) when such conduct breached an existing, valid labor contract.[21]

"MAMA AND PAPA SHOPS." The New York courts have maintained that an employment relationship must exist between an employer and employees, otherwise the act does not apply. In those small shops operated solely by husband and wife, the courts have enjoined all union picketing. Even when the shops have been owned and operated by individuals only related to each other the courts have refused to permit picketing.[22] However, when a group of relatives organized a corporation for the purpose of conducting business and when the corporation was owned and operated by four brothers and their mother, the court held that these individuals were employees; the New York Court of Appeals sustained a ruling of the lower court that the "Mama Papa" doctrine was inapplicable and permitted picketing.[23] In another case the owner of a restaurant being picketed by a union invited his seven workers to become owners of the business, offering them a partnership; an application made for an injunction to restrain the picketing was granted.[24]

CHARITABLE INSTITUTIONS. One of the earliest cases on this subject developed in 1945.[25]

In this case the court held that a charitable, nonprofit hospital was entitled to an injunction restraining its employees or the union from striking or organizing for the purpose of striking. The injunction was directed against the concerted activities which supported the strike and not against the right of any employee to quit his job. In 1946 another court held that peaceful picketing against a nonprofit hospital could be exercised so long as it did not interfere with the ordinary conduct and operation of the hospital.[26] In a 1959 case a strike against a voluntary hospital was held to be illegal.[27]

SECONDARY BOYCOTTS. The New York law applicable to secondary boycotts has been presented in Chapter 4.

COMPETING UNIONISM. One of the most difficult problems for New York courts has concerned attempts by one union to oust another union that has a collective agreement with an employer. In the Stillwell

---

21. J. Rodley Metzger Co. v. Fay, 4 App. Div. (2d) 436 (1957).
22. For cases, see Rubin v. Choina, 26 N.Y.S. (2d) 10 (1941); Lyons v. Myerson, 18 N.Y.S. (2d) 363 (1940).
23. Boro Park Sanitary Live Poultry Market Inc. v. Heller, 280 N.Y. 481 (1939).
24. Angelos v. Mesevitch, 289 N.Y. 498 (1943); the U.S. Supreme Court overruled the court of appeals and sustained the right to picket peacefully; see 320 U.S. 293 (1943).
25. Society of N.Y. Hospitals v. Hanson, 59 N.Y.S. (2d) 91 (1945).
26. Beth-El Hospital v. Robbins (1946), 10 LC 62,944.
27. Jewish Hospital of Brooklyn v. Davis, 37 LC 65,722 (1959); affirmed, 38 LC 65,729.

case [28] the court of appeals ruled that a rival union could peacefully picket an employer who had entered into a contract with another union. The court reasoned that picketing by one union to publicize that the conduct of an employer was socially objectionable to it was not persuasion to induce a breach of contract, and that the possibility of the picketing resulting in damage to the employer did not in itself constitute the basis for injunctive relief.

In 1937 the State Labor Relations Act was passed. This is referred to as the "baby" Wagner Act. New York has also an anti-injunction law, Section 876(a) of the Civil Practice Act. In 1942 the much cited Florsheim case [29] was decided by the court of appeals and the court reversed its ruling in the Stillwell case. After the State Labor Relations Board had certified an AFL clerks' union as the collective bargaining representative, and after this union and Florsheim had entered into a collective agreement, a CIO union picketed the employer's stores seeking recognition as the bargaining agent. An injunction against picketing was sustained on the principle that retaliatory cross-picketing did not create a "labor dispute" under New York law.

There is no doubt that the State Labor Relations Act of 1937 and the anti-injunction law, Section 876(a), have reduced the number of applications for injunctive relief in labor controversies. Union activities have become more vulnerable to equitable relief when employers have been able to satisfy courts that the matter in controversy does not constitute a "labor dispute" within the provisions of the New York law.

May the Norris-LaGuardia Act Be Invoked Against the U.S. Government When It Acts as an Employer?

In 1946 the UMW contested the right of the federal government to obtain an injunction to stop them from calling a strike. The union contended that the Norris-LaGuardia Act imposed on the government the same disability in obtaining injunctions as was imposed on private employers. The Supreme Court upheld the issuance of the injunction.

The facts in the case [30] are:

In October 1946 the United States was in possession of and was operating the major part of the country's bituminous coal mines. Under

28. Stillwell v. Kaplan, 259 N.Y. 405 (1932).
29. Florsheim Shoe Store Co. Inc. v. Retail Shoe Salesmen's Union, Local 287, 288 N.Y. 188 (1942).
30. U.S. v. Lewis and UMW, 330 U.S. 258 (1947). An interesting discussion of this case can be found in R. F. Watt, The Divine Right of Government by Judiciary, 14 *U. Chi. L. Rev.* 409 (1947).

date of May 29, 1946 the government and John L. Lewis, president of the miners, entered into a collective bargaining agreement and the terms of employment were controlled "for the period of government possession." On October 21, 1946 Lewis wrote a letter to the government asking for a conference to negotiate new wage terms beginning November 1, 1946. The government refused to meet with Lewis on the ground that terms and conditions were not negotiable under the existing agreement. Lewis then notified the government that the union would terminate the agreement as of November 20, 1946.

On November 18, 1946 the government filed a petition in the federal court of the District of Columbia and, among other things, asked that the strike threat be enjoined. The court granted the injunction. Notwithstanding the injunction, the strike began on November 18. By November 20 the walkout was in full swing.

On November 21 the government filed a petition to show cause why Lewis and the union should not be punished for contempt, alleging a willful violation of the injunction.

The union raised the point that under the Norris-LaGuardia Act no injunction could be issued because the controversy constituted a labor dispute, and no injunction could be granted even though the government was the employer.

After trial of the matter, both Lewis and the union were found guilty. Lewis was fined $10,000 and the union $3,500,000.

The Supreme Court, in affirming the decision, held that it could not construe the general term "employer" under the Norris-LaGuardia Act, to include the United States since there was no express reference to the United States and no evident affirmative grounds for believing that Congress intended to withhold an otherwise available remedy from the government as well as from a specified class of private persons. The Supreme Court reduced the fine against the union to $700,000.

Mr. Justice Murphy in his dissenting opinion said:

An objective reading of the Norris-LaGuardia Act removes any doubts as to its meaning and as to its applicability to the facts of this case. Section 4 provides in clear unmistakable language that "No court of the United States shall have jurisdiction to issue any restraining order or temporary or permanent injunction in any case involving or growing out of any labor dispute. . . ." That language, which is repeated in other sections of the act, is sufficient by itself to dispose of this case without further ado. . . .

. . . The federal equity power to issue restraining orders and injunctions simply cannot be invoked in this case, since it grows out of a private labor dispute. And it makes no difference that the party seeking the proscribed relief is the government rather than a private employer. . . . To permit the government to obtain an injunction where there has been a seizure would equally flout the language and policy of the act.

One of the basic rules of law provides that the judgment of an equity court must be obeyed and that any relief sought against the judgment must rest on the right to appeal. When a man defies an order of the court he does so at his own peril and must assume every risk. Otherwise the authority of our courts would be flaunted with impunity with the result that their effectiveness would be destroyed.

Although many agree that Mr. Lewis' leadership and dedication did much to provide economic justice to the coal miners, there is also general agreement and approval with the Supreme Court's judgment that Mr. Lewis' disobedience of the district court's injunction order called for the punishment meted out to him and his union. Certainly no man, however powerful, should be above the law in this country where law, and not man, is supreme.

State Anti-Injunction Laws

Seventeen states have adopted "baby" Norris-LaGuardia Acts. These laws patterned on the federal statute are important enough to warrant our attention. New York enacted such a law in 1935; [31] we shall give it some consideration.[32] This law did not purport to bar absolutely the issuance of labor injunctions; a significant number have been granted since 1935.

In granting labor injunctions the New York courts have relied on the expressed language of the statute or have assumed that the cases did not come within the purview of the act.

A state court may assert jurisdiction over an action initiated by an interstate employer to enjoin illegal picketing when the illegal activity did not constitute an unfair labor practice within the meaning of the National Labor Relations Act.[33] In this case, the New York court held that the picketing violated state public policy over which the state retained jurisdiction.

Despite the statutory language, a court banned picketing when a union and its members pursued a violent campaign against an employer.[34] The court found the union had been guilty of violence, intimi-

31. Chapter 477 of the Laws of 1935 (adding Section 876(a) to the Civil Practice Act.)
32. For a comprehensive treatment of Section 876(a) see Jacob Seidenberg, *The Labor Injunction in New York City, 1935–1950,* Cornell Studies in Industrial and Labor Relations, (1952) Cornell Univ., Ithaca, N.Y., vol. 4.
33. McLean Trucking Co. v. Doyle, N.Y., 36 LC 65,192 (1959).
34. Busch Jewelry Co. v. United Retail Union, Local 830, 5 N.Y.S.(2d) 575 (1938), affirmed 281 N.Y. 151.

dation, false propaganda, appeals to build up class hatred, and false, deceitful, and misleading statements.

Summary

Before 1932 the labor injunction had become a popular judicial device to thwart effective forms of self-help such as the picket line, the strike, and the boycott. In the name of protecting property, employers obtained injunctions which forbade virtually all picketing, boycotting, and strikes. The result was that employees had hardly any bargaining power.

The Norris-LaGuardia Act of 1932 placed restrictions on the issuance of injunctions in labor dispute cases, and for the first time the right to picket, to boycott, and to strike was legislatively protected. Labor unions for a long time had insisted that picketing, boycotting, and striking were justified, and the justification was asserted on the ground that these weapons were essential for workers who sought economic and social improvements. In addition, these economic weapons were necessary to combat the employer who, by paying low wages, and by maintaining substandard working conditions, threatened the economic gains made by unionized workers.

This act gave the worker more freedom of action in the economic arena than he had ever enjoyed before. This unparalleled freedom continued until 1947 when legislative curbs were placed on the use of the strike, the picket line, and the boycott. In later chapters we discuss the development of a more restricted labor philosophy.

CHAPTER SIX

Picketing and Free Speech

PICKETING is a means of publicly appealing to as much of the public as may be influenced by the facts to withhold its patronage from the picketed. It is a concomitant of a strike. When a strike ends the controversy ends and there is no longer any need for picketing. The general principle has been that picketing must be conducted peacefully and truthfully, and for a lawful object.

What possible objective does picketing seek? In our illustration, U has called a strike against E and has established a picket line at his place of business. The picketing seeks to:

(1) Publicize the facts of the controversy.

(2) Persuade nonunion workers, customers, and raw-material and

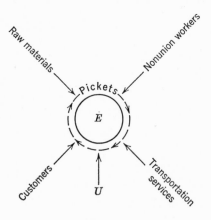

Figure 8

transportation suppliers to take action that will cause a falling off in the employer's business sufficient to induce him to negotiate a settlement of the controversy.

(3) To maintain striker morale.

The chances of getting a quick settlement will depend on how much cooperation the third parties are willing to give to the pickets. If the blockade is sufficiently tight the employer may be compelled to make good concessions to the union.

At common law one difficulty has arisen when the courts were required to determine the legality or illegality of the picketing's objective. In other instances the problem centered around the question of whether or not the picketing was coercive. What is lawful and what is coercive were questions reserved for the court alone.

Picketing that threatened persons seeking to deal with a struck employer; picketing resulting in a breach of the peace, and picketing motivated by malice alone were unlawful at common law.

Picketing with the objectives of the closed shop, the abandonment by an employer of technological innovations, the breach of a contract, and the interruptions of business relations between the struck employer and third parties by coercive means was considered illegal.

Even when labor unions were meticulously careful to see that picketing was carried on peacefully it was frequently enjoined, and it was not uncommon for some courts to declare all picketing unlawful on the ground that there could be no such thing as peaceful picketing. In 1905 [1] a federal court stated ". . . there is and can be no such thing as peaceful picketing, any more than there can be chaste vulgarity, or peaceful mobbing, or lawful lynching. . . ."

As late as 1926 a New Jersey court had this to say about picketing:

Obviously, the line of demarcation between peaceful picketing, if there is any such thing, and that which is threatening, intimidating and coercive, is so finely drawn as to be almost imperceptible. While the great weight of authority is to the effect that "peaceful picketing" for a lawful purpose is legal, I have found no case in which the term has been so defined that it may be universally applied. . . .[2]

The archaic common law doctrine, which condemned practically all picketing, was modified somewhat in 1921 when the U.S. Supreme Court handed down its decision in the Tri-City [3] case. Mr. Chief Justice Taft delivered the opinion of the court. The plant of the American Steel Foundries in Granite City, Illinois, was struck by the thirty-seven

1. A.T. and S.F.Ry. v. Gee, 139 Fed. 582 (1905).
2. Gevas v. Greek Restaurant Workers Club, 99 N.J. Eq. 770 (1926).
3. American Steel Foundries v. Tri-City Central Trades Council, 257 U.S. 184 (1921).

craft unions that made up the Tri-City Central Trades Council. Following the strike call the council established pickets on streets leading to the plant, instructing them to notify all persons entering the plant that a strike had been called because of a reduction of wages and to use all honorable means to persuade such persons not to take the places of the men on strike. In May 1914, the employer filed a bill seeking an injunction against the picketing. It asserted that the pickets were engaged in violent activities, were making threats to any who approached the plant, and were interfering with the petitioner's right to conduct business. The defendants admitted the picketing but denied that they were responsible for the violence which had admittedly occurred, and they denied that the pickets had made any threats against persons who sought to enter the plant. The district court granted the injunction and part of the decree recited that the defendants were enjoined

. . . from inducing or attempting to compel or induce by persuasion, threats, intimidation, force or violence or putting in fear or suggestions of danger any of the employees of the American Steel Foundries or persons seeking employment with it so as to cause them to refuse to perform any of their duties as employees of the American Steel Foundries. . . .

The injunction also forbade the defendant unions from picketing the plant of the employer. The circuit court of appeals modified the decree by striking out the word "persuasion" in the four places in which it occurred, and by inserting after the clause restraining picketing the following: "in a threatening or intimidating manner." This modification reinstated the picket line.

In 1921, when the case reached the U.S. Supreme Court, the decree was further modified. This court reversed that part of the decree allowing wide picketing and upheld that part permitting peaceful persuasion by no more than one representative for each point of ingress and egress in the plant.

Labor circles labeled this "pink-tea" picketing. Although this decision adhered closely to the view that picketing was odious and suspect, the Supreme Court did show some tolerance for this type of labor union activity when it said:

. . . Labor unions are recognized by the Clayton Act as legal when instituted for mutual help and lawfully carrying out their legitimate objects. They have long been thus recognized by the courts. They were organized out of the necessities of the situation. A single employee was helpless in dealing with an employer. He was dependent ordinarily on his daily wage for the maintenance of himself and family. If the employer refused to pay him the wages that he thought fair, he was nevertheless unable to leave the employ and to resist arbitrary and unfair treatment. Union was essential to give laborers opportunity to deal on equality with their employer. They united to exert influence upon him and to leave him in a body in order by this inconvenience to induce him to make better terms with them. . . .

Unions did not rejoice over the decision in the Tri-City case, but they found some hope in the Supreme Court's sanction of a single picket patrol at each entrance to the plant. This was no major victory but it was a heartening breakthrough. Section 20 of the Clayton Act had authorized lawful persuasion, according to the Supreme Court.

Organized labor was disheartened and doubted that complete victory would ever come through any modernization of the common law; great progress began in 1932, however, with the passage of the Norris-La-Guardia Act. Section 4 explicitly allowed peaceful picketing. Section 13, as we have already seen, placed a broad interpretation on the term "labor dispute." The Senn and the New Negro Alliance decisions recognized the rights of pickets to publicize the nature of a labor controversy, although the U.S. Supreme Court did not explicitly state that picketing was a form of speech.

In 1940 [4] the U.S. Supreme Court held that publicizing a labor controversy was constitutionally protected speech of public concern. Later, several other decisions followed more clearly equating picketing with free speech. More recently however, the Supreme Court has retreated from its language in the Thornhill case; now picketing may be enjoined when a determination has been made that it violates the expressed public policy of the federal or state government.

A discussion of picketing and free speech will gain meaning from a brief general discussion of free speech.

Free Speech and Peaceful Assembly

The First Amendment to the United States Constitution reads:

Congress shall make no law respecting an establishment of religion or prohibiting the free exercise thereof; or abridging the freedom of speech or of the press; or the right of people peaceably to assemble, and to petition the government for a redress of grievances.

The Fourteenth Amendment, Section 1, states:

All persons born or naturalized in the United States, and subject to the jurisdiction thereof, are citizens of the United States and of the State wherein they reside. No State shall make or enforce any law which shall abridge the privileges or immunities of citizens of the United States, nor

4. Thornhill v. Alabama, 310 U.S. 88 (1940).

shall any State deprive any person of life, liberty or property, without due process of law, nor deny to any person within its jurisdiction the equal protection of the laws.

Thus, free speech and peaceful assembly are explicit guarantees which neither Congress nor the states may annul. Free speech has been the subject matter of several celebrated cases that have reached the U.S. Supreme Court. In each case abridgment of speech was alleged and the abridgment resulted from action initiated by either the federal or a state government.

Does every abridgment of speech violate the Constitution? The Supreme Court answered this question negatively in the often-cited Schenck case [5] when it said:

. . . The character of every act depends upon the circumstances in which it was done. The most stringent protection of free speech would not protect a man in falsely shouting fire in a theatre, and causing a panic. It does not even protect a man from an injunction against uttering words that may have the effect of force. The question in every case is whether the words used are used in such circumstances and are of such a nature as to create a clear and present danger that will bring about the substantive evils that Congress has a right to prevent. It is a question of proximity and degree. . . .

Governments possess inherent powers to protect constituted authority and citizens against the substantial evils which may reasonably flow from the exercise of speech. Therefore, if speech meets the "clear and present danger rule," abridgment is constitutional according to the Supreme Court.

The U.S. Supreme Court stated the meaning of the "clear and present danger rule" in Bridges v. California.[6] While a motion for a new trial was pending in a labor controversy in a California court, Bridges sent a telegram to the state Secretary of Labor which referred to the trial judge's decision as "outrageous" and stated that any attempt to enforce the decision would result in a paralyzing strike. Bridges made certain other utterances to newspapers concerning the pending litigation. Because of his telegram and statements, Bridges was adjudged guilty of contempt of the state court. The conviction was upheld by the highest court in the state. Bridges challenged the court's action as an abridgment of freedom of speech and of the press prohibited by the Constitution. After reviewing the decision, the U.S. Supreme Court reversed the conviction. Mr. Justice Black summarized the court's argument in the following passages:

. . . A public utterance or publication is not to be denied the constitutional protection of freedom of speech and press merely because it concerns

5. Schenck v. U.S., 249 U.S. 47 (1918).
6. 314 U.S. 352 (1941).

a judicial proceeding still pending in the courts, upon the theory that in such a case it must necessarily tend to obstruct the orderly and fair administration of justice. . . . *No clear and present danger* of interference with the orderly administration of justice in a case pending before a court involving a criminal prosecution of members of a labor union, justifying the impairment of the constitutional right of freedom of speech and press through commitment for contempt, is shown in a case of a newspaper editorial which entitled "Probation for Gorillas?", states that the judge will make a serious mistake if he grants probation to the defendants. . . . Where there is *clear and present danger* of substantial evil flowing from indiscriminate criticism of a judicial proceeding, the constitutional freedoms of speech and press may be impaired only if the evils are extremely serious and the degree of imminence is extremely high. . . .

A few of the states have enacted laws regulating such matters as the distribution of literature, the assemblage of persons, and the solicitation of new union members by labor leaders. It was clear that the principal objective of these statutes was discouragement of labor union activity within the state. These laws were challenged several times on the ground that they unlawfully abridged the constitutional right of free speech and peaceful assembly. Thomas v. Collins [7] was one of the cases reviewed by the U.S. Supreme Court. Thomas, a labor leader, was scheduled to speak at a meeting to be held in Houston, Texas. The purpose of the meeting was to organize the workers of Humble Oil Company. A few hours before he was scheduled to speak Thomas was served with a restraining order. A Texas statute required a person to obtain a license before soliciting workers to join a union. Although Thomas had no such license he made his speech. He was thereafter convicted of a contempt of court. Throughout the contempt proceedings, Thomas claimed that the statute and the injunction were unconstitutional restraints on free speech and free assembly. The Supreme Court of Texas sustained the conviction. On appeal to the U.S. Supreme Court the conviction was set aside. Mr. Justice Rutledge, who delivered the court's opinion, said:

. . . The case confronts us again with the duty our system places on this Court to say where the individual's freedom ends and where the State's power begins. Choice on that border is perhaps more so where the usual presumption supporting legislation is balanced by the preferred place given in our scheme to the great, the indispensable democratic freedoms secured by the First Amendment. That priority gives these liberties a sanctity and a sanction not permitting dubious intrusions. And it is the character of the right, not of the limitation which determines what standard governs the choice. For these reasons any attempt to restrict those liberties must be justified by clear public interest, threatened not doubtfully or remotely, but

7. R. J. Thomas v. Collins, Sheriff, 323 U.S. 516 (1945).

by clear and present danger. . . . Only the gravest abuses, endangering paramount interests, give occasion for permissible limitations. . . . That the State has power to regulate labor unions with a view to protecting the public interest is . . . hardly to be doubted. Such regulation however, whether aimed at fraud or other abuses, must not trespass upon the domains set apart for free speech and free assembly. . . .

Justice Roberts wrote a dissenting opinion in which Chief Justice Warren, Justice Reed, and Justice Frankfurter concurred. Part of Justice Roberts' opinion follows.

. . . Since its (statute) requirements are not obviously burdensome, we cannot void the statute as an unnecessary or excessive exercise of the State's police power on any a priori reasoning. The State Supreme Court has found that conditions exist in Texas which justify and require such identification of paid organizers as the law prescribes. There is not a word of evidence in the record to contradict these conclusions. In the absence of a showing against the need for the statute this court ought not incontinently to reject the State's considered views of policy. . . . I think that if anyone pursues solicitation as a business for profit, of members for any organization, religious, secular or business, his calling does not bar the state from requiring him to identify himself as what he is,—a paid solicitor. . . .[8]

After this discussion of the common law status of picketing and the review of the constitutional privilege of free speech and peaceful assembly, we may consider major decisions in which the sole issue litigated was the constitutionalty of legislation seeking to abridge picketing, one of labor's self-help devices. Our attention will be centered on the Thornhill decision.

8. In Staub v. City of Baxley, 355 U.S. 313 (1958) a labor union organizer was convicted in Baxley, Georgia, of violating a municipal ordinance providing that persons seeking to solicit members of any organization requiring payment of dues shall first obtain a permit. The conviction was upheld by the Supreme Court of Georgia. Throughout the state proceedings the defendant claimed that the ordinance infringed upon his right of free speech. On appeal to the U.S. Supreme Court seven members of the court held that this ordinance violated the Fourteenth Amendment and the conviction was reversed.

Mr. Justice Whittaker wrote the opinion for the court and said ". . . it will be noted that appellant was not accused of any act against the peace, good order, or dignity of the community, nor of any particular thing he said in soliciting employees of the manufacturing company to join the union . . . It is undeniable that the ordinance authorized the Mayor and the Council of the City of Baxley to grant 'or refuse to grant' the required permit in their uncontrolled discretion. It thus makes enjoyment of speech contingent upon the will of the Mayor and the Council of the City, although that fundamental right is made free from congressional abridgment by the First Amendment and is protected by the Fourteenth Amendment from invasion by state action. . . ."

Justice Frankfurter dissented without reaching the constitutional issue.

The Thornhill Case, 1940

In 1923 the state of Alabama enacted a law prohibiting picketing. Byron Thornhill, a union leader, was convicted under this statute and was sentenced to imprisonment for 59 days in default of payment of a fine of $100 and costs. Thornhill appealed from the conviction on the ground that picketing was a form of speech protected under the First and Fourteenth Amendments of the Constitution. The appeal reached the U.S. Supreme Court in 1940 when the court held the statute unconstitutional and reversed the conviction.

Mr. Justice Murphy delivered the opinion of the court.

Petitioner, Byron Thornhill, was convicted in the Circuit Court of Tuscaloosa County, Alabama, of the violation of Section 3448 of the State Code of 1923. The Code Section reads as follows:

SECTION 3448. Loitering or picketing forbidden.—Any person or persons who, without a just cause or legal excuse therefor, go near to or loiter about the premises or place of business of any other person, firm, corporation, or association of people, engaged in a lawful business, for the purpose, or with the intent of influencing, or inducing other persons not to trade with, buy from, sell to, have business dealings with, or be employed by such persons, firm, corporation, or association, or who picket the works or place of business of such other persons, firms, corporations, or associations of persons, for the purpose of hindering, delaying, or interfering with or injuring any lawful business or enterprise of another, shall be guilty of a misdemeanor; but nothing herein shall prevent any person from soliciting trade or business for a competitive business.

The complaint against petitioner . . . is phrased substantially in the very words of the statute. The first and second counts charge that petitioner, without just cause or legal excuse, did "go near to or loiter about the premises" of the Brown Wood Preserving Company with the intent or purpose of influencing others to adopt one of enumerated courses of conduct. In the third count, the charge is that petitioner "did picket" the works of the Company "for the purpose of hindering, delaying or interfering with or injuring (its) lawful business." Petitioner demurred to the complaint on the grounds among others, that Section 3448 was repugnant to the Constitution of the United States in that it deprived him of "the right of peaceful assemblage," "the right of freedom of speech," and "the right to petition for redress." The demurrer, so far as the record shows, was not ruled upon and petitioner pleaded not guilty. The Circuit Court then proceeded to try the case without a jury, one not being asked for or demanded. Thornhill was found guilty. The court held the law constitutional, as did the Court of Appeals of Alabama on the authority of two previous decisions in the Alabama courts.

O'Rourke v. City of Birmingham, 27 Ala. App. 133, 168 So. 206, cert. denied, 232 Ala. 355, 168 So. 209; Hardie-Tynes Mfg. Co. v. Cruise, 189 Ala. 66, 66 So. 657. A petition for certiorari was denied by the Supreme Court of the State. The case is here on certiorari granted because of the importance of the question presented.

The proofs consist of the testimony of two witnesses for the prosecution. It appears that petitioner on the morning of his arrest was seen "in company with six or eight other men" "on the picket line" at the plant of the Brown Wood Preserving Company. Some weeks previously a strike order had been issued by a Union, apparently affiliated with the American Federation of Labor, which had as members all but four of the approximately one hundred employees of the plant. Since that time a picket line with two picket posts of six to eight men each had been maintained around the plant twenty-four hours a day. The picket posts appear to have been on Company property, "on a private entrance of employees, and not on any public road." One witness explained that practically all of the employees live on Company property and get their mail from a post office on Company property and that the Union holds its meetings on Company property. No demand was ever made upon the men not to come on the property. There is no testimony indicating the nature of the dispute between the Union and the Preserving Company, or the course of events which led to the issuance of the strike order, or the nature of the efforts of conciliation.

The Company scheduled a day for the plant to resume operations. One of the witnesses, Clarence Simpson, who was not a member of the Union, on reporting to the plant on the day indicated, was approached by petitioner who told him that "they were on strike and did not want anybody to go up there to work." None of the other employees said anything to Simpson, who testified: "Neither Mr. Thornhill nor any other employee threatened me on the occasion testified to. Mr. Thornhill approached me in a peaceful manner, and did not put me in fear; he did not appear to be mad." "I then turned and went back to the house, and did not go to work." The other witness, J. M. Walden, testified: "At the time Mr. Thornhill and Clarence Simpson were talking to each other, there was no one else present, and I heard no harsh words and saw nothing threatening in the manner of either man." For engaging in some or all of these activities, petitioner was arrested, charged, and convicted as described.

FIRST. The freedom of speech and of the press, which are secured by the First Amendment against abridgment by the United States, are among the fundamental personal rights and liberties which are secured to all persons by the 14th Amendment against abridgment by a state. . . .

SECOND. The section in question must be judged upon its fact. . . . Proof of an abuse of power in the particular case has never been deemed a requisite for attack on the constitutionality of a statute purporting to license the dissemination of ideas. Schneider v. State, 308 U.S. 147, 162–165; Hague v. C.I.O. 307 U.S. 496, 516; Lovell v. Griffin, 303 U.S. 444, 451. The cases when interpreted in the light of their facts indicate that the rule is not based upon any assumption that application for the license would be refused or would result in the imposition of other unlawful regulations. Rather it derives from an appreciation of the character of the evil inherent in a licensing system. The power of the licensor against which John Milton directed his assault by his "Appeal for the Liberty of Unlicensed Printing" is pernicious not merely by reason of the threat to censure comments on matters of public concern. It is not merely the sporadic abuse of power by the censor but the pervasive threat inherent in its very existence that constitutes the danger to freedom of discussion. See Near v. Minnesota, 283 U.S. 697, 713. One who might have had a license for the asking may therefore call into question the whole scheme of licensing when he is prosecuted for failure to procure it. . . .

THIRD. Section 3448 has been applied by the State courts so as to prohibit a single individual from walking slowly and peacefully back and forth on the public sidewalk in front of the premises of an employer, without speaking to anyone, carrying a sign or placard on a staff above his head stating only the fact that the employer did not employ union men affiliated with the American Federation of Labor; the purpose of the described activity was concededly to advise customers and prospective customers of the relationship existing between the employer and its employees and thereby to induce such customers not to patronize the employer. O'Rourke v. City of Birmingham, 27 Ala. App. 133, 168 So. 206, cert. denied, 232 Ala. 355, 168 So. 209. The statute as thus authoritatively construed and applied leaves room for no exceptions based upon either the number of persons engaged in the proscribed activity, the peaceful character of their demeanor, the nature of their dispute with an employer, or the restrained character and the accurateness of the terminology used in notifying the public of facts of the dispute . . ."

FOURTH. We think that Section 3448 is invalid on its face.

The freedom of speech and of the press guaranteed by the Constitution embraces at least the liberty to discuss publicly and truthfully all matters of public concern without previous restraint or fear of subsequent punishment. . . .

In the circumstances of our times the dissemination of information concerning the facts of a labor dispute must be regarded as within that area of free discussion that is guaranteed by the Constitution. Hague v. C.I.O. 307 U.S. 496; Schneider v. State, 308 U.S. 147, 155, 162–63. . . . See Senn v. Tile Layers Union, 301 U.S. 468, 478. It is recognized now that satisfactory hours and wages and working conditions in industry and a bargaining position which makes these possible have an importance which is not less than the interests of those in the business of industry directly concerned. The health of the present generation and of those as yet unborn may depend on these matters, and the practices in a single factory may have economic repercussions upon a whole region and affect widespread systems of marketing. . . .

The State urges that the purpose of the challenged statute is the protection of the community from the violence and breaches of the peace, which, it asserts, are the concomitants of picketing. The power and the duty of the

State to take adequate steps to preserve the peace and to protect the privacy, the lives, and the property of its residents cannot be doubted. But no clear and present danger of destruction of life or property, or invasion of the right of privacy, or breach of the peace can be thought to be inherent in the activities of every person who approaches the premises of an employer and publicizes the facts of a labor dispute involving the latter. . . .[9]

The Thornhill decision left no doubt about the right of workers to engage in peaceful picketing for lawful objectives without molestation on the part of any state. The U.S. Supreme Court stated these propositions:

(1) That the publicizing of a labor dispute is constitutionally protected speech of *public concern*. Labor disputes were no longer merely private disputes, the public, as consumers, were seen to have an important interest in labor controversies.

(2) That picketing is inclusive of nearly every practicable and effective means of such publicizing.

(3) That the possible economic loss to the concern picketed is neither so serious, or so imminent, as to justify abridgment of liberty and discussion. If the picketing passes the "clear and present danger" test successfully, it may not be abridged.

(4) That the doctrine that violence and breaches of the peace are inevitable concomitants of picketing is unfounded in fact.

Two interesting cases followed the Thornhill decision. In both the U.S. Supreme Court approved state interference with picketing activities. It has long been a rule of law that the guarantees enumerated in the U.S. Constitution are not absolute. Each right carries with it corresponding responsibilities.

9. The U.S. Supreme Court on the same day and on the same grounds invalidated an antipicketing ordinance of Shasta County, California, in Carlson v. California, 310 U.S. 106 (1940).

In 1938 after a siege of boycotting of CIO wood by AFL carpenters, Oregon by referendum adopted a stringent antipicketing law. It put penalties on (1) unionists and unions which obstructed lawful buying, selling, or transporting, (2) unionists and unions which picketed in the absence of a labor dispute, or boycotted an employer not directly involved in a labor dispute, (3) unions which collected so much in dues as to accumulate a fund larger than was necessary for the purposes of the organization, and (4) unionists and unions which interfered with anyone seeking employment.

"Labor dispute" was defined as a dispute of employees with the immediate employer over wages, hours, or working conditions in his shop. Excluded were representation questions and rival-union disputes. This definition showed the application of the antipicketing law, and also modified the Oregon anti-injunction law, which had contained the usual definition of "labor dispute" as is found in the Norris-LaGuardia Act.

In October 1940 the Oregon Supreme Court held the statute void, on the authority of Thornhill v. Alabama, AFL v. Bain, and C.I.O. v. Bain, 106 Pac. (2d) 544.

The first case in which the Supreme Court allowed a state to interfere with picketing by a labor union was heard by the court in 1940. It was the Meadowmoor [10] case. During a strike conducted by the Teamsters throughout the entire city of Chicago retail stores and milk products distributors were picketed. Some of the picketing was peaceful and some involved acts of terrorism. The violence was intermittent; it would occur in one part of the city, stop, and then erupt in another part of the city. The Meadowmoor Dairy filed a petition in the Supreme Court of Illinois seeking an injunction against all the picketing. The court issued an injunction. The issue in the case presented to the U.S. Supreme Court was whether a state can authorize its courts to enjoin peaceful acts of picketing when they are accompanied by contemporaneously violent, concededly outlawed conduct.

Mr. Justice Frankfurter delivered the opinion of the court.

The "vendor system" for distributing milk in Chicago gave rise to the dispute. Under that system, which was fully analyzed in Milk Wagon Drivers' Union v. Lake Valley Farm Products, 311 U.S. 91, milk is sold by the dairy companies to vendors operating their own trucks who resell to retailers. These vendors departed from the working standards theretofore achieved by the Union for its members as dairy employees. The Union, in order to compel observance of the established standards, took action against dairies using the vendor system. The present respondent, Meadowmoor Dairies, Inc., brought suit against the Union and its officials to stop interference with the distribution of its products. A preliminary injunction restraining all union conduct, violent and peaceful, was promptly issued, and the case was referred to a master for report. Besides peaceful picketing of the stores handling Meadowmoor's products, the master found that there had been violence on a considerable scale. Witnesses testified to more than fifty instances of window-smashing; explosive bombs caused substantial injury to the plants of Meadowmoor and another dairy using the vendor system and to five stores; stench bombs were dropped in five stores; three trucks of vendors were wrecked, seriously injuring one driver, and another was driven into a river; a store was set on fire and in large measure ruined; two trucks of vendors were burned; a storekeeper and a truck driver were severely beaten; workers at a dairy which, like Meadowmoor, used the vendor system, were held with guns and severely beaten about the head while being told "to join the union"; carloads of men followed vendors' trucks, threatened the drivers, and in one instance shot at the truck and driver. In more than a dozen of these occurrences, involving window-smashing, bombings, burnings, the wrecking of trucks, shootings and beatings, there was testimony to identify the wrongdoers as union men. In the light of his findings, the master recommended that all picketing, and not merely violent acts, should be enjoined. The trial court, however, accepted the recommendations only as to acts of violence and permitted peaceful picketing. The reversal of this ruling by the

10. Milk Wagon Drivers' Union of Chicago v. Meadowmoor Dairies, Inc., 312 U.S. 287 (1940).

Supreme Court, 371 Ill. 377, 21 N.E. (2d) 308, directing a permanent injunction as recommended by the master, is now before us.

The question which thus emerges is whether a state can choose to authorize its courts to enjoin acts of picketing in themselves peaceful when they are enmeshed with contemporaneously violent conduct which is concededly outlawed. The Constitution is invoked to deny Illinois the power to authorize its courts to prevent the continuance and recurrence of flagrant violence, found after an extended litigation to have occurred under specific circumstances, by the terms of a decree familiar in such cases. Such a decree, arising out of a particular controversy and adjusted to it, raises totally different constitutional problems from those that would be presented by an abstract statute with an overhanging and undefined threat to free utterance. To assimilate the two is to deny to the states their historic freedom to deal with controversies through the concreteness of individual litigation rather than through the abstractness of a general law.

The starting point is Thornhill's case. That case invoked the constitutional protection of free speech on behalf of a relatively modern means for "publicizing, without annoyance or threats of any kind, the facts of a labor dispute." 310 U.S. 100. The whole series of cases defining the scope of free speech under the Fourteenth Amendment are facets of the same principle in that they all safeguard modes appropriate for assuring the right to utterance in different situations. Peaceful picketing is the workingman's means of communication.

It must never be forgotten, however, that the Bill of Rights was the child of the Enlightenment. Back of the guarantee of free speech lay faith in the power of an appeal to reason by all the peaceful means for gaining access to the mind. It was in order to avert force and explosions due to restrictions upon rational modes of communication that the guarantee of free speech was given a generous scope. But utterance in a context of violence can lose its significance as an appeal to reason and become part of an instrument of force. Such utterance was not meant to be sheltered by the Constitution.

. . . No one will doubt that Illinois can protect its storekeepers from being coerced by fear of window-smashings or burnings or bombings. And acts which in isolation are peaceful may be part of a coercive thrust when entangled with acts of violence. The picketing in this case was set in a background of violence. In such a setting it could justifiably be concluded that the momentum of fear generated by past violence would survive even though future picketing might be wholly peaceful. So the Supreme Court of Illinois found. We cannot say that such a finding so contradicted experience as to warrant our rejection. Nor can we say that it was written into the Fourteenth Amendment that a state through its courts cannot base protection against future coercion on an inference of the continuing threat of past misconduct.

. . . We do not qualify the Thornhill and Carlson decisions. We reaffirm them. They involved statutes baldly forbidding all picketing near an employer's place of business. Entanglement with violence was expressly out of those cases. The statutes had to be dealt with on their face, and therefore we struck them down. Such an unlimited ban on free communication declared as the law of a state by a state court enjoys no greater protection here. But just as a state through its legislature may deal with specific circumstances menacing the peace by appropriately drawn acts, Thornhill v. Alabama, *supra*, so the law of a state may be fitted to a concrete situation through the authority given by the state to its courts. . . .

The injunction which we sustain is "permanent" only for the temporary period for which it may last. It is justified only by the violence that induced it and only so long as it counteracts a continuing intimidation. Familiar equity procedure assures opportunity for modifying or vacating an injunction when its continuance is no longer warranted. Here again, the state courts have not the last say. They must act in subordination to the duty of this Court to enforce constitutional liberties even when denied through spurious findings of fact in a state court. Compare Chambers v. Florida, 309 U.S. 227. Since the union did not urge that the coercive effect had disappeared either before us or, apparently, before the state court, that question is not now here.

A final word. Freedom of speech and freedom of the press cannot be too often invoked as a basis to our scheme of society. But these liberties will not be advanced or even maintained by denying to the states with all their resources, including the instrumentality of their courts, the power to deal with coercion due to extensive violence. Affirmed.

The common sense manifested by the Supreme Court in this case must be approved. Here the picketing started peacefully for a lawful purpose and then exploded into a reign of terror. Under its inherent police power, the state of Illinois was required to exercise necessary authority to protect property owners, workers, and pedestrians against unlawful acts resulting from the violent picketing. Without this power, the state would be rendered impotent and Chicago would have become a vast battleground where unlawfulness reigned. The most important facet of this case is the position taken by the Supreme Court that state courts may enjoin isolated instances of picket line violence, but they have no authority to issue injunctions so broad as to prohibit the peaceful phase of picketing. The state court injunction was upheld in this case only because the good and the bad part of the picketing were so enmeshed that it was impossible to separate the lawful from the unlawful acts.

A companion case also concerned with the authority of a state to intervene and enjoin picketing activities was the Ritter [11] case. This is an extremely important decision. Unlike the Meadowmoor case, no violence whatever developed in the Ritter case. A dispute arose between the carpenters' union and a building contractor engaged to put up a new structure for Ritter. The dispute developed when the contractor employed nonunion carpenters. The union, attempting to get the contractor to hire union carpenters, established a picket line, not at the construction site, but in front of Ritter's Café, located a mile and a half

11. Carpenters and Joiners Union of America v. Ritter's Café, 315 U.S. 722 (1942).

from the construction job. Obviously, the reason for picketing the café was to get Ritter to put pressure on the contractor to unionize the construction job. The café and the new building were completely unrelated and there was no community of interest. Ritter's business declined about 60 per cent as a result of the picket line. Ritter's application for an injunction restraining the picketing was granted by a Texas State Court, and the highest appellate state court sustained the lower court's judgment. The decision was based on the ground that the union had violated the state antitrust statute. The union appealed to the U.S. Supreme Court, which sustained the decision of the Texas courts. Throughout the court proceedings the union had contended that the Texas courts had violated the right of free speech as guaranteed by the First and Fourteenth Amendments. The injunction which forbade picketing in front of Ritter's Café did not phohibit the union from picketing the construction site.

Mr. Justice Frankfurter delivered the opinion of the U.S. Supreme Court.

. . . In the circumstances of the case before us Texas has declared that its general welfare would not be served if, in a controversy between a contractor and building workers' unions, the unions were permitted to bring to bear the full weight of familiar weapons of industrial combat against a restaurant business, which, as a business, has no nexus with the building dispute but which happens to be owned by a person who contracts with the builder. The precise question is, therefore, whether the Fourteenth Amendment prohibits Texas from drawing this line in confining the area of unrestricted industrial warfare.

. . . It is true that by peaceful picketing workingmen communicate their grievances. As a means of communicating the facts of a labor dispute peaceful picketing may be a phase of the constitutional right of free utterance. But recognition of peaceful picketing as an exercise of free speech does not imply that the states must be without power to confine the sphere of communication to that directly related to the dispute. Restriction of picketing to the area of the industry within which a labor dispute arises leaves open to the disputants other traditional modes of communication. To deny to the states the power to draw this line is to write into the Constitution the notion that every instance of peaceful picketing—anywhere and under any circumstances—is necessarily a phase of the controversy which provoked the picketing. Such a view of the Due Process Clause would compel the states to allow the disputants in a particular industrial episode to conscript neutrals having no relation to either the dispute or the industry in which it arose.

. . . It is not for us to assess the wisdom of the policy underlying the law of Texas. Our duty is at an end when we find that the Fourteenth Amendment does not deny her the power to enact that policy into law.

Three Justices dissented in this case. Justice Black, in his dissent, said in part

. . . Whatever injury the respondent suffered here resulted from the peaceful and truthful statements made to the public that he had employed a non-union contractor to erect a building. This information, under the Thornhill case, the petitioners were privileged to impart and the public was entitled to receive. It is one thing for a state to regulate the use of its streets and highways so as to keep them open and available for movement of people and property, or to pass general regulations as to their use in the interest of public safety, peace, comfort or convenience. . . . . It is quite another thing, however, to "abridge the constitutional liberty of one rightfully upon the street to impart information through speech or the distribution of literature."

The Ritter decision indicates some departure from the holding which the Supreme Court made in the Thornhill case when it stated,

. . . The State urges that the purpose of the challenged statute is the protection of the community from the violence and breaches of the peace, which, it asserts, are the concomitants of picketing. The power and the duty of the State to take adequate steps to preserve the peace and to protect the privacy, the lives, and the property of its residents cannot be doubted. But no clear and present danger of destruction of life or property, or invasion of the right of privacy, or breach of the peace can be thought to be inherent in the activities of every person who approaches the premises of an employer and publicizes the facts of a labor dispute involving the latter. . . . . The streets are natural and proper places for the dissemination of information and opinion; and one is not to have the exercise of his liberty of expression in appropriate places abridged on the plea that it may be exercised in some other place. . . .

It was clear the court felt that since picketing was declared to be a form of communication, the states might not abridge it except where there was "clear and present danger" to life or property. Certainly in the Ritter case there was no "clear and present danger" that continued picketing in front of the café would result in any damage to life or property. In departing from this rule, the Supreme Court applied a new test in the Ritter case; that picketing must be confined to the immediate area where the labor dispute has arisen.[12]

Several other important cases decided by the U.S. Supreme Court between 1940 and 1950 covered the subjects of picketing, free speech, and anti-injunction acts. Illinois was the situs of another precedent-setting case.[13] A union of beauty shop workers unsuccessfully tried to organize Swing's Beauty Parlor. Picketing of the shop followed. To enjoin this

12. See Goldfinger v. Feintuch, 276 N.Y. 281 (1937), in which the New York Court of Appeals allowed picketing of all those having a "unity of interest" with a struck manufacturer. This case was decided under the "baby" Norris-LaGuardia Act of New York, known as Section 876(a), Civil Practice Act.
13. AFL v. Swing, 312 U.S. 321 (1940).

interference with his business, and with the freedom of his workers not to join a union, Swing and his employees began an action to enjoin the picketing. The trial court denied the injunction. On appeal the judgment was reversed and the injunction was permitted on three grounds: (1) there was no dispute between the employer and his immediate employees; (2) the placards were libelous; (3) there were acts of violence.[14] However, the appellate court's action did not appear to rest on grounds (2) and (3) but rather on (1), for it said

. . . that this Court and the Supreme Court of this State have held in this case, that, under the law of this State, peaceful picketing or peaceful persuasion are unlawful when conducted by strangers to the employer (i.e., where there is not a proximate relation of employees and employer), and that appellants are entitled in this case to relief by injunction against the threat of such peaceful picketing or persuasion by appellees. . . .

The main issue in the Swing case was whether the relationship of employer-employee must exist before peaceful picketing will be permitted.

The U.S. Supreme Court vacated the injunction in this case. Justice Frankfurter, who wrote the opinion for the court, said that if a labor dispute existed, strangers having no relation with the employer might exercise the right of free speech by picketing. Part of the opinion follows.

. . . Such a ban of free communication is inconsistent with the guarantee of freedom of speech. That a state has ample power to regulate the local problems thrown up by modern industry and to preserve the peace is axiomatic. But not even these essential powers are unfettered by the requirements of the Bill of Rights. The scope of the Fourteenth Amendment is not confined by the notion of a particular state regarding the wise limits of an injunction in an industrial dispute, whether those limits be defined by statute or by the judicial organ of the state. A state cannot exclude workingmen from peacefully exercising the right of free communication by drawing the circle of economic competition between employers and workers so small as to contain only an employer and those directly employed by him. The right of free communication cannot therefore be mutilated by denying it to workers, in a dispute with an employer, even though they are not in his employ. . . . Members of a union might, without special statutory authorization by a State, make known the facts of a labor dispute, for freedom of speech is guaranteed by the Federal Constitution. . . .

14. In Angelos v. Mesevich, 320 U.S. 293 (1942), the U.S. Supreme Court said that the right to picket may not be taken away "merely because there may have been isolated incidents of abuse falling far short of violence occurring in the course of that picketing." In this case, members of a labor union picketed cafeterias operated solely by their owners in an attempt to organize them. The Supreme Court vacated an injunction granted by the New York state courts.

The U.S. Supreme Court was asked to pass on another important case [15] in which the issue was whether secondary picketing was entitled to protection as speech under the Constitution.

The facts in the Wohl dispute appear in the court's opinion, written by Mr. Justice Jackson.

. . . The union has for some years been engaged in obtaining collective bargaining agreements prescribing the wages, hours and working conditions of bakery drivers. Five years before the trial there were in New York City comparatively few peddlers or so-called independent jobbers—fifty at most, consisting largely of men who had a long established retail trade. About four years before the trial the social security and unemployment compensation laws, both of which imposed taxes on payrolls, became effective in the State of New York. Thereafter the number of peddlers of bakery products increased from year to year until at the time of hearing they numbered more than five hundred. In the eighteen months preceding the hearings, bakery companies which operated routes through employed drivers had notified the union that at the expiration of their contracts they would no longer employ drivers but would permit the drivers to purchase trucks for nominal amounts, in some instances fifty dollars, and thereupon to continue to distribute their baked goods as peddlers. Within such period a hundred and fifty drivers who were members of the union and had previously worked under union contracts and conditions were discharged and required to leave the industry unless they undertook to act as peddlers. . . .

. . . The union became alarmed at the aggressive inroads of this kind of competition upon the employment and living standards of its members. The trial court found that if employers with union contracts are forced to adopt the peddler system, "the wages, hours, and working conditions, six-day week, etc., attained by the union after long years of struggle will be destroyed and lost." In the spring of 1938 the union made an effort in good faith to persuade the peddlers to become members, and those who desired were admitted to membership. . . . When Wohl and Platzman refused to either join the union or employ a union relief man, and continued to work seven days each week, the union took the measures which led to this litigation. On January 23, 1939, the union caused two pickets to walk in the vicinity of the bakery which sold products to Wohl and Platzman, each picket carrying a placard, one bearing the name of Wohl and the other that of Platzman, and under each name appeared the following statement: "A bakery route driver works seven days a week. We ask employment for a union relief man for one day. Help us spread employment and maintain a union wage, hours and conditions. . . ." The picketing lasted less than two hours. Again on the 25th of January, the union caused two pickets to display the same placards in the vicinity for less than an hour; and on the same day a picket with a placard bearing the name of Wohl over the same statement, picketed for a very short time in the vicinity of another bakery from which

15. Bakery and Pastry Drivers and Helpers Local 802, Teamsters, v. Wohl, 315 U.S. 769 (1942).

Wohl had purchased baked products. It was also found that a member of the union had followed Platzman as he was distributing his products and called on two or three customers, advising them that the union was seeking to persuade Platzman to work but six days per week and employ a union driver as a relief man, and stating to one that in the event he continued to purchase from Platzman a picket would be placed in the vicinity on the following day with a placard reading as set forth above. It does not appear that this threat was carried out. . . .

. . . The trial court found that the placards were truthful and accurate in all respects; that the picketing consisted of no more than two pickets at any one time and was done in a peaceful and orderly manner, without violence or threat thereof. . . .

The trial court issued injunctions which restrained the union from picketing the places of business of manufacturing bakers who sell to the respondents or the places of business of their customers. The granting of the injunction was sustained by the New York appellate courts, including the court of appeals. Although a "baby" Norris-LaGuardia Act exists in New York, the injunction was issued here on the court's finding that a labor dispute did not exist; therefore the state anti-injunction law was inapplicable.

Throughout the court proceedings in New York the union contended that it had a constitutional right to advise the public accurately, truthfully, and without violence that Wohl and Platzman worked seven days a week and that the union was trying to secure employment from Wohl and Platzman for unemployed members of the union one day a week. The New York courts rejected this constitutional argument.

The U.S. Supreme Court reversed the decision of the New York Court of Appeals, vacated the injunction, and defending its action, stated:

. . . So far as we can ascertain from the opinions delivered by the state courts in this case, those courts were concerned only with the question whether there was involved a labor dispute within the meaning of the New York statutes and assumed that the legality of the injunction followed from a determination that such a dispute was not involved. Of course that does not follow: one need not be in a "labor dispute" as defined by state law to have a right under the Fourteenth Amendment to express a grievance in a labor matter by publication unattended by violence, coercion, or conduct otherwise unlawful or oppressive. . . .

. . . We ourselves can perceive no substantial evil of such magnitude as to mark a limit to the right of free speech which the petitioners sought to exercise. The record in this case does not contain the slightest suggestion of embarrassment in the task of governance; there are no findings and no circumstances from which we can draw the inference that the publication was attended or likely to be attended by violence, force or coercion, or conduct otherwise unlawful or oppressive; and it is not indicated that there was an actual or threatened abuse of the right to free speech through the use of excessive picketing. A state is not required to tolerate in all places and all circumstances even peaceful picketing by an individual. But so far as we can tell, respondents' mobility and their insulation from the public as middlemen made it practically impossible for petitioners to make known their legitimate grievances to the public whose patronage was sustaining the peddler system except by means here employed and contemplated; and those means are such as to have slight, if any, repercussions upon the interests of strangers to the issue . . .

The Wohl case declares that since picketing of a peaceful nature is speech and is constitutionally protected, a state is not free to define a labor controversy so narrowly as to accomplish indirectly what it may not accomplish directly. This decision is an extension of the Thornhill ruling, which allowed peaceful picketing.

The "Objectives" Test

We now direct our attention to a series of cases passed on by the Supreme Court, in which state court injunctions were sustained in labor controversies on the ground that the peaceful picketing was directed toward an unlawful end. In other words, whenever the picketing by unions is directed to objectives which are contrary to the state public policy expressed by state legislatures, or by state courts, the Supreme Court has sustained the constitutionality of injunctive relief against picketing, notwithstanding its peaceful conduct.

The Giboney Case

This "objectives" test was used by the U.S. Supreme Court for the first time in the Giboney [16] case, which concerned ice peddlers. The union's membership included about two hundred retail ice peddlers who drove their own trucks, selling ice from door to door in Kansas City. The union started a drive to organize all the nonunion peddlers. When the drive stalled the union obtained agreements from wholesale ice distributors under which they agreed not to sell ice to the nonunion peddlers. When Empire Storage and Ice Company became the only ice distributor continuing to sell ice to nonunion peddlers, the union picketed its place of business. The sole purpose of the picket line was to compel Empire to stop selling ice to nonunion peddlers. Under a Missouri antitrust statute, the trial court issued an injunction against

16. Giboney v. Empire Storage and Ice Co., 336 U.S. 490 (1948).

the picketing, after finding that the union was illegally restraining intra-state commerce. The highest appellate court in the state affirmed the decision.

The union carried the case to the Supreme Court, claiming that its picketing was directed toward the objective of improving the wages and working conditions of union members. The union claimed further that the picketing was free speech stemming from the First and Fourteenth Amendments, and that the state of Missouri had improperly interfered with these constitutional guarantees.

Before we examine the decision of the Supreme Court, let us go back to the Missouri antitrust statute. It provided that a violation thereof was punishable by a fine of not more than $5000 and imprisonment in the penitentiary for not more than 5 years. Had Empire consented to the agreement sought by the union, it would have been liable for viola-tion of this criminal statute, which also provided that competing ice distributors could bring a civil action against Empire and recover treble damages.

The U.S. Supreme Court upheld the judgment of the Missouri state court and said:

. . . Neither Thornhill v. Alabama, nor Carlson v. California, 310 U.S. 106, both decided the same day, supports the contention that conduct other-wise unlawful is always immune from state regulation because an integral part of that conduct is carried on by display of placards by peaceful picketers. In both these cases this Court struck down statutes which banned all dis-semination of information by people adjacent to certain premises, pointing out that the statutes were so broad that they could not only be utilized to punish conduct plainly illegal but could also be applied to ban all truthful publications of the facts of a labor controversy. . . .

We hold that the state's power to govern this field is paramount and that nothing in the constitutional guaranties of speech or press compels a state to apply or not to apply its anti-trade restraint law to groups of workers, busi-nessmen or others. . . .

The Giboney case holds that whenever a state statute imposes crimi-nal liability on a picketed employer for consenting to do what a union seeks, then the picketing may be enjoined even though it is carried on in an orderly and nonviolent manner. Some feel that this decision cir-cumvents the Thornhill ruling. The feeling that the Giboney decision, for all practical purposes, brought about the demise of the 1940 free speech doctrine, assumed the states were completely privileged now to use their legislative authority to create laws which could destroy the Thornhill doctrine by the indirect method. This assumption is question-able, since the Supreme Court by its decision approved only valid and reasonable state laws which would prohibit peaceful picketing only

when the unions failed the "objectives test." State legislation to encourage rather than discourage business competition was held to be a
valid law. To permit a union to exert economic pressure, however peaceful, which would, if effective, force an employer to violate a valid state
law, and open itself to grave punishment, would seem to warrant appropriate court action to remove the pressure.

We shall conclude this last series of cases dealing with peaceful picketing, and the "objectives" test, with a presentation of the Gazzam [17]
and Hanke [18] cases.

The Gazzam and Hanke Cases

In the Gazzam case the employer, Mr. Gazzam, employed about fifteen persons at Enetai Inn, a small hotel operated in Bremerton, Washington. In April 1946, a union demanded that Gazzam sign a union
contract which would require his employees to join the union. Gazzam
replied that this was a matter for the employees to decide and he gave
the union permission to solicit his employees for membership. The
union held meetings with the employees who unanimously refused to
join the union. Again Gazzam was asked to sign the union shop contract and when he refused, the union installed a single picket in front
of the hotel. Gazzam filed suit for an injunction, and for damages
against the union. The union claimed that its picketing was constitutionally protected as free speech. The state of Washington has a "little"
Norris-LaGuardia Act which bars its courts from issuing injunctions in
those cases where a "labor dispute" exists. The statute sets forth the
public policy of the state with relation to labor controversies. In its
declared public policy the state legislature has condemned all forms of
employer coercion to require employees to join a union against their
will. The trial court in September 1948, entered a judgment in favor of
Gazzam for the "wrongful picketing" in the sum of $500 and perma-
nently enjoined the union from picketing. The Supreme Court of
Washington affirmed the judgment. The union appealed to the U.S.
Supreme Court.

The issue before the U.S. Supreme Court was this: Do the First and
Fourteenth Amendments to the Constitution permit a state, in reliance
on its public policy, to enjoin peaceful picketing carried on for the purpose of compelling an employer to sign a contract with a labor union
which coerces his employees' choice of the bargaining representative?

This court, upholding the decision, said:

17. Building Service Employees v. Gazzam, 339 U.S. 532 (1950).
18. Teamsters v. Hanke, 339 U.S. 470 (1950).

. . . We are of the opinion that Giboney v. Empire Storage & Ice Co., 336 U.S. 490, controls the disposition of this case and that it therefore must be affirmed. In the Giboney case it is true that the state law which made the objectives of the picketing unlawful had criminal sanctions. The Washington Statute here has no criminal sanctions. Here, as in Giboney, the union was using its economic power with that of its allies to compel respondent to abide by union policy rather than by the declared policy of the state. That state guarantees workers free choice of representatives for bargaining purposes. If respondent had complied with petitioners' demands and had signed one of the tendered contracts and lived up to its terms, he would thereby have coerced his employees. . . .

The Hanke case concerns Mr. Hanke and his three sons, who as co-partners operated an auto repair and used-car business in Seattle, Washington. They had no employees. Local 309 of the Teamsters negotiated an agreement with the Auto Dealers Association, to which Hanke did not belong, providing that used car lots be closed at 6 P.M. on weekdays, all day Saturday and Sunday, and on eight specified holidays. This agreement was intended to be applicable to 115 car dealers in Seattle, all except 10 of whom were self-employers with no employees. It was the practice of the Hankes to remain open nights, weekends, and holidays. The senior Mr. Hanke possessed a union card in Local 309. The union urged the Hankes to respect the limitation on business hours. The Hankes refused. The union put a single picket to patrol peacefully in front of the Hankes' business. As a result of the picketing Hankes' business fell off heavily, and they brought suit against the union seeking to restrain the picketing. The trial court granted a permanent injunction against the picketing after rejecting the union's contention that the picketing was speech protected under the Constitution. The Supreme Court of Washington affirmed the judgment. The union took the case to the U.S. Supreme Court.

The issue was: Does the Fourteenth Amendment of the Constitution bar a state from the use of the injunction to prohibit the picketing of a business conducted by the owner himself without employees in order to secure compliance with a demand to become a union shop?

The U.S. Supreme Court, refusing to disturb the decision of the Washington courts, said, in part:

. . . Here, as in Hughes v. Superior Court, 339 U.S. 460, we must start with the fact that while picketing is an ingredient of communication, it cannot dogmatically be equated with the constitutionally protected freedom of speech. Our decisions reflect recognition that picketing is "indeed a hybrid." . . . The effort in the cases has been to strike a balance between the constitutional protection of the element of communication in picketing and the power of the State to set the limits of permissible contest open to industrial combattants [sic] . . . . it is not for this Court to question a State's judgment in regulating only where an evil seems to it most conspicuous . . .

Washington here concluded that even though the relief afforded the Hankes entailed restriction upon communication that the union sought to convey through picketing, it was more important to safeguard the value which the State placed upon self employers, leaving all other channels of communications open to the union. . . .[19]

Refuge under the Fourteenth Amendment was sought in another picketing case.[20] The facts are included in the opinion of the U.S. Supreme Court, delivered by Mr. Justice Frankfurter as follows:

Does the Fourteenth Amendment of the Constitution bar a State from use of the injunction to prohibit picketing of a place of business solely in order to secure compliance with a demand that its employees be in proportion to the racial origin of its then customers? Such is the broad question of this case.

The petitioners, acting on behalf of a group calling themselves Progressive Citizens of America, demanded of Lucky Stores, Inc., that it hire Negroes at its grocery store near the Canal Housing Project in Richmond, California, as white clerks quit or were transferred, until the proportion of Negro to white customers was reached. At the time in controversy about 50 per cent of the customers of the Canal store were Negroes. Upon refusal of this demand and in order to compel compliance, the Canal store was systematically patrolled by pickets carrying placards stating that Lucky refused to hire Negro clerks in proportion to Negro customers.

Suit was begun by Lucky to enjoin the picketing on appropriate allegations for equitable relief. The Superior Court of Contra Costa County issued a preliminary injunction restraining petitioners and others from picketing any of Lucky's stores to compel "the selective hiring of Negro clerks, such hiring to be based on the proportion of white and Negro customers who patronize plaintiff's stores." In the face of this injunction, petitioners continued to picket the Canal store, carrying placards reading: "Lucky Won't Hire Negro Clerks in Proportion to Negro Trade—Don't Patronize." In conformity with State procedure, petitioners were found guilty of contempt for "willfully disregarding" the injunction and were sentenced to imprisonment for two days and fined $20 each. They defended their conduct by challenging the injunction as a deprivation of the liberty assured them by the Due Process Clause of the Fourteenth Amendment. The intermediate appellate court annulled the judgment of contempt, 186 P. (2d) 756, but it was reinstated on review by the Supreme Court of California. That court held that the conceded purpose of the picketing in this case—to compel the hiring of Negroes in proportion to Negro customers—was unlawful even though pursued in a peaceful manner. Having violated a valid injunction petitioners were properly punishable for contempt. . . .

19. The U.S. Supreme Court, relying on this and other previous decisions, also held that peaceful picketing for an objective in violation of a state right-to-work statute could be constitutionally enjoined. See Plumbers Local 10 v. Graham, 345 U.S. 192 (1953).
20. Hughes v. Superior Court, 339 U.S. 460 (1950).

These considerations are most pertinent in regard to a population made up of so many diverse groups as ours. To deny to California the right to ban picketing in the circumstances of this case would mean that there could be no prohibition of the pressure of picketing to secure proportional employment on ancestral grounds of Hungarians in Cleveland, of Poles in Buffalo, of Germans in Milwaukee, of Portuguese in New Bedford, of Mexicans in San Antonio, of the numerous minority groups in New York, and so on through the whole gamut of racial and religious concentrations in various cities. States may well believe that such constitutional sheltering would inevitably encourage use of picketing to compel employment on the basis of racial discrimination. In disallowing such picketing, States may act under the belief that otherwise community tensions and conflicts would be exacerbated. The differences in cultural traditions, instead of adding flavor and variety to our common citizenry, might well be hardened into hostilities by leave of law. The Constitution does not demand that the element of communication in picketing prevail over the mischief furthered by its use in these situations. . . .

The injunction here was drawn to meet what California deemed the evil of picketing to bring about proportional hiring. We do not go beyond the circumstances of the case. Generalizations are treacherous in the application of large constitutional concepts. . . . The fact that California's policy is expressed by the judicial organ of the State rather than by the legislature we have repeatedly ruled to be immaterial. . . . For the Fourteenth Amendment leaves the States free to distribute the powers of government as they will between their legislative and judicial branches. Affirmed.

This is the law because the Supreme Court says it is; many believe it unfortunate, however. When a legislative body has under consideration a bill declaring public policy, there is generally opportunity for expression of views either at public hearings or directly to legislators and later to protest if dissatisfied by use of the ballot. Further, a statute gives advance warning as to what action is prohibited and what sanctions are prescribed. When judges declare something is against public policy, they do so after the fact and devise their own sanctions. It is also arguable that judges have less feel for public opinion then legislators.

The Thornhill Doctrine Radically Modified

Mr. Justice Frankfurter contributed some interesting statements in the case of Teamsters v. Vogt,[21] in which the retreat from the pronouncements of the Thornhill case is readily apparent. In this case the defendant unions, after having failed in their efforts to induce some of the plaintiff's employees to join them, picketed at the entrance of the

21. 354 U.S. 284 (1957).

plaintiff's gravel pit. A Wisconsin state court enjoined the picketing, and the decision was affirmed by the supreme court of the state on the ground that the picketing was planned to coerce the employer to interfere with its employees in their right to join or not to join a union.

On an appeal to the U.S. Supreme Court the decision was affirmed. This court held that a state may, consistent with the Fourteenth Amendment, enjoin union conduct in violation of a valid policy of the state. Mr. Justice Frankfurter said:

. . . The mere fact that there is picketing does not automatically justify its restraint without an investigation into its conduct and purposes; neither state courts nor state legislatures can enact blanket prohibitions against picketing. . . . The policy of a state prohibiting a union from picketing to coerce an employer to put pressure on his employees to join a union is valid. . . .

Referring to the court's opinion in the Thornhill decision Justice Frankfurter added the following comments, which appear in his opinion:

. . . Soon the Court came to realize that the broad pronouncements, but not the specific holding of Thornhill, had to yield to the impact of the facts "unforeseen" or at least not fully appreciated. . . . Implied reassessments of the broad language of the Thornhill case were finally generalized in a series of cases sustaining injunctions against peaceful picketing when arising in the course of a labor dispute, when such picketing was counter to valid state policy in a domain open to state regulation.

Mr. Justice Douglas, in his dissent, said that he accepted the Thornhill principle and did not want to retreat from it. An excerpt from his opinion follows.

. . . of course, we have always recognized that picketing has aspects which make it more than speech. . . . That difference underlies our decision in Giboney v. Empire Storage & Ice Co., 336 U.S. 490. There picketing was an essential part of a "single and integrated course of conduct, which was in violation of Missouri's valid law." We emphasized that "there was clear danger, imminent and immediate, that unless restrained, appellants would succeed in making the state policy a dead letter . . . But where, as here, no violence, no disorder, no fisticuffs, no coercion—indeed nothing but speech—the principles announced in Thornhill and Swing should give the advocacy of one side of a dispute First Amendment protection. . . . Today the Court signs the formal surrender. State courts and state legislatures cannot fashion blanket prohibitions on all picketing. But for practical purposes, now is as it was when Senn v. Tile Layers Union, 301 U.S. 468 was decided [sic]. State courts and state legislatures are free to decide whether to permit or suppress any particular picket line for any reason other than a blanket policy against all picketing. I would adhere to the principle announced in Thornhill. . . .

The peaceful-picketing–free-speech doctrine interpreted by the U.S. Supreme Court in the Giboney, Hanke, Gazzam, Hughes, and Vogt cases provides that picketing in labor controversy cases does not get blanket protection under the Fourteenth Amendment. This court has ruled that state courts and state legislatures may enjoin peaceful picketing when it has been determined that the objectives sought are unlawful, or whenever the objective contravenes valid state policy. The path of retreat from Thornhill to the unlawful objective doctrine is unfortunate. What is the objective of picketing? Sometimes it is clear, but in complicated situations it may not be, and then the objective may well be whatever the judges say it is. What is public policy? State statutes may explicitly define it, but where the law is silent public policy may be left to the whim of the judge.

When lawful objectives have been sought through violent picketing on a grand scale, restraining orders have been sustained by the U.S. Supreme Court. In other cases, when isolated incidents of violence have occurred, the court, reluctant to ban picketing completely, has modified the broad injunction to prohibit only the violent phase of picketing. The peaceful picketing in such cases has been protected under the free-speech doctrine.

Does the constitutional privilege of free speech protect peaceful picketing which is accompanied by false and misleading representations? This question was answered by the U.S. Supreme Court and by a few state courts. In Cafeteria Employees v. Angelos [22] the plaintiffs had in 1939 organized a partnership and conducted a business called The World Cafeteria. The partners carried on the firm without any outside assistance. The union, seeking to unionize the business, established a picket line outside the plaintiffs' premises. The plaintiffs sought a restraining order to enjoin the picketing on the ground that no labor dispute existed since the firm had no employees. The trial court found that the pickets carried false and misleading signs; that pickets approached customers and told them that plaintiffs' restaurant was giving bad food; that by patronizing the restaurant they were aiding the cause of Fascism; and that the pickets directed the customers about to enter plaintiffs' premises to a cafeteria across the street which was a competitor of the plaintiffs'.

An injunction was issued restraining the stationing of pickets "at or near the plaintiffs' place of business and from interfering with plaintiffs' customers, or from interfering in any wise with the plaintiffs' business." The decree was upheld by the New York Court of Appeals on the ground that no labor dispute could exist under Section 876(a) of the Civil Practice Act ("little" Norris-LaGuardia Act) unless there was employment.

22. 320 U.S. 293 (1943).

On the issue of free speech raised by the defendant union, this court said:

. . . The defendants had a constitutional right accurately and truthfully and without violence, force or coercion, or conduct otherwise unlawful or oppressive to make their grievances known to the public. But, a citizen is not required to tolerate peaceful picketing accompanied by untruthful representations, interference with his business or coercive conduct designed to injure or destroy his business whether a labor dispute exists or not. . . .

On appeal to the U.S. Supreme Court the judgment was reversed. Mr. Justice Frankfurter delivered the opinion of the court. A part of the opinion follows.

. . . That the picketing under review was peaceful is not questioned. And to use loose language or undefined slogans that are part of the conventional give-and-take in our economic and political controversies—like "unfair" or "fascist"—is not to falsify facts. In a setting like the present, continuing representations unquestionably false and acts of coercion going beyond the mere influence exerted by the fact of picketing are of course not constitutional prerogatives. But here we have no attempt by the state through its courts to restrict conduct justifiably found to be an abusive exercise of the right to picket. We have before us a prohibition as unrestricted as that which we found in A.F. of L. v. Swing, 312 U.S. 321. . . . A state cannot exclude working men in a particular industry from putting their case to the public in a peaceful way by drawing the circle of economic competition between employers and workers so small as to contain only an employer and those directly employed by him. . . . Right to free speech in the future cannot be forfeited because of dissociated acts of past violence. Still less can the right to picket itself be taken away merely because there may have been isolated incidents of abuse falling far short of violence occurring in the course of that picketing. . . .

In the Meadowmoor Dairies case,[23] cited in the Angelos opinion, the U.S. Supreme Court had affirmed the right of the state to ban all picketing when the large volume of violence resulting was so enmeshed with the peaceful picketing that it was impossible to separate the good from the bad. In the Angelos case, however, the court struck down the broad injunction that had enjoined all picketing, first because the picketing was admittedly peaceful, and secondly because the Supreme Court was not satisfied that the pickets had engaged in false and misleading representations. Therefore the court held that the Angelos case did not fit into the doctrine pronounced in the Meadowmoor opinion. Mr. Justice Frankfurter adhered to the Thornhill doctrine which recognized picketing as a form of speech to be protected under the First and Fourteenth Amendments of the Constitution. No state, he said, could properly issue

23. *Supra.*

a blanket prohibition against picketing unless it fell within the rule pronounced in Meadowmoor.

Facts similar to those existing in the Angelos case occurred in Magill Bros. v. Building Service Employees,[24] decided by the California Supreme Court. Since this case did not get to the U.S. Supreme Court it is probable, under the Angelos rule, that the decision would not have been disturbed in view of the court's position on the blanket prohibition of picketing by state courts. In Magill, none of the plaintiffs' employees was a member of the defendant union which had urged the employer to sign a closed shop agreement. After repeated refusals on the part of the plaintiff the union stationed pickets outside plaintiffs' premises. The pickets carried signs stating, "This house on strike AFL." At the time none of the plaintiffs' employees were on strike and no labor dispute existed between the employer and the employees. The trial court granted a temporary injunction which it later vacated. On appeal the California Supreme Court reversed the judgment. In its decision it provided that the plaintiff was entitled to a decree restraining the union from the use of false or untruthful statements in the exercise of their right to picket.

Throughout these court proceedings the union had contended that the constitutional guarantee of freedom of speech prohibited the intervention of equity even where untruthful picketing was involved. In rejecting the claim of the union the California court said:

> . . . The right to restrain the use of false or untruthful statements made in connection with picketing does not restrict the right to picket peacefully and honestly. It is a familiar doctrine of equity that the scope of the injunction will be limited to the wrongful acts sought to be prevented. The effect of the decree is to protect every legitimate right of the defendants, and at the same time prevent unlawful interference with the rights of the plaintiffs. The policy of this State which characterizes the use of false or fraudulent statements in picketing as unlawful is within the permissible limits which a state may impose upon industrial combatants without impairing the right of free speech. . . .

The contrast between Angelos and Magill is quite clear. In the Angelos case the New York court, conceding the picketing peaceful, had issued a blanket prohibition on its continuance because some of the disseminated information was allegedly false and misleading. In Magill, the restraining order enjoined only that part of the picketing found to be objectionable. In Magill, moreover, the falsity of the information could be objectively determined.

The subjects of free speech, picketing, and injunctions will be brought up to include the Labor Management Relations Act of 1947 and the

24. 6 LC 61,194, 20 Cal.(2d) 506 (1942).

Reporting and Disclosure Act of 1959 in later chapters. After these statutes and the cases flowing from them have been analyzed, it may become more clear that picketing and the free-speech doctrine first spelled out in Thornhill have been so emasculated that they can hardly be recognized. Certainly, there is much support for the contention that the "objectives" test has replaced the free-speech doctrine in picketing cases.

CHAPTER SEVEN

Labor and the Antitrust Laws after 1932

BETWEEN 1890 and 1932 labor unions were vulnerable to legal actions initiated under the Sherman Act and its amendment, the Clayton Act. The most distasteful feature of these proceedings after 1914 was the capriciousness of some federal judges in granting employers' applications for injunctions to restrain strikes, particularly those occurring during organizing campaigns. The usual ground for issuing the injunction was the court's declaration that the labor techniques utilized interfered illegally with interstate commerce.[1]

Congress met the unfavorable decisions of the Supreme Court with the enactment of the Norris-LaGuardia Act of 1932. This law, when read with the Sherman and Clayton Acts, gives specific labor activities considerable immunity from the provisions of the antitrust laws, a protection that labor unions had hoped for when Congress passed the Clayton Act in 1914. These three statutes, when considered together, plus the application of a more liberal attitude of the Supreme Court toward labor objectives, resulted in four important decisions, which for all practical purposes repealed the precedent-setting Danbury Hatters, Duplex, and Coronado cases.

In the cases that follow the activities of the unions were challenged on the ground that they constituted antitrust violations. In three of the cases the Supreme Court decided that the unions had not violated the antitrust laws.

1. See *The Labor Injunction*, F. Frankfurter, N. Greene, *supra*, for an excellent review of judicial abuses of the injunction in labor cases.

The Apex Case

In the Apex case [2] a long, violent sit-down strike closed down the plant of a large hosiery manufacturer. The union had sought a closed-shop agreement, which the employer had rejected. During its strike the union took over complete physical possession of the factory. Apex employed 2500 persons and manufactured more than $5,000,000 worth of hosiery, of which more than 80 per cent was shipped in interstate commerce. The manufacturing and shipping ceased completely during the long period of the strike. The employer brought an action against the union to recover treble the damages inflicted by the union during the conduct of its strike. It charged that the union had illegally restrained interstate commerce. The proceedings were initiated under Sections 1 and 7 of the Sherman Act. The trial court rendered a judgment in favor of Apex in the sum of $237,310, which the judged trebled to $711,932.55. The Circuit Court of Appeals reversed on the ground that the interstate commerce restrained was not substantial.

Apex appealed to the U.S. Supreme Court. Mr. Justice Stone delivered the opinion of the court.

. . . The facts are undisputed. There was evidence from which the jury could have found as follows. Petitioner employs at its Philadelphia factory about 2500 persons in the manufacture of hosiery, and manufactures annually merchandise of the value of about $5,000,000. Its principal raw materials are silk and cotton, which are shipped to it from points outside the state. It ships interstate more than 80 per cent of its finished product, and in the last eight months of 1937 it shipped in all 274,791 dozen pairs of stockings. In April, 1937, petitioner was operating a nonunion shop. A demand of the respondent Federation at that time for a closed shop came to nothing. On May 4, 1937, when only eight of petitioner's employees were members of the Federation, it ordered a strike. Shortly after midday on May 6, 1937, when petitioner's factory was shut down, members of the union, employed in other factories in Philadelphia, who had stopped work, gathered at petitioner's plant. Respondent Leader, president of the Federation, then made a further demand for a closed shop agreement. When this was refused, Leader declared a "sit-down strike." Immediately acts of violence against petitioner's plant and the employees in charge of it were committed by the assembled mob. It forcibly seized the plant, whereupon, under union leadership, its members were organized to maintain themselves as sit-down strikers in possession of the plant, and it remained in possession until June 23, 1937, when the strikers were forcibly ejected pursuant to an injunction ordered by the Court of Appeals for the Third Circuit in Apex

2. Apex Hosiery Co. v. Leader, 310 U.S. 469 (1940).

Hosiery Co. v. Leader, 90 F. (2d) 155, 159; reversed and dismissal ordered as moot in Leader v. Apex Hosiery Co., 302 U.S. 656.

The locks on all gates and entrances of petitioner's plant were changed; only strikers were given keys. No others were allowed to leave or enter the plant without permission of the strikers. During the period of their occupancy, the union supplied them with food, blankets, cots, medical care, and paid them strike benefits. While occupying the factory, the strikers wilfully wrecked machinery of great value, and did extensive damage to other property and equipment of the company. All manufacturing operations by petitioner ceased on May 6th. As the result of the destruction of the company's machinery and plant, it did not resume even partial manufacturing operations until August 19, 1937. The record discloses a lawless invasion of petitioner's plant and destruction of its property by force and violence of the most brutal and wanton character, under leadership and direction of respondents, and without interference by the local authorities.

For more than three months, by reason of respondents' acts, manufacture was suspended at petitioner's plant and the flow of petitioner's product into interstate commerce was stopped. When the plant was seized there were on hand 130,000 dozen pairs of finished hosiery, of a value of about $800,000, ready for shipment on unfilled orders, 80 per cent of which were to be shipped to points outside the state. Shipment was prevented by the occupation of the factory by the strikers. Three times in the course of the strike respondents refused requests made by petitioner to be allowed to remove the merchandise for the purpose of shipment in filling the orders. . . .

. . . In this suit, in which no diversity of citizenship of the parties is alleged or shown, the federal courts are without authority to enforce state laws. Their only jurisdiction is to vindicate such federal right as Congress has conferred on petitioner by the Sherman Act and violence, as will appear hereafter, however reprehensible, does not give the federal courts jurisdiction.

At the outset, and before considering the more substantial issues which we regard as decisive of this cause, it is desirable to remove from the field of controversy certain questions which have been much argued here and below, but which we think, in the circumstances of the present case, are irrelevant to the decision. We find abundant support for petitioner's contention that the effect of the sit-down strike was to restrict substantially the interstate transportation of its manufactured product, so as to bring the acts of respondents by which the restriction was effected within the reach of the commerce power if Congress has seen fit to exercise it . . . recently, where the statute was by its terms applicable and the question was of Congressional power, we have sustained the application of the Wagner Act . . . regulating labor relations "affecting" interstate commerce to situations no more closely related to the commerce than these, and where the interstate commerce affected was no greater in volume. And in the application of the Sherman Act, as we have recently had occasion to point out, it is the nature of the restraint and its effect on interstate commerce and not the amount of the commerce which are the tests of violation. . . .

. . . It is not seriously contended here that a conspiracy to derail and rob an interstate train, even though it were laden with 100,000 dozen pairs of stockings, necessarily would involve a violation of the Sherman Act. This Court has never applied the Act to laborers or to others as a means of policing interstate transportation, and so the question to which we must address ourselves is whether a conspiracy of strikers in a labor dispute to stop the operation of the employer's factory in order to enforce their demands against the employer is the kind of restraint of trade or commerce at which the Act is aimed, even though a natural and probable consequence of their acts and the only effect on trade or commerce was to prevent substantial shipments interstate by the employer.

A point strongly urged in behalf of respondents in brief and argument before us is that Congress intended to exclude labor organizations and their activities wholly from the operation of the Sherman Act. To this the short answer must be made that for the 32 years which have elapsed since the decision of Loewe v. Lawlor, 208 U.S. 274, this Court, in its efforts to determine the true meaning and application of the Sherman Act has repeatedly held that the words of the act, "Every contract, combination . . . or conspiracy in restraint of trade or commerce" do embrace to some extent and in some circumstances labor unions and their activities. . . .

. . . this Court has never applied the Sherman Act in any case, whether or not involving labor organizations or activities, unless the Court was of opinion that there was some form of restraint upon commercial competition in the marketing of goods or services and finally this Court has refused to apply the Sherman Act in cases like the present in which local strikes conducted by illegal means in a production industry prevented interstate shipment of substantial amounts of the product but in which it was not shown that the restrictions on shipments had operated to restrain commercial competition in some substantial way. First Coronado [case, reported in Chapter 3]; Leather Workers case [265 U.S. 457]. Levering and G. Co. v. Morrin, 289 U.S. 103. . . .

The question remains whether the effect of the combination or conspiracy among respondents was a restraint of trade within the meaning of the Sherman Act. This is not a case of labor organization being used by combinations of those engaged in an industry as the means of instrument for suppressing competition or fixing prices. See United States v. Brims, 272 U.S. 549 [reported in Chapter 3]; Local 167 v. United States, 291 U.S. 293. Here it is plain that the combination or conspiracy did not have as its purpose restraint upon competition in the market for petitioner's product. Its object was to compel petitioner to accede to the union demands and an effect of it, in consequence of the strikers' tortious acts, was the prevention of the removal of petitioner's product from interstate shipment. So far as appears the delay of these shipments was not intended to have and had no effect on prices of hosiery in the market. . . .

A combination of employees necessarily restrains competition among themselves in the sale of their services to the employer; yet such a combination was not considered an illegal restraint of trade at common law when the Sherman Act was adopted, either because it was not thought to be unreasonable or because it was not deemed a "restraint of trade." Since the enactment of the declaration in Sec. 6 of the Clayton Act that "the labor of a human being is not a commodity or article of commerce . . . nor shall such (labor) organizations or the members thereof be held or construed to be illegal combinations or conspiracies in the restraint of trade under the Anti-Trust Laws," it would seem plain that restraints on the sale of employee's services to the employer, however much they curtail the competition among employees, are not in themselves combinations or conspiracies in restraint of trade or commerce under the Sherman Act.

Strikes or agreements not to work, entered into by laborers to compel employers to yield to their demands, may restrict to some extent the power of employers who are parties to the dispute to compete in the market with those not subject to such demands. But under the doctrine applied to non-labor cases, the mere fact of such restrictions on competition does not in itself bring the parties to the agreement within the condemnation of the Sherman Act. Appalachian Coals, Inc. v. United States, 288 U.S. 344, 360. Furthermore, successful union activity, as for example consummation of a wage agreement with employers, may have some influence on price competition by eliminating that part of such competition which is based on differences in labor standards. Since, in order to render a labor combination effective it must eliminate the competition from non-union made goods, see American Steel Foundries V. Tri-City Central Trades Council, 257 U.S. 184, 209, an elimination of price competition based on differences in labor standards is the objective of any national labor organization. But this effect on competition has not been considered to be the kind of curtailment of price competition prohibited by the Sherman Act. See Levering and G. Co. v. Morrin, *supra*; cf. American Foundries Case, 257 U.S. 184, 209; Window Glass Manufacturers v. United States, 263 U.S. 403. And in any case, the restraint here is, as we have seen, of a different kind and has not been shown to have any actual or intended effect on price or price competition.

. . . This Court was first called on to consider a case like the present in the First Coronado [case], *supra*. There a local branch of a national labor union sought to unionize a coal mine which was shipping its product interstate to the extent of more than 5000 tons a week. Members of the union compelled the mine to shut down, by force and violence, including murder and arson. By reason of their forcible action all work at the mine was prevented, it filled with water, shipments of coal which were regularly moving in interstate commerce as mined, ceased, and the strikers burned more than ten cars, three of them loaded with coal and some billed for movement interstate. This Court, notwithstanding the admittedly substantial effect of the strike on the interstate movement of the coal, and the admittedly illegal and outrageous acts of the strikers, held that it was not a restraint of trade or commerce prohibited by the Sherman Act. It rested its decision specifically on two grounds: that "obstruction to coal mining is not a direct obstruction to interstate commerce in coal," and that the intent to obstruct the mining of coal and to burn the loaded cars, did not necessarily imply an intent to restrain the commerce, although concededly interstate shipments and the filling of interstate orders for coal were necessarily ended by the stoppage of mining operations and the destruction of the loaded cars. It perhaps suffices for present purposes to say that if the strike in the Coronado case was not within the Sherman Act because its effect upon the commerce was "indirect" and because the "intention" to shut down the mine and destroy the cars of coal destined for an interstate shipment, did not imply an "intention to obstruct interstate commerce," then the like tests require the like decision here.

But we are not relegated to so mechanical an application of these cryptic phrases in the application of the Sherman Anti-Trust Act, for the Court has since so interpreted them as to give to the phrase "restraint of trade or commerce" a meaning and content consonant with the legislative and judicial history of the Act to which we have referred. In the Leather Workers case, *supra,* the Court was again called on to determine whether a local strike in a factory which prevented shipment of its product in filling interstate orders of substantial volume violated the Sherman Act. As in the First Coronado [case] the Court held that the restraint was not one prohibited by the Sherman Act. It pointed out [in the Leather Workers case] . . . that there has been no attempt, as in Loewe v. Lawlor, to boycott the sale of complainant's products in other states, and that if the interruption of interstate shipments resulting from a local factory strike aimed at compelling the employer to yield to union demands were deemed within the sweep of the Sherman Act, "The natural, logical and inevitable result will be that every strike in any industry or even in any single factory will be within the Sherman Act and subject to Federal jurisdiction providing any appreciable amount of its product enters into interstate commerce," . . . .

. . . in the Second Coronado [case], *supra,* . . . it appeared that "the purpose of the destruction of the mines was to stop the production of non-union coal and prevent its shipment to markets of other states than Arkansas, where it would by competition tend to reduce the price of the commodity and affect injuriously the maintenance of wages for union labor in competing mines. . . ."

These cases show that activities of labor organizations not immunized by the Clayton Act are not necessarily violations of the Sherman Act. Underlying and implicit in all of them is recognition that the Sherman Act was not enacted to police interstate transportation, or to afford a remedy for wrongs, which were actionable under state law, and resulted from combinations and conspiracies which fall short, both in their purpose and effect, of any form of market control of a commodity, such as to "monopolize the supply, control its price, or discriminate between its would-be purchasers." These elements of restraint of trade, found to be present in the Second Coronado [case] and alone to distinguish it from the First Coronado [case] and the Leather Workers case, are wholly lacking here. We do not hold that conspiracies to obstruct or prevent transportation in interstate commerce can in no circumstances be violations of the Sherman Act. Apart from the Clayton Act it makes no distinction between labor and non-labor cases. We only hold now, as we have previously held both in labor and non-labor cases, that such restraints are not within the Sherman Act unless they are intended to have, or in fact have the effects on the market on which the Court relied to establish a violation in the Second Coronado case. Unless the principle of these cases is now to be discarded, an impartial application of the Sherman Act to the activities of industry and labor alike would seem to require that the Act be held inapplicable to the activities of respondents which had an even less substantial effect on the competitive conditions in the industry than the combinations of producers in the Appalachian Coal case and in others on which it relied.

If, without such effects on the market, we were to hold that a local factory strike, stopping production and shipment of its product interstate, violates the Sherman Law, practically every strike in modern industry would be brought within the jurisdiction of the federal courts, under the Sherman Act, to remedy local law violations. The Act was plainly not intended to reach such a result, its language does not require it, and the course of our decisions precluded it. The maintenance in our federal system of a proper distribution between state and national governments of police authority and of remedies private and public for public wrongs is of far-reaching importance. An intention to disturb the balance is not lightly to be imputed to Congress. The Sherman Act is concerned with the character of the prohibited restraints and with their effect on interstate commerce. It draws no distinction between the restraints effected by violence and those achieved by peaceful but oftentimes quite as effective means. Restraints not within the Act, when achieved by peaceful means, are not brought within its sweep merely because, without other differences, they are attended by violence. Affirmed.

Although the Supreme Court recognized that the criminal laws of Pennsylvania had been violated, it said that this was a matter exclusively of state concern. The Sherman Act condemns attempts to control prices, and all attempts to restrict competition in the market, but these evils, said the Supreme Court, were absent in the Apex case. The Supreme Court differentiated this and the second Coronado case by setting forth that in the Coronado case the union destroyed coal mines with the intent of stopping production for markets in several states, whereas in the Apex case there was no evidence to indicate that the motivating force behind the mob seizure of the factory was to prevent the company from manufacturing and shipping its product in interstate trade in order to reduce competitive pressures on unionized shops. The intent was clear; it was to force unionization on the nonunion plant.

The Hutcheson Case

In 1939 the U.S. Department of Justice issued a statement dealing with the application of the Sherman Act to labor unions. It said that any strike or boycott which interfered with an established system of collective bargaining (a jurisdictional dispute) and affected interstate commerce was a violation of the act. Following this declaration a number of indictments were brought against unions, and these cases were pressed despite the Supreme Court's opinion in the Apex case. One of the cases reached the Supreme Court. This was the Hutcheson case,[3] which involved a jurisdictional dispute between the Carpenters' Union and the Machinists' Union. Officers and employees of the Carpenters' Union were indicted, charged with conspiring to violate the Sherman Act. Generally speaking, a jurisdictional dispute involves two autonomous unions and is a dispute in which one union claims complete control over specfic work assignments to the exclusion of the other union. We shall have more to say about this type of dispute when the Taft-Hartley Law of 1947 is covered.

The issue in the Hutcheson case was whether a union's use of conventional, peaceful activities in a dispute with a rival union over certain jobs is a violation of the Sherman Act.

The facts are covered fully in Mr. Justice Frankfurter's opinion, delivered on behalf of the U.S. Supreme Court.

. . . Anheuser-Busch Inc., operating a large plant in St. Louis, contracted with Borsari Tank Corp. for the erection of an additional facility. The Gaylord Container Corp., a lessee of adjacent property from Anheuser-Busch, made a similar contract for a new building with the Stocker Company. Anheuser-Busch obtained the materials for its brewing and other operations and sold its finished products largely through interstate shipments. The Gaylord Corp. was equally dependent on interstate commerce for marketing its goods, as were the construction companies for their building materials. Among the employees of Anheuser-Busch were members of the United Brotherhood of Carpenters and Joiners of America and of the International Association of Machinists. The conflicting claims of these two organizations, affiliated with the American Federation of Labor, in regard to the erection and dismantling of machinery had long been a source of controversy between them. Anheuser-Busch had had agreements with both organizations whereby the Machinists were given the disputed jobs and the Carpenters agreed to submit all disputes to arbitration. But in 1939 the president of the Carpenters, their general representative, and two officials of the Carpenters' local organization, the four men under indictment, stood on the claims of the Carpenters for the jobs. Rejection by the employer of the Carpenters' demand and the refusal of the latter to submit to arbitration were followed by a strike of the Carpenters, called by the defendants against Anheuser-Busch and its tenant, and a request through circular letters and the official publication of the Carpenters that union members and their friends refrain from buying Anheuser-Busch beer.

These activities on behalf of the Carpenters formed the charge of the indictment as a criminal combination and conspiracy in violation of the Sherman Law. . . .

3. U.S. v. Hutcheson, 312 U.S. 219 (1940).

The Norris-LaGuardia Act removed the fetters upon trade union activities, which according to judicial construction section 20 of the Clayton Act had left untouched, by still further narrowing the circumstances under which the federal courts could grant injunctions in labor disputes. More especially, the Act explicitly formulated the "public policy of the United States" in regard to the industrial conflict, and by its light established that the allowable area of union activity was not to be restricted, as it had been in the Duplex case, to an immediate employer-employee relation. Therefore, whether trade union conduct constitutes a violation of the Sherman Law is to be determined only by reading the Sherman Law and Section 20 of the Clayton Act and the Norris-LaGuardia Act as a harmonizing test of outlawry of labor conduct.

Were, then, the acts charged against the defendants prohibited, or permitted, by these three interlacing statutes?

The refusal of the Carpenters to work for Anheuser-Busch or on construction work being done for it and its adjoining tenant, and the peaceful attempt to get members of other unions similarly to refuse to work, are plainly within the free scope accorded to workers by section 20 for "terminating any relation of employment," or "ceasing to perform any work or labor," or "recommending, advising or persuading others by peaceful means so to do." The picketing of Anheuser-Busch premises with signs to indicate that Anheuser-Busch was unfair to organized labor, a familiar practice in these situations, came within the language "attending at any place where any such persons may lawfully be, for the purpose of peacefully obtaining or communicating information, or from peacefully persuading any person to work or to abstain from working." Finally, the recommendation to union members and their friends not to buy or use the product of Anheuser-Busch is explicitly covered by "ceasing to patronize . . . any party to such dispute, or from recommending, advising, or persuading others by peaceful and lawful means so to do."

Clearly, then, the facts here charged constitute lawful conduct under the Clayton Act unless the defendants cannot invoke that Act because outsiders to the immediate dispute also shared in the conduct . . .

The relation of the Norris-LaGuardia Act to the Clayton Act is not that of a tightly drawn amendment to a technically phrased tax provision. The underlying aim of the Norris-LaGuardia Act was to restore the broad purpose which Congress thought it was formulating in the Clayton Act but which was frustrated, so Congress believed, by unduly restrictive judicial construction. This was authoritatively stated by the House Committee on the Judiciary. "The purpose of the bill is to protect the rights of labor in the same manner that Congress intended, when it enacted the Clayton Act, October 15, 1914, 38 Stat. L. 738, which Act, by reason of its construction and application by the Federal Courts, is ineffectual to accomplish the congressional intent." . . . The Norris-LaGuardia Act reasserted the original purpose of the Clayton Act by infusing into it the immunized trade union activities as redefined by the later Act. In this light, section 20 removes all such allowable conduct from the taint of being "violations of any law of the United States," including the Sherman Law.

The U.S. Supreme Court held that the Carpenters' Union, pursuing a labor dispute, and acting independently of any employer group, engaged in activities sanctioned by the Clayton and Norris-LaGuardia Acts. These activities, the court stated, were not in conflict with the antitrust laws. This case comes within the so-called collusion doctrine, which declared unions exempt from the provisions of the antitrust laws so long as they act in their own interest and do not conspire with nonunion groups. As more cases developed, it became apparent that the basic criterion of misconduct was the act of joining with employers to fix prices, restrict output, or limit competition in the product market.

The Hunt Case

In the Hunt case, another suit [4] under the Sherman Act, the U.S. Supreme Court allowed a union to drive an employer completely out of the field of interstate business. The employer had charged that the union's refusal to accept membership applications from its employees forced the employer to give up its business, which loss the employer claimed to result solely from a conspiracy to restrain interstate trade illegally.

The facts are clearly set forth in Mr. Justice Black's opinion.

For about fourteen years prior to 1939, the petitioner, a business partnership engaged in motor trucking, carried freight under a contract with the Great Atlantic & Pacific Tea Co. (A & P). Eighty-five per cent of the merchandise thus hauled by petitioner was interstate, from and to Philadelphia, Pennsylvania. The respondent union, composed of drivers and helpers, was affiliated with other A.F. of L. unions whose members worked at loading and hauling of freight by motor truck. In 1937, the respondent union called a strike of the truckers and haulers of A & P in Philadelphia for the purpose of enforcing a closed shop. The petitioner, refusing to unionize its business, attempted to operate during the strike. Much violence occurred. One of the union men was killed near union headquarters, and a member of the petitioner partnership was tried for the homicide and acquitted. A & P and the union entered into a closed-shop agreement, whereupon all contract haulers working for A & P, including the petitioner, were notified that their employees must join and become members of the union. All of the other contractor haulers except petitioner either joined the union or made closed-shop agreements with it. The union, however, refused to negotiate with the petitioner, and declined to admit any of its employees to membership. Although petitioner's services had been satisfactory, A & P, at the union's instigation, cancelled its contract with petitioner in accordance with the obligations of its closed-shop agreement with the union. Later, the petitioner

4. Hunt v. Crumboch, 325 U.S. 821 (1945).

obtained a contract with a different company, but again at the union's instigation, and upon the consummation of a close-shop contract by that company with the union, petitioner lost that contract and business. Because of the union's refusal to negotiate with the petitioner and to accept petitioner's employees as members, the petitioner was unable to obtain any further hauling contracts in Philadelphia. The elimination of the petitioner's service did not in any manner affect the interstate operations of A & P or other companies.

The petitioner then instituted this suit in a federal district court against respondents, the union and its representatives, praying for an injunction and asking for treble damages. . . . Both the trial court and Circuit Court of Appeals agreed that the union had not violated the Act.

The "destruction" of petitioner's business resulted from the fact that the union members, acting in concert, refused to accept employment with the petitioner, and refused to admit to their association anyone who worked for petitioner. The petitioner's loss of business is therefore analogous to the case of a manufacturer selling goods in interstate commerce who fails in business because union members refuse to work for him. Had a group of petitioner's business competitors conspired and combined to suppress petitioner's business by refusing to sell goods and services to it, such a combination would have violated the Sherman Act. . . . The only combination here, however, was one of workers alone and what they refused to sell petitioner was their labor.

It is not a violation of the Sherman Act for laborers in combination to refuse to work. They can sell or not sell their labor as they please, and upon such terms and conditions as they choose, without infringing the anti-trust laws. A worker is privileged under congressional enactments, acting either alone or in concert with his fellow workers, to associate or to decline to associate with other workers, to accept, refuse to accept, or to terminate a relationship of employment, and his labor is not to be treated as "a commodity or article of commerce." . . .

It is argued that their exercise falls within the condemnation of the Sherman Act, because . . . the union members' refusal to accept employment was due to personal antagonism against the petitioner arising out of the killing of a union man. But Congress in the Sherman Act and the legislation which followed it manifested no purpose to make any kind of refusal to accept personal employment a violation of the anti-trust laws. Such an application of those laws would be a complete departure from their spirit and purpose. Moreover, "So long as a union acts in its self-interest and does not combine with non-labor groups, the licit and illicit under Sec. 20 are not to be distinguished by any judgment regarding the wisdom or unwisdom, the rightness or wrongness, the selfishness or unselfishness of the end of which the particular union activities are the means." U.S. v. Hutcheson, 312 U.S. 232.

The controversy in the instant case, between a union and an employer, involves nothing more than a dispute over employment, and the withholding of labor services. It cannot therefore be said to violate the Sherman Act, as amended. That Act does not purport to afford remedies for all torts com-

mitted by or against persons engaged in interstate commerce. "The maintenance in our federal system of a proper distribution between state and national governments of police authority and of remedies private and public
for public wrongs is of far-reaching importance. An intention to disturb
the balance is not lightly to be imputed to Congress." Apex Hosiery Co. v.
Leader, 310 U.S. 469, 513. Whether the respondents' conduct amounts to
an actionable wrong subjecting them to liability for damages under Pennsylvania law is not our concern. Affirmed.

The court refused to find that the union's activities were proscribed
by the Sherman Act, and it ruled that workers may sell or withhold their
labor as they please. Furthermore, they may singly or in concert with
their fellow workers accept, refuse to accept, or terminate their employment, and this labor is not to be regarded as a "commodity or article of
commerce." In the Hunt case, the union refused to have anything to do
with the employer and with its employees. Since the union was justified
in pursuing its objective of nonassociation, the fact that the employer
was forced out of business did not bring about a violation of the anti-
trust laws. Many have felt that the employer received the harshest type
of treatment in this case. Some have condoned the union's action on
the ground that there was sufficient cause for the destruction it inflicted.

The Allen Bradley Case

The last of the antitrust cases to be presented concerns market control
of electrical commodities through joint action of a union and a group
of employers. The Allen Bradley case [5] resulted in the federal government getting the Supreme Court to enjoin the union and the employers
from engaging in activities where the charge embraced the claim that
the parties were illegally restraining trade. The facts in the case appear
in Mr. Justice Black's opinion.

The question presented is whether it is a violation of the Sherman Anti-
trust Act for labor unions and their members, prompted by a desire to get
and hold jobs for themselves at good wages and under high working standards, to combine with employers and with manufacturers of goods to restrain
competition in, and to monopolize the marketing of, such goods.

Upon the complaint of petitioners (Allen Bradley Company) and after
a lengthy hearing the District Court held that such a combination did violate the Sherman Act, entered a declaratory judgment to that effect, and
entered an injunction restraining respondents (Local Union No. 3, International Brotherhood of Electrical Workers) from engaging in a wide range
of specified activities. The Circuit Court of Appeals reversed the decision

5. Allen Bradley Co. v. Local 3, I.B.E.W., 325 U.S. 797 (1945).

and dismissed the cause, holding that combinations of unions and business men which restrained trade and tended to monopoly were not in violation of the Act where the bona fide purpose of the unions was to raise wages, provide better working conditions, and bring about better conditions of employment for their members. . . .

. . . Petitioners are manufacturers of electrical equipment. Their places of manufacture are outside of New York City, and most of them are outside of New York State as well. They have brought this action because of their desire to sell their products in New York City, a market area that has been closed to them through the activities of respondents and others.

Respondents are a labor union, its officials and its members. The union . . . has jurisdiction only over the metropolitan area of New York City. It is therefore impossible for the union to enter into a collective bargaining agreement with petitioners. Some of petitioners do have collective bargaining agreements with other unions, and in some cases even with other locals of the I.B.E.W.

Some of the members of respondent union work for manufacturers who produce electrical equipment similar to that made by petitioners; other members of respondent union are employed by contractors and work on the installation of electrical equipment, rather than in its production.

The union's consistent aim for many years has been to expand its membership, to obtain shorter hours and increased wages, and to enlarge employment opportunities for its members. To achieve this latter goal—that is, to make more work for its own members—the union realized that local manufacturers, employers of the local members, must have the widest possible outlets for their product. The union therefore waged aggressive campaigns to obtain closed shop agreements with all local electrical equipment manufacturers and contractors. Using conventional labor union methods, such as strikes and boycotts, it gradually obtained more and more closed shop agreements in the New York City area. Under these agreements, contractors were obliged to purchase equipment from none but local manufacturers who also had closed shop agreements with Local No. 3; manufacturers obligated themselves to confine their New York City sales to contractors employing the Local's members. In the course of time, this type of individual employer-employee agreement expanded into industry-wide understandings, looking not merely to terms and conditions of employment but also to price and market control. Agencies were set up composed of representatives of all three groups to boycott recalcitrant local contractors and manufacturers and to bar from the area equipment manufactured outside its boundaries. The combination among the three groups, union, contractors, and manufacturers, became highly successful from the standpoint of all of them. The business of New York City manufacturers had a phenomenal growth, thereby multiplying the jobs available for the Local's members. Wages went up, hours were shortened, and the New York electrical equipment prices soared, to the decided financial profit of local contractors and manufacturers. The success is illustrated by the fact that some New York manufacturers sold their goods in the protected city market at one price and sold identical goods outside of New York at a far lower price. All of this took place, as the Circuit Court of Appeals declared, "through the stifling of competition," and because the three groups, in combination as "co-partners," achieved "a complete monopoly which they used to boycott the equipment manufactured by the plaintiffs." Interstate sale of various types of electrical equipment has, by this powerful combination, been wholly suppressed.

Quite obviously, this combination of business men has violated both sec. (1) and (2) of the Sherman Act, unless its conduct is immunized by the participation of the union. For it intended to and did restrain trade in and monopolize the supply of electrical equipment in the New York City area to the exclusion of equipment manufactured in and between its would-be customers. Apex Hosiery Co. v. Leader. Our problem in this case is therefore a very narrow one—do labor unions violate the Sherman Act when, in order to further their own interests as wage earners, they aid and abet business men to do the precise things which that Act prohibits? . . .

Aside from the fact that the labor union here acted in combination with the contractors and manufacturers, the means it adopted to contribute to the combination's purpose fall squarely within the "specified acts" declared by section 20 not to be violations of federal law. For the union's contribution to the trade boycott was accomplished through threats that unless their employers bought their goods from local manufacturers the union laborers would terminate the "relation of employment" with them and cease to perform "work or labor" for them; and through their "recommending, advising, or persuading others by peaceful and lawful means" not to "patronize" sellers of the boycotted electrical equipment. Consequently, under our holdings in the Hutcheson case and other cases which followed it, had there been no union-contractor-manufacturer combination the union's actions here, coming as they did within the exemptions of the Clayton and Norris-La Guardia Acts, would not have been violations of the Sherman Act. We pass to the question of whether unions can with impunity aid and abet business men who are violating the Act. . . .

It is true that victory of the union in its disputes, even had the union acted alone, might have added to the cost of goods, or might have resulted in individual refusals of all of their employers to buy electrical equipment not made by Local No. 3. So far as the union might have achieved this result acting alone, it would have been the natural consequence of labor union activities exempted by the Clayton Act from the coverage of the Sherman Act. Apex Hosiery Co. v. Leader. But when the unions participated with a combination of business men who had complete power to eliminate all competition among themselves and to prevent all competition from others, a situation was created not included within the exemptions of the Clayton and Norris-LaGuardia Acts.

It must be remembered that the exemptions granted the unions were special exceptions to a general legislative plan. The primary objective of all the Anti-trust legislation has been to preserve business competition and to proscribe business monopoly. It would be a surprising thing if Congress, in order to prevent a misapplication of that legislation to labor unions, had bestowed upon such unions complete and unreviewable authority to aid business groups to frustrate its primary objective. For if business groups, by combining with labor unions, can fix prices and divide up markets, it was little more than a futile gesture for Congress to prohibit price fixing by business groups themselves. Seldom, if ever, has it been claimed before, that by permitting labor unions to carry on their own activities, Congress intended completely to abdicate its constitutional power to regulate interstate commerce and to empower interested business groups to shift our society from a competitive to a monopolistic economy. Finding no purpose of Congress to immunize labor unions who aid and abet manufacturers and traders in violating the Sherman Act, we hold that the district court correctly concluded that the respondents had violated the Act.

Our holding means that the same labor union activities may or may not be in violation of the Sherman Act, dependent upon whether the union acts alone or in combination with business groups. This, it is argued, brings about a wholly undesirable result—one which leaves labor unions free to engage in conduct which restrains trade. But the desirability of such an exemption of labor unions is a question for the determination of Congress. Apex Hosiery Co. v. Leader. It is true that many labor union activities do substantially interrupt the course of trade and that these activities, lifted out of the prohibitions of the Sherman Act, include substantially all, if not all, of the normal peaceful activities of labor unions. It is also true that the Sherman Act "draws no distinction between the restraints effected by violence and those achieved by peaceful . . . means," Apex Hosiery Co. v. Leader, . . . and that a union's exemption from the Sherman Act is not to be determined by a judicial "judgment regarding the wisdom or unwisdom, the rightness or wrongness, the selfishness or unselfishness of the end of which the particular union activities are the means." United States v. Hutcheson. Thus, these congressionally permitted union activities may restrain trade in and of themselves. There is no denying the fact that many of them do so, both directly and indirectly. Congress evidently concluded, however, that the chief objective of Anti-trust legislation, preservation of business competition, could be accomplished by applying the legislation primarily only to those business groups which are directly interested in destroying competition. The difficulty of drawing legislation primarily aimed at trusts and monopolies so that it could also be applied to labor organizations without impairing the collective bargaining and related rights of those organizations has been emphasized both by congressional and judicial attempts to draw lines between permissible and prohibited union activities. There is, however, one line which we can draw with assurance that we follow the congressional purpose. We know that Congress feared the concentrated power of business organizations to dominate markets and prices. It intended to outlaw business monopolies. A business is no less such because a union participates, and such participation is a violation of the Act.

. . . The judgment of the Circuit Court of Appeals ordering this action dismissed is accordingly reversed and the cause is remanded to the District

Court for modification and clarification of the judgment and injunction, consistent with this opinion.[6]

Other cases indicate that unions are vulnerable to attack even if an employers' group asks the union to enforce uniformly a long-standing but frequently ignored provision in its international constitution. Such an attack took place in Philadelphia Record Co. v. Manufacturing Photoengravers' Association.[7] In this case, judgment was given to the plaintiff on the ground that the request of the employers' group for enforcement of a "no night work" provision against the plaintiff's photoengraving department was actually a scheme to limit competition. The court held that the exempt status of the union could not be used as a blind to gain immunity for otherwise unlawful acts.

Another area in which immunity has been denied to unions occurs where there is some question concerning the good faith of the union. In Columbia River Packers v. Hinton [8] a union of independent fishermen attempted to impose uniform prices and other conditions of sale on a fish packers' group. The fishermen's union claimed immunity from the antitrust laws on the ground that the controversy constituted a labor dispute within the meaning of the Norris-LaGuardia Act. The Supreme Court rejected the claim and said:

. . . That a dispute . . . over the terms of a contract for the sale of fish is something different from a controversy concerning terms and conditions of employment . . . calls for no extended discussion. . . . The controversy here is altogether between fish sellers and fish buyers. . . .

There is no doubt that unions are beyond the reach of the Sherman and Clayton Acts so long as their activities are clearly unilateral in origin and untainted by subsequent employer participation. Another important requisite is that the activities must grow out of a labor dispute as defined under the Norris-LaGuardia Act.[9]

The Taft-Hartley Act of 1947 and the Reporting and Disclosure Act of 1959 have made various union activities such as the secondary boycott and the jurisdictional dispute unfair practices subject to injunctive

6. For other cases following the Allen Bradley decision, *see* Carpenters v. U.S., 330 U.S. 395 (1947) (agreement not to work on competitive lumber products); U.S. v. Fur Workers, 100 Fed. (2d) 541 (1938); and Lystad v. Teamsters Local 223, 135 F. Supp. 337 (1955) (agreement limiting installation of amusement devices to those owned by recognized union operators).
7. 155 Fed. (2d) 799 (1946).
8. 315 U.S. 143 (1942).
9. American Medical Ass'n v. U.S., 317 U.S. 519 (1943). (Where a medical association attempted to keep physicians from working on a full-time basis for a group health association, the Supreme Court held no labor dispute existed, and therefore the immunity provided by the Clayton and Norris-LaGuardia Acts was unavailable to the Medical Association.)

relief. The unions' immunity gained under the antitrust laws does not protect them against charges that they have committed unfair union practices. A detailed discussion of unfair practices will be made in a later chapter.

Summary

The Supreme Court, in the Apex Hosiery Company case, stated that labor unions are still subject to the Sherman Act to "some extent not defined." Its opinion clearly said that the Sherman Act was enacted in an era of trusts; that combinations of businesses and of capital were then organized and directed to control the market by suppression of competition in the marketing of goods and services; and that the resulting monopolistic tendency had become a matter of public concern. One of the objectives of the act was to protect consumers and the public from these monopolistic practices. The court went on to say that labor union activities violated the act only when the intent to restrain commerce illegally was clear and definite.

The Hutcheson decision declared that the Sherman, Clayton, and Norris-LaGuardia Acts had to be jointly considered in arriving at a conclusion as to whether labor union activities ran counter to the antitrust legislation. Conduct which these laws permitted was not to be declared a violation of federal law. The decision held also that the rulings in the Duplex Printing and Bedford Cut Stone Company cases were inconsistent with the Congressional policy set out in the three "interlacing statutes."

In the Hunt case the Supreme Court ruled that "it is not a violation of the Sherman Act for laborers in combination to refuse to work." This decision actually allowed the union to drive an employer out of business when it refused to provide workers to the employer. The court felt that as long as the union acted in its own self-interest, and did not cooperate with nonlabor groups, any restraint of commerce which might occur was permissible and not a violation of the antitrust laws.

The last important case discussed in this chapter was Allen Bradley. The union's activities here came within the proscribed provisions of the antitrust laws not only because these activities involved a restraint upon interstate commerce, but also because the labor union cooperated with an employer group in interfering with commerce. The court was careful to point out that the labor union, acting alone, might have legally boycotted certain goods from entering the New York market, but that when it went outside its own group, and assisted employers in bringing about the boycott, then the joint venture became an illegal combination in restraint of trade. Other factors must be considered in determining whether unions shall enjoy exemption from the antitrust laws. The Supreme Court demands that the union be a bona fide organization of workers, and that the activities grow out of a labor dispute as defined under Section 13 of the Norris-LaGuardia Act of 1932.

State Antitrust Laws

Several states have enacted antitrust legislation that is frequently used in prosecuting cases involving illegal restraints of trade. Labor unions have been the subject of state action under these statutes.[10] Where, however, union contracts incorporate provisions which violate state antitrust statutes, state prosecution may not be initiated if the contracts conform with the mandatory provisions of the National Labor Relations Act, and the amendments thereto.[11]

10. Giboney v. Empire Storage and Ice Co., 336 U.S. 490 (1949); Red Owl Inc. v. Meat Cutters Union, 109 F. Supp. 629 (1953).
11. Teamsters Local 24 v. Oliver, 358 U.S. 283 (1959) and 40 LC 66,511 (1960).

CHAPTER EIGHT

The Railway Labor Act of 1926

THE first law dealing with railway labor relations was enacted by Congress in 1888. It provided for voluntary arbitration and investigation of labor disputes that threatened to interrupt interstate commerce. During the ten years of its existence the arbitration provisions were never used. In 1898 the Erdman Act was passed; it relied on government mediation and conciliation for the prevention of railroad labor disputes, with a temporary board to be appointed in each case. Arbitration procedures were later improved, when mediation failed. The Newland Act of 1913 established a full-time Board of Mediation and Conciliation. The Adamson Act of 1916 attempted to settle a labor dispute by limiting the hours of work to eight. In 1920 the Transportation Act created the United States Railroad Labor Board with nine members (three to represent, respectively, carriers, unions, and the public), with authority to hear and decide all disputes. Compliance with board decisions was not obligatory.

The Railway Labor Act of 1926 applies to railroads and their employees and was the culmination of 38 years of experience with federal legislation regulating the labor relations of employers and employees engaged in this industry.[1] In 1936 an amendment brought airlines within the scope of the act.

The act imposes positive duties on carriers and employers alike, defines rights and makes provision for their protection, prescribes methods of settling various types of disputes, and sets up agencies for adjusting differences.

Employees are given the right to join unions of their own choice, and

1. See *Administration of the Railway Labor Act, 1934–1957*, U.S. Government Printing Office, Washington, D.C., 1957.

they and the employers have the duty of making every reasonable effort to enter into written contracts covering wages, rules, and working conditions.

The National Mediation Board set up by the act is composed of three members appointed by the President of the United States. Cases subject to board jurisdiction fall into two classes:

(1) Differences between carriers and employees regarding changes in rate of pay, rules, or working conditions.

(2) Disputes among employees as to who shall be their duly designated and authorized representatives. By elections, or by other means, it certifies who shall represent the workers in their collective bargaining.

Under Section 5 of the act, if a dispute between a carrier and its employees is not adjusted through mediation, the board may recommend voluntary arbitration. Under Section 10, if such a dispute arises and arbitration is rejected, and should the mediation board feel that interstate commerce may be so threatened that essential transportation service may be interrupted, the board shall notify the President, who may create an emergency board to investigate and report to him facts relating to the dispute. The emergency board has 30 days to investigate and report, and the President is given an additional period of 30 days to study the report. During this interval, which is frequently called the "cooling-off" period, the union may not lawfully strike, nor may the employer effectuate a change in conditions.

The National Railroad Adjustment Board and Compulsory Arbitration

In 1934 the Railway Labor Act was amended by Section 3, which provided for the creation of the National Railroad Adjustment Board. This board has power to render judicially enforcible decisions in disputes growing out of grievances or out of the interpretation or applications of agreements concerning rates of pay, rules, or working conditions.

The adjustment board consists of thirty-six members, eighteen selected by the rail carriers and eighteen by national labor unions. Each member receives compensation from the party or parties he represents. Section 3(h) provides that the board shall be composed of four divisions, each consisting of an equal number of management members and labor members; the jurisdiction is divided as follows.

The first division has jurisdiction over disputes involving train and yard service employees; i.e., engineers, firemen, hostlers and outside hostler helpers, conductors, trainmen, and yard service employees. This division consists of ten members.

The second division has jurisdiction over disputes involving machinists, boilermakers, blacksmiths, sheetmetal workers, electrical workers, carmen, and apprentices of all the foregoing; coach cleaners, powerhouse employees, and railroad shop laborers. This division consists of ten members.

The third division has jurisdiction over disputes involving station, tower, telegraph employees, train dispatchers, maintenance-of-way men, clerical employees, freight handlers, express, station, store employees, signalmen, sleeping-car conductors, and porters, maids, and dining car employees. This division consists of ten members.

The fourth division has jurisdiction over disputes involving employees of carriers directly or indirectly engaged in transportation of passengers or property by water, and all other employees of carriers over which jurisdiction is not given to the first, second, and third divisions. This division consists of six members.

The act provides that if any division fails to agree on an award because of a deadlock, or is unable to secure a majority vote of the division members, the division appoints a neutral to make the award.

The awards must be made in writing. If the carrier does not comply with the award, the U.S. District Court may be petitioned to enforce or set aside the award.

There is no adjustment board to cover labor disputes for the air carriers, although Section 205 of the act permits the National Mediation Board to establish a board for them when in its judgment the necessity exists.

The compulsory arbitration of certain types of labor disputes between rail carriers and their employees is a feature existing only in the federal Railway Labor Act. If either party submits a dispute to the National Railroad Adjustment Board, the award is final and binding on both parties. A strike by a union to prevent the board's settling a dispute which has been submitted to it may be enjoined since the specific provisions of the Railway Labor Act take precedence over the more general provisions of the Norris-LaGuardia Act.[2] On this point Chief Justice Warren said:

We hold that the Norris-LaGuardia Act cannot be read alone in matters dealing with railway labor disputes. There must be an accommodation of that statute and the Railway Labor Act so that the obvious purpose in the enactment of each is preserved. We think that the purposes of these Acts are reconcilable. . . .

In adopting the Railway Labor Act, Congress endeavored to bring about

2. Brotherhood of Railroad Trainmen v. Chicago River and Ind. R.R., 353 U.S. 30 (1957).

stable relationships between labor and management in the most important national industry. It found from the experience between 1926 and 1934 that the failure of voluntary machinery to resolve a large number of minor disputes called for a strengthening of the Act to provide an effective agency, in which both sides participated, for the final adjustment of such controversies. Accumulation of these disputes had resulted in the aggregate being serious enough to threaten disruption of transportation. Hence, with the full consent of the Brotherhoods, the 1934 amendment became law.

The constitutionality of the act was sustained by the Supreme Court in Texas and New Orleans R.R. v. Brotherhood of Railway Clerks.[3]

A federal court has authority to issue a mandatory injunction compelling an employer to comply with the collective-bargaining requirements of the act.[4]

The Steele and Michel Cases

The problem of race discrimination developed into a major case that resulted in a historic decision. This is the Steele case,[5] involving a Negro fireman employed on a railroad which was required to bargain with the Brotherhood of Firemen, a labor organization which excluded Negroes from membership. The Negro asked the brotherhood to process a grievance on his behalf. The union refused. Chief Justice Stone, speaking on behalf of the Supreme Court, said:

. . . The question is whether the Railway Labor Act . . . imposes on a labor organization, acting by authority of the statute as the exclusive bargaining representative of a craft or class of railway employees, the duty to represent all the employees in the craft without discrimination because of their race, and, if so, whether the courts have jurisdiction to protect the minority of the craft or class from the violation of such obligation. . . .

The allegations of the bill of complaint, so far as now material, are as follows: Petitioner, a Negro, is a locomotive fireman in the employ of respondent railroad, suing on his own behalf and that of his fellow employees who, like petitioner, are Negro firemen employed by the Railroad. Respondent Brotherhood, a labor organization, is, as provided under Sec. 2, Fourth, of the Railway Labor Act, the exclusive bargaining representative of the craft of firemen employed by the Railroad and is recognized as such by

3. 281 U.S. 548 (1930); See also Virginian Ry. v. System Federation 40, 300 U.S. 515 (1937), in which constitutional questions were raised concerning specific provisos in the act.
4. 300 U.S. 515, *supra*.
5. Steele v. Louisville and Nashville R.R., 323 U.S. 192 (1944). For other cases involving discrimination, see Williams v. Central of Georgia, 124 F. Supp. (2d) 164 (1954); Richardson v. Texas R.R., 242 Fed. (2d) 230 (1957).

it and the members of the craft. The majority of the firemen employed by the Railroad are white and are members of the Brotherhood, but a substantial minority are Negroes who by the constitution and ritual of the Brotherhood, are excluded from its membership. As the membership of the Brotherhood constitutes a majority of all firemen employed on respondent Railroad, and as under Sec. 2, Fourth, the members because they are the majority have the right to choose and have chosen the Brotherhood to represent the craft, petitioner and other Negro firemen on the road have been required to accept the Brotherhood as their representative for the purposes of the Act. . . .

Until April 8, 1941, the petitioner was in a "passenger pool," to which one white and five Negro firemen were assigned. These jobs were highly desirable in point of wages, hours, and other considerations. Petitioner had performed and was performing his work satisfactorily. Following a reduction in the mileage covered by the pool, all jobs in the pool were, about April 1, 1941, declared vacant. The Brotherhood and the Railroad, acting under the agreement, disqualified all the Negro firemen and replaced them with four white men, members of the Brotherhood, all junior in seniority to petitioner and no more competent or worthy. As a consequence petitioner was deprived of employment for sixteen days and then was assigned to more arduous, longer, and less remunerative work in local freight service. In conformity to the agreement, he was later replaced by a Brotherhood member junior to him, and assigned work on a switch engine, which was still harder and less remunerative, until January 3, 1942. On that date, after the bill of complaint in the present suit had been filed, he was reassigned to passenger service.

Protests and appeals of petitioner and his fellow Negro firemen, addressed to the Railroad and the Brotherhood, in an effort to secure relief and redress, have been ignored. Respondents have expressed their intention to enforce the agreement of February 18, 1941, and its subsequent modifications. The Brotherhood has acted and asserts the right to act as exclusive bargaining representative of the firemen's craft. It is alleged that in that capacity it is under an obligation and duty imposed by the Act to represent the Negro firemen impartially and in good faith; but instead, in its notice to and contracts with the railroads, it has been hostile and disloyal to the Negro firemen, has deliberately discriminated against them, and has sought to deprive them of their seniority rights and to drive them out of employment in their craft, all in order to create a monopoly of employment of Brotherhood members. . . .

The Supreme Court of Alabama took jurisdiction of the cause but held on the merits that petitioner's complaint stated no cause of action. It pointed out that the Act places a mandatory duty on the Railroad to treat with the Brotherhood as the exclusive representative of the employees in a craft, imposes heavy criminal penalties for willful failure to comply with its command, and provides that the majority of any craft shall have the right to determine who shall be the representative of the class for collective bargaining with the employer, see Virginia R. Co. v. System Federation, 300 U.S. 515, 545, 57 Sup. Ct. 592, 598, 81 L. Ed. 789. It thought that the Brotherhood was empowered by the statute to enter into the agreement of February 18, 1941, and that by virtue of the statute the Brotherhood has power by agreement with the Railroad both to create the seniority rights of petitioner and his fellow Negro employees and to destroy them. It construed the statute, not as creating the relationship of principal and agent between the members of the craft and the Brotherhood, but as conferring on the Brotherhood plenary authority to treat with the Railroad and enter into contracts fixing rates of pay and working conditions for the craft as a whole without any legal obligation or duty to protect the rights of minorities from discrimination or unfair treatment, however gross. Consequently it held that neither the Brotherhood nor the Railroad violated any rights of petitioner or his fellow Negro employees by negotiating the contracts discriminating against them. . . .

But we think that Congress, in enacting the Railway Labor Act and authorizing a labor union chosen by a majority of a craft, to represent the craft, did not intend to confer plenary power upon the union to sacrifice for the benefit of its members rights of the minority of the craft without imposing on it any duty to protect the minority. Since petitioner and the other Negro members of the craft are not members of the Brotherhood or eligible for membership, the authority to act for them is derived not from their action or consent but wholly from the command of the Act. Section 2, Fourth, provides: "Employees shall have the right to organize and bargain collectively through representatives of their own choosing. The majority of any craft or class of employees shall have the right to determine who shall be the representative of the craft or class for the purpose of this Act. . . .

By the terms of the Act, Sec. 2, Fourth, the employees are permitted to act "through" their representative, and it represents them "for the purpose of" the Act. Sections 2, Third, Fourth, Ninth. The purposes of the Act declared by Sec. 2 are the avoidance of "any interruption to commerce or to the operation of any carrier engaged therein," and this aim is sought to be achieved by encouraging "the prompt and orderly settlement of all disputes concerning rates of pay, rules, or working conditions." Compare Texas and N.O.R. Co. v. Brotherhood of Railway and S.S. Clerks, 281 U.S. 548, 569, 50 Sup. Ct. 427, 433, 74 L. Ed. 1034. These purposes would hardly be attained if a substantial minority of the craft were denied the right to have their interests considered at the conference table and if the final result of the bargaining process were to be the sacrifice of the interests of the minority by the action of a representative chosen by the majority. The only recourse of the minority would be to strike, with the attendant interruption of commerce, which the Act seeks to avoid. . . .

The labor organization chosen to be the representative of the craft or class of employees is thus chosen to represent all of its members, regardless of their union affiliations or want of them. As we have pointed out with respect to the like provision of the National Labor Relations Act, 29 U.S.C.A. Sec. 151 et seq., in J. I. Case Co. v. National Labor Relations Board, *supra*, 321 U.S. 338, 64 Sup. Ct. 580, "The very purpose of providing by statute for the collective agreement is to supersede the terms of separate agreements of employers with terms which reflect the strength and bargaining power and serve the welfare of the group. Its benefits and advantages are open to every employee of the represented unit. . . ." The purpose of providing for a representative is to secure . . . these benefits for those who are represented and not to deprive them or any of them of the benefits of collective bargaining for the advantage of the representative or those members of the craft who selected it. . . .

We think that the Railway Labor Act imposes upon the statutory representative of a craft at least as exacting a duty to protect equally the interests of the members of the craft as the Constitution imposes upon a legislature to give equal protection to the interests of those for whom it legislates. Congress has seen fit to clothe the bargaining representative with powers comparable to those possessed by a legislative body both to create and restrict the rights of those whom it represents, cf. J. I. Case Co. v. National Labor Relations Board, *supra*, 321 U.S. 335, 64 Supt. Ct. 579, but it has also imposed on the representative a corresponding duty. We hold that the language of the Act to which we have referred, read in the light of the purposes of the Act, expresses the aim of Congress to impose on the bargaining representative of a craft or class of employees the duty to exercise fairly the power conferred upon it in behalf of all those for whom it acts, without hostile discrimination against them.

This does not mean that the statutory representative of a craft is barred from making contracts which may have unfavorable effects on some of the members of the craft represented. Variations in the terms of the contract based on differences relevant to the authorized purposes of the contract in conditions to which they are to be applied, such as differences in seniority, the type of work performed, the competence and skill with which it is performed, are within the scope of the bargaining representative of a craft, all of whose members are not identical in their interest or merit. . . . Without attempting to mark the allowable limits of differences in the terms of contracts based on differences of conditions to which they apply, it is enough for present purposes to say that the statutory power to represent a craft and to make contracts as to wages, hours and working conditions does not include the authority to make among members of the craft discriminations not based on such relevant differences. Here the discriminations based on race alone are obviously irrelevant and invidious. Congress plainly did not undertake to authorize the bargaining representative to make such discriminations. . . .

So long as a labor union assumes to act as the statutory representative of a craft, it cannot rightly refuse to perform the duty, which is inseparable from the power of representation conferred upon it, to represent the entire membership of the craft. While the statute does not deny to such a bargaining labor organization the right to determine eligibility to its membership, it does require the union, in collective bargaining and in making contracts with the carrier, to represent non-union or minority union members of the craft without hostile discrimination, fairly, impartially, and in good faith. Wherever necessary to that end, the union is required to consider requests of non-union members of the craft and expressions of their views with respect to collective bargaining with the employer and to give to them notice of and opportunity for hearing upon its proposed action. . . .

We conclude that the duty which the statute imposes on a union representative of a craft to represent the interests of all its members stands on no different footing and that the statute contemplates resort to the usual judicial remedies of injunction and award of damages when appropriate for breach of that duty. The judgment is accordingly reversed and remanded for further proceedings not inconsistent with this opinion. Reversed.

In any matter where the National Railroad Adjustment Board does not have exclusive jurisdiction, as for example in the case of a dispute over the propriety of an employee's discharge, the employee may institute a common law action for damages. However, such an employee may not seek court relief after having lost his case before the board. In the Michel case [6] an employee brought suit in a federal court, after failing to get the right of reinstatement from the N.R.A.B. Judge Russell, in dismissing the suit, said:

. . . The primary question in the case is whether the voluntary submission of the employee's claim to the Division of the Railroads Adjustment Board having jurisdiction thereof, the prosecution of which was had with the full approval of the employee, and the determination of the claim upon the merits and adverse to the employee's contentions, presented a bar to a subsequent suit upon the same employment contract between the claimant against the carrier [sic] in a suit at law for damages. We are of the opinion that under these circumstances the proceeding before the National Railroad Adjustment Board evidenced an election of inconsistent remedies in that it was an acceptance of one of the two means afforded by law for redress for any grievances or claim arising out of the alleged unjustified discharge of the then claimant, now appellant, Michel. . . .

Consequently, there would appear no reason for not enforcing in such instances the fundamental principle that where one of two inconsistent remedies are available, the election of one precludes recourse to the other. This has been the uniform holding, correctly we think, of the Courts which have considered this question. It follows therefore that in the present case it appears from the uncontradicted facts that the question of whether the discharge of the appellant, Michel, was justified, on the one hand, or constituted a violation of the employment agreement on the other, has, in proceedings in effect instituted and prosecuted by appellant, been determined adversely to his contentions, he is therefore not legally entitled to maintain the present suit upon the same claim. . . .

The 1951 Amendment

The last amendment to the Railway Labor Act occurred in 1951, when Congress amended Section 2 so as to permit the union shop to

6. Michel v. L. and N.R.R., 188 Fed. (2d) 224 (1951).

be negotiated between carriers and the employees' bargaining representatives. The act does not make union shop agreements ineffective or illegal in those states which have enacted right-to-work laws. This amendment supersedes all state laws which seek to guarantee the right to work without regard to membership or lack of membership in a labor union. The leading case on the 1951 amendment is Railway Employees' Dept. v. Hanson.[7] The plaintiffs were not members of any union and had no desire to join one. Their employer and the union entered into a union shop agreement under which the plaintiffs were required to join the union as a condition of continued employment. The employees claimed that the union shop agreement violated the right-to-work provision of the Nebraska Constitution. They asked for an injunction restraining the railroad company from enforcing and applying the union shop agreement. The Nebraska state court granted the injunction. On appeal to the U.S. Supreme Court the injunction was vacated and the union shop agreement was upheld. Justice Douglas, speaking for the court, said:

The union shop provision of the Railway Labor Act is only permissive. Congress has not compelled nor required carriers and employees to enter into union shop agreements. The Supreme Court of Nebraska nevertheless took the view that justifiable questions under the First and Fifth Amendments were presented since Congress by the union shop provision of the Railway Labor Act, sought to strike down inconsistent laws in 17 States. The Supreme Court of Nebraska said, "Such action on the part of Congress is a necessary part of every union shop contract entered into on the railroads as far as these 17 States are concerned for without it such contracts could not be enforced therein."

We agree with that view. If private rights are being invaded, it is by force of an agreement made pursuant to federal law which expressly declares that state law is superseded. Cf. Smith v. Allwright, 321 U.S. 649, 663, In other words, the federal statute is the source of the power and authority by which any private rights are lost or sacrificed. The enactment of the federal statute authorizing union shop agreements is the governmental action on which the Constitution operates, though it takes a private agreement to invoke the federal sanction.

As already noted, the 1951 amendment, permitting the negotiation of union shop agreements, expressly allows those agreements notwithstanding any law "of any State." Section 2, Eleventh. A union agreement made pursuant to the Railway Labor Act has, therefore, the imprimatur of the federal law upon it and, by force of the Supremacy Clause of Article VI of the Constitution, could not be made illegal nor vitiated by any provision of the laws of a State.

We come then to the merits.

In the absence of conflicting legislation, there can be no doubt that it

7. 351 U.S. 225 (1956).

is within the police power of a State to prohibit the union or the closed shop. We so held in Lincoln Union v. Northwestern Co., 335 U.S. 525.

But the power of Congress to regulate labor relations in interstate industries is likewise well-established. Congress has authority to adopt all appropriate measures to "facilitate the amicable settlement of disputes which threaten the service of the necessary agencies of interstate transportation."

The choice by the Congress of the union shop as a stabilizing force seems to us to be an allowable one. Much might be said pro and con if the policy issue were before us. Powerful arguments have been made here that the long-run interests of labor would be better served by the development of democratic traditions in trade unionism without the coercive element of the union or the closed shop. Mr. Justice Brandeis, who had wide experience in labor-management relations prior to his appointment to the Court, wrote forcefully against the closed shop. He feared that the closed shop would swing the pendulum in the opposite extreme and substitute "tyranny of the employee" for "tyranny of the employer." But the question is one of policy with which the judiciary has no concern, as Mr. Justice Brandeis would have been the first to concede. Congress, acting within its constitutional powers, has the final say on policy issues.

Wide-ranged problems are tendered under the First Amendment. It is argued that the union shop agreement forces men into ideological and political associations which violate their right to freedom of conscience, freedom of association, and freedom of thought protected by the Bill of Rights. It is said that once a man becomes a member of these unions he is subject to vast disciplinary control and that by force of the federal Act unions now can make him conform to their ideology.

On the present record, there is no more an infringement or impairment of First Amendment rights than there would be in the case of a lawyer who by state law is required to be a member of an integrated bar. It is argued that compulsory membership will be used to impair freedom of expression. But that problem is not presented by this record. Congress endeavored to safeguard against that possibility by making explicit that no conditions to membership may be imposed except as respects "periodic dues, initiation fees, and assessments." If other conditions are in fact imposed, or if the exaction of dues, initiation fees, or assessments is used as a cover for forcing ideological conformity or other action in contravention of the First Amendment, this judgment will not prejudice the decision in that case. For we pass narrowly on Section 2, Eleventh, of the Railway Labor Act. We only hold that the requirement for financial support of the collective-bargaining agency by all who receive the benefits of its work is within the power of Congress under the Commerce Clause and does not violate either the First or the Fifth Amendment. We express no opinion on the use of other conditions to secure or maintain membership in a labor organization operating under a union or closed shop agreement. Reversed.

A relatively peaceful record has been maintained in the railroad and commercial air transport industries. The sound labor policies for these industries were formulated by Congress in the Railway Labor Act. Of course it ought to be made clear that the carriers and the labor unions are well aware of the great public responsibility which they hold, and —that they are cognizant also of the dire consequences which would follow an extensive shutdown of this essential transportation system. Strikes therefore on major lines have occurred only rarely, and the few which developed were settled quickly by pressure from the President of the United States.

CHAPTER NINE

The National Labor Relations Act of 1935

THE National Industrial Recovery Act of 1933 [1] was an effort of the national government to overcome the economic depression by removing the prohibitions set up by antitrust laws, permitting business to organize, and controlling prices. One of the act's purposes was "to reduce and relieve unemployment, and to improve standards of labor." As a concession to the AFL for its support of this economic program, Congress provided certain guarantees for workers, which appear in Section 7(a). This section reads as follows:

. . . That employees shall have the right to organize and bargain collectively through representatives of their own choosing, and shall be free from the interference, restraint or coercion of employers of labor, or their agents, and in the designation of such representatives or in self-organization or in other concerted activities for the purpose of collective bargaining or other mutual aid or protection.

A National Labor Board was created to administer Section 7(a). Employer hostility to the law and to the decisions of the board brought only chaos in the labor field, especially when the board found itself without the power to force defiant employers to abide by its decisions. The fatal blow to the N.I.R.A. program came in 1935 when the Supreme Court declared the law unconstitutional in Schechter Poultry Corp. v. U.S. [2] The specific fault of the law, according to the Supreme Court, was the attempt to regulate hours and wages of workers in intrastate business, an invalid exercise of federal power. Further, the decision struck down what the court called an improper delegation of legislative

1. Public Law No. 67 (73d. Cong.) approved June 16, 1933.
2. 295 U.S. 495 (1935).

powers. These points are covered in detail in the case, which follows. Mr. Chief Justice Hughes delivered the opinion of the court.

. . . A. L. A. Schechter Poultry Corporation and Schechter Live Poultry Market are corporations conducting wholesale poultry slaughterhouse markets in Brooklyn, New York City. Joseph Schechter operated the latter corporation and also guaranteed the credits of the former corporation, which was operated by Martin, Alex and Aaron Schechter.

[They] ordinarily purchase their live poultry from commission men at the West Washington Market in New York City or at the railroad terminals serving the city but occasionally they purchase from commission men in Philadelphia. They buy the poultry for slaughter and resale. After the poultry is trucked to their slaughterhouse markets in Brooklyn, it is there sold, usually within twenty-four hours, to retail poultry dealers and butchers who sell directly to consumers. The poultry purchased from [them] is immediately slaughtered, prior to delivery, by schochtim in [their] employ. [They] do not sell poultry in interstate commerce.

The "Live Poultry Code" was promulgated under Section 3 of the National Industrial Recovery Act. That section . . . authorizes the President to approve "codes of fair competition." Such a code may be approved for a trade or industry, upon application by one or more trade or industrial associations or groups, if the President finds (1) that such associations or groups "impose no inequitable restrictions on admission to membership therein and are truly representative," and (2) that such codes are not designed "to promote monopolies or to eliminate or oppress small enterprises and will not operate to discriminate against them, and will tend to effectuate the policy" of Title I of the Act.

Such codes "shall not permit monopolies or monopolistic practices." As a condition of his approval, the President may "impose such conditions (including requirements for the making of reports and the keeping of accounts) for the protection of consumers, competitors, employees and others, and in furtherance of the public interest, and may provide such exceptions to and exemptions from the provisions of such code as the President in his discretion deems necessary to effectuate the policy herein declared."

Where such a code has not been approved, the President may prescribe one, either on his own motion or on complaint. Violation of any provision of a code (so approved or prescribed) "in any transaction in or affecting interstate or foreign commerce" is made a misdemeanor punishable by a fine of not more than $500 for each offense, and each day the violation continued is to be deemed a separate offense.

The "Live Poultry Code" was approved by the President on April 13, 1934. Its divisions indicate its nature and scope. The code has eight articles entitled (1) purposes, (2) definitions, (3) hours, (4) wages, (5) general labor provisions, (6) administration, (7) trade practice provisions, and (8) general. . . .

The Code fixes the number of hours for workdays. It provides that no employe, with certain exceptions, shall be permitted to work in excess of forty (40) hours in any one week, and that no employe, save as stated, "shall be paid in any pay period less than at the rate of fifty (50) cents per hour."

The article containing "general labor provisions" prohibits the employment of any person under 16 years of age, and declares that employes shall have the right to "collective bargaining" and freedom of choice with respect to labor organizations, in the terms of 7(a) of the act.

The minimum number of employes who shall be employed by slaughterhouse operators is fixed, the numbers being graduated according to the average volume of weekly sales.

The question of chief importance relates to the provisions of the Code as to the hours and wages of those employed in defendants' slaughterhouse markets. It is plain that these requirements are imposed in order to govern the details of defendants' management of their local business. The persons employed in slaughtering and selling in local trade are not employed in interstate commerce. Their hours and wages have no direct relation to interstate commerce. . . .

If the Federal Government may determine the wages and hours of employes in the internal commerce of a State, because of their relation to cost and prices and their indirect effect upon interstate commerce, it would seem that a similar control might be exerted over other elements of cost, also affecting prices, such as the number of employes, rents, advertising, methods of doing business, etc.

All the processes of production and distribution that enter into cost could likewise be controlled. If the cost of doing an intrastate business is in itself the permitted object of Federal control, the extent of the regulation of cost would be a question of discretion and not of power.

The Government also makes the point that efforts to enact State legislation establishing high labor standards have been impeded by the belief that unless similar action is taken generally, commerce will be diverted from the States adopting such standards, and that this fear of diversion has led to demands for Federal legislation on the subject of wages and hours.

The apparent implication is that the Federal authority under the commerce clause should be deemed to extend to the establishment of rules to govern wages and hours in intrastate trade and industry generally throughout the country, thus overriding the authority of the States to deal with domestic problems arising from labor conditions in their internal commerce.

It is not the province of the Court to consider the economic advantages or disadvantages of such a centralized system. It is sufficient to say that the Federal Constitution does not provide for it. Our growth and development have called for wide use of the commerce power of the Federal Government in its control over the expanded activities of interstate commerce and in protecting that commerce from burdens, interferences and conspiracies to restrain and monopolize it.

But the authority of the Federal Government may not be pushed to such an extreme as to destroy the distinction, which the commerce clause itself establishes, between commerce "among the several States" and the internal concerns of a State. The same answer must be made to the contention that is based upon the serious economic situation which led to the passage of the Recovery Act—the fall in prices, the decline in wages and employment, and the curtailment of the market for commodities.

Stress is laid upon the great importance of maintaining wage distributions which would provide the necessary stimulus in starting "the cumulative forces making for expanding commercial activity." Without in any way disparaging this motive, it is enough to say that the recuperative efforts of the Federal Government must be made in a manner consistent with the authority granted by the Constitution.

We are of the opinion that the attempt through the provisions of the Code to fix the hours and wages of employes of defendants in their intrastate business was not a valid exercise of Federal power.

Following the failure of the National Industrial Recovery Act to survive the constitutional test, Senator Robert Wagner of New York introduced the National Labor Relations Act,[3] which both Houses of Congress approved on June 27, 1935, and which was signed by President Roosevelt on July 5, 1935.[4]

The chief positive aids which labor organizations received under the Wagner Act were protection against intimidation by employer agents, protection against discharge or discrimination for union activity, and a seat at a conference table.

The act created a National Labor Relations Board and gave it administrative authority to carry out the public policy as expressed in the statute. This policy was to encourage collective bargaining, which could develop only where the right of workers to join unions of their own

3. 49 Stat. L. (I) 449 (1935).

4. After signing the act, the President said: "This Act defines, as part of our substantive law, the right of self-organization of employees in industry for the purpose of collective bargaining, and provides methods by which the Government can safeguard that legal right. It establishes a National Labor Relations Board to hear and determine cases in which it is charged that this legal right is abridged or denied, and to hold fair elections to ascertain who are the chosen representatives of the employees. . . .

"A better relationship between labor and management is the high purpose of this Act. By assuring the employees the right of collective bargaining, it fosters the development of the employment contract on a sound and equitable basis. It aims to remove one of the chief causes of wasteful economic strife. By preventing practices which tend to destroy the independence of labor, it seeks, for every worker within its scope, that freedom of choice and action which is justly his.

"The National Labor Relations Board will be an independent quasi-judicial body. It should be clearly understood that it will not act as mediator or conciliator in labor disputes. The function of mediation remains, under this Act, the duty of the Secretary of Labor and of the Conciliation Service of the Department of Labor. It is important that the judicial function and the mediation function should not be confused. Compromise, the essence of mediation, has no place in the interpretation and enforcement of the law." (*Public Papers and Addresses of Franklin D. Roosevelt*, (1938) Random House, New York, Vol. IV, pp. 294–295.)

choice was protested. The heart of this new law, more often called the Wagner Act, will be found in Sections 7, 8, and 9. Section 7 reads:

Employees shall have the right of self-organization, to form, join, or assist labor organizations, to bargain collectively through representatives of their own choosing, and to engage in concerted activities, for the purpose of collective bargaining or other mutual aid or protection.

Section 8 of the act backs up the guarantees appearing in Section 7 by listing five proscriptions against specific forms of employer activity called "unfair labor practices." Although an unfair labor practice is not a crime, it is a statutory wrong akin to a common law tort. Neither fine nor imprisonment is incurred by the commission of an unfair labor practice. All employer unfair practices will be found in subsections 1 to 5 of Section 8, and they are referred to as (1) interference, restraint, and coercion; (2) domination of labor unions; (3) encouragement or discouragement of membership in labor unions by discrimination in hire or in tenure, terms, or conditions of employment; (4) discrimination against employees for filing charges or giving testimony against the employer, and (5) refusing to bargain collectively with the agent designated by the employees.

Section 9 of the act sets forth the principle of majority rule for the selection of bargaining representatives. The board determines the appropriate bargaining unit, the representative is selected by a secret ballot of the employees, or the board may utilize any other suitable method to ascertain such representatives.

Section 10 gives power to the board to "prevent any person from engaging in any unfair labor practice (listed in Section 8) affecting commerce." Section 10(b), (c), and (d) provide for a complaint, hearing, and answer. Testimony must be reduced to writing, and oral arguments before the board may be requested. The board issues findings of fact from which it may order either a dismissal of the complaint, or it may order the employer to cease and desist in the commission of the unfair practice. Because the board has been given no enforcement authority, this section allows both it and the aggrieved person recourse to the U.S. Circuit Court of Appeals for a review. The next and final appeal is to the U.S. Supreme Court.

The Constitutionality of the Act

In 1937, five decisions were handed down by the Supreme Court answering constitutional questions concerning the Wagner Act. Many authorities had believed the act would suffer the same fate as the National Industrial Recovery Act. Some of the best constitutional lawyers were very hopeful that the Supreme Court would strike down the Wagner Act, and their optimism was so high that they instructed their employer clients to conduct their labor relations affairs as though no law existed. Between the enactment of the law in 1935, and 1937 when the court passed on the constitutional questions raised, few of the larger corporations gave any practical recognition to the Wagner Act.

The constitutionality of the act was upheld by a margin of one vote of the nine Justices of the U.S. Supreme Court. The authoritative case is NLRB v. Jones & Laughlin Steel Corp.[5] Chief Justice Hughes, speaking for the court, said:

. . . In a proceeding under the National Labor Relations Act of 1935, the National Labor Relations Board found that the respondent, Jones & Laughlin Steel Corporation had violated the Act by engaging in unfair labor practices affecting commerce. The proceeding was instituted by the Beaver Valley Lodge No. 200, affiliated with the Amalgamated Association of Iron, Steel and Tin Workers of America, a labor organization. The unfair labor practices charged were that the corporation was discriminating against members of the union with regard to hire and tenure of employment, and was coercing and intimidating its employees in order to interfere with their self-organization. The discriminatory and coercive action alleged was the discharge of certain employees. . . .

The scheme of the National Labor Relations Act may be briefly stated. The first section (29 U.S.C.A. Par. 151) sets forth findings with respect to the injury to commerce resulting from the denial by employers of the right of employees to organize and from the refusal of employers to accept the procedure of collective bargaining. There follows a declaration that it is the policy of the United States to eliminate these causes of obstruction to the free flow of commerce. The Act then defines the terms it uses, including the terms "commerce" and "affecting commerce." Section 2 (29 U.S.C.A. Par. 152). It creates the National Labor Relations Board and prescribes its organization. Sections 3–6 (29 U.S.C.A. Pars. 153–156). It sets forth the right of employees to self-organization and to bargain collectively through representatives of their own choosing. Section 7 (29 U.S.C.A. Par. 157). It defines "unfair labor practices." Section 8 (29 U.S.C.A. Par. 158). It lays down rules as to the representation of employees for the purpose of collective bargaining. Section 9 (29 U.S.C.A. Par. 159). The Board is empowered to prevent the described unfair labor practices affecting commerce and the act prescribes the procedure to that end. The Board is authorized to petition designated courts to secure the enforcement of its order. The findings of the Board as to the facts, if supported by evidence, are to be conclusive. If either party on application to the court shows that additional evidence is material and that there were reasonable grounds for the failure to adduce such evidence in the hearing before the Board, the court may order the additional evidence to be taken. Any person aggrieved by a final order of the Board

5. 301 U.S. 1 (1937).

may obtain a review in the designated courts with the same procedure as in the case of an application by the Board for the enforcement of its order. Section 10 (29 U.S.C.A. Par. 160). The Board has broad powers of investigation. Section 11 (29 U.S.C.A. Par. 161). Interference with members of the Board or its agents in the performance of their duties is punishable by fine and imprisonment. Section 12 (29 U.S.C.A. Par. 162). Nothing in the act is to be construed to interfere with the right to strike. Section 13. (29 U.S.C.A. Par. 163). . . .

Thus, in its present application, the statute goes no further than to safeguard the right of employees to self-organization and to select representatives of their own choosing for collective bargaining or other mutual protection without restraint or coercion by their employer.

That is a fundamental right. Employees have as clear a right to organize and select their representatives for lawful purposes as the respondent has to organize its business and select its own officers and agents. Discrimination and coercion to prevent the free exercise of the right of employees to self-organization and representation is a proper subject for condemnation by competent legislative authority. Long ago we stated the reason for labor organizations. We said that they were organized out of the necessities of the situation; that a single employee was helpless in dealing with an employer; that he was dependent ordinarily on his daily wage for the maintenance of himself and family; that, if the employer refused to pay him the wages that he thought fair, he was nevertheless unable to leave the employ and resist arbitrary and unfair treatment; that union was essential to give laborers opportunity to deal on an equality with their employer. American Steel Foundries v. Tri-City Central Trades Council, 257 U.S. 184, 209, 66 L. ed. 189, 199, 42 S. Ct. 72, 78, 27 A.L.R. 360. We reiterated these views when we had under consideration the Railway Labor Act of 1926, 44 Stat. 577. Fully recognizing the legality of collective action on the part of employees in order to safeguard their proper interests, we said that Congress was not required to ignore this right but could safeguard it. Congress could seek to make appropriate collective action of employees an instrument of peace rather than of strife. We said that such collective action would be a mockery if representation were made futile by interference with freedom of choice. Hence the prohibition by Congress of interference with the selection of representatives for the purpose of negotiation and conference between employers and employees, "instead of being an invasion of the constitutional right of either, was based on the recognition of the rights of both." Texas & N.O.R. Co. v. Railway & S.S. Clerks, 281 U.S. 548, 74 L. ed. 1034, 50 S. Ct. 427. We have reasserted the same principle in sustaining the application of the Railway Labor Act as amended in 1934. Virginian Railway Co. v. System Federation No. 40, *supra*.

FOURTH. EFFECTS OF THE UNFAIR LABOR PRACTICE IN RESPONDENT'S ENTERPRISE. Giving full weight to respondent's contention with respect to a break in the complete continuity of the "stream of commerce" by reason of respondent's manufacturing operations, the fact remains that the stoppage of those operations by industrial strife would have a most serious effect upon interstate commerce. In view of respondent's far-flung activities, it is idle to say that the effect would be indirect or remote. It is obvious that it would be immediate and might be catastrophic. We are asked to shut our eyes to the plainest facts of our national life and to deal with the question of direct and indirect effects in an intellectual vacuum. Because there may be but indirect and remote effects upon interstate commerce in connection with a host of local enterprises throughout the country, it does not follow that other industrial activities do not have such a close and intimate relation to interstate commerce as to make the presence of industrial strife a matter of the most urgent national concern. . . .

Experience has abundantly demonstrated that the recognition of the right of employees to self-organization and to have representatives of their own choosing for the purpose of collective bargaining is often an essential condition of industrial peace. Refusal to confer and negotiate has been one of the most prolific causes of strife. This is such an outstanding fact in the history of labor disturbances that it is a proper subject of judicial notice and requires no citation of instances. The opinion in the case of Virginian Railway Co. v. System Federation No. 40, *supra*, points out that, in the case of carriers, experience has shown that before the amendment, of 1934, of the Railway Labor Act, "when there was no dispute as to the organizations authorized to represent the employees, and when there was willingness of the employer to meet such representative for a discussion of their grievances, amicable adjustment of differences had generally followed and strikes had been avoided."

FIFTH. THE MEANS WHICH THE ACT EMPLOYS—QUESTIONS UNDER THE DUE PROCESS CLAUSE AND OTHER CONSTITUTIONAL RESTRICTIONS. Respondent asserts its right to conduct its business in an orderly manner without being subjected to arbitrary restraints. What we have said points to the fallacy of the argument. Employees have their correlative right to organize for the purpose of securing the redress of grievances and to promote agreements with employers relating to rates of pay and conditions of work.

The Act does not compel agreements between employers and employees. It does not compel any agreements whatever. . . . The theory of the Act is that free opportunity for negotiation with accredited representatives of employees is likely to promote industrial peace and may bring about the adjustments and agreements which the Act in itself does not attempt to compel. . . . The Act does not interfere with the normal exercise of the right of the employer to select its employees or to discharge them. The employer may not under cover of that right, intimidate or coerce its employees with respect to their self-organization and representation, and, on the other hand, the Board is not entitled to make its authority a pretext for interference with the right of discharge when that right is exercised for other reasons than such intimidation and coercion. The true purpose is the subject of investigation with full opportunity to show the facts. It would seem that when employers freely recognize the right of their employees to their own organizations and their unrestricted right of representation, there will be much less occasion for controversy in respect to the free and appropriate exercise of the right of selection and discharge.

The Act has been criticized as one-sided in its application; that the employer to supervision and restraint and leaves untouched for which employees may be responsible; that it fails to provide prehensive plan,—with better assurances of fairness to both sides and increased chances of success in bringing about, if not compelling, equitable solutions of industrial disputes affecting interstate commerce. But, we are dealing with the power of Congress, not with a particular policy or with the extent to which policy should go. We have frequently said that the legislative authority, exerted within its proper field, need not embrace all the evils within its reach. The Constitution does not forbid "cautious advance," step by step, in dealing with the evils which are exhibited in activities within the range of legislative power. . . .

Our conclusion is that the order of the Board was within its competency and that the Act is valid as here applied. The judgment of the Circuit Court of Appeals is reversed and the cause is remanded for further proceedings in conformity with this opinion. It is so ordered. Reversed.

The determination of the constitutionality of the act rested on the interpretation of federal power to regulate interstate commerce. In this case, as others [6] decided in 1937, the Supreme Court ruled that the National Labor Relations Act was predicated on a proper conception of the power of Congress to regulate this commerce.

This act, guaranteeing workers the right to organize and be recognized, represents a radical departure from the legal standing of labor unions at common law.

Unfair Labor Practices

Labor unions regard the Wagner Act as a true Magna Charta largely because of the guarantees provided workers in Section 7 of the act.

Section 8 of the act constitutes a protective shield over these guarantees and prohibits specific types of employer activities which, if permitted, would nullify the rights in Section 7.

There is no provision in the act making rights for workers enforcible in federal courts independently of action by the board.[7]

The right to organize and engage in collective bargaining and concerted activities depends on the existence of employee status within the meaning of the act. A unit made up of a single employee will not be given protection, since Section 7 gives rights exclusively to employees.[8]

6. Associated Press v. NLRB, 301 U.S. 103 (1937); NLRB v. Friedman-Harry Marks Clothing Co., 301 U.S. 58 (1937); NLRB v. Fruehauf Trailer Co., 301 U.S. 49 (1937).
7. Blankenship v. Kurfman, 96 Fed. (2d) 450 (1938).
8. Panaderia Succession Alonso, 87 NLRB 877 (1949).

Independent contractors [9] and agricultural workers are not employees under the act.[10] The Wagner Act allowed supervisors all the rights enumerated in Section 7,[11] although later legislation excluded supervisors from the definition of the term "employee."

The term "employer" includes any person acting in the interest of an employer but excluding the following employers: [12]

(1) Federal, state, or municipal corporations.

(2) Railroad carriers and airlines covered under the Railway Labor Act.

(3) Labor unions in their representative capacities (other than when acting as employers).

If a firm is engaged in trade, traffic, commerce, transportation, or communication, any labor dispute in that firm brings the case within the coverage of the act.

Coverage of disputes "affecting" commerce is far broader than coverage of disputes in interstate commerce. Under the "affecting-commerce" criterion the act becomes applicable, in many instances, to businesses which have generally been considered as strictly "local," such as mining, manufacturing, and some phases of construction and retailing. The act has been applied to a bus company, a garment manufacturer, a non-profit press association, and local automobile dealers.

Because many cases developed, the board entered into agreements with various State Labor Relations Boards under which the national board ceded jurisdiction in cases of definitely local character, permitting the state boards to handle these cases and apply state labor laws.

We may now proceed to discuss the first of the unfair labor practices.

Section 8(1) reads: "It shall be an unfair labor practice for an employer to interfere with, restrain, or coerce employees in the rights guaranteed in Section 7."

Concrete acts which fall within the category of "interference" are bribery, espionage, threats, blacklisting, "runaway shops," promises to reward workers who reject unionization, and, in general, all activities designed to obstruct, thwart, or interfere with free organizational activities by employees. One of the most deliberate violations of this subsection occurred in the Remington Rand [13] case, where a series of unfair labor practices laid the foundation for charges filed against the

9. Newman v. Newsvendors Local 75, 14 LC 64,426 (C.Ch.) (1948).
10. Citizen News Co., 97 NLRB 428 (1951).
11. Packard Motor Co. v. NLRB 330 U.S. 485 (1947). The Taft-Hartley Act of 1947 has withdrawn the legislative protection given to supervisors under the Packard decision.
12. Wholly owned government corporations, Federal Reserve banks, and nonprofit hospitals were exempted by the 1947 amendments.
13. *In the matter of* Remington Rand Inc., 2 NLRB 626 (1937); NLRB v. Remington Rand Co., 94 Fed. (2d) 862 (1938), cert. denied, 304 U.S. 576 (1938).

employer. The charges actually covered violations of subsection (1) as well as other subsections. In all, the filed charges embraced espionage, violence, strikebreaking, and refusal to bargain with the designated agent of the workers. Although the decision came early after the passage of the Wagner Act, it remains a classic in labor law. The opinion and decision of the National Labor Relations Board follows.

. . . From the thousands of pages of testimony in this proceeding there may be distilled two very plain facts: The unwavering refusal of the respondent to bargain collectively with its employees and the cold, deliberate ruthlessness with which it fought the strike which its refusal to bargain had precipitated. If the provisions of the Act, 29 U.S.C.A. sec. 151 et seq., ever required justification, one need go no further than the facts of this case. Over 6000 employees, with their families and dependents, are subjected to the miseries of a prolonged strike, the people of six communities experience the economic hardships that inevitably result when an accustomed source of income is suddenly withdrawn, these same communities are turned into warring camps and unreasoning hatreds are created that lead to abuses alien to a sane civilization—all because the respondent refused to recognize the rights of six thousand employees. A decent respect for the rights of human beings demands that no employer be free to ignore his employees in such fashion, but that, as provided by the Act, they be entitled through the procedure of collective bargaining to have a voice in shaping their destinies. Human rights aside, even a calculating dollars and cents approach to the situation would require that an employer confer with the representatives of his employees, for here six manufacturing plants are rendered idle and the channels of commerce dislocated, at a cost of millions of dollars, simply because the respondent could not bring itself to meet with its employees. In the legal phraseology of the Act the respondent, from April, 1936 to the strike on May 26, and again from the strike to the time of the hearings in this case, has continuously refused to bargain collectively with the representatives of its employees as required by Section 8, subdivision (5). In the language of the average person, the respondent, through Rand, its president, has exhibited a callous, imperturbable disregard of the rights of its employees that is medieval in its assumption of power over the lives of men and shocking in its concept of the status of the modern industrial worker.

To draw attention from its determined refusals to bargain collectively with the representatives of its employees and as part of its "back to work" movements, the respondent secretly formed employees' associations which it exhibited to the public as genuine employee organizations dealing with the respondent at arm's length. These associations—the Middletown Remrand Employees' Back-to-Work Association, the Ilion Typewriter Employees Protective Association, and the Syracuse Employees' Independent Association—were "labor organizations" within the technical definition given that phrase in Section 2 subdivision (5) of the Act, for they were organizations in which employees participated and which existed for the purpose of dealing with employers concerning labor disputes and conditions of work, here the reopening of the plant. In view of that status, the respondent was forbidden by Section 8, subdivision (2) to dominate or interfere with their formation or administration or to contribute financial or other support to them. From the facts found above, the conclusion is inescapable that the respondent has deliberately flouted that provision of the Act. All three associations were nothing more than dummy organizations operated by the respondent to further the "back to work" movement and break the strike. All three associations operated in an identical manner—advertisements, offices, telephone numbers, requests to the respondent to open the plant, mass meetings and celebrations of employees at such openings. In each city where the associations operated the advertisements were in the same pattern—and moreover, were skillfully written. Moreover, in Norwood, where the respondent did not choose to create such an association but instead conducted the "back to work" movement entirely in its own name, the mechanics were nevertheless identical. The appearance of each association coincided with a drive on the respondent's part to create a "back to work" breach in union ranks and they were admirably suited to that end. The use of telephones, while permitting the respondent to ascertain the number of employees ready to return to work, as pointed out before also enabled it to keep secret the number of such employees, and, through the fear occasioned by such secrecy, prompted many more to telephone. In addition, the very presence of these associations would induce the public to believe that there was a large body of employees who did not belong to the unions, and that the strike was supported by only a small minority of employees. The associations also offered a basis for requests for heavy police protection and a medium for the dissemination of propaganda, which, if handed out by the respondent in its own name, might be held suspect by the public. It is apparent that these associations had many expenses—offices, telephones, advertisements, printed literature, offers of trips to Ilion, etc. Yet there is no indication of any means whereby the associations themselves obtained the large funds necessary to defray such expenses. There were no dues, no requests for contributions. The money obviously came from the respondent. Bergoff's testimony in regard to the Ilion association and Ellis' activities on behalf of the Middletown association, would in themselves indicate that these associations were alter egos of the respondent. It should be noted that at the Board's hearing in this case, Ellis was introduced by Simson as the "attorney for the Remington Rand at Middletown." Ellis had, as pointed out above, represented both strikebreakers employed by the respondent and the respondent itself in legal proceedings arising during the strike, so that his intimate relationship to the respondent is beyond question. Yet we also find Ellis preparing application blanks for the Middletown association and attempting to secure office space for it. We therefore find that the respondent organized and operated these associations and defrayed their expenses in violation of Section 8, subdivision (2). At Ilion, and later at Middletown, there was an attempt to capitalize on the results of these "back to work" associations by using them as a basis in the formation of company-controlled organizations among the employees that had returned to work. The successor organizations are tainted with the illegality of their predecessors and are likewise in violation of the Act.

We turn to a consideration of the other unfair labor practices. The strike was caused by the respondent's unqualified and determined refusal to meet with the representatives of its employees. Thus when the strike came the respondent knew it was not to be settled by collective bargaining or mediation. Outside agencies, unaware of the quality of the respondent's determination, and seeing only a costly and bitter strike, would make efforts to mediate the dispute. Governors, Industrial Commissioners, Mayors, State Mediation Boards, Federal Conciliators would attempt in turn to end the strike by the peaceful method of conferences. But all were predestined to failure in the face of that unyielding resolve to fight the strike rather than to compromise ever so little through the concession of a conference. And in the execution of that resolve the respondent exhibited even a greater disregard for human rights and values than that which characterized its earlier refusals to bargain. It immediately engaged not one, but four strikebreaking agencies and with their aid charted its campaign. That campaign, as we have shown, was built around "back to work" movements, created systematically by the respondent and operated for the most part through associations formed by it, which culminated in some cases in reopenings of the plants attended by celebrations and the return of massed groups of employees or thugs masquerading as such. These movements were built up through an intensive propaganda drive, openly in advertisements and news articles, covertly through the work of "missionaries." They were buttressed by threats to move the plants, and in some cases by actual movements of machinery, designed to create fear of loss of employment on the part of employees and fear of economic starvation on the part of whole communities. These threats presented a bewildering maze to both the employee and the man in the street—the Norwood and Syracuse plants were moving to Ilion, yet the Ilion plant was for sale. The Tonawanda and Middletown plants were also to be moved, and yet where could they be moved to if the other plants were also in the process of being transferred? The answer of course is that such confusion best served the respondent's interests, for no one community could feel sure of not being the victim. Keeping pace with these "back to work" movements was the respondent's constant drive to obtain the presence of large forces of police and guards, not only for the intimidation that their presence would work upon the average employee, but also because of the psychological effect such forces possess to turn the average citizen against a strike and the tendency of police and guards to indulge in excesses of force and arrest against employees on strike. Where the "back to work" movements did not result in inducing a sufficient number of employees to return, the respondent hired thousands of strikebreakers to operate its plants, describing them to the public as "loyal employees."

Such was the main attack. It was supported by a variety of manoeuvres and devices. Spies were planted in the various towns. The company attempted to bribe union leaders and to influence public officials. Individual bargaining was resorted to through bonuses, personal telegrams, and visits of foremen and "missionaries" in order to undermine the solidarity of the union members. Union leaders were discharged and others arrested for the purpose of demoralizing the union. We have previously discussed in detail these discharges of union leaders at Ilion, Syracuse and Tonawanda. All of the individuals discharged, whose names appear in the Conclusions of Law, were discharged because of their union membership and activity, and their discharges, and each of them, thus constitute discrimination in regard to hire and tenure of employment to discourage membership in a labor organization contrary to Section 8, subdivision (3) of the Act. These individuals, who were employees at the time of their discharge, thus ceased work as a consequence of unfair labor practices on the part of the respondent and therefore continued to be employees of the respondent within the meaning of the Act. Scenes of disorder and violence, to be described to the public as riots, were staged so that they could serve as the basis for injunctions, requests for police protection and "law and order" tirades in the press. In the planning of these disorders, the respondent exhibited the small value it placed on human life, for with even-handedness it stood willing to sacrifice the lives of the men whom it hired to break the strike as well as those of the strikers. Likewise, in having its agents commit acts of violence in such a fashion as to ascribe the guilt to the strikers and in its deliberate provocation of disorders by the strikers, it was not deterred by the knowledge that innocent men would be arrested and fined, that a citizenry, made almost hysterical through the respondent's subtle playing on its emotions and thoughts, would inflict excessive punishment upon men acting under infuriating provocation. Nor did the respondent stop at making dupes of the civil authorities or the leading citizens, as at Ilion, so that they would do the job for the respondent.

But all of these stratagems demanded for their success a public opinion favorable to the respondent and opposed to the strikers. The respondent appreciated that today the success or failure of a strike of such magnitude may ultimately depend upon the reaction of the public. It also recognized that a public fully informed of the tactics the respondent was employing and of its firm refusal to meet with its employees would in all probability condemn their use. Finally, it realized that the public is nearly entirely dependent upon the press and the radio for its information. Consequently, the respondent proceeded to wage a publicity campaign designed both to cloak its ruthlessness toward its employees and the public and to swing opinion against the unions. To this end numerous advertisements in the names of the respondent and its "back to work" associations were inserted in which the facts were distorted or completely falsified, the unions and their leaders maligned, and the communities' dependence upon the respondent's payrolls stressed. Radio speeches of the same nature were made at frequent intervals. Release after release was handed out by the respondent from its executive offices and from its various plants, such practice to be varied at times by suddenly shutting off that source of news and forcing the papers to turn to the advertisements or to the associations when such sources better served the respondent's immediate needs. Harding kept constant watch over the various press association reports so that the respondent could remedy impressions in the reports contrary to its ends, or supply through releases and advertisements information which it thought the public should be handed and which those reports did not carry. Replies to offers of mediation were so framed as to be no more than a means of conveying to the public some particular item of propaganda that the respondent was desirous of spreading. Aspects that were sure to evoke a desired response were continually stressed, such as violence and threats of the likelihood of loss of a particular plant through closing and moving elsewhere.

It must be remembered that by striking the employees did not sever their status as such with the respondent. Section 2, subdivision (3) of the Act defines the term "employee" to include "any individual whose work has ceased as a consequence of, or in connection with, any current labor dispute or because of any unfair labor practice." Here the strike was caused by the respondent's refusal to bargain collectively, and hence the employees ceased work as a consequence of an unfair labor practice. Moreover, the strike was obviously a "labor dispute" within the meaning of Section 2 subdivision (9) of the Act, since it was a controversy concerning conditions of employment and the association and representation of persons seeking to arrange terms and conditions of employment, and hence the employees also ceased work in connection with a current labor dispute. Thus, those employees who have not returned to work but who have remained on strike and who have not obtained employment elsewhere (between three and four thousand at the time of the hearing) have been since May 26, and still are, the employees of the respondent in view of the unfair labor practice that caused the strike and the currency of the labor dispute. These employees were, of course, within their rights in striking, for Section 13 of the Act declares that "Nothing in this Act shall be construed so as to interfere with or impede or diminish in any way the right to strike." Under Section 8, subdivision (1) of the Act, the respondent was forbidden to interfere, restrain or coerce these employees in the exercise of their rights guaranteed in Section 7—among others, to bargain collectively and to engage in concerted activities for that purpose and for mutual aid and protection. The activities of the respondent which we have described in detail were all designed to and did in fact interfere with, coerce and restrain its employees in the exercise of their rights. To put it concisely, those activities were employed to defeat the strike, to end the strike by breaking it rather than by settling it through collective bargaining. As the strike was in the first instance directly caused by the respondent's refusal to bargain collectively in violation of Section 8, subdivision (5), and was thereafter perpetuated through further refusals, also in violation of that Section, all of those activities must be regarded as contrary to Section 8, subdivision (1). While many, if not all, of those activities would likewise constitute unfair labor practices even though the strike and its continuation were not themselves the results of unfair labor practices, such a determination need not be made in this proceeding. Here, by its illegal refusal to bargain collectively, the respondent caused and perpetuated a strike and consequently any activities on its part designed to end that strike by defeating it, in contrast to settling it by the method of collective bargaining, are in violation of Section 8, subdivision (1). Each step taken so to defeat the strike constituted an assertion that the respondent would illegally continue to refuse to settle the strike through collective bargaining as provided by the Act—they were but the opposite faces of the same coin. We find that by its refusal to bargain collectively, and by its other acts, the respondent interfered with, coerced and restrained its employees in the exercise of the rights guaranteed in Section 7 of the Act.

Our previous decisions point the general remedy for these illegal acts. We have required in cases of strikes caused by a refusal to bargain collectively that the employer both bargain collectively with the representatives of his employees, and restore as far as possible the status quo that existed at the time of the strike. Normally, such restoration of the status quo is accomplished by the reinstatement of all employees on the payroll at the time of the strike, any new employees hired since that date to be dismissed if such action is necessary. If, because of curtailed production or other reasons, there are not a sufficient number of positions available to take care of all of the employees on the payroll at the time of the strike, the initial reinstatement is to be made on the basis of seniority by classifications, and those not reinstated are to be placed, on a similar basis, on a preferential list. However, the respondent's acts of closing one of its plants, the Norwood plant, opening another, the Elmira plant, and shifting the equipment of still other plants, have introduced factors which make solution of the problem more difficult. While the total number of individuals now employed is approximately equal to the number employed at the date the strike was called, there has been a radical alteration in the location of the jobs for these employees. Thus, the Norwood plant has been closed and its equipment moved to Ilion and Elmira plants, so that while no jobs are available at Norwood, additional jobs are available at Ilion and Elmira. Similarly, 45 per cent of the Syracuse operations and a substantial percentage of the Middletown operations have been transferred to Elmira, so that although the number of available positions in Syracuse and Middletown has been greatly reduced, a corresponding number of positions is now available at Elmira. Consequently, if all of the employees on the payroll of May 26, 1936, are to be reinstated, many will find it necessary to move from their present homes to other parts where positions are available. With nearly 4000 employees to be reinstated under such conditions, the complexity of the problem created by the respondent's act is readily realized.

The respondent will be ordered to reinstate all those production and maintenance employees involved who were employed on May 26, 1936, and who have not since received regular and substantially equivalent employment elsewhere. As the first step in carrying out this general order, such production and maintenance employees shall be reinstated to their former classifications, on the basis of seniority by classifications, where positions in such classifications are now open or have been filled by individuals employed since May 26, 1936, who were not employed on that date, the respondent dismissing such individuals if that is necessary to accomplish the reinstatement so ordered. In this fashion as far as possible employees will be reinstated in the plants in their own towns and will not be required to move elsewhere. But after such reinstatement there will still be a large group of employees, composed almost exclusively of Norwood, Syracuse, and Middletown exployees, who will have to move to other cities in order to obtain reinstatement. Consequently, all such production and maintenance employees not reinstated in the plant in their own towns shall be grouped together, regardless of the plant in which they were previously employed, on a single preferential list on the basis of seniority by classifications, to be offered the positions at the Elmira plant, and any positions still available at any of the other plants after those who struck at such plants have been reinstated. At Elmira, as well as elsewhere, individuals employed since May 26, 1936, who were not employed on that date must be dismissed if such action is necessary to effectuate such reinstatement. Thereafter, this list shall be drawn upon whenever further employees are needed at any of the plants involved, including the Elmira plant, preference being given to employees on the list then residing in the locality in which employment is available. The respondent will be ordered to pay the transportation expenses of any employee and his family who is forced to move in order to obtain reinstatement under these conditions. As can be gathered, the Board has attempted to keep such moving to a minimum by ordering that available positions at each plant be filled by employees residing in the locality. Finally, as many of the employees who had prior to the strike, designated the Joint Board as their representative for collective bargaining will thus be reinstated to the Elmira plant instead of to the plants where they had worked on May 26, 1936, we will include the Elmira plant together with the other plants in the unit which we have found to be appropriate for collective bargaining.

The employees who were individually discharged will be reinstated to their former positions, and in addition be awarded back pay on the following basis: (1) those who were discharged when they sought reinstatement during the continuance of the strike, designated as Group A in the Conclusions of Law, will receive back pay from the date of such discharge; (2) those who were discharged before the strike commenced or during the continuance of the strike, but not as a consequence of applications for reinstatement, designated as Group B in the Conclusions of Law, will receive back pay from the date of discharge to the date of the strike if the plant was operating in that period, and again from the date on which operations in their department began after the reopening of the plants involved to the date of offer of reinstatement.

Blacklisting union members by circulating their names among employers constitutes a violation of subsection (1). The antiunion potency of the blacklist was recognized by the U.S. Circuit Court of Appeals when it declared: "A long experience had shown that one of the most provocative and effective means by which employers sought to impede the organization of workers was the blacklisting of union men." [14]

Threats by employers or their agents which interfere with any of the rights protected by Section 7 are unfair labor practices. A leading case on this point is NLRB v. Virginia Electric and Power Co.[15]

14. NLRB v. Waumbec Mills, 114 Fed. (2d) 226 (1940). For other cases of blacklisting and threat of blacklisting, see Moss Planing Mill Co., 116 NLRB 8 (1956); NLRB v. Indiana Dish Co., 149 Fed. (2d) 987 (1945); Birmingham Post Co., 49 NLRB 206 (1943).
15. 314 U.S. 469 (1941).

Mr. Justice Murphy delivered the opinion of the court.

Upon the usual proceedings had pursuant to section 10 of the National Labor Relations Act, 29 U.S.C.A. section 160, the Board made substantially the following findings of fact:

For years prior to the events in this case the Virginia Electric and Power Company (hereinafter called the Company) was hostile to labor organizations. From 1922, when a strike was unsuccessful by a nationally affiliated union, until the formation of the Independent Organization of Employees (hereinafter called the Independent) in 1937, there was no labor organization among its employees. Shortly after the enactment of the National Industrial Recovery Act in 1933, 48 Stat. 195, Holtzclaw, the president of the Company, spoke to the employees and stated that any organization among them was "entirely unnecessary." Until his death in May 1937, the Company utilized the services of one Walters, an employee of the Railway Audit and Inspection Company, who prior to the effective date of the Act, admittedly furnished a report on the labor activity of the employees to the Company. In 1936, Bishop, Superintendent of Transportation in Norfolk, interrogated employees concerning union activities. On April 26, 1937, shortly after the Act was upheld, and an A.F. of L. organizer had appeared, the Company posted a bulletin throughout its operations appealing to the employees to bargain with the Company directly, without the intervention of an "outside" union, and thereby coerced its employees. In response to this bulletin several requests for increased wages and better working conditions were received. The Company decided to withhold action on those requests and directed its employees to select representatives to attend meetings at which Company officials would speak on the Wagner Act. These representatives met in Norfolk and Richmond on May 24 and were addressed by high Company officials, who read identical speeches stressing the desirability of forming a bargaining agency. . . .

While the Independent [union] was in the process of organization, Edwards, a supervisor, kept meetings of a rival C.I.O. union under surveillance and warned employees that they would be discharged for "messing with the C.I.O." On June 1, Mann, a member of the C.I.O. who had openly protested against an "inside" union at one of the May 11 meetings . . . attended by Superintendent Bishop's son, Warren, was discharged for union activities. . . .

Upon the basis of these findings and the entire record in the case the Board concluded that the Company had committed unfair labor practices within the meaning of section 8(1), (2) and (3) of the Act. Its order directed the Company to cease and desist from its unfair labor practices and from giving effect to its contract with the Independent, to withdraw recognition from and disestablish that organization, to reinstate with back pay the four wrongfully discharged employees, to reimburse each of its employees who was a member of the Independent in the amount of the dues and assessments checked off his wages by the Company on behalf of the Independent, and to post appropriate notices.

The Company and the Independent filed separate petitions in the court below to review and set aside the Board's order. The Board answered and requested enforcement of its order against the Company. The court below denied enforcement to any part of the Board's order, completely setting it aside. We granted the petition for writs of certiorari because the case was thought to present important questions in the administration of the Act. 312 U.S. 677, 61 S. Ct. 826, 85 L. Ed. 1117. . . .

The Board specifically found that the bulletin of April 26 and the speeches of May 24 "interfered with, restrained and coerced" the Company's employees in the exercise of their rights guaranteed by Section 7 of the Act. The Company strongly urges that such a finding is repugnant to the First Amendment. Neither the Act nor the Board's order here enjoins the employer from expressing its view on labor policies or problems, nor is a penalty imposed upon it because of any utterances which it has made. The sanctions of the Act are imposed not in punishment of the employer but for the protection of the employees. The employer in this case is as free now as ever to take any side it may choose on this controversial issue. But, certainly, conduct, though evidenced in part by speech may amount, in connection with other circumstances, to coercion within the meaning of the Act. If the total activities of an employer restrain or coerce his employees in their free choice, then those employees are entitled to the protection of the Act. And in determining whether a course of conduct amounts to restraint or coercion, pressure exerted vocally by the employer may no more be disregarded than pressure exerted in other ways. For "Slight suggestions as to the employer's choice between unions may have telling effect among men who know the consequences of incurring that employer's strong displeasure."

If the Board's order here may fairly be said to be based on the totality of the Company's activities during the period in question, we may not consider the findings of the Board as to the coercive effect of the bulletin and the speeches in isolation from the findings as respects the other conduct of the Company. If the Board's ultimate conclusion is based upon a complex of activities, such as the anti-union background of the Company, the activities of Bishop, Edwards' warning to the employees that they would be discharged for "messing with the C.I.O.," the discharge of Mann, the quick formation of the Independent, and the part which the management may have played in that formation, the conclusion would not be vitiated by the fact that the Board considered what the Company said in conjunction with what it did. The mere fact that language merges into a course of conduct does not put that whole course without the range of otherwise applicable administrative power. In determining whether the Company actually interfered with, restrained, and coerced its employees, the Board has a right to look at what the Company has said, as well as what it has done. . . .

The Board was of the view that the speeches delivered in the meetings of May 24 provided the impetus for the formation of a system-wide organization, that they re-emphasized the Company's distaste for "outside" organizations by referring to the bulletin, and that, after quoting the provision of the Act forbidding employer domination of labor organizations, they suggested that the employees select their "own" officers, and adopt their "own" by-laws and rules. The Board's finding was: "We find that at the May 24 meetings the respondent urged its employees to organize and to do so independently of 'outside' assistance, and that it thereby interfered with, restrained, and coerced its employees in the exercise of the rights guaranteed in Section 7 of the Act." . . .

The Supreme Court remanded the case to the NLRB for clarification of its determination that the independent union was employer-dominated. The court did not disturb the board's finding that subsections (1) and (3) were violated by the employer.

A foreman's statement that the employee who talked about a union "would be sticking his neck out" was considered a threat, unlawful under subsection (1).[16]

It was considered an interference with the employees' right of self-organization for a plant superintendent to threaten the probable loss of bonuses and other privileges if the employees joined the union.[17]

The following acts were held to be unlawful:

(1) An employer's threat to move his plant to another city if the union came in.[18]

(2) Threat to evict employees from company-owned houses because of their union membership.[19]

(3) Threat to isolate ("Like a rotten apple") pro-union employees.[20]

We now consider some other forms of employer interference, restraint, and coercion.

Economic Pressure

An employer commits an unfair labor practice under this subsection when he grants or withholds benefits from employees for the purpose of discrediting a labor union. For example, increasing wages to keep employees from joining a union is a violation. Giving employees bonuses, paid vacations, insurance benefits, etc., where the intent is to influence them against a union, constitutes a violation.[21] It is an unfair practice for an employer to withdraw a benefit or privilege in retaliation against

16. Hartland Plastics Inc., 93 NLRB 439 (1951).
17. Wolverine Shoe and Tanning Corp., 49 NLRB 881 (1943). See Freedom of Speech and the National Labor Relations Act, 48 *Yale L.J.* 54 (1938) for comments on employer's free speech.
18. Rugcrafters of Puerto Rico Inc., 112 NLRB 724 (1955).
19. Good Coal Co., 12 NLRB 136 (1939); U.S. Gypsum Co., 90 NLRB 964 (1950).
20. Montgomery Ward Co., 93 NLRB 640 (1951).
21. See Queen City Valve Inc., 93 NLRB 1576 (1951); West Point Mfg. Co., 115 NLRB 448 (1956).

the workers joining a union.[22] Where an employer offered a union leader a well-paying job if he would discontinue his organizing activities, the board held this to constitute a bribe and violation of the act.[23]

Runaway Shops

Removal of an existing business to another locality, or a threat of removal, may interfere with the free exercise of the employees' rights. This activity warrants the issuance of a complaint if the removal is motivated by a desire to thwart union or employee activity. In labor parlance, this antiunion tactic is known as the runaway shop. Of course, if an employer can prove that the removal was made in good faith, for example, that competitive conditions made it necessary, there is no statutory violation. The National Labor Relations Board will delve into the intent of the employer. If the purpose was found to be an evasion of a legal obligation established under the act, the board will declare the removal unlawful; it may order the employer to reestablish the business at the place from which the runaway occurred. In addition, the union may institute a civil suit for damages resulting from the employer's breach of a labor contract.

In the Brooks Shoe Manufacturing Company case,[24] the union sought damages from the employer for breaching a labor agreement provision barring removal of the plant during the life of the contract. The action was brought under Section 301 of the Taft-Hartley Law. A federal district court in Pennsylvania ruled that the employer's removal of the plant had violated the terms of the existing collective bargaining agreement, and that the employer was therefore liable for compensatory damages to the union. These damages consisted of loss of dues which would have been paid to the union by its members both during the remainder of the contract's term and during the 20 years following its expiration. A calculation of the probable loss accruing to the union in

22. A. S. Beck Shoe Corp., 92 NLRB 1457 (1951); Rein Co., 114 NLRB 694 (1955).
23. E. A. Laboratories Inc., 80 NLRB 625 (1948).
24. United Shoe Workers v. Brooks Shoe Mfg. Co., 187 F. Supp. 509 (1960). For other cases where actual removal was declared unlawful, see Tennessee-Carolina Transp., 108 NLRB 1369 (1954); Hopwood Retinning Co., 4 NLRB 922 (1938); Tredway and Taylor, 109 NLRB 1045 (1954).

For cases where unlawful threats of removal were made to discourage unionization, see Nina Dye Works Co., 95 NLRB 826 (1951); Winona Textile Mills Inc. v. NLRB, 160 Fed. (2d) 201 (1947); NLRB v. Kobritz, 193 Fed. (2d) 8 (1951).

For cases where the board found removal justifiable, see Fiss Corp., 43 NLRB 125 (1942); Brown Truck and Trailer Mfg. Co., 106 NLRB 999 (1953).

the future was warranted by the facts that the union had represented the employees consistently for the last 20 years, the employer's business had a minimum "life expectancy" of 20 more years, and it was reasonable to assume that the union would have continued to represent the employees for such a period had the employer not relocated his plant in breach of the contract. The court held further that by deliberately relocating his plant in breach of the union's contract, the employer also violated the national labor policy, as expressed in the National Labor Relations Act, when he ran away from his responsibility to bargain with the lawfully designated representative of his employees. The sum of $50,000 was awarded to the union.

Strikebreaking

Under Section 7 of the act the right to strike is a protected concerted activity. Therefore, the use of strike breakers during a strike violates Section 8(1). The use of strike guards, private police, strikebreaking agencies, and regular police when controlled by the employer, has been held to constitute interference.[25]

Where an employer induced a chamber of commerce committee to meet with strikers to persuade them to quit the strike, a violation of the act was found.[26]

In another case the employer sent employees an antiunion letter intended to undermine union strength and sent subsequent literature exhorting the employees to turn against their union leaders, which resulted in a back-to-work movement. This form of propaganda was construed to be an interference.[27]

Favoritism toward Unions

Employer favoritism or partiality toward a union constitutes interference with the employees' right to select a union of their own choice.[28] Akin to this violation is domination or unlawful support of a union by an employer; however, this constitutes an unfair labor practice under Section 8(2) rather than Section 8(1), which we are presently discussing. If an employer solicits members for a favored union, he com-

25. For cases, see NLRB v. West Ky. Coal Co., 116 Fed. (2d) 816 (1940); Sterling Corset Co., 9 NLRB 858 (1938); Remington Rand Co., 2 NLRB 626 (1937).
26. NLRB v. Hamilton Brown Shoe Co., 104 Fed. (2d) 49 (1939).
27. Reed and Prince Mfg. Co., 12 NLRB 944 (1939).
28. Cleveland Graphite Bronze Co., 75 NLRB 481 (1947); Colonial Fashions, 110 NLRB 1197 (1954).

mits an unfair labor practice.[29] Likewise, negotiating with a union other than the one representing the employees is an unfair practice.[30]

Interference with Elections [31]

An employer's interference with a representation election may constitute an unfair labor practice under Section 8(1). An example of prohibited activity is the employer's encouragement of an antiunion demonstration before the election takes place. Coercive speeches, malicious falsehoods, and threats are violations. The selection of a bargaining agent is the exclusive concern of the employees; therefore the employer should observe a policy of scrupulous neutrality before and during the election.

Barring Union Organizational Activities on Employer's Property [32]

Employers feel they have a right to adopt rules that bar any activity not connected with work, and so help to assure efficiency of plant operation. Employers consider union organizational drives a hindrance to the desired efficiency. On the other hand, unions feel that the best place to organize workers is at their place of work where they can be approached easily, and where the selling feature of unions can be presented more effectively. Many cases have developed under this subheading. A general no-solicitation rule is invalid when it covers the employees' nonworking time. Lunch and rest periods, even though paid for by the employer, belong to the employees, and to bar solicitation during these periods constitutes an unlawful interference. Lawful union activity does not include holding formal union meetings on company property. In the interest of keeping the plant clean and orderly, it is not unreasonable for an employer to prohibit at all times the distribution of union literature on the company's premises. When the employer's property is the

29. Coal Creek Co., 97 NLRB 14 (1951); Salant and Salant Inc., 92 NLRB 417 (1950).
30. NLRB v. Atlantic Stages, 180 Fed. (2d) 727 (1950).
31. For cases, see Crosley Corp., 60 NLRB 623 (1945); Morris Paper Mills, 73 NLRB 553 (1947); Reliance Mfg. Co., 56 NLRB 1083 (1944); Onondaga Pottery Co., 103 NLRB 770 (1953); NLRB v. Ind. Dish Co., 149 Fed. (2d) 987 (1945).
32. For cases, see Johnston Lawn Motor Corp., 110 NLRB 1955 (1954); No. Am. Aviation, 56 NLRB 959 (1944); George C. Knight Co., 102 NLRB 1198 (1953); W. T. Carter, 90 NLRB 2020 (1950); NLRB v. Republic Aviation Corp., 142 Fed. (2d) 193 (1944).

only available place to hold union meetings in a company-owned town, it was held to be unlawful for the employer to refuse to permit outdoor union meetings. In the Republic Aviation case, to be cited, the National Labor Relations Board sought an enforcement order to direct the employer to "cease and desist" from discouraging membership in a union and, as affirmative action, to reinstate four employees.

The question submitted to the circuit court of appeals was whether an employer could apply a rule generally forbidding solicitation of any kind in his plant to union electioneering during the employees' lunch hour without being guilty of an unfair labor practice. The court, granting the order, held that this was a "mixed question of law and fact" involving determination of a fact, which was wholly for the board. The court stated that a determination by the board that the employer was guilty of unfair labor practices in applying its general rule against solicitation so as to prevent electioneering for a union during the lunch hour, though specific animus against unions was not shown, was proper in view of the presumptive validity of the board's decision based in part on special acquaintance with the industrial relations in the plant.

The Republic Aviation case involved solicitation of union membership by employees of the company. In another leading case [33] the issue concerned solicitation by union organizers who were not employees of the company. In the Seamprufe matter, the National Labor Relations Board brought an action in the U.S. Circuit Court of Appeals, 10th District, to enforce an order prohibiting the employer from forbidding use of its private parking lot in an adjacent area by nonemployee union organizers who sought to distribute union literature and solicit union membership during the employees' nonworking hours. The court denied enforcement of the order. Justice Murrah, speaking for the court, said:

> . . . the fundamental basis for permitting the solicitation of union membership on company property is to vouchsafe the guaranteed right of self-organization. . . . When conducted by employees the solicitation amounts to the exercise of a right subject only to the correlative right of the employer to maintain plant production and discipline. An employee on company property exercising the right of self-organization does not violate a company no-trespass rule. . . . But a non-employee labor organizer who comes upon company property in violation of a non-discriminatory no-trespass role can justify his presence there only insofar as it bears a cogent relationship to the exercise of the employees' guaranteed right of self-organization. Here the union which the employee solicitors represented was not the bargaining agent for the employees. . . . Indeed the employees did not belong to any union, and the solicitors were therefore strangers to the right of self-organization, absent a showing of non-accessibility amounting to a handicap to self-organization. The Board found special circumstances of

33. NLRB v. Seamprufe, 222 Fed. (2d) 858 (1955).

inaccessibility. But we do not think that conclusion is legally justified by the facts.[34]

The union solicitation rule involving department stores falls into a special category. They may prohibit union solicitation on selling floors, even during nonworking hours, because of the presence of customers and the possible loss of business.[35]

When the board finds that the employer's conduct violates the interference, restraint, or coercion section of the Wagner Act, a cease and desist order is issued, which requires the employer to discontinue specific unfair practices. In effect, a cease and desist order is an injunction. Failure of the employer to obey the order may bring about a contempt of court proceeding.

Domination of Unions

Section 8(2) makes it an unfair labor practice for an employer to dominate or interfere with the formation or administration of any labor organization, or to contribute financial or other support to it.

Section 7 guarantees employees complete freedom in the selection of their representatives. One of the chief methods by which employers interfered with this freedom was to create company unions—unions which were mere puppets manipulated by employers. The board considers many factors in determining whether an employer has been guilty of domination, support of a union, or interference in the formation of a union. It is generally held that when an employer has control over the union sitting on the other side of the bargaining table, collective bargaining is a farce and a delusion.

We should note at the outset that an organization of workers limited to the workers of a single employer is lawful provided the employer has not dominated, supported financially, or interfered with the formation of the union.[36]

One of the leading cases on this subject of domination is NLRB v. Pennsylvania Greyhound Lines.[37] Mr. Justice Stone delivered the opinion of the court.

The main question for decision is whether, upon a finding that an employer has created and fostered a labor organization of employees and dom-

34. For other cases dealing with solicitation of union membership, see NLRB v. LeTourneau Co., 324 U.S. 793 (1941); Marshall Field and Co. v. NLRB, 200 Fed. (2d) 375 (1952); Bonwit Teller Inc. v. NLRB, 197 Fed. (2d) 640 (1952).
35. J. L. Hudson Co., 67 NLRB 1403 (1946); Meier and Frank Co., 89 NLRB 1016 (1950).
36. Greif and Bro. Inc. v. NLRB, 108 Fed. (2d) 551 (1939).
37. 303 U.S. 261 (1938).

inated its administration in violation of section 8(1), (2) of the National Labor Relations Act, the NLRB, in addition to ordering the employer to cease these practices, can require him to withdraw all recognition of the organization as the representative of its employees and to post notices of such withdrawal.

Upon charges filed by Local Division No. 1063, Amalgamated Association of Street, Electric Railway and Motor Coach Employees of America, a labor organization, the Board issued its complaint. . . . After notice to respondents, and hearing, the Board found that they had engaged in unfair labor practices by interfering with, restraining, and coercing employees in the exercise of their rights, guaranteed by section 7, 29 U.S.C.A. sec. 157, in that they had dominated and interfered with the formation and administration of a labor organization of their employees, Employees Association of the Pennsylvania Greyhound Lines, Inc., and had contributed financial and other support to it in violation of section 8(1), (2), 29 U.S.C.A. sec. 158 (1, 2).

The Board ordered that respondents cease each of the specified unfair labor practices. It further ordered that they withdraw recognition from the Employees Association as employee representative authorized to deal with respondents concerning grievances, terms of employment, and labor disputes, and that they post conspicuous notices in all the places of business where such employees are engaged, stating that the "Association is so disestablished and that respondents will refrain from any such recognition thereof." 1 N.L.R.B. 1. . . .

The history of the Act and its language show that its ruling purpose was to protect interstate commerce by securing to employees the rights established by section 7, 29 U.S.C.A. sec. 157, to organize, to bargain collectively through representatives of their own choosing, and to engage in concerted activities for that and other purposes. . . .

Before enactment of the National Labor Relations Act this Court had recognized that the maintenance of a "company union," dominated by the employer, may be a ready and effective means of obstructing self-organization of employees and their choice of their own representatives for the purpose of collective bargaining. . . .

The Board's subsidiary findings of fact fully sustain its conclusion that respondents had engaged in unfair labor practices, by active participation in the organization and administration of the Employees Association, which they dominated throughout its history, and to whose financial support they had contributed; in that they had interfered with, restrained and coerced their employees in the exercise of the rights confirmed by section 7 to form for themselves a labor organization and to bargain collectively through representatives of their own choosing.

It is unnecessary to repeat in full detail the facts disclosed by the findings. They show that before the enactment of the National Labor Relations Act, respondents, whose employees were unorganized, initiated a project for their organization under company domination. In the course of its execution officers or other representatives of respondent were active in promoting the

plan, in urging employees to join, in the preparation of the details of organization, including the by-laws, in presiding over organization meetings, and
in selecting employee representatives of the organization.

The by-laws and regulations provided that all motorbus operators, maintenance men and clerical employees, after three months service, automatically became members of the Association, and that only employees were
eligible to act as employee representatives. No provisions were made for
meetings of members, nor was a procedure established whereby employees
might instruct their representatives, or whereby those representatives might
disseminate information or reports. Grievances were to be taken up with
regional committees with final review by a Joint Reviewing Committee made
up of an equal number of regional chairmen and of management representatives, but review in those cases could not be secured unless there was a joint
submission of the controversy by employee and management representatives.

Change of the by-laws without employer consent was precluded by a provision that amendment should be only on a two-thirds vote of the Joint
Reviewing Committee, composed of equal numbers of employer and employee representatives. Employees paid no dues, all the Association expenses
being borne by the management.

Although the Association was in terms created as a bargaining agency for
the purpose of "providing adequate representation" for respondents' employees by "securing for them satisfactory adjustment of all controversial
matters," it has functioned only to settle individual grievances. On the one
recorded occasion when the employees sought a wage increase, the company
representatives prevented its consideration by refusing to join in the submission to the Joint Reviewing Committee.

In May, 1935, shortly before the passage of the Act, certain of respondents' Pittsburgh employees organized a local union, Local Division No. 1063
of the Amalgamated Association of Street, Electric Railway and Motor
Coach Employees of America, affiliated with the American Federation of
Labor, and continued to hold meetings of the organization after the passage
of the Act on July 5, 1935, 29 U.S.C.A. sec. 151 et seq. Before and after
that date, respondents' officers were active in warning employees against
joining the union and in threatening them with discharge if they should
join and in keeping the union meetings under surveillance. . . .

We may assume that there are situations in which the Board would not
be warranted in concluding that there was any occasion for withdrawal of
employer recognition of an existing union before an election by employees
under section 9(c), 29 U.S.C.A. sec. 159(c), even though it had ordered
the employer to cease unfair labor practices. But here respondents, by unfair
labor practices, have succeeded in establishing a company union so organized
that it is incapable of functioning as a bargaining representative of employees. With no procedure for meetings of members or for instructing employee
representatives, and with no power to bring grievances before the Joint Reviewing Committee without employer consent, the Association could not
without amendment of its by-laws be used as a means of the collective bar-

gaining contemplated by section 7; and amendment could not be had without the employer's approval.[38]

Many acts of the employer are considered in determining whether or not he dominated or interfered with a labor union.

The following illustrate a variety of proscribed employer activities.

(1) Outright formation of a company union by an employer or his agent.[39]

(2) The employer expressing hostility toward an affiliated or "outside" union, assisted its company-union rival.[40]

(3) An employer inducing employees to withdraw their membership in a rival union and encouraging them to join a favored union.[41]

(4) Solicitation of memberships in a company union by supervisory employees constitutes unlawful domination.[42]

(5) A gift of $400 and the right to operate a canteen which made a profit of $50 to $100 monthly was considered evidence of domination.[43]

(6) When employer paid membership dues for every employee who joined the favored union, the board considered this as evidence of domination.[44]

(7) Evidence that all meetings and organizational activities were held on the company property and that officers were paid for time spent in organizing an independent union was found to be evidence of illegality.[45]

(8) When the employer favored an AFL union over a CIO union, gave a list of employees to the AFL union to facilitate their solicitation, and ordered that hiring would be done only through the AFL hiring hall, the board held that the AFL had received illegal assistance.[46]

(9) Absence of any constitution, bylaws, or membership require-

---

38. In NLRB v. Ed. Friedrich Inc., 116 Fed. (2d) 888 (1940), the Circuit Court of Appeals, 5th District, upheld a board finding that the Ed. Friedrich Inc. Employees' Union was company dominated and supported, that a closed-shop agreement between the company and the union was therefore void, and of no effect, and that the company was guilty of unfair labor practices in dominating and supporting the union and in discharging Frank Baranek because he refused to join it, all in violation of Section 8 of the act. The board ordered the company to cease and desist from its unfair labor practices, to withdraw recognition from and disestablish the union as the employees' representative, to reinstate Baranek with back pay without deduction for sums earned by Baranek on work relief projects, and to post the usual notices.

39. Wilson and Co. v. NLRB, 103 Fed. (2d) 243 (1939).

40. Horton-Hubbard Mfg. Co., 94 NLRB 920 (1951).

41. NLRB v. Jack Smith Beverages, 202 Fed. (2d) 100 (1953).

42. Dow Chemical Co. v. NLRB, 117 Fed. (2d) 455 (1941).

43. Connor Foundry Co., 199 NLRB 146 (1952).

44. *Ibid.* 3.

45. Standard Oil Co. of Calif. 62 NLRB 449 (1945).

46. NLRB v. Rooney, 206 Fed. (2d) 730 (1953).

ment, other than employment in the plant in the employee representation plan was considered domination.[47]

(10) Lack of the union's financial independence was evidence of domination.[48]

(11) Complete absence of collective bargaining between a company union and the employer was held evidence of employer domination.[49]

(12) Where the independent associations allowed the employer's personnel director to dispose of employees' grievances unilaterally, the board held it to be illegal.[50]

Whenever the board finds that an employer dominates a union, a disestablishment order is issued, which means that the employer may not deal with the union. When a collective bargaining contract exists between the parties, the board orders that the contract be given no effect.

Where domination has not been proved, but evidence clearly indicates some employer support of the union, the board orders that no recognition be given the union until it has been sanctioned, and certified by the board. Certification usually results after the employees have participated in a secret election conducted by the board.

Discrimination against Unions, Union Activity, and Union Membership

Section 8(3) provides that it is an unfair labor practice for an employer, by discrimination in regard to hire or tenure of employment or any term or condition of employment, to encourage or discourage membership in any labor organization. (There follows authorization for employers to enter into union and closed-shop agreements.)

Discrimination against a person because of his union activities or membership is unlawful because it infringes on the statutorily guaranteed right of workers to join unions and to promote the union movement.

This subsection proscribes discriminatory discharges, layoffs, and demotions, as well as discriminatory withholding of employee benefits such as bonuses, insurance and pension benefits, and wage increases. It is also unlawful to refuse to hire a worker because he is a union member or engaged in union activities. Of course it is necessary to provide evidence that the employer was motivated by antiunion considerations in denying benefits to the employee. It should be noted also that sub-

47. Corson Mfg. Co., 112 NLRB 323 (1955).
48. NLRB v. Continental Box Co., 113 Fed. (2d) 93 (1940).
49. NLRB v. Aluminum Products Co., 120 Fed. (2d) 567 (1941).
50. NLRB v. Kinner Motors Inc., 152 Fed. (2d) 816 (1945).

section (3) makes it unlawful to encourage membership in a particular union as well as to discourage union membership.

The Peoples Motor Express [51] decision is a good example of the employer's violation of this subsection. It should be noted that the facts in the case cover violations of other subsections in Section 8.

DOBIE, C. J. . . . . We are called on to decide whether there was substantial evidence in the record to support the following findings of the Board: (1) That petitioner refused to bargain collectively with Local Union No. 71 of the International Brotherhood of Teamsters, Chauffeurs, Warehousemen and Helpers, affiliated with the American Federation of Labor (hereinafter called the union) in violation of Section 8(5) of the Act; (2) That petitioner, by threats of economic reprisal and other acts and statements indicating hostility to the union and tending to discourage membership therein, restrained and coerced petitioner's employees in violation of Section 8(3) of the Act, discriminatorily discharged employees Humphries, Britt and Moyer, because of their leadership and activities in the union.

Much of the evidence bears on all three of these findings and particularly the first two. On April 2, 1946, seven out of ten of petitioner's employees signed membership application cards designating the union as their collective bargaining representative. On April 6, 1946, employees Humphries, Britt and Moyer, at the request of all the employees, called on James Thrower, petitioner's president and manager, to discuss improvements in working conditions. Thrower immediately manifested anger and said: "If you don't want to work the way I am working, you can get out"; and then to Humphries, spokesman of the group, Thrower stated: "I feel like you are responsible for the whole entire thing, and you are fired now." Britt, upon admitting that he, too, was in the union, was also discharged by Thrower. Moyer then disclosed his union membership and Humphries stated that all of petitioner's drivers and the mechanic had signed union cards. Whereupon Thrower said: "Well, you are all fired. Every man who has his name on a card is fired." Thrower also declared: "Before I will go to a union, I'll park my trucks, close up my warehouse because I have all the money I need."

On April 8, 1946, when Humphries reported the results of this interview with Thrower to petitioner's other employees, they promptly quit work. Upon his arrival at the Charlotte, North Carolina, Terminal that morning, Thrower was informed by Humphries that the men were on strike and that only through the union could the strike be settled. Thrower again expressed his feelings against the union and threatened that he would sell out the business before he would deal with the union. Thrower, however, told Humphries that if the employees would drop any connection with the union then Thrower would sign individual 1-year contracts with them; but when this offer was referred to the employees by Humphries, they rejected the offer and Thrower was told of this rejection.

Later that same day, Herndon (an agent of the Union), accompanied

51. Peoples Motor Express v. NLRB, 165 Fed. (2d) 903 (1948).

by Humphries, Britt and Moyer, went to Thrower's office, identified himself and sought union recognition. There were then 10 employees in the appropriate unit and Herndon showed Thrower union designation of 8 of these employees. Thrower once more refused to recognize, or deal with, the union, reiterating his previous statements that he did not wish his employees to join the union.

Herndon thereupon sought the aid of the United States Conciliation Service. That night, a representative of the Conciliation Service arranged for a conference between the union and Thrower, to take place the following day. At this meeting, held on April 9, 1946, it was agreed to hold a consent election. All eight of the eligible employees voted in this election, held on April 30, 1946, when five employees voted against, and three employees in favor of, the union.

Even in the brief period between Thrower's first interview with Herndon on April 8 and the conference held the next morning, April 9, Thrower endeavored with some success to persuade his employees to sign individual 1-year contracts which provided for better jobs and increased salaries and were conditioned upon the abandonment of the union by these employees. Between the conference and the election, Thrower actively renewed (again with some success) his anti-union tactics, by threats and offer of favorable individual contracts to those employees who would desert the union. On the ground that Thrower's coercive practices had prevented a free election, timely objection to the election of April 30 was filed by the union, and after an investigation, the Regional Director, on June 26, 1946, set aside the election.

Upon such a record, we must hold that there was substantial evidence to support the first two findings of the Board: (1) That petitioner refused to bargain collectively with the union in violation of Section 8(5) of the Act; and (2) That petitioner, by threats of economic reprisal and other anti-union acts and statements, coerced its employees in violation of Section 8(1) of the Act. We, therefore, must uphold these findings and we must grant the enforcement of these parts of the Board's order which directed the petitioner to bargain collectively with the union and to cease and desist from its unfair labor practices, discouraging membership in the union. . . .

This brings us to our last question—(3) Was there substantial evidence to support the Board's finding that petitioner, in violation of Section 8(3) of the Act, discriminatorily discharged employees Humphries, Britt and Moyer because of their activities in the union? Since these three men were discharged at different times, under somewhat different circumstances, we take up each discharge separately.

Humphries was the unquestioned leader of, and spokesman for, the union. That he, to a greater extent than any other employee, vexed Thrower, is hardly open to doubt. At the time of his discharge, May 1, 1946, he had been employed by petitioner as a driver for seven years. On the very day after the election, he was assigned to drive a tractor which was older and less satisfactory than the tractor he had been accustomed to drive. Upon his return from his first run with this inferior tractor, the day after the election,

Humphries reported to Thrower at the Charlotte Terminal and was forth-with discharged by Thrower, who gave no reason for the discharge beyond the bare remark: "I can't use you any more."

Petitioner, at the hearing, for the first time contended that Humphries had been discharged because he had damaged the transmission on the tractor he had been driving. There was nothing in the evidence to show that Humphries had a bad record as a careless driver. During his seven-year term of employment he had been only in very minor (and not unusual) road accidents; furthermore, it was never proved that Humphries was responsible for the damage to the transmission of the tractor.

The long arm of circumstances cannot here be overlooked. A study of the record convinces us that there is substantial evidence to support the Board's finding that Humphries was discriminatorily discharged by petitioner for his union activities. See National Labor Relations Board v. Harris-Woodson Co., 162 F. (2d) 97, 100; North Carolina Finishing Co. v. National Labor Relations Board, 133 F. (2d) 714, 717.

The discharge of Britt occurred on May 4, 1946, only three days after the discharge of Humphries. Next to Humphries, Britt seems to have been the most active supporter of the union. On May 4, Thrower showed Britt a manifest dated January 31 and inquired about four tires listed in the manifest, which (according to the allegations of Thrower) had never been delivered. Once before, prior to the advent of the union into the picture, Britt had been questioned by Thrower concerning these tires and his explanation (which was corroborated) had apparently been accepted by Thrower.

After a brief argument, when this old affair was revived by Thrower on May 4 (four days after the election), Thrower remarked that he, himself, would have to drive the truck assigned to Britt as he was not making any money on it, and he forthwith discharged Britt upon the spot. Britt's offer to check the manifest was summarily rejected and when Britt returned to the terminal two days later (the following Monday) with the purpose of tracing the shipment in question, he was told that petitioner could not find this manifest and that Thrower had issued instructions that Humphries and Britt were not to be permitted on the premises of petitioner.

The evidence here does not satisfactorily prove that these tires were actually lost, much less that any negligent conduct of Britt contributed to the loss. No documentary evidence whatever was introduced to support Thrower's allegations about the tires. The Board doubted that Thrower even believed that Britt was responsible for the loss of the tires. There is real significance in the time that Thrower elected to revive an ancient (and apparently forgotten) complaint, and make it serve as the proffered excuse or reason for Britt's discharge.

We must hold, therefore, that the Board's finding as to Britt, of discriminatory discharge due to union activity, has substantial support in the evidence. See National Labor Relations Board v. Fairmont Creamery Co., 143 F. (2d) 668, 672, cert. denied, 323 U.S. 752; Hartsell Mills Co. v. National Labor Relations Board, 111 F. (2d) 291, 292.

Finally we come to the discharge of Moyer, whose employment by petitioner covered the period from January to June, 1946. His treatment by

Thrower, in the period right after the election, is in striking contrast to the treatment handed out to Humphries and Britt. A more desirable job was given to Moyer with a weekly salary increase from $45 to $65. After Moyer had been working at this new job for about three weeks, the truck he was driving was involved in a traffic accident which resulted in a dented fender. Thrower was not satisfied with Moyer's explanation of the accident.

Had Thrower been waiting for a pretext for Moyer's discharge, here it was. Moyer, however, was taken off the road and put to work, at a reduced salary, in the garage of the Charlotte Terminal. A few days later, Thrower permitted Moyer to resume his work on the road. Thrower then learned that Moyer had communicated some complaint against petitioner to the Interstate Commerce Commission and Thrower questioned Moyer about this.

On the next Saturday night, which was pay day, Moyer received only $44.70, whereupon he protested to Thrower concerning this alleged underpayment. Thrower then discharged Moyer, and as an excuse or reason for the discharge, Thrower stated that Moyer was unable to get along with Yandal, manager of petitioner's Charlotte Terminal. When Moyer himself was questioned at the hearing as to the reason for his discharge, he testified:

Q. You have testified that you were let go on account of personal reasons between you and Mr. Yandal, it that right, Mr. Moyer? That is all I want to know.

A. You heard what I said first?

Q. What do you say, now?

A. I said Mr. Thrower fired me because me and Mr. Yandal couldn't get along together.

The discharge of Moyer did not occur until the lapse of five weeks from the election and more than four weeks after the discharge of Humphries and Britt. The record discloses no unusual union activity on Moyer's part during the period preceding his discharge. The election, which the Union had lost, had not then been set aside, and with Humphries and Britt out of Thrower's way, his fears as to union domination appear to have been, temporarily at least, lulled into security, and there was no iminent reason demanding the dismissal of Moyer.

We cannot hold that, as to Moyer, there is substantial evidence to support the finding of a majority of the Board that Moyer was discriminatorily discharged for union activities. We agree with the contrary finding of Chairman Herzog of the Board.

Said Circuit Judge Wilber, in National Labor Relations Board v. Citizen-News Co., 134 F. (2d) 970, 974:

Circumstances that merely raise a suspicion that an employer may be activated by unlawful motives (in discharging an employee) are not sufficiently substantial to support a finding.

The request of the Board for the enforcement of its order is granted, save as to that portion of the order which requires the reinstatement with back pay of the employee Moyer; the petition of Peoples Motor Express, Inc., to set aside the Board's order is granted only as to that part of the order dealing with Moyer. The Board's order as to Moyer must be deleted and, with that modification, the order will be enforced.

Order modified and enforced.

The U.S. Supreme Court passed on the issue as to whether an employer might refuse to hire men solely because of their union membership. The decision was rendered in the Phelps Dodge case.[52]

FRANKFURTER, J. The dominating question which this litigation brings here for the first time is whether an employer subject to the National Labor Relations Act may refuse to hire employees solely because of their affiliations with a labor union. . . .

The source of the controversy was a strike, begun on June 10, 1935, by the International Union of Mine, Mill and Smelter Workers at Phelps Dodge's Copper Queen Mine, Bisbee, Arizona. Picketing of the mine continued until August 24, 1935, when the strike terminated. During the strike, the National Labor Relations Act came into force. . . . The basis of the Board's conclusion that the Corporation had committed unfair labor practices in violation of Sec. 8(3) of the Act was a finding, not challenged here, that a number of men had been refused employment because of their affiliations with the Union. Of these men, two, Curtis and Daugherty, had ceased to be in the Corporation's employ before the strike but sought employment after its close. The others, thirty-eight in number, were strikers. To "effectuate the policies" of the Act, Sec. 10(c), the Board ordered the Corporation to offer Curtis and Daugherty jobs and to make them whole for the loss of pay resulting from the refusal to hire them, and it ordered thirty-seven of the strikers reinstated with back pay, and the other striker made whole for loss in wages up to the time he became unemployable. Save for a modification presently to be discussed, the Circuit Court of Appeals enforced the order affecting the strikers but struck down the provisions relating to Curtis and Daugherty. . . .

It is no longer disputed that workers cannot be dismissed from employment because of their union affiliations. Is the national interest in industrial peace less affected by discrimination against union activity when men are hired? The contrary is overwhelmingly attested by the long history of industrial conflicts, the diagnosis of their causes by official investigations, the conviction of public men, industrialists and scholars. Because of the Pullman strike, Congress in the Erdman Act of 1898 prohibited inroads upon the workingman's right of association by discriminatory practices at the point of hiring. Kindred legislation has been put on the statute books of more than half the states. And during the late war the National War Labor Board concluded that discrimination against union men at the time of hiring violated its declared policy that "The right of workers to organize in trade-unions and to bargain collectively . . . shall not be denied, abridged, or interfered with by the employers in any manner whatsoever." Such a policy is an inevitable corollary of the principle of freedom of organization. Discrimination

52. Phelps Dodge Corp. v. NLRB, 313 U.S. 177 (1941).

against union labor in the hiring of men is a dam to self-organization at the source of supply. The effect of such discrimination is not confined to the actual denial of employment; it inevitably operates against the whole idea of the legitimacy of organization. In a word, it undermines the principle which, as we have seen, is recognized as basic to the attainment of industrial peace.

These are commonplaces in the history of American industrial relations. But precisely for that reason they must be kept in the forefront in ascertaining the meaning of a major enactment dealing with these relations. To be sure, in outlawing unfair labor practices Congress did not leave the matter at large. The practices condemned "are strictly limited to those enumerated in Section 8," S. Rep. No. 573, 74th Cong., 1st Sess., P. 8. Section 8(3) is the foundation of the Board's determination that in refusing employment to the two men because of their union affiliations Phelps Dodge violated the Act. And so we turn to its provisions that "It shall be an unfair labor practice for an employer . . . by discrimination in regard to hire or tenure of employment or any term or condition of employment to encourage or discourage membership in any labor organization."

. . . We are asked to read "hire" as meaning that wages paid to an employee so as to make the statute merely forbid discrimination in one of the terms of men who have secured employment. So to read the statute would do violence to a spontaneous textual reading of Sec. 8(3) in that "hire" would serve no function because, in the sense which is urged upon us, it is included in the prohibition against "discrimination in regard to . . . any term or condition of employment." Contemporaneous legislative history, and, above all, the background of industrial experience, forbid such textual mutilation.

The natural construction which the text, the legislative setting and the function of the statute command, does not impose an obligation on the employer to favor union members in hiring employees. He is as free to hire as he is to discharge employees. The statute does not touch "the normal exercise of the right of the employer to select its employees or to discharge them." It is directed solely against the abuse of that right by interfering with the countervailing right of self-organization. . . .

Reinstatement is the conventional correction for discriminatory discharges. Experience having demonstrated that discrimination in hiring is twin to discrimination in firing, it would indeed be surprising if Congress gave a remedy for the one which it denied for the other. The powers of the Board as well as the restrictions upon it must be drawn from 10(c), which directs the Board "to take such affirmative action, including reinstatement of employees with or without back pay, as will effectuate the policies of this Act." It could not be seriously denied that to require discrimination in hiring or firing to be "neutralized," Labor Board v. Mackay Co., 304 U.S. 333, 348, by requiring the discrimination to cease not abstractly but in the concrete victimizing instances, is an "affirmative action" which "will effectuate the policies of this Act." Therefore, if Sec. 10(c) had empowered the Board to "take such affirmative action as will effectuate the policies of this Act," the right to restore to a man employment which was wrongfully denied him could hardly be doubted. Even without such a mandate from Congress this Court compelled reinstatement to enforce the legislative policy against discrimination represented by the Railway Labor Act. Texas & N.O.R. Co. v. Railway Clerks, 281 U.S. 548. . . . To differentiate between discrimination in denying employment and in terminating it, would be a differentiation not only without substance but in defiance of that against which the prohibition of discrimination is directed.

As part of its remedial action against the unfair labor practices, the Board ordered that workers who had been denied employment be made whole for their loss of pay. In specific terms, the Board ordered payment to the men of a sum equal to what they normally would have earned from the date of the discrimination to the time of employment less their earnings during this period. The court below added a further deduction of amounts which the workers "failed without excuse to earn," and the Board here challenges this modification.

Making the workers whole for losses suffered on account of an unfair labor practice is part of the vindication of the public policy which the Board enforces. . . .

The decree below should be modified in accordance with this opinion.

OTHER FORMS OF UNLAWFUL DISCRIMINATION. (1) Where a strike has been caused by the employer's unfair labor practices, it is guilty of discrimination when it hires new employees in preference to strikers who are willing to return.[53]

(2) Failure to reinstate locked-out employees who failed to sign loyalty cards to the company constitutes discrimination.[54]

(3) An employer may not condition reinstatement on renunciation of employee's union affiliation.[55]

(4) The transfer of an employee to a position for which he is not fitted or which is less desirable is discriminatory where such action is taken because of union activities.[56]

(5) When an employer locked out employees allegedly because of low inventory and poor business conditions, it acted discriminatorily when the primary reason for the lockout was discouragement of union membership.[57]

(6) The employer's claim that the employee was discharged for falsifying his employment application and denying a criminal record was a pretext in view of the employer's antiunion bias and his knowledge of the employee's union activities.[58]

UNLAWFUL DISCRIMINATION FOR FILING CHARGES OR GIVING TESTIMONY AGAINST AN EMPLOYER. The act gives power to the

53. NLRB v. Stilley Plywood Co., 199 Fed. (2d) 319 (1952).
54. L. B. Hosiery Co., 88 NLRB 1000 (1950).
55. Mathews Lumber Co., 96 NLRB 322 (1951).
56. Ford Motor Co., 50 NLRB 534 (1943).
57. American Radiator Co., 7 NLRB 1127 (1938).
58. Photoswitch, 99 NLRB 1366 (1952).

NLRB to subpoena witnesses and provides that the board shall protect such witnesses. Section 8, subsection (4), makes it an unfair labor practice for an employer "to discharge or otherwise discriminate against an employee because he has filed charges or given testimony under this Act."

The circuit court of appeals ruled on this section in the case of NLRB v. Northwestern Mutual Fire Ass'n.[59]

HEALY, C. J. This is a petition of the National Labor Relations Board for the enforcement of an order entered upon the Board's determination that respondents had engaged in unfair labor practices affecting commerce. . . .

One Sylvester, a salaried salesman of respondent insurance companies, undertook to organize a union of the home office employees as an affiliate of the American Federation of Labor. The work of recruiting membership proceeded quietly and with a considerable measure of success. Plans were announced for the holding of a general meeting of all employees at a local [Seattle] hotel on the evening of December 4, 1940, for the purpose of perfecting the organization. When news of the proposed meeting reached the respondents' governing staff, directions were given to two supervisory employees—the assistant treasurer and the personnel manager—to attend and report their observations to Mr. Brill, the secretary of the companies. The two appeared at the meeting, at which a large group of employees were in attendance as was also a representative of the AFL. During the course of the meeting the two supervisors were requested to leave and did so. Following their departure a number of those present signed membership application cards.

Next morning the supervisory employees reported the results of their surveillance to the governing staff, giving the names of those present at the meeting and describing its course. The staff then directed to the various department heads a written notice stating that if their views were asked with reference to the forming of the union the reply was to be that "under the law the company is not permitted to give advice on the subject." The notice was not . . . communicated to the employees themselves.

During the course of the morning of December 5th, Crisman, the sales agency manager, was informed by Sylvester of the formation of the union. When told who some of the joining members were, Crisman observed to Sylvester, "You sure got a low-minded bunch in that union." This conversation was shortly reported to Fletcher, Crisman's superior in the agency department, and later to respondents' secretary, Brill. Fletcher at once telephoned Sylvester's wife and brother in a patent effort to exert outside pressure on Sylvester. The wife in effect declined to intercede, but the brother, who was an attorney representing several insurance companies, immediately got in touch with Sylvester and sought to persuade him to drop the union, saying that a continuance of his activities would embarrass the brother. The pressure, so the Board found, was renewed later in the day through respondent Greenwood, the manager of the building occupied by respondent companies. Greenwood appears to have gone to considerable lengths, by threats

59. 142 Fed. (2d) 866 (1944).

and otherwise, to dissuade Sylvester from further participation in the union movement and his efforts were not without the desired effect. In the course of the evening Greenwood telephoned Brill at the latter's home stating, in substance, that Sylvester was at his office, that he, Sylvester, had been doing some work "that he was not particularly proud of and that he wanted to come out and make amends and apologize and forget the whole business." Brill assented to the proposed visit of the two men and at Greenwood's telephoned suggestion had a fire lit in the fireplace when they arrived. At the session of the three in Brill's house, Sylvester produced the union cards signed by some 95 employees and burned all but a few of them in the fireplace.

From the testimony relating to the session in Brill's home it is plain that this high official was aware of the pressure being exerted by Greenwood upon Sylvester and that Brill did nothing to discourage it. As Sylvester was leaving the house Brill patted him on the back and told him to forget it, "that we all make mistakes some time or other." There is undisputed evidence that Greenwood had long been closely associated with the officials of respondent companies and was deeply in the latter's debt financially and otherwise. The Board inferred, and the inference is a fair one, that Greenwood's activities in squelching Sylvester had Brill's approval and at least his passive cooperation. Since Greenwood was found to have acted in the interest of the companies, the Board determined that he was an employer within the meaning of Sec. 2(2) of the Act, 29 U.S.C.A. Sec. 152(2).

With the collapse of Sylvester, the unionization movement subsided, and there followed immediately a counter drive to set up an independent association among the employees. The Board found that the establishment of the latter association was aided by the respondents' demonstrated antagonism toward the AFL union and its leader and by their active assistance in soliciting members for the association; also that the administration of the so-called independent union was completely dominated and controlled by representatives of the respondents. . . . The propriety of the cease and desist order is not open to serious doubt.

We have felt some hesitation as to a third provision of the order. This relates to the reinstatement of an employee named O'Connell. O'Connell had been in the employ of respondents since 1934, and for more than four years had been assistant cashier of the companies. He was one of the leaders —second only to Sylvester—in the abortive AFL movement. In January, 1941, with the establishment of the independent association or company union, O'Connell became chairman of a small remnant still adhering to the AFL group. In the spring of that year he was transferred to the auditing department over his protest that he had no training in that work and that his transfer would result in loss of compensation he had been receiving for overtime. Thereafter the post of assistant treasurer became vacant several times, but requests of O'Connell to be restored to the post were disregarded. There is no evidence that O'Connell had not performed efficiently the duties of assistant treasurer, and it is clear that his removal from that position was a demotion. The Board inferred that he had been demoted and refused reinstatement because of his lack of interest in the independent association and because of his activities in behalf of the AFL union. We think the inference is substantially supported.

When the present proceeding was being heard before an examiner, O'Connell was called as a Board witness and testified in a manner unfavorable to the respondents. On cross-examination he was asked whether he had not, a few days earlier, supplied a list of the names and addresses of company employees to one Hughes, an AFL organizer. He denied having done so. He also said that he had had nothing to do with the sending of notices for a proposed meeting of the AFL. After the noon recess O'Connell returned to the stand at his own request and stated that, in the interest of shielding a fellow employee who had aided him, he had earlier given incorrect testimony; that he had in fact submitted an employee mailing list to an AFL organizer named Lamberton; that he had compiled the list in part from a file in the mailing room of the respondent companies; and that Lamberton had used the list in mailing notices of a meeting at which the existing employee association was to be attacked as company-dominated.

Next morning Brill summoned O'Connell and informed him that he was being discharged immediately, Brill stating that he would not "tolerate an untruthful employee in my office." The following day Brill recalled O'Connell and said "I want you to know that we are not dismissing you because you told a lie in court; but the reason is because you gave information in our records to others."

From the evidence before it, the Board was not persuaded that the list obtained and given out by O'Connell was in fact confidential matter. It found that in any event "the unexplained inconsistency of the respondents' reasons for discharging O'Connell negatives the claim that he was discharged for either of these reasons," and that his employment was terminated because the companies had learned from his testimony that he "was taking an active part in the (AFL) Union's attempt to revive interest among their employees." Respondents were ordered to reinstate O'Connell upon request and to make him whole for any loss of pay he might have suffered by reason of his discharge.

On the whole record we are not able to say that the finding is unsupported or the order improper. It is the province of the Board, not of the courts, to determine what affirmative action will effectuate the policies of the Act.

Decree will be entered enforcing the Board's order in all respects.

OTHER UNLAWFUL DISCRIMINATORY ACTS UNDER SECTION 8, SUBSECTION (4). (1) Although supervisory officials are not covered under this subsection, the subpoena power given to the board allowed it to protect supervisors who were called as witnesses.[60]

(2) When an employer discharged a woman immediately following her husband's filing of charges against the employer, the discharge was discriminatory.[61]

60. Pedersen v. NLRB, 234 Fed. (2d) 417 (1956).
61. Serv-Air Aviation, 111 NLRB 689 (1955).

(3) The demotion of an employee following his testimony before the board was unlawful.[62]

(4) An employee's layoff a few days after he had given testimony before the board was discriminatory.[63]

(5) The act was violated when the employee was threatened with physical harm and legal action if he gave testimony to the board against his employer.[64]

(6) Singling out an employee who had testified at a board proceeding, and transferring him to a less desirable job was unlawful.[65]

(7) The employer's belief that the charges filed with the board were false was no justification for discharging the employee who filed them.[66]

Whenever the NLRB determines that an employer has violated Section 8, subdivision (1), (3), or (4), a remedial order under Section 10(c) is issued requiring the employer to:

(1) Reinstate the employee to his former position with all benefits formerly enjoyed by the employee.

(2) Cease and desist in committing unlawful acts.

(3) Pay all wages lost by the employee as a result of the unfair labor practice. (This is known as a "back-pay award.") The period for which the board grants back pay is from the discharge date to the date of the employer's reinstatement offer. In a back-pay order the board attempts as nearly as possible to have the employer reimburse the employee to the amount he would have earned if the employer had not committed the unfair practice.

(4) Post notices prepared by the board in conspicious places about the employer's premises that he will not engage in any of the specific unfair labor practices.

Employer's Refusal to Bargain Collectively

It is an unfair labor practice for an employer "To refuse to bargain collectively with the representatives of his employees, subject to the provisions of Section 9(a)."

The two basic rights the act seeks to protect are the right to organize and the right to bargain collectively. The preamble of the act emphasizes that a principal objective is to promote collective bargaining, which Congress believed minimized industrial conflict and reduced interference with interstate commerce. Congress also believed that compelling

---

62. NLRB v. American Rolbal Corp., 141 Fed. (2d) 1023 (1944).
63. Calif. Cotton Cooperative Ass'n, 110 NLRB 1494 (1954).
64. Mansfield Mills, 3 NLRB 901 (1937).
65. South Jersey Coach Lines, 92 NLRB 791 (1950).
66. Kramer Co., 29 NLRB 921 (1941).

an employer to bargain would help eliminate recurring business depressions and give workers uninterrupted purchasing power.

What employer activities constitute a refusal to bargain collectively?

One of the leading cases on the subject is H. J. Heinz Co. v. NLRB [67] which was reviewed by the Supreme Court.

Mr. Justice Stone delivered the opinion of the court.

Three questions are presented by the petition for certiorari in this case. . . .

THIRD. Whether the Board could validly find that petitioner's refusal to join with representatives of the labor organization authorized to represent its employees in collective bargaining, in signing a written contract embodying the terms of their agreement concerning wages, hours and working conditions, constituted a refusal to bargain collectively in violation of section 8(5) of the Act, and whether the Board exceeded its authority in ordering petitioner to join in signing the agreement. . . .

The Board found that during April and May, 1937, the two rival labor organizations, the Association and the Union, sought to organize petitioner's employees at its Pittsburgh plant. Petitioner's proposal that an election be held to determine which organization represented a majority of its employees was rejected by the Union which called a strike on May 24, 1937. The strike was ultimately settled by a written contract signed by petitioner, the Union, and the Association, which provided for an election, by the employees, under the supervision of a regional director of the National Labor Relations Board for the choice of an organization to represent them in collective bargaining. Meanwhile, and before the election, a majority of petitioner's two thousand employees at the Pittsburgh plant had signed petitions for membership in the Association, but upon the election held June 8, 1937, a majority of the employees cast their ballots for the Union. Petitioner has since recognized and bargained with the Union, but has refused to embody its agreement with the Union in a written contract. . . .

THE EMPLOYER'S REFUSAL TO SIGN A WRITTEN AGREEMENT. It is conceded that although petitioner has reached an agreement with the Union concerning wages, hours and working conditions of the employees, it has nevertheless refused to sign any contract embodying the terms of the agreement. The Board supports its order directing petitioner, on request of the Union, to sign a written contract embodying the terms agreed upon on the ground, among others, that a refusal to sign is a refusal to bargain within the meaning of the Act.

In support of this contention it points to the history of the collective bargaining process showing that its object has long been an agreement between employer and employees as to wages, hours and working conditions evidenced by a signed contract of statement in writing, which serves both as recognition of the union with which the agreements is reached and as a permanent memorial of its terms. This experience has shown that refusal to sign a written contract has been a not infrequent means of frustrating the

67. 311 U.S. 514 (1941).

bargaining process through the refusal to recognize the labor organization as a party to it and the refusal to provide an authentic record of its terms which could be exhibited to employees, as evidence of the good faith of the employer. Such refusals have proved fruitful sources of dissatisfaction and disagreement. Contrasted with the unilateral statement by the employer of his labor policy, the signed agreement has been regarded as the effective instrument of stabilizing labor relations and preventing, through collective bargaining, strikes and industrial strife.

We think that Congress, in thus incorporating in the new legislation the collective bargaining requirement of the earlier statutes, included as a part of it the signed agreement long recognized under the earlier acts as the final step in the bargaining process. It is true that the National Labor Relations Act, while requiring the employer to bargain collectively, does not compel him to enter into an agreement. But it does not follow, as petitioner argues, that, having reached an agreement, he can refuse to sign it, because he has never agreed to sign one. He may never have agreed to bargain but the statute requires him to do so. To that extent his freedom is restricted in order to secure the legislative objective of collective bargaining as the means of curtailing labor disputes affecting interstate commerce. The freedom of the employer to refuse to make an agreement relates to its terms in matters of substance and not, once it is reached, to its expression in a signed contract, the absence of which, as experience has shown, tends to frustrate the end sought by the requirement for collective bargaining. A business man who entered into negotiations with another for an agreement having numerous provisions, with the reservation that he would not reduce it to writing or sign it, could hardly be thought to have bargained in good faith. This is even more so in the case of an employer who, by his refusal to honor, with his signature, the agreements which he has made with a labor organization, discredits the organization, impairs the bargaining process and tends to frustrate the aim of the statute to secure industrial peace through collective bargaining.

Petitioner's refusal to sign was a refusal to bargain collectively and an unfair labor practice defined by Section 8(5). The Board's order requiring petitioner at the request of the Union to sign a written contract embodying agreed terms is authorized by Section 10(c). This is the conclusion which has been reached by five of the six courts of appeals which have passed upon the question. Affirmed.

Some of the subject matters on which an employer was required to bargain are wages, seniority rights, rates of pay, hours of employment, merit increases, incentive pay, holidays, vacations, bonuses, working conditions, welfare benefits, pensions, insurance plans, profit-sharing, layoffs, and grievance procedures.

In an authoritative case [68] involving subjects for collective bargaining, the employer insisted that its collective bargaining contract include (1) a "ballot clause calling for a pre-strike secret vote of the employees

68. NLRB v. Wooster Division of Borg Warner Corp., 356 U.S. 342 (1958).

(union and non-union) as to acceptance or rejection of the employer's last offer," and (2) a "recognition clause which excluded, as a party to the contract, the International Union which had been certified by the National Labor Relations Board as the employees' exclusive bargaining agent, and substituted for it the agent's uncertified local affiliate." The board held that the employer's insistence upon either of such clauses amounted to a refusal to bargain in violation of Section 8(a)(5) of the act.

The question was whether either of these clauses came within the scope of mandatory collective bargaining as defined in Section 8(d) of the act, as amended. The U.S. Supreme Court agreed with the National Labor Relations Board's decision that neither clause came within that definition. The court ruled that under the National Labor Relations Act establishing the obligation of employers and employee-designated unions to meet and bargain, the duty to bargain was limited to subjects which fall within the categories of "wages, hours, and other terms and conditions of employment," and, as neither party was legally obligated to reach an agreement or yield to the other party's demand, either party might insist on the adoption of its position on a subject within this area of mandatory bargaining as a condition to the execution of a written contract. Mr. Justice Burton, who wrote the court's opinion, stated that the clauses sought to be incorporated into the agreement by the employer's insistence were not subjects within the statutory phrase "wages, hours, and other terms and conditions of employment." However, the court did point out that when parties desire to bargain voluntarily on nonobligatory matters, and include them in a labor contract, such clauses are enforcible.

The following employer activities have been construed to be refusals to bargain:

(1) The employer refusing to furnish a union with salary information.[69]

(2) The employer ignoring the union's request to bargain.[70]

(3) The employer stating to the union representative that he would meet with the union, but nothing would be accomplished, was indicative of bad faith.[71]

(4) Denying the union the right to represent employees in grievance matters.[72]

(5) Failing to reply to a union letter requesting that the time and place of a meeting be set for negotiations.[73]

69. 57,456 C.Ch. (1960).
70. NLRB v. Somerville Brick Co., 194 Fed. (2d) 56 (1952).
71. Maurice Embroidery Works, 111 NLRB 1143 (1955).
72. Gagon Plating and Mfg. Co., 103 NLRB 263 (1953).
73. Republican Publishing Co., 73 NLRB 1085 (1947).

(6) When the employer was too busy to give the union a few days of his time, it was his duty to appoint a fully authorized representative to negotiate in his place.[74]

(7) The failure of the employer over a 15-month bargaining period to make one written counter-proposal to the union when the union had submitted three drafts of a contract was construed to be bad faith.[75]

(8) When the company submitted counter-proposals which served only to create unnecessary issues and to delay negotiations leading to a contract, the board held that such conduct indicated the employer at no time intended to bargain in good faith with the union.[76]

(9) The failure of the employer and the union to reach an agreement because of an impasse with respect to check-off, super-seniority, and union liability for strikes did not establish a refusal to bargain where the parties had reached agreement with respect to other issues.[77]

(10) Employer unlawfully insisted that the contract permit it to have unilateral control over wages, hours, conditions of employment, and grievances. The board held that no subject for collective bargaining would have remained.[78]

(11) The employer's insistence on a "settlement clause," which was equivalent to the demand that the union abandon its unfair practice charges, was unlawful.[79]

(12) The employer may not condition bargaining negotiations on return of strikers to work.[80]

(13) When the employer informed the union that he would deal with the union only after it organized the employer's competitors, the board sustained charges of refusal to bargain.[81]

(14) The union had a right to bargain for strikers as well as non-strikers. The employer's refusal to bargain was unlawful when he insisted on bargaining for nonstrikers only.[82]

(15) The employer's insistence on anti-Communist pledges from union officials and on their recognition of the free-enterprise system was unlawful.[83]

(16) The employer's insistence that he would have to know what the union's demands were before he would bargain was an unjustified condition.[84]

74. Paterson Steel and Forge Co., 96 NLRB 129 (1951).
75. Benson Produce Co., 71 NLRB 888 (1946).
76. NLRB v. Norfolk Shipbuilding and Drydock Corp., 172 Fed. (2d) 813 (1949).
77. Anchor Rome Mills, 86 NLRB 1120 (1949).
78. Dixie Corp., 105 NLRB 49 (1953).
79. Heider Mfg. Co., 91 NLRB 1185 (1950).
80. West Coast Luggage Co., 105 NLRB 414 (1953).
81. Newton Chevrolet Co., 37 NLRB 334 (1941).
82. Knight Morley Corp., 116 NLRB 140 (1956).
83. Standard Generator Service Co., 90 NLRB 790 (1950).
84. Palm Beach Broadcasting Corp., 63 NLRB 597 (1945).

(17) A union was entitled to information in employer's possession as to wage rates and increases, since it obviously could not intelligently bargain without this knowledge.[85]

(18) If employer claims financial inability to meet the union's demands, employer has duty to provide proof of its lack of ability.[86]

(19) A unilateral wage increase constituted a refusal to bargain.[87]

(20) Granting a bonus during negotiations without notifying or consulting the union constituted a refusal to bargain in good faith.[88]

(21) The employer's refusal to process pending grievances with the union acting as the employee's representative was unlawful.[89]

(22) Discriminatory discharge of the union negotiator during contract negotiations was considered as determining that the employer was not bargaining in good faith.[90]

(23) The employer was guilty of refusing to bargain when it supported and assisted an employee committee and bargained directly with employees during negotiations for new contract with the incumbent union.[91]

The NLRB has statutory discretion in determining the necessary measures to neutralize the employer's refusal to bargain in good faith. Its order may require the employer to cease and desist from its refusal. If the unfair practice has resulted in a strike, the board may order the strikers reinstated with back pay.

Since interference, restraint, and coercion is a catch-all unfair labor practice, a finding that the employer violated one of the other subdivisions of Section 8(a) will also support the inference that it interfered in contravention of Section 8(a)(1). For example, an employer who violates the act by refusing to bargain in good faith is ordinarily guilty of unlawful interference as well, since the refusal to bargain has an adverse effect on the right of employees to bargain collectively.

Employee Representation

Section 9 of the Wagner Act has four subdivisions, (a) to (d).

Subsection (a) provides that the majority of an appropriate bargaining unit shall select the bargaining representative. (This is known as the majority rule doctrine.)

85. Electric Auto-Lite Co., 89 NLRB 1192 (1950).
86. Truitt Mfg. Co. v. NLRB, 351 U.S. 149 (1956).
87. Hexton Furniture Co., 111 NLRB 342 (1955).
88. De Diego Taxi Cabs Inc., 107 NLRB 1026 (1954).
89. U.S. Gypsum Co., 90 NLRB 964 (1950).
90. *Ibid.*, 7.
91. Multi-Color Co., 114 NLRB 1129 (1955).

Subsection (b) vests authority in the board to determine the appropriate bargaining unit.

Subsection (c) gives the board the power to investigate and certify bargaining representatives and allows the board to use the secret ballot or "any other suitable method" to ascertain the employees' choice of a bargaining representative.[92]

Subsection (d) provides that whenever a board order arising out of an unfair labor practice is filed for action with the circuit court of appeals a transcript of the board record shall become part of the record on appeal.

The board's two functions are:

(1) to prevent and remedy unfair labor practices of employers.

(2) to determine on application whether or not employees want a union, and, when two or more unions are seeking to become the bargaining agent, to determine which union shall have the exclusive right to act as the representative. (Only one union may represent the workers in a specific bargaining unit.)

Whenever a union obtains a board certification it is assured representative status for at least one year, during which a rival union may not seek bargaining rights.

An election is preceded by a group of employees or a union filing a certification petition with the board. The petition is investigated by the board; if it meets board requirements and discloses that a representation question does exist, the board calls in the employer and the union to ascertain the method of resolving the representation issue. If both parties agree to an election, the board conducts a consent election. If either party objects to a consent election, the matter is set down for a formal hearing in the office of the regional director.

Whenever a hearing takes place the parties are permitted to present their respective positions supported by evidence, written or oral. Oral arguments before the board often conclude the hearing, although written briefs are frequently filed. During the period when the Wagner Act was effective, strict rules of evidence were not adhered to by the parties; quite frequently petitions were processed without benefit of legal counsel. Since the 1947 amendments legal formalities have been required.

On the conclusion of the board hearing, an order is issued directing an election or dismissing the petition; when an election is directed, the board selects the time and place for the election. Usually it is conducted at the employer's place of business, and the employer provides the board with a list of employees on his payroll as of a certain date. Prior to the election the union, and frequently the employer, engages in a propa-

92. Prior to 1939 the board would recognize union membership cards and other written or oral proof under the majority rule, and certification would be based on this proof. After 1939 the board has relied upon elections, particularly when a contesting union or an employer requested an election.

ganda campaign. On the day of the election the parties may designate election observers to oversee the election, and the employees now have the opportunity to vote for or against union representation. When the election has been concluded, a tally of votes is made and the result is disclosed to all the parties on the ballot.

If a union receives a majority of the votes cast in the election, it receives board certification. If a majority of the voters cast votes for no union, the board will certify that no union was chosen by the employees.

After the election either party may file objections for a multitude of reasons. For example, a union losing an election may seek to nullify the result by charging that the employer increased wages the day before the election, or that the employer coerced the workers into voting against the union.

The board's representation determinations are not subject to court review and only infrequently do the courts disturb bargaining-unit decisions made by the board.

Filing Petition for Election: Bargaining Units

In representation cases the board machinery begins operation only when a verified petition is filed by an employee, an employer, or a labor union acting for the employees. The petition indicates that interstate commerce is involved, the bargaining unit seeking representation, the percentage of employees the petitioner claims to represent,[93] and other relevant information.

Intervening parties are permitted to participate in certification elections if they show a contractual or other representative interest. An intervenor seeking a unit other than that sought by the petitioner must make a showing.

The sufficiency of a party's showing of interest is determined administratively and may not be litigated at the representation hearing.[94]

The board has kept in force its long-standing policy not to direct an election among employees presently covered by a valid collective-bargaining contract, except when certain conditions exist.[95] The contract must be in writing and executed. It must be broad enough in scope to promote the day-to-day bargaining relationship. Finally, the

93. Under the Wagner Act no specific percentage of interest was required. Since 1947 the board has required that the petitioner, other than an employer, show that at least 30% of those in the unit favor the petitioner.
94. Plains Cooperative Oil Mill, 123 NLRB 1709 (1959).
95. For exceptions to the general rule, see The Grand Union Co., 123 NLRB 1665 (1959); Appalachian Shale Products Co., 121 NLRB 1160 (1957); General Extrusion Co. Inc., 121 NLRB 1165 (1957); Pacific Coast Ass'n of Pulp and Paper Mfrs., 121 NLRB 990 (1957); Hershey Chocolate Corp., 121 NLRB 901 (1957); Nelson Name Plate Co., 122 NLRB 467 (1958).

contract must cover a proper bargaining unit and the employees who have sought to be represented by a bargaining agent.

The act provides that the NLRB must determine the unit appropriate for collective bargaining; whether it shall be industrial, including practically every worker in the plant; craft, including one group of skilled workers; or some other group which includes only a part of the workers. The board must decide also whether the bargaining unit shall include only one plant of the employer, or all the company's plants, or a group of separate and independent companies.

Whenever the board conducts a hearing to resolve a unit problem, it considers the history of collective bargaining in the plant and in similar plants of the industry and the common employment interests of the group involved, as well as the desires of the employees.

CRAFT UNITS. Requests for the establishment of craft units, or the severance of craft groups from existing larger units, must meet the following tests: [96] (1) The unit must be composed of true craft employees, and (2) a union seeking to sever a craft group from a broader existing unit must have traditionally devoted itself to serving the special interests of the type of employee involved. One of the earliest, landmark cases concerned with a craft bargaining unit is *In the matter of* Globe Machine and Stamping Co.[97]

On May 13, 1937, Metal Polishers Union, Local No. 3, herein called the Polishers Union, International Association of Machinists, District No. 54, herein called the I.A.M., and Federal Labor Union 18788, herein called the Federal Local, filed separate petitions with the Regional Director for the Eighth Region (Cleveland, Ohio), alleging that questions affecting commerce had arisen concerning the representation of employees. . . .

The three unions who filed petitions in this proceeding are all labor organizations affiliated with the American Federation of Labor. Local No. 3 of the Polishers Union includes members who are working in various plants in Cleveland. It claims jurisdiction over the polishers and buffers at the Company's plant. The I.A.M. limits its jurisdiction to the punch press operators. Its members at the Company's plant are in five or six different locals, all within District No. 54. The Federal Local claims the balance of the production and maintenance workers. Its membership is apparently restricted to men working at the Company's plant.

The U.A.W.A. is a labor organization affiliated with the Committee for Industrial Organization. It admits to membership all of the employees of the Company who are included within the three groups claimed by the petitioning unions. It appears to have a separate Local, No. 243, for employees of the Company.

96. For a leading case see American Potash and Chemical Corp., 107 NLRB 1418 (1954).
97. 3 NLRB 294 (1937).

During the period from 1933 to late in 1936, practically all of the employees engaged in production and maintenance were in one of the three unions. . . .

The Polishers Union, the I.A.M., and U.A.W.A. placed membership lists in evidence. No list was submitted by or for the Federal Local. The Polishers Union list includes members in good standing who were working for the Company as of the beginning of 1937. It has 59 names. The I.A.M. list contains 95 names of members who were working at the plant on May 13, the date of the petitions. The U.A.W.A. list includes all paid up members of the local at the Company's plant. It lists 35 polishers, and 119 in the press room. The total for all departments is 687. . . .

The petitioning unions claim that there are three separate units for collective bargaining in this plant. The U.A.W.A. contends that the plant cannot be subdivided as claimed and that it should be treated as one unit. All parties are agreed that there should be an election. They are also all agreed that eligibility should be based on the payroll for the week including May 13, 1937, the date of the petitions, and such a payroll has been supplied by the Company.

The Company's plant has numerous departments, major and minor, through which its products flow in the course of production. A representative of the Company testified that all products go through at least three departments and that a tie-up of one department would tie up the whole plant. A classification list which was placed in evidence shows that many different types of work are done at the plant. . . .

There is a great deal of testimony as to the degree of skill required for polishing and press room work. With regard to polishing it appears that some degree of skill is required for the work done at the Company's plant, although the operations are relatively simple and can be learned rather quickly. A man may become sufficiently adept at the tasks required in the plant without becoming an all-round polisher. However polishers are paid higher wages than are men on the assembly line, and in general, when taking on new men, experienced polishers are sought. Much the same applies to the punch press men. They are termed specialists by the I.A.M. They are not all-round machinists, but rather operators of a particular kind of machine. There was testimony to the effect that a new man would have to work very slowly and the product of his early labor would not be worth very much. There was also evidence, however, that a specialist at one machine within the press room would not necessarily be able to operate any other punch press machine.

In view of the facts described above, it appears that the Company's production workers can be considered either as a single unit appropriate for the purposes of collective bargaining, as claimed by the U.A.W.A., or as three such units, as claimed by the petitioning unions. The history of successful separate negotiations at the Company's plant, and also the essential separateness of polishing and punch press work at that plant, and the existence of a requirement of a certain amount of skill for that work are proof of the feasibility of the latter approach. The successful negotiation of a plant-wide agreement on May 20, 1937, as well as the interrelation and interdependence of the various departments at the Company's plant, are proof of the feasibility of the former.

In such a case where the considerations are so evenly balanced, the determining factor is the desire of the men themselves. On this point, the record affords no help. There has been a swing toward the U.A.W.A. and then away from it. The only documentary proof is completely contradictory. We will therefore order elections to be held separately for the men engaged in polishing and those engaged in punch press work. We will also order an election for the employees of the Company engaged in production and maintenance, exclusive of the polishers and punch press workers and of clerical and supervisory employees.

On the results of these elections will depend the determination of the appropriate unit for the purposes of collective bargaining. Such of the groups as do not choose the U.A.W.A. will constitute separate and distinct appropriate units, and such as do choose the U.A.W.A. will together constitute a single appropriate unit.

Directed that, as part of the investigation authorized by the Board to ascertain representatives for collective bargaining with The Globe Machine and Stamping Co., elections by secret ballot shall be conducted within fifteen (15) days from the date of this Direction, under the direction and supervision of the Regional Director for the Eighth Region, acting in this matter as agent for the National Labor Relations Board, and subject to Article III, Section 9 of said Rules and Regulations, among those employees of The Globe Machine and Stamping Co., who fall within the groups described below who were on the payroll of the Company for the week which included May 13, 1937:

a. Those engaged in polishing and buffing to determine whether they desire to be represented by the Metal Polishers Union, Local No. 3, affiliated with the American Federation of Labor, or the United Automobile Workers of America, affiliated with the Committee for Industrial Organization, for the purposes of collective bargaining.

b. Those engaged in the press room in the operation of punch press machines to determine whether they desire to be represented by International Association of Machinists, District No. 54, affiliated with the American Federation of Labor, or the United Automobile Workers of America, affiliated with the Committee for Industrial Organization, for the purposes of collective bargaining.

c. All other employees engaged in production and maintenance, except supervisory and clerical employees, to determine whether they desire to be represented by Federal Labor Union 18788, affiliated with the American Federation of Labor, or the United Automobile Workers of America, affiliated with the Committee for Industrial Organization, for the purposes of collective bargaining.

A history of collective bargaining on a craft unit basis was sufficient reason for the board's designation of crafts as separate units over the contentions by a rival union for industrial units.[98]

98. Toledo Scale Co., 45 NLRB 472 (1942).

SINGLE- OR MULTIPLE-PLANT UNITS. When the employer operates several plants, the bargaining unit may include the workers (1) in all the plants, (2) in some of the plants, or (3) in one of the plants.

In the case of Hygrade Food Products Corp.,[99] the board held for a single plant unit, rather than one consisting of 13 out of the employer's 60 plants, on the ground that previous labor contracts left much to be negotiated at the local plant level and that there was no clear indication that the parties intended to effect the consolidation of the 13 plant units.

When it held a multiplant-bargaining history to be controlling, even though the bargaining unit did not correspond to any area of the employer's operations, the board stated that it was "reluctant to disturb a pattern of bargaining which has been established with the consent of the employer and without regard for administrative lines over a period of five years.[100]

MULTIPLE-EMPLOYER UNITS. The board has held that a multi-employer unit is appropriate when two companies, although separate legal entities, are closely connected physically, maintain an interchange of employees, and handle labor problems through one person.[101]

In another case it was held that a single two-employer unit was appropriate in view of a common mailing address, telephone listing, office building, and adjacency of plants.[102]

The board has pointed out that to find any multi-employer unit appropriate the following things are essential: (1) a controlling history of bargaining on a multi-employer basis for a substantial period of time, and (2) an unequivocal manifestation by the individual employers of a desire to be bound in future collective bargaining by group rather than individual action.[103]

Investigation and Hearing on Representation Petition

If the petition meets the statutory requirements of the act, the board seeks in an informal conference to get the parties to consent to an election. When the informal settlement fails a formal hearing is scheduled and all questions are resolved then.

99. 85 NLRB (1949).
100. Underwood Corp., 101 NLRB 25 (1952).
101. South Georgia Pecan Co., 85 NLRB 591 (1949).
102. Clay and Bailey Mfg. Co., 106 NLRB 210 (1953).
103. American Publishing Co., 121 NLRB 115 (1958).

Elections

Once the board determines that a representation issue exists, the question must be resolved through a secret ballot election. The election details are left to the broad. Such matters as voting eligibility, timing of elections, and standards of election conduct are subject to rules laid down in the board's Rules and Regulations and in its decisions.

VOTING ELIGIBILITY. A voter must have employee status in the voting unit both on the applicable payroll date and on the date of the election.[104] However, this rule is not applicable in the case of employees who are ill, on vacation, temporarily laid off, or who, in the military service, appear in person at the polls. Strikers are eligible to vote.

In industries where employment is intermittent or seasonal eligibility is adjusted to the particular circumstances.[105]

TIMING OF ELECTIONS. The board directs that elections be held within 30 days from the date of the direction of election. In seasonal industries the election will be timed so as to occur at or near the first peak season following the direction of election.[106]

BALLOTS. The board gives employees both the right to bargain through representatives of their own free choosing and the right to refrain from collective bargaining. Therefore the ballot gives the employees the right to vote "yes" or "no" on the question of representation by a union. Where two or more unions appear on the ballot, the voter has a choice of voting for either union or "none." Ballots are furnished by the board.

STANDARDS OF ELECTION CONDUCT. The board seeks to assure participating employees a free choice in selecting or rejecting a bargaining representative. Any party to an election who believes that board standards were not met may, within five days of the election, file objections to the election with the board. The issues raised by such objections are finally determined by the board.[107]

Election details such as time, place, and notice of an election are left to the board. Invariably the election is held on the premises of the employer, unless the union objects. Utmost care is taken to preserve the secrecy of the ballot by guarding blank ballots and ballot boxes. A board

104. Post Falls Lumber Co., 122 NLRB 157 (1958).
105. Toledo Marine Terminals Inc., 121 NLRB 583 (1957); Independent Motion Picture Producers Ass'n Inc., 123 NLRB 1942 (1959).
106. Tropicana Products Inc., 122 NLRB 121 (1958).
107. See Section 102.69 of the board's *Rules and Regulations*, Series 7 (1961) for procedure in filing objections.

employee acts as custodian of the ballots and is responsible for assuring a fair election.

An election will be set aside if it was accompanied by conduct which, in the board's view, created an atmosphere of confusion or fear of reprisals and thus interfered with the employees' free and untrammeled choice of a representative, as guaranteed by the act.[108]

To insure an atmosphere conducive to a free election the board prohibits the participating parties from making pre-election speeches on company time and property to assemblies of employees within 24 hours of the time scheduled for the election.[109] Solicitation by a union agent of individual employees at their work stations to attend a union meeting, and requests that they vote for the union, were held not to contravene the rule.[110]

The board bars the use of reproductions of the board's official ballot as campaign propaganda, and will set aside an election where this rule is violated.[111]

To insure the employees' right to select or reject collective bargaining representatives in an atmosphere conducive to free expression, the board will set aside elections accompanied by propaganda prejudicial to such expression.[112]

If the board finds that campaign tactics resorted to by a party impaired the employees' free choice, the election will be voided.[113]

Elections have been set aside where attempts were made to influence the results by threats of reprisals or promises of benefits.[114]

WHAT CONSTITUTES A MAJORITY? The act provides that the majority of the appropriate unit shall designate the exclusive bargaining representative. A majority of those voting is sufficient to designate the representative, provided a substantial number of the eligible voted. This rule was adhered to in NLRB v. Standard Lime and Stone Co.[115] The facts of this case are set forth in the decision, which follows.

PARKER, C. J. This is a petition to enforce an order of the National Labor Relations Board directing the Standard Lime and Stone Company to bargain collectively with an A.F. of L. union as the bargaining representative of its employees. The company resists enforcement on the ground that the union has not been chosen as bargaining representative because (1) a ma-

108. Doughboy Plastic Production Inc., 122 NLRB 338 (1958).
109. Peerless Plywood Co., 107 NLRB 427 (1953).
110. Globe Motors Inc., 123 NLRB 30 (1959).
111. Custom Molders of P.R. and Shaw Harrison Corp., 121 NLRB 1007 (1958).
112. Celanese Corp. of America, 121 NLRB 303 (1958).
113. Jasper Wood Products Co., 123 NLRB 28 (1959).
114. Benjamin Elec. Co., 122 NLRB 1517 (1959).
115. 149 Fed. (2d) 435 (1945).

jority of eligible employees did not participate in the election at which the union was chosen, (2) the election was not representative of the choice of the majority, and (3) opportunity was not given, in a run-off election between two unions, to vote against representation by either.

The facts are that a United Mine Workers union petitioned the Board to make an investigation and certify a bargaining representative for the employees of the company. An A.F. of L. union intervened in this proceeding and on April 13, 1943, the Board proceeded to hold an election at which the company's employees were allowed to indicate by secret ballot their choice of the U.M.W. union, the A.F. of L. union or "neither" as bargaining representative. 439 employees were eligible to vote in this election, but only 218 votes were cast. 99 of these were cast for the A.F. of L. union, 62 for the U.M.W. union, and 57 for "neither." The company then asked that the petition be dismissed, but both unions asked that a run-off election be held and, on May 14, 1943, one was held between the two unions, with the "neither" choice eliminated. At the time of the run-off election, 409 employees were eligible and 166 voted, one of the ballots being void. 137 votes were cast for the A.F. of L. union and 28 for the U.M.W. union.

Both elections were fairly advertised and properly held and there is no evidence of coercion or interference on the part of the company or anyone else, and nothing to indicate that they were not fairly representative of the sentiment of the employees. The Board found that the vote was "substantial and representative" and certified the A.F. of L. union as the bargaining representative. The Company's refusal to bargain with the union was found by the Board to be an unfair labor practice and the usual order was entered directing the company to bargain with it.

On the first and principal question, that presented by lack of majority participation in either of the elections, we think that the conclusive answer is found in the decision of the Supreme Court in Virginian Railway v. System Federation No. 40, 300 U.S. 515, affirming the decision of this Court reported in 84 F. 2d 641.

Although there is no decision of the Supreme Court holding that a majority of the votes cast in an election is sufficient for the choice of a bargaining representative under the National Labor Relations Act, this is the holding of the Labor Board and of all the Circuit Courts of Appeals which have had occasion to pass upon the question. . . .

The company seeks to distinguish the Virginian Railway case and certain other of the decisions above cited on the ground that a majority of the employees participated in the elections there; but nothing in the statute furnishes the basis for such distinction. . . .

There is every reason to apply the sensible political rule to elections of this sort, and no reason that we can see to the contrary. The elections are held, not for the purpose of choosing representatives for the employees in their private and personal capacities, but for the purposes of collective bargaining, i.e., for the purpose of setting up industrial democracy by choosing some one to represent the interest of the employee in determining the rate of wages, hours of work, living conditions, etc., for the plant. The establishment of such industrial democracy is the avowed purpose of the National Labor Relations Act, which declares it to be in the public interest because of its tendency to preserve industrial peace and prevent interference with interstate commerce. . . . This being true, it would be as absurd to hold that collective bargaining is defeated because a majority of employees fail to participate in an election of representatives as it would be to hold that the people of a municipality are without officers to represent them because a majority of the qualified voters do not participate in an election held to choose such officers. In the one case, as in the other, the representative is being chosen to represent a constituency because it is in the public interest that the constituency be represented; all that should be necessary is that the election be properly advertised and fairly held and that the settled principle of majority rule be applied to the result. If the employees do not wish to be represented in collective bargaining they can so declare in the election; but where, as here, only a comparatively small number so express themselves the result should not be the same as if a majority had so voted. We pointed out in the Virginian Railway case the disadvantages and dangers which would follow from failure to apply the political rule in such elections.

The contention that the election was not representative is without merit. The Board found that the vote was substantial and representative, and there is nothing in the record to the contrary. The Company's argument on the point resolves itself into a contention that an election should not be permitted to determine a choice unless there is affirmative showing that a majority either participated or was prevented in some way from participating; but there is nothing in the statute or in reason to support such a position. It is for the Board, not us, to say whether an election is fair and representative; and where the record shows that over forty per cent of the company's employees participated in it and that it was fairly advertised and conducted, we cannot say that the Board's finding that it was representative is arbitrary and unreasonable or without support in the record.

And we are not impressed with the contention that the Board's certification may be ignored because "neither" was omitted from the choices submitted in the run-off election. On the first election only 57 of the votes cast registered that choice, which was less than the votes cast for either of the unions. It could not be unreasonable to drop in the run-off the choice which had received the lowest number of votes. This is quite usual procedure in other elections and we can see nothing unfair in applying it here. . . . Order enforced.

RUNOFF ELECTION. When none of the choices on the ballot gets a majority of the votes cast a runoff election is conducted. This election gives employees an opportunity to select either of two choices. For example, if 600 votes were cast in an election in which "Union A," "Union B," and "No Union" were the participants, one of the three choices would have to receive at least 301 votes to win certification. If, on the other hand, Union A received 200 votes, Union B 150 votes, and No Union 250 votes, the runoff election would be contested by A and

B, even though *A* and *No* Union, respectively, received the largest and second largest number of votes cast. The board reasoned that the 350 votes cast for both unions indicated a desire on the part of the employees to bargain collectively.[116]

The board will conduct a runoff election when a tie vote results between the first two choices.[117]

The runoff election eliminates the possibility that an insignificant minority of employees which happens to hold the balance between two or more competing unions can indefinitely forestall the selection of a bargaining agent.[118]

Certification of Bargaining Representative

The final step in a representation proceeding is:

(1) Certification of a union as the exclusive bargaining representative for all the workers in the bargaining unit, or

(2) Dismissal of the petition, based on the union's failure to attain majority status.

Once a union is certified, the employer is legally bound to recognize it for bargaining purposes for at least a year, and for longer if the union's bargaining status has not been successfully challenged in an ensuing election. When the certified union and the employer have negotiated a two- or even three-year collective-bargaining agreement, the board will not normally conduct another representation proceeding until the contract is close to its expiration date.

National Labor Relations Board Procedure

The board has a statutory duty to investigate all unfair practice complaints filed with it, and it has the authority to process representation petitions. In addition, the board has been given authority to issue subpoenas requiring attendance of witnesses to testify at board hearings; it may require the production of evidence such as records, correspondence, and documents. Failure of a witness to appear and failure to comply with information requested in a subpoena tecum will allow the board, through its counsel, to seek compliance by seeking an order in the federal district court.

116. The 1947 Amendment requires that Union *A* and *No* Union engage in the runoff election. Only the participants receiving the largest and second largest are now recognized.
117. NLRB *Rules and Regulations*, Sec. 102.70(d).
118. Coos Bay Lumber Co., 16 NLRB 476 (1939).

Under the Wagner Act, the National Labor Relations Board consisted of three members appointed by the President and confirmed by the Senate. The board delegates power to its counsel, regional directors, trial examiners, and hearing officers.

The board issues and processes complaints charging unfair labor practices. These complaints are investigated by the regional director. If there is no merit in the complaint, the matter is dismissed. However, when evidence supports the complaint, the board attempts to have the employer agree informally to discontinue the unfair practice and take any other affirmative action that is necessary. If the employer refuses to accept an informal settlement, a formal complaint is prepared. It is served with a right to file a formal answer. Now issue has been joined, and the matter is set down for a hearing presided over by a trial examiner. Until the 1947 act was passed, hearings were conducted without too much regard to the rules of evidence applying in federal courts. When the hearing is concluded, the trial examiner files his findings and recommendation for review by the board at its Washington, D.C., headquarters. A copy of the examiner's report is given to the employer, who may file exceptions thereto with the board, and who may request an opportunity to present oral argument before the board members. More frequently, the employer presents a legal brief seeking to have the board reject or modify the examiner's report. The NLRB renders the final decision.

After its review, the board may adopt, modify, or reject the recommendations made by the examiner. The board is authorized to order the employer guilty of an unfair practice to cease and desist therefrom and to take affirmative action such as posting notices that the employer will refrain from committing specific unfair practices. When the board has found that employees have been fired unlawfully, the order will provide for reinstatement without prejudice; in most discharge cases, the employer will be required to pay the employees all wages lost by reason of the employer's unfair practice.

Summary

The Wagner Act has been characterized justifiably as the worker's Magna Charta. Congress has stated that the worker's individual bargaining is hopeless and ineffective when pitted against giant corporate enterprises, and therefore a principal objective of the act has been to encourage collective bargaining. Collective bargaining, it was said, would eliminate low wages and poor working conditions. Wages, hours, and other conditions of employment would be established by mutual consent rather than by the employer's unilateral determination. Collective bargaining agreements would develop an industrial jurisprudence regulating both the employers' and the employees' rights and duties, and such regulation would tend to reduce industrial conflict. Of course, effective collective bargaining can develop only when employees have been given the right to join unions and to engage in specific concerted activities. These rights are enumerated in Section 7 and shielded in Section 8, which forbids employers to interfere with the guarantees provided in Section 7. Union membership increased phenomenally after the passage of the act, and collective bargaining became highly institutionalized, despite early employer hostility.

A National Labor Relations Board was created to administer the act. It has been given power to prevent employer unfair labor practices and to conduct representation elections in which the collective bargaining representative, if any, is determined. The board was given authority to issue rulings, but the act reserves to the federal courts the enforcement of these rulings.

The twelve-year period during which the Wagner Act was in effect resulted in approximately one hundred thousand cases dealing with unfair labor practices and employee representation.

The most common complaint raised against the act was that it brought about an imbalance in collective bargaining power which favored labor organizations. Critics of the law stated that although employers were required to respect the statutory rights of workers, the workers were immune from any statutory responsibilities concerning indiscriminate picketing, boycotts, strikes, or conduct at the bargaining table. It is true that some unions frequently adopted coercive methods in their organizing campaigns, used secondary boycotts indiscriminately, and at times bargained on a take-it-or-leave-it basis. Since these abuses did exist, it was only a question of time until the political climate became favorable for those who demanded statutory restrictions on labor union conduct. The time came in 1947 when Congress held labor unions principally responsible for the serious interruptions in production that followed the termination of World War II. Congress believed that the legislation enacted in 1947 would improve the collective bargaining process by regulating specific economic and political activities of labor organizations.

CHAPTER TEN

The Labor-Management Relations Act of 1947 (The Taft-Hartley Act)[1]

IN 1946, one year after the end of World War II, 4700 strikes occurred. They involved 4,650,000 workers, who lost 113,000,000 mandays of work. During that year the United States was twice faced with threats of a railroad strike, and two strikes were called in the coal fields.

In addition to this unprecedented amount of industrial conflict there were several other factors that encouraged opponents of the Wagner Act to push for legislative curbs on labor union activities. When price and wage controls were lifted inflation became relatively acute, and the wage-price spiral which followed the removal of controls was blamed on the unions' wage demands. During the war labor organizations had obtained government assistance in securing maintenance-of-membership clauses in labor contracts, which gave unions a modified form of union shop. This concession allowed by the federal authorities, in conjunction with the full employment existing throughout the war, contributed to the building up of the strongest trade union movement in American history. Leading members of Congress believed that this labor power would be used indiscriminately to the detriment of the economy. Communist infiltration into positions of prominence in labor unions was another growing concern in Congress.

The Democratic Party had had uninterrupted control of the federal legislature from 1933 to 1946, and during that period had given its complete support to organized labor. The Eightieth Congress that met in January 1947 was controlled by the Republicans, for the first time in

1. Act of June 23, 1947, 80th Congress, 1st Session, c. 120, 61 Stat. 136, 29 U.S.C. 141–144, 171–188.

fifteen years. The Republicans accepted the 1946 Congressional elections as a mandate to place needed restrictions on labor union power.

Early in 1947 a Senate committee headed by the late Senator Robert F. Taft conducted hearings to determine what amendments to the Wagner Act would bring about greater stability in the field of labor relations. Neither the AFL nor the CIO appeared at the hearings—although invited—lest their participation be interpreted as agreement that new legislation was needed. The top officials of both labor federations stated publicly that the Wagner Act was working well and that any changes in it would result only in weakening the organized labor movement.

The hearings concluded, Congress debated the Taft-Hartley bill and it became law in June 1947 over the veto of President Truman.

The Taft-Hartley Act is far longer and considerably more complex than the Wagner Act. It incorporates five titles, which we shall take up in order.

Title I is the only title directly concerned with the Wagner Act. It may be considered as a group of amendments to the 1935 law; it covers employer and union unfair labor practices, bargaining representatives, elections, and state laws.

Titles II–V create several provisions that are independent of the National Labor Relations Act. They are extremely important and are a complete law in themselves quite separate from Title I's amendments to the Wagner Act.

Title II establishes a Federal Mediation and Conciliation Service to assist employers and unions in minimizing major labor disputes, including those affecting the national health and welfare, and provides the machinery of the service.

Title III allows federal courts to entertain suits by and against labor organizations on such matters as collective-bargaining contracts and specific types of strikes and secondary boycotts. Other provisions under Title III include restrictions on the checkoff system and the administration of welfare and pension trust funds. The title bans political contributions by employers and unions in federal elections and imposes penalties on striking federal employees.

Title IV creates a Congressional committee to study and report on problems of labor relations and productivity.

Title V defines terms used in the act and is concerned with the individual worker's right to quit his job without penalty.

Title I. Amendments to the Wagner Act

The findings and policies of the 1947 act are substantially those of the 1935 law. We quote one new paragraph, however, because it reveals a principal objective sought by this new legislation:

Experience has further demonstrated that certain practices by some labor organizations, their officers, and members have the intent or the necessary effect of burdening or obstructing commerce by preventing the free flow of goods in such commerce through strikes and other forms of industrial unrest or through concerted activities which impair the interest of the public in the free flow of such commerce. The elimination of such practices is a necessary condition to the assurance of the rights herein guaranteed.

Several of the amendments deal with objectionable union practices and activities. The Taft-Hartley Act seeks to bring unions as well as employers under government regulation, thereby eliminating what some called the inherent imbalance of the Wagner Act.

The NLRB is retained as the chief administrative agency for processing unfair labor practices and for handling representation proceedings, with its membership increased from three to five members. A separate office called the General Counsel investigates unfair practices and determines whether or not a complaint should be entertained by the board. Along with authority to issue cease and desist orders, the board is now permitted to seek court injunctions pending the investigation of specific unfair cases. The new law requires the board to seek injunctions in cases involving secondary boycotts and jurisdictional disputes.

Exclusion of Supervisors

SECTION 2(3) of the Taft-Hartley Act, by defining the term "employee," excludes supervisory personnel, including foremen, from the protection of the law. Employers therefore need not recognize or bargain collectively with supervisory employees. Under the Wagner Act supervisors had been protected and could avail themselves of board action.[2]

2. *Matter of* Packard Motor Car Co., 61 NLRB 4 (1945).

Section 7. Nonparticipation in Concerted Activities

The guarantees enumerated in Section 7 of the Wagner Act are left undisturbed; however, the following language has been added:

. . . and shall also have the right to refrain from any and all of such activities except to the extent that such right may be affected by an agreement requiring membership in a labor organization as a condition of employment as authorized in section 8(a)(3).

This amendment allows employees the right to refrain from joining a union and engaging in concerted activities, except when the union and employer agree to a union-shop security clause; then the employee is bound to pay dues and initiation fees to the union even if he refuses to join it. The Wagner Act permitted the closed shop, under which membership in a union was required as a condition of employment. Moreover, the employer was required to fire any employee who failed to maintain good standing in the union at the union's request. The closed shop is the most extreme type of union security, since it gives the union considerable control over hiring. Under the Taft-Hartley Act, the closed shop is prohibited.

The 1935 Wagner Act allowed employees to join unions, assist in forming unions, and engage in concerted activities. It is appropriate now to point out the employees' right to refrain from exercising any of these statutory rights.

Employees have a right to work during a strike.[3]

When a union stated that "somebody might get hurt," the board held that such a statement was unlawful since it was sufficient to deter drivers of a struck employer from working to avoid physical harm.[4]

Section 8. Employer and Union Unfair Labor Practices

The five employer unfair labor practice acts are included in Section 8, subsections (a)(1) to (a)(5). These practices were discussed in Chapter 9.

Subsections (b)(1) to (b)(6) have been added to Section 8; they cover six proscribed union practices.

SECTION 8(B)(1) provides that it shall be an unfair labor practice for a labor organization or its agents

3. Sunset Line and Twine Co., 79 NLRB 1487 (1948).
4. NLRB v. Highway Truck Drivers, Local 107, 273 Fed. (2d) 815 (1959).

to restrain or coerce employees in the exercise of the rights guaranteed in Section 7: Provided, That this paragraph shall not impair the right of a labor organization to prescribe its own rules with respect to the acquisition or retention of membership therein; or . . . an employer in the selection of his representatives for the purpose of collective bargaining or the adjustment of grievances.

This subsection bars union conduct that involves actual or threatened violence, intimidation, or reprisals directed at employees. Labor unions are prohibited also from interfering with the employer's right to select its bargaining representative.

CASES AND RULINGS. When a union sent a letter to employees demanding that they join the union as a condition of employment, the board found a violation of Section 8(b)(1).[5]

It is unlawful for a union to make a final determination on seniority although its contract gives it this unilateral right.[6]

Refusing employees union membership under a policy restricting new membership to eldest sons of deceased members is not unlawful if no employment discrimination results.[7]

Administration of a health and welfare trust fund for the benefit only of union members constitutes unlawful union coercion.[8]

The following conduct by pickets on the picket line and elsewhere is unlawful: (1) threats of violence against nonstrikers, (2) blocking entrances, (3) trailing nonstrikers, (4) assaulting nonstrikers, and (5) damaging the house of a nonstriker.[9]

Violence by pickets against supervisors and independent contractors in the presence of strikers is unlawful coercion even though no nonstrikers are present.[10]

A direct interference with the activities of employees during working hours, demonstrating union power, is unlawful, even when it does not tend directly to enrolling employees in the union.[11]

Union threats of reprisals against employees subpoenaed to testify against the union at a board proceeding are unlawful.[12]

A union unlawfully coerced an employer by refusing to meet with him and threatening strike action because the employer's attorney would be present.[13]

5. Perry Coal Co., 125 NLRB (No. 110) (1959).
6. Miranda Fuel Co., 125 NLRB (No. 53) (1959).
7. Administrative Decision of NLRB General Counsel, Case 538 (1942).
8. Local 229, Textile Workers, 120 NLRB 1700 (1958).
9. Packinghouse Workers, 123 NLRB (No. 53) (1959); Steelworkers, 123 NLRB (No. 35) (1959); Eagle Mfg. Corp., 112 NLRB 74 (1955); Tungsten Mining Corp., 106 NLRB 903 (1953).
10. Communications Workers, 120 NLRB 684 (1958).
11. Gimbel Bros., 100 NLRB 870 (1952).
12. Personal Products Co., 108 NLRB 1129 (1954).
13. Local 294, Teamsters, 126 NLRB (No. 2) (1960).

A union engaged in a proscribed practice when it refused to deal with former union officers who represented employers.[14]

A union was justified in refusing to process an employee's grievance when it believed the grievance was without merit.[15]

One of the most important cases in which the Supreme Court considered Section 8(b)(1) was NLRB v. Teamsters Union 639 (the Curtis case).[16] Here the question was whether peaceful picketing by a union that does not represent a majority of the employees, to compel immediate recognition as the employees' exclusive bargaining agent, was conduct of the union that would "restrain or coerce" the employees in the exercise of rights guaranteed in Section 7 and thus an unfair labor practice act under Section 8(b)(1)(A) of the National Labor Relations Act as amended by the Taft-Hartley Act.

The court held that the provisions of the act prohibiting union tactics that coerce or restrain employees in the exercise of their right to join or refrain from joining a union cannot properly be construed as rendering recognition picketing by a minority union unlawful, since such prohibition is limited to acts of violence, intimidation, and reprisal, or threats of such acts. There was no language in the statute or in its legislative history giving the National Labor Relations Board authority to regulate recognition picketing except when another union was certified or when its object was a secondary boycott or to force employers and self-employed persons to join a union. The court held the board's determination that a minority union's picketing for recognition unlawfully coerced and restrained employees by impairing their job opportunities as a result of the economic pressure on their employer to be an unauthorized restriction on the right to strike. The court concluded that to give such a broad application to the proscription against union pressures on employees would permit the National Labor Relations Board to proceed against peaceful picketing in disregard of the safeguards against interference with legitimate picketing which were established in the amendments contained in the Labor-Management Reporting and Disclosure Act of 1959.

SECTION 8(B)(2) makes it a union unfair labor practice

to cause or attempt to cause an employer to discriminate against an employee in violation of subsection (a)(3) or to discriminate against an employee with respect to whom membership in such organization has been denied or terminated on some ground other than his failure to tender the periodic dues and initiation fees uniformly required as a condition of acquiring or retaining membership.

14. Int'l Typographical Union, AFL-CIO, 123 NLRB 806 (1959).
15. General Counsel, Case I-784 (1958).
16. 362 U.S. 274 (1960).

Unions are prohibited from causing or attempting to cause employers to discriminate against employees so as to encourage or discourage union membership. Employers are free to hire any workers of their choice whether or not they meet a union's membership qualifications. A union violates the law when it seeks to persuade an employer to give hiring preference to union members.

When a valid union-shop contract exists, employees who join the union must remain members in good standing; i.e., they must meet their initiation fee and dues obligations. This is a condition of employment; when the employee fails to meet this requirement the union may lawfully demand his discharge. However, for the union to demand the discharge of a worker who offers his initiation fees and dues which are rejected by the union is unlawful.

Discrimination is not limited to hiring and discharges. It is unlawful for a union to encourage or force an employer to discriminate against a worker with respect to layoffs, wage increases, transfers, vacation and welfare benefits, overtime, promotions, and seniority rights.

CASES AND RULINGS. When evidence showed that several unions coerced employers to agree to closed-shop conditions, a board finding that the unions not only created the possibility of future discrimination but actually caused discrimination against nonunion employees or applicants, was upheld.[17]

Picketing to compel an employer to encourage employees to join the union, or to discharge nonunion employees and replace them with union members, is a violation of Section 8(b)(2).[18]

Free-speech provisions of the act do not protect a union request that causes employer discrimination.[19]

Causing an employer to replace members of one union with members of another union in a work assignment dispute is unlawful.[20]

A union's practice of requiring all jobs to be cleared through it and its refusal to give clearance to applicants not in good standing is unlawful.[21]

Section 8(b)(2) is violated when the union engages in threats, slowdowns, and strikes to force an employer to give preference in hiring to union members over nonmembers.[22]

To cause an employer to discriminate against a nonunion employee in re-employment after a layoff is violative of the act.[23]

---

17. American Newspaper Publishers' Ass'n v. NLRB, 193 Fed. (2d) 782 (1951).
18. Werb v. Local 200, Teamsters, 66 N.W. (2d) 318 (1954).
19. NLRB v. Jarka Corp., 198 Fed. (2d) 618 (1952).
20. Frank P. Slater, 102 NLRB 153 (1953).
21. Morrison-Knudsen Co. v. NLRB, 39 LC 66,308 (1960).
22. N.Y. Times Co., 101 NLRB 589 (1952).
23. Local 170, Teamsters, 110 NLRB 850 (1954).

Causing an employer to lay off a worker who resigned his union membership is unlawful.[24]

Compelling an employer to drop the name of a union member to the bottom of the seniority list because he did not attend union meetings or engage in picket duty is unlawful.[25]

A union violated the act when it required an employer to deny promotion to a nonunion employee and grant it to a union member.[26]

The case [27] which follows illustrates a violation of Section 8(b)(2), as well as a violation of Section 8(a)(3). Both the union and the employer are charged in this case with unlawful discrimination.

DENMAN, C. J. This is a petition by the National Labor Relations Board to enforce certain orders of the Board against respondent company and respondent union.

A. THE BOARD'S ORDER AGAINST THE COMPANY. This order is based on a claimed violation of Section 8(a)(3)(B) of the Labor Management Act, hereafter called the Act, which provides "That no employer shall justify any discrimination against an employee for nonmembership in a labor organization. . . . (B) if he has reasonable grounds for believing that membership was denied or terminated for reasons other than the failure of the employee to tender the periodic dues and the initiation fees uniformly required as a condition of acquiring or retaining membership."

That is to say, that when a union shop agreement is entered into under Section 8(a)(3) of the Act, the Company could not discharge a member of the Union on the Union's demand if it had reasonable grounds for believing that the Union's demand for his discharge was on grounds other than for nonpayment of periodic dues and required initiation fees. The Company does not question that the "periodic dues" are those due the Union, subsequent to the making of the union-shop contract. N.L.R.B. v. International Union, 194 F. (2d) 698, 701. Colonial Fibre Co. v. N.L.R.B. 163 F. (2d) 65.

The facts, in brief, are: In 1944, one Marl, then working for the Company, refused to pay a Union political assessment and thereupon left the Union and paid no more dues. Under the Union rules he remained a member until he was "dropped" by some affirmative act of the Union, which was not taken. He remained a "suspended" member of the Union.

In 1948, he returned to work with the Company and was working there when on April 25, 1950, the Union entered into a union-shop contract providing that:

"All employees shall be required, as a necessary condition of continued employment, to become members of the Union in good standing not later than thirty (30) days from the effective date of this agreement or the

24. Packinghouse Workers, Local 267, 114 NLRB 1279 (1955).
25. Minneapolis Star Tribune Co., 109 NLRB 727 (1954).
26. Brodsky and Son, 144 NLRB 819 (1955).
27. NLRB v. Eclipse Lumber Co., 199 Fed. (2d) 684 (1952).

beginning date of their first employment, whichever occurs later, and to maintain such membership in good standing thereafter.

"The Union shall notify the Employer in writing of any employee who fails to become or remain a member of the Union in good standing, and the Employer shall, immediately upon receipt of such notification, dismiss any such employee from employment."

The Union had a constitutional provision to the effect that a delinquent member could be reinstated upon payment of the regular new member initiation fee of $10 and six months' back dues of $2.50 a month, and one month's dues at the increased rate of $2.75, totaling $27.75. On inquiry of the Union, Marl was told the amount he had to pay was the sum of $85.25, consisting of $70.50 past dues, $10 initiation fee, one month's advanced dues of $2.75, and a $2 fine for non-picketing in a prior strike.

When Marl protested, he was told by the Union treasurer that if he did not pay ". . . at the end of 30 days you know what happens." After thirty days had expired the Union notified the Company to dismiss Marl, which the Company did. . . .

We agree with the finding of both the Board and trial examiner, that Carpenter, a company executive, knew that the Union's demand for Marl's discharge was for Union obligations other than current dues or initiation fees.

We are of the opinion that the evidence supports the Board's finding that Carpenter, who told Marl, "We will have to let you go," was a supervisory employee of a rank to charge the Company with knowledge that Marl's discharge was in violation of Section 8(a)(3)(B) of the Act. Carpenter's title was General Sales Manager, but "with reference to the company's operations he was the next responsible person" to General Manager Stuchell. . . .

We order enforced the Board's orders against the Company. . . .

It is obvious from the above evidence that the Union violated Section 8(b)(2) of the Act. . . .

The Board's order respecting the Union is ordered enforced.

C. THE BOARD'S ORDER AGAINST THE UNION BECAUSE OF COERCIVE STATEMENTS TO UNION MEMBERS REQUIRING THEM TO PAY EXCESSIVE AMOUNTS TO REMAIN IN PROPER STANDING FOR EMPLOYMENT UNDER THE UNION SHOP AGREEMENT. The evidence amply supports the findings of the Board that such coercion by the Union caused some fourteen members of the Union to pay it sums in excess of $12.75 required to be in good standing under the Union shop agreement.

The Board's order respecting the fourteen Union members is ordered enforced.

SECTION 8(B)(3) sets forth that it shall be an unfair practice for a union "to refuse to bargain collectively with an employer, provided it is the representative of his employees subject to the provisions of Section 9(a)."

Section 8(d) of the act defines bargaining as:

the performance of the mutual obligation of the employer and the representative of the employees to meet at reasonable times and confer in good faith with respect to wages, hours, and other terms and conditions of employment, or the negotiation of an agreement or any question arising thereunder.

The NLRB has said:

The language of the amended Act, as well as its legislative history, indicate that Congress intended to impose upon labor organizations the same duty to bargain which had been imposed upon employers in Section 8(5) of the Wagner Act.[28]

The next case [29] is illustrative of a union's violation of this section when it chose not to bargain with the employer's representative.

HATCH, D. J. This cause came on to be heard upon the verified petition of Edwin A. Elliott, Regional Director of the Sixteenth Region of the National Labor Relations Board (herein called the Board), for a temporary injunction pursuant to Section 10(j) of the National Labor Relations Act, as amended (herein called the Act), pending the final disposition of the matters pending before the Board on a complaint of the General Counsel of the Board and upon the issuance of an order to show cause why injunctive relief should not be granted as prayed for in said petition. Respondents filed an answer to said petition and a preliminary motion to dismiss. The motion to dismiss was denied, and a hearing on the issue raised by the petition and answer was duly held on May 8, 1958. All parties were afforded an opportunity to be heard, to examine and cross examine witnesses, to present evidence bearing on the issues, and to argue on the evidence and the law. The Court has fully considered the petition, answer, evidence and arguments of counsel. Upon the entire record, the Court makes the following:

Findings of Fact

1. Petitioner is Regional Director of the Sixteenth Region of the Board, an agency of the United States, and files this petition for and on behalf of the Board.

2.(a) Respondent, Local Union 49, Sheet Metal Workers' International Association, AFL-CIO, (herein called Local 49), an unincorporated association, is a labor organization within the meaning of Sections 2(5), 8(b), 8(d) and 10(j) of the Act, and is engaged within this judicial district in transacting business and in promoting and protecting the interests of its employee members.

(b) At all time material herein, respondent E. D. Brooks has been busi-

28. Rabouin, doing business as Conway's Express, 87 NLRB 972 (1949).
29. Elliott v. Sheet Metal Workers, Local 49, 34 LC 71,553 (1958).

ness agent of Local 49, and its agent within the meaning of Sections 2(13), 8(b), 8(d) and 10(j) of the Act.

3. Jurisdiction of this proceeding is conferred upon this Court by Section 10(j) of the Act.

4. On or about March 24, 1958, New Mexico Sheet Metal Contractors Association, Inc. (herein called Association), pursuant to the provisions of the Act, filed a charge with the Board alleging that respondents have engaged in, and are engaging in unfair labor practices within the meaning of Sections 8(b)(1)(B), 8(b)(3) and 8(d) of the Act.

5. Said charge was referred to petitioner as Regional Director of the Sixteenth Region of the Board for investigation and was investigated by petitioner and under his supervision. After such investigation, the General Counsel of the Board on behalf of the Board, by petitioner, issued a complaint pursuant to Section 10(b) of the Act on April 29, 1958, charging that respondents have engaged in, and are engaging in, unfair labor practices within the meaning of Sections 8(b)(1)(B), 8(b)(3) and 8(d) of the Act, and affecting commerce within the meaning of Section 2, subsections (6) and (7) of the Act.

6. There is, and petitioner has reasonable cause to believe that:

(a) At all times material herein Association, a corporate membership association with its principal office and place of business in Albuquerque, New Mexico, was organized for, and engaged in, collective bargaining with collective bargaining representatives of employees on behalf of member employers and other employers in the State of New Mexico.

(b) At all times material herein Association has been designated by its member sheet metal contractors and certain other sheet metal contractors in the State of New Mexico as their collective bargaining representative for the purpose of collective bargaining with collective bargaining representatives of employees of the said member employers and other said employers with respect to wages, hours and other working conditions.

(c) At all times material herein Lydick Roofing Company (herein called Lydick), a sheet metal contractor, has been a member of Association, and has been engaged in the sale and installation of sheet metal and roofing products. During the calendar year 1957 the value of its sales of such products and services in connection therewith was approximately $1,000,000. Sales of these products and services outside the State of New Mexico accounted for approximately $250,000 of this material.

(d) At all times material herein respondent Local 49 has been and is the exclusive collective bargaining representative with respect to wages, hours, and other working conditions, pursuant to Section 9 of the Act, of the sheet metal worker employees of the sheet metal employer members of Association and the other sheet metal employers who have designated Association as their collective bargaining representative.

(e) Since . . . January, 1956, Association and respondent Local 49 have engaged in collective bargaining with respect to wages, hours and other working conditions for the said employees, and have negotiated collective bargaining contracts with respect to said matters and covering said employees. The last contract (herein called existing contract) was effective March 31,

1956, for a two year period with provision for an automatic renewal on a year to year basis unless written notice of change was given by either party 90 days prior to March 31, 1958, or the March 21 terminal date thereafter. The existing contract also provides that it continue in effect after such notice of change is served until the parties confer and the conferences are terminated by either party.

(f) On or about December 27, 1957, respondent Local 49 by respondent Brooks notified Association in writing that it was terminating the existing contract as of March 31, 1958.

(g) Neither on December 27, 1957, nor thereafter, have respondents, although requested to do so, offered to meet and confer with Association for the purpose of negotiating a contract change, nor have they met and conferred for such purpose with Association.

(h) Neither on December 27, 1957, nor thereafter, have respondents notified the Federal Mediation Service or the New Mexico State Labor and Industrial Commission of the notice by respondent Local 49 to Association of its termination of the existing contract effective March 31, 1958.

(i) Since on or about April 1, 1958, respondents have refused to continue in force or effect the terms and conditions of the existing contract, and have engaged in strikes against the Association and its members and the other contractors represented by Association in connection with this refusal.

(j) Since on or about December 27, 1957, although requested to do so, respondent Local 49 has refused to recognize, meet or bargain with Association as the selected representative of sheet metal employer members of Association and the other sheet metal employers who selected Association as its collective bargaining representative, has attempted to bargain directly with the said sheet metal employers, and since April 1, 1958, has engaged in strikes against Association members and the other said employers because of their selection of Association as their collective bargaining representative.

(k) The strikes by respondent Local 49 commencing on or about April 1, 1958, and continuing thereafter, have impaired and are impairing the construction in New Mexico of facilities for the production of uranium concentrate by Phillips Petroleum Company for the Atomic Energy Commission, and the construction of facilities for other National Defense projects at Los Alamos, New Mexico, and at other places in New Mexico.

(l) By their acts and conduct set forth above in findings of fact 6(g), 6(j) and 6(k), respondents have restrained or coerced employer members of Association and other employers in the selection of Association as their representative for the purpose of collective bargaining or the adjustment of grievances within the meaning of Section 8(b)(1)(B) of the Act.

(m) By their acts and conduct set forth above in findings of fact 6(g), 6(h), 6(i), 6(j) and 6(k), respondents have refused to bargain collectively with the meaning of Sections 8(b)(3) and 8(d) of the Act.

7. The acts and conduct of respondents set forth above in the findings of fact 6(g), 6(h), 6(i), 6(j) and 6(k), occurring in connection with the operations of the Association and its members and the other sheet metal contractors who have selected Association as their collective bargaining representative, have a close, intimate, and substantial relation to trade, traffic and

commerce among the several states and tend to lead and do lead to labor disputes burdening and obstructing commerce and the free flow of commerce.

8. It may be fairly anticipated that, unless restrained, respondents will continue and repeat the acts and conduct set forth above in the findings of fact . . . . or similar or like acts and conduct.

Conclusions of Law

1. This Court has jurisdiction of the parties and the subject matter of this proceeding, and under Section 10(j) of the Act, has jurisdiction to grant injunctive relief.

2. Respondent Local 49 is a labor organization within the meaning of Sections 2(5), 8(b) and 10(j) of the Act, and respondent Brooks is an agent of respondent Local 49 within the meaning of Sections 2(13), 8(b), 8(d) and 10(j) of the Act.

3. There is reasonable cause to believe that respondents have engaged in, and are engaging in unfair labor practices within the meaning of Section 8(b)(1)(B) and Sections 8(b)(3) and 8(d) of the Act, and affecting commerce within the meaning of Section 2, subsections (6) and(7) of the Act, and that a continuation of these practices will impair the policies of the Act as set forth in Section 1(b) thereof.

4. To preserve the issues for the determination of the Board as provided in the Act, it is appropriate, just and proper that, pending the final adjudication by the Board of the matters involved herein, respondents, their officers, agents, servants, employees, attorneys, and all members or persons acting in concert or participation with them, be enjoined and restrained from the commission and continuation of the acts and conduct set forth in findings of fact . . . or like or related acts or conduct, the commission of which in the future is likely or may be likely or fairly expected from respondent's acts and conduct in the past.

SECTION 8(B)(4), (A) AND (B). SECONDARY BOYCOTTS AND SECONDARY STRIKES. The fourth unfair union practice is found in this section. The primary objective of this section is the prohibition of secondary boycotts and unlawful strikes. The language used is complex and confusing, and the considerable amount of litigation revolving around the section's interpretation and application has added more confusion. Some degree of clarity has resulted from the enactment in 1959 of amendments to the Taft-Hartley Law. These more recent legislative enactments and the rulings and decisions made since 1959 will be discussed in Chapter 11.

Subsection (A) is directed against secondary action intended to disrupt the business relations of separate employers. It also prohibits secondary as well as primary strikes whose purpose is to force an employer or self-employed person to join any labor or employer organization. Subsection (B) contains the prohibition of strike action against an employer for the purpose of forcing another employer to recognize a labor organization not certified by the National Labor Relations Board.

CASES AND RULINGS. Cases under this section present questions whether the persons allegedly approached by the union were employees for secondary-boycott purposes; whether alleged work stoppages were unlawfully induced or encouraged within the meaning of the section, and whether the action engaged in by the union in fact constituted a strike. During the fiscal year of 1959,[30] the board adhered to the view that union inducement of strike action by secondary employees did not violate Section 8(b)(4) unless the employees were those of an employer within the definition of Section 2(2) of the act. Therefore a secondary strike by railroad employees [31] and employees of a Railway Express Agency subject to the Railway Labor Act [32] were held not to have violated Section 8(b)(4).

The words "induce and encourage" in Section 8(b)(4) have been held broad enough to include every form of influence and persuasion; [33] whether a union's conduct induced or encouraged a cessation of work depends "on the factual situation" in each case.[34]

Informing truck drivers that "they did not have to pull (struck) freight if they did not want to" was unlawful inducement.[35]

Unions have been held to have induced employees of secondary employers not to handle struck goods or nonunion materials by such conduct as veiled threats of bodily harm "if this is kept up." [36]

Inducement or encouragement may result from a union representative's silence. A failure to reply to questions regarding the purpose of a picket line was found to have caused the refusal of employees to cross it.[37]

Statements of a union representative seeking support of employees in a strike against an employer other than their own are no less violative of Section 8(b)(4) because they are made in the confines of a union meeting.[38]

---

30. See *Twenty-Fourth Annual Report*, NLRB, 1959.
31. Seafarers' Int'l Union of No. Am. (Superior Derrick Corp.), 122 NLRB 52 (1958); Local 1205 and Local 707, Teamsters (Atlantic-Pacific Mfg. Corp.), 122 NLRB 1215 (1959).
32. United Hatters Union (Louisville Cap Co.), 121 NLRB 1154 (1958).
33. United Marine Division, Local 333 (N.Y. Shipping Ass'n) 107 NLRB 686 (1954).
34. Phelps Dodge Corp. v. NLRB, 313 U.S. 177 (1941).
35. Local 984, Teamsters (The Humko Co. Inc.), 121 NLRB 1414 (1958).
36. Local 107, Teamsters (Virginia-Carolina Freight Line Inc.), 123 NLRB 551 (1959).
37. Seafarers' Int'l Union (Superior Derrick Corp.), 122 NLRB 52 (1958).
38. Amalgamated Meat Cutters Union (Western Inc.), 93 NLRB 336 (1951).

NEUTRALITY OF SECONDARY EMPLOYER. The prohibition against secondary boycotts is intended to protect neutral employers against being drawn into a dispute between a union and another employer. When a union charged with secondary-boycott action shows that the employer to whom it extended its primary strike was an "ally" of the primary employer, rather than a neutral, the board will dismiss the complaint.

Separate employers have been held to be "allies" for secondary-boycott purposes on the basis either of their corporate relationship [39] or of the performance of "struck work" turned over by the primary employer to the secondary employer.[40] In the Coors case the National Labor Relations Board ruled that the union had engaged in an unlawful secondary boycott in violation of Section 8(b)(4)(A) of the act. The board sought enforcement of its order directing the union to cease and desist from boycotting the Coors Company. The circuit court of appeals denied enforcement. The reasons for the denial appear in Justice Murrah's opinion, which follows.

. . . Section 8(b)(4)(A) provides, in presently material part, "It shall be an unfair labor practice for a labor organization or its agents . . . to induce or encourage the employees of any employer to engage in . . . a concerted refusal in the course of their employment to use . . . commodities or to perform any services, where an object thereof is: (A) forcing or requiring any employer . . . to cease using, selling, handling, transporting, or otherwise dealing in the products of any other producer. . . ." Consistent with its dual purposes of preserving to unions their right to strike and of shielding unoffending employers from employee pressures in disputes not their own, the Act does not proscribe peaceful picketing or related agitation at or near the premises of neutral employers, so long as it is neither directed toward, nor has the effect of inducing the neutral employees to a concerted refusal to perform some of their duties.

Coors customarily distributes its product to its Denver retailers in its own trucks from a Denver warehouse. When, during the collective bargaining for a new contract in April 1957, the warehouse and delivery personnel struck, Coors leased its Denver trucks to certain of its independent distributors and thus continued to operate the warehouse and service its Denver accounts. In May, 1957, the strikers began following the delivery trucks on their routes, and during the time of each delivery engaged in picketing and distributing pamphlets in and about the retail establishment, and on certain occasions conversed with retail establishment personnel, discouraging acceptance of the delivery. The pickets generally patrolled near the truck, the delivery en-

39. Warehouse and Distribution Workers Union (Bachman Machine Co.), 121 NLRB 1229 (1958).
40. Int'l Union of Brewery Workers (Adolph Coors Co.), 121 NLRB 271 (1958); enforcement of board order denied, 272 Fed. (2d) 817 (1959).

trance, and the main entrance. Their signs carried the legend, "To the beer drinking public—Coors Brewery—ON STRIKE—don't buy Coors beer," followed by the name of the union local. Only the words "on strike" were larger than the others, and all of the message was easily readable. The strikers also frequently told the retailer that they were not picketing him, but only the truck. The pamphlets carried a bold-lettered exhortation, "Don't buy Coors beer," and generally appealed for support of the strikers' cause. In several instances, oral pleas not to buy Coors and pamphlet distributions were made to employees as well as customers of the retailers. As for the entreaties to employees not to accept the delivery, three specific instances are described: At a drug store, the pharmacist was at first persuaded not to accept delivery, but after phoning the store owner, did accept; at another drug store, the clerk at the liquor department was similarly encountered but he referred the strikers to the store manager; and in a market, the entreaty was made to a person behind the counter. No refusals to accept any delivery were shown.

To be sure, we recognize that picketing frequently involves potent implications absent in other modes of communication. But here we find in the evidence neither any attempt to influence retailers' employees not to cross picket lines, which were of only momentary duration anyway, nor any work stoppage among these employees from which such an influence could be inferred. Indeed, we find in the union's picketing, pamphlet distribution, and exhortation of beer consumers, nothing more than legitimate embarrassment of the strike-breaking Coors driver and the advocacy of a consumer boycott of Coors beer.

And we fail to see where the encouragement of retail personnel to refuse to accept deliveries, even if directed at "employees" within the meaning of the Act, was intended or had the effect of invoking "concerted" action any more than in N.L.R.B. v. International Rice Milling Co., *supra*. In that case, the Court held that isolated efforts directed at "secondary" employees did not constitute an unfair labor practice, recognizing that only efforts to promote concerted action by the secondary employees are condemned.

We of course recognize the primary function of the Board to find facts, draw inferences, and construe the Act to effectuate its purposes. But we nevertheless have the "ultimate responsibility for the rationality of the Board's decision," and we will not enforce it if upon the whole record we are convinced that it is not justified in fact and law.

Upon consideration of this record, we are convinced that the undisputed facts do not justify the inference that the unions encouraged or induced employees of any retailer to engage in a concerted refusal to perform any service with the object of forcing any such retailer-employer to cease selling, handling or dealing in Coors products. The petition for enforcement must therefore be denied.

In this case [41] however the board held that the employer to whom the union extended its strike activities was not a neutral because it became voluntarily involved in the union's primary dispute by taking over

41. Int'l Union of Brewery Workers (Adolph Coors Co.), *supra*.

delivery of the struck employer's goods in accordance with a prestrike arrangement.

AMBULATORY AND COMMON SITUS PICKETING. The cases under the secondary-boycott provisions of the act have continued to present questions regarding the legality of picketing activities away from the primary employer's premises in connection with a primary dispute.

Ambulatory picketing results when strikers follow a struck employer's delivery trucks and picket when the truck arrives at its destination. Such picketing has been held unlawful and a violation of Section 8(b)(4) when the picketing at the delivery points was conducted so as to constitute an appeal to neutral employees to strike.[42] However, the board made it clear that the mere following of trucks by strikers does not, by itself, constitute prohibited inducement.[43]

The board has adhered to its former ruling[44] that ambulatory picketing at the premises of a secondary employer is per se for an unlawful object when a primary employer has a permanent place of business at which a union can adequately publicize its labor dispute.

"HOT-CARGO" AGREEMENTS. When unions had defended their secondary-boycott action by invoking agreements with the respective employers relieving employees of the duty to handle "hot cargo," the unions were uniformly found to have violated Section 8(b)(4) as it was interpreted by the U.S. Supreme Court in the Sand Door case.[45]

The Sand Door case is of great importance on the issue of secondary boycotts. The Sand Door Company was the exclusive distributor in southern California of doors manufactured by the Paine Lumber Company of Wisconsin, which employed nonunion workers. One of its customers was Watson and Dreps, a firm of millwork contractors. At the time of the dispute Watson and Dreps was supplying doors to Havstad and Jensen, a general contracting firm constructing a hospital in Los Angeles. Havstad and Jensen was party to a master labor agreement negotiated with the United Brotherhood of Carpenters and Joiners of America on behalf of its affiliated district councils and locals, including the unions that became the petitioners in this case; it contained a provision that the carpenters should "not be required to handle nonunion material."

In August 1954 doors manufactured by Paine and purchased by Sand were delivered to the hospital construction site by Watson and Dreps. On the morning of August 17, Fleisher, business agent of petitioner

42. Local 688, Teamsters (Acme Paper Co.), 121 NLRB 702 (1958).
43. *Ibid.*
44. Washington Coca-Cola Bottling Works, 107 NLRB 299 (1953); enforced, 220 Fed. (2d) 380 (1955).
45. Local 1976, United Bhd. of Carpenters (Sand Door and Plywood Co.) v. NLRB, 241 Fed. (2d) 147 (1957); affirmed, 357 U.S. 93 (1958).

Local 1976, came to the construction site and notified Havstad and Jensen's foreman, a union member, that the doors were nonunion and could not be hung. The foreman therefore ordered employees to cease handling the doors. When Havstad and Jensen's general superintendent appeared on the job and asked Fleisher why the workers had been prevented from handling the doors, he stated that they had been stopped until it could be determined whether the doors were union or nonunion. Subsequent negotiations between officers of Sand and the union failed to produce an agreement that would permit the doors to be installed.

On the basis of charges filed by Sand and a complaint duly issued the National Labor Relations Board found that petitioners had induced and encouraged employees to engage in a strike or concerted refusal to handle Paine's doors in order to force Havstad and Jensen and Sand to cease doing business with Paine, all in violation of Section 8(b)(4)(A).

The circuit court of appeals enforced the board's cease and desist order. Its reasoning follows.

. . . In our view, there was inducement to a concerted refusal in the statutory sense, not authorized by the contract between Havstad and Jensen and the Union. An employer may well remain free to decide, as a matter of business policy, whether he will accede to a union's boycott demands, or, if he has already agreed to do so, whether he will fulfill his agreement. An entirely different situation, however, is presented under Section 8(b)(4)(A) of the Act (29 USCA Section 8(b)(4)(A), *supra*) when it is sought to influence the employer's decision by a work stoppage of his employees. Such a work stoppage, Congress has plainly declared, is unlawful, when the object —clearly present here—"is . . . forcing or requiring any employer . . . to cease using . . . the products of any other . . . manufacturer, or to cease doing business with any other person."

In the instant case, we have seen that, despite the "hot cargo" provision in the contract, *supra*, the employees had actually been handling Paine doors. They ceased doing so only upon Fleisher's and Steiner's orders. Those orders, we think, were in direct contravention of the mandate.

We hold that the Board was correct in holding that the union, through its foreman Steinert and its business agent Fleisher, violated Section 8(b)(4)(A) by ordering employees of Havstad and Jensen to refuse to install Paine doors.

The case [46] that follows gives another leading interpretation of Section 8(b)(4).

BURTON, J., delivered the opinion of the Court.

The principal question here is whether a labor organization committed an unfair labor practice, within the meaning of Sec. 8(b)(4)(A) of the National Labor Relations Act, 49 Stat. 449, 29 U.S.C. Sec. 151, as amended by the Labor Management Relations Act, 1947, by engaging in a strike, an object of which was to enforce the general contractor on a construction proj-

46. NLRB v. Denver Bldg. Council, 341 U.S. 675 (1951).

ect to terminate its contract with a certain subcontractor on the project. For the reasons hereafter stated, we hold that such an unfair labor practice was committed.

In September, 1947, Doose and Lintner was the general contractor for the construction of a commercial building in Denver, Colorado. It awarded a subcontract for electrical work on the building, in an estimated amount of $2300, to Gould and Preisner, a firm which for 20 years had employed non-union workmen on construction work in that city. The latter's employees proved to be the only non-union workmen on the project. Those of the general contractor and of the other subcontractors were members of unions affiliated with the respondent Denver Building and Construction Trades Council (here called Council). . . .

Representatives of the Council and each of the respondent unions visited the project and reminded the contractor that Gould and Preisner employed non-union workmen and said that union men could not work on the job with non-union men. They further advised that if Gould and Preisner's men did work on the job, the Council and its affiliates would put a picket on it to notify their members that non-union men were working on it and that the job was unfair. All parties stood their ground.

January 9, the Council posted a picket at the project, carrying a placard stating "This Job Unfair to Denver Building and Construction Trades Council." He was paid by the Council and his picketing continued from January 9 through January 22. . . . Gould and Preisner were notified to get off the job so that Doose and Lintner could continue with the project. January 23, the Council removed its picket and shortly thereafter the union employees resumed work on the project. Gould and Preisner protested this treatment, but its workmen were denied entrance to the job. . . .

THE SECONDARY BOYCOTT. We now reach the merits of this case. They require a study of the objectives of the strike and a determination whether the strike came within the definition of an unfair labor practice stated in Section 8(b)(4)(A). . . .

While Sec. 8(b)(4) does not expressly mention "primary" or "secondary" disputes, strikes, or boycotts, the section often is referred to in the Act's legislative history as one of the Act's "secondary boycott sections." The other is Sec. 303, 61 Stat. 158, 29 U.S.C. (Supp. III), Sec. 187. . . .

At the same time that Sections 7 and 13 safeguard collective bargaining, concerted activities, and strikes between the primary parties to a labor dispute, Section 8(b)(4) restricts a labor organization and its agents in the use of economic pressure where an object of it is to force an employer or other person to boycott someone else.

We must first determine whether the strike in this case had a proscribed object. The conduct which the Board here condemned is readily distinguishable from that which it declined to condemn in the Rice Milling case, *ante*, p. 665. There the accused union sought merely to obtain its own recognition by the operator of a mill, and the union's pickets near the mill sought to influence two employees of a customer of the mill not to cross the picket line. In that case we supported the Board in its conclusion that such conduct was no more than was traditional and permissible in a primary strike. The union did not engage in a strike against the customer. It did not encourage concerted action by the customer's employees to force the customer to boycott the mill. It did not commit any unfair labor practice proscribed by Section 8(b)(4).

In the background of the instant case there was a long-standing labor dispute between the Council and Gould and Preisner due to the latter's practice of employing non-union workmen on construction jobs in Denver. The respondent labor organizations contend that they engaged in a primary dispute with Doose and Lintner alone, and that they sought simply to force Doose and Lintner to make the project an all-union job. If there had been no contract between Doose and Lintner and Gould and Preisner there might be substance in their contention that the dispute involved no boycott. If, for example, Doose and Lintner had been doing all the electrical work in this project through its own non-union employees, it could have replaced them with union men and thus disposed of the dispute. However, the existence of the Gould and Preisner subcontract presented a materially different situation. The non-union employees were employees of Gould and Preisner. The only way that respondents could attain their purpose was to force Gould and Preisner itself off the job. This, in turn, could be done only through Doose and Lintner's termination of Gould and Preisner's subcontract. The result is that the Council's strike, in order to attain its ultimate purpose, must have included among its objects that of forcing Doose and Lintner to terminate that subcontract. . . .

. . . For these reasons we conclude that the conduct of respondents constituted an unfair labor practice within the meaning of Section 8(b)(4)(A). The judgment of the Court of Appeals accordingly is reversed, and the case is remanded to it for procedure not inconsistent with this opinion.

So ordered.

DOUGLAS, J., dissenting:

The employment of union and non-union men on the same job is a basic protest in trade union history. That was the protest here. The union was not out to destroy the contractor because of his anti-union attitude. The union was not pursuing the contractor to other jobs. All the union asked was that union men not be compelled to work alongside non-union men on the same job. As Judge Rifkind stated in an analogous case, "The union was not extending its activity to a front remote from the immediate dispute but to one intimately and indeed inextricably united to it."

The picketing would undoubtedly have been legal if there had been no subcontractor involved—if the general contractor had put non-union men on the job. The presence of a subcontractor does not alter one whit the realities of the situation; the protest of the union was trying to protest the job on which union men were employed. If that is forbidden, the Taft-Hartley Act makes the right to strike, guaranteed by Section 13, dependent on fortuitous business arrangements that have no significance so far as the evils of the secondary boycott are concerned. . . .

STRIKES FOR RECOGNITION AGAINST CERTIFICATION. Section 8 (b) (4) (c) forbids a union to engage in strike activity in order to force an employer to recognize or bargain with one labor organization as the representative of the employer's employees when another union has been certified by the National Labor Relations Board as such representative.

The activity proscribed by this subsection is frequently referred to as jurisdictional picketing. This type of picketing occurred more frequently between 1935 and 1955, when the AFL and the CIO were rival federations, and two or more affiliates of each federation would fight one another for the right to represent the employees of a firm. In such a dispute, the employer was caught in the middle of a controversy in which he had no interest and over which he exercised no control. The employer's business sometimes came to a standstill until one of the unions won the jurisdictional battle. Subsection (C) seeks to remedy this situation.

In one case [47] the board found that the union's picketing activities after the certification of another union were unlawful within the meaning of Section 8(b)(4)(C) in that they implemented previous threats of the union that all measures would be taken to enforce the union's rights under a contract it had with the employer before the certification. In another case [48] the board rejected the contention of the union that its activities were for organizational purposes only. This contention could not be reconciled with the fact that the employer was placed on the union's unfair list and was picketed in order to force it to bring up wages and other employment conditions to the union's "area standard."

SECTIONS 8(B)(4)(D) AND 10(K). JURISDICTIONAL DISPUTES. Section 8(b)(4)(D) forbids a labor organization to engage in or induce strike action for the purpose of forcing any employer to assign particular work tasks to "employees in a particular labor organization, or in a particular trade, craft, or class rather than to employees in another labor organization or in another trade, craft, or class, unless such employer is failing to conform to an order or certification of the National Labor Relations Board determining the bargaining representative for employees performing such work."

An unfair labor practice charge under this section, however, must be handled differently from charges alleging any other type of unfair labor practice. Section 10(k) of the act requires that parties to a jurisdictional dispute be given ten days after notice of the filing of charges with the board to adjust their dispute. If, at the end of that time, they are unable to "submit to the Board satisfactory evidence that they have adjusted,

47. National Maritime Union (Moore-McCormack Lines Inc.), 121 NLRB 69 (1958).
48. District Lodge 24, Int'l Ass'n of Machinists (Industrial Chrome Plating Co.), 121 NLRB 1298 (1958).

or agreed upon methods for the voluntary adjustment of the dispute," the board is empowered to hear and determine the dispute.

Section 10(k) further provides that charges shall be dismissed when the board's determination of the underlying dispute has been complied with or when the parties have voluntarily adjusted the dispute. A complaint issues if the party charged fails to comply with the board's determination. A complaint may also be issued by the General Counsel in case of failure of the method agreed on to adjust the dispute.

For the board to proceed with a determination under Section 10(k) the record made at the hearing must show that a work assignment dispute within the meaning of Sections 8(b)(4)(D) and 10(k) exists; that there is reasonable cause to believe that the union has induced a work stoppage in connection with the dispute; and that the parties have not adjusted their dispute or agreed on methods for its voluntary adjustment. The board has held that it may properly take cognizance of a dispute arising from disagreement between two unions over which of two existing bargaining units appropriately includes disputed work, and that it may resolve such dispute by making the necessary unit determination.[49] A primary dispute between an employer and a union about hiring additional employees for a particular job comes within Section 10(k).[50]

When a union charged with a section 8(b)(4)(D) violation is found to have no valid claim to the disputed work, it is the board's practice to issue a determination to the effect that the union is not lawfully entitled to require the employer to assign the work to its members, rather than to the employer's own employees, whether members of another or of no labor organization. In this type of case, the board has consistently refrained from making an affirmative assignment of the work "to (the other party of the jurisdictional dispute), or to any other trade, craft, or class of employees." [51] The board has declined to adopt the view of one federal court that held that Section 10(k) requires such an affirmative award.[52] In 1961 the U.S. Supreme Court [53] upheld the view of the lower federal court, and the National Labor Relations Board is now required, in a jurisdictional-dispute case, to make an award to one union to the exclusion of another union.[54]

49. Window Glass Cutters League (Libbey-Owens-Ford Co.), 123 NLRB 1183 (1959).
50. Local 472, Int'l Laborers Union (Ernest Renda Contracting Co.), 123 NLRB 1176 (1959).
51. Int'l Bhd. of Electrical Workers (Southern New Eng. Tel. Co.), 121 NLRB 1061 (1958).
52. NLRB v. United Ass'n of Journeymen and Apprentices of the Plumbing, etc. (Frank W. Hake), 242 Fed. (2d) 722 (1957).
53. NLRB v. Local 1212, Int'l Bhd. Electrical Workers, 364 U.S. 573 (1961).
54. Violation of Section 8(b) (4) (D) was found in the following cases: Car-

EXCESSIVE OR DISCRIMINATORY FEES FOR UNION MEMBERSHIP.
Section 8 (b) (5) makes it an unfair labor practice for a union to
charge employees covered by a valid union security agreement a membership fee "in an amount which the Board finds excessive or discriminatory under all the circumstances." This section further provides that
"in making such a finding, the Board shall consider, among other relevant factors, the practices and customs of labor organizations in the
particular industry, and the wages currently paid to the employees affected."

In one case under this section the board held that the union acted
unlawfully when increasing its membership initiation fee fivefold and
requiring employees covered by a union security agreement to pay a
$250 initiation fee.[55] The fee was held both discriminatory and exces-
sive. The evidence in the case showed that the fee increase was for the
illegal purpose of maintaining a closed shop through the imposition
of an initiation fee in an amount calculated to discourage entrance into
the industry. There was no showing that the increase was prompted by
financial necessity, the cost of providing increased benefits, or any other
reason beyond the union's desire to promote a closed union. For the
purpose of remedying the unfair labor practice, the board directed
the union to cease giving effect to the $250 initiation fee requirement,
and to return to the employees all sums paid in excess of the former $50
fee.

In another case the board held that the union's uniform requirement
of a reinstatement fee for former members that was higher than the
initiation fee for new members was not discriminatory within the meaning of Section 8(b)(5).[56]

SECTION 8(B)(6). FEATHERBEDDING. The last of the six unfair
union practices is featherbedding.

Section 8(b)(6) makes it an unfair labor practice for a union to cause
an employer to pay, or deliver any money or other thing of value, in
the nature of an exaction for services which are not performed or will
not be performed.

The term featherbedding describes the practice demanding payment
of a wage for work which is not performed or of the union insisting on
the employment of more workers than are necessary.

The "bogus work" practice in the newspaper industry, which consists
of setting type to duplicate advertisements received from outside the

penters and Joiners Union (W. H. Condo), 121 NLRB 308 (1958); Radio and
Tel. Engrs. Union, Int'l Bhd. of Elec. Workers (Columbia Broadcasting Co.), 121
NLRB 1207 (1958).
55. Motion Picture Screen Cartoonists, Local 839, 121 NLRB 1196 (1958).
56. Local 173, Int'l Molders and Foundry Workers Union (Hubley Mfg. Co.),
121 NLRB 170 (1958).

shop in the form of mats, is not featherbedding, even though the type is not used and is destroyed. A union does not violate the act by insisting on pay for the "bogus work," even though the work is of no economic value to the employers and is not wanted by them.[57] A full text of the American Newspaper Publishers Association case, in which these points were made, follows.

The question here is whether a labor organization engages in an unfair labor practice, within the meaning of Sec. 8(b)(6) of the National Labor Relations Act, as amended by the Labor Management Relations Act, 1947, when it insists that newspaper publishers pay printers for reproducing advertising matter for which the publishers ordinarily have no use. For the reasons hereafter stated, we hold that it does not.

Petitioner, American Newspaper Publishers Association, is a New York corporation the membership of which includes more than 800 newspaper publishers. They represent over 90 per cent of the circulation of the daily and Sunday newspapers in the U.S. and carry over 90 per cent of the advertising published in such papers.

In November, 1947, petitioner filed with the National Labor Relations Board charges that the International Typographical Union, here called ITU, and its officers were engaging in unfair labor practices within the meaning of Sec. 8(b)(1), (2) and (6) of the National Labor Relations Act, as amended by the Labor Management Relations Act, 1947, here called the Taft-Hartley Act. . . .

Printers in newspaper composing rooms have long sought to retain the opportunity to set up in type as much as possible of whatever is printed by their respective publishers. In 1872, when printers were paid on a piecework basis, each diversion of composition was at once reflected by a loss in their income. Accordingly, ITU, which had been formed in 1852 from local typographical societies, began its long battle to retain as much typesetting work for printers as possible.

With the introduction of the linotype machine in 1890, the problem took on a new aspect. When a newspaper advertisement was set up in type, it was impressed on a cardboard matrix, or "mat." These mats were used by their makers and also were reproduced and distributed, at little or no cost, to other publishers who used them as molds for metal casting from which to print the same advertisement. This procedure by-passed all compositors except those who made up the original form. Facing this loss of work, ITU secured the agreement of newspaper publishers to permit their respective compositors, at convenient times, to set up duplicate forms for all local advertisements in precisely the same manner as though the mat had not been used. For this reproduction work the printer received their regular pay. The doing of this "made work" came to be known in the trade as "setting bogus." It was a wasteful procedure. Nevertheless, it has become a recognized idiosyncrasy of the trade and a customary feature of the wage structure and work schedule of newspaper printers. . . .

57. American Newspaper Publishers Ass'n v. NLRB 345 U.S. 100 (1953).

On rare occasions the reproduced compositions are used to print the advertisement when rerun, but, ordinarily, they are promptly consigned to the "hell box" and melted down. . . .

However desirable the elimination of all industrial featherbedding practices may have appeared to Congress, the legislative history of the Taft-Hartley Act, 29 U.S.C.A. Sec. 141 et seq., demonstrates that when the legislation was put in final form Congress decided to limit the practice but little by law.

A restraining influence throughout this congressional consideration of featherbedding was the fact that the constitutionality of the Lea Act penalizing featherbedding in the broadcasting industry was in litigation. That Act, known also as the Petrillo Act, had been adopted April 16, 1946, as an amendment to the Communications Act of 1934, 47 U.S.C.A. Sec. 151 et seq. . . .

On December 2, 1946, the U.S. District Court for the Northern District of Illinois held that it violated the First, Fifth, and Thirteenth Amendments to the Constitution of the U.S. United States v. Petrillo, D.C., 68 F. Supp. 845. The case was pending here on appeal throughout the debate on the Taft-Hartley bill. Not until June 23, 1947, on the day of the passage of the Taft-Hartley bill over the President's veto, was the constitutionality of the Lea Act upheld. United States v. Petrillo, 332 U.S. 1, 67 S. Ct. 1538, 91 L. Ed. 1877.

The purpose of the sponsors of the Taft-Hartley bill to avoid the controversial features of the Lea Act is made clear in the written statement which Senator Taft, co-sponsor of the bill and Chairman of the Senate Committee on Labor and Public Welfare, caused to be incorporated in the proceedings of the Senate, June 1947. . . .

The act now limits its condemnation to instances where a labor organization or its agents exact pay from an employer in return for services not performed or not to be performed. Thus, where work is done by an employee, with the employer's consent, a labor organization's demand that the employee be compensated for time spent in doing the disputed work does not become an unfair labor practice. The transaction simply does not fall within the kind of featherbedding defined in the statute. In the absence of proof to the contrary, the employee's compensation reflects his entire relationship with his employer. . . .

Accordingly, the judgment of the Court of Appeals sustaining dismissal of the complaint, insofar as it was based upon Sec. 8(b)(6), is affirmed."

When the musicians' union demanded that a local orchestra be hired wherever a traveling orchestra performs, and be paid for actual services which are not mere token services, it has been held that no violation of the act occurs even where such services are neither needed or desired by a theatre.[58]

It seems clear from the cases that this section is violated only when workers demand pay without working or offering to perform any work.

58. NLRB v. Gamble Enterprises Inc., 345 U.S. 117 (1953).

Then it is possible that the Hobbs Anti-Racketeering Act [59] would also be violated. The Hobbs Act seeks to prevent anyone from obstructing, delaying, or affecting interstate commerce by robbery or extortion.

SECTION 8 (C). THE FREE-SPEECH AMENDMENT. The First Amendment of the United States Constitution provides that Congress shall pass no law abridging the right of free speech. Section 7 of the Wagner Act provides that employees shall have the right to organize and join unions of their own choosing. Section 8 provides that employers may not interfere with the rights guaranteed workers in Section 7. Unquestionably employers do enjoy the right of free speech, yet, like all other constitutional rights, responsibilities flow from it. Congress created new rights through the enactment of the Wagner Act, and employers may not invade them or engage in activities which would lead to nullifying the prescribed worker rights. Therefore the question of free speech exercised by the employer must be considered in light of the rights granted workers under the 1935 act. It is very clear from the cases that any speech, or writing delivered by an employer that threatens the workers with economic loss if they join a union, or any promise of an economic benefit conditional on the workers' promise not to join a union, constitutes a violation of the act. On the other hand, an employer may express an opinion on the subject of unionism, and so long as coercion or interference is absent the communication is generally considered privileged.

CASES AND RULINGS. Between 1935 when the Wagner Act was passed, and 1947 when the Taft-Hartley Law was enacted, free speech became a frequently litigated issue. Since the Wagner Act was silent on free speech, the NLRB developed the policy that an employer might lawfully make antiunion statements provided they were not threatening or coercive. Nevertheless, during the early Wagner Act period, the board seemed to rule that every antiunion speech was intrinsically threatening or coercive or both. This policy was premised on the belief that the employer was in an economically superior position and had constantly to be supervised lest he take undue advantage of this position. In a major decision in 1941 the Supreme Court upheld a board ruling [60] which declared that antiunion speeches and literature were not privileged as free speech. In this case, while a union organizing drive was going on, the employer issued a bulletin and one of its officials delivered an antiunion speech before the workers. The court held that the employer's statements in themselves, when considered independently of their background, were privileged. However, when the employer's statements were considered in the context of its long history

59. Sec. 1951, Title 18, U.S. Code, Act of July 3, 1946, amending Act of June 18, 1934.
60. NLRB v. Va. Electric and Power Co., 314 U.S. 469 (1941).

of antiunion activities, the court held that the employer's words were coercive. On this point the court said:

. . . The employer . . . is as free now as ever to take any side it may choose on this controversial issue. But, certainly, conduct, though evidenced in part by speech, may amount, in connection with other circumstances, to coercion within the meaning of the Act.

In 1946 an interesting development concerning free speech occurred in a case [61] which developed the "captive-audience" doctrine. The employer involved in this case called together his employees on company time and property and delivered antiunion speeches directed against one of the two unions seeking representation rights. The employees constituted a captive audience inasmuch as they were forced to listen to the speeches. The board ruled that the company interfered with the employees' rights of self-organization. The circuit court of appeals upheld the board's finding that the speech made to a captive audience constituted coercion and interference even though the statements in themselves were not coercive. This court indicated in its opinion that the objection to the captive-audience device could be avoided if the employer accorded a similar opportunity to the union to address the employees on company property and time.

Employer groups were dissatisfied with the freedom of speech rulings handed down by the board and the courts. They expressed views that an imbalance existed between union and employer rights of free speech. Unions, they said, were permitted unlimited right to speak their minds and were completely free of the limitations imposed on employers. Congress was persuaded to include among the many amendments to the Wagner Act a provision dealing with free speech. Section 8(c) resulted. It reads as follows:

The expressing of any views, argument, or opinion, or the dissemination thereof, whether in written, printed, graphic, or visual form shall not constitute or be evidence of an unfair labor practice under any of the provisions of this Act, if such expression contains no threat of reprisal or force or promise of benefit.

In 1953 [62] the board reversed the position it took in the Clark [63] case and held that so long as the employer did not make a coercive antiunion speech to a captive audience it could lawfully deny the union's request for an opportunity to reply.

In another case [64] the board set an election aside when the employer assembled its workers on company time and property, less than 24 hours

61. NLRB v. Clark Bros. Co., 163 Fed. (2d) 373 (1947).
62. Livingston Shirt Corp., 107 NLRB 400 (1935).
63. *Supra.*
64. NLRB v. Peerless Plywood Co., 107 NLRB 427 (1953).

before the election, to listen to a noncoercive, antiunion speech. The operative circumstance was the fact that the speech was given less than 24 hours before the time scheduled for the representation election. The board established the following ruling:

. . . employers and unions alike will be prohibited from making election speeches on company time to massed assemblies of employees within twenty-four hours before the scheduled time for conducting an election.

In the Peerless Plywood case it was held that the 24-hour rule is designed to avoid the "unwholesome and unsettling effect" of last-minute election speeches on company time. This rule is inapplicable to other legitimate campaign media such as distribution of literature [65] or the posting of signs in the plant soliciting a pro-union vote.[66]

In the Falmouth case [67] the board refused to invalidate an election when the employer made a speech to its employees during the 24-hour period preceding the election. In this case the speech was given on the employees' own time, and they were advised that they were free to leave at any time. Furthermore, the speech was not coercive.

The free-speech rulings have been equally applicable to unions since 1947 when union unfair practices were incorporated into the Taft-Hartley Act. Coercive and threatening statements made to employees by a union are not privileged. The following union statements [68] were held to be violative of the act.

"Those who do not join the union will eventually lose their job."

"We have ways of handling people like you that argue against the union."

The free-speech provision in the act does not protect a union which coerces, intimidates, or threatens employees.[69] However, vile, obscene, and insulting remarks made by pickets to nonstrikers were considered protected statements under Section 8(c).[70]

Labor unions are quite unhappy with the amount of freedom given employers under Section 8(c). There is no question that employers have taken full advantage of the privileges given them to undermine or dislodge unions. Short of outright threats or promises of benefits, employers have become less inhibited in their antiunion expressions. Many unions feel that since 1947 this freedom of speech has blunted union efforts to organize new territory. The repeated failures to organize Southern textile mills and the slow union progress in organizing white-

---

65. U.S. Radium Corp., 122 NLRB 468 (1958).
66. Fisher Radio Corp., 123 NLRB 879 (1959).
67. Falmouth Co., 115 NLRB 1533 (1956).
68. Lane v. NLRB, 186 Fed. (2d) 671 (1951).
69. See NLRB v. I.L.W.U., 210 Fed. (2d) 581 (1954).
70. Textile Workers Union, 123 NLRB (No. 72) (1959).

collar workers are laid primarily at the door of board policy under Section 8(c) by most union officials.

SECTION 8(D). DUTIES OF PARTIES IN COLLECTIVE BARGAINING. We have already seen that Section 8(b)(3) makes it a union unfair practice to refuse to bargain with an employer if the union is the authorized bargaining agent. This obligation matches the one required by the employer under Section 8(a)(5) of the act.

Section 8(d) states that the duty to bargain means that the parties must confer in good faith but are under no legal obligation to reach an agreement. Collective bargaining is defined as the

performance of the mutual obligation of the employer and the representative of the employees to meet at reasonable times and confer in good faith with respect to wages, hours, and other terms and conditions of employment, or in the negotiation of an agreement, or any question arising thereunder, and the execution of a written contract incorporating any agreement reached if requested by either party, but such obligation does not compel either party to agree to a proposal or require the making of a concession.

Under this statutory duty to bargain labor unions and employers are required, reciprocally, to give 60-day notice of contract disputes to federal and state conciliation services. Section 8(d) further provides that, during a specified 60-day period, the existing contract must be kept in effect without resort to strikes or lock-outs by the parties. These provisions have slowed down the calling of strikes, enabled mediators to intervene before it is too late to help, and have generally provided an orderly method for resolving disputes and reaching final settlements.

In the leading case [71] on this point the U.S. Supreme Court held that the National Labor Relations Act had a dual purpose: To substitute collective bargaining for economic warfare and to protect the right of employees to engage in concerted activities for their own benefit. Chief Justice Warren delivered the opinion of the court.

. . . In particular we are concerned with Section 8(d)(4), which provides that a party who wishes to modify or terminate a collective bargaining contract must continue "in full force and effect, without resorting to strike or lockout, all the terms and conditions of the existing contract for a period of sixty days after . . . notice (of his wish to modify or terminate) is given or until the expiration date of such contract, whichever occurs later." Since Section 8(d) defines the duty to bargain collectively, a violation of Section 8(d)(4) constitutes a refusal to bargain, an unfair labor practice for employers, Section 8(a)(5), and unions, Section 8(b)(3). The last sentence of Section 8(d) contains an additional sanction: an employee who strikes within the specified 60-day period loses his status as an employee for the purposes of Section 8, 9 and 10 of the Act. The sole question presented by the petition for certiorari is:

71. NLRB v. Lion Oil Co., 352 U.S. 282 (1957).

Whether the requirement of this Section is satisfied where a contract provides for negotiation and adoption of modifications at an intermediate date during its term, and a strike in support of modification demands occurs after the date on which such modifications may become effective—and after the 60-day notice period has elapsed—but prior to the terminal date of the contract.

We are told by the Solicitor General that the question is of major importance in the negotiation and administration of hundreds of collective bargaining agreements throughout the country; that there is a decided trend among unions and employers to execute contracts of longer duration than formerly and to include provisions for reopening to negotiate changes during the contract term. Because of the importance of the question, we granted certiorari, 350 U.S. 986, to review a decision of the Court of Appeals for the Eighth Circuit to the effect that Section 8(d)(4) bans strikes to obtain modifications of a contract until the contract by its terms or by the action of the parties has terminated.

On October 23, 1950, respondent Lion Oil Co. and the Oil Workers International Union, CIO, entered into a contract which provided:

"This agreement shall remain in full force and effect for the period beginning October 23, 1950, and ending October 23, 1951, and thereafter until canceled in the manner hereinafter in this Article provided.

"This agreement may be canceled and terminated by the Company or the Union as of a date subsequent to October 23, 1951, by compliance with the following procedure:

"(a) If either party to this agreement desires to amend the terms of this agreement, it shall notify the other party in writing of its desire to that effect, by registered mail. No such notice shall be given prior to August 24, 1951. Within the period of 60 days immediately following the date of the receipt of said notice by the party to which notice is so delivered, the Company and the Union shall attempt to agree as to the desired amendments to this agreement.

"(b) If an agreement with respect to amendment of this agreement has not been reached within the 60-day period mentioned in the sub-section immediately preceding, either party may terminate this agreement thereafter upon not less than sixty days' written notice to the other. Any such notice of termination shall state the date upon which the termination of this agreement shall be effective."

On August 24, 1951, the union served written notice on the company of its desire to modify the contract. Negotiations began on the contractual changes proposed by the union. The union members voted for a strike on February 14, 1952, but the strike, thrice postponed as negotiations continued, did not actually begin until April 30, 1952. The union never gave notice to terminate the contract as contemplated by the quoted contractual provision. Therefore, at all relevant times a collective bargaining agreement was in effect. On August 3, a new contract was executed, and the strikers began to return to work the following day. Certain actions of the company during the strike were the basis of unfair labor practice charges by the union upon which a complaint issued.

The Labor Board found that the company was guilty of unfair labor practices under Section 8(a)(1), (3) and (5) of the Act. The company defended on the ground that the strike, because it occurred while the contract was in effect, was in violation of Section 8(d)(4).

The Board held that since, under the contract in dispute, October 23, 1951, was such an "agreed date," the notice given August 24, followed by a wait of more than 60 days, satisfied the statute. The company was ordered to cease and desist and, affirmatively, to make whole employees found to have been discriminated against.

On the company's petition for review, the Court of Appeals set aside the Board's order, 221 F. 2d 231. The court held that the "expiration date" of the contract was the date on which all rights and obligations under it would cease; that the second notice required to bring about this termination not having been given, the strike violated Section 8(d)(4) and the strikers therefore lost their status as employees entitled to the protection of the Act.

We find our guide to the general context of the statute in Mastro Plastics. In that case we recognized a "dual purpose" in the Taft-Hartley Act—to substitute collective bargaining for economic warfare and to protect the right of employees to engage in concerted activities for their own benefit. 350 U.S., at 284. A construction which serves neither of these aims is to be avoided unless the words Congress has chosen clearly compel it. The restriction on employees' concerted activities which would result from the construction placed upon Section 8(d)(4) by the Court of Appeals is obvious. Too, we think it would discourage the development of long-term bargaining relationships. Unions would be wary of entering into long-term contracts with machinery for reopening them for modification from time to time, if they thought the right to strike would be denied them for the entire term of such a contract, though they imposed no such limitations on themselves.

Applying that construction to the facts of this case, we hold that the notice and waiting requirements of Section 8(d) were fully satisfied. October 23, 1951 was the first date upon which the contract by its terms was subject to amendment. Notice of proposed amendments was served 60 days in advance. The strike did not occur until long afterward. The fact that on October 23 the contract became terminable upon further notice by either party is immaterial.

Here the strike occurred at a time when the parties were bargaining over modifications after notice and in accordance with the terms of the contract. Where there has been no express waiver of the right to strike, a waiver of the right during such a period is not to be inferred. We do not believe that the two-phase provision for terminating this contract means that it was not within the contemplation of the parties that economic weapons might be used to support demands for modification before the notice to terminate was given.

The judgment below is reversed and the case remanded for proceedings not inconsistent with this opinion.

Section 9. *Bargaining Units, Representation Proceedings, and Elections*

The Taft-Hartley Act requires that an employer bargain with representatives selected by a majority of his employees in a unit appropriate for collective bargaining.

Section 9, which has been discussed in Chapter 9, establishes the machinery necessary for determining which bargaining representative, if any, shall represent the employees for collective-bargaining purposes. The following discussion is devoted to the major changes resulting from amendments made to Section 9 by the Taft-Hartley Law of 1947.

SECTION 9(A) has been amended to allow an individual employee or group of employees to present grievances to their employer for adjustment without union intervention, provided the adjustment is not inconsistent with the bargaining contract, and provided further that the union has been invited to be present at the adjustment conference.[72] Under the Wagner Act of 1935 a labor contract prevented an individual employee from presenting grievances under any procedure except that provided in the contract, and the union was allowed to negotiate the actual disposition of the grievance.[73]

SECTION 9(B) has been significantly changed. Professional employees may not be placed in a bargaining unit with nonprofessionals unless a majority of the professionals vote in a National Labor Relations Board election to be included in the group.[74] The reason for this change can be found in the great contrast of interests between professionals and nonprofessionals, as well as the desire of the professionals to adhere to specific standards of performance and conduct. Section 2(12), of the act defines a "professional employee as one who is engaged in work predominantly intellectual as opposed to routine, mental, manual, mechanical or physical work and involving consistent exercise of discretion and judgment in its performance."

Craftsmen may petition to be placed in a bargaining unit separate from the larger industrial unit provided that the craftsmen belong to a union that has traditionally devoted itself to serving the special interests of the particular employees.[75]

72. West Texas Utilities Co. v. NLRB, 206 Fed. (2d) 442 (1953); Dazey Corp., 106 NLRB 553 (1953).
73. Hughes Tool Co., 147 Fed. (2d) 69.
74. For rulings, see Leedom v. Kyne, 308 U.S. 184 (1958); Standard Oil Co., 107 NLRB 1524 (1954).
75. See Am. Potash and Chemical Corp., 107 NLRB 1418 (1954); Plastic Film Co. Inc., 123 NLRB 1635 (1959); Dana Corp., 122 NLRB 365 (1958); General Electric Co., 123 NLRB 884 (1959).

Plant guards employed to protect the property of an employer or to protect the safety of persons on the employer's premises may not be included in any bargaining unit in which nonguard employees are included. In addition, the board may not certify as the representative of plant guards any union that either represents nonguard employees or is affiliated directly or indirectly with a union representing nonguard employees.[76]

REPRESENTATION PROCEEDINGS. SECTION 9(c)(1), (A) AND (B). Under the original National Labor Relations Act of 1935, a union was able to gain board approval as the bargaining representative in two ways: By obtaining a majority vote in a secret, board-conducted election, or by having the board examine union membership and dues lists to determine whether a majority of those on the employer's payroll were union members of fairly recent standing. In 1939 the board discontinued this card-check system. It has since adhered to an election in every case of a union making a claim for representation. The 1947 amendment provides that the board may formally certify a collective-bargaining representative only on the basis of the results of a board-conducted election. Sometimes unions bypass the board and seek representation status by demanding recognition from the employer; when its demand is rejected, the union may strike. When this type of strike is successful the legality of the means is seldom contested. However, the union will receive no official board recognition as the certified agent except as the result of a secret election. The recognition strike will be discussed in the next chapter.

Generally, board certification gives the labor organization bargaining status for no less than one year, during which its bargaining status may not be challenged by a rival union. Without certification, this security against a contest by another union does not hold.

A representation proceeding begins with filing a representation petition at the board offices. Under the amended act, an employer may file a petition when one or more labor organizations have asked it for recognition as the bargaining representative. A hearing follows the filing of the petition, and the board, after determining that a representation question exists, will direct the holding of an election by secret ballot and will certify the result.

If the petition has been filed by a labor organization, there must be a showing that at least 30 per cent of the employees involved have indicated that they wish to be represented by the petitioning union. No showing of employee interest is required when the employer files the petition.

76. For rulings, see Ohio Chemical Mfg. Co., 76 NLRB 1328 (1948); A.D.T. Co., 90 NLRB 154 (1955); Mack Mfg. Corp., 107 NLRB 209 (1953).

A question of representation may also be raised under Section 9(c)(1)(A) by petitioning for decertification of a bargaining agent which has been certified, or is currently recognized by the employer.[77] A showing of at least 30 per cent interest of the employees in the bargaining unit must accompany the decertification petition.

Evidence that a decertification petition was filed under the encouragement of an employer will result in a rejection of the petition.[78] The processing of this type of petition is similar to that of petitions for certification. If the union loses the decertification election, its bargaining status is nullified by the board.

SECTION 9(c)(3) provides that when a union loses a certification or decertification election 12 months must elapse before another representation election may take place. Another major provision in this amendment bars the economic strikers who are not entitled to reinstatement from participating in a representation election.[79]

The board will not direct an election among employees covered by a valid collective-bargaining agreement except under certain circumstances. The contract-bar rule insists that for the contract to be effective it must be in writing,[80] properly executed and binding on the parties, and of no more than reasonable duration.[81] This rule has been devised by the board to promote the statutory objective of stabilizing labor relations.

Section 9(c)(3) requires a runoff election where none of the choices on the ballot receives a majority of the votes cast. In this election employees must select one of the two choices that received the largest and second largest number of votes cast. "No union," will participate in the runoff election as a choice if it received either the largest or the second largest number of votes. This was not true under the Wagner Act. For example: If 400 votes were cast in a representation election, a total of at least 201 votes would be necessary to win. If Union A received 180 votes, Union B received 100 votes, and No Union received 120 votes, the ballot choices for the runoff election under the 1935 Act would be Union A and Union B. The board reasoned that since 280 persons wanted a union as against 120 who wanted no union, the employees should be permitted to select between Union A and Union B. Under the 1947 amendment, the runoff election would include Union A and No Union since they received the largest and second largest number of votes in the first election.

---

77. See Oakwood Tool and Engineering Co., 122 NLRB 812 (1958).
78. Georgia Kraft Co., 120 NLRB 806 (1958).
79. The 1959 Labor Management Reporting and Disclosure Act repealed this provision. Economic strikers may now participate in representation elections.
80. Appalachian Shale Products Co., 121 NLRB 1160 (1958).
81. Pacific Coast Ass'n, 121 NLRB 990 (1958).

SECTION 9 (E) (1). Another amendment of note is Section 9(e)(1). Under Section 8(a)(3), a union may validly make a union-shop agreement if it has a majority status in an appropriate bargaining unit and if the majority of the employees eligible to vote authorize it to make such an agreement in a secret board-conducted election. In 1951 [82] the National Labor Relations Act was amended by striking the election requirement out of this provision; now unions are permitted to enter into union-shop agreements provided the employer is willing to accept this type of security clause.

Under Section 9(e)(1) employees who have been subject to compulsory unionization may request a deauthorization election to rescind the union's authority to execute union-shop agreements. At least 30 per cent of the employees in the bargaining unit covered by the union shop agreement must join in the deauthorization petition. The revocation of the union's authority to execute a union-shop agreement must be approved by a majority of the employees in the bargaining unit, and not merely by a majority of those voting in the election.

SECTIONS 9 (F), 9 (G), AND 9 (H). Sections 9(f), 9(g), and 9(h) were repealed by the Labor Management Reporting and Disclosure Act of 159. These sections had required unions to file certain reports, including an annual financial statement, with the Secretary of Labor before the board was permitted to act upon any representation petition or unfair labor practice complaint filed by labor organizations. Also required as a condition for the use of the board's machinery was the filing of a non-Communist affidavit by every union officer in which he was required to swear "that he is not a member of the Communist party or affiliated with such party, and that he does not believe in or teach the overthrow of the United States Government by force or by any illegal or unconstitutional methods."

The 1959 act has several sections which compel labor unions to file financial and other types of reports with union members and with the Secretary of Labor. Communists are denied the right to hold union office under the new act. This law will be analyzed in the next chapter.

Section 10

THE FEDERAL PREEMPTION DOCTRINE. Section 10(a) of the Taft-Hartley Law provides:

. . . That the Board is empowered by agreement with any agency of any State or Territory to cede to such agency jurisdiction over any cases in any

82. Public Law 189, 82nd Congress, 1st Session, c. 534 approved Oct. 22, 1951.

industry (other than mining, manufacturing, communications and transportation, except where predominantly local in character) even though such cases may involve labor disputes affecting commerce, unless the provision of the State or Territorial statute applicable to the determination of such cases by such agency is inconsistent with the corresponding provision of this Act or has received a construction inconsistent therewith.

Article VI, Section 2 of the United States Constitution reads:

This Constitution, and the laws of the United States, which shall be made in pursuance thereof . . . shall be the Supreme Law of the Land; and the judges in every state shall be bound thereby, anything in the Constitution or Laws of any state to the contrary notwithstanding.

Under this constitutional principle of federal supremacy, state regulation, either statutory or judge-determined, becomes inoperative whenever Congress legislates in a specific field. Either by choice or because of insufficient funds, the board failed to exercise fully its statutory jurisdiction over all labor disputes affecting interstate commerce. Its failure encouraged the states to intervene in those labor disputes neglected by the federal board. With only a few exceptions, federal-state conflicts never became a major difficulty between 1935 and 1953. One of the earliest labor cases in which the U.S. Supreme Court was called on to invoke the preemption doctrine was Bethlehem Steel Co. v. N.Y. State Labor Relations Board.[83] The issue developed when the NLRB asserted jurisdiction over unions of foremen employed by industries subject to the Wagner Act. The board had refused to certify such unions as collective bargaining representatives. When the New York State Labor Relations Board attempted to certify these unions, the federal board challenged the action on the ground that certification of the unions conflicted with provisions of the Wagner Act, and that under the constitutional supremacy clause the state of New York was preempted. The U.S. Supreme Court agreed with the board and compelled New York to withdraw.

Since the enactment of the Taft-Hartley Act in 1947, the Supreme Court has delivered several decisions concerning the preemption doctrine. These rulings are important because they point out the broad jurisdictional power of the NLRB and the circumscribed area in which the states may assume authority.

In December 1953, the Supreme Court handed down a precedent-setting decision in the case of Garner v. Teamsters Union.[84] This was the first of a series of rulings based on the Taft-Hartley Act. In this case, the state of Pennsylvania attempted to assert jurisdiction and sought to

83. 330 U.S. 767 (1947). See also 315 U.S. 740 (1942); 338 U.S. 953 (1950); Hill v. Florida, 325 U.S. 538 (1945).
84. 346 U.S. 488 (1953).

enjoin peaceful and orderly picketing. The purpose of the picketing was to force an employer to encourage his employees to join a labor union. The Supreme Court held that state courts were without authority to pass on the legality of peaceful picketing, and whether a particular course of peaceful conduct was protected or proscribed may be decided only by the federal board.

In Weber v. Anheuser-Busch [85] the Supreme Court extended the application of the preemption doctrine. In this case the employer obtained an injunction in a state court barring picketing on the ground that its purpose was unlawful under the state antitrust laws. The employer had contended that the relief was sought under a general law dealing with restraint of trade, and not for any reason dealing with a labor dispute. On this argument, the employer succeeded in getting the state court to assert jurisdiction. The U.S. Supreme Court rejected the argument and vacated the injunction. It stated:

. . . where the facts reasonably bring the controversy within the sections (of the Taft-Hartley Law) prohibiting these practices, and where the conduct, if not prohibited by the federal Act, may be reasonably deemed to come within the protection afforded by the Act, the state court must decline jurisdiction in deference to the tribunal which Congress has selected for determining such issues in the first instance.

The importance of the doctrine of preemption became clear in three decisions handed down by the U.S. Supreme Court on March 25, 1957. These cases presented the same issue, the question of state jurisdiction over labor disputes affecting interstate commerce in which the National Labor Relations Board had declined jurisdiction because of the predominantly local character of the controversies. Guss v. Utah Labor Relations Board [86] involved an employer's refusal to bargain with a union which represented a majority of its employees.

Amalgamated Meat Cutters' Union v. Fairlawn Meats Inc.[87] and San Diego Building Trades Council v. Garmon [88] involved appeals from state court injunctions against picketing for recognition by nonrepresentative unions. The Supreme Court held, in each case, that the state board or state court had no jurisdiction over the matter even though the National Labor Relations Board had refused to act.

On the point of preemption, Justice Frankfurter said, in the second Garmon case:

. . . When it is clear or may fairly be assumed that the activities which a State purports to regulate are protected by section 7 of the National Labor

85. 348 U.S. 469 (1955); compare the Giboney case, *supra*, an antitrust case where no question of effect on interstate commerce was presented.
86. 353 U.S. 1 (1957).
87. 353 U.S. 20 (1957).
88. 353 U.S. 26 (1957); second Garmon case, 359 U.S. 236 (1959).

Relations Act, or constitute an unfair labor practice under section 8, due regard for the federal enactment requires that state jurisdiction must yield. To leave the State free to regulate conduct so plainly within the central aim of federal regulation involves too great a danger of conflict between power asserted by Congress and requirements imposed by state law. Nor has it mattered whether the States have acted through laws of broad general application rather than laws specifically directed towards the governance of industrial relations. Regardless of the mode adopted, to allow the States to control conduct which is the subject of national regulation would create potential frustration of national purposes.

At times it has not been clear whether the particular activity regulated by the States was governed by section 7 or section 8 or was, perhaps, outside both these sections. But courts are not primary tribunals to adjudicate such issues. It is essential to the administration of the Act that these determinations be left in the first instance to the National Labor Relations Board. What is outside the scope of this Court's authority cannot remain within a State's power and state jurisdiction too must yield to the exclusive primary competence of the Board.

At this point in our discussion of the preemption doctrine, we may conclude that a state may not decide questions of representation which are within the federal jurisdiction, nor may a state deal with certain conduct protected or prohibited by federal labor legislation. However, the state may, under Supreme Court rulings,[89] exercise jurisdiction over conduct involving violence and threats of violence. This power is granted because the state has the responsibility to preserve public safety and order. The states have the power not only to enjoin the violent conduct, but also to award tort damages for the consequences of such conduct even where such conduct may constitute a violation of the federal labor law. In 1958 an interesting decision[90] came down from the Supreme Court in which state authority was upheld. In this, the Gonzales, case, the plaintiff sued the union in a California state court for breach of contract. Gonzales contended that his expulsion from the union was contrary to the union by-laws. The union challenged the jurisdiction of the state court to entertain this suit by invoking the preemption doctrine. The California court granted judgment to Gonzales, ordered his reinstatement in the union, and awarded him money damages to cover the losses he had sustained. On an appeal to the U.S. Supreme Court, the state court judgment was sustained. Mr. Justice Frankfurter, speaking for the court, said:

. . . to preclude a state court from exerting its traditional jurisdiction to determine and enforce the rights of union membership would in many cases leave an unjustly ousted member without remedy for the restoration of his

89. See U.A.W. v. Wisconsin Emp. Rel. Bd., 351 U.S. 271 (1956); United Construction Workers v. Laburnum Construction Corp., 347 U.S. 656 (1954).
90. I.A.M. v. Gonzales, 356 U.S. 617 (1958).

important union rights. Such a drastic result, on the remote possibility of some entanglement with the Board's enforcement of the national policy, would require a more compelling indication of Congressional will than can be found in the interstices of the Taft-Hartley Act. . . . The National Labor Relations Board could not have given respondent the relief that California gave him according to its law of contracts and damages. Although, if the union's conduct constituted an unfair labor practice, the Board might possibly have been empowered to award back pay, in no event could it mulct in damages for mental and physical suffering. And the possibility of partial relief from the Board does not in such a case as is here presented, deprive a party of available state remedies for all damages suffered.

Chief Justice Warren and Justice Douglas dissented.

. . . In Garner, we rejected an attempt to secure preventive relief under state law for conduct over which the Board had remedial authority. We held that the necessity for uniformity in the regulation of labor relations subject to the Federal Act forbade recourse to potentially conflicting state remedies. . . . Since the majority's decision on the permissibility of a state-court damage award is at war with the policies of the Federal Act and contrary to the decisions of this Court, it is not surprising that the bulk of its opinion is concerned with the comforting irrelevancy of the State's conceded power to reinstate the wrongfully expelled. But it will not do to assert that the "possibility of conflict with federal policy" is as "remote" in the case of damages as with reinstatement.

The majority draws satisfaction from the fact that this was a suit for breach of contract, not an attempt to regulate or remedy union conduct designed to bring about an employer discrimination. But the presence or absence of pre-emption is a consequence of the effect of state action on the aims of federal legislation, not a game that is played with labels or an exercise in artful pleading. In a pre-emption case decided upon what now seem to be discarded principles, the author of today's majority opinion declared: "Controlling and therefore superseding federal power cannot be curtailed by the State even though the ground of intervention be different than that on which federal supremacy has been exercised." Weber v. Anheuser-Busch, *supra*, at 480. I would adhere to the view of pre-emption expressed by that case and by Garner v. Teamsters C. & H. Local Union, *supra*, and reverse the judgment below.

In another important case [91] the Supreme Court upheld the right of an employee to sue a union in a state court for damages under state law, even though the union's conduct constituted an unfair labor practice under the National Labor Relations Act. An award of $10,000 was made in the state court to compensate one Russell, the plaintiff, for the loss of earnings, mental suffering, and punitive damages occurring when mass picketing and threats of violence kept him from work during a strike. A majority of the Supreme Court said there was no conflict be-

91. Russell v. U.A.W., 356 U.S. 634 (1958).

tween the state court action and the National Labor Relations Act. Justice Burton, speaking for the court, said:

This action was instituted in the Circuit Court of Morgan County, Alabama, in 1952, by Paul S. Russell, the respondent, against the petitioners, International Union, United Automobile, Aircraft and Agricultural Implement Workers of America, CIO, an unincorporated labor organization, here called the union, and its agent, Volk, together with other parties not now in the case. Russell was a maintenance electrician employed by Calumet and Hecla Consolidated Copper Company (Wolverine Tube Division) in Decatur, Alabama, at $1.75 an hour and earned approximately $100 a week. The union was the bargaining agent for certain employees of the Division but Russell was not a member of the union nor had he applied for such membership. .

The allegations of his amended complaint may be summarized as follows: The union, on behalf of the employees it represented, called a strike to commence July 18, 1951. To prevent Russell and other hourly paid employees from entering the plant during the strike, and to thus make the strike effective, petitioners maintained a picket line from July 18 to September 24, 1951. This line was located along and in the public street which was the only means of ingress and egress to the plant. The line consisted of persons standing along the street or walking in a compact circle across the entire traveled portion of the street. Such pickets, on July 18, by force of numbers, threats of bodily harm to Russell and of damage to his property, prevented him from reaching the plant gates. At least one striker took hold of Russell's automobile. Some of the pickets stood or walked in front of his automobile in such a manner as to block the street and make it impossible for him, and others similarly situated, to enter the plant. The amended complaint also contained a second count to the same general effect but alleging that petitioners unlawfully conspired with other persons to do the acts above described.

The amended complaint further alleged that petitioners willfully and maliciously caused Russell to lose time from his work from July 18 to August 22, 1951, and to lose the earnings which he would have received had he and others not been prevented from going to and from the plant. Russell, accordingly, claimed compensatory damages for his loss of earnings and for his mental anguish, plus punitive damages, in the total sum of $50,000.

Petitioners filed a plea to the jurisdiction. They claimed that the National Labor Relations Board had jurisdiction of the controversy to the exclusion of the state court. The trial court overruled Russell's demurrer to the plea. However, the Supreme Court of Alabama reversed the trial court and upheld the jurisdiction of that court, even though the amended complaint charged a violation of Section 8(b)(1)(A) of the Federal Act. 258 Ala. 615, 64 So. 2d 384.

On remand, petitioners' plea to the jurisdiction was again filed but this time Russell's demurrer to it was sustained. The case went to trial before a jury and resulted in a general verdict and a judgment for Russell in the amount of $10,000 including punitive damages. On appeal, the Supreme Court of Alabama reaffirmed the Circuit Court's jurisdiction. It also affirmed the judgment for Russell on the merits, holding that Russell had proved the tort of wrongful interference with a lawful occupation. 264 Ala. 456, 88 So. 2d 175. Because of the importance of the jurisdictional issue, we granted certiorari. 352 U.S. 915.

There was much conflict in the testimony as to what took place in connection with the picketing but those conflicts were resolved by the jury in favor of Russell. Accepting a view of the evidence most favorable to him, the jury was entitled to conclude that petitioners did, by mass picketing and threats of violence, prevent him from entering the plant and from engaging in his employment from July 18 to August 22.

At the outset, we note that the union's activity in this case clearly was not protected by federal law. Indeed the strike was conducted in such a manner that it could have been enjoined by Alabama courts.

To the extent that a back pay award may provide relief for victims of an unfair labor practice, it is a partial alternative to a suit in the state courts for loss of earnings. If the employee's common-law rights of action against a union tortfeasor are to be cut off, that would in effect grant to unions a substantial immunity from the consequences of mass picketing or coercion such as was employed during the strike in the present case.

The situation may be illustrated by supposing, in the instant case, that Russell's car had been turned over resulting in damage to the car and personal injury to him. Under state law presumably he could have recovered for medical expenses, pain and suffering and property damages. Such items of recovery are beyond the scope of present Board remedial orders. Following the reasoning adopted by us in the Laburnum case, we believe that state jurisdiction to award damages for these items is not preempted. Nor can we see any difference, significant for present purposes, between tort damages to recover lost wages. We conclude that an employee's right to recover, in the state courts, all damages caused him by this kind of tortious conduct cannot fairly be said to be preempted without a clearer declaration of congressional policy than we find here. Of course, Russell could not collect duplicate compensation for lost pay from the state courts and the Board.

Punitive damages constitute a well-settled form of relief under the law of Alabama when there is a willful and malicious wrong. To the extent that such relief is penal in its nature, it is all the more clearly not granted to the Board by the Federal Acts. Accordingly, the judgment of the Supreme Court of Alabama is affirmed.

We have now seen that Congress has conferred on the National Labor Relations Board alone the power to regulate certain labor activities affecting interstate commerce by proscribing them or granting them protection. When the board declines jurisdiction, neither state boards nor state courts may take over. Only through a cession agreement as provided for in Section 10(a) of the Taft-Hartley Act may a state take jurisdiction over labor activities which involve, or affect, interstate commerce. No such agreements have ever been made. The reason for preempting the states in certain types of labor disputes is the desire of Congress to develop a uniform federal regulation of these disputes. The failure of the federal board to assert jurisdiction in certain labor cases and the states' preemption from entertaining these cases developed a vast "no-man's land." The Supreme Court was quite aware of this large area of inactivity, but it said that the problem created was one to be considered by Congress [92] and not by the courts.

We should not fail to note however, that the preemption doctrine does not bar any state from exercising regulatory power in those labor cases in which violence, threats of violence, or mass picketing may be present.

PROCEDURE IN UNFAIR LABOR PRACTICE ACTS. The National Labor Relations Board and its General Counsel have the duty of prosecuting and enforcing unfair labor practice charges.

Sections 10(b) to 10(j) inclusive empower the board:

(1) To issue complaints and to notice hearings.

(2) To conduct hearings.

(3) To take testimony in writing.

(4) To apply to the circuit court of appeals for enforcement of its order.

(5) To apply for injunctions against those charged with engaging in an unfair labor practice.

SECTION 10(K). HEARINGS ON JURISDICTIONAL STRIKES. We have seen that Section 8(b)4(D) of the act makes it an unfair labor practice for a union to force an employer to assign work to employees in a particular union rather than to employees in another labor union. Where the forcing union strikes an employer for control of work, the act provides that this is a jurisdictional strike and therefore constitutes an unfair practice.

Section 10(k) gives the board authority to hear and determine a jurisdictional dispute, unless within 10 days after notice that a jurisdictional-dispute charge has been filed with the board the parties to the dispute have submitted evidence of an adjustment of the problem. After concluding a 10(k) hearing, the board's policy has been to dismiss the unfair charge or to rule that one of the unions had engaged in a prohibited act. As late as 1961 the board had never ordered that one union shall have exclusive control of the disputed work. The board has adhered to this policy because of the closed-shop prohibition in the act. It has always felt that giving one union control of jobs in preference to another would be inconsistent with the ban on the closed shop.

In January 1961 the Supreme Court for the first time rendered a de-

---

92. Section 701(c), (1) and (2) of the 1959 Landrum-Griffin Act has eliminated the "no-man's land" problem.

cision [93] stating that the NLRB has a duty under the act to settle jurisdictional disputes. The court said:

> . . . We agree . . . that 10(k) requires the Board to decide jurisdictional disputes on their merits, and conclude that in this case that requirement means that the Board should affirmatively have decided whether the technicians or the stage employees were entitled to the disputed work.

SECTIONS 10(L) AND 10(M). Section 10(l) empowers the board to investigate a complaint involving a jurisdictional dispute, and if the board has reasonable cause to believe that the charges against the union are true, the board must apply to the U.S. District Court for a temporary injunction seeking to restrain the jurisdictional strike or other illegal conduct set forth in Section 8(b)4, (A), (B), or (C) of the act. The court may grant the injunction for 5 days ex parte, i.e., no notice need be given of the board's application to the union against whom the injunction is sought. Following the expiration of the 5-day period, the board usually applies for a permanent injunction at which time the union has the right to defend itself against the charge.

Section 10(m) provides that whenever any person is charged with engaging in an unfair labor practice within the meaning of subsection (a)(3) (discrimination; union shop agreement) or (b)(2) (coercion or discrimination) the charge shall be given priority over all other cases except cases of like character.

Sections 11 and 12

Sections 11(1) to 11(6) inclusive authorize the National Labor Board:

(1) To investigate all complaints filed with the board.

(2) To issue subpoenas requiring the attendance of witnesses and the production of books, records, and other evidence necessary in the conduct of investigations and trials, and

(3) To seek assistance from federal courts and federal administrative agencies relating to matters before the board.

Section 12 provides that any person who resists, prevents, impedes, or interferes with the business of the National Labor Relations Board shall be punished by fine or imprisonment or both.

The Right to Strike

Section 13 preserves the right of workers to engage in lawful strikes. Examples of unlawful strikes are sit-down strikes, strikes involving sec-

93. NLRB v. Electrical Workers Local 1212, 364 U.S. 573 (1961).

ondary boycotts, strikes to force acceptance of featherbedding practices, and strikes that amount to unfair union practices.

The U.S. Supreme Court has held unconstitutional a state law which
denied public utilities employees the right to strike.[94]

When a labor contract contains a step-by-step grievance procedure,
but has no "no-strike" provision, workers who strike without first resorting to the grievance procedure may be fired.[95]

The Mastro Plastics case [96] established a very interesting precedent.
The Supreme Court ruled that a strike in violation of a no-strike contract provision was lawful where it had been provoked by the employer's
unfair practices. Justice Burton delivered the opinion of the court.

This case presents two principal questions: (1) whether, in the collective-
bargaining contract before us, the union's undertaking "to refrain from
engaging in any strike or work stoppage during the term of this agreement"
waives not only the employees' right to strike for economic benefits but also
their right to strike solely against unfair labor practices of their employers,
and (2) whether section 8(d) of the National Labor Relations Act, as
amended, deprives individuals of their status as employees if, within the
waiting period prescribed by section 8(d)(4), they engaged in a strike
solely against unfair labor practices of their employers. For the reasons
hereafter stated, we answer each in the negative.

Mastro Plastics Corp. and French-American Reeds Manufacturing Co.,
Inc., petitioners herein, are New York corporations which, in 1949 and
1950, were engaged in interstate commerce, manufacturing, selling and distributing plastic articles, including reeds and other accessories for musical
instruments. They operated in the City of New York within the same plant,
under the same management and with the same employees. For collective
bargaining, their employees were represented by Local 22045, American
Federation of Labor, or by Local 3127, United Brotherhood of Carpenters
and Joiners of America, AFL. These locals occupied the same office and
used the services of the same representatives. During the period in question,
the right of representation of petitioners' employees was transferred back
and forth between them for reasons not material here. Accordingly, they
are referred to in this opinion as the "Carpenters."

In August 1950, Local 65 of the Wholesale and Warehouse Workers
Union began a campaign among petitioners' employees in an effort to become their collective-bargaining representative. Petitioners bitterly opposed
the movement, believing Local 65 to be Communist-controlled. Feeling
that the Carpenters were too weak to cope successfully with Local 65,
petitioners asked the Carpenters to transfer their bargaining rights to
Local 318, International Brotherhood of Pulp, Sulphite and Paper Mill
Workers, AFL. When the Carpenters declined to do so, petitioners selected
a committee of employees to visit 318, obtain membership cards and seek

94. Motor Coach Employees v. Wisconsin Emp. Rel. Board, 340 U.S. 383 (1951).
95. Mead Inc., 113 NLRB 1040 (1955).
96. NLRB v. Mastro Plastics Corp., 350 U.S. 270 (1956).

members for that union. The cards were distributed during working hours and petitioners paid their employees for time spent in the campaign, including attendance at a meeting of 318. Petitioners' officers and supervisors instructed employees to sign these cards and indicated that those refusing to do so would be "out."

September 28, Local 65 filed with the National Labor Relations Board its petition for certification as bargaining representative. October 24, Local 318 intervened in the representation proceedings and asked that it be certified. However, many employees revoked their applications for membership in 318 and reaffirmed their adherence to the Carpenters. This was followed on October 31 by the Carpenters' refusal to consent to an election on the ground that petitioners had unlawfully assisted 318 in the campaign.

November 10, 1950, a crisis developed when the president of petitioners summarily discharged Frank Ciccone, an employee of over four years' standing, because of the latter's activity in support of the Carpenters and his opposition to 318. We accept the finding of the National Labor Relations Board that petitioners "discriminatorily discharged, and thereafter refused to reinstate, Frank Ciccone because of his organizational activities in support of the . . . (Carpenters)." This discharge at once precipitated the strike which is before us and which the Board found "was clearly caused and prolonged by the cumulative effects of the (petitioners') unfair labor practices culminating in the discriminatory discharge of Ciccone." There was no disorder but the plant was virtually shut down until December 11 and it was March 9, 1951, before the Carpenters, on behalf of petitioners' employees, made an unconditional request to return to work. Petitioners ignored that request and neither Ciccone nor any of the other 76 striking employees has been reinstated.

In January 1951, the Carpenters initiated the present proceedings before the National Labor Relations Board by charging petitioners with unfair labor practices. Acting on those charges, the Board's general counsel filed a complaint alleging petitioners' support of Local 318 and discharge of numerous employees, including Ciccone, as violations of section 8(a) (1), (2) and (3) of the Act.

Petitioners admitted that they had discharged the employees in question and had not rehired them. They denied, however, that in so doing they had committed any unfair labor practices. Their first affirmative defense was that the waiver of the right to strike, expressed by their employees in their collective-bargaining contract, applied to strikes not only for economic benefits but to any and all strikes by such employees, including strikes directed solely against unfair labor practices of the employer.

Petitioners' other principal defense was that the existing strike began during the statutory waiting period initiated by the employees' request for modification of the contract and that, by virtue of section 8(d) of the Act, the strikers had lost their status as employees. That defense turned upon petitioners' interpretation of section 8(d), applying it not only to strikes for economic benefits but to any and all strikes occurring during the waiting period, including strikes solely against unfair labor practices of the employer.

The trial examiner made findings of fact sustaining the complaint and recommended that petitioners be ordered to cease and desist from the interference complained of and be required to offer to Ciccone and the 76 other discharged employees full reinstatement, together with back pay for Ciccone from November 10, 1950, and for the other employees from March 9, 1951. See, 103 N.L.R.B. 511, 526–563. With minor modifications, the Board adopted the examiner's findings and conclusions and issued the recommended order. 103 N.L.R.B. 511. The chairman and one member dissented in part.

The Court of Appeals, with one judge dissenting in part, accepted the Board's findings of fact and conclusions of law and enforced the Board's order.

Apart from the issues raised by petitioners' affirmative defenses, the proceedings reflect a flagrant example of interference by the employers with the expressly protected right of their employees to select their own bargaining representative. The findings disclose vigorous efforts by the employers to influence and even to coerce their employees to abandon the Carpenters as their bargaining representatives and to substitute Local 318. Accordingly, unless petitioners sustain at least one of their affirmative defenses, they must suffer the consequences of their unfair labor practices violating section 8(a) (1), (2) or (3) of the Act, as amended.

The waiver in the contract before us, upon which petitioners rely, is as follows:

"5. The Union agrees that during the term of this agreement, there shall be no interference of any kind with the operations of the Employers, or any interruptions or slackening of production of work by any of its members. The Union further agrees to refrain from engaging in any strike or work stoppage during the term of this agreement."

Petitioners argue that the words "any strike" leave no room for interpretation and necessarily include all strikes, even those against unlawful practices destructive of the foundation on which collective bargaining must rest. We disagree. We believe that the contract, taken as a whole, deals solely with the economic relationship between the employers and their employees. It is a typical collective-bargaining contract dealing with terms of employment and the normal operations of the plant. It is for one year and assumes the existence of a lawfully designated bargaining representative. Its strike and lockout clauses are natural adjuncts of an operating policy aimed at avoiding interruptions of production prompted by efforts to change existing economic relationships.

To adopt petitioners' all-inclusive interpretation of the clause is quite a different matter. That interpretation would eliminate, for the whole year, the employees' right to strike, even if petitioners, by coercion, ousted the employees' lawful bargaining representative and, by threats of discharge, caused the employees to sign membership cards in a new union.

The Supervisor's Right to Join a Union

The Wagner Act of 1935 gave supervisors all the rights allowed workers in Section 7.[97] Under Section 14(a) of the amended act these rights have been withdrawn. Section 2(11) of the 1947 act defines a supervisor as "any individual having authority to hire, transfer, suspend, lay-off, recall, promote, discharge, assign, reward, or discipline employees, responsibly to direct them, adjust their grievances, or effectively recommend such action; provided, that the exercise of such authority is not of a merely routine or clerical nature but requires the use of independent judgment."

Engineers in over-all charge of an engine room and its equipment, but with no employees to supervise, were held nonsupervisors since mere responsibility for physical property did not constitute supervisory authority.[98]

Section 14(a) does not prohibit a supervisor from becoming or remaining a member of a labor organization. It merely relieves employers from any compulsion by the NLRB to accord the status of employees to the front line of management.

A supervisor may not be discharged for failing to keep a union from organizing a plant, since such discrimination could lead rank-and-file workers to believe that they would also be discriminated against if they took part in union activities.[99]

State Laws on Closed and Union Shops

Although the 1947 National Labor Relations Act bans the closed shop, the law permits an employer and a labor organization to execute a union-shop agreement. Under a closed-shop agreement a person had to be a union member in good standing when he was hired, and the employer customarily got all his workers directly from the union. The union shop requires all employees to join the union within a specified period, usually 30 days, as a condition of continued employment. Under the union-shop arrangement the employer need not call upon the union for new workers; he may hire them from the open labor market. Another form of union security is the agency shop, in which nonunion employees are required to contribute to the financial support of the union, usually in a sum equal to union dues.

97. Packard Motor Co. v. NLRB, 330 U.S. 485 (1947).
98. Graham Transportation Co., 124 NLRB 960 (1959).
99. NLRB v. Talladega Cotton Factory, 213 Fed. (2d) 209 (1954).

In 1961 [100] the National Labor Relations Board declared lawful an agency-shop provision which required nonunion workers and newly hired employees, as a condition of employment, to pay the union, within 30 days following the date of the labor contract or of initial employment (whichever was later), a sum of money equivalent to union dues and initiation fees. The board upheld the provision because all the employees had the option of becoming, or refraining from becoming, union members.

Section 14(b) permits state laws to determine the validity of a contract containing a union security provision. Eighteen states (with one or two exceptions, they are in the South and Southwest) forbid all types of union security agreements, and employers covered by the federal act may not enter into any such agreement except the agency shop. This prohibition is permitted even though the union shop is lawful under the amended National Labor Relations Act. Employers engaged only in intrastate commerce, and hence not covered by the federal act, are free to execute any type of compulsory-unionism agreement allowed by the state law. New York allows all forms of union security agreements, including the closed shop.

State laws prohibiting union security agreements are called "right-to-work" laws; supporters of this type of legislation claim that these laws protect the worker's legal and moral right to refuse to join a union without losing employment. Opponents of right-to-work laws argue that the real purpose of such laws is to break and destroy unions and thus lower wages and other conditions of employment. They contend that some form of union security is essential for the survival of unions and the economic betterment of the worker and society.[101]

Union-Shop Agreements under the Railway Labor Act

A 1951 amendment [102] to the Railway Labor Act of 1926 specifically authorizes union-shop contracts. In a leading case [103] Nebraska attempted to invoke a right-to-work amendment of the Nebraska constitution against a union-shop agreement entered into by a railroad and a labor union. The U.S. Supreme Court struck down the action of the

100. General Motors Corp., (1961), 133 NLRB (No. 21).
101. For some interesting articles on right-to-work laws, see The Right to Work, *The Guaranty Survey*, p. 1 (1956); M. C. Benewitz, The Right-to-Work Case, 7 *Lab. L.J.* 9 (1956); J. A. McClain, Compulsory Freedom to Join a Union, 42 A.B.A.J. 723 (1956); and R. W. Gilbert, The Right to Work Revisited, 43 A.B.A.J. 231 (1957).
102. Public Law 914, 81st Congress, c. 1220, approved Jan. 10, 1951.
103. Railway Employees' Dept. v. Hanson, 351 U.S. 225 (1955).

state and held that Congress had the right to find the union shop a stabilizing force in maintaining industrial peace in the arteries of interstate commerce. The preemption doctrine has forbidden state regulation of union security clauses incorporated in bargaining agreements covering workers on interstate railroads.

Sections 15, 16, and 17

Section 15 of the amended National Labor Relations Act provides that when conflict between the act and the bankruptcy laws may exist, the provisions of the act shall prevail unless its provisions cannot be validly enforced; a federal bankruptcy court has no authority to stay a representation proceeding before the National Labor Relations Board,[104] and a back pay order issued by the NLRB may be enforced against a bankrupt employer.[105]

Section 16 provides that if any provision of the act is held to be invalid, the remaining provisions shall not be affected thereby. This separability clause is frequently referred to as a saving clause.

Section 17 provides that the act shall be cited as the National Labor Relations Act.

Section 17 concludes Title I and the amendments to the National Labor Relations Act of 1935. We shall now consider Title II, which establishes the Federal Mediation and Conciliation Service.

Title II. Conciliation of Labor Disputes in Industries Affecting Commerce; National Emergencies

SECTION 201. Congress believes that sound, stable industrial relations and the advancement of the general welfare of the nation can be secured by settling issues between employers and employees through conference and collective bargaining between employers and unions. Mediation and conciliation are methods used by government agents to help disputing unions and employers reach an agreement. Mediation is the act of a third-party intermediary, directed toward inducing the parties to a labor dispute to resume negotiations that have been terminated by their inability to agree on a labor contract. Conciliation is an attempt by a third party to bring about an amicable solution of the differences involved, but without authority to settle them. When the employer and the union, after having submitted their dispute to a mediation board,

104. *Matter of* American Buslines, 242 F. (Supp.) 877 (1957).
105. Nathanson v. NLRB 334 U.S. 25 (1952).

also agree to abide by the decision of a third party, the procedure is called arbitration.

SECTION 202. An independent agency known as the Federal Mediation and Conciliation Service has been created under this section. The service has its principal office in Washington, D.C.; regional offices are located in all important industrial areas of the United States. The service is headed by a Director who is authorized to cooperate with state and local mediation services whenever they exist.

The service provides mediators only in those disputes affecting national health and safety and in other serious labor disputes that substantially affect interstate commerce. In disputes affecting intrastate commerce, mediation services offered by the Federal Mediation and Conciliation Service are duplicated in a few states by similar state agencies. One of the best-known state mediation services is the New York State Board of Mediation and, like the federal service, its aid is invoked only on voluntary submission to mediation.

Functions of the Federal Mediation and Conciliation Service

SECTION 203 provides that it shall be the duty of the service, in order to prevent or minimize interruptions of the free flow of commerce growing out of labor disputes, to assist parties to labor controversies to settle them through conciliation and mediation. The services may be offered on motion of the service or on the request of one or more of the parties to the dispute. The service is cautioned in the statute to avoid attempting to mediate disputes that would have only a minor effect on interstate commerce.

If conciliation fails, the Director may seek to induce the parties to try arbitration as a means of settling the dispute without resort to a strike or lock-out. The disputants are under no statutory obligation to accept the recommendations of the service.

Duty of Employers and Employees

SECTION 204 seeks to prevent or minimize interruptions of the free flow of commerce growing out of labor disputes by calling upon employers and unions to

(1) Exert every reasonable effort to make and maintain collective bargaining agreements.

(2) Provide adequate notice to each other of any proposed change in the terms of such agreements.

(3) Submit all disputes to conference meetings called by either party.

(4) Refer the dispute to the service promptly when the conference method has failed.

National Labor Management Panel

SECTION 205 creates the National Labor Management Panel, composed of six persons outstanding in the field of management and six outstanding in the field of labor. It is the duty of the panel, at the request of the Director of the service, to advise on the avoidance of industrial controversies and the manner in which mediation and voluntary adjustment shall be administered, particularly with reference to controversies affecting the general welfare of the United States.

National Emergencies. Boards of Inquiry

SECTIONS 206 AND 207 provide that whenever the President of the United States believes a threatened or actual strike [106] or lock-out affecting an entire or substantial part of an industry will imperil the national health or safety, he may appoint a board of inquiry to inquire into the issues involved in the dispute and make a written report to him. The board has power to sit and act in any place and to conduct public or private hearings to ascertain the facts of the dispute. The board has subpoena power and may compel the attendance of witnesses. It has no authority to offer recommendations for settlement of the controversy.

Injunctions against Work Stoppages

SECTION 208 provides that after receiving a report from a board of inquiry the President may direct the Attorney General to petition any U.S. District Court to enjoin the threatened or actual strike, or the lock-out, provided the court finds that such strike or lock-out affects an entire industry, or a substantial part of it, and provided that the court determines that such a strike or lock-out will imperil the national health or safety.

Voting on the Employer's Last Offer of Settlement

SECTION 209 provides that whenever a U.S. District Court has enjoined a strike or lock-out the parties to the labor dispute have a duty

106. See, Emergency Strikes, Jay Kramer, 11 *Lab. L.J.*, 227 (1960).

to make every effort to settle the dispute with the assistance of the Federal Mediation and Conciliation Service.

After the injunction has issued, the board of inquiry is reconvened, and at the end of a 60-day period the board reports the current position of the parties and the efforts which have been made for the settlement of the dispute to the President. In its report, the board includes a statement of the employer's last offer of settlement. Within the succeeding 15 days, the National Labor Relations Board is required to take a secret ballot of the employees involved in the dispute on the question of whether they wish to accept the final offer of settlement, and the results of the balloting are certified to the Attorney General within 5 days after the voting has been completed. Since 1947 the National Labor Relations Board has conducted thirteen secret elections on the last offer of settlement. Without exception, the employees have supported their leaders in rejecting the last offer. All the national labor disputes subjected to this Taft-Hartley procedure, except two, were settled either through the immediate personal intervention of the President, or after the injunction was vacated. It would appear that the resumption of the strike increased the pressure to compromise.[107]

Terminating the Injunction

Under Section 210, the Attorney General must move in the U.S. District Court to vacate the injunction as soon as he receives the balloting certification. The President of the United States is authorized to make a report of the proceedings to Congress and give it his recommendations, which may include new legislation.

Unless the dispute has been settled during the 80-day injunction period, the parties are free to engage in a strike or a lock-out.

On June 26, 1961,[108] when President Kennedy invoked Section 206 of the Taft-Hartley Law, it was the eighteenth time since Congress established it in 1947 that this emergency machinery has been used.[109]

When the unions have opposed the Attorney General's application for an injunction it has usually been on the ground that the evidence did not support the government's charge that the national health or safety of the United States was endangered. The Supreme Court has upheld the issuance of the injunction in every case brought before it.[110] Fol-

107. For an informative article on this point, see L. Rehmus, Operation of the National Emergency Provisions of the LMRA, 62 *Yale L.J.* 1047 (1953).

108. U.S. v. Nat'l Maritime Union, U.S. District Ct., So. Dist. 61 Civ. 2347 (1961).

109. See *The N.Y. Times*, June 27, 1961.

110. See Steelworkers v. U.S., 361 U.S. 39 (1959).

lowing the issuance of the injunction by the district court in another case, the Steelworkers union appealed the decision to the United States Court of Appeals, 3rd Circuit.[111] Although this appellate court affirmed the lower court's decision by a vote of two to one, the dissenting opinion of Justice Hastie is worth noting, particularly on the point raised by the union that the strike did not affect the national health or safety. Judge Hastie said:

To put the matter somewhat differently, there is no legislative mandate that a court shall grant an injunction whenever a strike is imperiling national health or safety, though such peril is essential to jurisdiction. Rather, a court sitting in equity is called upon to balance all equitable considerations inherent in the statutory scheme or disclosed by the evidence in a given case. Under this analysis a primary and essential equitable consideration must be whether the underlying public purpose of the statute to promote and facilitate more effective bargaining would be served. Indeed, in my judgment some utility in accomplishing this primary purpose of the legislation should provide the principal equitable justification of injunctive relief.

Thus, a court, before issuing an injunction under Section 178 of Title 29, should satisfy itself that there is a reasonable basis for belief that a forced suspension of the strike will aid and accelerate the process of collective bargaining. In terms of the present case, has it been made to appear here that the parties are more likely to settle their dispute within the next eighty days if the strike is suspended for that period by court order than they are to accomplish this result while the strike continues?

Examining the pleadings and proof in the present record it appears that neither the government which seeks the injunction nor the steel companies whose employees are striking has shed any light on this critical question. Certainly there is no indication that violence or any other exacerbating conduct in the course of the strike is creating a climate harmful to negotiation. There is no suggestion that any tension or hostility inimical to negotiation would be relieved or any impediment to settlement removed by a suspension of the strike. There is simply nothing before us which warrants a conclusion that the objective of more productive bargaining would be served by an injunction.

The U.S. Supreme Court affirmed the decision. Rejecting the union's contention, the court said:

The statute imposes upon the courts the duty of finding, upon the evidence adduced, whether a strike or lockout meets the statutory conditions of breadth of involvement and peril to the national health or safety. We have accordingly reviewed the concurrent findings of the two lower courts. Petitioner here contests the findings that the continuation of the strike would imperil the national health and safety. The parties dispute the meaning of the statutory term "national health"; the Government insists that the term comprehends the country's general well-being, its economic

111. U.S. v. Steelworkers, 271 Fed. (2d) 67 (1959).

health; petitioner urges that simply the physical health of the citizenry is meant. We need not resolve this question, for we think the judgment below is amply supported on the ground that the strike imperils the national safety. Here we rely upon the evidence of the strike's effect on specific defense projects; we need not pass on the Government's contention that "national safety" in this context should be given a broader construction and application.

The Constitutionality of Sections 206–210

The constitutionality of Sections 206–210 has been upheld by the U.S. Supreme Court.[112] In the 1959 Steelworkers case, the court said:

We are of the opinion that the provision in question as applied here is not violative of the constitutional limitation prohibiting courts from exercising power of a legislative or executive nature, powers not capable of being conferred upon a court exercising solely "the judicial power of the United States." . . . Petitioner contends that the statute is constitutionally invalid because it does not set up any standard of lawful or unlawful conduct on the part of labor or management. But the statute does recognize certain rights in the public to have unimpeded for a time production in industries vital to the national health or safety. It makes the United States the guardian of these rights in litigation. The availability of relief, in the common judicial form of an injunction, depends on findings of fact, to be judicially made. Of the matters decided judicially, there is no review by other agencies of the Government. We conclude that the statute entrusts the courts only with the determination of a "case or controversy," on which the judicial power can operate, not containing any element capable of only legislative or executive determination. We do not find that the termination of the injunction after a specified time, or the machinery established in an attempt to obtain a peaceful settlement of the underlying dispute during the injunction's pendency, detracts from this conclusion.

Compilation of Collective-Bargaining Agreements

SECTION 211 requires that the Bureau of Labor Statistics of the U.S. Department of Labor "shall maintain a file of copies of all available collective bargaining agreements and other available agreements and actions thereunder settling or adjusting labor disputes."

The file is open for inspection, except for any information submitted in confidence, which must not be disclosed. Finally, the section provides that the bureau may furnish the information on file, except in-

---

112. Steelworkers v. U.S., 361 U.S. 39 (1959); U.S. v. Steelworkers, 202 Fed. (2d) 132; U.S. v. Mineworkers, 77 F. Supp. 563 (1948).

formation submitted in confidence, to employers, employees, and unions. It is the expressed intent that the information will aid in settling labor disputes.

Exemption of the Railway Labor Act

SECTION 212 states that the provisions of Title II of the act shall not be applicable to any matter subject to the provisions of the Railway Labor Act, as amended from time to time.

The ban against the secondary boycott does not apply when the union seeks to induce a boycott by railroad employees who are subject to the Railway Labor Act since, by definition, they are not employees within the meaning of Section 2(3) of the National Labor Relations Act.[113]

Title III. Suits by and against Labor Organizations

SECTION 301 of the Labor Management Relations Act provides that "suits for violation of contracts between an employer and a labor organization representing employees in an industry affecting commerce . . . may be brought in any district court of the United States." This section has established the principle that a labor contract is a legally enforcible agreement. At common law labor unions were treated as aggregates of individuals, each of whom would have to be named a party to the lawsuit.

In the Lincoln Mills case [114] the U.S. Supreme Court held that Section 301 requires the creation of a new body of federal substantive law governing rights and remedies under labor contracts in industries involving interstate commerce. This requires federal courts to create and apply federal law, but where none is available, state law may be appropriate. As a result of this far-reaching decision, courts now have authority to compel the enforcement of the arbitration clause in a labor agreement affecting interstate commerce.[115] The text of the Lincoln Mills decision follows. Justice Douglas delivered the opinion.

Petitioner-union entered into a collective bargaining agreement in 1953 with respondent-employer, the agreement to run one year and from year to year thereafter, unless terminated on specified notices. The agreement provided that there would be no strikes or work stoppages and that griev-

113. NLRB v. Locals 1205 and 707, Teamsters, 122 NLRB (No. 148) (1959).
114. Textile Workers v. Lincoln Mills, 353 U.S. 448 (1957).
115. See A. Cox, Reflections Upon Labor Arbitration, 72 *Harv. L. Rev.* 1482 (1959).

ances would be handled pursuant to a specified procedure. The last step in the grievance procedure—a step that could be taken by either party—was arbitration.

This controversy involves several grievances that concern work loads and work assignments. The grievances were processed through the various steps in the grievance procedure and were finally denied by the employer. The union requested arbitration, and the employer refused. Thereupon the union brought this suit in the District Court to compel arbitration.

The District Court concluded that it had jurisdiction and ordered the employer to comply with the grievance arbitration provisions of the collective bargaining agreement. The Court of Appeals reversed by a divided vote, 230 F. 2d 81. It held that, although the District Court had jurisdiction to entertain the suit, the court had no authority founded either in federal or state law to grant the relief.

The starting point of our inquiry is section 301 of the Labor Management Relations Act of 1947 which provides:

"(b) Any labor organization which represents employees in an industry affecting commerce as defined in this chapter and any employer whose activities affect commerce as defined in this chapter shall be bound by the acts of its agents. Any such labor organization may sue or be sued as an entity and in behalf of the employees whom it represents in the courts of the United States. Any money judgment against a labor organization in a district court of the United States shall be enforceable only against the organization as an entity and against its assets, and shall not be enforceable against any individual member or his assets."

From the face of the Act it is apparent that section 301(a) and section 301(b) supplement one another. Section 301(b) makes it possible for a labor organization, representing employees in an industry affecting commerce, to sue and be sued as an entity in the federal courts. Section 301(b) in other words provides the procedural remedy lacking at common law. Section 301(a) certainly does something more than that. Plainly, it supplies the basis upon which the federal district courts may take jurisdiction and apply the procedural rule of Section 301(b). The question is whether Section 301(a) is more than jurisdictional.

Plainly the agreement to arbitrate grievance disputes is the quid pro quo for an agreement not to strike. Viewed in this light, the legislation does more than confer jurisdiction in the federal courts over labor organizations. It expresses a federal policy that federal courts should enforce these agreements on behalf of or against labor organizations and that industrial peace can be best obtained only in that way.

To be sure there is a great medley of ideas reflected in the hearings, reports, and debates on this Act. Yet, to repeat, the entire tenor of the history indicates that the agreement to arbitrate grievance disputes was considered as quid pro quo of a no-strike agreement. And when in the House the debate narrowed to the question whether section 301 was more than jurisdictional, it became abundantly clear that the purpose of the section was to provide the necessary legal remedies.

The question then is, what is the substantive law to be applied in suits under Section 301(a)? We conclude that the substantive law to apply in suits under Section 301(a) is federal law which the courts must fashion from the policy of our national labor laws. Federal interpretation of the federal law will govern, not state law. But state law, if compatible with the purpose of Section 301, may be resorted to in order to find the rule that will best effectuate the federal policy. Any state law applied, however, will be absorbed as federal law and will not be an independent source of private rights.

The judgment of the Court of Appeals is reversed and the cause is remanded to that court for proceedings in conformity with this opinion.

Reversed.

The last part of Section 301 provides that any money judgment rendered against a union is enforcible only against the union as an entity and against its assets and that the property of individual union members may not be taken to satisfy the judgment.

CASES AND RULINGS. Federal and state courts have concurrent jurisdiction in actions under the Labor Management Relations Act based on violations of labor contracts. When a state court entertains an action under Section 301, the court must apply federal substantive law.[116]

Any right of recovery under Section 301 rests on a contract and its asserted violation.[117]

Individual employees or union members are given no right to sue for breach of contract under Section 301.[118]

When a union sued to recover wages due to employees who breached the contract, a federal court dismissed the suit on the ground that the action was based on the individual rights of employees and not on any duty owed to the union. The court's judgment was upheld by the U.S. Supreme Court.[119]

This section may not be invoked in a breach of contract action that stems from a jurisdictional dispute between two unions.[120]

An action to ascertain the validity of a union contract will be entertained by a federal court.[121]

An oral collective-bargaining agreement is valid under the Labor Management Relations Act and may become the subject of an action under Section 301.[122]

116. Anchor Motor Freight v. Local 445, Teamsters, 5 App. Div. (2d) 869 (1958).
117. Schatte v. Int'l Alliance Employees Union, 182 Fed. (2d) 158 (1949).
118. Capra v. Suro, 236 Fed. (2d) 107 (1956).
119. Ass'n of Westinghouse Salaried Employees v. Westinghouse Electric Corp., 348 U.S. 437 (1955).
120. Int'l Union of Operating Engrs. v. Pfeiffer Brewing Co., 115 F. Supp. 650 (1953).
121. Lima-Hamilton Corp. v. U.A.W., 19 LC 66,166 (1950).
122. Hamilton Foundry and Machine Co. v. Int'l Molders and Foundry Workers, 193 Fed. (2d) 209 (1951).

A strike provoked by unfair practices committed by the employer does not violate the no-strike provision in the contract.[123]

It is clear that Section 301 allows actions for money damages for the breach of a labor contract. Whether or not a federal court has authority to grant injunctions under Section 301 is not as clear. In one case,[124] however, the U.S. Supreme Court upheld the right of the federal court to enforce an arbitration agreement.

In other cases it has been held that Section 301 does not grant federal district courts authority to grant injunctive relief in breach of contract actions.[125]

Restrictions on Payments to Employee Representatives

SECTIONS 302(A) AND 302(B). These subsections make it unlawful for any employer to pay or deliver any money or other thing of value to any representative of any of his employees. It is also unlawful for any representative of any employees to receive or accept from the employer any money or other thing of value. This is a criminal statute which is enforced by the courts and not by the National Labor Relations Board. Fines and imprisonment may be imposed for proven violations.

SECTIONS 302(C)(1), 302(C)(2), AND 302(C)(3). Section 302(c)(1) states that the provisions of this section are not applicable if an employer pays money to a union representative as compensation for services rendered by him as an employee.

Section 302(c)(2) permits a union representative to accept money from an employer in satisfaction of judgment, and subsection (c)(3) allows a union representative to pay money to an employer in consideration for the purchase from him of a commodity, provided the purchase price conforms to the prevailing market price.

CHECKOFFS. Section 302 (c) (4) provides that an employer may deduct money from the wages of employees in payment of the employees' membership dues in the union. This is the checkoff provision. Checkoff of union dues is a device under which employers agree in a labor contract to deduct monthly dues from the wages of employees.

---

123. Mastro Plastics Corp. v. NLRB, 350 U.S. 270 (1956).

124. Goodall-Sanford v. Textile Workers Union 353 U.S. 550 (1957); see also, General Electric Co. v. Electrical Workers, 353 U.S. 547 (1957); Steelworkers v. Galland-Henning Mfg. Co., 354 U.S. 906 (1957).

125. Mead v. Local 25, Teamsters, 217 Fed. (2d) 6 (1954); Pilot Freight Carriers Inc. v. Bayne, 26 LC 68,744 (1954); Fitzgerald v. Haynes, 31 LC 70,456 (1956).

The money withheld by the employer is usually forwarded by check to the office of the union. Employers have found the checkoff system more satisfactory than allowing union representatives to visit employees on the job to make collections. These visits result in the interruption of production with loss of efficiency.

Section 302(c)(4) allows the checkoff when the employer has received from each employee a written assignment which shall not be irrevocable for a period of more than one year, or beyond the termination date of the labor contract, whichever occurs sooner. No state may prohibit or regulate the checkoff, because Congress has preempted the field.

CASES AND RULINGS. Under date of July 10, 1947, the Attorney General expressed the opinion "that initiation fees and assessments, being incidents of membership, should be considered as falling within the classification of membership dues." [126]

Although an employer need not agree to a checkoff, the subject matter is a proper subject for collective bargaining under Section 8(a)(5) of the National Labor Relations Act.[127]

When an employee refuses to execute the needed assignment allowing for the checkoff, the union may require the employee, under a union shop agreement, to pay his dues at the union office. However, a union attempt to force an employee to travel to another city to pay his union dues was construed by the NLRB as unlawful coercion.[128]

In one case an employer forced employees to join a company-dominated union and submit to a checkoff. The U.S. Supreme Court upheld the right of the NLRB to reimburse the employees the amount of the checked-off dues.[129]

WELFARE FUNDS. Section 302 (c) (5) provides that it shall not be unlawful for an employer to contribute money or other thing of value to a trust fund established by a labor union. The fund must meet the following conditions:

(1) The trust fund must be for the benefit of employees, their families, and their dependents.

(2) The fund must be jointly administered by the employer or employers, the representatives of employees, and neutral representatives, the latter acting only when a voting deadlock occurs.

(3) The fund must provide only medical or hospital care, pensions, disability, sickness, or unemployment benefits, or accident, sickness, or life insurance.

126. Opinion letter of Assistant Attorney General to Assistant Solicitor General, dated May 13, 1948.
127. U.S. Gypsum Co., 94 NLRB 112 (1951).
128. American Screw Co., 122 NLRB 485 (1958).
129. Va. Electric and Power Co. v. NLRB, 319 U.S. 353 (1943).

(4) The fund must be established through a written agreement with the employer or employers.

(5) The fund must be audited annually and the results made available to interested persons.

(6) If payments are to be used for pensions, a separate trust fund must be established out of which payments may be made only for pensions.

SECTION 302 (E) provides that federal courts shall have jurisdiction to restrain violations of Section 302 without regard to the statutory limitations placed on the issuance of injunctions by the Clayton Act of 1914 and the Norris-LaGuardia Act of 1932.

SECTION 302 (G) states that the administrative provisions of the statute do not apply to payments to trust funds established by a labor contract prior to January 1, 1946, if such trust funds are otherwise lawful. Nor do the requirements contained in the act as to the purposes of the fund prohibit payments to such trust funds if prior to January 1, 1947, the trust agreement contained provisions for pooled vacation benefits.

SECTION 302 (D) provides that any person who willfully violates any of the provisions of Section 302 shall, on conviction, be guilty of a misdemeanor, and be subject to a fine of not more than $10,000 or to imprisonment for not more than one year, or both.

Prior to the enactment of the 1947 Taft-Hartley Law some welfare and pension benefits were administered unilaterally by labor unions. This control resulted in abuses. Some labor union officials did not hesitate to draw from these funds monies for personal advantages; at times, trust funds were used for political purposes. In many cases audits were made haphazardly if at all, and the beneficiaries of the funds were given little or no information concerning the financial condition of the trust accounts. These and other abuses contributed to the enactment of Section 302.

CASES AND RULINGS. Any collective-bargaining agreement, or any pension or welfare trust fund agreement that provides that benefits shall go to union members but not to nonunion members violates the National Labor Relations Act.[130]

The trustees of a pension or welfare fund have power to establish eligibility requirements on which benefits are to be considered, and any judicial review of an adverse decision is limited to passing on the trustees' interpretation of the law and determining whether the evidence supported the trustees' ruling.[131]

130. Indiana Gas and Chemical Corp., C.Ch. NLRB 9802 (1961).
131. Bolgar v. Lewis, 41 LC 16,578 (1960); Pavlovscak v. Lewis, 41 LC 16,694 (1960); Sceuck v. Lewis, 41 LC 16,695 (1960).

A union's breach of contract does not excuse an employer's failure to contribute to a welfare fund.[132]

Unpaid employers' contributions to a union welfare or pension fund do not constitute wages under the federal bankruptcy law and are not entitled to priority in a proceeding against the estate of the bankrupt.[133]

A federal court may not enjoin union picketing that seeks to compel an employer to meet its welfare fund contributions.[134]

Pension rights that accrue to employees continue during the lives of the pensioners, regardless of the termination of the contract.[135]

Trustees of a pension or welfare fund have the right to sue for unpaid contributions.[136]

Boycotts and Other Unlawful Combinations

SUITS FOR DAMAGES. Section 303 allows any aggrieved person to sue in a federal court and to recover damages against a union that has engaged in conduct proscribed by this section. The unlawful conduct is the same as the unfair labor practices which are described in Section 8(b)(4), (A), (B), (C), and (D).

SECONDARY BOYCOTTS. Section 303(a)(1) prohibits strikes when the purpose is:

(a) To force an employer or a self-employed person to join any labor or employer organization.

(b) To force one employer to cease dealing with another employer. This subsection outlaws the secondary boycott, which may be described as the refusal to work for employer A unless he stops doing business with employer B, with whom the union has its real dispute. The act seeks to protect the unconcerned neutral employer. Neither in this subsection, nor in any part of Section 8(b)(4) of the act, does the term secondary boycott appear. This unlawful practice can be determined only by a close reading of the statute. Most damage suits under Section 303 have been based on charges that the union had engaged in an unlawful secondary boycott.

Despite the ban on the secondary boycott, a union may enter into a hot-cargo [137] agreement with an employer. The hot-cargo clause is a

132. Napoli v. Unkel, N.Y. County Court, 38 LC 66,009 (1959).
133. U.S. v. Embassy Restaurant, 359 U.S. 29; *Matter of* Sleep Products, 141 F. Supp. 463 (1956).
134. William Dunbar Company Inc. v. Painters and Glaziers, 129 F. Supp. 417 (1955).
135. New York City Omnibus Corp. v. Quill, 297 N.Y. 832 (1947).
136. Lewis v. Quality Coal Corp., 207 Fed. (2d) 140 (1959).
137. From 1949 to 1954 the NLRB permitted unions to use the "hot-cargo" clause as a defense against secondary boycotts. See Teamsters Local 294 (Rabouin doing

part of the collective-bargaining agreement and provides that the employer will not require his employees to handle goods coming from another employer or perform services for another employer which the union has labeled unfair. Since this subsection forbids only the use of force, a hot-cargo agreement voluntarily entered into does not violate the secondary-boycott prohibition.[138]

The section also prohibits strikes of which the purpose is:

(c) To force an employer to recognize or bargain with a labor union, unless it has been certified as the representative of the employees seeking representation.

(d) To force an employer to recognize or bargain with a particular union if another union has already been certified as the bargaining representative of the employees.

These prohibitions were deemed necessary to protect the principle of majority rule during the period for which a certification bars a new election. Generally, the protected period runs for one year; however, there are a few exceptions, which have already been discussed under the contract-bar rule.

The section further outlaws strikes when the intent is:

(e) To force any employer to assign work to employees in a particular union rather than to employees in another labor union, unless the employer has failed to conform to a National Labor Relations Board certification order.

JURISDICTIONAL STRIKES. Subsection (e) seeks to curb jurisdictional strikes, which generally do considerable economic damage to an employer's business. It should be noted here that this subsection protects the right of employees to refuse to cross a lawful picket line established in front of the premises of an employer other than their own employer.

Cases and Rulings

COMPELLING MEMBERSHIP IN AN EMPLOYER OR A LABOR ORGANIZATION. There are no reported cases under this subsection.

business as Conway's Express), 87 NLRB 972 (1949), affirmed, 195 Fed. (2d) 906 (1952). In 1954 the board changed its position and held that "hot-cargo" contracts could not be used as a valid defense against secondary boycotts if the employer reneged on his contract and ordered his employees to work on the unfair material. This position was upheld by the U.S. Supreme Court in AFL-CIO Carpenters and Joiners, Local 1976 (Sand Door and Plywood Co.), 357 U.S. 93 (1958).
138. The Landrum-Griffin Act of 1959, Section 8(e), has declared it an unfair labor practice for an employer and a labor union to enter into a "hot-cargo" agreement.

FORCING ONE EMPLOYER TO CEASE DEALING WITH ANOTHER EMPLOYER. We have pointed out that most Section 303 damage suits have been started under this subsection. The ultimate objective of a secondary boycott is generally organizational: The labor union is attempting to organize the employees of the primary employer.

Unions commonly use the picket line as a means of encouraging a secondary work stoppage. At times unions have appealed directly to supervisors or executives of secondary employers to stop dealings with the primary employer with whom the union has a dispute. If such a request is made and consented to by the employer, no violation of Section 303 has occurred.[139] A violation occurs when force is used to back up the appeal, or when the appeal for a work stoppage is made to employees of secondary employers.[140]

When a union established a picket line at the premises of an employer while a trucking company was delivering goods purchased from a struck employer and actually caused a stoppage of business between the trucking firm and its customer, a Utah court held that the union had no defense to a claim for damages which resulted from the lost business.[141]

A state court has jurisdiction to award damages based on a violation of Section 303 provided the unlawful conduct also violates state law.[142]

When the activities of a union attempting to organize a nonunion mine included secondary boycotts and other unlawful means, an appellate federal court upheld a damage award of $300,000 in compensatory damages in addition to $100,000 in punitive damages.[143] The text of this, the Meadow Creek Coal Co., case follows.

In 1944, two International Representatives of defendant called upon and informed Mr. W. T. Ray, president of plaintiff, that defendant represented a majority of plaintiff's employees, and that it wanted to negotiate a labor contract with the plaintiff. Mr. Ray did not believe that defendant represented a majority of his company's employees, and, therefore, a consent election was held under the supervision of the National Labor Relations Board, with the result that less than one-third of the legal votes cast were in favor of the defendant.

In the fall of 1946, defendant sent J. W. Ridings, a member of the International Board, L. H. Bell, an International Representative, Hugh Brown,

139. Local 1976, Carpenters and Joiners Union v. NLRB, 357 U.S. 93 (1958); Ferro-Co Corp., 102 NLRB 1660 (1953).
140. NLRB v. Musicians; Local 802, 226 Fed. (2d) 900 (1955); NLRB v. Denver Bldg. and Constr. Trades Council, 193 Fed. (2d) 421 (1952).
141. Dairy Distributors Inc. v. Local 976, Teamsters, Utah, 329 P. (2d) 414 (1958).
142. Benton Inc. v. Painters' Union, Cal., 291 P. (2d) 13 (1955).
143. U.M.W. v. Meadow Creek Coal Co., U.S. District Court, Tenn. Civil No. 1821, Oct. 28, 1957; affirmed, 263 Fed. (2d) 52 (1959).

an International Representative, and Ernest (Spooner) Stultz, an International Representative of District 19, into Putnam County, Tennessee, and adjacent counties to carry on an organization campaign at all mines not having a contract with defendant.

These men representing the defendant succeeded in organizing the workers in several mines and spent much of their time in and around Monterey, which was only two miles from the mine of plaintiff, in an effort to organize plaintiff's employees.

Sometime in late December 1947 the defendant, having failed to recruit the majority of plaintiff's employees, determined to close down plaintiff's mine by force. Through its representatives in the area and with the aid of many of its members generally in that part of Tennessee and Kentucky, defendant conspired to go on the property of plaintiff in force and in large numbers on January 12, 1948. In furtherance of such conspiracy, approximately 200 members of defendant met at the town of Sparta, Tennessee, about 22 miles from the mine of plaintiff, on the morning of January 12, 1948, and formed a motorcade from there to plaintiff's property, arriving in a body at about 2:30 P.M., just as the night and day shifts were changing.

Defendant, acting through its representatives and members, blockaded plaintiff's private road and placed guards at a point between the intersection of this road with the public highway and the mine, and would not allow customers to enter the property. These 200 men, some of whom were armed, intercepted plaintiff's employees and by persuasion and threats of bodily harm to them and their families sought to get them to join the United Mine Workers of America.

The mob crowded into, in front of, and around the commissary, where J. W. Ridings, Hugh Brown and Howard Madewell made speeches from the bed of a truck backed up in front of the commissary. In these speeches, they told those assembled, including the employees of the plaintiff, both the night and day shifts, 169 in number, among other things, that the plaintiff's mine would not run another day unless the company signed a contract with the union.

Upon arriving at plaintiff's mine on January 12, 1948, Ernest (Spooner) Stultz, a representative of District 19 of defendant, and Howard Madewell, president of the United Mine Workers Union Local at Wilder, Tennessee, who were in the first car of some 75 cars in the motorcade, told Manuel Powell, a supervisory employee of plaintiff, that they had come to shut down the mine and that it would stay closed until the company signed a contract with the union.

As a result of the action of the mob in trespassing upon plaintiff's property, and threatening its employees and officers, the night shift workers did not enter the mine that night, and on the following day only 8 to 12 men of the normal crew of approximately 160 men reported for work. Plaintiff was unable to operate the mine with this small number of men, and although it kept the mine in operable condition by the use of supervisory employees, it was unable to recruit a sufficient force of workers to resume mining.

The purpose of defendant in organizing and directing the march on the plaintiff's mine was to close its operation by force and to keep it closed until plaintiff signed a labor contract with defendant.

There were some trucks which went to the mine on January 12, 1948, for coal, which were forced to leave empty because they were prevented by the mob assembled by the defendant at the mine on that day from entering the property.

Trucks approaching the mine for coal were met on a private road which was blocked by representatives of the defendant, some of whom were armed with guns; and the truck drivers were told by the members of the United Mine Workers of America to "get to hell out of there" and not to come back until the management of the company had signed a contract.

One truck was at the bin being loaded with coal when the crowd arrived. Some of the members of the mob climbed upon the running board of the truck and told the driver that that would be the last load of coal that would come away from the mine until the union contract was signed by the management.

On June 23, 1948, a portion of the railroad track running from the main line of the Tennessee Central Railroad to the plaintiff's mine was destroyed by a dynamite explosion. This act placed the employees of the Tennessee Central Railroad in fear of great bodily harm and caused them to refuse to transport coal from the plaintiff's mine.

The evidence concerning the dynamiting of the railroad track on plaintiff's property shows that members of the United Mine Workers of America had possessed, handled, and transported dynamite on the same night the railroad track was blown up near to the point where the dynamiting took place. . . .

The material and operative facts supporting the plaintiff's federal claim of secondary boycott are substantially the same as the facts supporting its non-federal or state claim of an unlawful conspiracy to injure its business.

The acts and conduct of the defendant as set forth in the Findings of Fact above constitute an unlawful interference with the plaintiff's business, in violation of the plaintiff's rights under the common law obtaining in Tennessee, thereby entitling the plaintiff to recover damages proximately resulting therefrom. The means employed by the defendant to accomplish its purpose were improper and unlawful, consisting of harassment, violence and threats of violence against the plaintiff, its employees, customers, and other persons doing business with it. The effect of such conduct was to drastically interfere with and curtail production of coal at the plaintiff's mine during the year 1948.

The defendant is responsible for the acts and conduct of its agents, servants, and representatives, in accordance with the general rules governing the relationship of master and servant or principal and agent. In this case the defendant is clearly shown to have been directly responsible for the conduct which brought about the wrongful closing of the plaintiff's mine and wrongful interference with its business to such extent as to make the defendant legally liable therefore.

The plaintiff is entitled to recover compensatory damages against the defendant in the amount of $300,000.00.

By reason of the wilful and malicious conduct of the defendant in closing the plaintiff's mine and interfering with its business, the Court is of the opinion that the plaintiff is entitled to recover, in addition, punitive damages in the amount of $100,000.00

FORCING AN EMPLOYER TO RECOGNIZE OR BARGAIN WITH A UNION THAT IS NOT THE CERTIFIED BARGAINING REPRESENTATIVE OF THE EMPLOYEES. In one case the union with intimidation and threats of violence demanded recognition to which it was not entitled. The union prevented the employer from using its regular employees and forced it to abandon a construction contract with a consequent loss of profits. A Virginia court awarded the employer damages in the amount of $130,000, representing compensatory as well as punitive damages. The U.S. Supreme Court sustained the damage award.[144]

It should be noted that the federal courts have ruled that punitive damages may not be awarded against a union for a violation of Section 303.[145] However, punitive damages may be made under state common law.

FORCING AN EMPLOYER TO RECOGNIZE OR BARGAIN WITH A PARTICULAR UNION IF ANOTHER UNION HAS ALREADY BEEN CERTIFIED AS THE BARGAINING REPRESENTATIVE OF THE EMPLOYEES. Where an incumbent union's certification was more than a year old, and a rival union struck to enforce a demand for recognition, a court held that the strike violated Section 303 of the act and that the employer was entitled to maintain an action for damages suffered as a result of the unlawful strike.[146]

FORCING ANY EMPLOYER TO ASSIGN PARTICULAR WORK TO EMPLOYEES IN A PARTICULAR UNION RATHER THAN TO EMPLOYEES IN ANOTHER LABOR UNION. We have stated that the purpose of this subsection is to curb work stoppages resulting from jurisdictional disputes.

In a recent case [147] the employer charged that the defendant union encouraged a work stoppage, threatened members of other craft unions, and prevented them from working for the employer. The court ruled that the conduct of the union violated Section 303 and that the plaintiff could maintain a damage action.

Section 303 seeks to make unions more responsible in their dealings with employers. There is no doubt that many Section 303 violations have occurred since 1947, yet relatively few damage suits have been

144. United Constr. Workers v. Laburnum Constr. Corp., 347 U.S. 656 (1954).
145. U.M.W. v. Patton, 211 Fed. (2d) 742 (1954).
146. Tungsten Mining Corp. v. U.M.W., District 50, 242 Fed. (2d) 84 (1957). See also Lewis Food Co. v. Drivers' Union, 159 F. Supp. 763 (1958).
147. Young Constr. Co. v. Plumbers' Union, U.S. District Ct., Eastern District of Ill. Civil No. 3311 (1957).

processed to judgment. Employers are quite reluctant to sue unions with which they deal; unions forced to pay damages might lose their entire assets, acquired over a long period, and the union members might well leave no stone unturned in an effort to retaliate against the employer.

Restrictions on Political Contributions

SECTION 304 prohibits political contributions by corporations or labor unions in connection with any federal election. It is also unlawful for a candidate or political committee to accept any contribution. A corporation or a labor union violating this section may be fined $5000, and any officer of a corporation or officer of a labor union violating this section may be fined $1000 or imprisoned for one year or both.

This section does not prohibit political activities engaged in and expenditures made by political groups of labor organizations, such as the Committee on Political Education (COPE), which is affiliated with the AFL-CIO. In one case [148] the U.S. Supreme Court dismissed an indictment based on a charge that the CIO had violated Section 304 when it expended its funds for the publication of its regular periodical containing statements supporting a candidate for federal office.

In another case [149] the Supreme Court upheld an indictment against the U.A.W. when they paid for a television broadcast supporting candidates for federal office.

Strikes by Government Employees

SECTION 305 makes it unlawful for any individual employed by the federal government to participate in any strike. Any such individual who strikes shall be discharged immediately, shall forfeit his civil service status, if any, and shall not be eligible for re-employment by any branch of the federal government for three years.

There is no record of any strike called by federal employees since the enactment of the Taft-Hartley Law. The activities of John L. Lewis and his Mineworkers' Union in 1946 undoubtedly contributed greatly to the inclusion of Section 305 in the act.

In a celebrated case,[150] Lewis called a strike which closed down prac-

148. U.S. v. CIO, 335 U.S. 106 (1948).
149. U.S. v. U.A.W., 352 U.S. 567 (1957).
150. U.S. v. U.M.W. and John L. Lewis, 330 U.S. 258 (1947). The union's principal defense, that the Norris-LaGuardia Act barred the issuance of the injunction in this case, is discussed in Chapter 5.

tically all the bituminous coal mines of the country. The federal government had been possession of these mines and had engaged in some conferences with Lewis concerning a new collective-bargaining contract. To forestall the strike, the government petitioned a federal court for an injunction restraining the strike call. The injunction was granted and ignored by Lewis and his union. Although Lewis questioned the court's authority to grant an injunction in the case, the court rejected his arguments and punished both Lewis and the union for criminal and civil contempt of court.

On appeal, the U.S. Supreme Court upheld, with some modification, the judgment of the district court. Chief Justice Vinson delivered the opinion of the court and held that the miners were government employees. He said:

. . . The defendants contended . . . that workers in mines seized by the Government are not employees of the Federal Government; that in operating the mines thus seized, the Government is not engaged in a sovereign function; and that, consequently, the situation in this case does not fall within the area which we have indicated as lying outside the scope of the Norris-LaGuardia Act. It is clear, however, that workers in the mines seized by the Government under the authority of the War Labor Disputes Act stand in an entirely different relationship to the Federal Government with respect to their employment from that which existed before the seizure was effected. That Congress intended such to be the case is apparent both from the terms of the statute and from the legislative deliberation preceding its enactment. Section 3 of the War Labor Disputes Act . . . calls for the seizure of any plant, mine or facility when the President finds that the operation thereof is threatened by strike or other labor disturbance and that an interruption in production will unduly impede the war effort. Congress intended that by virtue of Government seizure, a mine should become, for purposes of production and operation, a Government facility in as complete a sense as if the Government held full title and ownership. . . .

It is descriptive of the situation to state that the Government, in order to maintain production and to accomplish the purposes of the seizure, has substituted itself for the private employer in dealing with those matters which formerly were the subject of collective bargaining between the union and the operators. The defendants by their conduct have given practical recognition to this fact. The union negotiated a collective agreement with the Government and has made use of the procedures provided by the War Labor Disputes Act to modify its terms and conditions. The Union has apparently regarded the Krug-Lewis agreement as a sufficient contract of employment to satisfy the mine workers' traditional demand of a contract as a condition precedent to their work. . . .

Although we have held that the Norris-LaGuardia Act did not render injunctive relief beyond the jurisdiction of the District Court, there are alternative grounds which support the power of the District Court to punish violations of its orders as criminal contempt.

In the case before us, the District Court had the power to preserve existing conditions while it was determining its own authority to grant injunctive relief. The defendants, in making their private determination of the law, acted at their peril. Their disobedience is punishable as criminal contempt. . . .

State courts have authority to grant injunctions in strikes by employees of state or local governments. The state of New York has enacted a statute [151] quite similar to Section 304 of the Taft-Hartley Act.[152]

Even in the absence of statutes prohibiting government employees from striking, state courts have been permitted to enjoin such strikes on the ground that essential state and local government services must not be impaired.[153]

Title IV. Joint Committee to Study and Report on Basic Labor Problems

Sections 401–407 of the Taft-Hartley Act created a joint committee made up of seven Senators and seven Congressmen, to be appointed by the President.

FUNCTIONS OF THE COMMITTEE. It shall conduct a thorough study and investigation of the entire field of labor-management relations, including but not limited to:

(1) The means by which permanent, friendly cooperation between employers and employees and stability of labor relations may be secured throughout the United States.

(2) The means by which the individual employee may achieve a greater productivity and higher wages, including plans for guaranteed annual wages, incentive profit sharing, and bonus systems.

(3) The internal organization and administration of labor unions, with special attention to the impact on individuals of collective agreements requiring membership in unions as a condition of employment.

(4) The labor relations policies and practices of employers and associations of employers.

(5) The desirability of welfare funds for the benefit of employees and their relation to the social-security system.

151. Sec. 22(a) of the Civil Service Law, as added by Ch. 391, L. 1947 (Condon-Wadlin Act) (1947).
152. For New York cases, see N.Y. Transit Authority v. Loos, 154 N.Y.S.(2d) 209 (1956); Jewish Hospital v. "John Doe," 252 App. Div. 581 (1937).
153. See Norwalk Teachers Ass'n v. Board of Education, City of Norwalk, 138 Conn. 269 (1951); City of Los Angeles v. Los Angeles Building and Constr. Trades Council, 210 P. (2d) 305 (1949).

(6) The methods and procedures for best carrying out the collective-bargaining processes, with special attention to the effects of industry-wide or regional bargaining on the national economy.

(7) The administration and operation of existing federal laws relating to labor relations; and

(8) Such other problems and subjects in the field of labor-management relations as the committee deems appropriate.

The committee has been given power to hold hearings, require by subpoena the attendance of witnesses and the production of books, and take testimony.

Reports of the committee are submitted to the Senate and the House of Representatives. The last statutory report was filed at the time the committee went out of existence on March 1, 1949. Since then, the regular Senate Committee on Labor and the House Committee on Education and Labor have been conducting periodical hearings and have proposed new legislation to both Houses. One major piece of recommended legislation that Congress has adopted is the Reporting and Disclosure Act of 1959 (Landrum-Griffin Act), which will be discussed in the next chapter.

Title V. Definitions and Individual Rights

SECTION 501. The term "industry affecting commerce" means any industry or activity in commerce or in which a labor dispute would burden or obstruct commerce or tend to burden or obstruct commerce or the free flow of commerce.

This definition is one of exclusion as well as of inclusion. The authority of the NLRB does not extend to the relationship of all employees and employers. It purports to reach only what may be deemed to burden and obstruct interstate and foreign commerce.

The board has adopted jurisdictional yardsticks for determining whether or not it will take control of representation election and unfair practice cases.[154] The NLRB may not decline cases meeting the yardsticks prevailing on August 1, 1959. They specify minimum gross annual sales or purchases for various business firms. For example, if a retail business affecting commerce does a gross yearly volume of business of $500,000 or more, the board must take jurisdiction over any representation or unfair labor practice case that occurs between the business and its employees or a union. Jurisdiction will be asserted over any

154. The Landrum-Griffin Act of 1959 provides that the jurisdictional yardsticks which prevailed on August 1, 1959 shall control.

controversy that has a substantial impact on national defense without any regard to the volume of business done by the business.

The term "strike" includes any strike or other concerted stoppage of work by employees (including a stoppage by reason of the expiration of a collective-bargaining agreement), and any concerted slow-down or other concerted interruption of operations by employees. A concerted walk-out because of dangerous work conditions is not a strike.[155]

SECTION 502 provides that an individual employee may quit his job and may not be compelled to work without his consent.

The Thirteenth Amendment to the Constitution of the United States provides that:

Neither slavery nor involuntary servitude, except as a punishment for crime whereof the party shall have been duly convicted, shall exist within the United States, or any place subject to their jurisdiction.

The U.S. Supreme Court has held that the prohibitions of the Thirteenth Amendment are not limited to slavery as such, but extend to any practice having the effect of coercing a party to work against his will.[156]

When 114 out of 115 employees quit work within two days, the board held this to be a concerted work stoppage rather than a simultaneous quitting of individual employees.[157]

Summary

The Taft-Hartley Act has had a great impact on substantive labor law. The law was enacted in 1947 after a period in which unions called an unprecedented number of strikes that resulted in economic turmoil and seriously affected the normal flow of interstate and foreign commerce and imperiled the national welfare. Congress proposed that this new law be a mechanism for freeing industry from alleged union abuses of economic and political power. Congress was also interested in protecting the individual unorganized worker from union pressure. For the first time, the law sought to impose on labor organizations statutory responsibilities which the lawmakers believed would equalize bargaining power and diminish labor conflict.

Section 8, one of the major provisions, makes unions as well as employers accountable for the commission of unfair practices. Unions are

155. NLRB v. Knight Morley Corp., 251 Fed. (2d) 753 (1957).
156. See Taylor v. Georgia, 315 U.S. 25 (1941).
157. Roane-Anderson Co., 82 NLRB 696 (1949); U.S. v. U.M.W., 177 Fed. (2d) 29 (1948).

forbidden to force workers to join a union, to compel employers to pressure workers to join a union, to force an employer to discriminate against an employee whom the union refuses to admit to union membership, to refuse to bargain in good faith with the employer, to engage in secondary boycotts, to charge excessive initiation fees, and to engage in featherbedding practices.

In addition, this section prohibits picketing or strikes to enforce secondary boycotts. Although the Norris-LaGuardia Act of 1932 brought about a great reduction in issuance of injunctions in labor dispute cases, the Taft-Hartley Law permits injunctive relief in specific types of labor controversies. The National Labor Relations Board is mandated to seek injunctions in secondary boycott cases. The statute also permits employers, both primary and secondary, to sue unions in federal court to recover damages resulting from the use of the secondary boycott. Employers may use the federal courts in bringing civil actions for damages against labor organizations charged with the unlawful breach of collective-bargaining agreements; however, judgments obtained against unions do not extend to the personal resources of union members. Prior to the enactment of this law, unions had long been liable in state courts on their contracts; nevertheless, only a few damage suits have been brought by employers against unions for breach of contract, and the small number of damage suits may be explained by the employers' realization that a money judgment recovered against a union will inevitably result in some form of retaliation by the union members.

Section 8(c) provides for freedom of speech and states that an expression of an opinion shall not be evidence of an unfair labor practice unless it contains promises or threats or can be said to be coercive. The courts have so liberally interpreted this section that labor unions have claimed that under it employers have seriously interrupted the extension of trade union membership, especially in the southern states.

The law has banned the closed-shop type of security clause, but the union shop has been permitted except those states in which right-to-work laws have been enacted. The checkoff of union dues, initiation fees, and assessments, which usually accompanies a security agreement, may be negotiated between an employer and a labor organization if the employee consents in writing to the deductions.

It was not until 1944 that supervisors were classified as employees and were allowed all the rights enumerated in the Wagner Act of 1935. The Taft-Hartley Law abrogated these rights when it stated that supervisors were not employees within the legislative definition of that term.

Employees have been permitted a wide choice of elections. The Wagner Act provided only for the representation election. The representation and certification procedures have undergone marked changes. An employer assumes some risk when he deals with a union claiming recognition if that union has not been certified after a board election. As to elections held on petition of the union, the statute now provides that a representation election will be held by the board only if the union demanding the election has at least 30 per cent of the employees in the union or pledged to join the union. A representation election generally may not be held for one year after a union has been certified, or during the term of a valid, written, collective-bargaining agreement, provided the agreement is for a reasonable length of time, usually not exceeding two years.

There has been a change in the runoff election procedure. Formerly, if there were two unions contesting for representation in a plant, the board would hold an election upon which three choices would appear, Union A, Union B, and No Union. If No Union got the largest number of votes, the runoff election would be held between No Union and the union that received more votes than the other union. However, if No Union got the second greatest number of votes, it was excluded from the runoff and the runoff would be held between the two unions. Under the new statute the runoff must be between the two choices that received the highest number of votes. Furthermore, the employer has been given the right to file for a representation election whenever a union demands bargaining recognition. This has created difficulties for unions seeking recognition as the bargaining agent for the employees but not completely accepted. The employer, by filing a representation petition, can forestall a renewal of the organizational campaign for one year if the union loses the election. The board may not certify professional employees as part of a major unit unless the professional employees vote to be included in that unit.

There are three other types of elections provided for in the act. Employees who are covered under a union-shop agreement may petition for an election to withdraw the union security agreement and bring about open-shop conditions. Employees may rid themselves of their union by filing a decertification petition with the board which is followed by a secret election to determine whether or not the employees desire the union to continue to act as the bargaining representative. The last type of election provided for under the statute is conducted by the board when actual or threatened strikes affect the national welfare or safety. In this election the employees are permitted to vote on acceptance or rejection of their employer's last offer. In every election that has been held on the employer's last offer the workers have voted to reject it. We might point out here that the statute requires the Attorney General, at the request of the President, to seek to enjoin a threatened or actual strike which affects the national welfare or safety.

Another major statutory provision concerns trust funds for the payment of welfare and pension benefits to employees. The welfare plan must be in writing, the trust fund must be administered bilaterally, and the funds held in trust must be for intended purposes, i.e., for the exclusive benefit of the employees and members of their families.

The statute sets up a mediation and conciliation service as an independent agency whose purpose is to provide assistance as a last resort in settling labor disputes when the collective-bargaining process has failed.

Labor organizations are prohibited from using union funds for political purposes when federal elections are involved. There have been a few cases dealing with union political activities, and generally the courts have permitted unions to advance the candidacy of men for national office provided the support emanates through union publications. The AFL-CIO has organized a political arm (COPE) which is very active in national elections and does not run afoul of the act.

The complexity of the Taft-Hartley Law cannot be overestimated. The U.S. Supreme Court has not yet passed on all the lower court decisions or on all NLRB rulings. Of course, as time passes, final decisions will have been made on every section of the act.

Whether or not the act has fulfilled its objectives is a matter of opinion. When the law became effective in June 1947 many labor representatives characterized it a "slave labor law." There were others, principally employer representatives, who believed the law did not go far enough in curbing labor union power and abuses. Events of the 1950's encouraged Congress to enact additional labor laws regulating labor union activities; they are incorporated in the 1959 Reporting and Disclosure Act (the Landrum-Griffin Act), which we cover in the next chapter.

CHAPTER ELEVEN

The Labor-Management Reporting and Disclosure Act of 1959 and Its Amendments to the Taft-Hartley Act

THIS law [1] was created after more than two years of public hearings held before the Select Committee on Investigation of Improper Activities in Labor-Management Relations, or as it was commonly called, the McClellan Committee. This committee, under the chairmanship of Senator McClellan of Arkansas, reached the following conclusions:

(1) Democratic freedom was lacking in the unions investigated.

(2) International unions abused their power to place local unions under trusteeship.

(3) There was misuse of union funds.

(4) Some employers engaged in collusion with unions and paid union officials to get "sweetheart" contracts.

(5) Illegal activities and violence continued to prevail in labor-management disputes.

(6) Certain employers and their representatives engaged in such unlawful activities in violation of the Taft-Hartley Law as granting business concessions and loans to union leaders in return for favors.

1. 73 Stat. 519 (1959), hereafter cited as L.M.R.D.A. This act is also known as the Landrum-Griffin Act.

(7) Organizational picketing was sometimes used as "blackmail" picketing to extort funds from management.

(8) Racketeers and gangsters had gained high positions in and complete control over some unions.

(9) Lawyers engaged in questionable conduct in their relationships with some corrupt union officials; for instance, protecting the interests of union officials when they were in conflict with the interests of the membership which paid their legal fees.

(10) Law enforcement agents were lax in investigating and prosecuting those responsible for violence in labor-management disputes.

(11) An extensive "no-man's land" existed on the matter of federal-state jurisdiction in labor dispute cases.

As a result of these findings, the McClellan Committee recommended that Congress expand federal labor legislation to eliminate the offenses as well as the unlawful conduct.

The committee's findings were accepted by Congress, after which a considerable amount of debate took place on the various reform bills introduced. Eventually Congress passed the L.M.R.D.A. Most of its provisions became effective on September 14, 1959.

This long and involved statute introduces a new concept in labor law; the direct intervention by the federal government into the internal structure and affairs of labor unions. The law has seven titles, each of several provisions. Titles I–V deal with union reforms. They guarantee a "bill of rights" to union members in the conduct of union affairs that is comparable to the first ten amendments to the United States Constitution. Periodic secret elections of union officers, free speech, rights of assembly, and detailed financial statements by labor organizations are prescribed rights of union members. Members of the Communist Party and persons convicted of specific crimes are barred from holding union offices until five years have elapsed after resignation from the Party after the person has completed his prison term. In addition, union members are permitted to sue in the federal courts for an accounting of union funds, to receive fair trials during disciplinary proceedings, to sue for the recovery of misappropriated union funds, and to sue for the enforcement of other specific rights listed in the five titles. Section 505 of Title V is a lengthy amendment to Section 302 of the Taft-Hartley Act.

Title VI comprises the following miscellaneous provisions:

(1) The Secretary of Labor has power to investigate complaints alleging violations of the act.

(2) Extortionate picketing is a federal crime.

(3) It is a crime for any person to use any violence or threat of violence against another person for the purpose of interfering with his exercise of any rights under the act.

(4) It is unlawful to discipline a union member who attempts to exercise his rights under the act.

Title VII contains amendments to the Taft-Hartley Law dealing with secondary boycotts and hot-cargo contracts, recognition and organizational picketing, federal-state jurisdiction, status of economic strikers in representation elections, and the special status given workers in the building construction and garment industries.

The act seeks its objectives by following two courses. It creates new federal crimes in order to punish dishonest union officials as well as those officials who willfully use violence or threaten violence against members who seek to exercise their newly created civil rights. In addition, every labor union subject to federal law must file with the Secretary of Labor detailed, annual financial statements which union members and other interested persons may examine.

Title I. The Bill of Rights of Union Members

SECTIONS 101–104 give members of labor organizations the following rights:

(1) Every union member has a right to speak freely at union meetings without fear of punishment by union officers, but the member must abide by any reasonable rules adopted by the union concerning the conduct of meetings.

(2) Every union member has the right to nominate candidates for union office, to vote in union elections, to attend membership meetings, and to have a voice in the business taken up at such meetings, subject only to such reasonable rules and regulations as are set forth in the union constitution and by-laws.

(3) No dues may be increased nor any assessments be levied by a local union unless a majority of the members in good standing who are present at a regular or special meeting vote for such increase, and all members must be given reasonable notice that this matter will be brought up for a vote at such meeting.

(4) A union member has the right to bring a court action without any union interference. However, the union members must exhaust reasonable remedies of appeal within the union before instituting a court proceeding against the union.

(5) A union may not fine, suspend, or expel a member (except for nonpayment of dues) unless the member has been served with specific written charges, given a reasonable time to prepare his defense, and allowed a fair hearing.

(6) Every person covered by a collective-bargaining agreement has the right to request the union for a copy of the agreement.

(7) Every labor union must inform its members of the provisions of this law.

Cases and Rulings

The constitutionality of the Bill of Rights constituting Title I has been upheld by a federal district court in Michigan.[2] In this case the court also ruled that nonunion employees, even though covered by a labor contract, have no right of free speech at union meetings.

In the Bennett case [3] a union fired one of its field representatives for being intoxicated. Bennett remained a member of the union. He brought an action against the union claiming he could not be fired without a hearing. The court dismissed the action on the ground that this was an employment relationship, and since union membership rights were not involved, Bennett had no right to a hearing.

In a similar situation [4] a union fired a business agent who had been convicted of robbery. He sued under Section 102 claiming a wrongful discharge had taken place without a hearing. The court held again that this involved an employer relationship, and therefore no hearing was required.

Courts have been very conservative in injecting themselves into the internal affairs of unions. The act is vague, and some believe that because it was poorly drafted, courts take great latitude in deciding cases. The courts have been insistent on one point; that union members must exhaust internal union remedies, provided they are reasonable, before court relief will be made available to them. This condition precedent appears in Section 101(a)(4). In Smith v. Local 467, Teamsters,[5] the plaintiff was given an honorable union withdrawal card in 1958. In 1959 he applied for reinstatement and was denied. Smith sued the local union, then appealed its decision to the Council of Teamsters. Smith claimed he had a right to have a lawyer present at his hearing. The court held that the act gave Smith the right of hearing, but that the law was silent on the right of counsel. The court held further that Title I created substantive rights, and since Smith left the union in

2. Johnson v. Local 58, Electrical Workers, 39 LC 66,260 (1960).
3. Bennett v. Engineers, 39 LC 66,183 (1960).
4. Strauss v. Teamsters, 45 LRRM 2348 (1959). See also Jackson v. Martin Co., 180 F. Supp. 475 (1960).
5. 181 F. Supp. 14 (1960). For articles on exhaustion of internal remedies, see B. Aaron, The Labor Management Reporting and Disclosure Act of 1959, 73 *Harv. L. Rev.* 851 (1960), and an article of the same title by R. A. Smith, 46 *Va. L. Rev.* 195 (1960).

1958, these rights were not retroactive. In 1959 he was not a member, and therefore he could not assert rights under the 1959 act. Finally, the court ruled that 101(a)(4) requires that a member exhaust union remedies before he goes to court.

In the Johnson case [6] the union members were successful in their action against the union. Dissident union members held separate union meetings seeking a separate international charter. When they sued the union officers who allegedly interfered with these meetings, the union sought to dismiss the action on the ground that members were required to exhaust their internal remedies. The court rejected the union defense on the ground that the union hearing procedures were unreasonable and would consume a considerable amount of time which would work against the dissidents.

In Allen v. Local 92, Bridgeworkers,[7] a U.S. District Court in Alabama ruled that the union had violated the statutory provisions safeguarding union members from improper disciplinary actions when it fined certain members without serving such members with any written charges and without granting them a hearing. On another complaint made by the union members in this same case relating to the inspection of union records, the court held that the members were entitled to a copy of the complete collective-bargaining agreement affecting the members. In another case [8] brought under Section 102 to enforce union membership rights, the court temporarily sustained the complaint, which alleged interference with the equal rights of union members and freedom of assembly. However, the single remaining issue was whether the complainant had exhausted the reasonable hearing procedures within the meaning of the act. Because the testimony on the subject matter was so rambling and so general, the court ordered that the proceeding be stayed in order to afford the plaintiff the opportunity of exhausting union hearing procedures.[9] Cases dealing with the necessity of exhaustion of internal remedies before beginning court action are not all in accord. In Connor v. Teamsters [10] the court found that immediate and irreparable damage would result if the union members were required to exhaust their internal remedies before court relief was permitted. It should be noted that in this case, however, threats of reprisal, violence, and other forms of disorder were present during the

6. *Supra.*
7. 41 LC 16,697 (1960).
8. Light v. Erskine, 41 LC 16,599 (1960).
9. See also Myers v. Operating Engineers, 40 LC 66,436 (1960), in which it was held that when a union member was seeking a postelection remedy for an allegedly improper election, the court had no jurisdiction if the complaining member had not exhausted his union remedies or applied to the Secretary of Labor for relief. The same ruling was given in Temko v. Hilbert 40 LC 66,757 (1960).
10. 39 LC 66,115 (1959). See also Allen v. Local 92, *supra.*

conduct of a union meeting called for the purpose of amending the union's by-laws and to nominate candidates for union office.

A New York District Court in the Figueroa case [11] held that the requirement that a union member exhaust his internal remedies is not absolute. Justifying this position, Justice Sugarman said: ". . . Whether reasonable hearing procedures were available and, if so, whether plaintiffs should have utilized them are matters which cannot be determined at this time." The court denied the union's motion to dismiss the complaint and sent the matter to trial.

Whether a union member has a right to be represented by counsel in a hearing before his union was answered in the Smith case.[12] Justice Yankwich of the District Court of California said:

. . . In effect, the complainant alleges that the Executive Board is biased against him and that no provision is made for representation by counsel in hearings before it. The answer to the contention lies in the statement of the fundamental principle that the right to be represented by counsel, guaranteed by the Sixth Amendment to the Constitution of the United States, does not apply to hearings before labor unions. The reason is obvious. All that a union member is entitled to in any controversy between him and the union is a fair hearing. This means only that before any action is taken against him he must be informed of the charges and be given an opportunity to hear them and refute them. This satisfies the constitutional concept as to all administrative proceedings. . . . By becoming a member of a union the worker in effect, makes a contract to be governed by the constitution and by-laws, and the rules of the organization.

Title II. Reporting by Labor Organizations, Officers, and Employees of Labor Organizations

The intended beneficiary of the act is the union member. Other rights, in addition to the substantive rights appearing in Title I, are guaranteed to the union member by Title II. These rights require unions to give each member various types of information, and permit him to protect and enforce these guarantees.

It was expected that given information about his union the union member would exercise his democratic rights, and participate more fully in the affairs of his union. Along with the right to information, the union member may "for just cause" sue to examine any of the union's books, records, and accounts that are needed to verify such reports. In some respects the union member enjoys a position analagous to that of a corporation stockholder. The union member may not press

11. Figueroa v. National Maritime Union, 42 LC 16,864 (1961).
12. Smith v. Local 467, *supra*.

his demand to inspect the books and records unless he can establish a bona fide reason for the inspection. The act does not intend to permit fishing expeditions; therefore it is expected that the union member will have to set forth some facts indicating that inaccuracies in the reports exist or that there have been statutory violations by union officers.

SECTIONS 201 AND 202 of Title II provide that every labor organization shall file with the Secretary of Labor the following information:

(1) A copy of its constitution and by-laws.

(2) Administrative reports that include the name and address of the union, names of officers, amount of dues, frequency of union meetings, type of financial auditing used, method of ratifying collective-bargaining agreements, and method of calling strikes.

(3) A detailed financial statement signed by the elected officers of the union.

(4) Each officer and employee of a labor union (other than an office clerk) must file annually a report listing securities and other property owned by him or any member of his household. He must also file a report on any business transaction he has had with an employer whose employees the union represents and must report any money or other thing of value received from such an employer.

SECTIONS 203(A) TO 203(G) of Title II concern reports required to be filed by employers with the Secretary of Labor. They must cover:

(1) Expenditures made for the purpose of interfering with, restraining, coercing, or persuading employees to exercise or not to exercise their concerted rights under the National Labor Relations Act.

(2) Any payment or loan made to a union or its officers.

(3) Any agreement with a labor relations consultant under which the consultant undertakes to influence employees in their choice of a bargaining representative or provides the employer with information in connection with a labor dispute.

The reports are filed annually and signed by the employer's principal officers. The Secretary of Labor may investigate reportable matters.

SECTIONS 204–210. Section 204 exempts attorneys from including in any of the reports required to be filed any information he has received by reason of the attorney-client relationship.

Section 205 allows the Secretary of Labor to make reasonable provision for public inspection of information contained in all reports filed in his office by labor unions and by union and employer officials.

Section 206 provides that every person required to file reports with the Secretary of Labor must preserve for no less than five years all records substantiating the statements made in the reports.

Section 209 makes it a new federal crime to wilfully refuse to file the required reports, or to make a false statement in the reports, or to withhold, conceal, or destroy books and records that are required to be kept for no less than five years. Conviction may bring a fine of $10,000 or one year imprisonment or both.

Section 210 provides that whenever a violation of the reporting requirements appears to have occurred the Secretary of Labor may bring a civil action in the federal court for a restraining order or for other appropriate relief.

Title II gives the federal government the role of a watchdog over the administrative and financial affairs of unions. The federal power also has authority to demand certain reports from employers who deal with labor organizations. It is clear that the reporting and disclosure features of Title II are directed toward protecting the union member beneficiary by imposing requirements which will severely punish dishonesty uncovered between unions or employers in their labor-management relationship.

Cases and Rulings

In a New York case [13] a union member who wanted to examine the union's books sent a letter to the union and received no answer. He brought an action to compel inspection. The court dismissed the action on the ground that the union member did not show just cause for examining the records.

In an Ohio case [14] the circuit court of appeals allowed a group of union members to examine the books, records, and accounts of their local union. According to the court, just cause for the examination existed because there was a reasonable basis to the belief that the report filed by the local with respect to the procedures for issuing work permits was incomplete, inexact, or amounted to an inadequate explanation of the detailed procedures actually followed by the local in referring applicants for employment.

Title III. Trusteeships

A trusteeship is any receivership or other method of supervision or control whereby a labor organization suspends the autonomy otherwise available to a subordinate body under its constitution or by-laws.[15]

The McClellan Committee hearings revealed that the international unions surveyed had flagrantly abused their power of placing local un-

13. Henderson v. Sarle, 197 N.Y.S. (2d) 920 (1960).
14. Allen v. Bridgeworkers Union, 41 LC 16,697 (1960).
15. Section 3(h) of the act.

ions under trusteeship. Some trusteeships had lasted for as long as thirty years, and attempts by the rank-and-file members to throw off the shackles had been met with violence and intimidation. Finally, the committee found that some locals under trusteeship had been plundered by the very officials entrusted with the management of their affairs.

SECTION 301 provides that a trusteeship may be established and administered by an international union only if it is for one of the following purposes, specified in Section 302:

(1) Correcting corruption or financial malpractices.

(2) Assuring the performance of union contracts or of the duties of a local union or district council as the collective-bargaining representative.

(3) Restoring democratic procedures.

(4) Carrying out the legitimate objects of the local union or other subordinate body.

During the continuance of a trusteeship the labor organization that has assumed supervision over the subordinate union shall file on behalf of the subordinate union the annual financial report required by Section 201. In addition, the trusteeship must file with the Secretary of Labor an administrative report including a statement of reasons for establishing the trusteeship and a full account of the financial condition of the subordinate body at the time the trusteeship was established.

Section 301 provides further that any person who is convicted of violating the provisions relating to trusteeships may be fined $10,000 or imprisoned for one year or both.

In one case [16] an international appointed a trustee over an affiliate that sought to disaffiliate. The court upheld the international's right to take over the property of the local union.

It was believed that dissident subordinate-union members were required to seek relief through the Secretary of Labor in trusteeship cases. However, in one case [17] a court disagreed and allowed a civil action to stand without seeking the Secretary's intervention.

A trusteeship properly established under a union's constitutional procedure is presumed to be valid for a period not exceeding eighteen months.[18]

The procedure through the Secretary of Labor affords the primary and principal remedy for the individual member of the local. The authorization for the bringing of suit by a member or by the local is a supplemental and accessory method of securing relief.[19]

16. Crocker v. Weil, 45 LRRM 2935 (1959).
17. Executive Board v. Local 28, I.B.E.W., 40 LC 66,514 (1960). Contrary holding: Flaherty v. McDonald, 40 LC 66,514 (1960).
18. Dawson v. Delaney, 39 LC 66,352 (1960).
19. See Rizzo v. Ammond, 40 LC 66,506 (1960).

Title IV. Elections: Terms of Office and
Election Procedures

Since one of the major goals of the act is to develop democracy in all labor organizations, the provisions of Section 401, which deals with free and democratic elections, are of great importance. The act does not set forth in detail the procedures for nomination and election of officers to be followed, but it sets up minimum requirements. Elections are to be conducted in accordance with the constitution and by-laws of each union so long as these laws do not conflict with provisions of the act.

All officers must be elected by secret ballot, even in uncontested elections. Officers of national and international labor organizations must be elected every five years, officers of intermediate posts, such as joint boards, joint councils, and conferences, every four years, and officers in local unions, every three years.

A reasonable opportunity must be given to members in good standing to nominate candidates of their own choice, and such members are eligible to be candidates and to hold officers, subject to reasonable qualifications uniformly imposed. The resources of the union are not to be used to support a favorite candidate for union office over other candidates; what is done for one candidate must be done for all bona fide candidates at their request, with equal expense. All reasonable requests of a candidate to distribute campaign literature by mail at the candidate's expense to all members in good standing must be honored, and if campaign literature is distributed without charge for one candidate, it must be distributed for all candidates without charge. Each candidate has a right to inspect the list containing the names and last known addresses of all members of the union who are subject to a labor agreement with an employer which requires membership in the union as a condition of employment.

The act provides that if, on application of a member, the Secretary of Labor finds after a hearing that the procedures for removal of elected local-union officers guilty of serious misconduct are not adequate, members may then, for cause shown, and after notice and hearing, remove any such officer by membership vote in a secret-ballot election conducted by the officers of the local union. A member of a labor organization may file a complaint with the Secretary of Labor alleging that the provisions of Title IV have been violated, but the complaint will not be acted on until the member has exhausted the remedies available to him under the laws of the local and international unions and has not obtained a final decision within three months after invoking them.

A labor union must give reasonable notice of the offices to be filled by an election, the time for submitting nominations, and the place for submitting them. The members must be given enough time to nominate candidates of their choice for office, and any qualifications imposed on members who choose to run for office must be reasonable. For example, a regulation that a person must have been a member of the union for not less than one year will be considered a reasonable eligibility requirement for nomination and election to a union office. A rule disqualifying all but a handful of members would be construed as unreasonable.

This title provides further that all delegates to national or international conventions must be elected by secret ballot. Finally, where the union constitution or by-laws conflict with the provisions of Title IV, the act gives the unions time to bring their laws and regulations into line with the provisions of the act.

This title states that all union officers must be elected periodically. An "officer" is defined as "any constitutional officer, any person authorized to perform the functions of president, vice-president, secretary, treasurer, or other executive functions of a labor organization, and any member of its executive board or similar governing body."

The Bureau of Labor Management,[20] U.S. Dept. of Labor, has ruled that when a union business agent has duties that result in his position falling within the definition of an officer, he must be elected by the membership.

Shop stewards need not be elected by secret ballot unless the union laws require it. If the shop steward exercises executive functions, a secret election for the office is required.[21]

A federal district court in Michigan[22] held that court relief will not be allowed a union member who seeks to prevent the sending of allegedly improperly elected delegates to a national convention when an application for the intervention of the Secretary of Labor had not been exhausted.

In a much litigated case[23] involving the eligibility of certain members to vote in an election of local-union officers, a federal court ruled that all members of the local union who had paid their quarterly dues before the end of the third quarter of 1960, and who paid their fourth-quarter dues as they became due on October 1, 1960, or at any time before the election were eligible to vote in the local-union election.

The Connor case[24] received a great deal of publicity in New Jersey

20. BLMR Technical Assistance Aid 5, *Electing Union Officers*, Washington, 1960.
21. Dept. of Labor Press Release, February 13, 1961.
22. Myers v. Operating Engineers, 40 LC 66,436 (1960).
23. Boggia v. Hoffa, 41 LC 16,732 (1960).
24. Connor v. Teamsters Local 560, 39 LC 66,115 (1959).

when a group of union members sought and were successful in getting a district court to issue an injunction restraining the union and its officers from holding a meeting to nominate candidates. A previous union meeting had resulted in violence and disorder during and after the meeting. Following the issuance of the injunction, the parties entered into a stipulation which guaranteed that any union nomination meetings and elections would be conducted in accordance with rules promulgated by the local's international union on recommendations of its board of monitors.

Federal courts will not generally afford relief to union members until the members have exhausted their internal remedies or have successfully brought about intervention by the Secretary of Labor. In a Delaware case,[25] however, the district court enjoined the holding of a union election on the application of a union member when the court felt that the injunctive relief was incidental to the member's primary claim that his rights under the Bill of Rights section of the act had been violated.

Title V. Safeguards for Labor Organizations

More than half a billion dollars a year are collected from union members; it is estimated that pension, health, and welfare funds total from twenty-five to thirty billion dollars. These funds, according to testimony given before the McClellan Committee, are increasing at the rate of five billion dollars a year. The committee received additional testimony that some union officials regarded union treasuries as their happy hunting grounds. Because Congress believed that union offices are positions of trust, and that officers hold union funds and other property for the exclusive benefit of the members, the act has imposed the same duty on union officers as is expected of other trustees. That is, the union officers are required to put their obligations to the union and its members ahead of any personal interest.

Certain principles have been settled by the new fiduciary provisions appearing in Section 501. Union officials are fiduciaries with regard to union funds and property. If a union official becomes involved in a conflict-of-interest situation, he will be held as a trustee and compelled by the courts to reimburse the union to the extent of any profit he gained by the breach of his trustee relationship, and this will hold whether or not the union has suffered an actual loss. When a union official accepts a bribe or other unlawful payment from the employer, he will be compelled to deposit his gain in the union treasury. Embez-

25. Sheridan v. Bhd. of Carpenters, 42 LC 16,781 (1961).

zlement, theft, or conversion of union money or property is made a federal crime by Section 501(c) that is punishable by a $10,000 fine or five years in prison or both.

Section 502 provides another safeguard. Officers, agents, and employees who handle the funds or property of any union or of any trust in which a union is interested must be bonded for not less than 10 per cent of the funds handled annually by the person. If the funds annually handled by the individual do not exceed $5000, no bond is required. The bond must be carried with corporate sureties approved by the Secretary of the Treasury. A violation of this section may lead to a fine of up to $10,000 or imprisonment for one year or both.

In a further attempt to safeguard union funds, labor unions are prohibited under Section 503(a) from making loans to officers and employees which result in an indebtedness in excess of $2000 for each person. Neither unions nor employers may pay the fines of any persons convicted of any willful violation of any part of the 1959 act. Improper loans or the payment of fines may subject violators to a $5000 fine or one year in prison or both.

Section 504 bars Communists and persons convicted of specific crimes from holding union office or working for a union in any capacity other than clerical or custodial. Nor may any such person act as a labor relations consultant for an employer or employer association. This disability is removed when five years have elapsed since the person terminated his membership in the Communist Party or since he completed his term of imprisonment. A willful violation of this section may lead to the imposition of a fine or prison sentence or both.

Section 505 amends Section 302 of the 1947 Labor Management Relations Act. Under Section 302 of the 1947 act, payments by employers to union officials and the taking of money by such officials constituted a federal crime. Of course, payments made in the course of employment and other legitimate transactions were excluded. These unlawful payment provisions have been broadened in the new act as follows:

(a) To cover payments made by consultants or other persons acting for employers.

(b) To include officers of any union.

(c) To include payments to employees to cause them to attempt to influence other employees in exercising their bargaining rights.

(d) To cover payment to any union officer with an intent to influence him in any of his actions.

In the leading case [26] decided under Section 501, the U.S. Court of Appeals, 3rd Circuit ruled that although the act does not expressly prohibit a union from paying the legal expenses of its officers in defending themselves in a suit charging them with misappropriation of union

26. Teamsters Local 107 v. Raymond Cohen, 284 Fed. (2d) 162 (1960).

funds, a resolution adopted by the union in advance of the trial authorizing such payment was invalid. The court reasoned that such payment of legal fees would be inconsistent with the aims and purposes of the act, which makes it the duty of union officers to hold labor organization money and property only for the benefit of the organization and its members. A general exculpatory provision in the laws of a labor organization purporting to relieve any such person of liability for breach of the duties declared by Section 501 is void as against public policy.

The Bill of Rights sections of the 1959 act should assist all union members in demanding faithful performance of the fiduciary duties of their elected officers. Democracy can now prevail in all unions and the political freedom of members is made secure by the act. These legislative rights can become fruitful only when union members manifest real interest in union affairs. By regularly attending meetings and exercising freedom of speech, union members can be sure that their rights will be safeguarded. As long as many trade unionists continue to view their unions as "slot machines" that provide dollar benefits in exchange for small monthly dues, true democratic self-government can never be realized.

The great majority of American trade unions, and more particularly the craft unions, have adhered continuously to the tradition of self-government. There is no question in the minds of informed persons that the autocracy and racketeering which existed in the very few unions investigated by the McClellan Committee resulted mainly from the apathetic attitude of the union membership. It is true, of course, that in a small number of unions abuses were tolerated by the members only because some union leaders used various types of violence, threats, and intimidation to prevent the exercise of democratic rights. By and large, union members, like members of a state, will enjoy the privileges which flow from democracy only in proportion to the number of responsibilities they are willing to accept.

Title VI. Miscellaneous Provisions

SECTION 601 provides that whenever the Secretary of Labor believes it necessary to determine whether any person has violated or is about to violate any provision of the act, except the Bill of Rights provisions appearing in Title I or the amendments to the 1947 Taft-Hartley Law, he may initiate any investigation and is given power to issue subpoenas for the production and inspection of records and the presence of witnesses. The Secretary is permitted under Section 607 to make agreements with other federal agencies for cooperation and mutual assistance in the performance of his functions under the act.

SECTION 602 creates another federal crime called extortionate picketing. Organizational picketing is a device sometimes used by labor unions to organize substandard firms. The McClellan Committee obtained testimony indicating that some unions used the organizational picket line as a criminal device to extort money from business firms. For example, a picket line would be established in front of the premises of a nonunion firm, and invariably truckmen and other secondary employees would refuse to cross the picket line. After the picketed employer had sustained serious economic losses, he would receive a visit from the persons who had established the picket line. These individuals were extortionists seeking not to organize workers but to obtain money from the distressed employer. Usually the employer paid the price demanded, after which the picket line was withdrawn. Section 602 seeks to prevent this racketeering by making it unlawful to picket for the personal profit or enrichment of any individual. Of course picketing to obtain wage increases and other bona fide employee benefits is lawful. The severe penalty of twenty years of imprisonment is provided, along with a $10,000 fine, or both.

SECTION 609 makes it unlawful for any labor union or union representative to discipline any member for exercising any right to which he is entitled. Union members may, under Section 102 of the act, bring federal court actions to enjoin any such discipline.

SECTION 610. This last important section of Title VI provides that it shall be unlawful for any person to use force or violence or to coerce or intimidate any union member for the purpose of interfering with his exercising or preventing him from exercising any of the rights provided to him under the 1959 act. Any person who is convicted under this section may be imprisoned for one year or fined $1000 or both.

Cases and Rulings

The most important decision [27] to be made under Title VI occurred in a case involving Teamsters Local 299 in Detroit. The issue involved the right of the Secretary of Labor to secure judicial enforcement of subpoenas duces tecum he had issued and served on union officers in connection with an investigation he was attempting under the authority of Section 601. The union contended that it was obligatory on the Secretary to establish probable cause for the investigation as a con-

27. Goldberg, Secretary of Labor v. Local 299, Teamsters, U.S. Ct. of App. 6th Circuit No. 14533, August 16, 1961.

dition precedent to obtaining enforcement of the subpoenas by the court. The district court in Michigan accepted the union's position and denied enforcement. The circuit court of appeals reversed and granted enforcement of the subpoenas issued by the Secretary. This court said in part:

. . . We believe Oklahoma Press Publishing Co. v. Walling, 327 U.S. 186 is dispositive of this issue. In upholding enforcement of a subpoena duces tecum issued by the Administrator of the Wage and Hour Division of the Department of Labor, the Court said:

"Congress has made no requirement in terms of any showing of "probable cause"; and, in view of what has already been said, any possible constitutional requirement of that sort was satisfied by the Administrator's showing in this case, including not only the allegations concerning coverage, but also that he was proceeding with his investigation in accordance with the mandate of Congress and that the records sought were relevant to that purpose. . . . The result therefore sustains the Administrator's position that his investigative function, in searching out violations with a view to securing enforcement of the Act, is essentially the same as the grand jury's or the court's, in issuing other pretrial orders for the discovery of evidence, and is governed by the same limitations. These are that he shall not act arbitrarily or in excess of his statutory authority, but this does not mean that his inquiry must be limited by forecasts of the probable result of the investigation. . . ."

Title VII. Amendments to the Labor-Management Relations Act of 1947

The new law enacted several amendments to the Taft-Hartley Act. They concern the following subject matter:

(1) Federal-state jurisdiction over labor cases involving or affecting interstate commerce. The "no-man's land" problem has been resolved.

(2) The National Labor Relations Board may delegate its authority.

(3) Economic strikers are now permitted to vote in representation elections.

(4) Secondary-boycott loopholes have been closed.

(5) Hot-cargo agreements are prohibited. Certain exceptions have been allowed for construction and garment unions.

(6) Consumer and publicity picketing has been made lawful under specific conditions.

(7) Statutory restrictions have been placed on recognition and organizational types of picketing.

(8) Exacting a fee or charge from an interstate motor carrier for unloading cargo carried by a vehicle is a crime.

Federal-State Jurisdiction

After the doctrine of federal preemption had been authoritively established by the U.S. Supreme Court in Garner v. Teamsters,[28] there was still some doubt whether a firm whose volume of business was too small to bring it within the jurisdictional standards of the NLRB could be made a party to an action started by a union in a state court or state administrative agency, or whether such an employer could get relief in the state court when faced with an illegal strike or picket line. In 1957 [29] the court held that where the NLRB had determined that the volume of business done by a firm was too small to warrant board action, and therefore refused to process a union's complaint against the employer, an order issued by the Utah State Labor Board was unenforcible because of the preemption rule.

The Guss case created a vast "no-man's land" which the Supreme Court said could best be remedied by Congressional action. The satisfactory solution to this problem came with the enactment of Section 701 of the 1959 Landrum-Griffin Act. This section authorizes the NLRB by rule or decision to decline jurisdiction over any dispute involving "any class or category of employers," where, in the opinion of the board, the effect of such dispute on commerce is not sufficiently substantial to warrant its exercising jurisdiction. It then permits state agencies and state courts to assume jurisdiction with respect to disputes the board has declined to hear. However, the dollar-volume jurisdictional standards employed by the board on August 1, 1959 are frozen into the law, and the board may not in the future change its jurisdictional standards. The long-overdue reform of eliminating "no-man's land" in labor law should go far to promote the expressed national labor policy.

Delegation of Board Authority

Another important provision in Section 701 allows the NLRB to delegate authority to its regional directors to determine appropriate bargaining units and other questions of representation, to direct elections, and to issue certifications. This decision-making authority is expected to reduce the great delay in disposing of cases that had resulted from the prior rule that all final decisions had to be made by the board members in Washington, D.C.

28. 346 U.S. 485 (1953).
29. Guss v. Utah Labor Board, 353 U.S. 1 (1957).

Economic Strikers

Under the Taft-Hartley Law economic strikers not entitled to rein-statement were ineligible to vote in a board representation election. Economic strikers are workers who refuse to return to work until such time as the employer agrees to grant the workers wage increases or other economic benefits. Such workers risk losing their jobs, since the em-ployer is permitted to replace the economic strikers. It was long felt that the 1947 law was too harsh and allowed employers to get rid of unions by deliberately and unjustly refusing to make any economic concessions and so encouraging the workers to strike. After the strike call, the strikers would be replaced, and the employer would ask the board to hold a representation election to determine whether or not the union represented his workers. Only the strike replacements were eligible to vote in the election. Obviously, the replacements would not vote for the striking union. The defeated union was thereafter barred from picketing and could not seek representation rights until twelve months had expired from the date the employer-requested election was held. This union-busting device was prominently used in the O'Sullivan Rubber Corporation case.[30] Section 702 of the 1959 act repeals Section 9(c)(3) of the 1947 Taft-Hartley Law, and under the amendment economic strikers as well as strike replacements are eligible to partici-pate in representation elections.

Secondary Boycotts

One of the principal objectives of the Taft-Hartley Act of 1947 was to prohibit all forms of secondary boycotts by labor unions. The appli-cation and interpretation of Section 8(b)(4), (A) and (B), which sought to make secondary types of economic pressure unlawful, allowed exceptions to develop. For example, it was found that a union could induce employees of a secondary employer that was not covered by the National Labor Relations Act, such as a railroad, not to handle goods of a primary employer with whom the union had a dispute.[31] Further-more, a union could lawfully threaten a secondary employer with re-prisals unless he stopped dealing with a primary employer, and a union could enter into a hot-cargo agreement with an employer. The agree-ment gave the union all the advantages of a secondary boycott. Finally,

30. NLRB v. United Rubber Workers, 269 Fed. (2d) 694 (1959).
31. Local 25, Teamsters v. N.Y., N.H., and H.R.R., 350 U.S. 155 (1956).

the 1947 act allowed a union to induce single employees of a secondary employer to withhold their labor.

Section 704 of the act seeks to close the exceptions which developed under Section 8(b)(4) of the Taft-Hartley Act. This section has been rewritten and Section 8(b)(4), (i) and (ii) list the type of activity banned when the object of such activity is proscribed. Section 8(b)(4), (A), (B), (C), and (D) enumerate the prohibited objectives. Furthermore, in the new 8(b)(4) section, Congress has substituted the word "individual" for the term "employees" and the term "concerted" has been eliminated, and by doing so has made unlawful any inducement directed by a union against a single employee of a secondary employer when the employee has been requested to stop working on goods originating from a primary employer with whom the union has a dispute. The new provisos in Section 8(b)(4) do not invalidate any primary strike or primary picketing that do not seek objectives prohibited in Section 8(b)(4), (A), (B), (C), or (D).

Cases and Rulings

COERCION AND THREATS TO EMPLOYERS. In the Gilmore Construction case,[32] the board held that Section 8(b)(4)(i) was violated when the union picketed a construction project because the general contractor had employed a nonunion subcontractor and informed the general contractor that the picketing would stop only if the subcontractor were removed from the job. The board pointed out that the picketing constituted "coercion and restraint" under the new amendment.

In another case [33] the union refused to allow its members to work for a primary contractor on a construction project until it had agreed to cease doing business with two nonunion subcontractors engaged in operations at the same project. An 8(b)(4)(i)(B) charge was filed with the board against the union. This section makes it unlawful for a union to induce its members to strike with an object of forcing the employer to discontinue doing business with nonunion firms. The board sustained the charge on the basis that the strike against the construction company necessarily restrained and coerced the company to force it to cease doing business with the nonunion employers.

It is therefore clear that any threats or coercion directed against

32. International Hod Carriers Union (Gilmore Constr. Co.), 127 NLRB (541) (1960).
33. Local 825, Teamsters (Carlton Bros. Co.), 131 NLRB (No. 67) (1961); a similar ruling was made in Local 457, Plumbers Union (Bomat Plumbing and Heating), 131 NLRB (No. 151) (1961).

secondary employers are unlawful. It is also clear that when a union seeks to induce secondary employees to stop working on goods coming from a struck primary employer such inducement is likewise unlawful.[34] However, if a union induces a managerial employee of a secondary employer to stop dealing with a primary employer, the board has held that such an inducement would not violate the law.[35] The board stated that it will be necessary in each case to examine the authority, responsibility, and background of the supervisors and their working conditions, duties, and functions on the job involved in the dispute to determine whether the supervisor is insulated from inducement.

"ALLY" DOCTRINE. A secondary employer whose employees perform work of a strike-bound employer which would otherwise have been performed by the strikers is an "ally" of the strike-bound employer. Economic pressure exerted by a striking union against the secondary employer is therefore not a violation of 8(b)(4)(A).[36] For secondary-boycott purposes, an employer has been held not a neutral but an ally when he and another company were commonly owned and controlled or engaged in integrated operations, or when the work performed by independent contractors was "farmed-out struck work."

A recent and important decision on the "ally" doctrine was made in the Milwaukee Plywood case.[37] The Milwaukee Plywood Company was a wholly owned subsidiary of Aetna Plywood of Chicago. In July 1958, Teamsters Local 743 struck Aetna and picketed its plant in Chicago. In August 1958 this union established a picket line at the Milwaukee Company plant in Milwaukee. Warehousemen employed at the Milwaukee Company plant refused to cross the picket line. Members of Local 200 of the Teamsters appeared from time to time to relieve pickets belonging to Local 743. Members of Local 200 were employees of carriers which served the Milwaukee Company, and they were instructed by officers of Local 200 not to go through the picket line. On two occasions, officers of Local 200 talked directly with the management of trucking companies about respecting the picket line at Milwaukee.

The Milwaukee Company filed an 8(b)(4)(A) complaint against Local 200, which was dismissed by the board after a hearing. The Milwaukee Company petitioned the U.S. Circuit Court of Appeals, 7th Circuit, to review and set aside the board's dismissal. The court, denying the petition, said:

. . . In view of the close inter-relationship between petitioner and Aetna Plywood, no point is made that the Board erred in considering them to be,

34. Local 299, Sheet Metal Workers Union (S.M. Kisner), 131 NLRB (No. 147) (1961).
35. Local 505, Teamsters (Carolina Lumber Co.), 130 NLRB (No. 148) (1961).
36. See Douds v. Metro. Fed. of Architects, 75 F. Supp. 672 (1948).
37. Milwaukee Plywood Co. v. NLRB, 285 Fed. (2d) 325 (1960).

in effect, one employer. . . . The instant case is no different in legal contemplation from the conventional situation where a union sets up a picket line at the premises of an employer with whom it has a dispute. . . . We hold that the picket line activities of Local 200, in endeavoring to persuade its members employed by other employers were inextricably interwoven elements of the primary picket line itself, and were lawful under the Act.[38]

In another case [39] of a union seeking refuge under the ally doctrine the board ruled that the union had unlawully threatened Mr. Chimento, the sole owner of Advance Trucking Corporation, by stating that it would stop the firm's operations if it did not refrain from transporting products distributed by Fein Can Corporation, against whom the union was on strike. The union had argued that Advance was an ally of the Fein Corporation. The board struck down this argument when it said that the two employers were separately owned and controlled and that the services performed on a cost-plus basis by Advance for Fein were the same both before and after the strike began.

COMMON SITUS PICKETING. The issue involved in a General Electric Company case [40] was whether or not a picket patrol before a company gate used exclusively by employees of independent contractors was conduct proscribed by Section 8(b) (4)(A) of the act.

The company operated a plant outside of Louisville, Kentucky known as Appliance Park. Since 1954 the company had sought to confine the employees of independent contractors who worked on the premises of the park to using Gate 3-A and confining its use to them. The company's purpose was to insulate General Electric employees from the frequent labor disputes in which the contractors were involved. Gate 3-A was 550 feet away from the nearest entrance available for General Electric employees, suppliers, and deliverymen. On July 27, 1958, the union representing General Electric employees called a strike at the park, and picketing took place at all the gates including Gate 3-A. Because of the picketing, almost all the employees of the independent contractors refused to enter the company's premises. The company contended that picketing at Gate 3-A sought to enmesh the employees of neutral employers in the dispute between the union and the company and that by so doing the union violated the secondary-boycott provision of the act.

Mr. Justice Frankfurter delivered the opinion for the court. He stated:

38. For a case in which the ally doctrine was rejected, see NLRB v. Local 516 Plant Guard Workers, 42 LC 16,822 (1960).
39. Local 810, Teamsters (Advance Trucking Corp.), 131 NLRB (No. 10) (1961).
40. Local 761, Electrical, Radio, and Machine Workers Union v. NLRB, U.S. Sup. C., Docket No. 321, May 1961.

. . . Section 8(b)(4)(A) of the Act provides that it shall be an unfair labor practice for a labor organization to engage in, or to induce or encourage the employees of any employer to engage in, a strike or a concerted refusal in the course of their employment to use, manufacture, process, transport, or otherwise handle or work on any goods, articles, materials, or commodities or to perform any services, where an object thereof is: (A) forcing or requiring any employer or other person, to cease doing business with any other person. . . . This provision could not be literally construed; otherwise it would ban most strikes historically considered to be lawful, so-called primary activity. While 8(b)(4) does not expressly mention primary or secondary disputes, strikes or boycotts, that section often is referred to in the Act's legislated history as one of the Act's secondary boycott sections. The impact of the section was directed toward what is known as the secondary boycott whose sanctions bear, not upon the employer who alone is a party to the dispute, but upon some third party who has no concern in it. . . . But not all so-called secondary boycotts were outlawed. The section does not speak generally of secondary boycotts. It describes and condemns specific union conduct directed towards specific objectives: they must be induced to engage in a strike or concerted refusal; an object must be to force or require their employer or another person to cease doing business with a third person. . . . The impact of new situations made the Board conscious of the complexity of the problem by reason of the protean form in which it appeared. This became clear in the common situs cases—situations where two employers were performing separate tasks on common premises. . . . The Board concluded that when the situs of the primary employer was "ambulatory" there must be a balance between the union's right to picket and the interest of the secondary employer in being free from picketing. It set four standards for picketing in such situations which would be presumptive of valid primary activity: (1) that the picketing be limited to times when the situs of the dispute was located on the secondary premises, (2) That the primary employer be engaged in his normal business at the situs, (3) that the picketing take place reasonably close to the situs, and (4) that the picketing clearly disclose that the dispute was only with the primary employer. . . .[41]

In a case similar to the one now before us, the Court of Appeals for the Second Circuit sustained the Board in its application of Section 8(b)(4)(A) to a separate-gate situation. "There must be a separate gate, marked and set apart from other gates; the work done by the men who use the gate must be unrelated to the normal operations of the employer, and the work must be of a kind that would not, if done when the plant were engaged in its regular operations, necessitate curtailing those operations." United Steel Workers v. Labor Board (1961) 42 LC 16, 939. The foregoing course of reasoning would require that the judgment below sustaining the Board's order be affirmed but for one consideration, even though this consideration may turn out not to effect the result. The legal path by which the Board and the Court of Appeals reached their decisions did not take into account

41. These evidentiary tests were established in the Moore Dry Dock case, 92 NLRB 547 (1950).

that if Gate 3-A was in fact used by employees of independent contractors who performed conventional maintenance work necessary to the normal operations of General Electric, the use of the gate would have been a mingled one outside the bar of Section 8(b)(4)(A). . . . For determination of the questions thus raised, the case must be remanded by the Court of Appeals to the Board.

Reversed.

PICKETING BY AN INDIVIDUAL WORKER—UNION RESPONSIBILITY. An interesting development [42] occurred when a member of the United Mine Workers Union named Hover lost his job after the Edna Coal Company subcontracted work to an independent trucking company. Hover was particularly outspoken in his criticism of the events which led to his layoff, and when a union agent told Hover that he could "fight for his job," Hover made a picket sign and began picketing the mining operation, alleging that the independent trucking company was unfair to organized labor. Mine workers honored the picket line; when the union agent was asked if the picket line should be honored, the agent told members that they should "let their conscience be their guide." The company filed a complaint with the board charging the union with inducing or encouraging primary employees to stop work. The board dismissed the complaint on the ground that the union did not induce or encourage a work stoppage. It held that the union did not cause the picketing and had no legal duty to stop its members from honoring the picket line, since Hover's purpose in picketing was to gain reinstatement.

INDUCEMENT OF SINGLE EMPLOYEE OF SECONDARY EMPLOYER. The primary purpose of the 1959 amendments to Section 8(b)(4) was to close certain so-called loopholes in the section which had become apparent during the course of litigation between the board and the courts. By changing "employees" to "any individual" and omitting the word "concerted" the revision of this section closed one loophole. The inducement of a single secondary employee now falls within the ban of the section. In the Perfection Mattress and Spring Company case [43] the board held that despite the fact that peaceful picketing conducted at the premises of neutral employers was for the purpose of informing the public of a primary dispute and was not intended to bring about any work stoppage among the neutral employees, it nevertheless was unlawful. Here the board ruled that the object of the picketing was to force the neutral employer to cease doing business with the primary employer, and that it had the proscribed effect of inducing and encouraging an individual employee to refuse to work.

42. District 15, U.M.W. (Edna Coal Co.), 132 NLRB (No. 42) (1961).
43. NLRB v. United Wholesale and Warehouse Employees Union, 129 NLRB (No. 125) (1960).

Hot-Cargo Agreements

Section 8(e) is new and makes it unlawful for a labor union and an employer to enter into a hot-cargo agreement under which the employer agrees that he will not ask his employees to work on goods or products originating from an employer engaged in a dispute with another union.

One of the provisos to Section 8(e) allows unions engaged in the construction and garment industries to enter into modified types of hot-cargo agreements under certain conditions without violating the law. For example, a construction union may make an agreement with an employer requiring him to refuse to have any work done at a job site by a nonunion contractor. Garment unions are permitted to enter into agreements which exclude the farming out of work to nonunion contractors. It should be noted, however, that these unions have not been immunized completely from the prohibition of secondary-boycott pressures.

Cases and Rulings

The board has had an opportunity in two cases [44] to indicate the kinds of agreements that are prohibited by the terms of Section 8(e) and the kinds of agreements that might be permissible under it. These cases involved demands by locals in Miami and San Francisco affiliated with the Amalgamated Lithographers Union for the inclusion of certain clauses in their new contracts. In its decisions, the board indicated that it intended to look behind the bare language of the clauses that were allegedly permissible under Section 8(e) to determine their true purpose. When the clause—no matter how artfully drafted—is nothing more than a roundabout way of compelling an employer not to handle struck or nonunion work, the board will find a violation of Section 8(e). On the other hand, the board will not find a violation if the clause simply spells out the board's ally doctrine by indicating that employees are not to be required to handle farmed-out struck work unless the contracting employer has customarily performed such work for the struck employer.

A hot-cargo agreement was the issue in another case [45] in which Gallagher, an employer, was engaged in the trucking business and per-

44. Amalgamated Lithographers of America, (the Employing Lithographers), 130 NLRB (No. 102) (1961); Amalgamated Lithographers of America (Miami Post), 130 NLRB (No. 107) (1961).
45. Local 107, Teamsters, (E. A. Gallagher and Sons), 131 NLRB (No. 117) (1961).

formed both over-the-road and local trucking functions. About 40 per cent of the employer's business was hauling steel. The majority of the steel hauling was performed by as many as forty independent owner-operators who picked up the steel at the mill in and on trucks and delivered it directly to the consignee. They were paid on the ton-mileage basis and were in no way connected with the employer other than as independent contractors. The independent owner-operators were generally not union members. However, the local drivers employed by Gallagher were union members. The union sought to eliminate the nonunion competition by demanding that Gallagher agree in a collective-bargaining agreement not to deal with the independent owner-operators. The employer refused to accept the union's proposal. The union then called a strike to compel the inclusion in the contract of clauses requiring that truck deliveries be made only by union members and that preference in hiring or leasing be given to employers having a union contract. The employer filed an 8(e) complaint with the board. The board sustained the complaint, stating that the proposals made by the local union were unlawful by virtue of the NLRB hot-cargo provisions, and that when the union sought to force a cessation of business between the struck employer and the independent owner-drivers, it violated the secondary-boycott provisions of the act as well.

Recognition and Organizational Picketing [46]

Another important amendment to the Taft-Hartley Act is Section 8(b)(7), which deals with recognition and organizational picketing. Recognition picketing is generally defined as picketing an employer's establishment to force the employer to recognize and bargain with the union. Organizational picketing is directed at employees and seeks to persuade them to join the union. Prior to the 1959 Landrum-Griffin Act federal statutes were silent on these forms of picketing. Both types of picketing came under severe criticism from the McClellan Committee. One of the most common complaints raised against them was their alleged interference with the individual right of a worker to join or not to join a union. It had been stated that this right was consistently violated when a picketed employer, in order to be relieved of damaging economic pressure exerted against him by a union, forced the workers to join the union. Other abuses occurred when "paper" local unions, with no members, used recognition or organizational picketing as a means of extorting money from the harassed employer.

Section 8(b)(7) has made it illegal in three situations for a labor union to picket or threaten to picket any employer with the object of

46. See Allen H. Duffy, Picketing By An Uncertified Union: The New Section 8(b) (7), 69 *Yale L.J.* 1393 (1960).

requiring him to recognize or bargain with a union or force employees to accept the union as their bargaining representative.

The first situation that makes such picketing unlawful and a new unfair labor practice is that in which the employer has lawfully recognized another union or in which a current labor contract between the employer and another union exists.

Second, a union may not picket if a National Labor Relations Board election has been held during the preceding twelve months.

The third situation is when no union is currently recognized and no election has been held within the preceding twelve months. Some major interpretative problems of Section 8(b)(7) are presented by subparagraph (C), which provides that recognition or organizational picketing may be lawfully conducted for a "reasonable period," not to exceed 30 days, after which such picketing becomes illegal unless a representation petition has been filed with the board. If the picketing continues beyond the 30 days without a representation petition having been filed, the picketing constitutes an unfair labor practice, and the board, on a complaint filed with it by the employer, is required to seek an injunction to enjoin the picketing. This is the sole remedy allowed an employer under the new section. Labor unions have criticized the 30-day limitation on this type of picketing, claiming that the period is too short a one in which to organize large numbers of employees.

It should be noted that the new restrictions on recognition and organizational picketing are not applicable when a union has been certified as the bargaining representative by the board. Another very important exemption to the 30-day picketing rule has resulted from a proviso in Section 8(b)(7)(C), which allows picketing "for the purpose of truthfully advising the public" that the employer does not employ members or have a contract with a labor union, unless an effect of such picketing is to cause employees to refuse to make pickups or deliveries or perform services. The consumer publicity proviso is discussed later in this chapter. Another proviso of Section 10(1) prohibits the board from seeking injunctive relief in a Section 8(b)(7) case whenever a meritorious charge has been filed alleging that the employer has dominated or interfered with a labor organization in violation of Section 8(a)(2) of the act.

Cases and Rulings

The Stork Club case [47] was one of the early decisions handed down by the board interpreting Section 8(b)(7). In this case the union con-

47. Local 89, Hotel and Restaurant Employees Union, 130 NLRB (No. 67) (1961).

ceded that one of the objects of the picketing from January 1957 to January 1960 was recognition. For approximately two months after the Landrum-Griffin Act became effective on November 13, 1959, the union picketed for recognition without filing a representation petition with the board. This was a violation of Section 8(b)(7)(C). The union contended that after January 15, 1960, the picketing became informational. The board ruled, however, that informational picketing is not a protected activity under the new law if it has the effect of inducing individuals employed by any other person not to pick up or deliver goods. The evidence adduced at the hearing showed that during a one-week period four drivers on five different occasions refused to deliver bottle goods to the Stork Club because of the picket line. Since the picket line encouraged and induced secondary workers not to deal with the primary employer, the Stork Club, the activity of the union was proscribed under Section 8(b)(7)(C) and constituted an unfair labor practice within the meaning of Section 2, (6) and (7) of the act.

In another case [48] a union was enjoined from picketing an employer on the ground that the picketing sought recognition as well as to disseminate information. The federal appellate court remanded the injunction for modification and held that the injunction should have reached only the illegal activity, namely, the recognition objectives.

In the Calumet Contractors Association case [49] the United States Court of Appeals, 7th Circuit, affirmed a district court order granting the NLRB temporary injunctive relief when the union was charged with having violated Section 8(b)(7)(C). In this case the association was made up of building contractors that did not have contracts with the hod carriers union. The union picketed a construction site, and the picket sign claimed that the masonry subcontractor on the job was not performing his work with qualified craftsmen or paying prevailing wages. The union distributed handbills advising the public that the union was not intending to induce employees of any employer to engage in a refusal to work and also stated that there was no intent on its part to seek recognition. The union contended, therefore, that the object of the picketing was not to seek recognition, but to show the public that the prevailing scale of wages and conditions were not being met. The district court concluded that there was reasonable cause to believe that the union had violated Section 8(b)(7)(C), although the evidence did not clearly establish such a violation. The appellate court said: "It is sufficient to sustain the District Court's findings and conclusion if there be any evidence which together with all the reasonable inferences that might be drawn therefrom supports a conclusion that

48. NLRB v. Local 89, Hotel and Restaurant Employees Union, 280 Fed. (2d) 760 (1960).
49. NLRB v. Hod Carriers Union, 277 Fed. (2d) 688 (1960).

there is a reasonable cause to believe that a violation had occurred." [50]

In Charlton Press [51] a union contended that it represented a majority of the employees in the unit in which recognition was being sought and that an election was unnecessary to establish the union's representative status because this could be ascertained by counting the employees who had refused to cross the picket line. The union believed that Congress did not intend Section 8(b)(7)(C) to be applicable in such circumstances. The district court, however, stated that "while the main thrust of this new amendment to the Act was to prevent recognition picketing by a union representing a minority of employees, or none at all, 8(b)(7)(C) simply sets up a procedure where by the factual qualifications of a union to act as the representative of a group of employees is to be determined by the NLRB at an early stage. The burden of going through the proceeding falls upon those who are in fact right as well as those who in fact are wrong."

In the Saturn case [52] the issue involved the reasonable period of time within which an election petition must be filed. Here the recognition picketing had been in progress for a number of months when Section (b)(7) went into effect on November 13, 1959. The charge under this section was filed with the board on November 23, 1959, and a petition for injunctive relief alleging that the picketing had continued for more than a reasonable period of time without the filing of an election petition was filed with the district court on December 2, 1959. The district court concluded that while "no act or conduct on the part of the respondent occurring prior to November 15, 1959 can be held or deemed to be an unfair labor practice such conduct could be considered for other purposes." The court found reasonable cause to believe that the picketing after November 13, 1959, had been conducted for more than a reasonable time prior to the filing of the petition for injunctive relief without the filing of an election petition.

In Sapulpa [53] a district court in Oklahoma found reasonable cause to believe that recognition picketing had been conducted for more than 15 days, an unreasonable period of time without the filing of a petition for a board election. In the Q.T. Shoe case,[54] a New Jersey district court found reasonable cause to believe that "ten days of violations, coercion, and intimidation in organizational picketing before filing of a petition for an election served to shorten the period for which the union may

50. Certiorari denied by the U.S. Sup. Ct., 364 U.S. 863 (1960).

51. Greene v. Int'l Typographical Union (Charlton Press Inc.), 182 F. Supp. 788 (1960).

52. 45 LRRM 2363, (1959).

53. Elliot v. Sapulpa Typographical Union (Sapulpa Daily Herald), 45 LRRM 2400 (1959).

54. Cuneo v. United Shoe Workers (Q.T. Shoe Mfg. Co.) 181 F. Supp. 324 (1960).

reasonably be allowed to picket before seeking the impartial intervention of the Board."

In an administrative decision [55] the General Counsel of the board refused to issue a complaint against the union charging it with an 8(b)(7) violation. The union had engaged in picketing and had failed to file an election petition within a reasonable time. Picketing had started when bargaining negotiations had broken down and the evidence showed that there had been a long history of bargaining between the union and the employer.

In the Woodward Motors case,[56] the union attempted to organize the Woodward employees. In January 1961 the board election was held and resulted in a rejection of the union. About two weeks after the election, the union placed signs at the entrances of the Woodward place of business advising the public that the employees were not protected by a labor union contract. Some of the union representatives spoke with persons about to enter the Woodward premises and some of these persons refused to enter the Woodward establishment. The union contended that it was picketing for informational purposes. The court disagreed and held that the union had violated Section 8(b)(7) of the act and issued an injunction restraining the picketing.

Consumer Picketing and Publicity

One of the most complex provisions of the amendments to the Taft-Hartley Act is found in the second general proviso of Section 8(b)(4), which states that nothing in this section "shall be construed to prohibit publicity, other than picketing," for the purpose of advising the public that a product produced by an employer with whom the union has a dispute is being distributed by another employer. This proviso also states that it does not apply if the publicity has "an effect of inducing any individual" to refuse to deliver goods at the establishment of the employer engaged in the distribution. Although the Taft-Hartley Act was silent on consumer boycotts, one case decided under that law had held consumer picketing unlawful when it was directed at the employees of the distributor.[57] It would appear that peaceful picketing directed only at customers and unaccompanied by other approaches to the retail establishment or its employees constitutes a lawful activity under the amended law. A request to customers conveyed by a picket sign to refrain from purchasing a particular product does not appear to

55. Case SR—1098, January 5, 1961.
56. NLRB v. Local 182, Teamsters, (1961) U.S. Dist. Ct., Northern Dist. N.Y., Civil No. 8481.
57. NLRB v. Dallas General Drivers, 264 Fed. (2d) 642 (1959).

violate the new law. Congress has permitted this new publicity device
to labor unions so that they may seek to protect their members and
unionized employers against competition originating in "sweat-shops"
and other places of employment where wages or working conditions are
considered substandard.

Cases and Rulings

APPEAL TO CUSTOMERS OF NEUTRAL EMPLOYERS—THE BLACK-
LIST—FREE SPEECH. A district court, in California,[58] held that a union
involved in a strike against a primary employer who operated a television
station engaged in an unlawful secondary boycott by (1) threatening
sponsors of the station with publication of their refusal to stop patronizing the struck station, (2) requesting members of other unions to stop
using the sponsors' products, and (3) sending letters to advertising
agencies and sponsors threatening them with "long-lasting resentment"
if they continued to advertise with the struck station. A temporary
injunction was issued pending final determination by the NLRB. This
same court ruled that the distribution of leaflets informing customers
of neutral retailers selling products of neutral sponsors advertising on
a struck TV station that the station was unfair and that the sponsors
were still advertising on the station was an unlawful consumer boycott
under the act. The appeal, said the court, was a tertiary boycott, since
it was directed not at the customers of the primary employer, but at
the customers of retailers handling the products of secondary employers.
The leaflets were not privileged either by "free-speech" guarantees or
by the provision in the act allowing publicity for the purpose of truthfully advising the public that the products produced by a primary employer were distributed by another employer.

An interesting development occurred in a case [59] involving ambulatory
picketing, which is carried on by a roving patrol of union members who
follow in separate cars the trucks of the struck employer; when the
trucks stop to make a pickup or delivery, the ambulatory pickets station
themselves in front of the customers' premises, with signs informing the
public that a dispute exists between the union and the owner of the
trucks. The right to engage in this type of picketing is frowned on by
the board and the courts because of its effect on secondary persons, and
it is allowed only under certain conditions. Picketing of the primary
employer at the place of business of the secondary employer will be
permitted when the primary employer has no permanent place of busi-

58. NLRB v. American Federation of Television and Radio Artists, 191 F. Supp.
676 (1961).
59. NLRB v. Local 868, Teamsters, 179 F. Supp. 921 (1960). The decision might
have been different if the 1959 act had applied.

ness at which a union can adequately publicize its labor dispute.[60] In this case a union struck in October 1959 for recognition as the bargaining representative of the employees of Metallurgical Processing Corporation. This company was in the service business and part of the service provided its customers was the pickup and delivery of parts which were treated at its plant. On October 29 and October 30 three employees of the company were followed by union representatives in separate cars as each employee made his pickups and deliveries. The union placed a single picket at the establishments of several of the company's customers who carried a sign reading that the union was on strike against the Metallurgical Corporation. The picket did not patrol more than twenty minutes at any of the customer's establishments.

The question presented was the applicability of the secondary-boycott provision contained in Section 8(b)(4), (A) and (B), of the act. The board petitioned for an injunction charging that the union sought to induce secondary employers and employees to withhold their services. The union contended that its picketing was purely informational. The district court, denying injunctive relief, said:

. . . Ambulatory picketing per se is not prohibited by the Act. . . . The essence of the problem here is whether the kind of picketing and related conduct employed in this case was in furtherance of a lawful or unlawful objective. If the objective was lawful, any adverse effect upon the secondary employers must necessarily be viewed as incidental to the lawful exercise of a statutory right. . . . The court finds that there was no effort here to induce or encourage a strike or a concerted refusal on the part of the secondary employees to cease working upon the primary employer's goods. The real purpose of the picketing was to advertise the dispute between the primary employer and the Union among the drivers of the station wagons. . . .

In Spar Builders [61] a union that had a dispute with one of the subcontractors picketed a housing development on both weekdays and weekends. The picketing took place in front of a model home but near a road utilized by employees of neutral employers working at the housing development. The court found that the picketing, insofar as it appealed to employees, constituted a violation of subparagraphs both (i) and (ii) of Section 8(b)(4), but refused to find that the publicity addressed to customers on weekends violated subparagraph (ii), and permitted the union to continue its picketing on weekends to reach potential homebuyers.[62]

60. For leading cases dealing with ambulatory picketing, see Moore Dry Dock Co., 92 NLRB 547 (1950); Washington Coca-Cola Bottling Works v. NLRB, 220 Fed. (2d) 380 (1955); Int'l Rice Milling Co. v. NLRB, 341 U.S. 665 (1951).
61. McLeod v. Local 1929 (Spar Builders), 183 F. Supp. 494 (1960).
62. Subsequently a trial examiner of the board found that the weekend picketing violated subparagraph (ii). See the board's decision to the same effect in Perfection Mattress and Spring Co., 129 NLRB (No. 125) (1960).

In an administrative decision [63] of the General Counsel, it was ruled that a union had lawfully distributed handbills at the customers' entrance of two retail stores urging the public not to buy products of a company with which the union had a labor dispute. The company had charged that the union had engaged in conduct proscribed by Section 8(b)(4)(ii)(B) of the act. There was no evidence that the union's activity interfered with store deliveries or caused any work stoppage by the store's personnel. The General Counsel concluded from the evidence that the activity of the union was protected under the act's publicity proviso since it did not induce a secondary work stoppage.

In another administrative decision [64] of the board, the General Counsel was asked to rule in a case in which a union had distributed leaflets at entrances of an employer's retail store stating that another employer's products were manufactured by nonunion labor and urging customers not to purchase them. Again the General Counsel concluded that the activity in question fell within the purview of the publicity proviso in Section 8(b)(4) of the act and constituted lawful activity since the distribution of the leaflets did not cause any stoppage of deliveries or refusal by employees of the retailer to handle the products involved.

In the Stan-Jay case [65] the board rejected the argument that in order to invalidate informational picketing it must be established not only that employees of a secondary employer refused to cross the picket line but also that this was the intended effect of such picketing. The board concluded that it was sufficient if this was the actual effect of the picketing.

Some of the most important decisions involving Section 8(b)(7)(C) were made in February 1961. The Stork Club case, already discussed, was one of the decisions in which informational and recognition picketing were considered. In the Crown Cafeteria case [66] the board decided that the informational-picket proviso applies only when publicity is the sole purpose of picketing. In this particular case the board felt that the picketing was not for the sole purpose of truthfully advising the public that the employer involved did not employ union members or have a union contract, and that it also had the object of recognition.

In another 8(b)(7)(C) case,[67] the board ruled that a union not cur-

---

63. Case 1299, May 16, 1961.
64. Case SR—1204, April 4, 1961.
65. Local 239, Teamsters (Stan-Jay Auto Parts), 127 NLRB 958 (1960). The U.S. Court of Appeals for the 2nd Circuit enforced the board's order in Stan-Jay in all respects, 289 Fed. (2d) 41 (1961).
66. 130 NLRB 68 (1961).
67. Blinne Construction Company, 130 NLRB 69 (1961); similar rulings were made in Local Joint Board, Hotel and Restaurant Workers and Peter Irwin, 130 NLRB 68 (1961); Local 705, Teamsters (Cartage and Terminal Management Corp.), 130 NLRB 70 (1961).

rently certified as the bargaining representative violated this section even though it was picketing to protest the employer's unfair labor practices. The picketing in this case had continued for more than 30 days without any representation petition being filed. The board was of the opinion that the union was actually engaged in recognition picketing.

In the Fowler case [68] a federal district court in Indiana denied the board's petition for injunctive relief when the board had based its petition on a charge that the picketing conducted by the union was illegal. The union contended that its picketing was purely for informational purposes. Since there were no stoppages of services or deliveries to the picketed employer, the court ruled for the union and supported its contention that it sought only to inform the public that the employer did not have a contract with the union.

Summary of Title VII: Boycotts; Picketing

There is no question that the new amendments to Section 8(b)(4) were enacted to make unlawful all economic pressures exerted by unions against secondary employers and secondary workers. Congress has, in effect, given these secondary persons the status of neutrals, deserving protection against a labor union which in the course of industrial warfare seeks to treat them as combatants. The term "secondary boycott" has considerable emotional appeal, and because of it, many persons have been inclined to sympathize and to support neutral employers who, against their wishes and interests, may become enmeshed in an economic war. Under the hot-cargo ban, an employer may no longer agree with a union to stop dealing with a neutral employer with whom the union has a dispute.[69]

When is a secondary employer a neutral and when is he a combatant? This is frequently a difficult question to answer, yet its answer should provide a more rational approach to the propriety or impropriety of the secondary boycott. Labor unions have consistently held that a secondary employer loses his neutrality when he does business with another employer with whom the union has a dispute. They reason that a secondary employer who sells a commodity or renders a service to a struck employer is actually helping the primary employer to bring about the

68. Getreu v. Hotel and Restaurant Employees Union (Fowler Hotel Inc.), 187 F. Supp. 738 (1960). For other cases dealing with informational picketing, see Meat Cutters, Local 391, 131 NLRB (No. 57) (1961); Brown v. Television and Radio Artists, 42 LC 16, 849 (1961); Green v. Typographical Union Local 285, 40 LC 66,782 (1960); Graham v. Retail Clerks, Local 57, 41 LC 16,678 (1960); Kennedy v. Retail Clerks, Local 324, 42 LC 16,964 (1961).
69. See D. Meyer, Ally or Neutral—The Secondary Boycott Dilemma, 34 *Tul. L. Rev.* 343 (1960).

defeat of the union's objectives. They claim, therefore, that the secondary employer ought to be a legitimate target for economic pressure. If the unions' argument is sound, and many believe it to be, the complete ban on all secondary boycotts is unfair and unjust because it denies the union the right to defend itself against an adversary. It is true that powerful unions in the past have at times used the secondary boycott indiscriminately and have damaged innocent business establishments. Laws are frequently directed to the elimination of abuses stemming from activities which are intrinsically good, and in order to reach the few abuses, all the activities must be sacrificed.

The statute provides that unless the ally doctrine is applicable in a given situation, all secondary employers and secondary employees have been immunized from labor union pressure. Labor leaders fear that the new secondary-boycott provisions will tend to reduce the effectiveness of all labor unions in the economic arena. All unions, with the exception of garment and construction unions, which have been given a partial statutory exemption from the ban on secondary boycotts, will have difficulty in protecting their high wages and good working conditions against the substandard conditions existing in many nonunion establishments.

The permissive feature in Section 8(b)(7) allowing consumer or informational publicity under specific conditions has doubtful value to labor unions. Unless picketing results in some degree of economic damage to the establishment being picketed, it seems that the pickets are wasting their time. Under the statute, the publicity is permissible provided no employee withholds his labor. It is extremely difficult to establish a picket patrol that encourages primary and secondary employees to continue their normal operations. Assuming that these employees could be persuaded to continue their normal working activities, will the publicity directed exclusively to prospective customers bring about the desired effect, i.e., a withholding of customer patronage? Here again great doubt exists. One thing is certain, however. If consumer publicity becomes ineffective, labor unions will inevitably demand remedial legislation.

The new restrictions placed on recognition and organizational picketing are certain to be challenged by labor unions on constitutional grounds. The 1940 Thornhill decision [70] made by the Supreme Court hailed picketing as the workingman's means of communication. Since picketing was a form of speech, its exercise by workers was believed to be unassailable by the courts. Following this historic decision, the Supreme Court, in a series of cases, narrowed the right of workers to picket, and the states were permitted to interfere with picketing. Under certain conditions, the states were permitted to ban picketing com-

70. Thornhill v. Alabama, 310 U.S. 88 (1940).

pletely.[71] Later, the court adopted an "objectives" test [72] which further curbed the right of workers to picket. It will be interesting to see what attitude the court will assume when the unions test the constitutionality of that part of Section 8(b)(7) relating to picketing. The radical changes during the last twenty years in the Supreme Court's attitude on picketing could reasonably lead us to predict that the court will uphold the new restrictions on picketing.[73] We know that testimony before the McClellan Committee, relating to blackmail and coercive picketing carried on by some labor unions, led to the enactment of the provisos. Forcing employers to recognize unions and forcing workers to join unions have been made unlawful, if the expressed Congressional intent is to be effective.

Another amendment to the Taft-Hartley Law is found in Section 302(b)(2) which provides that it is unlawful for any labor organization or for any person acting on behalf of such organization to demand or accept from the operator of an interstate motor carrier any money or other thing of value as a fee or charge for the unloading of the cargo carried by the vehicle. This section is a derivative from the Hobbs Act,[74] frequently called the Anti-Racketeering Act. The Hobbs Act makes it a federal crime to obstruct or delay the movement of any article of commerce by robbery or extortion. The criminal penalties imposed by this law are imprisonment for up to twenty years, a fine of $10,000, or both.[75]

71. Milk Wagon Drivers' Union v. Meadowmoor Dairies, 312 U.S. 287 (1941).
72. See Giboney v. Empire Storage and Ice Co., 336 U.S. 490 (1948).
73. See G. Farmer and C. Williamson, Picketing and the Injunctive Power of State Courts—From Thornhill to Vogt, 35 *U. Det. L.J.* 431 (1958), concerning the changing attitude of the Supreme Court on picketing by workers as free speech.
74. Title 18, U.S. Code, Act of July 3, 1946, c. 537, 79th Congress, 60 Stat. 420, amending Act of July 18, 1934.
75. For leading cases under the Hobbs Act, see U.S. v. Green, 350 U.S. 415 (1957); U.S. v. Stirone, 361 U.S. 312 (1960); Bianchi v. U.S., 219 Fed. (2d) 182 (1955); U.S. v. Sweeney, 262 Fed. (2d) 272 (1959).

CHAPTER TWELVE

Conciliation, Mediation, and Arbitration

CONCILIATION is an attempt by a third party to bring about an amicable solution of the differences involved between two parties, but without power to settle them. Mediation is just another term for conciliation. The mediator or conciliator, usually in the employ of a federal or state agency, acts as a peacemaker whose primary function is to keep the disputants together for the purpose of "talking out" their differences and ultimately arriving at an agreement.

Arbitration is a process in which parties voluntarily submit all matters in dispute to the judgment of a neutral person, known as an arbitrator, who decides the controversy. The decision is called the award. The question is as conclusively determined as it would have been by a court of justice.

At common law courts frowned upon the arbitration process and refused to compel parties to adhere to their agreement to arbitrate. Once an award was made, however, courts would enforce it. Courts felt that only judges trained in the law were sufficiently qualified to deal with the intricacies of disputes. Another reason for this narrow judicial attitude was the traditional position that every person had a right to a day in court. It is obvious that courts desired to keep all the business they could get. Today, arbitration has been accepted as a peaceful method of settling disputes and is widely promoted by the legal profession as a whole.

One of the earliest arbitration statutes [1] was enacted by the English Parliament. It provided:

. . . that all merchants and others, who desire to end any controversy, suit or quarrel (for which there is no other remedy but by personal action

1. 9 & 10 Wm. 3, c. 15 (1703).

or suit in equity) may agree that their submission of the suit to arbitration or umpirage shall be made a rule of any of the king's courts of record, and may insert such agreement in their submission, or promise, on condition of the arbitration bond; which agreement being proved upon oath by one of the witnesses thereto, the court shall make a rule that such submission and award shall be conclusive; and, after such rule is made, the parties disobeying the award shall be liable to be punished, as for a contempt of court; unless such award shall be set aside for corruption, or other misbehavior in the arbitrators or umpire, proved on oath to the court, within one term after the award is made.[2]

Although most states have enacted arbitration statutes allowing for the submission of labor disputes to this form of adjudication, the federal government has not followed suit. The United States Arbitration Act of 1925 specifically exempts labor controversies. The federal laws that deal with labor arbitration are the 1934 amendment to the Railway Labor Act, under which the National Railroad Adjustment Board has been given jurisdiction to make judicially enforcible awards, and Section 301 of the Labor Management Relations Act (The Taft-Hartley Act) of 1947.

Since the end of World War II arbitration of labor disputes has become an important part of our industrial life. Over 90 per cent of the more than 150,000 collective-bargaining contracts now in existence in the United States provide for arbitration as the terminal step in grievance procedure. Although voluntarily entered into, these contracts call for compulsory arbitration. In the absence of any contractual obligation, submission of disputes to arbitration can be effected by the consent of the parties. With some exceptions, the arbitration of labor disputes is limited to those disputes concerning the interpretation and application of existing contracts. On infrequent occasions, when the employer and the union have reached an impasse and are seeking to avoid a strike, an arbitrator has been allowed to settle an "interest" controversy, such as one over wage rates or other important conditions to be incorporated in a new labor agreement. For most purposes, we may agree that arbitration is a tool or device used to resolve labor disputes arising during the term of an existing labor contract.

There are many reasons why arbitration has become an acceptable and popular method for the settling of labor disputes. Its greatest advantage rests in the desire on the part of employer and union alike to maintain an uninterrupted continuity of production. The arbitration clause in a bargaining agreement suspends for the entire term of the contract all strikes and lock-outs, the most potent weapons of industrial warfare. Obviously, the elimination of conflict encourages a more peace-

2. English arbitration statutes were amended and consolidated in 1889, 52 & 53 Vict., c. 49.

ful employer-union relationship. Another advantage inherent in the process of arbitration is the low financial cost of the proceeding. In arbitration, cases are presented with less need for lawyers and this results in substantial savings to small unions and business firms. The principal, and usually only, expense incurred in the arbitration of a labor dispute is the fee paid to the arbitrator, and this is generally shared equally by the parties. When the issues are complex, the services of competent attorneys may be necessary and desirable. Many labor arbitrators are not lawyers and therefore do not adhere to rigid rules of evidence, thus avoiding excessive legalism.

Since most states have enacted arbitration statutes, they have established agencies that provide lists of arbitrators from which the selection is made and cases are heard in free offices provided by the agencies. The Federal Mediation and Conciliation Service will, on request, provide the necessary machinery for the arbitration of labor disputes. Finally, private associations like the American Arbitration Association furnish competent personnel and excellent physical facilities for the arbitration of disputes. Frequently there are fewer legal problems than social and economic ones to be solved in labor disputes, and it may be more desirable to employ the arbitration process than judicial acumen.

One basic feature of arbitration is that awards, in most cases, are not reviewable by the courts, nor are the facts found by the arbitrator, his interpretation and application of the terms and conditions of the contracts, and finally any law he may apply in the case. This principle was well defined in a leading New York decision [3] in which several brewing companies sought to confirm the award of the arbitrator and the union cross-moved to set aside the award.

Justice Desmond, speaking for the court of appeals, which affirmed the judgment for the companies, said:

The principal law points argued by appellants dispute the authority of the arbitrator to order an injunction against appellants.

Arbitration and adjustment procedures are prescribed by Part V and Part VI of the general collective bargaining agreement between the breweries and the unions and the collective bargaining agreement, among other things, forbids any "slowdown" (or any lockout or strike). On March 1, 1956, the brewery companies, alleging that the unions and the workers were engaging in a slowdown, demanded of the American Arbitration Association that the association proceed immediately with the appointment of an arbitrator and with the scheduling of a hearing to be held within 24 hours. This was a resort to the so-called "speedy arbitration" procedure which is described in the collective bargaining agreement in section 1(b) of Part VI. Earlier parts of this agreement, being Part V and section 1 of Part VI, describe possible proceedings before an adjustment committee and

3. Ruppert v. Teamsters, 3 N.Y. (2d) 576 (1956).

before a board of arbitration. However, Part VI, in sections 1(b) and 2, makes it clear that whenever a violation of the prohibition against strikes, slowdowns, etc., is alleged, either party may waive the adjustment and arbitration provisions referred to in earlier parts of the agreement and thereupon the dispute shall be submitted to arbitration within 24 hours after receipt of notice by the American Arbitration Association, and the award in such cases shall be issued not later than 48 hours after the conclusion of the hearing. Those speedy procedures were carried out in this instance with the result that on March 2, 1956, the next day after the companies invoked the speedy procedure, hearings were held before the arbitrator. On March 4, 1956, the arbitrator handed up his opinion and award in which he found that there were slowdowns at the breweries in violation of the agreement. He therefore enjoined the local unions from continuing the slowdowns and directed the local unions to make necessary steps to stop the slowdowns.

Besides questioning the power of the arbitrator to issue an injunction, the unions, appellants, make two other points: first, that there was failure to comply with a condition precedent to arbitration; and, second, that there was no sufficient proof before the arbitrator that the unions had ordered and conducted a slowdown.

The first and most important question is as to whether the arbitrator exceeded his powers in including an injunction in his award. The collective bargaining agreement does not directly affirm or deny such a power but in general terms authorizes arbitration and says that the arbitrators' decision "shall be final and binding upon all parties to the given dispute." However, it is apparent that nothing short of an injunction would have accomplished the evident intent of these parties that there be speedy and immediately effective relief against strikes, lockouts and slowdowns. True, we find no decision in this Court confirming an arbitration award containing an injunction but we have upheld awards which commanded employers to rehire or retain employees—that is, mandatory injunctions (Matter of Devery Daniels & Kennedy, Inc., 292 N.Y. 596; Matter of United Culinary Bar and Grill Employees Schiffman, 299 N.Y. 577). The whole question is as to the intent of the parties (see Dodds v. Hakes, 114 N.Y. 260). Traditionally, arbitrators have been licensed to direct such conduct of the parties as is necessary to the settlement of the matters in dispute (see 6 Williston on Contracts rev. ed., p. 5392 et seq.; see authorities cited in 5 C.J., Arbitration and Award, p. 131, n. 34, and in 6 C.J.S., Arbitration and Award, p. 225).

On this injunction question, appellants say further that, even if injunctions are not necessarily and always unlawful in arbitration awards, this particular injunction was forbidden by section 876-a of the Civil Practice Act. That well-known statute forbids the issuance of an injunction by a court or judge in a labor dispute except after the making of findings not made here. This award was confirmed by Special Term (and affirmed by the Appellate Division) and so in the broadest sense, although not in the sense of the statute, the courts have ordered this particular injunction. But, once we have held that this particular employer-union agreement not only did not forbid but contemplated the inclusion of an injunction in such an award, no ground remains for invalidating this injunction. Section 876-a, like its prototype the Federal Norris-LaGuardia Act, was the result of union resentment against the issuance of injunctions in labor strifes. But arbitration is voluntary and there is no reason why unions and employers should deny such powers to the special tribunals they themselves create. Section 876-a and article 84 (Arbitration) are both in our Civil Practice Act. Each represents a separate public policy and by affirming here we harmonize those two policies.

The last position taken by appellants is that there was no proof of a slowdown and no proof that if there was a slowdown it was caused by the unions. However, the transcript in this record of the proceedings before this arbitrator, while containing no common-law proof that there had been a slowdown, does show what amounts to testimony by representatives of all the brewing companies that there had been a slowdown with no denial by the unions. A reading of the transcript shows that this fact was not really in dispute at all and the present contention of appellants that there was no sufficient proof of a slowdown seems to be an afterthought.

The judgment appealed from should be affirmed with costs.

Legal issues do sometimes flow from arbitration, but they deal largely with procedural objections rather than substantive law. These legal issues will be given consideration now.

Judicial Review of Arbitration

Action to Compel Arbitration

At common law agreements to arbitrate were not enforcible in suits seeking to compel arbitration. This rule was uniformly followed prior to the enactment of state laws authorizing arbitration.

An action to compel an employer to arbitrate will not be entertained if the union failed to adhere to the grievance procedures in the labor contract.[4] The grievance machinery in the labor agreement must be exhausted before the right to arbitration may be enforced.

Individual employees, although beneficiaries under a collective bargaining contract, may not demand arbitration. When a discharged employee attempted to invoke the arbitration clause in an agreement, the court rejected the employee's application for enforcement of the clause on the ground that there was no clear evidence showing bad faith on the part of the union in its belief that the discharge was justified.[5] In a similar New York case, the court suggested that if the union

4. Cotter v. Ansco, 118 N.Y.S. (2d) 500 (1952).
5. *Matter of* Wright and Ruppert, 182 N.Y.S. (2d) 102 (1953).

had inadequately or unfairly represented the employee, he might sue the union for damages sustained.[6] An attempt by an employee to force the union and the employer to arbitrate his grievance was rejected since "the proper exercise of discretion over grievances and the interpretation of the collective bargaining agreement in the interest of all its members is vested in the authorized representatives of the union." [7]

FEDERAL COURT POWER TO COMPEL ARBITRATION. Section 301(a) of the Taft-Hartley Law of 1947 provides that employers and unions may institute an action in the federal district courts for any violation of a collective-bargaining agreement. It was not clear whether an action to compel arbitration was feasible under this section until 1956, when the U.S. Supreme Court answered the question affirmatively in the Lincoln Mills case.[8] In this litigation, the union had entered into a collective-bargaining agreement in 1953 with the employer, the agreement to run one year and from year to year thereafter unless terminated on specified notices. The agreement provided that there would be no strikes or work stoppages and that grievances would be handled pursuant to a specified procedure. The last step in the grievance procedure was arbitration. This controversy involved several grievances that concerned work loads and work assignments. The grievances were processed and were finally denied by the employer. The union requested arbitration and the employer refused. The union brought suit under Section 301(a) to compel arbitration. In sustaining the union's demand, Mr. Justice Douglas, speaking for the court, said:

. . . Plainly, the agreement to arbitrate grievance disputes is the quid pro quo for an agreement not to strike. Viewed in this light, the legislation does more than confer jurisdiction in the federal courts over labor organizations. It expresses a federal policy that federal courts should enforce these agreements on behalf of or against labor organizations and that industrial peace can be best obtained only in that way . . . It seems, therefore, clear to us that Congress adopted a policy which placed sanctions behind agreements to arbitrate grievance disputes by implication rejecting the common law rule . . . against enforcement of executory agreements to arbitrate.

The case holds also that federal substantive law, when it exists, must be applied to this type of action. Where such law does not exist, the federal courts may adopt rules of state law and these rules will be absorbed into a body of federal law.

6. *Matter of* Calka and Tobin Packing Co., (New York), 9 A.D. (2d) 820 (1959).
7. Renzi v. Oertel Brewing Co., 36 LC 65,141 (1958).
8. Textile Workers of America v. Lincoln Mills, 353 U.S. 448 (1956).

Action to Stay Arbitration

It has long been the policy of most states that when parties enter into an agreement and one of its provisions provides that any dispute arising out of or in connection with it shall be settled by arbitration, the dispute must be arbitrated. Any controversy that arises within the compass of that provision must also go to arbitration.

In a leading New York case [9] an employer sought a proceeding to stay arbitration on the ground that the contract which it had made with the employee seeking arbitration was void and unenforcible in that it was lacking in mutuality. The employer contended that the contract obligated it to engage the employee for his entire lifetime and permitted him to terminate his employment at will. All the courts in New York, including the court of appeals, denied the motion for a stay. In ordering the employer to comply with the request to arbitrate, the highest New York court said in part:

. . . In our view, the question whether the contract lacked mutuality of obligation, depending as it does primarily on a reading and construction of the agreement, and involving, as is obvious from the disagreement amongst judges of this Court and the courts below, substantial difficulties of interpretation, is to be determined by the arbitrators, not the court. Once it be ascertained that the parties broadly agreed to arbitrate a dispute "arising out of or in connection with" the agreement, it is for the arbitrators to decide what the agreement means and to enforce it according to the rules of law which they deem appropriate in the circumstances.

A court will stay arbitration when fraud or duress practiced against one of the parties renders the agreement voidable.[10]

If there is no bona fide dispute between the parties, i.e., if the asserted claim is frivolous, the court will stay arbitration.[11]

When a condition precedent to arbitration under a contract or an applicable statute has not been fulfilled, a stay will be granted.[12]

Action to Vacate an Award on the Ground That the Arbitrator Erred in Judgment

In a leading case on this point, the New York Court of Appeals, in rejecting a motion to vacate an award,[13] said:

9. Exercycle Corp. v. Maratta, 11 A.D. (2d) 677 N.Y. (1960).
10. *Matter of* Lipman, 289 N.Y. 76 (1942).
11. *Matter of* General Electric Co., 300 N.Y. 262 (1949).
12. *Matter of* Cauldwell-Wingate Co., 262 A.D. (N.Y.) (1941).
13. Exercycle Corp. v. Maratta, 9 N.Y. (2d) 329 (1961).

. . . The arbitrator is a judge appointed by the parties; he is by their consent invested with judicial functions in the particular case; he is to determine the right as between the parties in respect to the matter submitted, and all questions of fact or law upon which the right depends are . . . deemed to be referred to him for decision. The court possesses no general supervisory power over awards, and if the arbitrators keep within their jurisdiction, their award will not be set aside because they have erred in judgment either upon the facts or the law.

When the arbitrator makes a mathematical error in arriving at his award, the court will not vacate the award but will modify it to the extent of correcting the error.

Action to Stay Arbitration or to Set Aside an Award on the Ground That the Matter in Dispute is Not Arbitrable Under the Contract

In a case when a union was alleged to have violated a no-strike clause in a collective-bargaining agreement, the United States Circuit Court of Appeals held that the question of whether the no-strike clause had been violated was for the courts to determine rather than the arbitrator.[14]

Despite the presence of a broad arbitration clause in a contract, the question often arises whether the parties regarded certain matters as being subject to arbitration. Whether the question of arbitrability of such disputes is to be determined by the court or left to the decision of the arbitrator is still one of the most controversial issues in labor-management arbitration.[15]

No arbitrable issue is involved when the contract itself contains specific provisions limiting arbitration and leaving no room for a dispute concerning its interpretation.[16]

Action to Vacate an Award on the Ground That a Fair Trial Was Denied

In one case [17] members of a union were discharged by their employer in pursuance of an award in an arbitration of a dispute between the union and the employer that concerned a collective-bargaining agree-

14. Drake Bakeries v. Confectionery Workers, Local 50, 287 Fed. (2d) 155 (1960).
15. See Local 205, United Electric Workers v. General Electric Co., 172 F. Supp. 53 (1959).
16. Pari-Mutuel Employees' Guild v. Los Angeles Turf Club Inc., 169 Cal. App. 2d 571, 337 P. 2d 575 (1959).
17. Fudickar v. Guardian Mutual Life Ins. Co., 62 N.Y. 399 (1875).

ment. The discharged workers moved to vacate the award on the ground that they were not permitted to be represented by counsel of their own choosing at the hearing before the arbitrators. The court denied the motion to vacate on the ground that the employees were not themselves parties to the agreement and consequently were not parties to the controversy or the arbitration. An order vacating an award may be made only on the application of a party to the controversy that was arbitrated; in this case, such a motion could be made only by the union or the employer.

Action to Enforce Awards

A motion to compel specific performance of an arbitrator's award will be entertained in all states which have enacted arbitration statutes.

Enforcement of labor arbitration awards under Section 301(a) of the Taft-Hartley Law is available in federal courts, since, as was stated in one case,[18] "authority to compel arbitration carries with it authority to enforce the resulting award."

On June 20, 1961, the United States Supreme Court rendered three significant decisions relating to the enforcement of arbitration provisions and awards under collective-bargaining agreements. The first case [19] is concerned with an application to compel a reluctant party to arbitrate. On this point, the court said:

. . . The Congress . . . has by Section 301 of the Labor Management Relations Act, assigned the courts the duty of determining whether the reluctant party has breached his promise to arbitrate. For arbitration is a matter of contract and a party cannot be required to submit to arbitration any dispute which he has not agreed so to submit. Yet, to be consistent with congressional policy in favor of settlement of disputes by the parties through the machinery of arbitration, the judicial inquiry under Section 301 must be strictly confined to the question whether the reluctant party did agree to arbitrate the grievance or did agree to give the arbitrator power to make the award he made. An order to arbitrate the particular grievance should not be denied unless it may be said with positive assurance that the arbitration clause is not susceptible to an interpretation that covers the asserted dispute. Doubts should be resolved in favor of coverage.

In the second case,[20] the employer refused to arbitrate on the ground that it had not violated the contract. The Supreme Court disagreed with the employer and ordered arbitration. It stated:

18. Kornman Co. v. Amalgamated Clothing Workers, 264 Fed. (2d) 733 (1959).
19. See also 45 *Va. L. Rev.* 739 (1959). Steelworkers v. Warrior and Gulf Co., 363 U.S. 574 (1961).
20. Steelworkers v. American Mfg. Co., 363 U.S. 564 (1961).

. . . The union claimed in this case that the company had violated a specific provision of the contract. The company took the position that it had not violated that clause. There was, therefore, a dispute between the parties as to the "meaning, interpretation and application of the collective bargaining agreement." Arbitration should have been ordered. When the judiciary undertakes to determine the merits of a grievance under the guise of interpreting the grievance procedure of collective bargaining agreements, it usurps a function which under that regime is entrusted to the arbitration tribunal.

In the third case,[21] the question concerned the refusal of the court to review the merits of an arbitration award. The Supreme Court, endorsing the refusal, had this to say:

. . . The refusal of courts to review the merits of an arbitration award is the proper approach to arbitration under collective bargaining agreements. The federal policy of settling labor disputes by arbitration would be undermined if courts had the final say on the merits of the awards. . . . When an arbitrator is commissioned to interpret and apply the collective bargaining agreement, he is to bring his informed judgment to bear in order to reach a fair solution to the problem. This is especially true when it comes to formulating remedies. . . . When the arbitrator's words manifest an infidelity to this obligation, courts have no choice but to refuse enforcement of the award.
. . . A mere ambiguity in the opinion accompanying an award, which permits the inference that the arbitrator may have exceeded his authority, is no reason for refusing to enforce the award. Arbitrators have no obligation to the court to give their reasons for an award. To require opinions free of ambiguity may lead arbitrators to play it safe by writing no supporting opinions.

These decisions clearly hold that the labor arbitrator's source of law is not confined to the express provisions of the contract, that judicial inquiry must be limited to whether the reluctant party agreed to arbitrate the dispute, that a dispute must be held to be arbitrable unless it can be said with positive assurance to be excluded by the contract, and that doubts are to be resolved in favor of arbitration. Another lesson learned from these Supreme Court cases is that courts should refuse to review the merits of an arbitration award. One last point is that courts will not overrule the arbitrator because they place a different construction on the contract from that of the arbitrator.

21. Steelworkers v. Enterprise Corp., 363 U.S. 593 (1961).

Action to Vacate an Award on the Ground That the Arbitrator Exceeded His Authority

When an employee was discharged for dereliction of his duty, a court [22] held that it was within the power of a board of arbitrators to rule that the discharge was too severe a penalty and to reinstate the employee. Such action did not interfere with the prerogatives of management or alter the contract.

A New York court [23] ruled that the vacating of an arbitration award must be sought in court within three months after the award is made. A lack of knowledge of the facts on which to challenge the award until the expiration of more than three months does not extend this limitation.

The United States Circuit Court of Appeals [24] vacated an arbitrator's award on the ground that the arbitrator exceeded his authority. In this case the arbitrator, as part of his decision, directed the union and the employer to negotiate on the subject of engineering surveys to be made on the production speed of an assembly line. The grievance before the arbitrator was whether or not the employer's increased speed of the assembly line was an unreasonable quota of production, and he decided that the union had not proved that it was. The contract specifically limited the arbitrator's function to deciding only the issues involved in the particular proceeding and expressly withheld from the arbitrator any authority to add to, ignore, or modify any of the contractual terms or to go beyond what was necessary for the interpretation and application of the contract.

A New York court [25] vacated an arbitrator's award on the ground that he had exceeded his authority. In this case, the labor contract provided for severance pay if any vessel owned by the employer was transferred to a foreign registry. When a ship went aground and was sold to a foreign company for scrap, the arbitrator awarded severance pay. The Supreme Court of New York held that the arbitrator had exceeded his authority when he placed his interpretation on the collective-bargaining agreement.

22. Overall v. Delta Refining Co., 40 LC 66,486 (1960).
23. *Matter of* Bhd. of Railway and Steamship Clerks, 42 LC 50,162 (1961).
24. Local 791, I.U.E., 41 LC 16,667 (1960).
25. Acolian Steamship Corp. v. Marine Engineers' Beneficial Ass'n, N.Y. Sup. Ct., 42 LC 50,215 (1961).

Action to Vacate an Award on the Ground That Federal Law Preempts the Arbitrator's Authority

Although the general rule is that arbitrator's awards may not be challenged because they misinterpret a law, the National Labor Relations Board voided an award which would have resulted in a violation of the National Labor Relations Act.[26] In this case the arbitrator had ruled that members of one union could be required to be members of another union following a schism. The board held this ruling to be repugnant to the provisions of the act.

A recent court ruling [27] declared that state courts have concurrent jurisdiction of actions involving the enforcement of union contracts in industries affecting commerce, but that they must apply federal substantive law in deciding such actions, and, more particularly, in determining the arbitrability of a dispute. The importance of this ruling warrants careful consideration of the case. Justice Worley of the Tennessee Court of Appeals delivered the decision, which follows.

This appeal brings under review a declaratory judgment construing a collective bargaining agreement between the litigating parties and decreeing that, under the facts of the case and the pertinent provisions of the contract, the appellee was under no duty to submit to arbitration the question of the layoff of thirteen of its employees on January 30, 1959, allegedly the result of a management decision to subcontract certain of its work.

Volunteer Electric Cooperative filed the original bill against defendants J. F. Gann and others (business manager and members of Local Union 846, International Brotherhood of Electrical Workers) alleging the existence of a currently binding collective bargaining contract between the parties containing provisions for arbitration of grievances which could not otherwise be adjusted, the bill reciting that a dispute had arisen as to "the action of complainant's management in determining the necessity for a reduction in its working force for economic reasons and thereafter making such reduction by separating thirteen employees from its payrolls on January 30, 1959." The bill further recites the position of the employer that this layoff of employees was solely a management decision under the contract, but that notwithstanding the contract provisions the labor union had demanded that "the question of the propriety and justification for the 'layoff' be submitted to the process of arbitration as provided in said contract." The bill further recited reasons for complainant's position that the dispute concerning the layoff is not subject to arbitration and prayed that the Court construe the agreement and determine whether or not the question referred to is properly arbitrable under the provisions thereof. The defendant Labor Union filed

26. Hershey Chocolate Corp., C.Ch., NLRB 9493 (1960).
27. Volunteer Electric Cooperative v. J. F. Gann, 41 LC 16,537 (1960).

answer and cross bill asserting in substance that the thirteen employees were laid off when there was work available and needing to be done, that other persons not covered by the collective bargaining agreement were employed to do such work, and that the layoff was wrongful and arbitrary and in violation of several cited provisions of the collective bargaining agreement. The Union, as cross complainant, asked that the Court "interpret and construe the issue, disputes or differences existing between the parties and that the defendant be ordered and required, in conformity with the collective bargaining agreement or contract, to submit all issues, differences and disputes to arbitration, as provided for" therein.

The pleadings in this case thus present to the Court for construction a collective bargaining agreement for the purpose of determining the arbitrability of a dispute between the parties thereunder. In the absence of some express provision in the agreement to the contrary the question of arbitrability is properly to be determined by the Court.

A matter of critical importance here, in the determination of the question of arbitrability, is the law to be applied. By the Labor Management Relations Act and the course of decision thereunder, there has been created a "new substantive law" dealing with the enforcement of collective bargaining agreements in industries "affecting commerce." Textile Workers Union v. Lincoln Mills, 353 U.S. 448.

By the terms of the statute cited such contracts are now enforceable by action brought in United States District Courts, without regard to amount in controversy or diversity of citizenship, but it has also been generally held that state courts have concurrent jurisdiction to deal with actions based on such collective bargaining agreements.

And while the question of what law is to be applied in such concurrent jurisdiction-state court actions is in the fringe area of this unique development of Federal substantive law by judicial decision (directed in Lincoln Mills, *supra*) the opinion is usually expressed that because of federal preemption of the field, and in order to effect the uniform national labor policy which is one of the objects of the National Labor Management Relations Act, federal law must be applied. If it was the intent of Congress to preempt the field, as has been held, we must accept the result that federal "substantive law" is controlling.

The pleadings in this case contain no averment that Volunteer Electric Cooperative is an industry "affecting commerce," although it has been generally held that similar utilities fall within this class.

Except for the body of law established under the federal act, it would seem that the common law rule to the effect that executory agreements to arbitrate are judicially unenforceable is still the law in Tennessee.

It is true that the contract we consider provides (paragraph 24) that "nothing in this agreement shall be construed to require the employer to hire any person not required in the proper and efficient operation of its properties" and that paragraph 25 declares Employer's "sole right" to lay off employees, but the Union has asserted that the layoff violated paragraph 15 guaranteeing full time employment to "employees covered by this agreement," under conditions there stated, paragraph 22 relating to regard of seniority in lay off, and paragraph 25 "in that this so-called 'layoff' was for the purpose of destroying the union." Can it be held that these Union charges relating to and growing out of the lay off, considered without regard to their merit, failed to create "questions, disputes, or grievances as to the interpretation, application, or performance of the terms of this agreement"?

In the light of these late United States Supreme Court decisions, of which the Chancellor did not have the "benefit," and which he certainly could not have foreseen, we must rule that the Union's complaints as to multiple breaches of the collective bargaining agreement created an arbitrable question under the broad arbitration provisions of this contract, despite the existence of the contract provisions which would make such layoff appear to have been the exercise of a reserved management function.

For the reasons stated, and under what we believe to be a mandate of controlling Federal decision in the field, we have concluded that the decree of the Chancellor must be reserved and a decree here entered declaring the dispute between the parties reflected by pleadings and proof to be arbitrable under the provisions of the applicable collective bargaining agreement. The costs will be adjudged against Appellee.

Reversed.

Summary

The fact that less than 10 per cent of collective-bargaining agreements now in effect fail to provide for the arbitration of contract disputes is substantial evidence of the desirability of this peaceful process over the alternatives of litigation, strikes, and lock-outs, which are the most costly methods of resolving the inevitable disputes that arise in the administration of labor agreements.

The great value of voluntary arbitration over judicial intervention and other means for settling disputes developing during the term of the collective bargaining contract, was admirably set forth in 1955 by Harry Shulman, the late Dean of Yale Law School, when he wrote: [28]

. . . Arbitration is a means of making collective bargaining work and thus preserving private enterprise in a free government. When it works fairly well, it does not need the sanction of the law of contracts or the law of arbitration. It is only when the system breaks down completely that the courts' aid in these respects is invoked. But the courts cannot, by occasional sporadic decision, restore the parties' continuing relationship; and their in-

28. H. Shulman, Reason, Contract, and Law in Labor Relations, 68 *Harv. L. Rev.* 999 (1955).

tervention in such cases may seriously affect the going systems of self-government. When their autonomous system breaks down, might not the parties better be left to the usual methods for adjustment of labor disputes rather than to court actions on the contract or on the arbitration award? I suggest that the law stay out—but, mind you, not the lawyers.

Appendix

The Railway Labor Act

Act of May 20, 1926, 69th Congress

An Act to provide for the prompt disposition of disputes between carriers and their employees, and for other purposes.

Be it enacted by the Senate and House of Representatives of the United States of America in Congress assembled,

Definitions

SECTION 1. When used in this Act and for the purposes of this Act:

First. The term "carrier" includes any express company, sleeping-car company, and any carrier by railroad, subject to the Interstate Commerce Act, including all floating equipment such as boats, barges, tugs, bridges and ferries; and other transportation facilities used by or operated in connection with any such carrier by railroad, and any receiver or any other individual or body, judicial or otherwise, when in the possession of the business of employers or carriers covered by this Act: *Provided, however,* That the term "carrier" shall not include any street, interurban, or suburban electric railway unless such a railway is operating as a part of a general steam railroad system of transportation, but shall not exclude any part of the general steam railroad system of transportation now or hereafter operated by any other motive power;

Second. The term "Adjustment Board" means one of the boards of adjustment provided for in this Act;

Third. The term "Board of Meditation" means the Board of Meditation created by this Act;

Fourth. The term "commerce" means commerce among the several States or between any State, Territory, or the District of Columbia and any foreign nation, or between any Territory or the District of Columbia and any State, or between any Territory and any other Territory, or between any Territory and the District of Columbia, or within any Territory or the District of Columbia, or between points in the same State but through any other State or any Territory or the District of Columbia or any foreign nation.

Fifth. The term "employee" as used herein includes every person in the service of a carrier (subject to its continuing authority to supervise and direct the manner of rendition of his service) who performs any work defined as that of an employee or subordinate official in the orders of the Interstate Commerce Commission now in effect, and as the same may be amended or interpreted by orders hereafter entered by the commission pursuant to the authority which is hereby conferred upon it to enter orders amending or interpreting such existing orders: *Provided, however,* That no occupational classification made by order of the Interstate Commerce Commission shall be construed to define the crafts according to which railway employees may be organized by their voluntary action, nor shall the jurisdiction or powers of such employee organizations be regarded as in any way limited or defined by the provisions of this Act or by the orders of the commission.

Sixth. The term "district court" includes the Supreme Court of the District of Columbia; and the term "circuit court of appeals" includes the Court of Appeals of the District of Columbia.

This Act may be cited as the Railway Labor Act.

General Duties

SEC. 2. First. It shall be the duty of all carriers, their officers, agents, and employees to exert every reasonable effort to make and maintain agreements concerning rates of pay, rules, and working conditions, and to settle all disputes, whether arising out of the application of such agreements or otherwise, in order to avoid any interruption to commerce or to the operation of any carrier growing out of any dispute between the carrier and the employees thereof.

Second. All disputes between a carrier and its employees shall be considered, and, if possible, decided, with all expedition, in conference between representatives designated and authorized so to confer, respectively, by the carriers and by the employees thereof interested in the dispute.

Third. Representatives, for the purposes of this Act, shall be designated by the respective parties in such manner as may be provided in their corporate organization or unincorporated association, or by other means of collective action, without interference, influence, or coercion exercised by either party over the self-organization or designation of representatives by the other.

Fourth. In case of a dispute between a carrier and its employees, arising out of grievances or out of the interpretation or application of agreements concerning rates of pay, rules, or working conditions, it shall be the duty of the designated representative or representatives of such carrier and of such employees, within ten days after the receipt of notice of a desire on the part of either party to confer in respect to such dispute, to specify a time and place at which such conference shall be held: *Provided,* (1) That the place so specified shall be situated upon the railroad line of the carrier involved unless otherwise mutually agreed upon; and (2) that the time so specified shall allow the designated conferees reasonable opportunity to reach such place of conference, but shall not exceed twenty days from the receipt of such notice: *And provided further,* That nothing in this paragraph shall be construed to supersede the provisions of any agreement (as to conferences) then in effect between the parties.

Fifth. Disputes concerning changes in rates of pay, rules, or working conditions shall be dealt with as provided in section 6 and in other provisions of this Act relating thereto.

Boards of Adjustment—Grievances—Interpretation of Agreements

sec. 3. First. Boards of adjustment shall be created by agreement between any carrier or group of carriers, or the carriers as a whole, and its or their employees.

The agreement

(a) Shall be in writing;

(b) Shall state the group or groups of employees covered by such adjustment board;

(c) Shall provide that disputes between an employee or group of employees and a carrier, growing out of grievances or out of the interpretation or application of agreements concerning rates of pay, rules, or working conditions, shall be handled in the usual manner up to and including the chief operating officer of the carrier designated to handle such disputes; but, failing to reach an adjustment in this manner, that the dispute shall be referred to the designated adjustment board by the parties, or by either party, with a full statement of the facts and all supporting data bearing upon the dispute;

(d) Shall provide that the parties may be heard either in person, by counsel, or by other representative, as they may respectively elect, and that adjustment boards shall hear and, if possible, decide promptly all disputes referred to them as provided in paragraph (c). Adjustment boards shall give due notice of all hearings to the employee or employees and the carrier or carriers involved in the dispute;

(e) Shall stipulate that decisions of adjustment boards shall be final and binding on both parties to the dispute; and it shall be the duty of both to abide by such decisions;

(f) Shall state the number of representatives of the employees and the number of representatives of the carrier or carriers on the adjustment board, which number of representatives, respectively, shall be equal;

(g) Shall provide for the method of selecting members and filling vacancies;

(h) Shall provide for the portion of expenses to be assumed by the respective parties;

(i) Shall stipulate that a majority of the adjustment board members shall be competent to make an award, unless otherwise mutually agreed;

(j) Shall stipulate that adjustment boards shall meet regularly at such times and places as designated; and

(k) Shall provide for the method of advising the employees and carrier or carriers of the decisions of the board.

Second. Nothing in this Act shall be construed to prohibit an individual carrier and its employees from agreeing upon the settlement of disputes through such machinery of contract and adjustment as they may mutually establish.

Board of Mediation

SEC. 4. There is hereby established, as an independent agency in the executive branch of the Government, a board to be known as the Board of Mediation and to be composed of five members appointed by the President, by and with the advice and consent of the Senate. The terms of office of the members first taking office shall expire, as designated by the President at the time of nomination, one at the end of the first year, one at the end of the second year, one at the end of the third year, one at the end of the fourth year, and one at the end of the fifth year, after January 1, 1926. The terms of office of all successors shall expire five years after the expiration of the terms for which their predecessors were appointed; but any member appointed to fill a vacancy occurring prior to the expiration of the term for which his predecessor was appointed shall be appointed only for the unexpired term of his predecessor. Vacancies in the board shall not impair the powers nor affect the duties of the board nor of the remaining members of the board. A majority of the members in office shall constitute a quorum for the transaction of the business of the board. Each member of the board shall receive a salary at the rate of $12,000 per annum, together with necessary traveling expenses and subsistence expenses, or per diem allowance in lieu thereof, subject to the provisions of law applicable thereto, while away from the principal office of the board on business required by this Act. No person in the employment of or who is pecuniarily or otherwise interested in any organization of employees or any carrier shall enter upon the duties of or continue to be a member of the board.

A member of the board may be removed by the President for inefficiency, neglect of duty, malfeasance in office, or ineligibility, but for no other cause.

Second. The board shall annually designate a member to act as chairman. The board shall maintain its principal office in the District of Columbia, but it may meet at any other place whenever it deems it necessary. The board may designate one or more of its members to exercise the functions of the board in mediation proceedings. Each member of the board shall have power to administer oaths and affirmations. The board shall have a seal which shall be judicially noticed. The board shall make an annual report to Congress.

Third. The board may (1) appoint such experts and assistants to act in a confidential capacity and, subject to the provisions of the civil service laws, such other officers and employees, and (2) in accordance with the Classification Act of 1923 fix the salary of such experts, assistants, officers, and employees, and (3) make such expenditures (including expenditures for rent and personal services at the seat of government and elsewhere, for law books, periodicals, and books of reference, and for printing and binding, and including expenditures for salaries and compensation, necessary traveling expenses and expenses actually incurred for subsistence, and other necessary expenses of boards of arbitration, in accordance with the provisions of section 7) as may be necessary for the execution of the functions vested in the board, or in the boards of arbitration, and as may be provided for by the Congress from time to time. All expenditures of the board shall be allowed and paid on the presentation of itemized vouchers therefor approved by the chairman.

Functions of Board of Mediation

SEC. 5. First. The parties, or either party, to a dispute between an employee or group of employees and a carrier may invoke the services of the Board of Mediation created by this Act, or the Board of Mediation may proffer its services, in any of the following cases:

(a) A dispute arising out of grievances or out of the interpretation or application of agreements concerning rates of pay, rules, or working conditions not adjusted by the parties in conference and not decided by the appropriate adjustment board;

(b) A dispute which is not settled in conference between the parties, in respect to changes in rates of pay, rules, or working conditions;

(c) Any other dispute not decided in conference between the parties.

In either event the said board shall promptly put itself in communication with the parties to such controversy, and shall use its best efforts, by mediation, to bring them to agreement. If such efforts to bring about an amicable adjustment through mediation shall be unsuccessful, the said board shall at once endeavor as its final required action (except as provided in paragraph third of this section and in section 10 of this Act), to induce the parties to submit their controversy to arbitration in accordance with the provisions of this Act.

Second. In any case in which a controversy arises over the meaning or the application of any agreement reached through mediation under the provisions of this Act, either party to the said agreement, or both, may apply to the Board of Mediation for an interpretation as to the meaning or application of such agreement. The said board shall upon receipt of such request notify the parties to the controversy, and after a hearing of both sides give its interpretation within thirty days.

Third. The Board of Mediation shall have the following duties with respect to the arbitration of disputes under section 7 of this Act:

(a) On failure of the arbitrators named by the parties to agree on the remaining arbitrator or arbitrators within the time set by section 7 of this Act, it shall be the duty of the Board of Mediation to name such remaining arbitrator or arbitrators. It shall be the duty of the board in naming such arbitrator or arbitrators to appoint only those whom the board shall deem wholly disinterested in the controversy to be arbitrated and impartial and without bias as between the parties to such arbitration. Should, however, the board name an arbitrator or arbitrators not so disinterested and impartial, then, upon proper investigation and presentation of the facts, the board shall promptly remove such arbitrator.

If an arbitrator named by the Board of Mediation, in accordance with the provisions of this Act, shall be removed by such board as provided by this Act, or if such an arbitrator refuses or is unable to serve, it shall be the duty of the Board of Mediation, promptly, to select another arbitrator, in the same manner as provided in this Act for an original appointment by the Board of Mediation.

(b) Any member of the Board of Mediation is authorized to take the acknowledgment of an agreement of arbitration under this Act. When so acknowledged, or when acknowledged by the parties before a notary public or the clerk of a district court or a circuit court of appeals of the United States, such agreement to arbitrate shall be delivered to a member of said board, or transmitted to said board, to be filed in its office.

(c) When an agreement to arbitrate has been filed with the Board of Mediation, or with one of its members, as provided by this section, and when the said board, or a member thereof, has been furnished the names of the arbitrators chosen by the parties to the controversy, it shall be the duty of the Board of Mediation to cause a notice in writing to be served upon said arbitrators, notifying them of their appointment, requesting them to meet promptly to name the remaining arbitrator or arbitrators necessary to complete the board of arbitration, and advising them of the period within which, as provided by the agreement to arbitrate, they are empowered to name such arbitrator or arbitrators.

(d) Either party to an arbitration desiring the reconvening of a board of arbitration to pass upon any controversy arising over the meaning or application of an award may so notify the Board of Mediation in writing, stating in such notice the question or questions to be submitted to such reconvened board. The Board of Mediation shall thereupon promptly communicate with the members of the board of arbitration, or a subcommittee of such board appointed for such purpose pursuant to a provision in the agreement to arbitrate, and arrange for the reconvening of said board or subcommittee, and shall notify the respective parties to the controversy of the time and place at which the board, or the subcommittee, will meet for hearings upon the matters in controversy to be submitted to it. No evidence other than that contained in the record filed with the original award shall be received or considered by such reconvened board or subcommittee, except such evidence as may be necessary to illustrate the interpretations suggested by the parties. If any member of the original board is unable or unwilling to serve on such reconvened board or subcommittee thereof, another arbitrator shall be named in the same manner and with the same powers and duties as such original arbitrator.

(e) The Interstate Commerce Commission, the Bureau of Labor Statistics, and the custodian of the records, respectively, of the Railroad Labor Board, of the mediators designated in the Act approved June 1, 1898, providing for mediation and arbitration, known as the Erdman Act, and of the

Board of Mediation and Conciliation created by the Act approved July 15, 1913, providing for mediation, conciliation, and arbitration, known as the Newlands Act, are hereby authorized and directed to transfer and deliver to the Board of Mediation created by this Act any and all papers and documents heretofore filed with or transferred to them, respectively, bearing upon the settlement, adjustment, or determination of disputes between carriers and their employees or upon mediation or arbitration proceedings held under or pursuant to the provisions of any Act of Congress in respect to such disputes; and the President is authorized to require the transfer and delivery to the Board of Mediation, created by this Act, of any and all such papers and documents filed with or in the possession of any agency of the Government. The President is authorized to designate a custodian of the records and property of the Railroad Labor Board, until the transfer and delivery of such records to the Board of Mediation and the disposition of such property in such manner as the President may direct.

Procedure in Changing Rates of Pay, Rules, and Working Conditions

SEC. 6. Carriers and the representatives of the employees shall give at least thirty days' written notice of an intended change affecting rates of pay, rules, or working conditions, and the time and place for conference between the representatives of the parties interested in such intended changes shall be agreed upon within ten days after the receipt of said notice, and said time shall be within the thirty days provided in the notice. Should changes be requested from more than one class or associated classes at approximately the same time, this date for the conference shall be understood to apply only to the first conference for each class; it being the intent that subsequent conferences in respect to each request shall be held in the order of its receipt and shall follow each other with reasonable promptness. In every case where such notice of intended change has been given, or conferences are being held with reference thereto, or the services of the Board of Mediation have been requested by either party, or said board has proffered its services, rates of pay, rules, or working conditions shall not be altered by the carrier until the controversy has been finally acted upon, as required by section 5 of this Act, by the Board of Mediation, unless a period of ten days has elapsed after termination of conferences without request for or proffer of the services of the Board of Mediation.

Arbitration

SEC. 7. First. Whenever a controversy shall arise between a carrier or carriers and its or their employees which is not settled either in conference between representatives of the parties or by the appropriate adjustment board or through mediation, in the manner provided in the preceding sections, such controversy may, by agreement of the parties to such controversy, be submitted to the arbitration of a board of three (or, if the parties to the controversy so stipulate, of six) persons: *Provided, however,* That the failure or refusal of either party to submit a controversy to arbitration shall not be construed as a violation of any legal obligation imposed upon such party by the terms of this Act or otherwise.

Second. Such board of arbitration shall be chosen in the following manner:

(a) In the case of a board of three the carrier or carriers and the representatives of the employees, parties respectively to the agreement to arbitrate, shall each name one arbitrator; the two arbitrators thus chosen shall select a third arbitrator. If the arbitrators chosen by the parties shall fail to name the third arbitrator within five days after their first meeting, such third arbitrator shall be named by the Board of Mediation.

(b) In the case of a board of six the carrier or carriers and the representatives of the employees, parties respectively to the agreement to arbitrate, shall each name two arbitrators; the four arbitrators thus chosen shall, by a majority vote, select the remaining two arbitrators. If the arbitrators chosen by the parties shall fail to name the two arbitrators within fifteen days after their first meeting, the said two arbitrators, or as many of them as have not been named, shall be named by the Board of Mediation.

Third. (a) When the arbitrators selected by the respective parties have agreed upon the remaining arbitrator or arbitrators, they shall notify the Board of Mediation; and, in the event of their failure to agree upon any or upon all of the necessary arbitrators within the period fixed by this Act, they shall, at the expiration of such period, notify the Board of Mediation of the arbitrators selected, if any, or of their failure to make or to complete such selection.

(b) The board of arbitration shall organize and select its own chairman and make all necessary rules for conducting its hearings: *Provided, however,* That the board of arbitration shall be bound to give the parties to the controversy a full and fair hearing, which shall include an opportunity to present evidence in support of their claims, and an opportunity to present their case in person, by counsel, or by other representative as they may respectively elect.

(c) Upon notice from the Board of Mediation that the parties, or either party, to an arbitration desire the reconvening of the board of arbitration (or a subcommittee of such board of arbitration appointed for such purpose pursuant to the agreement to arbitrate) to pass upon any controversy over the meaning or application of their award, the board, or its subcommittee, shall at once reconvene. No question other than, or in addition to, the questions relating to the meaning or application of the award, submitted by the party or parties in writing, shall be considered by the reconvened board of arbitration or its subcommittee.

Such rulings shall be acknowledged by such board or subcommittee thereof in the same manner, and filed in the same district court clerk's office, as the original award and become a part thereof.

(d) No arbitrator, except those chosen by the Board of Mediation, shall be incompetent to act as an arbitrator because of his interest in the controversy to be arbitrated, or because of his connection with or partiality to either of the parties to the arbitration.

(e) Each member of any board of arbitration created under the provisions of this Act named by either party to the arbitration shall be compensated by the party naming him. Each arbitrator selected by the arbitrators or named by the Board of Mediation shall receive from the Board of Mediation such compensation as the Board of Mediation may fix, together with his necessary traveling expenses and expenses actually incurred for subsistence, while serving as an arbitrator.

(f) The board of arbitration shall furnish a certified copy of its award to the respective parties to the controversy, and shall transmit the original, together with the papers and proceedings and a transcript of the evidence taken at the hearings, certified under the hands of at least a majority of the arbitrators, to the clerk of the district court of the United States for the district wherein the controversy arose or the arbitration is entered into, to be filed in said clerk's office as hereinafter provided. The said board shall also furnish a certified copy of its award, and the papers and proceedings, including testimony relating thereto, to the Board of Mediation, to be filed in its office; and in addition a certified copy of its award shall be filed in the office of the Interstate Commerce Commission: *Provided, however,* That such award shall not be construed to diminish or extinguish any of the powers or duties of the Interstate Commerce Commission, under the Interstate Commerce Act, as amended.

(g) A board of arbitration may, subject to the approval of the Board of Mediation, employ and fix the compensation of such assistants as it deems necessary in carrying on the arbitration proceedings. The compensation of such employees, together with their necessary traveling expenses and expenses actually incurred for subsistence, while so employed, and the necessary expenses of boards of arbitration, shall be paid by the Board of Mediation.

Whenever practicable, the board shall be supplied with suitable quarters in any Federal building located at its place of meeting or any place where the board may conduct its proceedings or deliberations.

(h) All testimony before said board shall be given under oath or affirmation, and any member of the board shall have the power to administer oaths or affirmations. The board of arbitration, or any member thereof, shall have the power to require the attendance of witnesses and the production of such books, papers, contracts, agreements, and documents as may be deemed by the board of arbitration material to a just determination of the matters submitted to its arbitration, and may for that purpose request the clerk of the district court of the United States for the district wherein said arbitration is being conducted to issue the necessary subpoenas, and upon such request the said clerk or his duly authorized deputy shall be, and he hereby is, authorized, and it shall be his duty, to issue such subpoenas. In the event of the failure of any person to comply with any such subpoena, or in the event of the contumacy of any witness appearing before the board of arbitration, the board may invoke the aid of the United States courts to compel witnesses to attend and testify and to produce such books, papers, contracts, agreements, and documents to the same extent and under the same conditions and penalties as provided for in the Act to regulate commerce approved February 4, 1887, and the amendments thereto.

Any witness appearing before a board of arbitration shall receive the same fees and mileage as witnesses in courts of the United States, to be paid by the party securing the subpoena.

sec. 8. The agreement to arbitrate

(a) Shall be in writing;

(b) Shall stipulate that the arbitration is had under the provisions of this Act;

(c) Shall state whether the board of arbitration is to consist of three or of six members;

(d) Shall be signed by the duly accredited representatives of the carrier or carriers and the employees, parties respectively to the agreement to arbitrate, and shall be acknowledged by said parties before a notary public, the clerk of a district court or circuit court of appeals of the United States, or before a member of the Board of Mediation, and, when so acknowledged, shall be filed in the office of the Board of Mediation;

(e) Shall state specifically the questions to be submitted to the said board for decision; and that, in its award or awards, the said board shall confine itself strictly to decisions as to the questions so specifically submitted to it;

(f) Shall provide that the questions, or any one or more of them, submitted by the parties to the board of arbitration may be withdrawn from arbitration on notice to that effect signed by the duly accredited representatives of all the parties and served on the board of arbitration;

(g) Shall stipulate that the signatures of a majority of said board of arbitration affixed to their award shall be competent to constitute a valid and binding award;

(h) Shall fix a period from the date of the appointment of the arbitrator or arbitrators necessary to complete the board (as provided for in the agreement) within which the said board shall commence its hearings;

(i) Shall fix a period from the beginning of the hearings within which the said board shall make and file its award: *Provided,* That the parties may agree at any time upon an extension of this period;

(j) Shall provide for the date from which the award shall become effective and shall fix the period during which the award shall continue in force;

(k) Shall provide that the award of the board of arbitration and the evidence of the proceedings before the board relating thereto, when certified under the hands of at least a majority of the arbitrators, shall be filed in the clerk's office of the district court of the United States for the district wherein the controversy arose or the arbitration was entered into, which district shall be designated in the agreement; and, when so filed, such award and proceedings shall constitute the full and complete record of the arbitration;

(l) Shall provide that the award, when so filed, shall be final and conclusive upon the parties as to the facts determined by said award and as to the merits of the controversy decided;

(m) Shall provide that any difference arising as to the meaning, or the application of the provisions, of an award made by a board of arbitration shall be referred back for a ruling to the same board, or, by agreement, to a subcommittee of such board; and that such ruling, when acknowledged in the same manner, and filed in the same district court clerk's office, as the original award, shall be a part of and shall have the same force and effect as such original award; and

(n) Shall provide that the respective parties to the award will each faithfully execute the same.

The said agreement to arbitrate, when properly signed and acknowledged as herein provided, shall not be revoked by a party to such agreement: *Provided, however,* That such agreement to arbitrate may at any time be revoked and canceled by the written agreement of both parties, signed by their duly accredited representatives, and (if no board of arbitration has yet been constituted under the agreement) delivered to the Board of Mediation or any member thereof; or, if the board of arbitration has been constituted as provided by this Act, delivered to such board of arbitration.

SEC. 9. First. The award of a board of arbitration, having been acknowledged as herein provided, shall be filed in the clerk's office of the district court designated in the agreement to arbitrate.

Second. An award acknowledged and filed as herein provided shall be conclusive on the parties as to the merits and facts of the controversy submitted to arbitration, and unless, within ten days after the filing of the award, a petition to impeach the award, on the grounds hereinafter set forth, shall be filed in the clerk's office of the court in which the award has been filed, the court shall enter judgment on the award, which judgment shall be final and conclusive on the parties.

Third. Such petition for the impeachment or contesting of any award so filed shall be entertained by the court only on one or more of the following grounds:

(a) That the award plainly does not conform to the substantive requirements laid down by this Act for such awards, or that the proceedings were not substantially in conformity with this Act;

(b) That the award does not conform, nor confine itself, to the stipulations of the agreement to arbitrate; or

(c) That a member of the board of arbitration rendering the award was guilty of fraud or corruption; or that a party to the arbitration practiced fraud or corruption which fraud or corruption affected the result of the arbitration: *Provided, however,* That no court shall entertain any such petition on the ground that an award is invalid for uncertainty; in such case the proper remedy shall be a submission of such award to a reconvened board, or subcommittee thereof, for interpretation, as provided by this Act: *Provided further,* That an award contested as herein provided shall be construed liberally by the court, with a view to favoring its validity, and that no award shall be set aside for trivial irregularity or clerical error, going only to form and not to substance.

Fourth. If the court shall determine that a part of the award is invalid on some ground or grounds designated in this section as a ground of invalidity, but shall determine that a part of the award is valid, the court shall set aside the entire award: *Provided, however,* That, if the parties shall agree thereto, and if such valid and invalid parts are separable, the court shall set aside the invalid part, and order judgment to stand as to the valid part.

Fifth. At the expiration of ten days from the decision of the district court upon the petition filed as aforesaid, final judgment shall be entered in accordance with said decision, unless during said ten days either party shall appeal therefrom to the circuit court of appeals. In such case only such portion of the record shall be transmitted to the appellate court as is necessary to the proper understanding and consideration of the questions of law presented by said petition and to be decided.

Sixth. The determination of said circuit court of appeals upon said questions shall be final, and, being certified by the clerk thereof to said district court, judgment pursuant thereto shall thereupon be entered by said district court.

Seventh. If the petitioner's contentions are finally sustained, judgment shall be entered setting aside the award in whole or, if the parties so agree, in part; but in such case the parties may agree upon a judgment to be entered disposing of the subject matter of the controversy, which judgment when entered shall have the same force and effect as judgment entered upon an award.

Eighth. Nothing in this Act shall be construed to require an individual employee to render labor or service without his consent, nor shall anything in this Act be construed to make the quitting of his labor or service by an individual employee an illegal act; nor shall any court issue any process to compel the performance by an individual employee of such labor or service, without his consent.

Emergency Board

SEC. 10. If a dispute between a carrier and its employees be not adjusted under the foregoing provisions of this Act and should, in the judgment of the Board of Mediation, threaten substantially to interrupt interstate commerce to a degree such as to deprive any section of the country of essential transportation service, the Board of Mediation shall notify the President, who may thereupon, in his discretion, create a board to investigate and report respecting such dispute. Such board shall be composed of such number of persons as to the President may seem desirable: *Provided, however,* That no member appointed shall be pecuniarily or otherwise interested in any organization of employees or any carrier. The compensation of the members of any such board shall be fixed by the President. Such board shall be created separately in each instance and it shall investigate promptly the facts as to the dispute and make a report thereon to the President within thirty days from the date of its creation.

There is hereby authorized to be appropriated such sums as may be necessary for the expenses of such board, including the compensation and the necessary traveling expenses and expenses actually incurred for subsistence, of the members of the board. All expenditures of the board shall be allowed and paid on the presentation of itemized vouchers therefor approved by the chairman.

After the creation of such board and for thirty days after such board has made its report to the President, no change, except by agreement, shall be made by the parties to the controversy in the conditions out of which the dispute arose.

General Provisions

SEC. 11. If any provision of this Act, or the application thereof to any person or circumstance, is held invalid, the remainder of the Act, and the application of such provision to other persons or circumstances, shall not be affected thereby.

SEC. 12. There is hereby authorized to be appropriated such sums as may be necessary for expenditure by the Board of Mediation in carrying out the provisions of this Act.

SEC. 13. (a) Paragraph "Second" of subdivision (b) of section 128 of the Judicial Code, as amended, is amended to read as follows:

"Second. To review decisions of the district courts, under section 9 of the Railway Labor Act."

(b) Section 2 of the Act entitled "An Act to amend the Judicial Code, and to further define the jurisdiction of the circuit court of appeals and of the Supreme Court, and for other purposes," approved February 13, 1925, is amended to read as follows:

"SEC. 2. That cases in a circuit court of appeals under section 9 of the Railway Labor Act; under section 5 of 'An Act to create a Federal Trade Commission, to define its powers and duties, and for other purposes,' approved September 26, 1914; and under section 11 of 'An Act to supplement existing laws against unlawful restraints and monopolies, and for other purposes,' approved October 15, 1914, are included among the cases to which sections 239 and 240 of the Judicial Code shall apply."

SEC. 14. Title III of the Transportation Act, 1920, and the Act approved July 15, 1913, providing for mediation, conciliation, and arbitration, and all Acts and parts of Acts in conflict with the provisions of this Act are hereby repealed, except that the members, secretary, officers, employees, and agents of the Railroad Labor Board, in office upon the date of the passage of this Act, shall receive their salaries for a period of 30 days from such date, in the same manner as though this Act had not been passed.

Approved, May 20, 1926.

The 1934 Amendment to the Railway Labor Act

An Act to amend the Railway Labor Act approved May 20, 1926, and to provide for the prompt disposition of disputes between carriers and their employees.

Be it enacted by the Senate and House of Representatives of the United States of America in Congress assembled, That section 1 of the Railway Labor Act is amended to read as follows:

"Definitions

"SECTION 1. When used in this Act and for the purposes of this Act

"First. The term 'carrier' includes any express company, sleeping-car company, carrier by railroad, subject to the Interstate Commerce Act, and any company which is directly or indirectly owned or controlled by or under common control with any carrier by railroad and which operates any equipment or facilities or performs any service (other than trucking service) in connection with the transportation, receipt, delivery, elevation, transfer in transit, refrigeration or icing, storage, and handling of property transported by railroad, and any receiver, trustee, or other individual or body, judicial or otherwise, when in the possession of the business of any such 'carrier': *Provided, however,* That the term 'carrier' shall not include any street, interurban, or suburban electric railway, unless such railway is operating as a part of a general steam-railroad system of transportation, but shall not exclude any part of the general steam-railroad system of transportation now or hereafter operated by any other motive power. The Interstate Commerce Commission is hereby authorized and directed upon request of the Mediation Board or upon complaint of any party interested to determine after hearing whether any line operated by electric power falls within the terms of this proviso.

"Second. The term 'Adjustment Board' means the National Railroad Adjustment Board created by this Act.

"Third. The term 'Mediation Board' means the National Mediation Board created by this Act.

"Fourth. The term 'commerce' means commerce among the several States

386

or between any State, Territory, or the District of Columbia and any foreign nation, or between any Territory or the District of Columbia and any State, or between any Territory and any other Territory, or between any Territory and the District of Columbia, or within any Territory or the District of Columbia, or between points in the same State but through any other State or any Territory or the District of Columbia or any foreign nation.

"Fifth. The term 'employee' as used herein includes every person in the service of a carrier (subject to its continuing authority to supervise and direct the manner of rendition of his service) who performs any work defined as that of an employee or subordinate official in the orders of the Interstate Commerce Commission now in effect, and as the same may be amended or interpreted by orders hereafter entered by the Commission pursuant to the authority which is hereby conferred upon it to enter orders amending or interpreting such existing orders: *Provided, however,* That no occupational classification made by order of the Interstate Commerce Commission shall be construed to define the crafts according to which railway employees may be organized by their voluntary action, nor shall the jurisdiction or powers of such employee organizations be regarded as in any way limited or defined by the provisions of this Act or by the orders of the Commission.

"Sixth. The term 'representative' means any person or persons, labor union, organization, or corporation designated either by a carrier or group of carriers or by its or their employees, to act for it or them.

"Seventh. The term 'district court' includes the Supreme Court of the District of Columbia; and the term 'circuit court of appeals' includes the Court of Appeals of the District of Columbia.

"This Act may be cited as the 'Railway Labor Act.' "

SEC. 2. Section 2 of the Railway Labor Act is amended to read as follows:

"General Purposes

"SEC. 2. The purposes of the Act are: (1) To avoid any interruption to commerce or to the operation of any carrier engaged therein; (2) to forbid any limitation upon freedom of association among employees or any denial, as a condition of employment or otherwise, of the right of employees to join a labor organization; (3) to provide for the complete independence of carriers and of employees in the matter of self-organization to carry out the purposes of this Act; (4) to provide for the prompt and orderly settlement of all disputes concerning rates of pay, rules, or working conditions; (5) to provide for the prompt and orderly settlement of all disputes growing out of grievances or out of the interpretation or application of agreements covering rates of pay, rules, or working conditions.

"General Duties

"First. It shall be the duty of all carriers, their officers, agents, and employees to exert every reasonable effort to make and maintain agreements concerning rates of pay, rules, and working conditions, and to settle all disputes, whether arising out of the application of such agreements or otherwise, in order to avoid any interruption to commerce or to the operation of any carrier growing out of any dispute between the carrier and the employees thereof.

"Second. All disputes between a carrier or carriers and its or their employees shall be considered, and, if possible, decided, with all expedition, in conference between representatives designated and authorized so to confer, respectively, by the carrier or carriers and by the employees thereof interested in the dispute.

"Third. Representatives, for the purposes of this Act, shall be designated by the respective parties without interference, influence, or coercion by either party over the designation of representatives by the other; and neither party shall in any way interfere with, influence, or coerce the other in its choice of representatives. Representatives of employees for the purposes of this Act need not be persons in the employ of the carrier, and no carrier shall by interference, influence, or coercion seek in any manner to prevent the designation by its employees as their representatives of those who or which are not employees of the carrier.

"Fourth. Employees shall have the right to organize and bargain collectively through representatives of their own choosing. The majority of any craft or class of employees shall have the right to determine who shall be the representative of the craft or class for the purposes of this Act. No carrier, its officers or agents, shall deny or in any way question the right of its employees to join, organize, or assist in organizing the labor organization of their choice, and it shall be unlawful for any carrier to interfere in any way with the organization of its employees, or to use the funds of the carrier in maintaining or assisting or contributing to any labor organization, labor representative, or other agency of collective bargaining, or in performing any work therefor, or to influence or coerce employees in an effort to induce them to join or remain or not to join or remain members of any labor organization, or to deduct from the wages of employees any dues, fees, assessments, or other contributions payable to labor organizations, or to collect or to assist in the collection of any such dues, fees, assessments, or other contributions: *Provided,* That nothing in this Act shall be construed to prohibit a carrier from permitting an employee, individually, or local representatives of employees from conferring with management during working hours without loss of time, or to prohibit a carrier from furnishing free transportation to its employees while engaged in the business of a labor organization.

"Fifth. No carrier, its officers, or agents shall require any person seeking employment to sign any contract or agreement promising to join or not to join a labor organization; and if any such contract has been enforced prior to the effective date of this Act, then such carrier shall notify the employees by an appropriate order that such contract has been discarded and is no longer binding on them in any way.

"Sixth. In case of a dispute between a carrier or carriers and its or their employees, arising out of grievances or out of the interpretation or application of agreements concerning rates of pay, rules, or working conditions, it shall be the duty of the designated representative or representatives of such carrier or carriers and of such employees, within ten days after the receipt of notice of a desire on the part of either party to confer in respect to such dispute, to specify a time and place at which such conference shall be held; *Provided,* (1) That the place so specified shall be situated upon the line of the carrier involved or as otherwise mutually agreed upon; and (2) that the time so specified shall allow the designated conferees reasonable opportunity to reach such place of conference, but shall not exceed twenty days from the receipt of such notice: *And provided further,* That nothing in this Act shall be construed to supersede the provisions of any agreement (as to conferences) then in effect between the parties.

"Seventh. No carrier, its officers or agents shall change the rates of pay, rules, or working conditions of its employees, as a class as embodied in agreements except in the manner prescribed in such agreements or in section 6 of this Act.

"Eighth. Every carrier shall notify its employees by printed notices in such form and posted at such times and places as shall be specified by the Mediation Board that all disputes between the carrier and its employees will be handled in accordance with the requirements of this Act, and in such notices there shall be printed verbatim, in large type, the third, fourth, and fifth paragraphs of this section. The provisions of said paragraphs are hereby made a part of the contract of employment between the carrier and each employee, and shall be held binding upon the parties, regardless of any other express or implied agreements between them.

"Ninth. If any dispute shall arise among a carrier's employees as to who are the representatives of such employees designated and authorized in accordance with the requirements of this Act, it shall be the duty of the Mediation Board, upon request of either party to the dispute, to investigate such dispute and to certify to both parties, in writing, within thirty days after the receipt of the invocation of its services, the name or names of the individuals or organizations that have been designated and authorized to represent the employees involved in the dispute, and certify the same to the carrier. Upon receipt of such certification the carrier shall treat with the representative so certified as the representative of the craft or class for the purposes of this Act. In such an investigation, the Mediation Board shall be authorized to take a secret ballot of the employees involved, or to utilize any other appropriate method of ascertaining the names of their duly designated and authorized representatives in such manner as shall insure the choice of representatives by the employees without interference, influence, or coercion exercised by the carrier. In the conduct of any election for the purposes herein indicated the Board shall designate who may participate in the election and establish the rules to govern the election, or may appoint a committee of three neutral persons who after hearing shall within ten days designate the employees who may participate in the election. The Board shall have access to and have power to make copies of the books and records of the carriers to obtain and utilize such information as may be deemed necessary by it to carry out the purposes and provisions of this paragraph.

"Tenth. The willful failure or refusal of any carrier, its officers or agents to comply with the terms of the third, fourth, fifth, seventh, or eighth paragraph of this section shall be a misdemeanor, and upon conviction thereof the carrier, officer, or agent offending shall be subject to a fine of not less than \$1,000 nor more than \$20,000 or imprisonment for not more than six months, or both fine and imprisonment, for each offense, and each day during which such carrier, officer, or agent shall willfully fail or refuse to comply with the terms of the said paragraphs of this section shall constitute a separate offense. It shall be the duty of any district attorney of the United States to whom any duly designated representative of a carrier's employees may apply to institute in the proper court and to prosecute under the direction of the Attorney General of the United States, all necessary proceedings for the enforcement of the provisions of this section, and for the punishment of all violations thereof and the costs and expenses of such prosecution shall be paid out of the appropriation for the expenses of the courts of the United States: *Provided,* That nothing in this Act shall be construed to require an individual employee to render labor or service without his consent, nor shall anything in this Act be construed to make the quitting of his labor by an individual employee an illegal act; nor shall any court issue any process to compel the performance by an individual employee of such labor or service, without his consent."

SEC. 3. Section 3 of the Railway Labor Act is amended to read as follows:

"National Board of Adjustment—Grievances— Interpretation of Agreements

"SEC. 3. First. There is hereby established a Board, to be known as the 'National Railroad Adjustment Board,' the members of which shall be selected within thirty days after approval of this Act, and it is hereby provided

"(a) That the said Adjustment Board shall consist of thirty-six members, eighteen of whom shall be selected by the carriers and eighteen by such labor organizations of the employees, national in scope, as have been or may be organized in accordance with the provisions of section 2 of this Act.

"(b) The carriers, acting each through its board of directors or its receiver or receivers, trustee or trustees or through an officer or officers designated for that purpose by such board, trustee or trustees or receiver or receivers, shall prescribe the rules under which its representatives shall be selected and shall select the representatives of the carriers on the Adjustment Board and designate the division on which each such representative shall serve, but no carrier or system of carriers shall have more than one representative on any division of the Board.

"(c) The national labor organizations, as defined in paragraph (a) of this section, acting each through the chief executive or other medium designated by the organization or association thereof, shall prescribe the rules under which the labor members of the Adjustment Board shall be selected and shall select such members and designate the division on which each member shall serve; but no labor organization shall have more than one representative on any division of the Board.

"(d) In case of a permanent or temporary vacancy on the Adjustment Board, the vacancy shall be filled by selection in the same manner as in the original selection.

"(e) If either the carriers or the labor organizations of the employees fail to select and designate representatives to the Adjustment Board, as provided in paragraphs (b) and (c) of this section, respectively, within sixty days after the passage of this Act, in case of any original appointment to office of a member of the Adjustment Board, or in case of a vacancy in any such office within thirty days after such vacancy occurs, the Mediation Board shall thereupon directly make the appointment and shall select an individual associated in interest with the carriers or the group of labor organizations of employees, whichever he is to represent.

"(f) In the event a dispute arises as to the right of any national labor organization to participate as per paragraph (c) of this section in the selection and designation of the labor members of the Adjustment Board, the Secretary of Labor shall investigate the claim of such labor organization to participate, and if such claim in the judgment of the Secretary of Labor has merit, the Secretary shall notify the Mediation Board accordingly, and within ten days after receipt of such advice the Mediation Board shall request those national labor organizations duly qualified as per paragraph (c) of this section to participate in the selection and designation of the labor members of the Adjustment Board to select a representative. Such representative, together with a representative likewise designated by the claimant, and a third or neutral party designated by the Mediation Board, constituting a board of three, shall within thirty days after the appointment of the neutral member, investigate the claims of the labor organization desiring participation and decide whether or not it was organized in accordance with section 2 hereof and is otherwise properly qualified to participate in the selection of the labor members of the Adjustment Board, and the findings of such boards of three shall be final and binding.

"(g) Each member of the Adjustment Board shall be compensated by the party or parties he is to represent. Each third or neutral party selected under the provisions of (f) of this section shall receive from the Mediation Board such compensation as the Mediation Board may fix, together with his necessary traveling expenses and expenses actually incurred for subsistence, or per diem allowance in lieu thereof, subject to the provisions of law applicable thereto, while serving as such third or neutral party.

"(h) The said Adjustment Board shall be composed of four divisions, whose proceedings shall be independent of one another, and the said divisions as well as the number of their members shall be as follows:

"First division: To have jurisdiction over disputes involving train- and yard-service employees of carriers; that is, engineers, firemen, hostlers, and outside hostler helpers, conductors, trainmen, and yard-service employees. This division shall consist of ten members, five of whom shall be selected and designated by the carriers and five of whom shall be selected and designated by the national labor organizations of the employees.

"Second division: To have jurisdiction over disputes involving machinists, boilermakers, blacksmiths, sheet-metal workers, electrical workers, car men, the helpers and apprentices of all the foregoing, coach cleaners, power-house employees, and railroad-shop laborers. This division shall consist of ten members, five of whom shall be selected by the carriers and five by the national labor organizations of the employees.

"Third division: To have jurisdiction over disputes involving station, tower, and telegraph employees, train dispatchers, maintenance-of-way men, clerical employees, freight handlers, express, station, and store employees, signal men, sleeping-car conductors, sleeping-car porters, and maids and dining-car employees. This division shall consist of ten members, five of whom shall be selected by the carriers and five by the national labor organizations of employees.

"Fourth division: To have jurisdiction over disputes involving employees of carriers directly or indirectly engaged in transportation of passengers or property by water, and all other employees of carriers over which jurisdiction is not given to the first, second, and third divisions. This division shall consist of six members, three of whom shall be selected by the carriers and three by the national labor organizations of the employees.

"(i) The disputes between an employee or group of employees and a carrier or carriers growing out of grievances or out of the interpretation or application of agreements concerning rates of pay, rules, or working conditions, including cases pending and unadjusted on the date of approval of this Act, shall be handled in the usual manner up to and including the chief operating officer of the carrier designated to handle such disputes; but, failing to reach an adjustment in this manner, the disputes may be referred by petition of the parties or by either party to the appropriate division of the Adjustment Board with a full statement of the facts and all supporting data bearing upon the disputes.

"(j) Parties may be heard either in person, by counsel, or by other representatives, as they may respectively elect, and the several divisions of the Adjustment Board shall give due notice of all hearings to the employee or employees and the carrier or carriers involved in any disputes submitted to them.

"(k) Any division of the Adjustment Board shall have authority to empower two or more of its members to conduct hearings and make findings upon disputes, when properly submitted, at any place designated by the division: *Provided, however,* That final awards as to any such dispute must be made by the entire division as hereinafter provided.

"(l) Upon failure of any division to agree upon an award because of a deadlock or inability to secure a majority vote of the division members, as provided in paragraph (n) of this section, then such division shall forthwith agree upon and select a neutral person, to be known as 'referee,' to sit with the division as a member thereof and make an award. Should the division fail to agree upon and select a referee within ten days of the date of the deadlock or inability to secure a majority vote, then the division, or any member thereof, or the parties or either party to the dispute may certify that fact to the Mediation Board, which Board shall, within ten days from the date of receiving such certificate, select and name the referee to sit with the division as a member thereof and make an award. The Mediation Board shall be bound by the same provisions in the appointment of these neutral referees as are provided elsewhere in this Act for the appointment of arbitrators and shall fix and pay the compensation of such referees.

"(m) The awards of the several divisions of the Adjustment Board shall be stated in writing. A copy of the awards shall be furnished to the respective parties to the controversy, and the awards shall be final and binding upon both parties to the dispute, except insofar as they shall contain a money award. In case a dispute arises involving an interpretation of the award the division of the Board upon request of either party shall interpret the award in the light of the dispute.

"(n) A majority vote of all members of the division of the Adjustment Board shall be competent to make an award with respect to any dispute submitted to it.

"(o) In case of an award by any division of the Adjustment Board in favor of petitioner, the division of the Board shall make an order, directed to the carrier, to make the award effective and, if the award includes a requirement for the payment of money, to pay to the employee the sum to which he is entitled under the award on or before a day named.

"(p) If a carrier does not comply with an order of a division of the Adjustment Board within the time limit in such order, the petitioner, or any person for whose benefit such order was made, may file in the District Court of the United States for the district in which he resides or in which is located the principal operating office of the carrier, or through which the carrier operates, a petition setting forth briefly the causes for which he claims relief, and the order of the division of the Adjustment Board in the premises. Such suit in the District Court of the United States shall proceed in all respects as other civil suits, except that on the trial of such suit the findings and order of the division of the Adjustment Board shall be prima facie evidence of the facts therein stated, and except that the petitioner shall not be liable for costs in the district court nor for costs at any subsequent stage of the proceedings, unless they accrue upon his appeal, and such costs shall be paid out of the appropriation for the expenses of the courts of the United States. If the petitioner shall finally prevail he shall be allowed a reasonable attorney's fee, to be taxed and collected as a part of the costs of the suit. The district courts are empowered, under the rules of the court governing actions at law, to make such order and enter such judgment, by writ of mandamus or otherwise, as may be appropriate to enforce or set aside the order of the division of the Adjustment Board.

"(q) All actions at law based upon the provisions of this section shall be begun within two years from the time the cause of action accrues under the award of the division of the Adjustment Board, and not after.

"(r) The several divisions of the Adjustment Board shall maintain headquarters in Chicago, Illinois, meet regularly, and continue in session so long as there is pending before the division any matter within its jurisdiction which has been submitted for its consideration and which has not been disposed of.

"(s) Whenever practicable, the several divisions or subdivisions of the Adjustment Board shall be supplied with suitable quarters in any Federal building located at its place of meeting.

"(t) The Adjustment Board may, subject to the approval of the Mediation Board, employ and fix the compensations of such assistants as it deems necessary in carrying on its proceedings. The compensation of such employees shall be paid by the Mediation Board.

"(u) The Adjustment Board shall meet within forty days after the approval of this Act and adopt such rules as it deems necessary to control proceedings before the respective divisions and not in conflict with the provisions of this section. Immediately following the meeting of the entire Board and the adoption of such rules, the respective divisions shall meet and organize by the selection of a chairman, a vice chairman, and a secretary. Thereafter each division shall annually designate one of its members to act as chairman and one of its members to act as vice chairman: *Provided, however,* That the chairmanship and vice-chairmanship of any division shall alternate as between the groups, so that both the chairmanship and vice-chairmanship shall be held alternately by a representative of the carriers and a representative of the employees. In case of a vacancy, such vacancy shall be filled for the unexpired term by the selection of a successor from the same group.

"(v) Each division of the Adjustment Board shall annually prepare and submit a report of its activities to the Mediation Board, and the substance of such report shall be included in the annual report of the Mediation Board to the Congress of the United States. The reports of each division of the Adjustment Board and the annual report of the Mediation Board shall state in detail all cases heard, all actions taken, the names, salaries, and duties of all agencies, employees, and officers receiving compensation from the United States under the authority of this Act, and an account of all moneys appropriated by Congress pursuant to the authority conferred by this Act and disbursed by such agencies, employees, and officers.

"(w) Any division of the Adjustment Board shall have authority, in its discretion, to establish regional adjustment boards to act in its place and stead for such limited period as such division may determine to be necessary. Carrier members of such regional boards shall be designated in keeping with rules devised for this purpose by the carrier members of the Adjustment Board and the labor members shall be designated in keeping with rules devised for this purpose by the labor members of the Adjustment Board. Any such regional board shall, during the time for which it is appointed, have the same authority to conduct hearings, make findings upon disputes and adopt the same procedure as the division of the Adjustment Board appointing it, and its decisions shall be enforceable to the same extent and under the same processes. A neutral person, as referee, shall be appointed for service in connection with any such regional adjustment board in the same circumstances and manner as provided in paragraph (1) hereof, with respect to a division of the Adjustment Board.

"Second. Nothing in this section shall be construed to prevent any individual carrier, system, or group of carriers and any class or classes of its or their employees, all acting through their representatives, selected in accordance with the provisions of this Act, from mutually agreeing to the establishment of system, group, or regional boards of adjustment for the purpose of adjusting and deciding disputes of the character specified in this section. In the event that either party to such a system, group, or regional board of adjustment is dissatisfied with such arrangement, it may upon ninety days' notice to the other party elect to come under the jurisdiction of the Adjustment Board."

Section 4 of the Railway Labor Act is amended to read as follows:

"National Mediation Board

"SEC. 4. First. The Board of Mediation is hereby abolished, effective thirty days from the approval of this Act and the members, secretary, officers, assistants, employees, and agents thereof, in office upon the date of the approval of this Act, shall continue to function and receive their salaries for a period of thirty days from such date in the same manner as though this Act had not been passed. There is hereby established, as an independent agency in the executive branch of the Government, a board to be known as the 'National Mediation Board,' to be composed of three members appointed by the President, by and with the advice and consent of the Senate, not more than two of whom shall be of the same political party. The terms of office of the members first appointed shall begin as soon as the members shall qualify, but not before thirty days after the approval of this Act, and expire, as designated by the President at the time of nomination, one on February 1, 1935, one on February 1, 1936, and one on February 1, 1937. The terms of office of all successors shall expire three years after the expiration of the terms for which their predecessors were appointed; but any member appointed to fill a vacancy occurring prior to the expiration of the term for which his predecessor was appointed shall be appointed only for the unexpired term of his predecessor. Vacancies in the Board shall not impair the powers nor affect the duties of the Board nor of the remaining members of the Board. Two of the members in office shall constitute a quorum for the transaction of the business of the Board. Each member of the Board shall receive a salary at the rate of $10,000 per annum, together with necessary traveling and subsistence expenses, or per diem allowance in lieu thereof, subject to the provisions of law applicable thereto, while away from the principal office of the Board on business required by this Act. No person in the employment of or who is pecuniarily or otherwise interested in any organization of employees or any carrier shall enter upon the duties of or continue to be a member of the Board.

"All cases referred to the Board of Mediation and unsettled on the date of the approval of this Act shall be handled to conclusion by the Mediation Board.

"A member of the Board may be removed by the President for inefficiency, neglect of duty, malfeasance in office, or ineligibility, but for no other cause.

"Second. The Mediation Board shall annually designate a member to act as chairman. The Board shall maintain its principal office in the District of Columbia, but it may meet at any other place whenever it deems it necessary so to do. The Board may designate one or more of its members to exercise the functions of the Board in mediation proceedings. Each member of the Board shall have power to administer oaths and affirmations. The Board shall have a seal which shall be judicially noticed. The Board shall make an annual report to Congress.

"Third. The Mediation Board may (1) appoint such experts and assistants to act in a confidential capacity and, subject to the provisions of the civil-service laws, such other officers and employees as are essential to the effective transaction of the work of the Board; (2) in accordance with the Classification Act of 1923, fix the salaries of such experts, assistants, officers, and employees; and (3) make such expenditures (including expenditures for rent and personal services at the seat of government and elsewhere, for law books, periodicals, and books of reference, and for printing and binding, and including expenditures for salaries and compensation, necessary traveling expenses and expenses actually incurred for subsistence, and other necessary expenses of the Mediation Board, Adjustment Board, Regional Adjustment Boards established under paragraph (w) of section 3, and boards of arbitration, in accordance with the provisions of this section and sections 3 and 7, respectively), as may be necessary for the execution of the functions vested in the Board, in the Adjustment Board and in the boards of arbitration, and as may be provided for by the Congress from time to time. All expenditures of the Board shall be allowed and paid on the presentation of itemized vouchers therefor approved by the chairman.

"Fourth. The Mediation Board is hereby authorized by its order to assign, or refer, any portion of its work, business, or functions arising under this or any other Act of Congress, or referred to it by Congress or either branch thereof, to an individual member of the Board or to an employee or employees of the Board to be designated by such order for action thereon, and by its order at any time to amend, modify, supplement, or rescind any such assignment or reference. All such orders shall take effect forthwith and remain in effect until otherwise ordered by the Board. In conformity with and subject to the order or orders of the Mediation Board in the premises, and such individual member of the Board or employee designated shall have power and authority to act as to any of said work, business, or functions so assigned or referred to him for action by the Board.

"Fifth. All officers and employees of the Board of Mediation (except the members thereof, whose offices are hereby abolished) whose services in the judgment of the Mediation Board are necessary to the efficient operation of the Board are hereby transferred to the Board, without change in classification or compensation; except that the Board may provide for the adjustment of such classification or compensation to conform to the duties to which such officers and employees may be assigned.

"All unexpended appropriations for the operation of the Board of Mediation that are available at the time of the abolition of the Board of Mediation shall be transferred to the Mediation Board and shall be available for its use for salaries and other authorized expenditures."

SEC. 5. Section 5 of the Railway Labor Act is amended to read as follows:

"Functions of Mediation Board

"SEC. 5. First. The parties, or either party, to a dispute between an employee or group of employees and a carrier may invoke the services of the Mediation Board in any of the following cases:

"(a) A dispute concerning changes in rates of pay, rules, or working conditions not adjusted by the parties in conference.

"(b) Any other dispute not referable to the National Railroad Adjustment Board and not adjusted in conference between the parties or where conferences are refused.

"The Mediation Board may proffer its services in case any labor emergency is found by it to exist at any time.

"In either event the said Board shall promptly put itself in communication with the parties to such controversy, and shall use its best efforts, by mediation, to bring them to agreement. If such efforts to bring about an amicable settlement through mediation shall be unsuccessful, the said Board shall at once endeavor as its final required action (except as provided in paragraph third of this section and in section 10 of this Act) to induce the parties to submit their controversy to arbitration, in accordance with the provisions of this Act.

"If arbitration at the request of the Board shall be refused by one or both parties, the Board shall at once notify both parties in writing that its mediatory efforts have failed and for thirty days thereafter, unless in the intervening period the parties agree to arbitration, or an emergency board shall be created under section 10 of this Act, no change shall be made in the rates of pay, rules, or working conditions or established practices in effect prior to the time the dispute arose.

"Second. In any case in which a controversy arises over the meaning or the application of any agreement reached through mediation under the provisions of this Act, either party to the said agreement, or both, may apply to the Mediation Board for an interpretation of the meaning or application of such agreement. The said Board shall upon receipt of such request notify the parties to the controversy, and after a hearing of both sides give its interpretation within thirty days.

"Third. The Mediation Board shall have the following duties with respect to the arbitration of disputes under section 7 of this Act:

"(a) On failure of the arbitrators named by the parties to agree on the remaining arbitrator or arbitrators within the time set by section 7 of this Act, it shall be the duty of the Mediation Board to name such remaining arbitrator or arbitrators. It shall be the duty of the Board in naming such arbitrator or arbitrators to appoint only those whom the Board shall deem wholly disinterested in the controversy to be arbitrated and impartial and without bias as between the parties to such arbitration. Should, however, the Board name an arbitrator or arbitrators not so disinterested and impartial, then, upon proper investigation and presentation of the facts, the Board shall promptly remove such arbitrator.

"If an arbitrator named by the Mediation Board, in accordance with the provisions of this Act, shall be removed by such Board as provided by this Act, or if such an arbitrator refuses or is unable to serve, it shall be the duty of the Mediation Board, promptly, to select another arbitrator, in the same manner as provided in this Act for an original appointment by the Mediation Board.

"(b) Any member of the Mediation Board is authorized to take the acknowledgment of an agreement to arbitrate under this Act. When so acknowledged, or when acknowledged by the parties before a notary public or the clerk of a district court or a circuit court of appeals of the United States, such agreement to arbitrate shall be delivered to a member of said Board or transmitted to said Board, to be filed in its office.

"(c) When an agreement to arbitrate has been filed with the Mediation Board, or with one of its members, as provided by this section, and when the said Board has been furnished the names of the arbitrators chosen by the parties to the controversy it shall be the duty of the Board to cause a notice in writing to be served upon said arbitrators, notifying them of their appointment, requesting them to meet promptly to name the remaining arbitrator or arbitrators necessary to complete the Board of Arbitration, and advising them of the period within which, as provided by the agreement to arbitrate, they are empowered to name such arbitrator or arbitrators.

"(d) Either party to an arbitration desiring the reconvening of a board of arbitration to pass upon any controversy arising over the meaning or application of an award may so notify the Mediation Board in writing, stating in such notice the question or questions to be submitted to such reconvened Board. The Mediation Board shall thereupon promptly communicate with the members of the Board of Arbitration, or a subcommittee of such Board appointed for such purpose pursuant to a provision in the agreement to arbitrate, and arrange for the reconvening of said Board of Arbitration or subcommittee, and shall notify the respective parties to the controversy of the time and place at which the Board, or the subcommittee, will meet for hearings upon the matters in controversy to be submitted to it. No evidence other than that contained in the record filed with the original award shall be received or considered by such reconvened Board or subcommittee, except such evidence as may be necessary to illustrate the interpretations suggested by the parties. If any member of the original Board is unable or unwilling to serve on such reconvened Board or subcommittee thereof, another arbitrator shall be named in the same manner and with the same powers and duties as such original arbitrator.

"(e) Within sixty days after the approval of this Act every carrier shall file with the Mediation Board a copy of each contract with its employees in effect on the 1st day of April 1934, covering rates of pay, rules, and working conditions. If no contract with any craft or class of its employees has been entered into, the carrier shall file with the Mediation Board a statement of that fact including also a statement of the rates of pay, rules, and working conditions applicable in dealing with such craft or class. When any new contract is executed or change is made in an existing contract with any class or craft of its employees covering rates of pay, rules, or working conditions, or in those rates of pay, rules, and working conditions of employees not covered by contract, the carrier shall file the same with the Mediation Board within thirty days after such new contract or change in existing contract has been executed or rates of pay, rules, and working conditions have been made effective.

"(f) The Mediation Board shall be the custodian of all papers and documents heretofore filed with or transferred to the Board of Mediation bearing upon the settlement, adjustment, or determination of disputes between carriers and their employees or upon mediation or arbitration proceedings held under or pursuant to the provisions of any Act of Congress in respect thereto; and the President is authorized to designate a custodian of the records and property of the Board of Mediation until the transfer and delivery of such records to the Mediation Board and to require the transfer and delivery to the Mediation Board of any and all such papers and documents filed with it or in its possession."

SEC. 6. Section 6 of the Railway Labor Act is amended to read as follows:

"SEC. 6. Carriers and representatives of the employees shall give at least thirty days' written notice of an intended change in agreements affecting rates of pay, rules, or working conditions, and the time and place for the beginning of conference between the representatives of the parties interested in such intended changes shall be agreed upon within ten days after the receipt of said notice, and said time shall be within the thirty days provided in the notice. In every case where such notice of intended change has been given, or conferences are being held with reference thereto, or the services of the Mediation Board have been requested by either party, or said Board has proffered its services, rates of pay, rules, or working conditions shall not be altered by the carrier until the controversy has been finally acted upon as required by section 5 of this Act, by the Mediation Board, unless a period of ten days has elapsed after termination of conferences without request for or proffer of the services of the Mediation Board."

SEC. 7. The Railway Labor Act is amended by striking out the words "Board of Mediation" wherever they appear in sections 7, 8, 10, and 12 of such Act, and inserting in lieu thereof the words "Mediation Board."

SEC. 8. If any section, subsection, sentence, clause, or phrase of this Act is for any reason held to be unconstitutional, such decision shall not affect the validity of the remaining portions of this Act. All Acts or parts of Acts inconsistent with the provisions of this Act are hereby repealed.

Approved, June 21, 1934.

The 1936 Amendment to the Railway Labor Act

An Act to amend the Railway Labor Act.

Be it enacted by the Senate and House of Representatives of the United States of America in Congress assembled, That the Railway Labor Act, approved May 20, 1926, as amended, herein referred to as "Title I," is hereby further amended by inserting after the enacting clause the caption "Title I" and by adding the following title II:

"TITLE II

"SECTION 201. All of the provisions of title I of this Act, except the provisions of section 3 thereof, are extended to and shall cover every common carrier by air engaged in interstate or foreign commerce, and every carrier by air transporting mail for or under contract with the United States Government, and every air pilot or other person who performs any work as an employee or subordinate official of such carrier or carriers, subject to its or their continuing authority to supervise and direct the manner of rendition of his service.

"SEC. 202. The duties, requirements, penalties, benefits, and privileges prescribed and established by the provisions of title I of this Act, except section 3 thereof, shall apply to said carriers by air and their employees in the same manner and to the same extent as though such carriers and their employees were specifically included within the definition of 'carrier' and 'employee,' respectively, in section 1 thereof.

"SEC. 203. The parties or either party to a dispute between an employee or a group of employees and a carrier or carriers by air may invoke the services of the National Mediation Board and the jurisdiction of said Mediation Board is extended to any of the following cases:

"(a) A dispute concerning changes in rates of pay, rules, or working conditions not adjusted by the parties in conference.

"(b) Any other dispute not referable to an adjustment board, as hereinafter provided, and not adjusted in conference between the parties, or where conferences are refused.

"The National Mediation Board may proffer its services in case any labor emergency is found by it to exist at any time.

"The services of the Mediation Board may be invoked in a case under this title in the same manner and to the same extent as are the disputes covered by section 5 of title I of this Act.

"sec. 204. The disputes between an employee or group of employees and a carrier or carriers by air growing out of grievances, or out of the interpretation or application of agreements concerning rates of pay, rules, or working conditions, including cases pending and unadjusted on the date of approval of this Act before the National Labor Relations Board, shall be handled in the usual manner up to and including the chief operating officer of the carrier designated to handle such disputes; but, failing to reach an adjustment in this manner, the disputes may be referred by petition of the parties or by either party to an appropriate adjustment board, as hereinafter provided, with a full statement of the facts and supporting data bearing upon the disputes.

"It shall be the duty of every carrier and of its employees, acting through their representatives, selected in accordance with the provisions of this title, to establish a board of adjustment of jurisdiction not exceeding the jurisdiction which may be lawfully exercised by system, group, or regional boards of adjustment, under the authority of section 3, Title I, of this Act.

"Such boards of adjustment may be established by agreement between employees and carriers either on any individual carrier, or system, or group of carriers by air and any class or classes of its or their employees; or pending the establishment of a permanent National Board of Adjustment as hereinafter provided. Nothing in this Act shall prevent said carriers by air, or any class or classes of their employees, both acting through their representatives selected in accordance with provisions of this title, from mutually agreeing to the establishment of a National Board of Adjustment of temporary duration and of similarly limited jurisdiction.

"sec. 205. When, in the judgment of the National Mediation Board, it shall be necessary to have a permanent national board of adjustment in order to provide for the prompt and orderly settlement of disputes between said carriers by air, or any of them, and its or their employees, growing out of grievances or out of the interpretation or application of agreements between said carriers by air or any of them, and any class or classes of its or their employees, covering rates of pay, rules, or working conditions, the National Mediation Board is hereby empowered and directed, by its order duly made, published, and served, to direct the said carriers by air and such labor organizations of their employees, national in scope, as have been or may be recognized in accordance with the provisions of this Act, to select and designate four representatives who shall constitute a board which shall be known as the 'National Air Transport Adjustment Board.' Two members of said National Air Transport Adjustment Board shall be selected by said carriers by air and two members by the said labor organizations of the employees, within thirty days after the date of the order of the National Mediation Board, in the manner and by the procedure prescribed by title I of this Act for the selection and designation of members of the National Railroad Adjustment Board. The National Air Transport Adjustment Board shall meet within forty days after the date of the order of the National Mediation

Board directing the selection and designation of its members and shall organize and adopt rules for conducting its proceedings, in the manner prescribed in section 3 of title I of this Act. Vacancies in membership or office shall be filled, members shall be appointed in case of failure of the carriers or of labor organizations of the employees to select and designate representatives, members of the National Air Transport Adjustment Board shall be compensated, hearings shall be held, findings and awards made, stated, served, and enforced, and the number and compensation of any necessary assistants shall be determined and the compensation of such employees shall be paid, all in the same manner and to the same extent as provided with reference to the National Railroad Adjustment Board by section 3 of title I of this Act. The powers and duties prescribed and established by the provisions of section 3 of title I of this Act with reference to the National Railroad Adjustment Board and the several divisions thereof are hereby conferred upon and shall be exercised and performed in like manner and to the same extent by the said National Air Transport Adjustment Board, not exceeding, however, the jurisdiction conferred upon said National Air Transport Adjustment Board by the provisions of this title. From and after the organization of the National Air Transport Adjustment Board, if any system, group, or regional board of adjustment established by any carrier or carriers by air and any class or classes of its or their employees is not satisfactory to either party thereto, the said party, upon ninety days' notice to the other party, may elect to come under the jurisdiction of the National Air Transport Adjustment Board.

"SEC. 206. All cases referred to the National Labor Relations Board, or over which the National Labor Relations Board shall have taken jurisdiction, involving any dispute arising from any cause between any common carrier by air engaged in interstate or foreign commerce or any carrier by air transporting mail for or under contract with the United States Government, and employees of such carrier or carriers, and unsettled on the date of approval of this Act, shall be handled to conclusion by the Mediation Board. The books, records, and papers of the National Labor Relations Board and of the National Labor Board pertinent to such case or cases, whether settled or unsettled, shall be transferred to the custody of the National Mediation Board.

"SEC. 207. If any provision of this title or application thereof to any person or circumstance is held invalid, the remainder of the Act and the application of such provision to other persons or circumstances shall not be affected thereby.

"SEC. 208. There is hereby authorized to be appropriated such sums as may be necessary for expenditure by the Mediation Board in carrying out the provisions of this Act."

Approved, April 10, 1936.

The Anti-Injunction Act

The Norris-LaGuardia Act
Act of March 23, 1932, 72d Congress

An Act to amend the Judicial Code and to define and limit the jurisdiction of courts sitting in equity, and for other purposes.

Be it enacted by the Senate and House of Representatives of the United States of America in Congress assembled,

[Injunctions in Labor Disputes]

SECTION 1. That no court of the United States, as herein defined, shall have jurisdiction to issue any restraining order or temporary or permanent injunction in a case involving or growing out of a labor dispute, except in a strict conformity with the provisions of this Act; nor shall any such restraining order or temporary or permanent injunction be issued contrary to the public policy declared in this Act.

[Public Policy of Act—Right of Collective Bargaining]

SEC. 2. In the interpretation of this Act and in determining the jurisdiction and authority of the courts of the United States, as such jurisdiction and authority are herein defined and limited, the public policy of the United States is hereby declared as follows:

Whereas under prevailing economic conditions, developed with the aid of governmental authority for owners of property to organize in the corporate and other forms of ownership association, the individual unorganized worker is commonly helpless to exercise actual liberty of contract and to protect his freedom of labor, and thereby to obtain acceptable terms and conditions of employment, wherefore, though he should be free to decline to associate with his fellows, it is necessary that he have full freedom of association, self-organization, and designation of representatives of his own choosing, to negotiate the terms and conditions of his employment, and that he shall be free from the interference, restraint, or coercion of employers of labor, or their agents, in the designation of such representatives or in self-organization or in other concerted activities for the purpose of collective bargaining or other mutual aid or protection; therefore, the following definitions of, and limitations upon, the jurisdiction and authority of the courts of the United States are hereby enacted.

[Enforcement of Contracts—Contracts Forbidding Membership in Labor Unions Unenforceable]

SEC. 3. Any undertaking or promise, such as is described in this section, or any other undertaking or promise in conflict with the public policy declared in section 2 of this Act, is hereby declared to be contrary to the public policy of the United States, shall not be enforceable in any court of the United States and shall not afford any basis for the granting of legal or equitable relief by any such court, including specifically the following:

Every undertaking or promise hereafter made, whether written or oral; express or implied, constituting or contained in any contract or agreement of hiring or employment between any individual, firm, company, association, or corporation, and any employee or prospective employee of the same, whereby

(a) Either party to such contract or agreement undertakes or promises not to join, become, or remain a member of any labor organization or of any employer organization; or

(b) Either party to such contract or agreement undertakes or promises that he will withdraw from an employment relation in the event that he joins, becomes, or remains a member of any labor organization or of any employer organization.

[Limitation upon the Jurisdiction of Federal Courts to Issue Injunctions in Labor Disputes]

SEC. 4. No court of the United States shall have jurisdiction to issue any restraining order or temporary or permanent injunction in any case involving or growing out of any labor dispute to prohibit any person or persons participating or interested in such dispute (as these terms are herein defined) from doing, whether singly or in concert, any of the following acts:

(a) Ceasing or refusing to perform any work or to remain in any relation of employment;

(b) Becoming or remaining a member of any labor organization or of any employer organization, regardless of any such undertaking or promise as is described in section 3 of this Act;

(c) Paying or giving to, or withholding from, any person participating or interested in such labor dispute, any strike or unemployment benefits or insurance, or other moneys or things of value;

(d) By all lawful means aiding any person participating or interested in any labor dispute who is being proceeded against in, or is prosecuting, any action or suit in any court of the United States or of any State;

(e) Giving publicity to the existence of, or the facts involved in, any labor dispute, whether by advertising, speaking, patrolling, or by any other method not involving fraud or violence;

(f) Assembling peaceably to act or to organize to act in promotion of their interests in a labor dispute;

(g) Advising or notifying any person of an intention to do any of the acts heretofore specified;

(h) Agreeing with other persons to do or not to do any of the acts heretofore specified; and

(i) Advising, urging, or otherwise causing or inducing without fraud or violence the acts heretofore specified, regardless of any such undertaking or promise as is described in section 3 of this Act.

[Unlawful Combination]

SEC. 5. No court of the United States shall have jurisdiction to issue a restraining order or temporary or permanent injunction upon the ground that any of the persons participating or interested in a labor dispute constitute or are engaged in an unlawful combination or conspiracy because of the doing in concert of the acts enumerated in section 4 of this Act.

[Responsibility of Labor Unions for Acts of Individuals]

SEC. 6. No officer or member of any association or organization, and no association or organization participating or interested in a labor dispute, shall be held responsible or liable in any court of the United States for the unlawful acts of individual officers, members, or agents, except upon clear proof of actual participation in, or actual authorization of, such acts, or of ratification of such acts after actual knowledge thereof.

[Procedure in Issuing Injunctions in Labor Disputes]

SEC. 7. No court of the United States shall have jurisdiction to issue a temporary or permanent injunction in any case involving or growing out of a labor dispute, as herein defined, except after hearing the testimony of witnesses in open court (with opportunity for cross-examination) in support of the allegations of a complaint made under oath, and testimony in opposition thereto, if offered, and except after findings of fact by the court, to the effect

(a) That unlawful acts have been threatened and will be committed unless restrained or have been committed and will be continued unless restrained, but no injunction or temporary restraining order shall be issued on account of any threat or unlawful act excepting against the person or persons, association, or organization making the threat of committing the unlawful act or actually authorizing or ratifying the same after actual knowledge thereof;

(b) That substantial and irreparable injury to complainant's property will follow;

(c) That as to each item of relief granted greater injury will be inflicted upon complainant by the denial of relief than will be inflicted upon defendants by the granting of relief;

(d) That complainant has no adequate remedy at law; and

(e) That the public officers charged with the duty to protect complainant's property are unable or unwilling to furnish adequate protection.

Such hearing shall be held after due and personal notice thereof has been given, in such manner as the court shall direct, to all known persons against whom relief is sought, and also to the chief of those public officials of the county and city within which the unlawful acts have been threatened or committed charged with the duty to protect complainant's property: *Provided, however,* That if a complainant shall also allege that, unless a temporary restraining order shall be issued without notice, a substantial and irreparable injury to complainant's property will be unavoidable, such a temporary restraining order may be issued upon testimony under oath, sufficient, if sustained, to justify the court in issuing a temporary injunction upon a hearing after notice. Such a temporary restraining order shall be effective for no longer than five days and shall become void at the expiration of said five days. No temporary restraining order or temporary injunction shall be issued except on condition that complainant shall first file an undertaking with adequate security in an amount to be fixed by the court sufficient to recompense those enjoined for any loss, expense, or damage caused by the improvident or erroneous issuance of such order or injunction, including all reasonable costs (together with a reasonable attorney's fee) and expense of defense against the order or against the granting of any injunctive relief sought in the same proceeding and subsequently denied by the court.

The undertaking herein mentioned shall be understood to signify an agreement entered into by the complainant and the surety upon which a decree may be rendered in the same suit or proceeding against said complainant and surety, upon a hearing to assess damages of which hearing complainant and surety shall have reasonable notice, the said complainant and surety submitting themselves to the jurisdiction of the court for that purpose. But nothing herein contained shall deprive any party having a claim or cause of action under or upon such undertaking from electing to pursue his ordinary remedy by suit at law or in equity.

[Complainant Must Comply with Legal Obligations and Attempt to Settle Dispute by Negotiation or Arbitration]

sec. 8. No restraining order or injunctive relief shall be granted to any complainant who has failed to comply with any obligation imposed by law which is involved in the labor dispute in question, or who has failed to make every reasonable effort to settle such dispute either by negotiation or with the aid of any available governmental machinery of mediation or voluntary arbitration.

[Specific Acts Enjoined]

sec. 9. No restraining order or temporary or permanent injunction shall be granted in a case involving or growing out of a labor dispute, except on the basis of findings of fact made and filed by the court in the record of the case prior to the issuance of such restraining order or injunction; and every restraining order or injunction granted in a case involving or growing out of a labor dispute shall include only a prohibition of such specific act or acts as may be expressly complained of in the bill of complaint or petition filed in such case and as shall be expressly included in said findings of fact made and filed by the court as provided herein.

[Expediting Appeals Where Temporary Injunction is Issued]

sec. 10. Whenever any court of the United States shall issue or deny any temporary injunction in a case involving or growing out of a labor dispute, the court shall, upon the request of any party to the proceedings and on his filing the usual bond for costs, forthwith certify as in ordinary cases the record of the case to the circuit court of appeals for its review. Upon the filing of such record in the circuit court of appeals, the appeal shall be heard and the temporary injunctive order affirmed, modified, or set aside with the greatest possible expedition, giving the proceeding precedence over all other matters except older matters of the same character.

[Jury Trial in Contempt Cases]

sec. 11. Repealed.

Act of June 25, 1948, c. 645, § 21, 62 Stat. 862, effective September 1, 1948, repealed Section 11, which read as follows:

"sec. 11. In all cases arising under this Act in which a person shall be charged with contempt in a court of the United States (as herein defined), the accused shall enjoy the right to a speedy and public trial by an impartial jury of the State and district wherein the contempt shall have been committed: *Provided*, That this right shall not apply to contempts committed in the presence of the court or so near thereto as to interfere directly with the administration of justice or to apply to the misbehavior, misconduct, or disobedience of any officer of the court in respect to the writs, orders, or process of the court."

In place of the repealed section, the Act of June 25, 1948, c. 645, 62 Stat.

862, enacted the following provision as Section 3692 of Title 18—Crimes and Criminal Procedures:

"SEC. 3692. JURY TRIAL FOR CONTEMPT IN LABOR DISPUTE CASES. In all cases of contempt arising under the laws of the United States governing the issuance of injunctions or restraining orders in any case involving or growing out of a labor dispute, the accused shall enjoy the right to a speedy and public trial by an impartial jury of the State and district wherein the contempt shall have been committed.

"This section shall not apply to contempts committed in the presence of the court or so near thereto as to interfere directly with the administration of justice nor to the misbehavior, misconduct, or disobedience of any officer of the court in respect to the writs, orders or processes of the court."

[Designation of New Judge in Certain Contempt Cases]

SEC. 12. Repealed.

Act of June 25, 1948, c. 645, § 21, 62 Stat. 862, effective September 1, 1948, repealed Section 12, which read as follows:

"SEC. 12. The defendant in any proceeding for contempt of court may file with the court a demand for the retirement of the judge sitting in the proceeding, if the contempt arises from an attack upon the character or conduct of such judge and if the attack occurred elsewhere than in the presence of the court or so near thereto as to interfere directly with the administration of justice. Upon the filing of any such demand the judge shall thereupon proceed no further, but another judge shall be designated in the same manner as is provided by law. The demand shall be filed prior to the hearing in the contempt proceeding."

The subject formerly covered by the repealed section is now covered by portions of Rule 42 of the Rules of Criminal Procedure, which rules were prescribed by the United States Supreme Court under the authority of the Act of June 29, 1940, c. 445, 18 U.S.C. 687 (Proceedings in criminal cases prior to and including verdict; power of Supreme Court to prescribe rules) and the Act of November 21, 1941, c. 492, 18 U.S.C. 689 (Proceedings to punish for criminal contempt of court; application to sections 687 and 688).

Rule 42 of the Rules of Criminal Procedure reads as follows:

"RULE 42. CRIMINAL CONTEMPT. (a) *Summary Disposition*. A criminal contempt may be punished summarily if the judge certifies that he saw or heard the conduct constituting the contempt and that it was committed in the actual presence of the court. The order of contempt shall recite the facts and shall be signed by the judge and entered of record.

"(b) *Disposition upon Notice and Hearing*. A criminal contempt except as provided in subdivision (a) of this rule shall be prosecuted on notice. The notice shall state the time and place of hearing, allowing a reasonable time for the preparation of the defense, and shall state the essential facts constituting the criminal contempt charged and describe it as such. The notice shall be given orally by the judge in open court in the presence of the defendant or, on application of the United States Attorney or of an attorney appointed by the court for that purpose, by an order to show cause or an order of arrest. The defendant is entitled to a trial by jury in any case in which an act of Congress so provides. He is entitled to admission to bail as provided in these rules. If the contempt charged involves disrespect to or criticism of a judge, that judge is disqualified from presiding at the trial or hearing except with the defendant's consent. Upon a verdict or finding of guilt the court shall enter an order fixing the punishment."

Application of Act; Definitions; "Labor Dispute"

SEC. 13. When used in this act and for the purposes of this act

(a) A case shall be held to involve or to grow out of a labor dispute when the case involves persons who are engaged in the same industry, trade, craft, or occupation; or have direct or indirect interests therein; or who are employees of the same employer; or who are members of the same or an affiliated organization of employers or employees; whether such dispute is (1) between one or more employers or associations of employers and one or more employees or associations of employees; (2) between one or more employers or associations of employers and one or more employers or associations of employers; (3) between one or more employees or associations of employees and one or more employees or associations of employees; or when the case involves any conflicting or competing interests in a "labor dispute" (as hereinafter defined) of "persons participating or interested" therein (as hereinafter defined).

(b) A person or association shall be held to be a person participating or interested in a labor dispute if relief is sought against him or it, and if he or it is engaged in the same industry, trade, craft, or occupation in which such dispute occurs, or has a direct or indirect interest therein, or is a member, officer, or agent of any association composed in whole or in part of employers or employees engaged in such industry, trade, craft, or occupation.

(c) The term "labor dispute" includes any controversy concerning terms or conditions of employment, or concerning the association or representation of persons in negotiating, fixing, maintaining, changing, or seeking to arrange terms or conditions of employment, regardless of whether or not the disputants stand in the proximate relation of employer and employee.

(d) The term "court of the United States" means any court of the United States whose jurisdiction has been or may be conferred or defined or limited by Act of Congress, including the courts of the District of Columbia.

[Unconstitutionality of Part of Act]

SEC. 14. If any provision of this Act or the application thereof to any person or circumstance is held unconstitutional or otherwise invalid, the remaining provisions of the Act and the application of such provisions to other persons or circumstances shall not be affected thereby.

[Repealing Clause]

SEC. 15. All Acts and parts of Acts in conflict with the provisions of this Act are hereby repealed.

The National Labor Relations Act

The Wagner Act
Act of July 5, 1935, 74th Congress

An Act to diminish the causes of labor disputes burdening or obstructing interstate and foreign commerce, to create a National Labor Relations Board, and for other purposes.

Be it enacted by the Senate and House of Representatives of the United States of America in Congress assembled,

Findings and Policy

SECTION 1. The denial by employers of the right of employees to organize and the refusal by employers to accept the procedure of collective bargaining lead to strikes and other forms of industrial strife or unrest, which have the intent or the necessary effect of burdening or obstructing commerce by (a) impairing the efficiency, safety, or operation of the instrumentalities of commerce; (b) occurring in the current of commerce; (c) materially affecting, restraining, or controlling the flow of raw materials or manufactured or processed goods from or into the channels of commerce, or the prices of such materials or goods in commerce; or (d) causing diminution of employment and wages in such volume as substantially to impair or disrupt the market for goods flowing from or into the channels of commerce.

The inequality of bargaining power between employees who do not possess full freedom of association or actual liberty of contract, and employers who are organized in the corporate or other forms of ownership association substantially burdens and affects the flow of commerce, and tends to aggravate recurrent business depressions, by depressing wage rates and the purchasing power of wage earners in industry and by preventing the stabilization of competitive wage rates and working conditions within and between industries.

Experience has proved that protection by law of the right of employees to organize and bargain collectively safeguards commerce from injury, impairment, or interruption, and promotes the flow of commerce by removing certain recognized sources of industrial strife and unrest, by encouraging practices fundamental to the friendly adjustment of industrial disputes arising out of differences as to wages, hours, or other working conditions, and by restoring equality of bargaining power between employers and employees.

It is hereby declared to be the policy of the United States to eliminate the causes of certain substantial obstructions to the free flow of commerce and to mitigate and eliminate these obstructions when they have occurred by encouraging the practice and procedure of collective bargaining and by protecting the exercise by workers of full freedom of association, self-organization, and designation of representatives of their own choosing, for the purpose of negotiating the terms and conditions of their employment or other mutual aid or protection.

Definitions

SEC. 2. When used in this Act

(1) The term "person" includes one or more individuals, partnerships, associations, corporations, legal representatives, trustees, trustees in bankruptcy, or receivers.

(2) The term "employer" includes any person acting in the interest of an employer, directly or indirectly, but shall not include the United States, or any State or political subdivision thereof, or any person subject to the Railway Labor Act, as amended from time to time, or any labor organization (other than when acting as an employer), or anyone acting in the capacity of officer or agent of such labor organization.

(3) The term "employee" shall include any employee, and shall not be limited to the employees of a particular employer, unless the Act explicitly states otherwise, and shall include any individual whose work has ceased as a consequence of, or in connection with, any current labor dispute or because of any unfair labor practice, and who has not obtained any other regular and substantially equivalent employment, but shall not include any individual employed as an agricultural laborer, or in the domestic service of any family or person at his home, or any individual employed by his parent or spouse.

(4) The term "representatives" includes any individual or labor organization.

(5) The term "labor organization" means any organization of any kind, or any agency or employee representation committee or plan, in which employees participate and which exists for the purpose, in whole or in part, of dealing with employers concerning grievances, labor disputes, wages, rates of pay, hours of employment, or conditions of work.

(6) The term "commerce" means trade, traffic, commerce, transportation, or communication among the several States, or between the District of Columbia or any Territory of the United States and any State or other Territory, or between any foreign country and any State, Territory, or the

District of Columbia, or within the District of Columbia or any Territory, or between points in the same State but through any other State or any Territory or the District of Columbia or any foreign country.

(7) The term "affecting commerce" means in commerce, or burdening or obstructing commerce or the free flow of commerce, or having led or tending to lead to a labor dispute burdening or obstructing commerce or the free flow of commerce.

(8) The term "unfair labor practice" means any unfair labor practice listed in section 8.

(9) The term "labor dispute" includes any controversy concerning terms, tenure or conditions of employment, or concerning the association or representation of persons in negotiating, fixing, maintaining, changing, or seeking to arrange terms or conditions of employment, regardless of whether the disputants stand in the proximate relation of employer and employee.

(10) The term "National Labor Relations Board" means the National Labor Relations Board created by section 3 of this Act.

(11) The term "old Board" means the National Labor Relations Board established by Executive Order Numbered 6763 of the President on June 29, 1934, pursuant to Public Resolution Numbered 44, approved June 19, 1934 (48 Stat. 1183), and reestablished and continued by Executive Order Numbered 7074 of the President of June 15, 1935, pursuant to Title I of the National Industrial Recovery Act (48 Stat. 195) as amended and continued by Senate Joint Resolution 133 [1] approved June 14, 1935.

National Labor Relations Board

sec. 3. (a) There is hereby created a board, to be known as the "National Labor Relations Board" (hereinafter referred to as the "Board"), which shall be composed of three members, who shall be appointed by the President, by and with the advice and consent of the Senate. One of the original members shall be appointed for a term of one year, one for a term of three years, and one for a term of five years, but their successors shall be appointed for terms of five years each, except that any individual chosen to fill a vacancy shall be appointed only for the unexpired term of the member whom he shall succeed. The President shall designate one member to serve as chairman of the Board. Any member of the Board may be removed by the President, upon notice and hearing, for neglect of duty or malfeasance in office, but for no other cause.

(b) A vacancy in the Board shall not impair the right of the remaining members to exercise all the powers of the Board, and two members of the Board shall, at all times, constitute a quorum. The Board shall have an official seal which shall be judicially noticed.

(c) The Board shall at the close of each fiscal year make a report in writing to Congress and to the President stating in detail the cases it has heard, the decisions it has rendered, the names, salaries, and duties of all

1. So in original.

employees and officers in the employ or under the supervision of the Board, and an account of all moneys it has disbursed.

SEC. 4. (a) Each member of the Board shall receive a salary of $10,000 a year, shall be eligible for reappointment, and shall not engage in any other business, vocation, or employment. The Board shall appoint, without regard for the provisions of the civil-service laws but subject to the Classification Act of 1923, as amended, an executive secretary, and such attorneys, examiners, and regional directors, and shall appoint such other employees with regard to existing laws applicable to the employment and compensation of officers and employees of the United States, as it may from time to time find necessary for the proper performance of its duties and as may be from time to time appropriated for by Congress. The Board may establish or utilize such regional, local, or other agencies, and utilize such voluntary and uncompensated services, as may from time to time be needed. Attorneys appointed under this section may, at the direction of the Board, appear for and represent the Board in any case in court. Nothing in this Act shall be construed to authorize the Board to appoint individuals for the purpose of conciliation or mediation (or for statistical work), where such service may be obtained from the Department of Labor.

(b) Upon the appointment of the three original members of the Board and the designation of its chairman, the old Board shall cease to exist. All employees of the old Board shall be transferred to and become employees of the Board with salaries under the Classification Act of 1923, as amended, without acquiring by such transfer a permanent or civil service status. All records, papers, and property of the old Board shall become records, papers, and property of the Board, and all unexpended funds and appropriations for the use and maintenance of the old Board shall become funds and appropriations available to be expended by the Board in the exercise of the powers, authority, and duties conferred on it by this Act.

(c) All of the expenses of the Board, including all necessary traveling and subsistence expenses outside the District of Columbia incurred by the members or employees of the Board under its orders, shall be allowed and paid on the presentation of itemized vouchers therefor approved by the Board or by any individual it designates for that purpose.

SEC. 5. The principal office of the Board shall be in the District of Columbia, but it may meet and exercise any or all of its powers at any other place. The Board may, by one or more of its members or by such agents or agencies as it may designate, prosecute any inquiry necessary to its functions in any part of the United States. A member who participates in such an inquiry shall not be disqualified from subsequently participating in a decision of the Board in the same case.

SEC. 6. (a) The Board shall have authority from time to time to make, amend, and rescind such rules and regulations as may be necessary to carry out the provisions of this Act. Such rules and regulations shall be effective upon publication in the manner which the Board shall prescribe.

Rights of Employees

SEC. 7. Employees shall have the right to self-organization, to form, join, or assist labor organizations, to bargain collectively through representatives of their own choosing, and to engage in concerted activities, for the purpose of collective bargaining or other mutual aid or protection.

SEC. 8. It shall be an unfair labor practice for an employer

(1) To interfere with, restrain, or coerce employees in the exercise of the rights guaranteed in section 7.

(2) To dominate or interfere with the formation or administration of any labor organization or contribute financial or other support to it: *Provided*, That subject to rules and regulations made and published by the Board pursuant to section 6(a), an employer shall not be prohibited from permitting employees to confer with him during working hours without loss of time or pay.

(3) By discrimination in regard to hire or tenure of employment or any term or condition of employment to encourage or discourage membership in any labor organization: *Provided*, That nothing in this Act, or in the National Industrial Recovery Act (U.S.C., Supp. VII, title 15, secs. 701–712), as amended from time to time, or in any code or agreement approved or prescribed thereunder, or in any other statute of the United States, shall preclude an employer from making an agreement with a labor organization (not established, maintained, or assisted by any action defined in this Act as an unfair labor practice) to require as a condition of employment membership therein, if such labor organization is the representative of the employees as provided in section 9(a), in the appropriate collective bargaining unit covered by such agreement when made.

(4) To discharge or otherwise discriminate against an employee because he has filed charges or given testimony under this Act.

(5) To refuse to bargain collectively with the representatives of his employees, subject to the provisions of Section 9(a).

Representatives and Elections

SEC. 9. (a) Representatives designated or selected for the purposes of collective bargaining by the majority of the employees in a unit appropriate for such purposes, shall be the exclusive representatives of all the employees in such unit for the purposes of collective bargaining in respect to rates of pay, wages, hours of employment, or other conditions of employment: *Provided*, That any individual employee or a group of employees shall have the right at any time to present grievances to their employer.

(b) The Board shall decide in each case whether, in order to insure to employees the full benefit of their right to self-organization and to collective bargaining, and otherwise to effectuate the policies of this Act, the unit appropriate for the purposes of collective bargaining shall be the employer unit, craft unit, plant unit, or subdivision thereof.

(c) Whenever a question affecting commerce arises concerning the representation of employees, the Board may investigate such controversy and certify to the parties, in writing, the name or names of the representatives that have been designated or selected. In any such investigation, the Board shall provide for an appropriate hearing upon due notice, either in conjunction with a proceeding under section 10 or otherwise, and may take a secret ballot of employees, or utilize any other suitable method to ascertin [1] such representatives.

(d) Whenever an order of the Board made pursuant to section 10(c) is based in whole or in part upon facts certified following an investigation pursuant to subsection (c) of this section, and there is a petition for the enforcement or review of such order, such certification and the record of such investigation shall be included in the transcript of the entire record required to be filed under subsections 10(e) or 10(f), and thereupon the decree of the court enforcing, modifying, or setting aside in whole or in part the order of the Board shall be made and entered upon the pleadings, testimony, and proceedings set forth in such transcript.

Prevention of Unfair Labor Practices

SEC. 10. (a) The Board is empowered, as hereinafter provided, to prevent any person from engaging in any unfair labor practice (listed in section 8) affecting commerce. This power shall be exclusive, and shall not be affected by any other means of adjustment or prevention that has been or may be established by agreement, code, law, or otherwise.

(b) Whenever it is charged that any person has engaged in or is engaging in any such unfair labor practice, the Board, or any agent or agency designated by the Board for such purposes, shall have power to issue and cause to be served upon such person a complaint stating the charges in that respect, and containing a notice of hearing before the Board or a member thereof, or before a designated agent or agency, at a place therein fixed, not less than five days after the serving of said complaint. Any such complaint may be amended by the member, agent, or agency conducting the hearing or the Board in its discretion at any time prior to the issuance of an order based thereon. The person so complained of shall have the right to file an answer to the original or amended complaint and to appear in person or otherwise and give testimony at the place and time fixed in the complaint. In the discretion of the member, agent or agency conducting the hearing or the Board, any other person may be allowed to intervene in the said proceeding and to present testimony. In any such proceeding the rules of evidence prevailing in courts of law or equity shall not be controlling.

(c) The testimony taken by such member, agent or agency or the Board shall be reduced to writing and filed with the Board. Thereafter, in its discretion, the Board upon notice may take further testimony or hear argu-

1. So in original.

ment. If upon all the testimony taken the Board shall be of the opinion that any person named in the complaint has engaged in or is engaging in any such unfair labor practice, then the Board shall state its findings of fact and shall issue and cause to be served on such person an order requiring such person to cease and desist from such unfair labor practice, and to take such affirmative action, including reinstatement of employees with or without back pay, as will effectuate the policies of this Act. Such order may further require such person to make reports from time to time showing the extent to which it has complied with the order. If upon all the testimony taken the Board shall be of the opinion that no person named in the complaint has engaged in or is engaging in any such unfair labor practice, then the Board shall state its findings of fact and shall issue an order dismissing the said complaint.

(d) Until a transcript of the record in a case shall have been filed in a court, as hereinafter provided, the Board may at any time, upon reasonable notice and in such manner as it shall deem proper, modify or set aside, in whole or in part, any finding or order made or issued by it.

(e) The Board shall have power to petition any circuit court of appeals of the United States (including the Court of Appeals of the District of Columbia), or if all the circuit courts of appeals to which application may be made are in vacation, any district court of the United States (including the Supreme Court of the District of Columbia), within any circuit or district, respectively, wherein the unfair labor practice in question occurred or wherein such person resides or transacts business, for the enforcement of such order and for appropriate temporary relief or restraining order, and shall certify and file in the court a transcript of the entire record in the proceeding, including the pleadings and testimony upon which such order was entered and the findings and order of the Board. Upon such filing, the court shall cause notice thereof to be served upon such person, and thereupon shall have jurisdiction of the proceeding and of the question determined therein, and shall have power to grant such temporary relief or restraining order as it deems just and proper, and to make and enter upon the pleadings, testimony, and proceedings set forth in such transcript a decree enforcing, modifying, and enforcing as so modified, or setting aside in whole or in part the order of the Board. No objection that has not been urged before the Board, its member, agent or agency, shall be considered by the court, unless the failure or neglect to urge such objection shall be excused because of extraordinary circumstances. The findings of the Board as to the facts, if supported by evidence, shall be conclusive. If either party shall apply to the court for leave to adduce additional evidence and shall show to the satisfaction of the court that such additional evidence is material and that there were reasonable grounds for the failure to adduce such evidence in the hearing before the Board, its member, agent, or agency, the court may order such additional evidence to be taken before the Board, its member, agent, or agency, and to be made a part of the transcript. The Board may modify its findings as to the facts, or make new findings, by reason of additional evidence so taken and filed, and it shall file such modified or new findings, which, if supported by evidence, shall be conclusive, and shall file its recommendations, if any, for the modification or setting aside of its original order. The jurisdiction of the court shall be exclusive and its judgment and decree shall be final, except that the same shall be subject to review by the appropriate circuit court of appeals if application was made to the district court as hereinabove provided, and by the Supreme Court of the United States upon writ of certiorari or certification as provided in sections 239 and 240 of the Judicial Code, as amended (U.S.C., title 28, secs. 346 and 347).

(f) Any person aggrieved by a final order of the Board granting or denying in whole or in part the relief sought may obtain a review of such order in any circuit court of appeals of the United States in the circuit wherein the unfair labor practice in question was alleged to have been engaged in or wherein such person resides or transacts business, or in the Court of Appeals of the District of Columbia, by filing in such court a written petition praying that the order of the Board be modified or set aside. A copy of such petition shall be forthwith served upon the Board, and thereupon the aggrieved party shall file in the court a transcript of the entire record in the proceeding, certified by the Board, including the pleading and testimony upon which the order complained of was entered and the findings and order of the Board. Upon such filing, the court shall proceed in the same manner as in the case of an application by the Board under subsection (e), and shall have the same exclusive jurisdiction to grant to the Board such temporary relief or restraining order as it deems just and proper, and in like manner to make and enter a decree enforcing, modifying, and enforcing as so modified, or setting aside in whole or in part the order of the Board; and the findings of the Board as to the facts, if supported by evidence, shall in like manner be conclusive.

(g) The commencement of proceedings under subsection (e) or (f) of this section shall not, unless specifically ordered by the court, operate as a stay of the Board's order.

(h) When granting appropriate temporary relief or a restraining order, or making and entering a decree enforcing, modifying, and enforcing as so modified or setting aside in whole or in part an order of the Board, as provided in this section, the jurisdiction of courts sitting in equity shall not be limited by the Act entitled "An Act to amend the Judicial Code and to define and limit the jurisdiction of courts sitting in equity, and for other purposes," approved March 23, 1932 (U.S.C., Supp. VII, title 29, secs. 101–115).

(i) Petitions filed under this Act shall be heard expeditiously, and if possible within ten days after they have been docketed.

Investigatory Powers

SEC. 11. For the purpose of all hearings and investigations, which, in the opinion of the Board, are necessary and proper for the exercise of the powers vested in it by section 9 and section 10

(1) The Board, or its duly authorized agents or agencies, shall at all reasonable times have access to, for the purpose of examination, and the

right to copy any evidence of any person being investigated or proceeded against that relates to any matter under investigation or in question. Any member of the Board shall have power to issue subpenas requiring the attendance and testimony of witnesses and the production of any evidence that relates to any matter under investigation or in question, before the Board, its member, agent, or agency conducting the hearing or investigation. Any member of the Board, or any agent or agency designated by the Board for such purposes, may administer oaths and affirmations, examine witnesses, and receive evidence. Such attendance of witnesses and the production of such evidence may be required from any place in the United States or any Territory or possession thereof, at any designated place of hearing.

(2) In case of contumacy or refusal to obey a subpena issued to any person, any District Court of the United States or the United States courts of any Territory or possession, or the Supreme Court of the District of Columbia, within the jurisdiction of which the inquiry is carried on or within the jurisdiction of which said person guilty of contumacy or refusal to obey is found or resides or transacts business, upon application by the Board shall have jurisdiction to issue to such person an order requiring such person to appear before the Board, its member, agent, or agency, there to produce evidence if so ordered, or there to give testimony touching the matter under investigation or in question; and any failure to obey such order of the court may be punished by said court as a contempt thereof.

(3) No person shall be excused from attending and testifying or from producing books, records, correspondence, documents, or other evidence in obedience to the subpena of the Board, on the ground that the testimony or evidence required of him may tend to incriminate him or subject him to a penalty or forfeiture; but no individual shall be prosecuted or subjected to any penalty of forfeiture for or on account of any transaction, matter, or thing concerning which he is compelled, after having claimed his privilege against self-incrimination, to testify or produce evidence, except that such individual so testifying shall not be exempt from prosecution and punishment for perjury committed in so testifying.

(4) Complaints, orders, and other process and papers of the Board, its member, agent, or agency, may be served either personally or by registered mail or by telegraph or by leaving a copy thereof at the principal office or place of business of the person required to be served. The verified return by the individual so serving the same setting forth the manner of such service shall be proof of the same, and the return post office receipt or telegraph receipt therefor when registered and mailed or telegraphed as aforsaid shall be proof of service of the same. Witnesses summoned before the Board, its member, agent, or agency, shall be paid the same fees and mileage that are paid witnesses in the courts of the United States, and witnesses whose depositions are taken and the persons taking the same shall severally be entitled to the same fees as are paid for like services in the courts of the United States.

(5) All process of any court to which application may be made under this Act may be served in the judicial district wherein the defendant or other person required to be served resides or may be found.

(6) The several departments and agencies of the Government, when

directed by the President, shall furnish the Board, upon its request, all records, papers, and information in their possession relating to any matter before the Board.

SEC. 12. Any person who shall willfully resist, prevent, impede, or interfere with any member of the Board or any of its agents or agencies in the performance of duties pursuant to this Act shall be punished by a fine of not more than $5,000 or by imprisonment for not more than one year, or both.

Limitations

SEC. 13. Nothing in this Act shall be construed so as to interfere with or impede or diminish in any way the right to strike.

SEC. 14. Wherever the application of the provisions of section 7(a) of the National Industrial Recovery Act (U.S.C., Supp. VII, title 15, sec. 707 (a)), as amended from time to time, or of section 77 B, paragraphs (1) and (m) of the Act approved June 7, 1934, entitled "An Act to amend an Act entitled 'An Act to establish a uniform system of bankruptcy throughout the United States' approved July 1, 1898, and Acts amendatory thereof and supplementary thereto" (48 Stat. 922, pars. (1) and (m)), as amended from time to time, or of Public Resolution Numbered 44, approved June 19, 1934 (48 Stat. 1183), conflicts with the application of the provisions of this Act, this Act shall prevail: *Provided,* That in any situation where the provisions of this Act cannot be validly enforced, the provisions of such other Acts shall remain in full force and effect.

SEC. 15. If any provision of this Act, or the application of such provision to any person or circumstance, shall be held invalid, the remainder of this Act, or the application of such provision to persons or circumstances other than those as to which it is held invalid, shall not be affected thereby.

SEC. 16. This Act may be cited as the "National Labor Relations Act." Approved, July 5, 1935.

Labor Management Relations Act, 1947

The Taft-Hartley Act
Act of June 23, 1947,[1] 80th Congress

An Act to amend the National Labor Relations Act, to provide additional facilities for the mediation of labor disputes affecting commerce, to equalize legal responsibilities of labor organizations and employers, and for other purposes.

Be it enacted by the Senate and House of Representatives of the United States of America in Congress assembled,

Short Title and Declaration of Policy

SECTION 1. (a) This Act may be cited as the "Labor Management Relations Act, 1947."

(b) Industrial strife which interferes with the normal flow of commerce and with the full production of articles and commodities for commerce, can be avoided or substantially minimized if employers, employees, and labor organizations each recognize under law one another's legitimate rights in their relations with each other, and above all recognize under law that neither party has any right in its relations with any other to engage in acts or practices which jeopardize the public health, safety, or interest.

It is the purpose and policy of this Act, in order to promote the full flow of commerce, to prescribe the legitimate rights of both employees and employers in their relations affecting commerce, to provide orderly and peaceful procedures for preventing the interference by either with the legitimate rights of the other, to protect the rights of individual employees in their relations with labor organizations whose activities affect commerce, to define and proscribe practices on the part of labor and management which affect commerce and are inimical to the general welfare, and to protect the rights of the public in connection with labor disputes affecting commerce.

1. Passed by Congress over the President's veto.

TITLE I. AMENDMENT OF NATIONAL LABOR RELATIONS ACT

SEC. 101. The National Labor Relations Act is hereby amended to read as follows:

"Findings and Policies

SECTION 1. The denial by some employers of the right of employees to organize and the refusal by some employers to accept the procedure of collective bargaining lead to strikes and other forms of industrial strife or unrest, which have the intent or the necessary effect of burdening or obstructing commerce by (a) impairing the efficiency, safety, or operation of the instrumentalities of commerce; (b) occurring in the current of commerce; (c) materially affecting, restraining, or controlling the flow of raw materials or manufactured or processed goods from or into the channels of commerce, or the prices of such materials or goods in commerce; or (d) causing diminution of employment and wages in such volume as substantially to impair or disrupt the market for goods flowing from or into the channels of commerce.

"The inequality of bargaining power between employees who do not possess full freedom of association or actual liberty of contract, and employers who are organized in the corporate or other forms of ownership association substantially burdens and affects the flow of commerce, and tends to aggravate recurrent business depressions, by depressing wage rates and the purchasing power of wage earners in industry and by preventing the stabilization of competitive wage rates and working conditions within and between industries.

"Experience has proved that protection by law of the right of employees to organize and bargain collectively safeguards commerce from injury, impairment, or interruption, and promotes the flow of commerce by removing certain recognized sources of industrial strife and unrest, by encouraging practices fundamental to the friendly adjustment of industrial disputes arising out of differences as to wages, hours, or other working conditions, and by restoring equality of bargaining power between employers and employees.

"Experience has further demonstrated that certain practices by some labor organizations, their officers, and members have the intent or the necessary effect of burdening or obstructing commerce by preventing the free flow of goods in such commerce through strikes and other forms of industrial unrest or through concerted activities which impair the interest of the public in the free flow of such commerce. The elimination of such practices is a necessary condition to the assurance of the rights herein guaranteed.

"It is hereby declared to be the policy of the United States to eliminate the causes of certain substantial obstructions to the free flow of commerce and to mitigate and eliminate these obstructions when they have occurred by encouraging the practice and procedure of collective bargaining and by protecting the exercise by workers of full freedom of association, self-organization, and designation of representatives of their own choosing, for the purpose of negotiating the terms and conditions of their employment or other mutual aid or protection.

"Definitions

"SEC. 2. When used in this Act

"(1) The term 'person' includes one or more individuals, labor organizations, partnerships, associations, corporations, legal representatives, trustees, trustees in bankruptcy, or receivers.

"(2) The term 'employer' includes any person acting as an agent of an employer, directly or indirectly, but shall not include the United States or any wholly owned Government corporation, or any Federal Reserve Bank or any State or political subdivision thereof, or any corporation or association operating a hospital, if no part of the net earnings inures to the benefit of private shareholder or individual, or any person subject to the Railway Labor Act, as amended from time to time, or any labor organization (other than when acting as an employer), or anyone acting in the capacity of officer or agent of such labor organization.

"(3) The term 'employee' shall include any employee, and shall not be limited to the employees of a particular employer, unless the Act explicitly states otherwise, and shall include any individual whose work has ceased as a consequence of, or in connection with, any current labor dispute or because of any unfair labor practice, and who has not obtained any other regular and substantially equivalent employment, but shall not include any individual employed in agriculture, or in the domestic service of any family or person at his home, or any individual employed by his parent or spouse, or any individual having the status of an independent contractor, or any individual employed as a supervisor, or any individual employed by an employer subject to the Railway Labor Act, as amended from time to time, or by any other person who is not an employer as herein defined.

"(4) The term 'representatives' includes any individual or labor organization.

"(5) The term 'labor organization' means any organization of any kind, or any agency or employee representation committee or plan, in which employees participate and which exists for the purpose, in whole or in part, of dealing with employers concerning grievances, labor disputes, wages, rates of pay, hours of employment, or conditions of work.

"(6) The term 'commerce' means trade, traffic, commerce, transportation, or communication among the several States, or between the District of Columbia or any Territory of the United States and any State or other Territory, or between any foreign country and any State, Territory, or the District of Columbia, or within the District of Columbia or any Territory, or between points in the same State but through any other State or any Territory or the District of Columbia or any foreign country.

"(7) The term 'affecting commerce' means in commerce, or burdening or obstructing commerce or the free flow of commerce, or having led or tending to lead to a labor dispute burdening or obstructing commerce or the free flow of commerce.

"(8) The term 'unfair labor practice' means any unfair labor practice listed in section 8.

"(9) The term 'labor dispute' includes any controversy concerning terms, tenure or conditions of employment, or concerning the association or representation of persons in negotiating, fixing, maintaining, changing, or seeking to arrange terms or conditions of employment, regardless of whether the disputants stand in the proximate relation of employer and employee.

"(10) The term 'National Labor Relations Board' means the National Labor Relations Board created by section 3 of this Act.

"(11) The term 'supervisor' means any individual having authority, in the interest of the employer to hire, transfer, suspend, lay off, recall, promote, discharge, assign, reward, or discipline other employees, or responsibly to direct them, or to adjust their grievances, or effectively to recommend such action if in connection with the foregoing the exercise of such authority is not of a merely routine or clerical nature, but requires the use of independent judgment.

"(12) The term 'professional employee' means

"(a) any employee engaged in work (i) predominantly intellectual and varied in character as opposed to routine mental, manual, mechanical, or physical work; (ii) involving the consistent exercise of discretion and judgment in its performance; (iii) of such a character that the output produced or the result accomplished cannot be standardized in relation to a given period of time; (iv) requiring knowledge of an advanced type in a field of science or learning customarily acquired by a prolonged course of specialized intellectual instruction and study in an institution of higher learning or a hospital, as distinguished from a general academic education or from an apprenticeship or from training in the performance of routine mental, manual, or physical processes; or

"(b) any employee, who (i) has completed the courses of specialized intellectual instruction and study described in clause (iv) of paragraph (a), and (ii) is performing related work under the supervision of a professional person to qualify himself to become a professional employee as defined in paragraph (a).

"(13) In determining whether any person is acting as an agent of another person so as to make such other person responsible for his acts, the question of whether the specific acts performed were actually authorized or subsequently ratified shall not be controlling.

"National Labor Relations Board

"SEC. 3. (a) The National Labor Relations Board (hereinafter called the 'Board') created by this Act prior to its amendment by the Labor Management Relations Act, 1947, is hereby continued as an agency of the

United States, except that the Board shall consist of five instead of three members, appointed by the President by and with the advice and consent of the Senate. Of the two additional members so provided for, one shall be appointed for a term of five years and the other for a term of two years. Their successors, and the successors of the other members, shall be appointed for terms of five years each, excepting that any individual chosen to fill a vacancy shall be appointed only for the unexpired term of the member whom he shall succeed. The President shall designate one member to serve as Chairman of the Board. Any member of the Board may be removed by the President, upon notice and hearing, for neglect of duty or malfeasance in office, but for no other cause.

"(b) The Board is authorized to delegate to any group of three or more members any or all of the powers which it may itself exercise. A vacancy in the Board shall not impair the right of the remaining members to exercise all of the powers of the Board, and three members of the Board shall, at all times, constitute a quorum of the Board, except that two members shall constitute a quorum of any group designated pursuant to the first sentence hereof. The Board shall have an official seal which shall be judicially noticed.

"(c) The Board shall at the close of each fiscal year make a report in writing to Congress and to the President stating in detail the cases it has heard, the decisions it has rendered, the names, salaries, and duties of all employees and officers in the employ or under the supervision of the Board, and an account of all moneys it has disbursed.

"(d) There shall be a General Counsel of the Board who shall be appointed by the President, by and with the advice and consent of the Senate, for a term of four years. The General Counsel of the Board shall exercise general supervision over all attorneys employed by the Board (other than trial examiners and legal assistants to Board members) and over the officers and employees in the regional offices. He shall have final authority, on behalf of the Board, in respect of the investigation of charges and issuance of complaints under section 10, and in respect of the prosecution of such complaints before the Board, and shall have such other duties as the Board may prescribe or as may be provided by law.

"SEC. 4. (a) Each member of the Board and the General Counsel of the Board shall receive a salary of $12,000 a year, shall be eligible for reappointment, and shall not engage in any other business, vocation, or employment. The Board shall appoint an executive secretary, and such attorneys, examiners, and regional directors, and such other employees as it may from time to time find necessary for the proper performance of its duties. The Board may not employ any attorneys for the purpose of reviewing transcripts of hearings or preparing drafts of opinions except that any attorney employed for assignment as a legal assistant to any Board member may for such Board member review such transcripts and prepare such drafts. No trial examiner's report shall be reviewed, either before or after its publication, by any person other than a member of the Board or his legal assistant, and no trial examiner shall advise or consult with the Board with respect to exceptions taken to his findings, rulings, or recommendations. The Board may establish or utilize such regional, local, or other agencies, and utilize such voluntary and uncompensated services, as may from time to time be needed. Attorneys appointed under this section may, at the direction of the Board, appear for and represent the Board in any case in court. Nothing in this Act shall be construed to authorize the Board to appoint individuals for the purpose of conciliation or mediation, or for economic analysis.

"(b) All of the expenses of the Board, including all necessary traveling and subsistence expenses outside the District of Columbia incurred by the members or employees of the Board under its orders, shall be allowed and paid on the presentation of itemized vouchers, therefor approved by the Board or by any individual it designates for that purpose.

"SEC. 5. The principal office of the Board shall be in the District of Columbia, but it may meet and exercise any or all of its powers at any other place. The Board may, by one or more of its members or by such agents or agencies as it may designate, prosecute any inquiry necessary to its functions in any part of the United States. A member who participates in such an inquiry shall not be disqualified from subsequently participating in a decision of the Board in the same case.

"SEC. 6. The Board shall have authority from time to time to make, amend, and rescind, in the manner prescribed by the Administrative Procedure Act, such rules and regulations as may be necessary to carry out the provisions of this Act.

"Rights of Employees

"SEC. 7. Employees shall have the right to self-organization, to form, join, or assist labor organizations, to bargain collectively through representatives of their own choosing, and to engage in other concerted activities for the purpose of collective bargaining or other mutual aid or protection, and shall also have the right to refrain from any or all of such activities except to the extent that such right may be affected by an agreement requiring membership in a labor organization as a condition of employment as authorized in section 8(a)(3).

"Unfair Labor Practices

"SEC. 8. (a) It shall be an unfair labor practice for an employer

"(1) to interfere with, restrain, or coerce employees in the exercise of the rights guaranteed in section 7;

"(2) to dominate or interfere with the formation or administration of any labor organization or contribute financial or other support to it: *Provided*, That subject to rules and regulations made and published by the Board pursuant to section 6, an employer shall not be prohibited from permitting employees to confer with him during working hours without loss of time or pay;

"(3) by discrimination in regard to hire or tenure of employment or any term or condition of employment to encourage or discourage membership in any labor organization: *Provided*, That nothing in this Act, or in any other statute of the United States, shall preclude an employer from making an agreement with a labor organization (not established, maintained, or assisted by any action defined in section 8(a) of this Act as un unfair labor practice) to require as a condition of employment membership therein on or after the thirtieth day following the beginning of such employment or the effective date of such agreement, whichever is the later, (i) if such labor organization is the representative of the employees as provided in section 9(a), in the appropriate collective-bargaining unit covered by such agreement when made; and (ii) if, following the most recent election held as provided in section 9(e) the Board shall have certified that at least a majority of the employees eligible to vote in such election have voted to authorize such labor organization to make such an agreement: *Provided further*, That no employer shall justify any discrimination against an employee for nonmembership in a labor organization (A) if he has reasonable grounds for believing that such membership was not available to the employee on the same terms and conditions generally applicable to other members, or (B) if he has reasonable grounds for believing that membership was denied or terminated for reasons other than the failure of the employee to tender the periodic dues and the initiation fees uniformly required as a condition of acquiring or retaining membership;

"(4) to discharge or otherwise discriminate against an employee because he has filed charges or given testimony under this Act;

"(5) to refuse to bargain collectively with the representatives of his employees, subject to the provisions of section 9(a).

"(b) It shall be an unfair labor practice for a labor organization or its agents

"(1) to restrain or coerce (A) employees in the exercise of the rights guaranteed in section 7: *Provided*, That this paragraph shall not impair the right of a labor organization to prescribe its own rules with respect to the acquisition or retention of membership therein; or (B) an employer in the selection of his representatives for the purposes of collective bargaining or the adjustment of grievances;

"(2) to cause or attempt to cause an employer to discriminate against an employee in violation of subsection (a)(3) or to discriminate against an employee with respect to whom membership in such organization has been denied or terminated on some ground other than his failure to tender the periodic dues and the initiation fees uniformly required as a condition of acquiring or retaining membership;

"(3) to refuse to bargain collectively with an employer, provided it is the representative of his employees subject to the provisions of section 9(a);

"(4) to engage in, or to induce or encourage the employees of any employer to engage in, a strike or a concerted refusal in the course of their employment to use, manufacture, process, transport, or otherwise handle or work on any goods, articles, materials, or commodities or to perform any services, where an object thereof is: (A) forcing or requiring any employer or self-employed person to join any labor or employer organization or any employer or other person to cease using, selling, handling, transporting, or otherwise dealing in the products of any other producer, processor, or manufacturer, or to cease doing business with any other person; (B) forcing or requiring any other employer to recognize or bargain with a labor organization as the representative of his employees unless such labor organization has been certified as the representative of such employees under the provisions of section 9; (C) forcing or requiring any employer to recognize or bargain with a particular labor organization as the representative of his employees if another labor organization has been certified as the representative of such employees under the provisions of section 9; (D) forcing or requiring any employer to assign particular work to employees in a particular labor organization or in a particular trade, craft, or class rather than to employees in another labor organization or in another trade, craft, or class, unless such employer is failing to conform to an order or certification of the Board determining the bargaining representative for employees performing such work: *Provided*, That nothing contained in this subsection (b) shall be construed to make unlawful a refusal by any person to enter upon the premises of any employer (other than his own employer), if the employees of such employer are engaged in a strike ratified or approved by a representative of such employees whom such employer is required to recognize under this Act;

"(5) to require of employees covered by an agreement authorized under subsection (a)(3) the payment, as a condition precedent to becoming a member of such organization, of a fee in an amount which the Board finds excessive or discriminatory under all the circumstances. In making such a finding, the Board shall consider, among other relevant factors, the practices and customs of labor organizations in the particular industry, and the wages currently paid to the employees affected; and

"(6) To cause or attempt to cause an employer to pay or deliver or agree to pay or deliver any money or other thing of value in the nature of an exaction, for services which are not performed or not to be performed.

"(c) The expressing of any views, argument, or opinion, or the dissemination thereof, whether in written, printed, graphic, or visual form, shall not constitute or be evidence of an unfair labor practice under any of the provisions of this Act, if such expression contains no threat of reprisal or force or promise of benefit.

"(d) For the purposes of this section, to bargain collectively is the performance of the mutual obligation of the employer and the representative of the employees to meet at reasonable times and confer in good faith with respect to wages, hours, and other terms and conditions of employment, or the negotiation of an agreement, or any question arising thereunder, and the execution of a written contract incorporating any agreement reached if requested by either party but such obligation does not compel either party to agree to a proposal or require the making of a concession: *Provided*, That where there is in effect a collective-bargaining contract covering employees in an industry affecting commerce, the duty to bargain collectively shall also mean that no party to such contract shall terminate or modify such contract, unless the party desiring such termination or modification

"(1) serves a written notice upon the other party to the contract of the proposed termination or modification sixty days prior to the expiration date thereof, or in the event such contract contains no expiration date, sixty days prior to the time it is proposed to make such termination or modification;

"(2) offers to meet and confer with the other party for the purpose of negotiating a new contract or a contract containing the proposed modifications;

"(3) notifies the Federal Mediation and Conciliation Service within thirty days after such notice of the existence of a dispute, and simultaneously therewith notifies any State or Territorial agency established to mediate and conciliate disputes within the State or Territory where the dispute occurred, provided no agreement has been reached by that time; and

"(4) continues in full force and effect, without resorting to strike or lock-out, all the terms and conditions of the existing contract for a period of sixty days after such notice is given or until the expiration date of such contract, whichever occurs later:

"The duties imposed upon employers, employees, and labor organizations by paragraphs (2), (3), and (4) shall become inapplicable upon an intervening certification of the Board, under which the labor organization or individual, which is a party to the contract, has been superseded as or ceased to be the representative of the employees subject to the provisions of section 9(a), and the duties so imposed shall not be construed as requiring either party to discuss or agree to any modification of the terms and conditions contained in a contract for a fixed period, if such modification is to become effective before such terms and conditions can be reopened under the provisions of the contract. Any employee who engages in a strike within the sixty-day period specified in this subsection shall lose his status as an employee of the employer engaged in the particular labor dispute, for the purposes of sections 8, 9, and 10 of this Act, as amended, but such loss of status for such employee shall terminate if and when he is reemployed by such employer.

"Representatives and Elections

"SEC. 9. (a) Representatives designated or selected for the purposes of collective bargaining by the majority of the employees in a unit appropriate for such purposes, shall be the exclusive representatives of all the employees in such unit for the purposes of collective bargaining in respect to rates of pay, wages, hours of employment, or other conditions of employment: *Provided*, That any individual employee or a group of employees shall have the right at any time to present grievances to their employer and to have such grievances adjusted, without the intervention of the bargaining representative, as long as the adjustment is not inconsistent with the terms of a collective-bargaining contract or agreement then in effect: *Provided further,* That the bargaining representative has been given opportunity to be present at such adjustment.

"(b) The Board shall decide in each case whether, in order to assure to employees the fullest freedom in exercising the rights guaranteed by this Act, the unit appropriate for the purposes of collective bargaining shall be the employer unit, craft unit, plant unit, or subdivision thereof: *Provided,* That the Board shall not (1) decide that any unit is appropriate for such purposes if such unit includes both professional employees and employees who are not professional employees unless a majority of such professional employees vote for inclusion in such unit; or (2) decide that any craft unit is inappropriate for such purposes on the ground that a different unit has been established by a prior Board determination, unless a majority of the employees in the proposed craft unit vote against separate representation or (3) decide that any unit is appropriate for such purposes if it includes, together with other employees, any individual employed as a guard to enforce against employees and other persons rules to protect property of the employer or to protect the safety of persons on the employer's premises; but no labor organization shall be certified as the representative of employees in a bargaining unit of guards if such organization admits to membership, or is affiliated directly or indirectly with an organization which admits to membership, employees other than guards.

"(c)(1) Whenever a petition shall have been filed, in accordance with such regulations as may be prescribed by the Board

"(A) by an employee or group of employees or any individual or labor organization acting in their behalf alleging that a substantial number of employees (i) wish to be represented for collective bargaining and that their employer declines to recognize their representative as the representative defined in section 9(a), or (ii) assert that the individual or labor organization, which has been certified or is being currently recognized by their employer as the bargaining representative, is no longer a representative as defined in section 9(a); or

"(B) by an employer, alleging that one or more individuals or labor organizations have presented to him a claim to be recognized as the representative defined in section 9(a);

the Board shall investigate such petition and if it has reasonable cause to believe that a question of representation affecting commerce exists shall provide for an appropriate hearing upon due notice. Such hearing may be conducted by an officer or employee of the regional office, who shall not make any recommendations with respect thereto. If the Board finds upon the record of such hearing that such a question of representation exists, it shall direct an election by secret ballot and shall certify the results thereof.

"(2) In determining whether or not a question of representation affecting commerce exists, the same regulations and rules of decision shall apply irrespective of the identity of the persons filing the petition or the kind of relief sought and in no case shall the Board deny a labor organization a place on the ballot by reason of an order with respect to such labor organization or its predecessor not issued in conformity with section 10(c).

"(3) No election shall be directed in any bargaining unit or any subdivision within which, in the preceding twelve-month period, a valid election shall have been held. Employees on strike who are not entitled to reinstatement shall not be eligible to vote. In any election where none of the choices on the ballot receives a majority, a run-off shall be conducted, the ballot providing for a selection between the two choices receiving the largest and second largest number of valid votes cast in the election.

"(4) Nothing in this section shall be construed to prohibit the waiving of hearings by stipulation for the purpose of a consent election in conformity with the regulations and rules of decision of the Board.

"(5) In determining whether a unit is appropriate for the purposes specified in subsection (b) the extent to which the employees have organized shall not be controlling.

"(d) Whenever an order of the Board made pursuant to section 10(c) is based in whole or in part upon facts certified following an investigation pursuant to subsection (c) of this section, and there is a petition for the enforcement or review of such order, such certification and the record of such investigation shall be included in the transcript of the entire record required to be filed under subsection 10(e) or 10(f), and thereupon the decree of the court enforcing, modifying, or setting aside in whole or in part the order of the Board shall be made and entered upon the pleadings, testimony, and proceedings set forth in such transcript.

"(e)(1) Upon the filing with the Board by a labor organization, which is the representative of employees as provided in section 9(a), of a petition alleging that 30 per centum or more of the employees within a unit claimed to be appropriate for such purposes desire to authorize such labor organization to make an agreement with the employer of such employees requiring membership in such labor organization as a condition of employment in such unit, upon an appropriate showing thereof the Board shall, if no question of representation exists, take a secret ballot of such employees, and shall certify the results thereof to such labor organization and to the employer.

"(2) Upon the filing with the Board by 30 per centum or more of the employees in a bargaining unit covered by an agreement between their employer and a labor organization made pursuant to section 8(a)(3)(ii), of a petition alleging they desire that such authority be rescinded, the Board shall take a secret ballot of the employees in such unit, and shall certify the results thereof to such labor organization and to the employer.

"(3) No election shall be conducted pursuant to this subsection in any bargaining unit or any subdivision within which, in the preceding twelve-month period, a valid election shall have been held.

"(f) No investigation shall be made by the Board of any question affecting commerce concerning the representation of employees, raised by a labor organization under subsection (c) of this section, no petition under section 9(e)(1) shall be entertained, and no complaint shall be issued pursuant to a charge made by a labor organization under subsection (b) of section 10, unless such labor organization and any national or international labor organization of which such labor organization is an affiliate or constituent unit

(A) shall have prior thereto filed with the Secretary of Labor copies of its constitution and bylaws and a report, in such form as the Secretary may prescribe, showing

"(1) the name of such labor organization and the address of its principal place of business;

"(2) the names, titles, and compensation and allowances of its three principal officers and of any of its other officers or agents whose aggregate compensation and allowances for the preceding year exceeded $5,000, and the amount of the compensation and allowances paid to each such officer or agent during such year;

"(3) the manner in which the officers and agents referred to in clause (2) were elected, appointed, or otherwise selected;

"(4) the initiation fee or fees which new members are required to pay on becoming members of such labor organization;

"(5) the regular dues or fees which members are required to pay in order to remain members in good standing of such labor organization;

"(6) a detailed statement of, or reference to provisions of its constitution and bylaws, showing the procedure followed with respect to, (a) qualification for or restrictions on membership, (b) election of officers and stewards, (c) calling of regular and special meetings, (d) levying of assessments, (e) imposition of fines, (f) authorization for bargaining demands, (g) ratification of contract terms, (h) authorization for strikes, (i) authorization for disbursement of union funds, (j) audit of union financial transactions, (k) participation in insurance or other benefit plans, and (l) expulsion of members and the grounds therefor;

and (B) can show that prior thereto it has

"(1) filed with the Secretary of Labor, in such form as the Secretary may prescribe, a report showing all of (a) its receipts of any kind and the sources of such receipts, (b) its total assets and liabilities as of the end of its last fiscal year, (c) the disbursements made by it during such fiscal year, including the purposes for which made; and

"(2) furnished to all of the members of such labor organization copies of the financial report required by paragraph (1) hereof to be filed with the Secretary of Labor.

"(g) It shall be the obligation of all labor organizations to file annually with the Secretary of Labor, in such form as the Secretary of Labor may prescribe, reports bringing up to date the information required to be supplied in the initial filing by subsection (f)(A) of this section, and to file with the Secretary of Labor and furnish to its members annually financial reports in the form and manner prescribed in subsection (f)(B). No labor organization shall be eligible for certification under this section as the representative of any employees, no petition under section 9(e)(1) shall be entertained, and no complaint shall issue under section 10 with respect to a charge filed by a labor organization unless it can show that it and any national or international labor organization of which it is an affiliate or constituent unit has complied with its obligation under this subsection.

"(h) No investigation shall be made by the Board of any question affecting commerce concerning the representation of employees, raised by a labor organization under subsection (c) of this section, no petition under section 9(e)(1) shall be entertained, and no complaint shall be issued pursuant to a charge made by a labor organization under subsection (b) of section 10, unless there is on file with the Board an affidavit executed contemporaneously or within the preceding twelve-month period by each officer of such labor organization and the officers of any national or international labor organization of which it is an affiliate or constituent unit that he is not a member of the Communist Party or affiliated with such party, and that he does not believe in, and is not a member of or supports any organization that believes in or teaches the overthrow of the United States Government by force or by any illegal or unconstitutional methods. The provisions of section 35A of the Criminal Code shall be applicable in respect to such affidavits.

"Prevention of Unfair Labor Practices.

"SEC. 10. (a) The Board is empowered, as hereinafter provided, to prevent any person from engaging in any unfair labor practice (listed in section 8) affecting commerce. This power shall not be affected by any other means of adjustment or prevention that has been or may be established by agreement, law, or otherwise: *Provided,* That the Board is empowered by agreement with any agency of any State or Territory to cede to such agency jurisdiction over any cases in any industry, (other than mining, manufacturing, communications, and transportation, except where predominantly local in character) even though such cases may involve labor disputes affecting commerce, unless the provision of the State or Territorial statute applicable to the determination of such cases by such agency is inconsistent with the corresponding provision of this Act or has received a construction inconsistent therewith.

"(b) Whenever it is charged that any person has engaged in or is engaging in any such unfair labor practice, the Board, or any agent or agency designated by the Board for such purposes, shall have power to issue and cause to be served upon such person a complaint stating the charges in that respect, and containing a notice of hearing before the Board or a member thereof, or before a designated agent or agency, at a place therein fixed, not less than five days after the serving of said complaint: *Provided,* That no complaint shall issue based upon any unfair labor practice occurring more than six months prior to the filing of the charge with the Board and the service of a copy thereof upon the person against whom such charge is made, unless the person aggrieved thereby was prevented from filing such charge by reason of service in the armed forces, in which event the six-month period shall be computed from the day of his discharge. Any such complaint may be amended by the member, agent, or agency conducting the hearing or the Board in its discretion at any time prior to the issuance of an order based thereon. The person so complained of shall have the right to file an answer to the original or amended complaint and to appear in person or otherwise and give testimony at the place and time fixed in the complaint. In the discretion of the member, agent, or agency conducting the hearing or the Board, any other person may be allowed to intervene in the said proceeding and to present testimony. Any such proceeding shall, so far as practicable, be conducted in accordance with the rules of evidence applicable in the district courts of the United States under the rules of civil procedure for the district courts of the United States, adopted by the Supreme Court of the United States pursuant to the Act of June 19, 1934 (U.S.C., title 28, secs. 723-B, 723-C).

"(c) The testimony taken by such member, agent, or agency or the Board shall be reduced to writing and filed with the Board. Thereafter in its discretion, the Board upon notice may take further testimony or hear argument. If upon the preponderance of the testimony taken the Board shall be of the opinion that any person named in the complaint has engaged in or is engaging in any such unfair labor practice, then the Board shall state its findings of fact and shall issue and cause to be served on such person an order requiring such person to cease and desist from such unfair labor practice, and to take such affirmative action including reinstatement of employees with or without back pay, as will effectuate the policies of this Act: *Provided,* That where an order directs reinstatement of an employee, back pay may be required of the employer or labor organization, as the case may be, responsible for the discrimination suffered by him: *And provided further,* That in determining whether a complaint shall issue alleging a violation of section 8(a)(1) or section 8(a)(2), and in deciding such cases, the same regulations and rules of decision shall apply irrespective of whether or not the labor organization affected is affiliated with a labor organization national or international in scope. Such order may further require such person to make reports from time to time showing the extent to which it has complied with the order. If upon preponderance of the testimony taken the Board shall not be of the opinion that the person named in the complaint has engaged in or is engaging in any such unfair labor practice, then the Board shall state its findings of fact and shall issue an order dismissing the said complaint. No order of the Board shall require the reinstatement of any individual as an employee who has been suspended or discharged, or the payment to him of any back pay, if such individual was suspended or discharged for cause. In case the evidence is presented before a member of the Board, or before an examiner or examiners thereof, such member, or such examiner or examiners, as the case may be, shall issue and cause to be served on the parties to the proceeding a proposed report, together with a recommended order, which shall be filed with the Board, and if no exceptions are filed within twenty days after service thereof upon such parties, or within such further period as the Board may authorize, such recommended order shall become the order of the Board and become effective as therein prescribed.

"(d) Until a transcript of the record in a case shall have been filed in a court, as hereinafter provided, the Board may at any time, upon reasonable notice and in such manner as it shall deem proper, modify or set aside, in whole or in part, any finding or order made or issued by it.

"(e) The Board shall have power to petition any circuit court of appeals of the United States (including the United States Court of Appeals for the District of Columbia), or if all the circuit courts of appeals to which application may be made are in vacation, any district court of the United States (including the District Court of the United States for the District of Columbia), within any circuit or district, respectively, wherein the unfair labor practice in question occurred or wherein such person resides or transacts business, for the enforcement of such order and for appropriate temporary relief or restraining order, and shall certify and file in the court a transcript of the entire record in the proceedings, including the pleadings and testimony upon which such order was entered and the findings and order of the Board. Upon such filing, the court shall cause notice thereof to be served upon such person, and thereupon shall have jurisdiction of the proceeding and of the question determined therein, and shall have power to grant such temporary relief or restraining order as it deems just and proper, and to make and enter upon the pleadings, testimony, and proceedings set forth in such transcript a decree enforcing, modifying, and enforcing as so modified, or setting aside in whole or in part the order of the Board. No objection that has not been urged before the Board, its member, agent, or agency, shall be considered by the court, unless the failure or neglect to urge such objection shall be excused because of extraordinary circumstances. The findings of the Board with respect to questions of fact if supported by substantial evidence on the record considered as a whole shall be conclusive. If either party shall apply to the court for leave to adduce additional evidence and shall show to the satisfaction of the court that such additional evidence is material and that there were reasonable grounds for the failure to adduce such evidence in the hearing before the Board, its member, agent, or agency, the court may order such additional evidence to be taken before the Board, its members, agent, or agency, and to be made a part of the transcript. The Board may modify its findings as to the facts, or make new findings, by reason of additional evidence so taken and filed, and it shall file such modified or new findings, which findings with respect to questions of fact if supported by substantial evidence on the record considered as a whole shall be conclusive, and shall file its recommendations, if any, for the modification or setting aside of its original order. The jurisdiction of the court shall be exclusive and its judgment and decree shall be final, except that the same shall be subject to review by the appropriate circuit court of appeals if application was made to the district court as hereinabove provided, and by the Supreme Court of the United States upon writ of certiorari or certification as provided in sections 239 and 240 of the Judicial Code, as amended (U.S.C., title 28, secs. 346 and 347).

"(f) Any person aggrieved by a final order of the Board granting or denying in whole or in part the relief sought may obtain a review of such order in any circuit court of appeals of the United States in the circuit wherein the unfair labor practice in question was alleged to have been engaged in or wherein such person resides or transacts business, or in the United States Court of Appeals for the District of Columbia, by filing in such court a written petition praying that the order of the Board be modified or set aside. A copy of such petition shall be forthwith served upon the

Board, and thereupon the aggrieved party shall file in the court a transcript of the entire record in the proceeding, certified by the Board, including the pleading and testimony upon which the order complained of was entered, and the findings and order of the Board. Upon such filing, the court shall proceed in the same manner as in the case of an application by the Board under subsection (e), and shall have the same exclusive jurisdiction to grant to the Board such temporary relief or restraining order as it deems just and proper, and in like manner to make and enter a decree enforcing, modifying, and enforcing as so modified, or setting aside in whole or in part the order of the Board; the findings of the Board with respect to questions of fact if supported by substantial evidence on the record considered as a whole shall in like manner be conclusive.

"(g) The commencement of proceedings under subsection (e) or (f) of this section shall not, unless specifically ordered by the court, operate as a stay of the Board's order.

"(h) When granting appropriate temporary relief or a restraining order, or making and entering a decree enforcing, modifying, and enforcing as so modified, or setting aside in whole or in part an order of the Board, as provided in this section, the jurisdiction of courts sitting in equity shall not be limited by the Act entitled 'An Act to amend the Judicial Code and to define and limit the jurisdiction of courts sitting in equity, and for other purposes,' approved March 23, 1932 (U.S.C., Supp. VII, title 29, secs. 101–115).

"(i) Petitions filed under this Act shall be heard expeditiously, and if possible within ten days after they have been docketed.

"(j) The Board shall have power, upon issuance of a complaint as provided in subsection (b) charging that any person has engaged in or is engaging in an unfair labor practice, to petition any district court of the United States (including the District Court of the United States for the District of Columbia), within any district wherein the unfair labor practice in question is alleged to have occurred or wherein such person resides or transacts business, for appropriate temporary relief or restraining order. Upon the filing of any such petition the court shall cause notice thereof to be served upon such person, and thereupon shall have jurisdiction to grant to the Board such temporary relief or restraining order as it deems just and proper.

"(k) Whenever it is charged that any person has engaged in an unfair labor practice within the meaning of paragraph (4)(d) of section 8(b), the Board is empowered and directed to hear and determine the dispute out of which such unfair labor practice shall have arisen, unless, within ten days after notice that such charge has been filed, the parties to such dispute submit to the Board satisfactory evidence that they have adjusted, or agreed upon methods for the voluntary adjustment of, the dispute. Upon compliance by the parties to the dispute with the decision of the Board or upon such voluntary adjustment of the dispute, such charge shall be dismissed.

"(l) Whenever it is charged any person has engaged in an unfair labor practice within the meaning of paragraph (4)(A), (B), or (C) of section 8(b), the preliminary investigation of such charge shall be made forthwith and given priority over all other cases except cases of like character in the office where it is filed or to which it is referred. If, after such investigation, the officer or regional attorney to whom the matter may be referred has reasonable cause to believe such charge is true and that a complaint should issue, he shall, on behalf of the Board, petition any district court of the United States (including the District Court of the United States for the District of Columbia) within any district where the unfair labor practice in question has occurred, is alleged to have occurred, or wherein such person resides or transacts business, for appropriate injunctive relief pending the final adjudication of the Board with respect to such matter. Upon the filing of any such petition the district court shall have jurisdiction to grant such injunctive relief or temporary restraining order as it deems just and proper, notwithstanding any other provision of law: *Provided further,* That no temporary restraining order shall be issued without notice unless a petition alleges that substantial and irreparable injury to the charging party will be unavoidable and such temporary restraining order shall be effective for no longer than five days and will become void at the expiration of such period. Upon filing of any such petition the courts shall cause notice thereof to be served upon any person involved in the charge and such person, including the charging party, shall be given an opportunity to appear by counsel and present any relevant testimony: *Provided further,* That for the purposes of this subsection district courts shall be deemed to have jurisdiction of a labor organization (1) in the district in which such organization maintains its principal office, or (2) in any District in which its duly authorized officers or agents are engaged in promoting or protecting the interests of employee members. The service of legal process upon such officer or agent shall constitute service upon the labor organization and make such organization a party to the suit. In situations where such relief is appropriate the procedure specified herein shall apply to charges with respect to section 8(b)(4)(D).

"Investigatory Powers

"SEC. 11. For the purpose of all hearings and investigations, which, in the opinion of the Board, are necessary and proper for the exercise of the powers vested in it by section 9 and section 10

"(1) The Board, or its duly authorized agents or agencies, shall at all reasonable times have access to, for purpose of examination, and the right to copy any evidence of any person being investigated or proceeded against that relates to any matter under investigation or in question. The Board, or any member thereof, shall upon application of any party to such proceedings, forthwith issue to such party subpenas requiring the attendance and testimony of witnesses or the production of any evidence in such proceeding or investigation requested in such application. Within five days after the service of a subpena or any person requiring the production of any evidence in his possession or under his control, such person may petition the Board to revoke, and the Board shall revoke such subpena if in its opinion the evidence whose production is required does not relate to any matter under investigation, or any matter in question in such proceedings, or if in its opinion such subpena does not describe with sufficient particularity the evidence whose production is required.

Any member of the Board, or any agent or agency designated by the Board for such purposes, may administer oaths and affirmations, examine witnesses, and receive evidence. Such attendance of witnesses and the production of such evidence may be required from any place in the United states or any Territory or possession thereof, at any designated place of hearing.

"(2) In case of contumacy or refusal to obey a subpena issued to any person, any district court of the United States or the United States courts of any Territory or possession, or the District Court of the United States for the District of Columbia, within the jurisdiction of which the inquiry is carried on or within the jurisdicton of which said person guilty of contumacy or refusal to obey is found or resides or transacts business, upon application by the Board shall have jurisdiction to issue to such person an order requiring such person to appear before the Board, its member, agent, or agency, there to produce evidence if so ordered, or there to give testimony touching the matter under investigation or in question; and any failure to obey such order of the court may be punished by said court as a contempt thereof.

"(3) No person shall be excused from attending and testifying or from producing books, records, correspondence, documents, or other evidence in obedience to the subpena of the Board, on the ground that the testimony or evidence required of him may tend to incriminate him or subject him to a penalty or forfeiture; but no individual shall be prosecuted or subjected to any penalty or forfeiture for or on account of any transaction, matter, or thing concerning which he is compelled, after having claimed his privilege against self-incrimination, to testify or produce evidence, except that such individual so testifying shall not be exempt from prosecution and punishment for perjury committed in so testifying.

"(4) Complaints, orders, and other process and papers of the Board, its member, agent, or agency may be served either personally or by registered mail or by telegraph or by leaving a copy thereof at the principal office or place of business of the person required to be served. The verified return by the individual so serving the same setting forth the manner of such service shall be proof of the same, and the return post office receipt or telegraph receipt therefor when registered and mailed or telegraphed as aforsaid shall be proof of service of the same. Witnesses summoned before the Board, its member, agent, or agency, shall be paid the same fees and mileage that are paid witnesses in the courts of the United States, and witnesses whose depositions are taken and the persons taking the same shall severally be entitled to the same fees as are paid for like services in the courts of the United States.

"(5) All process of any court to which application may be made under this Act may be served in the judicial district wherein the defendant or other person required to be served resides or may be found.

"(6) The several departments and agencies of the Government, when directed by the President, shall furnish the Board, upon its request, all records, papers, and information in their possession relating to any matter before the Board.

"SEC. 12. Any person who shall willfully resist, prevent, impede, or interfere with any member of the Board or any of its agents or agencies in the performance of duties pursuant to this Act shall be punished by a fine of not more than $5,000 or by imprisonment for not more than one year, or both.

"Limitations

"SEC. 13. Nothing in this Act, except as specifically provided for herein, shall be construed so as either to interfere with or impede or diminish in any way the right to strike, or to affect the limitations or qualifications on that right.

"SEC. 14. (a) Nothing herein shall prohibit any individual employed as a supervisor from becoming or remaining a member of a labor organization, but no employer subject to this Act shall be compelled to deem individuals defined herein as supervisors as employees for the purpose of any law, either national or local, relating to collective bargaining.

"(b) Nothing in this Act shall be construed as authorizing the execution or application of agreements requiring membership in a labor organization as a condition of employment in any State or Territory in which such execution or application is prohibited by State or Territorial law.

"SEC. 15. Wherever the application of the provisions of section 272 of chapter 10 of the Act entitled 'An Act to establish a uniform system of bankruptcy throughout the United States,' approved July 1, 1898, and Acts amendatory thereof and supplementary thereto (U.S.C., title 11, sec. 672), conflicts with the application of the provisions of this Act, this Act shall prevail: *Provided,* That in any situation where the provisions of this Act cannot be validly enforced, the provisions of such other Acts shall remain in full force and effect.

"SEC. 16. If any provision of this Act, or the application of such provision to any person or circumstances, shall be held invalid, the remainder of this Act, or the application of such provision to persons or circumstances other than those as to which it is held invalid, shall not be affected thereby.

"SEC. 17. This Act may be cited as the 'National Labor Relations Act.'"

Effective Date of Certain Changes

SEC. 102. No provision of this title shall be deemed to make an unfair labor practice any act which was performed prior to the date of the enactment of this Act which did not constitute an unfair labor practice prior thereto, and the provisions of section 8(a)(3) and section 8(b)(2) of the National Labor Relations Act as amended by this title shall not make an unfair labor practice the performance of any obligation under a collective-bargaining agreement entered into prior to the date of the enactment of this Act, or (in the case of an agreement for a period of not more than one year) entered into on or after such date of enactment, but prior to the effective date of this title, if the performance of such obligation would not have constituted an unfair labor practice under section 8(3) of the National Labor Relations Act prior to the effective date of this title, unless such agreement was renewed or extended subsequent thereto.

SEC. 103. No provisions of this title shall affect any certification of representatives or any determination as to the appropriate collective-bargaining unit, which was made under section 9 of the National Labor Relations Act prior to the effective date of this title until one year after the date of such certification or if in respect of any such certification, a collective-bargaining contract was entered into prior to the effective date of this title, until the end of the contract period or until one year after such date, whichever first occurs.

SEC. 104. The amendments made by this title shall take effect sixty days after the date of the enactment of this Act, except that the authority of the President to appoint certain officers conferred upon him by section 3 of the National Labor Relations Act as amended by this title may be exercised forthwith.

TITLE II. CONCILIATION OF LABOR DISPUTES IN INDUSTRIES AFFECTING COMMERCE; NATIONAL EMERGENCIES

SEC. 201. That it is the policy of the United States that

(a) sound and stable industrial peace and the advancement of the general welfare, health, and safety of the Nation and of the best interests of employers and employees can most satisfactorily be secured by the settlement of issues between employers and employees through the processes of conference and collective bargaining between employers and the representatives of their employees.

(b) the settlement of issues between employers and employees through collective bargaining may be advanced by making available full and adequate governmental facilities for conciliation, mediation, and voluntary arbitration to aid and encourage employers and the representatives of their employees to reach and maintain agreements concerning rates of pay, hours, and working conditions, and to make all reasonable efforts to settle their differences by mutual agreement reached through conferences and collective bargaining or by such methods as may be provided for in any applicable agreement for the settlement of disputes; and

(c) certain controversies which arise between parties to collective-bargaining agreements may be avoided or minimized by making available full and adequate governmental facilities for furnishing assistance to employers and the representatives of their employees in formulating for inclusion within such agreements provision for adequate notice of any proposed changes in the terms of such agreements, for the final adjustment of grievances or questions regarding the application or interpretation of such agreements, and other provisions designed to prevent the subsequent arising of such controversies.

SEC. 202. (a) There is hereby created an independent agency to be known as the Federal Mediation and Conciliation Service (herein referred to as the "Service" except that for sixty days after the enactment of this Act such term shall refer to the conciliation service of the Department of Labor). The Service shall be under the direction of a Federal Mediation and Conciliation Director (hereinafter referred to as the "Director"), who shall be appointed by the President by and with the advice and consent of the Senate. The Director shall receive compensation at the rate of $12,000 per annum. The Director shall not engage in any other business, vocation, or employment.

(b) The Director is authorized, subject to the civil-service laws, to appoint such clerical and other personnel as may be necessary for the execution of the functions of the Service, and shall fix their compensation in accordance with the Classification Act of 1923, as amended, and may, without regard to the provisions of the civil-service laws and the Classification Act of 1923, as amended, appoint and fix the compensation of such conciliators and mediators as may be necessary to carry out the functions of the Service. The Director is authorized to make such expenditures for supplies, facilities, and services as he deems necessary. Such expenditures shall be allowed and paid upon presentation of itemized vouchers therefor approved by the Director or by any employee designated by him for that purpose.

(c) The principal office of the Service shall be in the District of Columbia, but the Director may establish regional offices convenient to localities in which labor controversies are likely to arise. The Director may by order, subject to revocation at any time, delegate any authority and discretion conferred upon him by this Act to any regional director, or other officer or employee of the Service. The Director may establish suitable procedures for cooperation with State and local mediation agencies. The Director shall make an annual report in writing to Congress at the end of the fiscal year.

(d) All mediation and conciliation functions of the Secretary of Labor or the United States Conciliation Service under section 8 of the Act entitled "An Act to create a Department of Labor," approved March 4, 1913 (U.S.C., title 29, sec. 51), and all functions of the United States Conciliation Service under any other law are hereby transferred to the Federal Mediation Service, together with the personnel, records, and unobligated balances of appropriations, allocations, or other funds of the United States Conciliation Service. Such transfer shall take effect upon the sixtieth day after the date of enactment of this Act. Such transfer shall not affect any proceedings pending before the United States Conciliation Service or any certification, order, rule, or regulation theretofore made by it or by the Secretary of Labor. The Director and the Service shall not be subject in any way to the jurisdiction or authority of the Secretary of Labor or any official or division of the Department of Labor.

Functions of the Service

SEC. 203. (a) It shall be the duty of the Service, in order to prevent or minimize interruptions of the free flow of commerce growing out of labor disputes, to assist parties to labor disputes in industries affecting commerce to settle such disputes through conciliation and mediation.

(b) The Service may proffer its services in any labor dispute in any industry affecting commerce, either upon its own motion or upon the request of one or more of the parties to the dispute, whenever in its judgment such dispute threatens to cause a substantial interruption of commerce. The Director and the Service are directed to avoid attempting to mediate disputes which would have only a minor effect on interstate commerce if State or other conciliation services are available to the parties. Whenever the Service does proffer its services in any dispute, it shall be the duty of the Service promptly to put itself in communication with the parties and to use its best efforts, by mediation and conciliation, to bring them to agreement.

(c) If the Director is not able to bring the parties to agreement by conciliation within a reasonable time, he shall seek to induce the parties voluntarily to seek other means of settling the dispute without resort to strike, lock-out, or other coercion, including the submission to the employees in the bargaining unit of the employer's last offer of settlement for approval or rejection in a secret ballot. The failure or refusal of either party to agree to any procedure suggested by the Director shall not be deemed a violation of any duty or obligation imposed by this Act.

(d) Final adjustment by a method agreed upon by the parties is hereby declared to be the desirable method for settlement of grievance disputes arising over the application or interpretation of an existing collective-bargaining agreement. The Service is directed to make its conciliation and mediation services available in the settlement of such grievance disputes only as a last resort and in exceptional cases.

SEC. 204. (a) In order to prevent or minimize interruptions of the free flow of commerce growing out of labor disputes, employers and employees and their representatives, in any industry affecting commerce, shall

(1) exert every reasonable effort to make and maintain agreements concerning rates of pay, hours, and working conditions, including provision for adequate notice of any proposed change in the terms of such agreements;

(2) whenever a dispute arises over the terms or application of a collective-bargaining agreement and a conference is requested by a party or prospective party thereto, arrange promptly for such a conference to be held and endeavor in such conference to settle such dispute expeditiously; and

(3) in case such dispute is not settled by conference, participate fully and promptly in such meetings as may be undertaken by the Service under this Act for the purpose of aiding in a settlement of the dispute.

SEC. 205. (a) There is hereby created a National Labor-Management Panel which shall be composed of twelve members appointed by the President, six of whom shall be selected from among persons outstanding in the field of management and six of whom shall be selected from among persons outstanding in the field of labor. Each member shall hold office for a term of three years, except that any member appointed to fill a vacancy occurring prior to the expiration of the term for which his predecessor was appointed shall be appointed for the remainder of such term, and the terms of office of the members first taking office shall expire, as designated by the President at the time of appointment, four at the end of the first year, four at the end of the second year, and four at the end of the third year after the date of appointment. Members of the panel, when serving on business of the panel, shall be paid compensation at the rate of $25 per day, and shall also be entitled to receive an allowance for actual and necessary travel and subsistence expenses while so serving away from their places of residence.

(b) It shall be the duty of the panel, at the request of the Director, to advise in the avoidance of industrial controversies and the manner in which mediation and voluntary adjustment shall be administered particularly with reference to controversies affecting the general welfare of the country.

National Emergencies

SEC. 206. Whenever in the opinion of the President of the United States, a threatened or actual strike or lock-out affecting an entire industry or a substantial part thereof engaged in trade, commerce, transportation, transmission, or communication among the several States or with foreign nations or engaged in the production of goods for commerce will, if permitted to occur or to continue, imperil the national health or safety, he may appoint a board of inquiry to inquire into the issues involved in the dispute and to make a written report to him within such time as he shall prescribe. Such report shall include a statement of the facts with respect to the dispute, including each party's statement of its position but shall not contain any recommendations. The President shall file a copy of such report with the Service and shall make its contents available to the public.

SEC. 207. (a) A board of inquiry shall be composed of a chairman and such other members as the President shall determine, and shall have power to sit and act in any place within the United States and to conduct such hearings either in public or in private, as it may deem necessary or proper, to ascertain the facts with respect to the causes and circumstances of the dispute.

(b) Members of a board of inquiry shall receive compensation at the rate of $50 for each day actually spent by them in the work of the board, together with necessary travel and subsistence expenses.

(c) For the purpose of any hearing or inquiry conducted by any board appointed under this title, the provisions of sections 9 and 10 (relating to the attendance of witnesses and the production of books, papers, and documents) of the Federal Trade Commission Act of September 16, 1914, as amended (U.S.C. 19, title 15, secs. 49 and 50, as amended), are hereby made applicable to the powers and duties of such board.

SEC. 208. (a) Upon receiving a report from a board of inquiry the

President may direct the Attorney General to petition any district court of the United States having jurisdiction of the parties to enjoin such strike or lock-out, or the continuing thereof, and if the court finds that such threatened or actual strike or lock-out (i) affects an entire industry or a substantial part thereof engaged in trade, commerce, transportation, transmission, or communication among the several States or with foreign nations, or engaged in the production of goods for commerce; and (ii) if permitted to occur or to continue, will imperil the national health or safety, it shall have jurisdiction to enjoin any such strike or lock-out, or the continuing thereof, and to make such other orders as may be appropriate.

(b) In any case, the provisions of the Act of March 23, 1932, entitled "An Act to amend the Judicial Code and to define and limit the jurisdiction of courts sitting in equity, and for other purposes," shall not be applicable.

(c) The order or orders of the court shall be subject to review by the appropriate circuit court of appeals and by the Supreme Court upon writ of certiorari or certification as provided in section 239 and 240 of the Judicial Code, as amended (U.S.C., title 29, secs. 346 and 347).

SEC. 209. (a) Whenever a district court has issued an order under section 208 enjoining acts or practices which imperil or threaten to imperil the national health or safety, it shall be the duty of the parties to the labor dispute giving rise to such order to make every effort to adjust and settle their differences, with the assistance of the Service created by this Act. Neither party shall be under any duty to accept, in whole or in part, any proposal of settlement made by the Service.

(b) Upon the issuance of such order, the President shall reconvene the board of inquiry which has previously reported with respect to the dispute. At the end of a sixty-day period (unless the dispute has been settled by that time), the board of inquiry shall report to the President the current position of the parties and the efforts which have been made for settlement and shall include a statement by each party of its position and a statement of the employer's last offer of settlement. The President shall make such report available to the public. The National Labor Relations Board, within the succeeding fifteen days, shall take a secret ballot of the employees of each employer involved in the dispute on the question of whether they wish to accept the final offer of settlement made by their employer as stated by him and shall certify the results thereof to the Attorney General within five days thereafter.

SEC. 210. Upon the certification of the results of such ballot or upon a settlement being reached, whichever happens sooner, the Attorney General shall move the court to discharge the injunction, which motion shall then be granted and the injunction discharged. When such motion is granted, the President shall submit to the Congress a full and comprehensive report of the proceedings, including the findings of the board of inquiry and the ballot taken by the National Labor Relations Board together with such recommendations as he may see fit to make for consideration and appropriate action.

Compilation of Collective Bargaining Agreements, Etc.

SEC. 211. (a) For the guidance and information of interested representatives of employers, employees, and the general public, the Bureau of Labor Statistics of the Department of Labor shall maintain a file of copies of all available collective bargaining agreements and other available agreements and actions thereunder settling or adjusting labor disputes. Such file shall be open to inspection under appropriate conditions prescribed by the Secretary of Labor, except that no specific information submitted in confidence shall be disclosed.

(b) The Bureau of Labor Statistics in the Department of Labor is authorized to furnish upon request of the Service, or employers, employees, or their representatives, all available data and factual information which may aid in the settlement of any labor dispute, except that no specific information submitted in confidence shall be disclosed.

Exemption of Railway Labor Act

SEC. 212. The provisions of this title shall not be applicable with respect to any matter which is subject to the provisions of the Railway Labor Act, as amended from time to time.

TITLE III. SUITS BY AND AGAINST LABOR ORGANIZATIONS

SEC. 301. (a) Suits for violation of contracts between an employer and a labor organization representing employees in an industry affecting commerce as defined in this Act, or between any such labor organizations, may be brought in any district court of the United States having jurisdiction of the parties, without respect to the amount in controversy or without regard to the citizenship of the parties.

(b) Any labor organization which represents employees in an industry affecting commerce as defined in this Act and any employer whose activities affect commerce as defined in this Act shall be bound by the acts of its agents. Any such labor organization may sue or be sued as an entity and in behalf of the employees whom it represents in the courts of the United States. Any money judgment against a labor organization in a district court of the United States shall be enforceable only against the organization as an entity and against its assets, and shall not be enforceable against any individual member or his assets.

(c) For the purposes of actions and proceedings by or against labor organizations in the district courts of the United States, district courts shall be deemed to have jurisdiction of a labor organization (1) in the district in which such organization maintains its principal office, or (2) in any

district in which its duly authorized officers or agents are engaged in representing or acting for employee members.

(d) The service of summons, subpena, or other legal process of any
court of the United States upon an officer or agent of a labor organization,
in his capacity as such, shall constitute service upon the labor organization.

(e) For the purposes of this section, in determining whether any person
is acting as an "agent" of another person so as to make such other person
responsible for his acts, the question of whether the specific acts performed
were actually authorized or subsequently ratified shall not be controlling.

Restrictions on Payments to Employee Representatives

SEC. 302. (a) It shall be unlawful for any employer to pay or deliver,
or to agree to pay or deliver, any money or other thing of value to any representative of any of his employees who are employed in an industry affecting
commerce.

(b) It shall be unlawful for any representative of any employees who are
employed in an industry affecting commerce to receive or accept, or to
agree to receive or accept, from the employer of such employees any money
or other thing of value.

(c) The provisions of this section shall not be applicable (1) with respect to any money or other thing of value payable by an employer to any
representative who is an employee or former employee of such employer, as
compensation for, or by reason of, his services as an employee of such employer; (2) with respect to the payment or delivery of any money or other
thing of value in satisfaction of a judgment of any court or a decision or
award of an arbitrator or impartial chairman or in compromise, adjustment,
settlement or release of any claim, complaint, grievance, or dispute in the
absence of fraud or duress; (3) with respect to the sale or purchase of an
article or commodity at the prevailing market price in the regular course
of business; (4) with respect to money deducted from the wages of employees in payment of membership dues in a labor organization: *Provided,*
That the employer has received from each employee, on whose account
such deductions are made, a written assignment which shall not be irrevocable for a period of more than one year, or beyond the termination date of
the applicable collective agreement, whichever occurs sooner; or (5) with
respect to money or other thing of value paid to a trust fund established by
such representative, for the sole and exclusive benefit of the employees of
such employer, and their families and dependents (or of such employees,
families, and dependents jointly with the employees of other employers
making similar payments, and their families and dependents): *Provided,*
That (A) such payments are held in trust for the purpose of paying, either
from principal or income or both, for the benefit of employees, their families
and dependents, for medical or hospital care, pensions on retirement or
death of employees, compensation for injuries or illness resulting from occupational activity or insurance to provide any of the foregoing, or unemploy-

ment benefits or life insurance, disability and sickness insurance, or accident insurance; (B) the detailed basis on which such payments are to be made is specified in a written agreement with the employer, and employees and employers are equally represented in the administration of such fund, together with such neutral persons as the representatives of the employers and the representatives of the employees may agree upon and in the event the employer and employee groups deadlock on the administration of such fund and there are no neutral persons empowered to break such deadlock, such agreement provides that the two groups shall agree on an impartial umpire to decide such dispute, or in event of their failure to agree within a reasonable length of time, an impartial umpire to decide such dispute shall, on petition of either group, be appointed by the district court of the United States for the district where the trust fund has its principal office, and shall also contain provisions for an annual audit of the trust fund, a statement of the results of which shall be available for inspection by interested persons at the principal office of the trust fund and at such other places as may be designated in such written agreement; and (C) such payments as are intended to be used for the purpose of providing pensions or annuities for employees are made to a separate trust which provides that the funds held therein cannot be used for any purpose other than paying such pensions or annuities.

(d) Any person who willfully violates any of the provisions of this section shall, upon conviction thereof, be guilty of a misdemeanor and be subject to a fine of not more than $10,000 or to imprisonment for not more than one year, or both.

(e) The district courts of the United States and the United States courts of the Territories and possessions shall have jurisdiction, for cause shown, and subject to the provisions of section 17 (relating to notice to opposite party) of the Act entitled "An Act to supplement existing laws against unlawful restraints and monopolies, and for other purposes," approved October 15, 1914, as amended (U.S.C., title 28, sec. 381), to restrain violations of this section, without regard to the provisions of sections 6 and 20 of such Act of October 15, 1914, as amended (U.S.C., title 15, sec. 17, and title 29, sec. 52), and the provisions of the Act entitled "An Act to amend the Judicial Code and to define and limit the jurisdiction of courts sitting in equity, and for other purposes," approved March 23, 1932 (U.S.C., title 29, secs. 101–115).

(f) This section shall not apply to any contract in force on the date of enactment of this Act, until the expiration of such contract, or until July 1, 1948, whichever first occurs.

(g) Compliance with the restrictions contained in subsection (c)(5)(B) upon contributions to trust funds, otherwise lawful, shall not be applicable to contributions to such trust funds established by collective agreement prior to January 1, 1946, nor shall subsection (c)(5)(A) be construed as prohibiting contributions to such trust funds if prior to January 1, 1947 such funds contained provisions for pooled vacation benefits.

Boycotts and Other Unlawful Combinations

sec. 303. (a) It shall be unlawful, for the purposes of this section only, in an industry or activity affecting commerce, for any labor organization to engage in, or to induce or encourage the employees of any employer to engage in, a strike or a concerted refusal in the course of their employment to use, manufacture, process, transport, or otherwise handle or work on any goods, articles, materials or commodities or to perform any services where an object thereof is

(1) forcing or requiring any employer or self-employed person to join any labor or employer organization or any employer or other person to cease using, selling, handling, transporting, or otherwise dealing in the products of any other producer, processor, or manufacturer, or to cease doing business with any other person;

(2) forcing or requiring any other employer to recognize or bargain with a labor organization as the representative of his employees unless such labor organization has been certified as the representative of such employees under the provisions of section 9 of the National Labor Relations Act;

(3) forcing or requiring any employer to recognize or bargain with a particular labor organization as the representative of his employees if another labor organization has been certified as the representative of such employees under the provisions of section 9 of the National Labor Relations Act;

(4) forcing or requiring any employer to assign particular work to employees in a particular labor organization or in a particular trade, craft, or class rather than to employees in another labor organization or in another trade, craft, or class unless such employer is failing to conform to an order of certification of the National Labor Relations Board determining the bargaining representative for employees performing such work. Nothing contained in this subsection shall be construed to make unlawful a refusal by any person to enter upon the premises of any employer (other than his own employer), if the employees of such employer are engaged in a strike ratified or approved by a representative of such employees whom such employer is required to recognize under the National Labor Relations Act.

(b) Whoever shall be injured in his business or property by reason of any violation of subsection (a) may sue therefor in any district court of the United States subject to the limitations and provisions of section 301 hereof without respect to the amount in controversy, or in any other court having jurisdiction of the parties, and shall recover the damages by him sustained and the cost of the suit.

Restriction on Political Contributions

sec. 304. Section 313 of the Federal Corrupt Practices Act, 1925 (U.S.C., 1940 edition, title 2, sec. 251; Supp. V, title 50, App., sec. 1509), as amended, is amended to read as follows:

"SEC. 313. It is unlawful for any national bank, or any corporation organized by authority of any law of Congress, to make a contribution or expenditure in connection with any election to any political office, or in connection with any primary election or political convention or caucus held to select candidates for any political office, or for any corporation whatever, or any labor organization to make a contribution or expenditure in connection with any election at which Presidential and Vice Presidential electors or a Senator or Representative in, or a Delegate or Resident Commissioner to Congress are to be voted for, or in connection with any primary election or political convention or caucus held to select candidates for any of the foregoing offices, or for any candidate, political committee, or other person to accept or receive any contribution prohibited by this section. Every corporation or labor organization which makes any contribution or expenditure in violation of this section shall be fined not more than $5,000; and every officer or director of any corporation, or officer of any labor organization, who consents to any contribution or expenditure by the corporation or labor organization, as the case may be, in violation of this section shall be fined not more than $1,000 or imprisoned for not more than one year, or both. For the purposes of this section 'labor organization' means any organization of any kind, or any agency or employee representation committee or plan, in which employees participate and which exists for the purpose, in whole or in part, of dealing with employers concerning grievances, labor disputes, wages, rates of pay, hours of employment, or conditions of work."

Strikes by Government Employees

SEC. 305. It shall be unlawful for any individual employed by the United States or any agency thereof including wholly owned Government corporations to participate in any strike. Any individual employed by the United States or by any such agency who strikes, shall be discharged immediately from his employment, and shall forfeit his civil service status, if any, and shall not be eligible for reemployment for 3 years by the United States or any such agency.

TITLE IV. CREATION OF JOINT COMMITTEE TO STUDY AND REPORT ON BASIC PROBLEMS AFFECTING FRIENDLY LABOR RELATIONS AND PRODUCTIVITY

SEC. 401. There is hereby established a joint congressional committee to be known as the Joint Committee on Labor-Management Relations (hereafter referred to as the committee), and to be composed of seven Members of the Senate Committee on Labor and Public Welfare, to be appointed by the President pro tempore of the Senate, and seven Members of the House of Representatives Committee on Education and Labor, to be appointed by the Speaker of the House of Representatives. A vacancy in membership of the committee shall not affect the powers of the remaining members to execute the functions of the committee, and shall be filled in the same manner as the original selection. The committee shall select a chairman and a vice chairman from among its members.

SEC. 402. The committee, acting as a whole or by subcommittee, shall conduct a thorough study and investigation of the entire field of labor-management relations, including but not limited to

(1) the means by which permanent friendly co-operation between employers and employees and stability of labor relations may be secured throughout the United States;

(2) the means by which the individual employee may achieve a greater productivity and higher wages, including plans for guaranteed annual wages, incentive profit-sharing and bonus systems;

(3) the internal organization and administration of labor unions, with special attention to the impact on individuals of collective agreements requiring membership in unions as a condition of employment;

(4) the labor relations policies and practices of employers and associations of employers;

(5) the desirability of welfare funds for the benefit of employees and their relation to the social-security system;

(6) the methods and procedures for best carrying out the collective-bargaining processes, with special attention to the effects of industry-wide or regional bargaining upon the national economy;

(7) the administration and operation of existing Federal laws relating to labor relations; and

(8) such other problems and subjects in the field of labor-management relations as the committee deems appropriate.

SEC. 403. The committee shall report to the Senate and the House of Representatives not later than March 15, 1948, the results of its study and investigation, together with such recommendations as to necessary legislation and such other recommendations as it may deem advisable and shall make its final report not later than January 2, 1949.

SEC. 404. The committee shall have the power, without regard to the civil-service laws and the Classification Act of 1923, as amended, to employ and fix the compensation of such officers, experts, and employees as it deems necessary for the performance of its duties, including consultants who shall receive compensation at a rate not to exceed $35 for each day actually spent by them in the work of the committee, together with their necessary travel and subsistence expenses. The committee is further authorized, with the consent of the head of the department or agency concerned to utilize the services, information, facilities, and personnel of all agencies in the executive branch of the Government and may request the governments of the several States, representatives of business, industry, finance, and labor, and such other persons, agencies, organizations, and instrumentalities as it deems appropriate to attend its hearings and to give and present information, advice, and recommendations.

SEC. 405. The committee, or any subcommittee thereof, is authorized to hold such hearings; to sit and act at such times and places during the sessions, recesses, and adjourned periods of the Eightieth Congress; to require by subpena or otherwise the attendance of such witnesses and the production of such books, papers, and documents; to administer oaths; to take such testimony; to have such printing and binding done; and to make such expenditures within the amount appropriated therefor; as it deems advisable. The cost of stenographic services in reporting such hearings shall not be in excess of 25 cents per one hundred words. Subpenas shall be issued under the signature of the chairman or vice chairman of the committee and shall be served by any person designated by them.

SEC. 406. The members of the committee shall be reimbursed for travel, subsistence, and other necessary expenses incurred by them in the performance of the duties vested in the committee, other than expenses in connection with meetings of the committee held in the District of Columbia during such times as the Congress is in session.

SEC. 407. There is hereby authorized to be appropriated the sum of $150,000, or so much thereof as may be necessary, to carry out the provisions of this title, to be disbursed by the Secretary of the Senate on vouchers signed by the chairman.

TITLE V. DEFINITIONS

SEC. 501. When used in this Act

(1) The term "industry affecting commerce" means any industry or activity in commerce or in which a labor dispute would burden or obstruct commerce or tend to burden or obstruct commerce or the free flow of commerce.

(2) The term "strike" includes any strike or other concerted stoppage of work by employees (including a stoppage by reason of the expiration of a collective-bargaining agreement) and any concerted slow-down or other concerted interruption of operations by employees.

(3) The terms "commerce," "labor disputes," "employer," "employee," "labor organization," "representative," "person," and "supervisor" shall have the same meaning as when used in the National Labor Relations Act as amended by this Act.

Saving Provision

SEC. 502. Nothing in this Act shall be construed to require an individual employee to render labor or service without his consent, nor shall anything in this Act be construed to make the quitting of his labor by an individual employee an illegal act; nor shall any court issue any process to compel the performance by an individual employee of such labor or service, without his consent; nor shall the quitting of labor by an employee or employees in good faith because of abnormally dangerous conditions for work at the place of employment of such employee or employees be deemed a strike under this Act.

Separability

SEC. 503. If any provision of this Act, or the application of such provision to any person or circumstance, shall be held invalid, the remainder of this Act, or the application of such provision to persons or circumstances other than those as to which it is held invalid shall not be affected thereby.

The 1951 Amendment to the
National Labor Relations Act

Be it enacted by the Senate and House of Representatives of the United States of America in Congress assembled, That the National Labor Relations Act, as amended, is hereby further amended as follows:

(a) By adding at the end of said Act the following new section:

"SEC. 18. No petition entertained, no investigation made, no election held, and no certification issued by the National Labor Relations Board, under any of the provisions of section 9 of the National Labor Relations Act, as amended, shall be invalid by reason of the failure of the Congress of Industrial Organizations to have complied with the requirements of section 9(f), (g), or (h) of the aforesaid Act prior to December 22, 1949, or by reason of the failure of the American Federation of Labor to have complied with the provisions of section 9(f), (g), or (h) of the aforesaid Act prior to November 7, 1947: *Provided,* That no liability shall be imposed under any provision of this Act upon any person for failure to honor any election or certificate, referred to above, prior to the effective date of this amendment: *Provided,* however, That this proviso shall not have the effect of setting aside or in any way affecting judgments or decrees heretofore entered under section 10(e) or (f) and which have become final."

(b) Subsection (a) (3) of section 8 of said Act is amended by striking out so much of the first sentence as reads "; and (ii) if, following the most recent election held as provided in section 9(e) the Board shall have certified that at least a majority of the employees eligible to vote in such election have voted to authorize such labor organization to make such an agreement": and inserting in lieu thereof the following: "and has at the time the agreement was made or within the preceding twelve months received from the Board a notice of compliance with sections 9(f), (g), (h), and (ii) unless following an election held as provided in section 9(e) within one year preceding the effective date of such agreement, the Board shall have certified that at least a majority of the employees eligible to vote in such election have voted to rescind the authority of such labor organization to make such an agreement:"

(c) Section 9(e) of such Act is amended by striking out all of subsections (1) and (2) and inserting in lieu thereof the following: "(1) Upon the filing with the Board, by 30 per centum or more of the employees in a bargaining unit covered by an agreement between their employer and a labor organization made pursuant to section 8(a)(3), of a petition alleging the desire that such authority be rescinded, the Board shall take a secret ballot of the employees in such unit and certify the results thereof to such labor organization and to the employer." Renumber subsection "(3)" as "(2)."

(d) Subsection (f), (g), and (h) of section 9 of such Act are amended by striking out the words "No petition under section 9(e)(1) shall be entertained," where they appear in each of such subsections.

The Labor-Management Reporting
and Disclosure Act of 1959

The Landrum-Griffin Act
Act of September 14, 1959, 86th Congress

An act to provide for the reporting and disclosure of certain financial transactions and administrative practices of labor organizations and employers, to prevent abuses in the administration of trusteeships by labor organizations, to provide standards with respect to the election of officers of labor organizations, and for other purposes.

Be it enacted by the Senate and House of Representatives of the United States of America in Congress assembled,

Short Title

SECTION 1. This Act may be cited as the "Labor-Management Reporting and Disclosure Act of 1959."

Declaration of Findings, Purposes, and Policy

SEC. 2. (a) The Congress finds that, in the public interest, it continues to be the responsibility of the Federal Government to protect employees' rights to organize, choose their own representatives, bargain collectively, and otherwise engage in concerted activities for their mutual aid or protection; that the relations between employers and labor organizations and the millions of workers they represent have a substantial impact on the commerce of the Nation; and that in order to accomplish the objective of a free flow of commerce it is essential that labor organizations, employers, and their officials adhere to the highest standards of responsibility and ethical conduct in administering the affairs of their organizations, particularly as they affect labor-management relations.

(b) The Congress further finds, from recent investigations in the labor and management fields, that there have been a number of instances of breach of trust, corruption, disregard of the rights of individual employees, and other failures to observe high standards of responsibility and ethical conduct which require further and supplementary legislation that will afford necessary protection of the rights and interests of employees and the public generally as they relate to the activities of labor organizations, employers, labor relations consultants, and their officers and representatives.

(c) The Congress, therefore, further finds and declares that the enactment of this Act is necessary to eliminate or prevent improper practices on the part of labor organizations, employers, labor relations consultants, and their officers and representatives which distort and defeat the policies of the Labor Management Relations Act, 1947, as amended, and the Railway Labor Act, as amended, and have the tendency or necessary effect of burdening or obstructing commerce by (1) impairing the efficiency, safety, or operation of the instrumentalities of commerce; (2) occurring in the current of commerce; (3) materially affecting, restraining, or controlling the flow of raw materials or manufactured or processed goods into or from the channels of commerce, or the prices of such materials or goods in commerce; or (4) causing diminution of employment and wages in such volume as substantially to impair or disrupt the market for goods flowing into or from the channels of commerce.

61 Stat. 136.
29 USC 141.
44 Stat. 577.
45 USC 151.

Definitions

SEC. 3. For the purposes of titles I, II, III, IV, V (except section 505), and VI of this Act

(a) "Commerce" means trade, traffic, commerce, transportation, transmission, or communication among the several States or between any State and any place outside thereof.

(b) "State" includes any State of the United States, the District of Columbia, Puerto Rico, the Virgin Islands, American Samoa, Guam, Wake Island, the Canal Zone, and Outer Continental Shelf lands defined in the Outer Continental Shelf Lands Act (43 U.S.C. 1331–1343).

67 Stat. 462.

(c) "Industry affecting commerce" means any activity, business, or industry in commerce or in which a labor dispute would hinder or obstruct commerce or the free flow of commerce and includes any activity or industry "affecting commerce" within the meaning of the Labor Management Relations Act, 1947, as amended, or the Railway Labor Act, as amended.

(d) "Person" includes one or more individuals, labor organizations, partnerships, associations, corporations, legal representatives, mutual companies, joint-stock companies, trusts, unincorporated organizations, trustees, trustees in bankruptcy, or receivers.

(e) "Employer" means any employer or any group or association of employers engaged in an industry affecting commerce (1) which is, with respect to employees engaged in an industry affecting commerce, an employer within the meaning of any law of the United States relating to the employment of any employees or (2) which may deal with any labor organization concerning grievances, labor disputes, wages, rates of pay, hours of employment, or conditions of work, and includes any person acting directly or indirectly as an employer or as an agent of an employer in relation to an employee but does not include the United States or any corporation wholly owned by the Government of the United States or any State or political subdivision thereof.

(f) "Employee" means any individual employed by an employer, and includes any individual whose work has ceased as a consequence of, or in connection with, any current labor dispute or because of any unfair labor practice or because of exclusion or expulsion from a labor organization in any manner or for any reason inconsistent with the requirements of this Act.

(g) "Labor dispute" includes any controversy concerning terms, tenure, or conditions of employment, or concerning the association or representation of persons in negotiating, fixing, maintaining, changing, or seeking to arrange terms or conditions of employment, regardless of whether the disputants stand in the proximate relation of employer and employee.

(h) "Trusteeship" means any receivership, trusteeship, or other method of supervision or control whereby a labor organization suspends the autonomy otherwise available to a subordinate body under its constitution or by-laws.

(i) "Labor organization" means a labor organization engaged in an industry affecting commerce and includes any organization of any kind, any agency, or employee representation committee, group, association, or plan so engaged in which employees participate and which exists for the purpose, in whole or in part, of dealing with employers concerning grievances, labor disputes, wages, rates of pay, hours, or other terms or conditions of employment, and any conference, general committee, joint or system board, or joint council so engaged which is subordinate to a national or international labor organization, other than a State or local central body.

(j) A labor organization shall be deemed to be engaged in an industry affecting commerce if it

(1) is the certified representative of employees under the provisions of the National Labor Relations Act, as amended, or the Railway Labor Act, as amended; or

61 Stat. 136.
29 USC 167.
44 Stat. 577.
45 USC 151.

(2) although not certified, is a national or international labor organization or a local labor organization recognized or acting as the representative of employees of an employer or employers engaged in an industry affecting commerce; or

(3) has chartered a local labor organization or subsidiary body which is representing or actively seeking to represent employees of employers within the meaning of paragraph (1) or (2); or

(4) has been chartered by a labor organization representing or actively seeking to represent employees within the meaning of paragraph (1) or (2) as the local or subordinate body through which such employees may enjoy membership or become affiliated with such labor organization; or

(5) is a conference, general committee, joint or system board, or joint council, subordinate to a national or international labor organization, which includes a labor organization engaged in an industry affecting commerce

within the meaning of any of the preceding paragraphs of this subsection, other than a State or local central body.

(k) "Secret ballot" means the expression by ballot, voting machine, or otherwise, but in no event by proxy, of a choice with respect to any election or vote taken upon any matter, which is cast in such a manner that the person expressing such choice cannot be identified with the choice expressed.

(l) "Trust in which a labor organization is interested" means a trust or other fund or organization (1) which was created or established by a labor organization, or one or more of the trustees or one or more members of the governing body of which is selected or appointed by a labor organization, and (2) a primary purpose of which is to provide benefits for the members of such labor organization or their beneficiaries.

(m) "Labor relations consultant" means any person who, for compensation, advises or represents an employer, employer organization, or labor organization concerning employee organizing, concerted activities, or collective bargaining activities.

(n) "Officer" means any constitutional officer, any person authorized to perform the functions of president, vice president, secretary, treasurer, or other executive functions of a labor organization, and any member of its executive board or similar governing body.

(o) "Member" or "member in good standing," when used in reference to a labor organization, includes any person who has fulfilled the requirements for membership in such organization, and who neither has voluntarily withdrawn from membership nor has been expelled or suspended from membership after appropriate proceedings consistent with lawful provisions of the constitution and bylaws of such organization.

(p) "Secretary" means the Secretary of Labor.

(q) "Officer, agent, shop steward, or other representative," when used with respect to a labor organization, includes elected officials and key administrative personnel, whether elected or appointed (such as business agents, heads of departments or major units, and organizers who exercise substantial independent authority), but does not include salaried nonsupervisory professional staff, stenographic, and service personnel.

(r) "District court of the United States" means a United States district court and a United States court of any place subject to the jurisdiction of the United States.

TITLE I. BILL OF RIGHTS OF MEMBERS OF LABOR ORGANIZATIONS

Bill of Rights

SEC. 101. (A) (1) EQUAL RIGHTS. Every member of a labor organization shall have equal rights and privileges within such organization to nominate candidates, to vote in elections or referendums of the labor organization, to attend membership meetings, and to participate in the deliberations and voting upon the business of such meetings, subject to reasonable rules and regulations in such organization's constitution and bylaws.

(2) FREEDOM OF SPEECH AND ASSEMBLY. Every member of any labor organization shall have the right to meet and assemble freely with other members; and to express any views, arguments, or opinions; and to express at meetings of the labor organization his views, upon candidates in an election of the labor organization or upon any business properly before the meeting, subject to the organization's established and reasonable rules pertaining to the conduct of meetings: *Provided,* That nothing herein shall be construed to impair the right of a labor organization to adopt and enforce reasonable rules as to the responsibility of every member toward the organization as an institution and to his refraining from conduct that would interfere with its performance of its legal or contractual obligations.

(3) DUES, INITIATION FEES, AND ASSESSMENTS. Except in the case of a federation of national or international labor organizations, the rates of dues and initiation fees payable by members of any labor organization in effect on the date of enactment of this Act shall not be increased, and no general or special assessment shall be levied upon such members, except

(A) in the case of a local labor organization, (i) by majority vote by secret ballot of the members in good standing voting at a general or special membership meeting, after reasonable notice of the intention to vote upon such question, or (ii) by majority vote of the members in good standing voting in a membership referendum conducted by secret ballot; or

(B) in the case of a labor organization, other than a local labor organization or a federation of national or international labor organizations, (i) by majority vote of the delegates voting at a regular convention, or at a special convention of such labor organization held upon not less than thirty days' written notice to the principal office of each local or constituent labor organization entitled to such notice, or (ii) by majority vote of the members in good standing of such labor organization voting in a membership referendum conducted by secret ballot, or (iii) by majority vote of the members of the executive board or similar governing body of such labor organization, pursuant to express authority contained in the constitution and bylaws of such labor organization: *Provided.* That such action on the part of the executive board or similar governing body shall be effective only until the next regular convention of such labor organization.

(4) PROTECTION OF THE RIGHT TO SUE. No labor organization shall limit the right of any member thereof to institute an action in any court, or in a proceeding before any administrative agency, irrespective of whether or not the labor organization or its officers are named as defendants or respondents in such action or proceeding, or the right of any member of a labor organization to appear as a witness in any judicial, administrative, or legislative proceeding, or to petition any legislature or to communicate with any legislator: *Provided,* That any such member may be required to exhaust reasonable hearing procedures (but not to exceed a four-month lapse of time) within such organization, before instituting legal or administrative proceedings against such organizations or any officer thereof: *And provided*

further, That no interested employer or employer association shall directly or indirectly finance, encourage, or participate in, except as a party, any such action, proceeding, appearance, or petition.

(5) SAFEGUARDS AGAINST IMPROPER DISCIPLINARY ACTION. No member of any labor organization may be fined, suspended, expelled, or otherwise disciplined except for nonpayment of dues by such organization or by any officer thereof unless such member has been (A) served with written specific charges; (B) given a reasonable time to prepare his defense; (C) afforded a full and fair hearing.

(b) Any provision of the constitution and bylaws of any labor organization which is inconsistent with the provisions of this section shall be of no force or effect.

Civil Enforcement

SEC. 102. Any person whose rights secured by the provisions of this title have been infringed by any violation of this title may bring a civil action in a district court of the United States for such relief (including injunctions) as may be appropriate. Any such action against a labor organization shall be brought in the district court of the United States for the district where the alleged violation occurred, or where the principal office of such labor organization is located.

Retention of Existing Rights

SEC. 103. Nothing contained in this title shall limit the rights and remedies of any member of a labor organization under any State or Federal law or before any court or other tribunal, or under the constitution and bylaws of any labor organization.

Right to Copies of Collective Bargaining Agreements

SEC. 104. It shall be the duty of the secretary or corresponding principal officer of each labor organization, in the case of a local labor organization, to forward a copy of each collective bargaining agreement made by such labor organization with any employer to any employee who requests such a copy and whose rights as such employee are directly affected by such agreement, and in the case of a labor organization other than a local labor organization, to forward a copy of any such agreement to each constituent unit which has members directly affected by such agreement; and such officer shall maintain at the principal office of the labor organization of which he is an officer copies of any such agreement made or received by such labor organization, which copies shall be available for inspection by any member or by any employee whose rights are affected by such agreement. The provisions of section 210 shall be applicable in the enforcement of this section.

ment; and such officer shall maintain at the principal office of the labor organization of which he is an officer copies of any such agreement made or received by such labor organization, which copies shall be available for inspection by any member or by any employee whose rights are affected by such agreement. The provisions of section 210 shall be applicable in the *Post,* p. 530. enforcement of this section.

Information as to Act

SEC. 105. Every labor organization shall inform its members concerning the provisions of this Act.

TITLE II. REPORTING BY LABOR ORGANIZATIONS, OFFICERS AND EMPLOYEES OF LABOR ORGANIZATIONS, AND EMPLOYERS

Report of Labor Organizations

SEC. 201. (a) Every labor organization shall adopt a constitution and bylaws and shall file a copy thereof with the Secretary, together with a report, signed by its president and secretary or corresponding principal officers, containing the following information

(1) the name of the labor organization, its mailing address, and any other address at which it maintains its principal office or at which it keeps the records referred to in this title;

(2) the name and title of each of its officers;

(3) the initiation fee or fees required from a new or transferred member and fees for work permits required by the reporting labor organization;

(4) the regular dues or fees or other periodic payments required to remain a member of the reporting labor organization; and

(5) detailed statements, or references to specific provisions of documents filed under this subsection which contain such statements, showing the provision made and procedures followed with respect to each of the following: (A) qualifications for or restrictions on membership, (B) levying of assessments, (C) participation in insurance or other benefit plans, (D) authorization for disbursement of funds of the labor organization, (E) audit of financial transactions of the labor organization, (F) the calling of regular and special meetings, (G) the selection of officers and stewards and of any representatives to other bodies composed of labor organizations' representatives, with a specific statement of the manner in which each officer was elected, appointed, or otherwise selected, (H) discipline or removal of officers or agents for breaches of their trust, (I) imposition of fines, suspensions, and expulsions of members, including the grounds for such action and any provision made for notice, hearing, judgment on the evidence, and appeal procedures, (J) authorization for bargaining demands, (K) ratification of contract terms, (L) authorization for strikes, and (M) issuance of work per-

mits. Any change in the information required by this subsection shall be reported to the Secretary at the time the reporting labor organization files with the Secretary the annual financial report required by subsection (b).

(b) Every labor organization shall file annually with the Secretary a financial report signed by its president and treasurer or corresponding principal officers containing the following information in such detail as may be necessary accurately to disclose its financial condition and operations for its preceding fiscal year

(1) assets and liabilities at the beginning and end of the fiscal year;

(2) receipts of any kind and the sources thereof;

(3) salary, allowances, and other direct or indirect disbursements (including reimbursed expenses) to each officer and also to each employee who, during such fiscal year, received more than $10,000 in the aggregate from such labor organization and any other labor organization affiliated with it or with which it is affiliated, or which is affiliated with the same national or international labor organization;

(4) direct and indirect loans made to any officer, employee, or member, which aggregated more than $250 during the fiscal year, together with a statement of the purpose, security, if any, and arrangements for repayment;

(5) direct and indirect loans to any business enterprise, together with a statement of the purpose, security, if any, and arrangements for repayment; and

(6) other disbursements made by it including the purposes thereof;

all in such categories as the Secretary may prescribe.

(c) Every labor organization required to submit a report under this title shall make available the information required to be contained in such report to all of its members, and every such labor organization and its officers shall be under a duty enforceable at the suit of any member of such organization in any State court of competent jurisdiction or in the district court of the United States for the district in which such labor organization maintains its principal office, to permit such member for just cause to examine any books, records, and accounts necessary to verify such report. The court in such action may, in its discretion, in addition to any judgment awarded to the plaintiff or plaintiffs, allow a reasonable attorney's fee to be paid by the defendant, and costs of the action.

61 Stat. 143.   (d) Subsections (f), (g), and (h) of section 9 of the National Labor
29 USC 159.   Relations Act, as amended, are hereby repealed.

(e) Clause (i) of section 8(a)(3) of the National Labor Relations Act,
29 USC 158.   as amended, is amended by striking out the following: "and has at the time the agreement was made or within the preceding twelve months received from the Board a notice of compliance with sections 9(f), (g), (h)."

Report of Officers and Employees of Labor Organizations

SEC. 202. (a) Every officer of a labor organization and every employee of a labor organization (other than an employee performing exclusively clerical or custodial services) shall file with the Secretary a signed report listing and describing for his preceding fiscal year

(1) any stock, bond, security, or other interest, legal or equitable, which he or his spouse or minor child directly or indirectly held in, and any income or any other benefit with monetary value (including reimbursed expenses) which he or his spouse or minor child derived directly or indirectly from, an employer whose employees such labor organization represents or is actively seeking to represent, except payments and other benefits received as a bona fide employee of such employer;

(2) any transaction in which he or his spouse or minor child engaged, directly or indirectly, involving any stock, bond, security, or loan to or from, or other legal or equitable interest in the business of an employer whose employees such labor organization represents or is actively seeking to represent;

(3) any stock, bond, security, or other interest, legal or equitable, which he or his spouse or minor child directly or indirectly held in, and any income or any other benefit with monetary value (including reimbursed expenses) which he or his spouse or minor child directly or indirectly derived from, any business a substantial part of which consists of buying from, selling or leasing to, or otherwise dealing with, the business of an employer whose employees such labor organization represents or is actively seeking to represent;

(4) any stock, bond, security, or other interest, legal or equitable, which he or his spouse or minor child directly or indirectly held in, and any income or any other benefit with monetary value (including reimbursed expenses) which he or his spouse or minor child directly or indirectly derived from, a business any part of which consists of buying from, or selling or leasing directly or indirectly to, or otherwise dealing with such labor organization;

(5) any direct or indirect business transaction or arrangement between him or his spouse or minor child and any employer whose employees his organization represents or is actively seeking to represent, except work performed and payments and benefits received as a bona fide employee of such employer and except purchases and sales of goods or services in the regular course of business at prices generally available to any employee of such employer; and

(6) any payment of money or other thing of value (including reimbursed expenses) which he or his spouse or minor child received directly or indirectly from any employer or any person who acts as a labor relations consultant to an employer, except payments of the kinds referred to in section 302(c) of the Labor Management Relations Act, 1947, as amended.   *Post*, p. 537.

(b) The provisions of paragraphs (1), (2), (3), (4), and (5) of subsection (a) shall not be construed to require any such officer or employee to report his bona fide investments in securities traded on a securities exchange registered as a national securities exchange under the Securities Exchange Act of 1934, in shares in an investment company registered under the Investment Company Act of 1940, or in securities of a public utility holding company registered under the Public Utility Holding Company Act of 1935, or to report any income derived therefrom.

48 Stat. 881.
15 USC 78a.
54 Stat. 789.
15 USC 80a–51
49 Stat. 803.
15 USC 79.

(c) Nothing contained in this section shall be construed to require any officer or employee of a labor organization to file a report under subsection (a) unless he or his spouse or minor child holds or has held an interest, has received income or any other benefit with monetary value or a loan, or has engaged in a transaction described therein.

Report of Employers

SEC. 203. (a) Every employer who in any fiscal year made

(1) any payment or loan, direct or indirect, of money or other thing of value (including reimbursed expenses), or any promise or agreement therefor, to any labor organization or officer, agent, shop steward, or other representative of a labor organization, or employee of any labor organization, except (A) payments or loans made by any national or State bank, credit union, insurance company, savings and loan association or other credit institution and (B) payments of the kind referred to in section 302(c) of the Labor Management Relations Act, 1947, as amended;

Post, p. 537.

(2) any payment (including reimbursed expenses) to any of his employees, or any group or committee of such employees, for the purpose of causing such employee or group or committee of employees to persuade other employees to exercise or not to exercise, or as the manner of exercising, the right to organize and bargain collectively through representatives of their own choosing unless such payments were contemporaneously or previously disclosed to such other employees;

(3) any expenditure, during the fiscal year, where an object thereof, directly or indirectly, is to interfere with, restrain, or coerce employees in the exercise of the right to organize and bargain collectively through representatives of their own choosing, or is to obtain information concerning the activities of employees or a labor organization in connection with a labor dispute involving such employer, except for use solely in conjunction with an administrative or arbitral proceeding or a criminal or civil judicial proceeding;

(4) any agreement or arrangement with a labor relations consultant or other independent contractor or organization pursuant to which such person undertakes activities where an object thereof, directly or indirectly, is to persuade employees to exercise or not to exercise, or persuade employees as to the manner of exercising, the right to organize and bargain collectively through representatives of their own choosing, or undertakes to supply such employer with information concerning the activities of employees or a labor organization in connection with a labor dispute involving such employer, except information for use solely in conjunction with an administrative or arbitral proceeding or a criminal or civil judicial proceeding; or

(5) any payment (including reimbursed expenses) pursuant to an agreement or arrangement described in subdivision (4);

shall file with the Secretary a report, in a form prescribed by him, signed by its president and treasurer or corresponding principal officers showing in detail the date and amount of each such payment, loan, promise, agreement, or arrangement and the name, address, and position, if any, in any firm or labor organization of the person to whom it was made and a full explanation of the circumstances of all such payments, including the terms of any agreement or understanding pursuant to which they were made.

(b) Every person who pursuant to any agreement or arrangement with an employer undertakes activities where an object thereof is, directly or indirectly

(1) to persuade employees to exercise or not to exercise, or persuade employees as to the manner of exercising, the right to organize and bargain collectively through representatives of their own choosing; or

(2) to supply an employer with information concerning the activities of employees or a labor organization in connection with a labor dispute involving such employer, except information for use solely in conjunction with an administrative or arbitral proceeding or a criminal or civil judicial proceeding;

shall file within thirty days after entering into such agreement or arrangement a report with the Secretary, signed by its president and treasurer or corresponding principal officers, containing the name under which such person is engaged in doing business and the address of its principal office, and a detailed statement of the terms and conditions of such agreement or arrangement. Every such person shall file annually, with respect to each fiscal year during which payments were made as a result of such an agreement or arrangement, a report with the Secretary, signed by its president and treasurer or corresponding principal officers, containing a statement (A) of its receipts of any kind from employers on account of labor relations advice or services, designating the sources thereof, and (B) of its disbursements of any kind, in connection with such services and the purposes thereof. In each such case such information shall be set forth in such categories as the Secretary may prescribe.

(c) Nothing in this section shall be construed to require any employer or other person to file a report covering the services of such person by reason of his giving or agreeing to give advice to such employer or representing or agreeing to represent such employer before any court, administrative agency, or tribunal of arbitration or engaging or agreeing to engage in collective bargaining on behalf of such employer with respect to wages, hours, or other terms or conditions of employment or the negotiation of an agreement or any question arising thereunder.

(d) Nothing contained in this section shall be construed to require an employer to file a report under subsection (a) unless he has made an expenditure, payment, loan, agreement, or arrangement of the kind described therein. Nothing contained in this section shall be construed to require any other person to file a report under subsection (b) unless he was a party to an agreement or arrangement of the kind described therein.

(e) Nothing contained in this section shall be construed to require any regular officer, supervisor, or employee of an employer to file a report in connection with services rendered to such employer nor shall any employer be required to file a report covering expenditures made to any regular officer, supervisor, or employee of an employer as compensation for service as a regular officer, supervisor, or employee of such employer.

(f) Nothing contained in this section shall be construed as an amendment to, or modification of the rights protected by, section 8(c) of the National Labor Relations Act, as amended.

29 USC 158.

(g) The term "interfere with, restrain, or coerce" as used in this section means interference, restraint, and coercion which, if done with respect to the exercise of rights guaranteed in section 7 of the National Labor Relations Act, as amended, would, under section 8(a) of such Act, constitute an unfair labor practice.

29 USC 157.

Attorney-Client Communications Exempted

SEC. 204. Nothing contained in this Act shall be construed to require an attorney who is a member in good standing of the bar of any State, to include in any report required to be filed pursuant to the provisions of this Act any information which was lawfully communicated to such attorney by any of his clients in the course of a legitimate attorney-client relationship.

Reports Made Public Information

SEC. 205. (a) The contents of the reports and documents filed with the Secretary pursuant to sections 201, 202, and 203 shall be public information, and the Secretary may publish any information and data which he obtains pursuant to the provisions of this title. The Secretary may use the information and data for statistical and research purposes, and compile and publish such studies, analyses, reports, and surveys based thereon as he may deem appropriate.

(b) The Secretary shall by regulation make reasonable provision for the inspection and examination, on the request of any person, of the information and data contained in any report or other document filed with him pursuant to section 201, 202, or 203.

(c) The Secretary shall by regulation provide for the furnishing by the Department of Labor of copies of reports or other documents filed with the Secretary pursuant to this title, upon payment of a charge based upon the cost of the service. The Secretary shall make available without payment of a charge, or require any person to furnish, to such State agency as is designated by law or by the Governor of the State in which such person has his principal place of business or headquarters, upon request of the Governor of such State, copies of any reports and documents filed by such person with the Secretary pursuant to section 201, 202, or 203, or of information and data contained therein. No person shall be required by reason of any law of any State to furnish to any officer or agency of such State any information included in a report filed by such person with the Secretary pursuant to the provisions of this title, if a copy of such report, or of the portion thereof containing such information, is furnished to such officer or agency. All moneys received in payment of such charges fixed by the Secretary pursuant to this subsection shall be deposited in the general fund of the Treasury.

Retention of Records

SEC. 206. Every person required to file any report under this title shall maintain records on the matters required to be reported which will provide in sufficient detail the necessary basic information and data from which the documents filed with the Secretary may be verified, explained or clarified, and checked for accuracy and completeness, and shall include vouchers, worksheets, receipts, and applicable resolutions, and shall keep such records available for examination for a period of not less than five years after the filing of the documents based on the information which they contain.

Effective Date

SEC. 207. (a) Each labor organization shall file the initial report required under section 201(a) within ninety days after the date on which it first becomes subject to this Act.

(b) Each person required to file a report under section 201(b), 202, 203(a), or the second sentence of 203(b) shall file such report within ninety days after the end of each of its fiscal years; except that where such person is subject to section 201(b), 202, 203(a), or the second sentence of 203(b), as the case may be, for only a portion of such a fiscal year (because the date of enactment of this Act occurs during such person's fiscal year or such person becomes subject to this Act during its fiscal year) such person may consider that portion as the entire fiscal year in making such report.

Rules and Regulations

SEC. 208. The Secretary shall have authority to issue, amend, and rescind rules and regulations prescribing the form and publication of reports required to be filed under this title and such other reasonable rules and regulations (including rules prescribing reports concerning trusts in which a labor organization is interested) as he may find necessary to prevent the circumvention or evasion of such reporting requirements. In exercising his power under this section the Secretary shall prescribe by general rule simplified reports for labor organizations or employers for whom he finds that by virtue of their size a detailed report would be unduly burdensome, but the Secretary may revoke such provision for simplified forms of any labor organization or employer if he determines, after such investigation as he deems proper and due notice and opportunity for a hearing, that the purposes of this section would be served thereby.

Criminal Provisions

sec. 209. (a) Any person who willfully violates this title shall be fined not more than $10,000 or imprisoned for not more than one year, or both.

(b) Any person who makes a false statement or representation of a material fact, knowing it to be false, or who knowingly fails to disclose a material fact, in any document, report, or other information required under the provisions of this title shall be fined not more than $10,000 or imprisoned for not more than one year, or both.

(c) Any person who willfully makes a false entry in or willfully conceals, withholds, or destroys any books, records, reports, or statements required to be kept by any provision of this title shall be fined not more than $10,000 or imprisoned for not more than one year, or both.

(d) Each individual required to sign reports under sections 201 and 203 shall be personally responsible for the filing of such reports and for any statement contained therein which he knows to be false.

Civil Enforcement

sec. 210. Whenever it shall appear that any person has violated or is about to violate any of the provisions of this title, the Secretary may bring a civil action for such relief (including injunctions) as may be appropriate. Any such action may be brought in the district court of the United States where the violation occurred or, at the option of the parties, in the United States District Court for the District of Columbia.

TITLE III. TRUSTEESHIPS

Reports

sec. 301. (a) Every labor organization which has or assumes trusteeship over any subordinate labor organization shall file with the Secretary within thirty days after the date of the enactment of this Act or the imposition of any such trusteeship, and semiannually thereafter, a report, signed by its president and treasurer or corresponding principal officers, as well as by the trustees of such subordinate labor organization, containing the following information: (1) the name and address of the subordinate organization; (2) the date of establishing the trusteeship; (3) a detailed statement of the reason or reasons for establishing or continuing the trusteeship; and (4) the nature and extent of participation by the membership of the subordinate organization in the selection of delegates to represent such organization in regular or special conventions or other policy-determining bodies and in the election of officers of the labor organization which has assumed trusteeship over such subordinate organization. The initial report shall also include a full and complete account of the financial condition of such subordinate organization as of the time trusteeship was assumed over it. During the continuance of a trusteeship the labor organization which has assumed trusteeship over a subordinate labor organization shall file on behalf of the subordinate labor organization the annual financial report required by section 201(b) signed by the president and treasurer or corresponding principal officers of the labor organization which has assumed such trusteeship and the trustees of the subordinate labor organization.

(b) The provisions of section 201(c), 205, 206, 208, and 210 shall be applicable to reports filed under this title.

(c) Any person who willfully violates this section shall be fined not more than $10,000 or imprisoned for not more than one year, or both.

(d) Any person who makes a false statement or representation of a material fact, knowing it to be false, or who knowingly fails to disclose a material fact, in any report required under the provisions of this section or willfully makes any false entry in or willfully withholds, conceals, or destroys any documents, books, records, reports, or statements upon which such report is based, shall be fined not more than $10,000 or imprisoned for not more than one year, or both.

(e) Each individual required to sign a report under this section shall be personally responsible for the filing of such report and for any statement contained therein which he knows to be false.

Purposes for Which a Trusteeship May Be Established

SEC. 302. Trusteeships shall be established and administered by a labor organization over a subordinate body only in accordance with the constitution and bylaws of the organization which has assumed trusteeship over the subordinate body and for the purpose of correcting corruption or financial malpractice, assuring the performance of collective bargaining agreements or other duties of a bargaining representative, restoring democratic procedures, or otherwise carrying out the legitimate objects of such labor organization.

Unlawful Acts Relating to Labor Organization Under Trusteeship

SEC. 303. (a) During any period when a subordinate body of a labor organization is in trusteeship, it shall be unlawful (1) to count the vote of delegates from such body in any convention or election of officers of the labor organization unless the delegates have been chosen by secret ballot in an election in which all the members in good standing of such subordinate body were eligible to participate, or (2) to transfer to such organization any current receipts or other funds of the subordinate body except the normal per capita tax and assessments payable by subordinate bodies not in trusteeship: *Provided,* That nothing herein contained shall prevent the distribution of the assets of a labor organization in accordance with its constitution and bylaws upon the bona fide dissolution thereof.

(b) Any person who willfully violates this section shall be fined not more than $10,000 or imprisoned for not more than one year, or both.

Enforcement

sec. 304. (a) Upon the written complaint of any member or subordinate body of a labor organization alleging that such organization has violated the provisions of this title (except section 301) the Secretary shall investigate the complaint and if the Secretary finds probable cause to believe that such violation has occurred and has not been remedied he shall, without disclosing the identity of the complainant, bring a civil action in any district court of the United States having jurisdiction of the labor organization for such relief (including injunctions) as may be appropriate. Any member or subordinate body of a labor organization affected by any violation of this title (except section 301) may bring a civil action in any district court of the United States having jurisdiction of the labor organization for such relief (including injunctions) as may be appropriate.

(b) For the purpose of actions under this section, district courts of the United States shall be deemed to have jurisdiction of a labor organization (1) in the district in which the principal office of such labor organization is located, or (2) in any district in which its dully authorized officers or agents are engaged in conducting the affairs of the trusteeship.

(c) In any proceeding pursuant to this section a trusteeship established by a labor organization in conformity with the procedural requirements of its constitution and bylaws and authorized or ratified after a fair hearing either before the executive board or before such other body as may be provided in accordance with its constitution or bylaws shall be presumed valid for a period of eighteen months from the date of its establishment and shall not be subject to attack during such period except upon clear and convincing proof that the trusteeship was not established or maintained in good faith for a purpose allowable under section 302. After the expiration of eighteen months the trusteeship shall be presumed invalid in any such proceeding and its discontinuance shall be decreed unless the labor organization shall show by clear and convincing proof that the continuation of the trusteeship is necessary for a purpose allowable under section 302. In the latter event the court may dismiss the complaint or retain jurisdiction of the cause on such conditions and for such period as it deems appropriate.

Report to Congress

sec. 305. The Secretary shall submit to the Congress at the expiration of three years from the date of enactment of this Act a report upon the operation of this title.

Complaint by Secretary

SEC. 306. The rights and remedies provided by this title shall be in addition to any and all other rights and remedies at law or in equity: *Provided,* That upon the filing of a complaint by the Secretary the jurisdiction of the district court over such trusteeship shall be exclusive and the final judgment shall be res judicata.

TITLE IV. ELECTIONS

Terms of Office; Election Procedures

SEC. 401. (a) Every national or international labor organization, except a federation of national or international labor organizations, shall elect its officers not less often than once every five years either by secret ballot among the members in good standing or at a convention of delegates chosen by secret ballot.

(b) Every local labor organization shall elect its officers not less often than once every three years by secret ballot among the members in good standing.

(c) Every national or international labor organization, except a federation of national or international labor organizations, and every local labor organization, and its officers, shall be under a duty, enforceable at the suit of any bona fide candidate for office in such labor organization in the district court of the United States in which such labor organization maintains its principal office, to comply with all reasonable requests of any candidate to distribute by mail or otherwise at the candidate's expense campaign literature in aid of such person's candidacy to all members in good standing of such labor organization and to refrain from discrimination in favor of or against any candidate with respect to the use of lists of members, and whenever such labor organizations or its officers authorize the distribution by mail or otherwise to members of campaign literature on behalf of any candidate or of the labor organization itself with reference to such election, similar distribution at the request of any other bona fide candidate shall be made by such labor organization and its officers, with equal treatment as to the expense of such distribution. Every bona fide candidate shall have the right, once within 30 days prior to an election of a labor organization in which he is a candidate, to inspect a list containing the names and last known addresses of all members of the labor organization who are subject to a collective bargaining agreement requiring membership therein as a condition of employment, which list shall be maintained and kept at the principal office of such labor organization by a designated official thereof. Adequate safeguards to insure a fair election shall be provided, including the right of any candidate to have an observer at the polls and at the counting of the ballots.

(d) Officers of intermediate bodies, such as general committees, system boards, joint boards, or joint councils, shall be elected not less often than once every four years by secret ballot among the members in good standing or by labor organization officers representative of such members who have been elected by secret ballot.

(e) In any election required by this section which is to be held by secret ballot a reasonable opportunity shall be given for the nomination of candidates and every member in good standing shall be eligible to be a candidate and to hold office (subject to section 504 and to reasonable qualifications uniformly imposed) and shall have the right to vote for or otherwise support the candidate or candidates of his choice, without being subject to penalty, discipline, or improper interference or reprisal of any kind by such organization or any member thereof. Not less than fifteen days prior to the election notice thereof shall be mailed to each member at his last known home address. Each member in good standing shall be entitled to one vote. No member whose dues have been withheld by his employer for payment to such organization pursuant to his voluntary authorization provided for in a collective bargaining agreement shall be declared ineligible to vote or be a candidate for office in such organization by reason of alleged delay or default in the payment of dues. The votes cast by members of each local labor organization shall be counted, and the results published, separately. The election officials designated in the constitution and bylaws or the secretary, if no other official is designated, shall preserve for one year the ballots and all other records pertaining to the election. The election shall be conducted in accordance with the constitution and bylaws of such organization insofar as they are not inconsistent with the provisions of this title.

(f) When officers are chosen by a convention of delegates elected by secret ballot, the convention shall be conducted in accordance with the constitution and bylaws of the labor organization insofar as they are not inconsistent with the provisions of this title. The officials designated in the constitution and bylaws or the secretary, if no other is designated, shall preserve for one year the credentials of the delegates and all minutes and other records of the convention pertaining to the election of officers.

(g) No moneys received by any labor organization by way of dues, assessment, or similar levy, and no moneys of an employer shall be contributed or applied to promote the candidacy of any person in an election subject to the provisions of this title. Such moneys of a labor organization may be utilized for notices, factual statements of issues not involving candidates, and other expenses necessary for the holding of an election.

(h) If the Secretary, upon application of any member of a local labor organization, finds after hearing in accordance with the Administrative Procedure Act that the constitution and bylaws of such labor organization do not provide an adequate procedure for the removal of an elected officer guilty of serious misconduct, such officer may be removed, for cause shown and after notice and hearing, by the members in good standing voting in a secret ballot conducted by the officers of such labor organization in accordance with its constitution and bylaws insofar as they are not inconsistent with the provisions of this title.

(i) The Secretary shall promulgate rules and regulations prescribing minimum standards and procedures for determining the adequacy of the removal procedures to which reference is made in subsection (h).

Enforcement

SEC. 402. (a) A member of a labor organization
(1) who has exhausted the remedies available under the constitution and bylaws of such organization and of any parent body, or
(2) who has invoked such available remedies without obtaining a final decision within three calendar months after their invocation,

may file a complaint with the Secretary within one calendar month thereafter alleging the violation of any provision of section 401 (including violation of the constitution and bylaws of the labor organization pertaining to the election and removal of officers). The challenged election shall be presumed valid pending a final decision thereon (as hereinafter provided) and in the interim the affairs of the organization shall be conducted by the officers elected or in such other manner as its constitution and bylaws may provide.

(b) The Secretary shall investigate such complaint and, if he finds probable cause to believe that a violation of this title has occurred and has not been remedied, he shall, within sixty days after the filing of such complaint, bring a civil action against the labor organization as an entity in the district court of the United States in which such labor organization maintains its principal office to set aside the invalid election, if any, and to direct the conduct of an election or hearing and vote upon the removal of officers under the supervision of the Secretary and in accordance with the provisions of this title and such rules and regulations as the Secretary may prescribe. The court shall have power to take such action as it deems proper to preserve the assets of the labor organization.

(c) If, upon a preponderance of the evidence after a trial upon the merits, the court finds
(1) that an election has not been held within the time prescribed by section 401, or
(2) that the violation of section 401 may have affected the outcome of an election,

the court shall declare the election, if any, to be void and direct the conduct of a new election under supervision of the Secretary and, so far as lawful and practicable, in conformity with the constitution and bylaws of the labor organization. The Secretary shall promptly certify to the court the names of the persons elected, and the court shall thereupon enter a decree declaring such persons to be the officers of the labor organization. If the proceeding is for the removal of officers pursuant to subsection (h) of section 401, the Secretary shall certify the results of the vote and the court shall enter a decree declaring whether such persons have been removed as officers of the labor organization.

(d) An order directing an election, dismissing a complaint, or designating elected officers of a labor organization shall be appealable in the same manner as the final judgment in a civil action, but an order directing an election shall not be stayed pending appeal.

Application of Other Laws

sec. 403. No labor organization shall be required by law to conduct elections of officers with greater frequency or in a different form or manner than is required by its own constitution or bylaws, except as otherwise provided by this title. Existing rights and remedies to enforce the constitution and bylaws of a labor organization with respect to elections prior to the conduct thereof shall not be affected by the provisions of this title. The remedy provided by this title for challenging an election already conducted shall be exclusive.

Effective Date

sec. 404. The provisions of this title shall become applicable
(1) ninety days after the date of enactment of this Act in the case of a labor organization whose constitution and bylaws can lawfully be modified or amended by action of its constitutional officers or governing body, or
(2) where such modification can only be made by a constitutional convention of the labor organization, not later than the next constitutional convention of such labor organization after the date of enactment of this Act, or one year after such date, whichever is sooner. If no such convention is held within such one-year period, the executive board or similar governing body empowered to act for such labor organization between conventions is empowered to make such interim constitutional changes as are necessary to carry out the provisions of this title.

TITLE V. SAFEGUARDS FOR LABOR ORGANIZATIONS

Fiduciary Responsibility of Officers of Labor Organizations

sec. 501. (a) The officers, agents, shop stewards, and other representatives of a labor organization occupy positions of trust in relation to such organization and its members as a group. It is, therefore, the duty of each such person, taking into account the special problems and functions of a labor organization, to hold its money and property solely for the benefit of the organization and its members and to manage, invest, and expend the same in accordance with its constitution and bylaws and any resolutions of the governing bodies adopted thereunder, to refrain from dealing with such organization as an adverse party or in behalf of an adverse party in any matter connected with his duties and from holding or acquiring any pecuniary or personal interest which conflicts with the interests of such organization, and to account to the organization for any profit received by him in whatever capacity in connection with transactions conducted by him or under his direction on behalf of the organization. A general exculpatory provision in the constitution and bylaws of such a labor organization or a general exculpatory resolution of a governing body purporting to relieve any such person of liability for breach of the duties declared by this section shall be void as against public policy.

(b) When any officer, agent, shop steward, or representative of any labor organization is alleged to have violated the duties declared in subsection (a) and the labor organization or its governing board or officers refuse or fail to sue or recover damages or secure an accounting or other appropriate relief within a reasonable time after being requested to do so by any member of the labor organization, such member may sue such officer, agent, shop steward, or representative in any district court of the United States or in any State court of competent jurisdiction to recover damages or secure an accounting or other appropriate relief for the benefit of the labor organization. No such proceeding shall be brought except upon leave of the court obtained upon verified application and for good cause shown which application may be made ex parte. The trial judge may allot a reasonable part of the recovery in any action under the subsection to pay the fees of counsel prosecuting the suit at the instance of the member of the labor organization and to compensate such member for any expenses necessarily paid or incurred by him in connection with the litigation.

(c) Any person who embezzles, steals, or unlawfully and willfully abstracts or converts to his own use, or the use of another, any of the moneys, funds, securities, property, or other assets of a labor organization of which he is an officer, or by which he is employed, directly or indirectly, shall be fined not more than $10,000 or imprisoned for not more than five years, or both.

Bonding

SEC. 502. (a) Every officer, agent, shop steward, or other representative or employee of any labor organization (other than a labor organization whose property and annual financial receipts do not exceed $5,000 in value), or of a trust in which a labor organization is interested, who handles funds or other property thereof shall be bonded for the faithful discharge of his duties. The bond of each such person shall be fixed at the beginning of the organization's fiscal year and shall be in an amount not less than 10 per centum of the funds handled by him and his predecessor or predecessors, if any, during the preceding fiscal year, but in no case more than $500,000. If the labor organization or the trust in which a labor organization is interested does not have a preceding fiscal year, the amount of the bond shall be, in the case of a local labor organization, not less than $1,000, and in the case of any other labor organization or of a trust in which a labor organization is interested, not less than $10,000. Such bonds shall be individual or schedule in form, and shall have a corporate surety company as surety thereon. Any person who is not covered by such bonds shall not be permitted to receive, handle, disburse, or otherwise exercise custody or control of the funds or other property of a labor organization or of a trust in which a labor organization is interested. No such bond shall be placed through an agent or broker or with a surety company in which any labor organization or any officer, agent, shop steward, or other representative of a labor organization has any direct or indirect interest. Such surety company shall be a corporate surety which holds a grant of authority from the Secretary of the Treasury under the Act of July 30, 1947 (6 U.S.C. 6–13), as an acceptable surety on Federal bonds.

61 Stat. 648.

(b) Any person who willfully violates this section shall be fined not more than $10,000 or imprisoned for not more than one year, or both.

Making of Loans; Payment of Fines

sec. 503. (a) No labor organization shall make directly or indirectly any loan or loans to any officer or employee of such organization which results in a total indebtedness on the part of such officer or employee to the labor organization in excess of $2,000.

(b) No labor organization or employer shall directly or indirectly pay the fine of any officer or employee convicted of any willful violation of this Act.

(c) Any person who willfully violates this section shall be fined not more than $5,000 or imprisoned for not more than one year, or both.

Prohibition against Certain Persons Holding Office

sec. 504. (a) No person who is or has been a member of the Communist Party or who has been convicted of, or served any part of a prison term resulting from his conviction of, robbery, bribery, extortion, embezzlement, grand larceny, burglary, arson, violation of narcotics laws, murder, rape, assault with intent to kill, assault which inflicts grievous bodily injury, or a violation of title II or III of this Act, or conspiracy to commit any such crimes, shall serve

(1) as an officer, director, trustee, member of any executive board or similar governing body, business agent, manager, organizer, or other employee (other than as an employee performing exclusively clerical or custodial duties) of any labor organization, or

(2) as a labor relations consultant to a person engaged in an industry or activity affecting commerce, or as an officer, director, agent, or employee (other than as an employee performing exclusively clerical or custodial duties) of any group or association of employers dealing with any labor organization,

during or for five years after the termination of his membership in the Communist Party, or for five years after such conviction or after the end of such imprisonment, unless prior to the end of such five-year period, in the case of a person so convicted or imprisoned, (A) his citizenship rights, having been revoked as a result of such conviction, have been fully restored, or (B) the Board of Parole of the United States Department of Justice determines that such person's service in any capacity referred to in clause (1) or (2) would not be contrary to the purposes of this Act. Prior to making any such determination the Board shall hold an administrative hearing and shall give notice of such proceeding by certified mail to the State, county, and Federal prosecuting officials in the jurisdiction or jurisdictions in which such person was convicted. The Board's determination in any such proceeding shall be final. No labor organization or officer thereof shall knowingly permit any person to assume or hold any office or paid position in violation of this subsection.

(b) Any person who willfully violates this section shall be fined not more than $10,000 or imprisoned for not more than one year, or both.

(c) For the purposes of this section, any person shall be deemed to have been "convicted" and under the disability of "conviction" from the date of the judgment of the trial court or the date of the final sustaining of such judgment on appeal, whichever is the later event, regardless of whether such conviction occurred before or after the date of enactment of this Act.

Amendment to Section 302, Labor Management Relations Act, 1947

SEC. 505. Subsections (a), (b), and (c) of section 302 of the Labor Management Relations Act, 1947, as amended, are amended to read as follows: 29 USC 186.

"SEC. 302. (a) It shall be unlawful for any employer or association of employers or any person who acts as a labor relations expert, adviser, or consultant to an employer or who acts in the interest of an employer to pay, lend, or deliver, or agree to pay, lend, or deliver, any money or other thing of value

"(1) to any representative of any of his employees who are employed in an industry affecting commerce; or

"(2) to any labor organization, or any officer or employee thereof, which represents, seeks to represent, or would admit to membership, any of the employees of such employer who are employed in an industry affecting commerce; or

"(3) to any employee or group or committee of employees of such employer employed in an industry affecting commerce in excess of their normal compensation for the purpose of causing such employee or group or committee directly or indirectly to influence any other employees in the exercise of the right to organize and bargain collectively through representatives of their own choosing; or

"(4) to any officer or employee of a labor organization engaged in an industry affecting commerce with intent to influence him in respect to any of his actions, decisions, or duties as a representative of employees or as such officer or employee of such labor organization.

"(b)(1) It shall be unlawful for any person to request, demand, receive, or accept, or agree to receive or accept, any payment, loan, or delivery of any money or other thing of value prohibited by subsection (a).

"(2) It shall be unlawful for any labor organization, or for any person acting as an officer, agent, representative, or employee of such labor organization, to demand or accept from the operator of any motor vehicle (as defined in part II of the Interstate Commerce Act) employed in the transportation of property in commerce, or the employer of any such operator, any money or other thing of value payable to such organization or to an officer, agent, representative or employee thereof as a fee or charge for the unloading, or in connection with the unloading, of the cargo of such vehicle: *Provided*, That nothing in this paragraph shall be construed to make unlawful any payment by an employer to any of his employees as compensation for their services as employees.

"(c) The provisions of this section shall not be applicable (1) in respect to any money or other thing of value payable by an employer to any of his employees whose established duties include acting openly for such employer in matters of labor relations or personnel administration or to any representative of his employees, or to any officer or employee of a labor organization, who is also an employee or former employee of such employer, as compensation for, or by reason of, his service as an employee of such employer; (2) with respect to the payment or delivery of any money or other thing of value in satisfaction of a judgment of any court or a decision or award of an arbitrator or impartial chairman or in compromise, adjustment, settlement, or release of any claim, complaint, grievance, or dispute in the absence of fraud or duress; (3) with respect to the sale or purchase of an article or commodity at the prevailing market price in the regular course of business; (4) with respect to money deducted from the wages of employees in payment of membership dues in a labor organization: *Provided*, That the employer has received from each employee, on whose account such deductions are made, a written assignment which shall not be irrevocable for a period of more than one year, or beyond the termination date of the applicable collective agreement, whichever occurs sooner; (5) with respect to money or other thing of value paid to a trust fund established by such representative, for the sole and exclusive benefit of the employees of such employer, and their families and dependents (or of such employees, families, and dependents jointly with the employees of other employers making similar payments, and their families and dependents): *Provided*, That (A) such payments are held in trust for the purpose of paying, either from principal or income or both, for the benefit of employees, their families and dependents, for medical or hospital care, pensions on retirement or death of employees, compensation for injuries or illness resulting from occupational activity or insurance to provide any of the foregoing, or unemployment benefits or life insurance, disability and sickness insurance, or accident insurance; (B) the detailed basis on which such payments are to be made is specified in a written agreement with the employer, and employees and employers are equally represented in the administration of such fund, together with such neutral persons as the representatives of the employers and the representatives of employees may agree upon and in the event the employer and employee groups deadlock on the administration of such fund and there are no neutral persons empowered to break such deadlock, such agreement provides that the two groups shall agree on an impartial umpire to decide such dispute, or in event of their failure to agree within a reasonable length of time, an impartial umpire to decide such dispute shall, on petition of either group, be appointed by the district court of the United States for the district where the trust fund has its principal office, and shall also contain provisions for an annual audit of the trust fund, a statement of the results of which shall be available for inspection by interested persons at the principal office of the trust fund and at such other places as may be designated in such written agreement; and (C) such payments as are intended to be used for the purpose of providing pensions or annuities for employees are made to a separate trust which provides that the funds held therein cannot be used for any purpose other than paying such pensions or annuities; or (6) with respect to money or other thing of value paid by any employer to a trust fund established by such representative for the purpose of pooled vacation, holiday, severance or similar benefits, or defraying costs of apprenticeship or other training programs: *Provided,* That the requirements of clause (B) of the proviso to clause (5) of this subsection shall apply to such trust funds."

TITLE VI. MISCELLANEOUS PROVISIONS

Investigations

SEC. 601. (a) The Secretary shall have power when he believes it necessary in order to determine whether any person has violated or is about to violate any provision of this Act (except title I or amendments made by this Act to other statutes) to make an investigation and in connection therewith he may enter such places and inspect such records and accounts and question such persons as he may deem necessary to enable him to determine the facts relative thereto. The Secretary may report to interested persons or officials concerning the facts required to be shown in any report required by this Act and concerning the reasons for failure or refusal to file such a report or any other matter which he deems to be appropriate as a result of such an investigation.

(b) For the purpose of any investigation provided for in this Act, the provisions of sections 9 and 10 (relating to the attendance of witnesses and the production of books, papers, and documents) of the Federal Trade Commission Act of September 16, 1914, as amended (15 U.S.C. 49, 50), are hereby made applicable to the jurisdiction, powers, and duties of the Secretary or any officers designated by him.

38 Stat. 717.

Extortionate Picketing

sec. 602. (a) It shall be unlawful to carry on picketing on or about the premises of any employer for the purpose of, or as part of any conspiracy or in furtherance of any plan or purpose for, the personal profit or enrichment of any individual (except a bona fide increase in wages or other employee benefits) by taking or obtaining any money or other thing of value from such employer against his will or with his consent.

(b) Any person who willfully violates this section shall be fined not more than $10,000 or imprisoned not more than twenty years, or both.

Retention of Rights under Other Federal and State Laws

sec. 603. (a) Except as explicitly provided to the contrary, nothing in this Act shall reduce or limit the responsibilities of any labor organization or any officer, agent, shop steward, or other representative of a labor organization, or of any trust in which a labor organization is interested, under any other Federal law or under the laws of any State, and, except as explicitly provided to the contrary, nothing in this Act shall take away any right or bar any remedy to which members of a labor organization are entitled under such other Federal law or law of any State.

(b) Nothing contained in titles I, II, III, IV, V, or VI of this Act shall be construed to supersede or impair or otherwise affect the provisions of the Railway Labor Act, as amended, or any of the obligations, rights, benefits, privileges, or immunities of any carrier, employee, organization, representative, or person subject thereto; nor shall anything contained in said titles (except section 505) of this Act be construed to confer any rights, privileges, immunities, or defenses upon employers, or to impair or otherwise affect the rights of any person under the National Labor Relations Act, as amended.

44 Stat. 577.
45 USC 151.

61 Stat. 136.
29 USC 167.

Effect on State Laws

sec. 604. Nothing in this Act shall be construed to impair or diminish the authority of any State to enact and enforce general criminal laws with respect to robbery, bribery, extortion, embezzlement, grand larceny, burglary, arson, violation of narcotics laws, murder, rape, assault with intent to kill, or assault which inflicts grievous bodily injury, or conspiracy to commit any of such crimes.

Service of Process

sec. 605. For the purposes of this Act, service of summons, subpena, or other legal process of a court of the United States upon an officer or agent of a labor organization in his capacity as such shall constitute service upon the labor organization.

Administrative Procedure Act

SEC. 606. The provisions of the Administrative Procedure Act shall be applicable to the issuance, amendment, or rescission of any rules or regulations, or any adjudication, authorized or required pursuant to the provisions of this Act.

60 Stat. 237.
5 USC 1001
note

Other Agencies and Departments

SEC. 607. In order to avoid unnecessary expense and duplication of functions among Government agencies, the Secretary may make such arrangements or agreements for cooperation or mutual assistance in the performance of his functions under this Act and the functions of any such agency as he may find to be practicable and consistent with law. The Secretary may utilize the facilities or services of any department, agency, or establishment of the United States or of any State or political subdivision of a State, including the services of any of its employees, with the lawful consent of such department, agency, or establishment; and each department, agency, or establishment of the United States is authorized and directed to cooperate with the Secretary and, to the extent permitted by law, to provide such information and facilities as he may request for his assistance in the performance of his functions under this Act. The Attorney General or his representative shall receive from the Secretary for appropriate action such evidence developed in the performance of his functions under this Act as may be found to warrant consideration for criminal prosecution under the provisions of this Act or other Federal law.

Criminal Contempt

SEC. 608. No person shall be punished for any criminal contempt allegedly committed outside the immediate presence of the court in connection with any civil action prosecuted by the Secretary or any other person in any court of the United States under the provisions of this Act unless the facts constituting such criminal contempt are established by the verdict of the jury in a proceeding in the district court of the United States, which jury shall be chosen and empaneled in the manner prescribed by the law governing trial juries in criminal prosecutions in the district courts of the United States.

Prohibition on Certain Discipline by Labor Organization

SEC. 609. It shall be unlawful for any labor organization, or any officer, agent, shop steward, or other representative of a labor organization, or any employee thereof to fine, suspend, expel, or otherwise discipline any of its members for exercising any right to which he is entitled under the provisions of this Act. The provisions of section 102 shall be applicable in the enforcement of this section.

Deprivation of Rights under Act by Violence

SEC. 610. It shall be unlawful for any person through the use of force or violence, or threat of the use of force or violence, to restrain, coerce, or intimidate, or attempt to restrain, coerce, or intimidate any member of a labor organization for the purpose of interfering with or preventing the exercise of any right to which he is entitled under the provisions of this Act. Any person who willfully violates this section shall be fined not more than $1,000 or imprisoned for not more than one year, or both.

Separability Provisions

SEC. 611. If any provision of this Act, or the application of such provision to any person or circumstances, shall be held invalid, the remainder of this Act or the application of such provision to persons or circumstances other than those as to which it is held invalid, shall not be affected thereby.

TITLE VII. AMENDMENTS TO THE LABOR MANAGEMENT RELATIONS ACT, 1947, AS AMENDED

Federal-State Jurisdiction

29 USC 164.   SEC. 701. (a) Section 14 of the National Labor Relations Act, as amended, is amended by adding at the end thereof the following new subsection:

"(c)(1) The Board, in its discretion, may, by rule of decision or by published rules adopted pursuant to the Administrative Procedure Act, decline to assert jurisdiction over any labor dispute involving any class or category of employers, where, in the opinion of the Board, the effect of such labor dispute on commerce is not sufficiently substantial to warrant the exercise of its jurisdiction: *Provided,* That the Board shall not decline to assert jurisdiction over any labor dispute over which it would assert jurisdiction under the standards prevailing upon August 1, 1959.

"(2) Nothing in this Act shall be deemed to prevent or bar any agency or the courts of any State or Territory (including the Commonwealth of Puerto Rico, Guam, and the Virgin Islands), from assuming and asserting jurisdiction over labor disputes over which the Board declines, pursuant to paragraph (1) of this subsection, to assert jurisdiction."

(b) Section 3(b) of such Act is amended to read as follows: 29 USC 153.

"(b) The Board is authorized to delegate to any group of three or more members any or all of the powers which it may itself exercise. The Board is also authorized to delegate to its regional directors its powers under sec- 29 USC 159. tion 9 to determine the unit appropriate for the purpose of collective bargaining, to investigate and provide for hearings, and determine whether a question of representation exists, and to direct an election or take a secret ballot under subsection (c) or (e) of section 9 and certify the results thereof, except that upon the filing of a request therefor with the Board by any interested person, the Board may review any action of a regional director delegated to him under this paragraph, but such a review shall not, unless specifically ordered by the Board, operate as a stay of any action taken by the regional director. A vacancy in the Board shall not impair the right of the remaining members to exercise all of the powers of the Board, and three members of the Board shall, at all times, constitute a quorum of the Board, except that two members shall constitute a quorum of any group designated pursuant to the first sentence hereof. The Board shall have an official seal which shall be judicially noticed."

Economic Strikers

SEC. 702. Section 9(c)(3) of the National Labor Relations Act, as 29 USC 159. amended, is amended by amending the second sentence thereof to read as follows: "Employees engaged in an economic strike who are not entitled to reinstatement shall be eligible to vote under such regulations as the Board shall find are consistent with the purposes and provisions of this Act in any election conducted within twelve months after the commencement of the strike."

Vacancy in Office of General Counsel

SEC. 703. Section 3(d) of the National Labor Relations Act, as 29 USC 153. amended, is amended by adding after the period at the end thereof the following: "In case of a vacancy in the office of the General Counsel the President is authorized to designate the officer or employee who shall act as General Counsel during such vacancy, but no person or persons so designated shall so act (1) for more than forty days when the Congress is in session unless a nomination to fill such vacancy shall have been submitted to the Senate, or (2) after the adjournment sine die of the session of the Senate in which such nomination was submitted."

Boycotts and Recognition Picketing

SEC. 704. (a) Section 8(b)(4) of the National Labor Relations Act, as amended, is amended to read as follows:

"(4)(i) to engage in, or to induce or encourage any individual employed by any person engaged in commerce or in an industry affecting commerce to engage in, a strike or a refusal in the course of his employment to use, manufacture, process, transport, or otherwise handle or work on any goods, articles, materials, or commodities or to perform any services; or (ii) to threaten, coerce, or restrain any person engaged in commerce or in an industry affecting commerce, where in either case an object thereof is

"(A) forcing or requiring any employer or self-employed person to join any labor or employer organization or to enter into any agreement which is prohibited by section 8(e);

"(B) forcing or requiring any person to cease using, selling, handling, transporting, or otherwise dealing in the products of any other producer, processor, or manufacturer, or to cease doing business with any other person, or forcing or requiring any other employer to recognize or bargain with a labor organization as the representative of his employees unless such labor organization has been certified as the representative of such employees under the provisions of section 9: *Provided,* That nothing contained in this clause (B) shall be construed to make unlawful, where not otherwise unlawful, any primary strike or primary picketing;

"(C) forcing or requiring any employer to recognize or bargain with a particular labor organization as the representative of his employees if another labor organization has been certified as the representative of such employees under the provisions of section 9;

"(D) forcing or requiring any employer to assign particular work to employees in a particular labor organization or in a particular trade, craft, or class rather than to employees in another labor organization or in another trade, craft, or class, unless such employer is failing to conform to an order or certification of the Board determining the bargaining representative for employees performing such work:

Provided, That nothing contained in this subsection (b) shall be construed to make unlawful a refusal by any person to enter upon the premises of any employer (other than his own employer), if the employees of such employer are engaged in a strike ratified or approved by a representative of such employees whom such employer is required to recognize under this Act: *Provided further,* That for the purposes of this paragraph (4) only, nothing contained in such paragraph shall be construed to prohibit publicity, other than picketing, for the purpose of truthfully advising the public, including consumers and members of a labor organization, that a product or products are produced by an employer with whom the labor organization has a primary dispute and are distributed by another employer, as long as such publicity does not have an effect of inducing any individual employed by any person other than the primary employer in the course of his employment to refuse to pick up, deliver, or transport any goods, or not to perform any services, at the establishment of the employer engaged in such distribution;".

(b) Section 8 of the National Labor Relations Act, as amended, is amended by adding at the end thereof the following new subsection: 29 USC 158.

"(e) It shall be an unfair labor practice for any labor organization and any employer to enter into any contract or agreement, express or implied, whereby such employer ceases or refrains or agrees to cease or refrain from handling, using, selling, transporting or otherwise dealing in any of the products of any other employer, or to cease doing business with any other person, and any contract or agreement entered into heretofore or hereafter containing such an agreement shall be to such extent unenforcible and void: *Provided,* That nothing in this subsection (e) shall apply to an agreement between a labor organizaton and an employer in the construction industry relating to the contracting or subcontracting of work to be done at the site of the construction, alteration, painting, or repair of a building, structure, or other work: *Provided further,* That for the purposes of this subsection (e) and section 8(b)(4)(B) the terms 'any employer,' 'any person engaged in commerce or an industry affecting commerce,' and 'any person' when used in relation to the terms 'any other producer, processor, or manufacturer,' 'any other employer,' or 'any other person' shall not include persons in the relation of a jobber, manufacturer, contractor, or subcontractor working on the goods or premises of the jobber or manufacturer or performing parts of an integrated process of production in the apparel and clothing industry: *Provided further,* That nothing in this Act shall prohibit the enforcement of any agreement which is within the foregoing exception."

(c) Section 8(b) of the National Labor Relations Act, as amended, is amended by striking out the word "and" at the end of paragraph (5), striking out the period at the end of paragraph (6), and inserting in lieu thereof a semicolon and the word "and," and adding a new paragraph as follows:

"(7) to picket or cause to be picketed, or threaten to picket or cause to be picketed, any employer where an object thereof is forcing or requiring an employer to recognize or bargain with a labor organization as the representative of his employees, or forcing or requiring the employees of an employer to accept or select such labor organization as their collective bargaining representative, unless such labor organization is currently certified as the representative of such employees:

"(A) where the employer has lawfully recognized in accordance with this Act any other labor organization and a question concerning representation may not appropriately be raised under section 9(c) of this Act,

"(B) where within the preceding twelve months a valid election under section 9(c) of this Act has been conducted, or

"(C) where such picketing has been conducted without a petition under section 9(c) being filed within a reasonable period of time not to exceed thirty days from the commencement of such picketing: *Provided,* That when such a petition has been filed the Board shall forthwith, without regard to the provisions of section 9(c)(1) or the absence of a showing of a substantial interest on the part of the labor organization, direct an election in such unit as the Board finds to be appropriate and shall certify the results thereof: *Provided further,* That nothing in this subparagraph (C) shall be construed to prohibit any picketing or other publicity for the purpose of truthfully advising the public (including consumers) that an employer does not employ members of, or have a contract with, a labor organization, unless an effect of such picketing is to induce any individual employed by any other person in the course of his employment, not to pick up, deliver or transport any goods or not to perform any services.

"Nothing in this paragraph (7) shall be construed to permit any act which would otherwise be an unfair labor practice under this section 8(b)."

29 USC 160.   (d) Section 10(l) of the National Labor Relations Act, as amended, is amended by adding after the words "section 8(b)," the words "or section 8(e) or section 8(b)(7)," and by striking out the period at the end of the third sentence and inserting in lieu thereof a colon and the following: "*Provided further,* That such officer or regional attorney shall not apply for any restraining order under section 8(b)(7) if a charge against the employer under section 8(a)(2) has been filed and after the preliminary investigation, he has reasonable cause to believe that such charge is true and that a complaint should issue."

29 USC 187.   (e) Section 303(a) of the Labor Management Relations Act, 1947, is amended to read as follows:

"(a) It shall be unlawful, for the purpose of this section only, in an industry or activity affecting commerce, for any labor organization to engage in any activity or conduct defined as an unfair labor practice in section 8(b)(4) of the National Labor Relations Act, as amended."

Building and Construction Industry

29 USC 158.   SEC. 705. (a) Section 8 of the National Labor Relations Act, as amended by section 704(b) of this Act, is amended by adding at the end thereof the following new subsection:

"(f) It shall not be an unfair labor practice under subsections (a) and (b) of this section for an employer engaged primarily in the building and construction industry to make an agreement covering employees engaged (or who, upon their employment, will be engaged) in the building and construction industry with a labor organization of which building and construction employees are members (not established, maintained, or assisted by any action defined in section 8(a) of this Act as an unfair labor practice) because (1) the majority status of such labor organization has not been established under the provisions of section 9 of this Act prior to the making of such agreement, or (2) such agreement requires as a condition of employment, membership in such labor organization after the seventh day following the beginning of such employment or the effective date of the agreement, whichever is later, or (3) such agreement requires the employer to notify such labor organization of opportunities for employment with such employer, or gives such labor organization an opportunity to refer qualified applicants for such employment, or (4) such agreement specifies minimum training or experience qualifications for employment or provides for priority in opportunities for employment based upon length of service with such employer, in the industry or in the particular geographical area: *Provided,* That nothing in this subsection shall set aside the final proviso to section 8(a)(3) of this Act: *Provided further,* That any agreement which would be invalid, but for clause (1) of this subsection, shall not be a bar to a petition filed pursuant to section 9(c) or 9(e)."

(b) Nothing contained in the amendment made by subsection (a) shall be construed as authorizing the execution or application of agreements requiring membership in a labor organization as a condition of employment in any State or Territory in which such execution or application is prohibited by State or Territorial law.

Priority in Case Handling

SEC. 706. Section 10 of the National Labor Relations Act, as amended, 29 USC 160. is amended by adding at the end thereof a new subsection as follows:

"(m) Whenever it is charged that any person has engaged in an unfair labor practice within the meaning of subsection (a)(3) or (b)(2) of section 8, such charge shall be given priority over all other cases except cases of like character in the office where it is filed or to which it is referred and cases given priority under subsection (l)."

Effective Date of Amendments

SEC. 707. The amendments made by this title shall take effect sixty days after the date of the enactment of this Act and no provision of this title shall be deemed to make an unfair labor practice, any act which is performed prior to such effective date which did not constitute an unfair labor practice prior thereto.

Approved September 14, 1959.

Index of Statutes

Index of Cases

Subject Index

NOTE : All cases are found in the Index of Cases beginning on page 490; an index of statutes appears on page 489. In this index, LMRA, LMRDA, NLRA, and NLRB refer, respectively, to the Labor-Management Relations Act, the Labor-Management Reporting and Disclosure Act, the National Labor Relations Act, and the National Labor Relations Board.